Maryland Marriage Evidences,
1634–1718

MARYLAND MARRIAGE EVIDENCES,

1634–1718

Robert W. Barnes

GENEALOGICAL PUBLISHING CO., INC.

Copyright © 2005
Genealogical Publishing Co., Inc.
3600 Clipper Mill Road, Suite 260
Baltimore, Maryland 21211
Library of Congress Catalogue Card Number 2005926651
International Standard Book Number 0-8063-1760-4
Made in the United States of America

*Dedicated to my colleagues in the Reference Department
at the Maryland State Archives*

Contents

Introduction

It is with great pleasure that I dedicate this book to my colleagues in the Reference Department at the Maryland State Archives. They are knowledgeable about Maryland records, dedicated to giving patrons in the Search Room the best possible service. They are supportive of each other and have patiently listened to me reporting the progress of this book.

When I published *Maryland Marriages, 1634-1777* in 1975, I attempted to compile all the marriages in existing church records for Maryland within that time frame. The resulting volume contained some 12,000 marriages.

The present volume contains marriage records taken from religious and civil sources and, in addition, marriage references taken from land, court, and probate records. As of this writing, I have found 2,007 actual marriage records from religious and civil sources (indicated by boldface type); 4,143 clues to marriages that have already taken place, found in land, court, and probate records; and another 267 entries that are actual marriage records, enhanced by other clues, making a total of 6,417 entries.

While compiling *Maryland Marriage Evidences 1634-1718*, I found errors in my first book of Maryland marriages that need to be corrected. For example, John Clary married on 30 Dec 1705 Elizabeth Haly (AAAN:1). His name has been misread by several transcribers as Cary but an examination of the original register shows the name was written as Clary.

Marriage records from civil and religious sources are in boldface type, while marriage references are in plain type. Civil sources include marriages recorded by clerks of the county courts, marriages noted in land records, banns posted in court and land records, marriage intentions and licenses, and marriages found in Bibles. Religious sources include the surviving church records.

A word of caution when dealing with transcriptions: 17th-century handwriting can be hard to read. I found this: "Morris, m. by 12 Oct 1696, Rachell, in whose right he was exec. of Abraham Sacote of CH Co." (INAC 14:72). The name may have been Abraham Laproate of CH Co. (MWB 3:404).

I decided to compare the published *Maryland Calendar of Wills* with the original Prerogative Court wills. In pages 1-100 of Will Book 1, I found five clues to marriages that did not appear in the published abstracts.

Laws Pertaining to Marriage

It is important to study the laws of the country pertaining to the time in which you are interested. For instance, in England in the 17th century the only legal marriages were those performed in parish churches, and the only burials were in the parish churchyard, so many Catholics have their marriages recorded in the Anglican registers.

A law in Virginia stipulated that marriages could be only performed in the mornings on weekdays.

In Maryland there were a number of laws pertaining to marriage and the recording of marriages.

In October 1640 the Assembly of Maryland enacted a law stating that no one could be married unless the banns had been published three days earlier in a chapel or some other public place (*Archives of Maryland* [hereafter *ARMD*] 1:97).

In April 1658 it was enacted by the Lord Proprietary "by and with the consent of this present General Assembly," that the clerks of each county court were to keep a register of all persons born, married, or died, and any person who waited more than two months to register such an event should be fined twenty pounds of tobacco. The act was to continue in effect for three years. Another act of the same session said that any persons desiring to be married should publish their intentions at any session of court, church, chapel, or meeting house, at a time when the meeting was full (*ARMD* 1:373, 374).

At the session ending May 1666 the Assembly described the form the marriage ceremony should take (*ARMD* 2:148).

At a meeting of the Council held in September 1685, it was ordered that "anyone, magistrate, priest, or minister, qualified to marry or join in matrimony should not perform such a ceremony to any persons 'strangers from Virginia or elsewhere' without a license or certificate from some Magistrate or other person within this Province thereunto legally authorized and empowered of having past due Examination, and that the parties desiring the same may lawfully be joined together" (*ARMD* 17:399).

At the session ending June 1692 it was enacted that all persons intending marriage could apply to a minister, pastor, or magistrate. Clerks were to keep a register of births, marriages, and burials in a fair and legible hand (*ARMD* 13:450, 530).

On a more somber note at that session, the Assembly enacted a law directing that if "any freeborn English or white woman should marry with any Negro or other Slave or any free Negro she should lose her freedom and become a servant during the term of seven years to the use and benefit of the Ministry or the Poor of the same Parish at the discretion of the Vestry men of the Parish to which the said Woman at the time of Marriage did belong, and if the man was a free Negro, he should forfeit his freedom and become a Servant to the use aforesaid during his natural life" (*ARMD* 13:547).

On 12 June 1694 Thomas Lawrence, Secretary of the Province, announcing Act of Assembly "to keep records of all births, marriages and deaths," wrote the following to Mr. John West, Clerk of Somerset County, to be read in Court in June Next.

"Whereas according to an Act of Assembly of this Province entitled an Act for the Registering of Births, Marriages & Burials. It is enacted that within two months after the birth of any Child, person married or the death of any person within this Province, that the Birth of the Child born by the Parents & the time of the marriage of any Person married, married & the time of the death of any person dying by the Extr or Admn[r] be entered upon Record by the Clerk of the County Court. And whereas the inhabitants of the several & respective Counties are very slack & negligent in entering the same according to the tenour of sd act these are to will and require the inhabitants of the several and respective Counties bring in a just & true account of the Children born, the persons married and the persons deceased and to enter the same upon record with the

Clerk of the County Court in which they doe inhabit & dwell & for the future to enter the same within the time limited as by the sd act is required whereof they are not to fail under the penalty in the sd Act mentioned & for default to be prosecuted accordingly whereof every person by their Ma'ties Special Command are to take notice. Given under [my?] hand this eleventh day of May Anno Domini 1694" (SOJU LD:97).

In July 1696 it was enacted by the "Authority aforesaid by and with the Advice and Consent aforesaid That if any Minister priest or Magistrate shall join in Marriage any persons Contrary to the Table of Marriages by this Act appointed to be Set up in every parish Church within this Province he or they shall forfeit the sum of five Thousand pounds of tobacco" (*ARMD* 19:430).

By May 1704 the registrars of the parish were to keep a register of all births, marriages, and burials within the parish (*ARMD* 24:268).

Types of Documents Used in This Volume

Direct records of marriages may be found in parish registers and administrative records of some denominations, in marriage licenses and allegations, in banns posted in the county court, and in pastoral registers.

Indirect references to marriages can be found in land records, probate and court records, marriage contracts, Maryland state papers, and court reports.

Marriages and marriage references may also be found in private records, such as newspapers, diaries, letters, family Bibles, and sometimes in the records of other states.

Acknowledgments

If it takes a whole village to raise a child, it certainly takes a good-sized community to bring a book like this to completion. Family, friends, and colleagues have offered support, encouragement, and technical advice.

My wife has shown endless patience while I have worked on this book.

I owe a debt of gratitude to Dolly Ziegler, who suggested the title of the book and who provided much helpful editorial assistance. Dolly, Patricia Dockman Anderson, Robert K. Headley, Jr., Martin Wasserman, and Allender Sybert have listened to my thoughts and made suggestions.

Thanks are due to Michael Tepper, Eileen Perkins, Joe Garonzik, and Marian Hoffman and the staff at Genealogical Publishing for publishing this work. Edward C. Papenfuse and the staff at the Maryland State Archives have maintained original records and created on-line sources that have been invaluable to researchers.

I want to thank the staff, volunteers, and patrons of the Maryland State Archives, who have encouraged me; and those, such as Vernon L. Skinner, Dr. Carson Gibb, John Polk, and John Lyon, who have suggested new sources and even shared some of their findings with me.

Dr. Beatriz Hardy and Francis O'Neill at the Maryland Historical Society have maintained a fine library in which to do research.

Additions and Corrections

There is an old saying that goes "We'd just sold the baby carriage when . . . ."
That principle has come to life in the compiling of this book. The author had finished
indexing the entries through the P's and Q's when Dr. Carson Gibb completed his
excellent work *Early Settlers of Maryland.* This revision of Skordas' earlier work of the
same name has been posted on the Maryland State Archives web site, and by searching
for the word "wife" in the "description" box, the compiler has found another 65 entries,
most of which had to be posted in the additions and corrections. Researchers owe
Carson Gibb a vote of thanks for this work, and another vote of thanks to Dr. Edward C,
Papenfuse, Archivist of the State of Maryland, for hosting Gibb's works.

Another recent publication also provided new entries: F. Edward Wright's *Quaker
Minutes of the Eastern Shore, 1676-1779.* Lewes: Delmarva Roots, 2003.

The Index

After the text there will be a full-name index of brides and others mentioned in
the text. In some cases I have consolidated variations in spellings under the most
commonly used form of the name. The variations were cross-referenced. Ann and Anne
have been combined as Ann(e). Eliza and Elizabeth are shown as Eliza(beth).

BIBLIOGRAPHY

Primary Sources and Abbreviations Used

AA Co.: Anne Arundel County.

AAAN: St. Anne's Parish, AA Co. MSA SC 15; MSA M 143; 175. (See MSA Card Index 27, AACR below.)

AAAL: All Hallow's Parish, AA Co. MSA SC 2458; AAAL 1: Register, 1669-1721; AALH 2: Register 1700-1724. (See MSA Card Index 27, AACR below.)

AAJA: St. James Parish, AA Co. MSA SC 2497. (See MSA Card Index 27, AACR below.)

AAJU: ANNE ARUNDEL CO. COURT (Judgment Record), MSA C 91. (See Hayman below.)

AALR: ANNE ARUNDEL CO. COURT (Land Records) MSA C 97. (See Dodd below.)

AAMA: St. Margaret's Parish, AA Co. MSA SC 2915. (See MSA Card Index 27, AACR below.)

admin.: administrator or administration.

admx: administratrix.

BA Co.: Baltimore County.

BAAD: BA CO. REGISTER OF WILLS (Administration Accounts) MSA C 261.

BACP: BA CO. COURT (Proceedings) MSA C 400.

BALR: BA CO. COURT (Land Records) MSA C 352. (See Scisco below.)

BAPA: St. Paul's Parish, BA Co. MSA SC 2652. (See Reamy below.)

BAWB: BA CO. REGISTER OF WILLS (Wills) MSA C 435, CM 188.

BINV: BA CO. REGISTER OF WILLS (Inventories) MSA C 340, CM 155.

CE Co.: Cecil Co.

CELR: CE CO. COURT (Land Records) MSA C 626, CM 343. (See also Brown, below.)

CENE: Northeast Parish, CE Co., MSA SC 2488. (See *CECH* below.)

CESS: St. Stephen's Parish, CE Co., MSA SC 2507. (See *CECH* below.)

CH Co.: Charles Co.

CH CO. COURT (Court Record), MSA C 658, CM 394.

CHLR: CH CO. COURT (Land Records) MSA C 670, CM 394. (See Jourdan below.)

CHPR: CH CO. REGISTER OF WILLS (Probate Records). (See King below.)

CHWB: CH CO. REGISTER OF WILLS (Wills) MSA C681, CM 412.

CV Co. Calvert Co.

CVCH: Christ Church Parish Register, CV Co.. MSA SC 2638. (See Jourdan below.)

DO Co.: Dorchester Co.

DOJR: DO CO. COURT (Judgment Record) MSA C 704, CM 438. (See Wright below.)

DOLR: DO CO. COURT (Land Records) MSA C 710, CM 440. (See McAllister below.)

exec.: executor.

extx.: executrix.

HAGE: St. George's Parish Register, HA Co. MSA SC 2459. (See Reamy below.)

INAC: PREROGATIVE COURT (Inventories and Accounts) MSA S536, SM 13. (See Skinner below.)

Judgements. (See PCJU below.)

KE Co.: Kent Co.

KECM or KECE: Cecil Monthly Meeting, Kent Co.; MSA SC 3120; Marriages, 1698-1784, MSA M 908. (See Carroll, *ESVR* 1 below.)

KELR: KE CO. COURT (Land Records). MSA C 1068, CM 662. (See Harper below.)

KESH: Shrewsbury Parish Register, Kent Co. MSA SC 2513. (See *ESVR* below.)

KESP: St. Paul's Parish Register, Kent Co. MSA SC 2650. (See Dunroche, *ESVR* below.)

LAND OFFICE (Rent Rolls): MSA S 18, SM 130. (See *MRR*, SMRR below.)

LAND OFFICE (Warrant Record): CB(#3)*, CB(#4)*; AA(#7)*, BB(#8)*.

MCHR: CHANCERY COURT (Chancery Record) MSA C 517, SM 1. (See Hooper below.)

MDAD: PREROGATIVE COURT (Accounts) MSA S 531, SM 7. (See Skinner below.)

MDCR: See MCHR.

MHS: Maryland Historical Society, Baltimore, MD.

MINV: PREROGATIVE COURT (Inventories) MSA S 536, SM 13. (See Skinner below.)

MM: Monthly Meeting, of the Society of Friends.

MPL: LAND OFFICE (Patent Record) MSA S 11, SM 2. (See Coldham, Gibb, Skordas below.)

MDTP: PREROGATIVE COURT (Testamentary Proceedings) MSA S 529 SM 15. (See Skinner below.)

MO Co.: Montgomery Co.

MOPG: Prince George's Parish Register, Montgomery Co. MSA SC 2637.

MSA: Maryland State Archives, Annapolis, MD. When used with C, CM, S, or SM, denotes a specific record series.

MWAR: See Warrants, Warrant Record below.

MWB: PREROGATIVE COURT (Wills) MSA S 539, SM 17. (See *MCW* below.)

PCJU: PROVINCIAL COURT (Judgment Record) MSA S 551, SM 20.

PCLR: PROVINCIAL COURT (Land Records) MSA S 552, SM 22.

PG Co.: Prince George's Co.

PGLR: PG CO. COURT (Land Records) MSA C 1237, CM 782. (See Jourdan below.)

PGKG: St. John's/Piscatway Parish/King George's Parish, PG Co. MSA SC 2227.

PGQA: Queen Anne's Parish, PG Co. MSA SC 2667.

PGWB: PG CO. REGISTER OF WILLS (Wills) MSA C 1326, CM 816.

PROPRIETARY RECORDS: See Skinner below.

QA Co.: Queen Anne's Co.

QAEJ: Queen Anne's Ejectment Papers (LAND OFFICE) 1636-1777, MSA S 549.

QAJR; QA CO. COURT (Judgment Records) MSA C 1416, CM 844. (QAJRh: See Harper, Wright below.)

QALR: QA CO. COURT (Land Records) MSA C 1426, CM 1163. (See Leonard below.)

Rent Rolls (LAND OFFICE), 1639-1776 MSA s18, sm130.

SJSG: St. John's and St. George's Parish, BA and HA Counties; MSA SC 1642. (See Peden below.)

SM Co.: St. Mary's Co.

SMAD: SM CO. REGISTER OF WILLS (Administration Accounts) MSA C1506, CM 908. (See Fresco below.)

SMWB: SM CO. REGISTER OF WILLS (Wills) MSA C 1720, CM 926. (See Fresco below.)

SO Co.: Somerset County.

SOJU: SO CO. COURT (Judicial Record). MSA C 1774, CM 962. (See Polk, Walczyk below.) (A liber designation followed by an "e" designates an electronic transcription as part of the *Archives of Maryland On Line.*)

SOLR: SO CO. COURT (Land Records) MSA C 1778, CM 963.

SOLR: Liber IKL: The Register of Births, Marriages and Deaths, 1649-1720, is interspersed with deeds in a volume of land records. Some of the pages are barely legible (MSA MdHR 6950; location 10/45/1/14). (See Torrence below.)

TA Co.: Talbot Co.

TAJR: TA CO. COURT (Judgment Record) MSA C 1875, MSA CM 1010. (See Wright below.)

TAJU: See TAJR (above).

TALR: TA CO. COURT (Land Records) MSA C 180, CM 1011. (See Leonard below.)

TAPE: St. Peter's Parish, TA Co. MSA SC 2640. (See Day, *ESVR* below.)

TATH: Third Haven Monthly Meeting, Society of Friends. MSA SC 2394. Marriage Book, Indexed, 1668-1935 on MSA M 286. (See Carroll, *ESVR*, vol. 1 below.)

Warrant Record. See LAND OFFICE (Warrant Record) MSA S 23/

Warrants. See LAND OFFICE (Warrants) MSA S1285.

WIST: Stepney Parish, WI Co.. MSA SC 2659. (See *ESVR* below).

WRMM (or WRMMa): West River Monthly Meeting, Society of Friends. MSA SC. (See AACR, *QRSM* below).

Secondary Sources

AACR: F. Edward Wright. *Anne Arundel Co. Church Records of the 17th and 18th Centuries.* Westminster, MD: Family Line Publications, no date.

AMG: Annapolis *Maryland Gazette.*

ARMD: *Archives of Maryland.* Volumes 1-70 exist in hard copy. Vols. 71- are located at the Maryland State Archives web site as *Archives of Maryland on-line.*

AWAP: Peter Wilson Coldham. *American Wills and Administrations in the Prerogative Court of Canterbury, 1610-1857.* Baltimore: Genealogical Publishing Co., 1989.

Barnes, Robert W. *Maryland Marriages, 1634-1777.* Baltimore: Genealogical Publishing Co., 1975.

Brown, June D. *Abstracts of Cecil County, Maryland, Land Records, 1673-1751.* Westminster, Md.: Family Line Publications, 1998.

Burns, Annie Walker, Maryland Marriage References, typescript, Maryland Historical Society.

Carroll: Kenneth Carroll. *Quakerism on the Eastern Shore of Maryland.* Baltimore: Maryland Historical Society.

CECH: Henry C. Peden, Jr. *Early Anglican Church Records of Cecil County.* Westminster, Md.: Family Line Publications, 1990.

CMSP: *Calendar of Maryland State Papers: The Black Books.* Publications of the Hall of Records Commission No. 1. 1942. Reprint, Baltimore: Genealogical Publishing Co., 1967.

CSM: *Chronicles of St. Mary's.*

Coldham, Peter Wilson. *Settlers of Maryland, 1679-1783. Consolidated Edition.* Baltimore: Genealogical Publishing Co., 2002.

Cotton, Jane Baldwin. "Extracts from the Early Records of Maryland." *MHM* 16:279-298, 369-385, 17:60-74, 292-308.

CV Co.: Calvert Co.

Day, Henry Hale. "Being a complete, full, and true list of all the marriages entered upon the Marriage Record of St. Peter's Parish of Talbot County, Maryland. Copied by the undersigned who was Registrar of the said Parish continuously from 1905 ... , and that said Marriages have been copied in order in which they were recorded in the original record books, many of which were entered out of order."

DO Co.: Dorchester Co.

Dodd, Rosemary B., and Patricia M. Bausell, eds. *Abstracts of Land Records of Anne Arundel County, Maryland.* 3 vols. Pasadena, Md.: The Anne Arundel Genealogical Society, n.d.

Dunroche, Rev. Chris T., Rector of St. Paul's Parish, Helen Arrowsmith, and Kate Rose (Mrs. George) Beck. Transcription of St. Paul's Parish, KE Co. July 1893. (The pages of the transcript through C are not numbered, so each section has been arbitrarily assigned a number, as A1, A2, B1, B2, etc. Beginning with D, the pages are clearly numbered. But the pages for the W's are not numbered; some of the folios are missing, and some of the page numbers are hard to decipher).

ESVR: F. Edward Wright. *Eastern Shore Vital Records.* 5 vols. 1642-1825. Westminster, Md.: Family Line Publications.

Fothergill, Augusta B. *Wills of Westmoreland County, Virginia, 1654-1800.* 1925. Reprint, Baltimore: Genealogical Publishing Co.

Fresco: Margaret K. Fresco, *Marriages and Deaths: St. Mary's County, Maryland, 1634 -1900.* Ridge, Md.: The Author, 1982.

Gibb: Carson Gibb. *Supplement to [Skordas'] Early Settlers of Maryland.* Electronic data base located on the Maryland State Archives web site.

HAGE: Bill and Martha Reamy. *St. George's Parish Registers, 1689-1793.* FLP, 1988. (Page numbers are to the original registers.)

Harper, Irma S. *First Kent, Second Kent, Third Kent.* 3 vols. Privately printed. [Abstracts of Kent Co. Land Records for the years 1648-1726.]

-------. *Maryland Marriage Clues.* 3 vols. Pub. by the Author.

-------. "Queen Anne's County Judgments Records." *Chesapeake Cousins* 24 (1) 22-25 (1710-1730), 24 (2) 26-29 (1730-1737), 25 (1) 22-24 (1737-1740).

Harris and McHenry [Court Reports]. 4 vols., 1700-1779. See *NGSQ* 53 (below).

Harrison: Lucy H. Harrison: official copyist of the Maryland Historical Society whose transcriptions of early parish registers were the basis of this author's *Maryland Marriages, 1634-1777.*

Hayman, Doug. "Orphans Cases in Anne Arundel County Court, Maryland, Judgment Record TB#1, March 1705-September 1709," *Readings* 7 (1) (Jan 2004) 3-8.

Headley, Robert Kirk, Jr. *Married Well and Often: Marriages of the Northern Neck of Virginia, 1649-1800.* Baltimore: Genealogical Publishing Co., 2003.

Heinegg, Paul. *Free African Americans of Maryland and Delaware from the Colonial Period to 1810.* Baltimore: Genealogical Publishing Co., 2000.

Hodges' Marriage References: Maryland State Archives Card Index 5. [It should be noted that some of her citations are obscure. "Liber 1" could refer to MWB 1 or MDTP 1.]

Hooper, Debbie. *Abstracts of Chancery Court Records of Maryland, 1669-1782.* Westminster, Md.: Family Line Publications.

Jourdan, Elise Greenup. *Abstracts of Charles County, Maryland, Land and Court Records, 1658-1722.* 3 vols. Westminster, Md.: Family Line Publications, 1993-1994.

-------. *Colonial Records of Southern Maryland.* Westminster, Md.: Family Line Publications, 1997.

-------. *Prince George's Co. Land Records, 1702-1743.* 6 vols. Westminster, Md.: Family Line Publications.

Judgments: probably Provincial Court Judgment Records (used by Hodges and Fresco).

King, Ruth, and Carol Mitchell, "Charles County, Maryland, Probate Records, Inventories, Part I, 1673-1753," *MGSB* 25 (1) 52- ; CHPR A: "Charles Co. Probate Records, 1677-1717," *MGSB* 25 (1) 52-62; CHPR B: "Charles Co. Probate Records, 1717-1735," *MGSB* 25 (1) 62-76; CHPR C: "Charles Co. Probate Records, 1737-1752," *MGSB* 25 (1) 76-91.

Leonard, Bernice. *Queen Anne's Co. Land Records.* St. Michael's, Md.: The Author.

-------. *Talbot County Land Records.* St. Michael's, Md.: The Author.

Liber: used by Hodges, possibly to refer to MWB.

Maryland Court of Appeals Reports. See *Harris and McHenry* above.

McAllister, James B. *Abstracts of Dorchester Co. Land Records.* Reprint, Westminster, Md.: Family Line Publications.

MCW: Maryland Calendar of Wills, 1634-1777. Various editions.

MG: Maryland Genealogies: A Consolidation of Articles from the Maryland Historical Magazine. 2 vols. Baltimore: Genealogical Publishing Co., 1980.

MGSB: Maryland Genealogical Society Bulletin.

MHM: Maryland Historical Magazine.

MM: Monthly Meeting.

MRR: Maryland Rent Rolls: Baltimore and Anne Arundel Counties. Baltimore: Genealogical Publishing Co., 1976.

MSA Card Index 27: An index of marriages recorded primarily in Protestant Episcopal Churches.

MWAR: MARYLAND LAND OFFICE Warrant Record, MSA S 23.

NFMP: Harry Wright Newman. *Flowering of the Maryland Palatinate.* 1961. Reprint, Baltimore: Genealogical Publishing Co.

NGSQ 53:199-204. Jean Stephenson, "Extracts from Maryland Court Records," *National Genealogical Society Quarterly* 53:199-204.

Peden, Henry C., Jr., *St. John's and St. George's Parish Register, Baltimore and Harford County, Maryland, 1696-1851.* Westminster, Md.: Family Line Publications, 1987). (Page numbers are to the original parish register.)

Polk, John, Electronic transcriptions of SOJU 1692-1693, 1693-1694, and 1695-1695, graciously made available to the author.

Provincial Court: term used by Fresco and Hodges; probably to refer to either Provincial Court Judgments or Provincial Court Land Records.

QMES: F. Edward Wright. *Quaker Minutes of the Eastern Shore of Maryland, 1676-1779.* Dover, Del.: Delmarva Roots, 2003.

QRNM: Henry C. Peden, Jr. *Quaker Records of Northern Maryland.* Westminster, Md.: Family Line Publications.

QRSM: Henry C. Peden, Jr., *Quaker Records of Southern Maryland.* Westminster, Md.: Family Line Publications, 1992.

Reamy, Bill, and Martha Reamy. *Records of St Paul's Parish.* Westminster, Md.: Family Line Publications. © by Martha Reamy.

-------. *St. George's Parish Registers, 1698-1793.* Westminster, Md.: Family Line Publications, 1988.

Russell, Donna Valley, "The Putative Daughters of John Larkin," *MGSB* 45 (1) (Winter 2004) 35-62.

Russell, George Ely, "Portuguese and Spanish Colonists in 17th Century Maryland." *TAG* 76 (April 2001).

Scisco, Louis Dow. *Baltimore County Land Records, 1665-1687.* Baltimore: Genealogical Publishing Co.

Sherwood, George [F. T.]. *American Colonists in English Records.* 1921, 1933. Reprint, Baltimore: Genealogical Publishing Co., 1969.

Skinner, V. L., Jr. *Abstracts of Administration Accounts of the Prerogative Court of Maryland. Libers 1-74, 1718-1777.* 11 vols. Westminster, Md.: Family Line Publications.

-------. *Abstracts of the Inventories of the Prerogative Court of Maryland, 1718-1777.* Westminster, Md.: Family Line Publications .

-------. *Abstracts of the Inventories and Accounts of the Prerogative Court of Maryland, 1674-1718.* Westminster, Md.: Family Line Publications .

-------. *Abstracts of the Proprietary Records of the Provincial Court of Maryland, 1637-1658.* Westminster, Md.: Willow Bend Books, 2002.

-------. *Abstracts of the Testamentary Proceedings of the Prerogative Court of Maryland. Volume I: 1658-1674.* Baltimore: Clearfield Publishing Co., 2004.

Skordas, Gust.: *Early Settlers of Maryland, 1633-1680*. Baltimore: Genealogical Publishing Co., 1979.

SMRR: St. Mary's Co. Rent Roll, 1707; transcribed by Christopher Johnston; microfilm of original is at MHS. Pages given are to the Johnston transcription.

SOLR:IKL: The Register of Births, Marriages and Deaths, 1649-1720, is interspersed with deeds in a volume of land records. Some of the pages are barely legible (MSA MdHR 6950; location 10/45/1/14). They have also been published in Clayton Torrence, *Old Somerset on the Eastern Shore of Maryland*. 1935. Reprint, Westminster, Md.: Family Line Publications, 1992, pp. 396-400.

TAG: The American Genealogist.

Torrence, Clayton. *Old Somerset on the Eastern Shore of Maryland*. 1935. Reprint, Westminster, Md.: Family Line Publications, 1992.

VMHB: Virginia Magazine of History and Biography.

Westmoreland Co., VA, Will Book. (See Fothergill above.)

Walczyk, Frank. *Somerset County, Maryland, Judicial Records, 1797-1711*. 4 vols. Coram, N.Y.: Peter's Row, 1998.

Wright, F. Edward. *Judgment Records of Dorchester, Queen Anne's & Talbot Counties*. Lewes, Del.: Delmarva Roots, 2001.

Maryland Marriage Evidences, 1634–1718

[-?-], m. on (date not given), Mary Bellica (KESP:20).

[-?-], m. on 23 April ---, Mary Cordwell (AAJA?).

[-?-], m. on 7 April 1713, Susanna Dryor (AAAL 2:10).

[-?-], Domingo, Negro man, m. by March 1677 in CV Co., Mary Davis, b. in Mark Lane, London, dau. of Richard Davis of that place, and sister of Joh. Davis. Domingo and Mary had two children: Thomas, b. 14 March 1677 in CV Co., and Rose, b. 11 Aug 1694 in SM Co. (AAJU VD#1).

[-?-]-**"Little" Robin, "Negro man," m. 1681 in SM Co. by a priest named Nicholas Geulick, Elizabeth Shorter, servant of William Roswell.** Rev. Geulick deposed on 15 June 1702 that he had performed the marriage (Heinegg:325, cites *Cases in the General Court and Court of Appeal of Maryland*:238-240, and *Cases in the Court of Appeals of Maryland*:359-362).

Thomas, m. on 13 April 1704, [-?-] [-?-] (AAAN:19).

Thomas, m. in 1714, Elizabeth Howard (AAAN:22).

AARON

Ambrose, m. by 1716, Ann Lewis, dau. of Glode Lewis of DO Co. (MWB 14:370; INAC 32B:65; MINV 18:209).

ABBINGTON. See ABINGTON.

ABBOT. See ABBOTT.

ABBOT(T)

James, m. by 1710, Elizabeth, dau. of Thomas Vickers of DO Co. (MWB 13:272, 14:657).

John, m. by 1707, Anne, dau. of John Barker of TA Co. (MWB 12:80, INAC 32A:28, 32C:87). She m. 2nd, John Brium (INAC 29:282).

John, m. on 10 Sep 1718, Elizabeth Norris (TAPE).

Samuel, m. on 3 Dec 1701, Eliner [-?-] (TAPE).

Samuel, m. on 30 Jan 1709, Margaret Shannahane (TAPE).

Silvester, m. on 10 Feb 1700, Elizabeth [-?-] (TAPE).

Simon, m. by 1651 Maudlin [-?-], and had daus. Deborah (MPL 4:68) and, after coming to MD, Dorcas. Maudlin m. 2nd, Edmund Townhill, 3rd, by 1661, George Nettlefold, and 4th. Thomas Smithwick (MWB 1:627, 2:363; MDTP 7:112, 9:331).

Thomas, m. on 13 June 1713, Elizabeth Gitboard (TAPE).

ABEL(L)

John, of SM Co., m. by 1714, [-?-], dau. of Edward Fisher (INAC 36B:75).

ABINGTON
 John, m. [-?-], widow, one of the execs of Geo. Noble (Hodges cites Judgments 29:232).
 John, m. on 20 Oct 1715, Mary Hutchinson (PGKG:248).She was the dau. of William Hutchinson of PG Co., and she m. 2nd, by 1746, Dr. Andrew Scott (*ARMD* 38:343; MWB 22:64; MCHR 5:235, 237; MDAD 19:469, 21:100, 23:167, 24:101; MDTP 28:308, 31:40, 32:122).

ABLE. See ABEL.

ABRAHAM(S)
 Hugh, m. by 14 Aug 1712, Hester, poss. widow of Humphrey Beckett; Abrahams named a son-in-law John Beckett, and daus.-in-law Elizabeth Becraft and Mary Rodecy, and Humphrey Beckett, son of Humphrey (MWB 13:571).
 Isaac, m. by 11 Dec 1660, Elizabeth, widow of Thomas Read (*ARMD* 41:379).
 Jacob, of TA Co., planter, m. on 28 May 1685 [*sic*], Isabel Omeli, of TA co., spinster, at Betty's Cove Meeting House (TATH).
 Richard, m. on 27 Jan 1714, Anne Clark (TAPE).

ACCARS
 James, m. on 15 Nov 1716, Elizabeth Abbott (TAPE).

ACKWITH
 Richard, m. by 11 June 1713, Elizabeth, extx. of John Hains of SO Co. (INAC 34:233).

ACKWORTH
 Richard, m. 6 Dec 1683, Sarah Hardy (SOLR:IKL).

ACTON
 Henry, m. by 12 Oct [1703?], Ann, widow and admx. of Richard Gambra, PG Co., dec. (MWB 3:72; PGLR F:71; INAC 27:262).
 Richard, m. on 11 Dec 1707, Ann Sewell (AAAN:1).

ACWORTH. See ACKWORTH.

ADAMS
 [-?-], m. by 12 Jan 1707, Anne, dau. of Samuel Collins [Collings?], bricklayer of Pocomoke, SO Co. (MWB 12:262). She was a sister of John Collins of SO Co. (MWB 12, pt. 2::88).
 Francis (Addams), m. by 13 Nov 1707, Mary, dau. of George Godfrey (CHLR C#2:89).
 Gabriel, m. on 20 Feb 1704/5, Ann Morton (AAJA:30 #16).
 Henry, of CH Co., m. by Jan 1671/2, Margaret, admx. of Oliver Balse (*ARMD* 60:361).

Henry, m. by 1686, Mary Cockshutt, dau. of John and Jane Cockshott of St. Inigoe's, SM Co. (MPL ABH:22, 59-61; *ARMD* 1:145, 4:164; MCHR 3:707; Prov. Court S:126-131).

John, m. by 1667, Joan [-?-] (MPL 10:637).

Philip, m. 9 July 1670, Anne Crewe (SOLR:IKL).

Philip, m. 1 Sep 1691, Mary Barry (SOLR:IKL:3).

Richard, m. by Dec 1671, Mary, admx. of John Stansby (BACP F#1:146).

ADDAMS. See ADAMS.

ADDASON

John, m. by March 1708/9, Mary, extx. of George Johnson, Jr. (SOJU 1707-1711:77).

ADDERSON

John, m. by 13 Nov 1710, [-?-], widow of Robert Coverthought (MCHR PC:675).

ADDERTON

Jeremiah, m. by 1702, Mary (Neale) Egerton, widow of Charles Egerton, and dau. of James Neale of CH Co. (MCHR 2:659-664; MDTP 28:474; MWB 15:90; MDAD 1:34, INAC 28:221, 32B:11).

Jeremiah, m. by 1714, Anne Luckett, dau. of Thomas Hussey and Anne [-?-] Luckett of CH Co. (Hodges cites Judgements 106:408; CHLR O#2:274).

ADDISON

Andrew, m. on 4 Nov 1708, Elizabeth Brittaine (AALR 1:36).

John, m. by 21 May 1677, Rebecca, relict and extx. of Thomas Dent (INAC 4:74; *ARMD* 66:391, 67:1, 68:69; CHLR Z:121)

Thomas, age 22, son of Hon. Col. John Addison, m. on 31 April 1701, Elizabeth Tasker, age 15, dau. of Thomas Tasker (Addison, Rev. Henry, Bible, *MGSB* 17:127; PGKG:243).

Thomas, m. on 17 June 1709, Elinor, age c19, 2nd dau. of Col. Walter Smith (Addison, Rev. Henry, Bible, *MGSB* 17:127; PGKG:243).

ADKEY

John, m. by 27 Nov 1700, Mary, dau. of John Bullock of SM Co. (MWB 3:502).

ADKINS

John, m. on 10 Nov 1717, Mary Murray (KESP:A1).

Robert, m. by 1717, Elizabeth Highway, sister of Jacob (MWB 14:407).

ADWICK

James, d. by May 1666, having m. Grace, sister of John Walker; she m. 2nd, by 1666, Thomas Winton (MWB 1:248; Hodges cites Liber 1, Part F: 2:88, 89).

AHERN
Daniel, m. on 13 Jan 1708/9, Elizabeth Walker (AAAN:1).
Patrick, m. on 31 Aug 1707, Sarah Dimond (AAAN:1).

AIDERY
William, m. by 23 Aug 1717 [poss. an error for 1727], Rachel, widow of Joseph Barron of TA Co. (MDAD 8:482).

AIRES. See AYRES.

AIRS. See AYRES.

AIRY
David, m. by Sep 1708, Susannah Jenkinson, extx. of John Jadwin (MDTP 21:56).

ALDERNE
William, m. by 11 Sep 1700, Catherine, extx. of David Blaney of TA Co. (INAC 20:54).

ALDERY
William, m. by 23 Aug 1717 [This may be an error for 1727], m. Rachel, widow of Joseph Barron (MDAD 8:482).

ALDRIDGE
[-?-], m. by 27 Sep 1703, Rebecca Hancock, admx. of Stephen Hancock of AA Co. (INAC 24:182).
Thomas, m. 15 July 1703, Elizabeth Purdy (AAAL 1:26). She was a dau. of John Purdy of All Hallows Parish, AA Co. (MWB 13:464).

ALDSBURY
Thomas, m. by Oct 1710, [-?-], extx. of William Hadden (MDTP 21:277).

ALEWARD
John, on 14 Nov 1676, banns of matrimony were published for him and Mary Dixon (SOLR O#7:62r).
Thomas, m. on 28 May 1702, Mary [-?-] (TAPE).

ALFORD
Edward, m. on 23 April 1716, by Rev. Mr. Manadier, Mary Dawson, both of DO Co. (TAPE).
Matthias (Alphord), m. on 25 Nov 1703, Ellen Grundy (TAPE).
Moses, m. by 1697, Christian, admx. of Elias Godward of DO Co. (Cotton cites INAC 15:167).
Moses, m. on 25 May 1704, Mary Staple (KESP:A1).
Moses (Alfred), m. by 15 June 1705, [-?-], widow of John Stavely of CE Co. (INAC 25:120, 300).

ALLEN

[-?-], m. by 20 March 1706/7, Mary, dau. of Murphy Warde of PG Co. (MWB 12:227).

Jasper, m. by 28 March 1670, Mary, dau. of Ishmael Wright (MDTP 4A:2).

Jasper, m. by 24 Feb 1675, Mary, widow and admx. of John Martin (INAC 4:376). Mary m. by 10 March 1676 [-?-] Taylor (INAC 2:187).

John, m. by 9 Jan 1692, Ellinor, dau. of John Lambert (CHLR D#2:35).

John, m. by 15 March 1705, Joane, admx. of Richard Moore of TA Co. (INAC 25:432).

John, m. on 12 Oct 1710, Jane Cox (AALR 1:37).

Joseph, m. by 1676/7, Mary, dau. of Ishmael and Margaret Wright of CV Co.; she m. 2nd, Robert Taylor (MDTP 2:161, 4:2, 8:496).

Joseph, m. on 8 Dec 1715, Eliza. Peck (AAJA:49#1).

Thomas, m. by 1718, Mary, admx. of Robert Craft of CH Co. (MDAD 1:301, 360).

William, m. on 30 Jan 1700, Elizabeth [-?-] (TAPE).

ALLERTON

Isaac, Gent., m. by Jan 1663, Dame Elizabeth, relict and admx. of Simon Overzee (CHLR D:16R; *ARMD* 49:466).

ALLINGSWORTH

Richard, m. 22 Oct 1672, Margaret Covington (SOLR:IKL).

ALLIS

John, m. in Oct 1705, Jane Blaksham (AAMA:82).

ALLMAN

Thomas, m. by 19 Sep 1701, Penelope, dau. of Thomasin Hayden of SM Co. (MWB 3:477, 11:270).

ALLNUTT

William, of CV Co., m. by 7 July 1712, Sarah [-?-], niece of that Sarah [-?-] who m. 1st, John Homewood, and 2nd, John Bennett (TALR RF#12:97).

ALLSEEN

James, m. on 27 Dec 1704, Joan Poor (KESP:A1).

ALLWELL

John, m. on 30 Nov 1704, Elizabeth Jeff, widow, (AAAN:19).

ALMAN

Abraham, m. by banns on 13 Jan 1717, by Mr. Sewell, Margaret Deane, spinster (*CESS*).

ALPHORD. See ALFORD.

ALTIN
   John (Alteen), m. on 7 Feb 1704, Joan Moore (TAPE; TAJR 1706-1708).

ALVEY
   [-?-], m. by 27 Nov 1700, Eliza, dau. of John Bullock of SM Co. (MWB 3:502).
   Pope, m. by 9 Feb 1663/4, Ann, admx. of John Hammond (*ARMD* 49:121-122;
MWB 10:17; MPL ABH:338, 12:550).

ALVRAY
   Joseph, of SM Co., m. by 1705, Elizabeth Bullock (MWB 3:502, 10:17).

AMBROSE
   [-?-], m. by April 1710, Ann, mother of Thomas and William Jackson (QALR
ETA:85, 86).
   Abraham, m. on 27 Aug 1704, Elinor Mason (KESP:A1).

AMOS
   Ludigate, m. on 2 March 1711, Mary Orange (AALR 1:38).
   Newdigate, m. on 4 Jan 1708/9, Honor Fitzgerald (AAAN:1).

AMPEY
   John, m. on 31 May ---, Mary Armstrong (KESP:A1).

ANDERSON
   [-?-], m. by 4 May 1679, Rebecca, dau. of Henry Woolchurch of TA Co. (MWB
7:120; INAC 10:426). She m. 2nd Stephen Darden or Durden (q.v.: See TATH).
   [-?-], m. by Feb 1679/80, Mary, widow of William [Pate?] (MDTP 11:301).
   Andrew (Enderson), m. by 23 Jan 1671, Eliza, mother of George Moore (MWB
1:484).
   Francis, d. by c1698 having m. Mary, sister of Jacob Abrahams of TA Co. (INAC
16:176).
   James, former admin. of John Lyon, d. by 21 Feb [1709], when his widow
Rebecca had m. William Rowly (INAC 30:327).
   James, m. by 1708, Margaret, widow of John Nicholes, Sr. (DOLR Old 6:121).
   John, m. on 21 Aug 1711, Ann Brookson (KESP:A1).
   Peter, m. by 8 July 1686, Ellinor, admx. of John Morris of TA Co. (INAC 9:49).
   Thomas, m. by 1692, Rebecca Barker (Hodges cites Liber 6, Pt. 2: 5).
   William, m. on 6 March 1698, Sarah [-?-] (TAPE).
   William, of TA Co., m. by 1698, Sarah, admx. of William Gwyn (INAC 17:94).
   William, m. on 2 Sep 1704, Margery Prise (TAPE). She was Margery, relict
and extx. of John Price of TA Co. (INAC 27:134, 30:165).
   William, m. by 18 June 1706, Mary, widow of John Davis and mother of Mary,
Elizabeth, and Anne Davis (INAC 25:418; AALR IH#I:263; AAJU IB#2:184).
   William, m. on 23 June 1709, Elizabeth Kilburn (AAAN:7).
   William, m. on 24 June 1715, Martha Carr (TAPE).

ANDERTON

[-?-], m. by 28 Feb 1658, [-?-] [poss. Sarah], dau. of Jane Eltonhead of SM Co. (MWB 1:94).

John, m. by 1667/8, Gertrude, dau. of Thomas Smith of KE Co. (*ARMD* 57:246-249).

John, m. Sarah, sister of Thomas Taylor of CV Co.; she m. 2nd, Thomas Courtney (*ARMD* 49:211).

Peter, of TA Co., m. by 1686, Eleanor, relict and admx. of Jno. Morris, dec. (MDTP 13:364).

Peter, m. by 24 Oct 1709, Mary, admx. of Thomas Kale of AA Co. (INAC 30:239).

ANDREW

George, m. on 22 Sep 1672, Thomason Hart or Hurt (SOLR:IKL).

Mr. Patrick, m. on 30 June 1715, Mrs. Ann Bigger (CVCH).

Thomas, m. by 1716, Elizabeth, widow of Thomas Ford (Hodges cites Judg. VD#1:419).

ANDREWS

[-?-], m. by 9 Nov 1707, Rachel, dau. of Teague Riggin, Sr., of SO Co. (MWB 12:223).

[-?-], m. by 5 April 1709, Ellen, dau. of Richard Adams of DO Co. (MWB 12, pt.2:119).

Christopher, of KE Co., m. by 7 Oct 1672, Mary, widow of William Stanley. He d. by Oct 1677 (*ARMD* 51:86; MDTP 9A:396-397).

John, m. by 1677, Eleanor, dau. of James Pattison; she m. 2nd, Wm. Harbut (MDTP 6:83, 85).

Patrick, m. by 25 April 1716, Ann, extx. of Col. Jno. Bigger of CV Co. (INAC 37A:25).

Thomas, m. on 25 July 1708, Dorothy Edwards (AAAN:7).

Thomas, m. on 2 Aug 1715, Elizabeth Guttheridge (AAAN:22).

ANGELL

John, d. by 23 Sep 1697, having m. Ellinor, dau. of James Pattison of SM Co.; she m. 2nd, William Herbert (MWB 6:85).

ANKRUM

Richard, m. by 10 Oct 1717, Mary, dau. of Ann, the widow of [-?-] Foester [*sic*] of CH Co. (MWB 14:424).

ANKTELL

Francis, m. on 19 Aug 1708, Elizabeth Evans (AAJA:26 #1). She was a dau. of Lewis Evans (MPL FF#7:292, PL#4:440).

ANNIS
    Thomas, m. by 30 April 1718, Elizabeth, extx. of Thomas Mackey of CH Co. (MDAD 1:60).

ARCHDALE
    [-?-], m. by 1717, Elizabeth, dau. of Lewis Evans of AA Co. (Warrant Record BB(#8):56).

ARCHER
    Jacob, m. by 24 Dec 1694, Mary, admx. of Jonas Maddox of CE Co. (INAC 13A:242, 243). She m. 2nd, by 20 Sep 1701, Yorke Yorkenson (INAC 20:271).
    Jacob, m. by lic. on 4 Oct 1713, by Richard Sewell, Mary Freeman, spinster (CESS).

ARDEN
    [-?-] (also Arding or Harding), m. by 1714, Mary, heir of Joseph Strawbridge (BAAD 1:7).

ARDERY
    William, m. by 23 Aug 1717, Rachel, widow of Joseph Barron of TA Co. (MDAD 8:482).

ARES
    John, m. on 25 Oct 1702, Eliz. [-?-] (TAPE).
    Jno., m. on 9 Dec 1704, Jane Hobbs (TAPE).
    William, m. on 16 Oct 1710, Elizabeth Chaplin (TAPE).

AREY
    David, of TA Co., planter, m. on 1 d. 11 m., 1695, Hannah Jadwin, spinster, dau. of John and Hannah Jadwin, of TA Co., at the meeting house near Tuckahoe (TATH).
    David, planter, m. on 12 d. 9 m., 1707, Elizabeth Cook, both of TA Co., at Tuckahoe Meeting House (TATH).
    Joseph, planter, m. on 10 d. 9 m., 1708, Mary Baynard, both of TA Co., at Tuckahoe Creek meeting (TATH).

ARGENT
    William, d. by 16 Jan 1666, having m. Margaret, who was the widow of Thomas Noabes [or Hobes], and mother of Bartholomew Herring (MDTP 2:77, 145).

ARGRASS
    John, m. on 7 Sep 1703, Margaret Jones (TAPE).

ARMIGER
    Thomas, m. by 1672, Ann, widow of Francis Trippus (MDTP 5:377).

ARMSTRONG
[-?-], m. by 20 Feb 1710, Mary, dau. of John Price of TA Co. (MWB 13:568).
Francis, m. by 1659, Frances, widow of Cornelius Abrahamson (MPL R:69b, 4:153).
John, m. on 26 Aug 1714, Rebeckah Hicks (SJSG:7).

ARNELL. See ARNOLD.

ARNOLD
Amania, m. on 16 Jan 1706, Elizabeth Baswassick (KESP:A1).
Anthony, m. by Aug 1686, Rachel, extx. of Thomas Maddox of AA Co. (MDTP 14:88).
Benjamin, m. by 1696, Susanna, widow of James Phillips, and mother of Anthony and James Phillips and Mary Carville (INAC 15:25; BAAD 2:63; MWB 6:81).
Lawrence, m. by 10 April 1674, Ann, dau. of Andrew Ellenor, a Spaniard (*ARMD* 51:113).

ARNOTT
William, m. by 24 Nov 1709, Mary, formerly wife of Thomas Michell (DOLR Old 6:143).

ARON
[-?-], m. by 2 May 1716, Anne, dau. of Glode Lewis, Sr., of DO Co. (MWB 14:730).

ARPE. See EARP.

ARRINGTON
Richard, m. by 23 March 1716, Mary, sister of Richard Shelvington (TALR RF#12:309).

ARTHERBURY
Thomas, m. by 1 June 1702, Martha, admins. of Basil Booth of CV Co. (INAC 22:1).

ARTHUR
Alexander (Athur), m. on 21 May 1704, Mary Smith (AAJA:28#17).
Archibald, of the Parish of St. Margaret Patents, m. by 22 Aug 1700, Ann, dau. of John Meekes, of Parish of St. Paul's Shadwell, chirurgeon, dec. (PGLR A:419, 422).
William, m. by April 1709, Grace, dau. of Thomas Thomas of SM Co. (PCJU TL#3:44).

ASA
[-?-], m. by 21 Feb 1710, Dinah, widow of 1st, [-?-] Nuthead, by whom she had a son William, and 2nd, Manus Devren of AA Co., carpenter (AALR PK:364).

ASBESTON
William, m. by 1 Jan 1654, Elizabeth, dau. of Robert Smith (*ARMD* 10:514, 515).

AS(H)COM(B)(E)
[-?-], d. by 1666 having m. Margery, widow of Wm. Batten. She m. 3rd John Bowles (MPL ABH: 202).
Nathaniel; 26 Dec 1706; Margaret Bigger (CVCH).
Richard, m. by 19 Dec 1688, Mary, dau. of John Hammond of BA Co., and widow of Samuel Brand, also of BA Co. (MDTP 14:124).

ASHCROFT
Thomas, m. by 1 July 1714, Susannah, extx. of William Hopkins of TA Co. (INAC 36A:39).

ASHFORD
Michael, m. by 13 Nov 1677, Rachel, dau. of Johanna, wife of Thomas Hussey (CHLR G:72).

ASHLEY/ASHLY
Isaac, m. on 9 July 1714, Mary Wroth (KESP:A1).
John, m. on 3 Aug 1714, Mary Wroth (See Isaac above) (KESP:A1).
John, m. on 14 Aug 1714, Martha Wroth (KESP:A1).
William, m. on 25 Jan 1718, Sarah ffuller (AAMA:85).

ASHMAN
George, m. by Feb 1685/6 Elizabeth, widow of William Cromwell, mother of Thomas Cromwell, and widow of William Ball (BAAD 1:349, 2:244; MDTP 13:294, 382).

ASKEN. See ASKIN.

ASKERS
John, m. 1659, Margaret Lane (MPL Q:70, 4:60).

ASKEW
John, m. by 1654, Margaret Sams (MPL 4:60, Q:70).
Michael, m. by 1699, Elizabeth, dau. of William and Priscilla Lisle (INAC 19:165, 166).
Richard, m. by 4 March 1690, Mary, widow and extx. of Edward Reeves (BALR IR#AM:68; BACP F#1:128; G#1:84; INAC 10:336; MDTP 15:8).

ASKIN
John (Askens), m. by c1654/9, Margaret Sams (MPL 4:60, Q:70).
John, m. by 25 Aug 1679, Rebecca, dau. of George Wright of SM Co., who named a grandson John Asken, Jr., in his will of that date (MWB 2:83).

John m. 2nd, by 1676, Rebecca, dau. of Daniel Clocker. She m. 2nd, Bryan Daly, and 3rd, Jno. Seamans (MWB 2:82; Liber 4:51; Hodges cites Pro. Court BB WRC:429; INAC 3:711; SMWB PC#1:99).

ASPENALL. See ASPINALL.

ASPINALL
Henry, m. by 8 March 1663/4, Mary, dau. of Walter Pakes (*ARMD* 49:168; PCJU BB:226, 287).
Capt. Henry, m. by 9 Dec 1676, Mary [-?-]; they were called brother and sister of the testator in the will of Henry Fletcher of CH Co. (MWB 5:138).
Henry, m. by Jan 1676/7, Mary, extx. of William Wilkinson of CH Co. (MDTP 8A:401).

ASTIN
John, and Sarah Pardoe, filed their intentions to marry on 26 d., 9 m., 1686 (WRMMa).

ATCHESON/ATCHISON
Vincent, m. by 1673, Hannah [-?-] (Hodges cites Warrants 17:579).
Vincent, m. by 11 Nov 1673, Hannah [-?-], whose sister Mary was wife and extx. of Lieut. William Smith and then of Garret Vansweringen (*ARMD* 65:127, 137; MPL 17:579).

ATCHINSON
Robert, m. by 2 Nov 1714, Elizabeth, admx. of Joseph Hull of KE Co. (INAC 36B:150).

ATHEY
John, m. on 4 June 1711, Margaret Lewis (PGKG:256).

ATHUR. See ARTHUR.

ATKINS
[-?-] (Attkins), m. after 1667, Ann, widow of Richard Pinner (*ARMD* 57:241; MPL GG:213, 11:235).
George, m. by 12 March 1666/7, [-?-], relict of Edward Pinner (*ARMD* 60:63).
John, m. by 10 April 1700, Mary, relict and extx. of Peter Sefferson [*sic*] of CE Co. (INAC 19½B:52)
John, m. on 20 Oct 1713, Mary Haynes (KESP:A1).
Joshua, m. on 28 Aug 1718, Mary Lyon (TAPE).
Robert (Attkins), m. on 10 June 1711, Eliza: Highway (WIST).

ATKINSON
Joseph, m. on 2 d. 2 m., 16599, Naomi Wright, both of DO Co., at the meeting house near Fishing Creek (TATH).

Richard, m. on 23 Jan 1705/6, Margaret Pickeren (AAAL 1:32(2)).

ATTAWAY/ATTOWAY
John, m. by Sep 1705, Susannah, extx. of Thomas Hatton of SM Co. (INAC 25:52, 111; Hodges cites Judg. 16:390).
Thomas (Atterway), m. by 1700, Joan, extx. of John Smith of CV Co. (Cotton cites INAC 19B:27).
Thomas (Attoway), of SM Co., m. by 19 Dec 1715, Susanna, dau. of Elizabeth Guibert of SM Co. (MWB 14:224).
Thos., of SM Co., d. by 20 May 1718, with Eliza Davis extx. (MDAD 1:48).

ATTERBERRY/ATTERBURY
Thomas, m. by 18 April 1700, Joan, admx. of John Smith (MDTP 18A:47; INAC 19½B:27).

ATTICK
John, m. on 4 Feb 1713, Elizabeth Barney (KESP:A1).

ATTKINS. See ATKINS.

ATTOWAY. See ATTAWAY.

ATWELL
John, m. on 11 Dec 1707, Margaret Horn (AAJA:35 #1).
Joseph, of TA Co., m. by 1707, Mary [-?-] (Hodges cites Judg. 11:80).

AURKHURT
Alexander, m. on 9 April 1705, Ann Barton (CVCH).

AUSTEN. See AUSTIN.

AUSTIN
Henry, m. by 1708, Eliza, widow of Robert Tyler (Hodges cites Judg. 11:139).
John, m. on 6 Jan 1712, Jane Sparks (CVCH).
Thomas, m. by Feb 1697, Susanna [-?-], mother of Humphrey, John and Susanna Posey (CHLR V#1:310). She m. 3rd, by 1690, Edward Philpot (CHLR Q#1:26; V#1:310).
William, of PG Co., m. by 1 Aug 1707, Ann, widow of [-?-] Walker (q.v.), and dau. of William Rought of CV Co. (PGLR C:210).
William, m. by 24 April 1714, [-?-], dau. of William Tippin, planter, of QA Co. (MWB 14:11).

AUTHORS
John, m. by 21 May 1714, Anne, admx. of John Cufney of SM Co., and by April 1715, [-?-], extx. of Henry Smith (INAC 36B:81; MDTP 22:460).

AVERY
John, 15 Feb 1674, prenuptial gift of land to Ann Daldson (DOLR 3 Old:124).

AVIS
Samuel, m. by 24 Jan 1715/6, Judith, admx. of George Husband of DO Co. (INAC 37A:34).

AXON
Matthew, m. by 23 Sep 1684, [Sarah], widow of Richard Bedworth and mother of Abraham, Richard, and John Thornberry (MWB 4:89).

AYLMER
Justinian, m. by April 1708, Isabella, admx. of William Reed (MDTP 21:18).

AYRES
Ambrose (Ayrris), m. on 18 Feb 1704/5, Margaret Pell (KESP:A1).
Edward, m. by 22 Nov 1666, Isabell, widow of Abraham Holman (MDTP 2:61).
George (Ayrs), m. by Dec 1699, Elenor, extx. of John Long (MDTP 18A:48).
Henry, m. by 11 Feb 1718, Comfort, dau. of Matthew Scarbrough of SO Co. (MWB 18:294).
John, m. by 30 Aug 1680, Ann, relict and admx. of Thomas Earle of TA Co. (INAC 7B:27).
Samuel (Airs), m. by Feb 1714/5, Judith, admx. of George Husband (MDTP 22:471).
Thomas, m. on 22 Jan 17--, Sarah Ingram (KESP:A1).
William, m. 1st, by June 1652, Sarah [-?-]; m. as his 2nd wife, Martha [-?-] (MPL ABH:348).
William (Aires), m. by 8 Nov 1717, Elizabeth, formerly the wife of James Chaplin, planter (TALR RF#12:305).

AYRRIS. See AYRES.

BACON
John, m. on 1 March 1714/5, Barbara Cruchly (AALR 1:38).

BAGBY
[-?-] (Baggaby), m. by 19 Oct 1709, Eliza, sister of Lawrence Riley of SO Co. (MWB 12, pt. 2:240).
John, m. on or about 10 Nov 1714, Mary, dau. of John Ford of CV Co. (*1 Harris and McHenry* 42, "Hemsley vs. Smith," *NGSQ* 53:109).

BAGGABY. See BAGBY.

BAGGOTT
[-?-], m. by 29 March 1714, Mary, dau of Thomas Hagoe (Hague?) of CH Co. (MWB 14:213).

BAGGS
    John, m. by 2 March 1708, Hannah, dau. of William Parrott (DOLR Old 6:131).

BAGNALL
    Ralph, m. by 7 July 1708, Rebecca, dau. of Samuel Vines, mentioned in account of John Holloway of CV Co. (INAC 28:158).

BAILEY/BAYLEY
    [-?-], m. by 22 Sep 1718, Anne, widow of Henry Lawrence of SM Co. (MDAD 2:327, 437).
    Charles (Bayley) of AA Co., m. by 7 Sep 1678, Mary (now dec'd), extx. of John Hawkins (AA) (MDTP 10:277).
    Henry (Bayly), m. on 21 July ---, Martha Harrell (PGKG:276).
    John, m. by 28 Aug 1680, Magdalen, widow and admx. of James Pean (INAC 7A:215).
    Richard, of AA Co., m. by Feb 1688/9, [-?-], widow of Mark Johnson (MDTP 14:135).
    Robert (Baly), m. in Aug 1714, Sarah Smith (AAMA:84).
    Thomas (Bayly), m. by 28 Sep 1694, Perseverance, dau. of Robert Wade of South R., AA Co. (MWB 7:6).
    Thomas (Bayly), m. on 30 Jan 1708/9, Catherine Mack---- (AAAN:1).
    William (Bayly), of PG Co., d. by 11 June 1703 when his extx. Jane had m. Richard Beven (INAC 24:16).
    William (Bayley), m. on 21 Oct 1705, Elizabeth Gill (AAAL).

BAINES
    Christopher, m. by 1671, Ann, sister of Charles Brooke of CV Co. (MPL 20:285).

BAISEY
    Michael, m. by 28 Jan 1652/3, [-?-], widow of Anthony Rawlings (the father of John Rawlings) (*ARMD* 10:213).

BAKER
    [-?-], m. by 26 Feb 1704, Martha, dau. of George Britt of CH Co. (MWB 3:485).
    Abraham, m. by 1682, [Mary], extx. of John Neck (*ARMD* 70:214, 328).
    Anthony, m. on 27 Oct 1714, Elizabeth Cassaday (KESP:B3).
    Charles, of SO Co., m. by 29 Jan 1666, Sarah, relict of John Elzey (*ARMD* 54:656).
    Charles, m. by 25 June 1711, [-?-], dau. of William Hawkins, Sr., of BA Co., who called Baker his son-in-law in his will of that date (MWB 13:213).
    John, m. by 1688, Elizabeth, admx. of John and Frances Catterton (Cotton cites INAC 10:183).
    John, m. on 18 May 1710, Hannah Williams (CVCH).
    John, m. by 1713 Ann [-?-] (SMWB HH: 237).
    John, m. by 18 Jan 1705, Ann, dau. of Thomas Courtney of SM Co. (MWB 12:54; INAC 37B:107).

Maurice, m. in Jan 1704, Sarah Nickels (AAMA:83).

Morris, m. on 9 Jan 1704/5, Sarah Nicholson, both of Westminster Parish (AAAN:19).

Thomas, of CH Co., d. by 10 Aug 1686 when his relict and extx. Ann had m. James Berry (INAC 9:131).

Thomas, m. by 15 Aug 1695, Elizabeth [-?-]; late of CH Co., but now of Richmond Co., VA (Hodges cites PCLR WRC: folio not given).

William, m. on 10 Jan 1704/5, Elizabeth Floyd (AAAN:19).

William, m. by 1709, Mary Merrill, dau. of Wm. and Eliza (MWB 13:137).

BALDING
[-?-], m. by 11 Aug 1684, Elizabeth, formerly Dorrell (AALR IH#1:225).

BALDRIDGE
Thomas, d. c1654, m. prob. in MD, Grace Beman; she m. 2nd, by 10 March 1655/6, John Tew (*NFMP*:171 cites Westmoreland Co., VA, Order Book 2:28).

BALDWIN
James, m. on 20 Jan 1714, Mary Tyler (PGQA:1).

John, m. after 12 Aug 1684, Hester, age 55 c1684, widow of 1st, William Gough, and 2nd, Nicholas Nicholson and dau. of John Larkin (MWB 14:30; INAC 7A:118, 10:225, 13A:313; *ARMD* 69:337-339, 70:292; AALR IT#5:18, 29; SY#1:62-63).

BALE
Anthony, m. on 18 June 1715, Ann Plummer (HAGE:33).

Thomas; At October Court 1697 Thomas Bale agreed to serve Wm. Hemsley for two years from the present because Hemsley allowed him to marry his servant Margrett Dehorty who had five years to serve, and whom Thomas Bale had gotten with child. Hemsley agreed to set them both free after the said two years and to keep the child (TAJU AB8:441).

BALE. See BALL.

BALL
Benjamin, m. by c1696, Martha, relict and extx. of Robert Freeland of CV Co. (INAC 13B:95).

Benjamin, m. by 2 Jan 1711, Susannah, widow of William, *als* Anthony Workman, and grandmother of Rhoda, Workman, and Susannah Harris, children of Isaac Harris (QALR ETA:96; MDTP 23:27).

Benjamin, of Kent Island, m. on 8 d., 5 m. (July), 1714, Elizabeth Richardson, dau. of William and Margaret, of AA Co. (WRMM).

Daniel, m. on 11 Aug 1718, Eleanor Gardner (AAJA:52#2).

Edward, m. by 9 Oct 1696, Priscilla, relict and admx. of William Lyle and of Henry Dikes (or Dukes), both of CV Co. (INAC 14:85, 86; 19:166, which gives Henry's name as Dukes).

Edward, of CV Co., m. by May 1699, Priscilla, relict of Col. William Lile (MDTP 17:323).

Hilary, m. by 2 Feb 1705, Ann, b. c1678/9, sister of James Wheeler; she m. 2nd, by 1726, [-?-] Scandall or Scandell [See Scandlen] (PGLR C:156, 175, M:28, RR:232).

John, m. on 19 Feb 17--, Sarah Johnston (PGKG:271).

John, m. on 14 Nov 1711, Anne Sash (AALR 1:38).

Richard, m. by 1 March 1661, Mary, wid. of Thomas Humphreys (*ARMD* 67:134 (says William Ball; BALR RM#HS:19).

BALLARD
Charles of SO Co., m. by 29 Jan 1666, Sarah, relict of John Elzey (*ARMD* 54:656).

BALLERIC
Francis (Ballery), m. by 22 April 1696, Elinor, admx. of Edward Frawner of CV Co. (INAC 13B:7).

BALLIN
William, m. by 24 Aug 1698, Margery, mother of Lydia who m. George Newman (MCHR PC:395).

BALSE
Oliver, d. by Jan 1671/2 when his admx. Margaret had m. Henry Adams of CH Co. (*ARMD* 60:361).

BALY. See BAILEY.

BANES
William, m. 26 Dec 1684, Anne Phesey (SOLR:IKL).

BANGALL
Alexander, m. in Jan ---, Elizabeth Viney (KESP:B1).

BANISTER
[-?-], m. by 7 mo., 1717, Mary, dau. of Alice Hall of SO Co. (MWB 18:253).

BANKS
George, m. by 1707, Catherine, admx. of Daniel Huntsman of SM Co. (INAC 26:303).

Henry, m. on 29 April 1716, Elizabeth Wickes (KESP:B3).

Nicholas, m. by 5 June 1676, [-?-], dau. of John Boon of TA Co. (MWB 7:232).

Lieut. Richard, m. by 10 April 1653, Margaret, widow of Richard Hatton, dec., who was bro. of Secretary Thomas Hatton (*ARMD* 10:259; MWB 1:65; MPL ABH:314, 422).

William, m. by 4 June 1717, Bridget, admx. of Daniel Shehawn of TA Co. (INAC 37B:45).

BARBER

Edward, joiner, of London, m. by 1683, Rebecca, dau. of Ralph Williams of AA Co., dec. (AALR IT#5:72-77).

James, m. on 18 d. 5 m., 1682, Mary Gush, both of TA Co., at the house of William Dixon (TATH).

John, m. 31 Aug 1680, Ann [Winne?] (SOLR:IKL).

John, m. on 23 April 1710, Sarah Pingston, *als.* James (AALR 1:37).

John, m. by June 1718, Frances, extx. of Matthew Ferrell (MDTP 23:194).

Dr. Luke (Barbour), d. by 6 Dec 1671, when his widow Elizabeth had m. John Blomfield (INAC 1:195; MWB 1:534; *ARMD* 5:102, 15:21, 51:334).

BARKER

[-?-], m. by 5 Sep 1698, Mary, admx. of Francis Watkins of BA Co (INAC 16:209).

Charles, m. on 13 Jan 1707/8, Anne Jones (AAAN:1).

John, m. by 25 Nov 1695, Mary, dau. and extx. of Henry Woolchurch of TA Co. (MWB 7:120; INAC 10:424, 426).

John, m. by 21 May 1706, Martha, dau. of Geo. and Eliza Brett (INAC 26:31; MWB 14:509; MDAD 26:31).

John, m. by 23 Jan 1712, Mary, extx. of Richard Way of CH Co. (INAC 34:184).

Richard, m. by 1708, Dorothy, widow of Thomas Hinton of CV Co. (INAC 29:400; MDTP 22:10; PCJU PL#2:704).

Samuel, m. on 15 Nov 1715, Mary Balard [Ballard?] (PGKG:242).

William, m. by 1685, Mary, dau. of Henry Woolchurch of TA Co. (MWB 7:120; Hodges cites PCJU 45:229, 242[?]).

William, m. by 1698, Mary, admx. of Francis Watkins of BA Co. (MDTP 17:202; INAC 16:209).

BARKLEY

Thomas, m. on 17 June 1709, Margrit Blaylock (WIST).

BARKSTON

Clement, m. by 23 Jan 1709, Katherine, extx. of Charles Sallyard (INAC 30:341).

BARLEIGH

Pasque, m. 21 Aug 1684, Hannah Keene (SOLR:IKL).

BARNES

[-?-], of CV Co., m. by June 1677, Sarah, widow of Nicholas Carre of CV Co. (MDTP 9A:263, 10:117).

[-?-], m. by 14 March 1702, Elinor, dau. of John Wilson of TA Co. (MWB 3:465).

[-?-], m. by 28 July 1702, Eliza, sister of James and John Ford of Herring Creek, AA Co. (MWB 11:272).

John, m. by 30 Aug 1672, [-?-], dau. of Walter Walterling (MWB 1:502).

John, m. by m. by 16 Nov 1678, Sarah, now age 18, dau. and coheir of Samuel Neale of SM Co. (MDTP 10:323).

John, m. by March 1705, [-?-], relict of William Viney (TAJR RF#10).

Matthew, m. by 18 July 1705, Elizabeth, dau. of Owen Jones; they had at least two children, Matthew, and Elizabeth (CHLR Z:208).

Matthew, m. by 23 July 1716, Sarah, admx. of Henry Guilford of CH Co. (INAC 37A:131).

Richard, m. 1 Feb 1672, Susanna Searle (SOLR:IKL).

Richard, m. on 28 July 1716, Sarah Stevens (AAAN:29).

William, m. on 18 Sep 1718, Susannah Davis (AAAN:40).

BARNETT

John, on 13 Nov 1683, banns of matrimony were published for him and Alce Taylor (SOJU O#7:11).

BARNEY

[-?-], m. by 16 Jan 1717, Elizabeth, dau. of Mary Stevenson (BALR TB#E:517).

Francis, m. on 3 Aug 1714, Ruth Alford (KESP:B3).

BARNWELL

James, m. by 8 March 1716, Elizabeth, sister of Lemmon John Catrup (TALR 12:273).

BARRATT

Darbey, m. on 21 Feb 1709, Catherine Vinton (TAPE). She was a dau. of Daniel Vinton (TALR RF#12:329).

Philip, m. by Oct 1686, Ann, relict of William Sinclair of CE or KE Co. (MDTP 13:426).

Phillip, m. by banns on 20 Feb 1710 by Mr. Sewell, Jane Merrit (CESS).

Philip, m. 3 May 1713, by Richard Sewell, Katherine Werrey, spinster (CESS).

William, m. on 13 Jan ---, Sarah Randal (KESP:B1).

BARRETT

John, m. by [c1700], Alice, extx. of Nicholas Corbin of BA Co. (INAC 20:47).

Thomas, m. on 5 Feb 1708, Mary Fossett (KESP:B2).

William, m. in Jan ---, Jane Rawlinson (KESP:B1).

BARRON

Joseph, d. by 23 Aug 1717 [This may be an error for 1727] when his widow Rachel had m. William Aldery (MDAD 8:482).

Robert, m. by 1717, Mary, dau. of Abraham Lemaster of SM Co. and CH Co. (SMWB PC#1:219; MWB 18:10).

Thomas (Barremand), m. by 9 Aug 1708, Elisabeth, admx. of Stephen Cheshire of SM Co. (INAC 28:293).

BARROW

[-?-], m. by 4 Aug 1718, Susanna, relict of Andrew Kinnimont (TALR RF#12:334).

Thomas, m. by 1710, Elizabeth, widow of Stephen Cheshire of SM Co. (SMWB HH:206).

BARRY

John, m. on 10 June 1712, Sarah Ridgely (AALR 1:38).

BARTLETT

Thomas (Barklett?), Jr., and Margaret Willson, who has children, filed their intentions to marry on 3 d., 9 m., 1704, and 1 d., 10 m., 1704 (WRMMa). She was Margaret, widow and extx. or admx. of Moses Wilson of AA Co. (INAC 25:419).

Thomas, m. by 28 Jan 1707, Elizabeth, extx. of James Ashbrook of CH Co. (INAC 28:99).

BARTON

John, m. on 1 June 1703, Hester Holmes (CVCH). She was extx. of Richard Holmes of CV Co. (INAC 25:366).

Richard, m. on 26 Dec 1705, Elizabeth Jyllingame (AAAL 1:32(2)).

William, m. by 1661, [-?-], relict of William Hungerford (*ARMD* 41:455).

William, m. by 1703, Sarah Waring, widow (MWB 3:643).

William, m. on 9 April 1705, Catherine Place (CVCH).

BARTWITH

[-?-], m. by 20 April 1717, Frances, dau. of Dorothy Taylor of DO Co. (MWB 14:527).

BASEY

Michael, of DO Co., m. by 3 Nov 1673, Joanna, mother of John Rawlings (DOLR 3 Old:25).

BASHTEEN

William, banns pub. March 1699/1700, Lydia Algood (HAGE:9).

BASSIL

Ralph, m. on 23 Sep 1697, Rose Hopper (AAAL 1:6).

BATCHELLOR

William, m. on 25 Dec 1714, Elizabeth Henricks (TAPE).

BATEMAN

George, m. by 15 March 1703, Mary, relict and admx. of William Jenkins of CH Co. (MWB 3:133).

Henry, m. on 22 Dec 1707, Sarah Powell (AAAN:1).

Ishmael, m. by 5 Oct 1704, Mary Boyd, dau. of John (MWB 3:635).

John, of London, m. by Nov 1662, d. by 24 Nov 1664; marriage settlement dated 14 Aug 1649, Mary, dau. of Margaret Perry of the City of Westminster, Mddx (*ARMD* 49:291, 57:50; MWB 1:192; MDTP 1D:138).

William, m. by May 1688, [-?-], admx. of John Wheeler (MDTP 14:78). In 1692 she was admx. of her son John Wheeler (MDTP15A:5).

William, m. 27 Jan 1696, Mary Wellen (AAAL).

William, m. on 14 Sep 1704, Elizabeth Westingcott or Westmycott) (KESP:B1).

William, m. by 2 Jan 1707, Abigail, dau. of Thomas Pierce of CE Co., who named their son William as his grandson (MWB 14:274).

BATES
John, m. by 1697, Sarah, widow of Roger Bishop of AA Co. (MDTP 16:118).

BATHERSHALL
Henry, m. in Dec ---, Rachel Rusk (KESP:B2).
Henry (Bathurshell), m. by 29 Oct 1711, [-?-], legatee of George Smith of KE Co. (INAC 33A:10).

BATIE
John, m. by Nov 1695, Sarah, extx. of Roger Bishop (INAC 15:180).

BATS
Thomas, m. in Aug ---, Prudence Passalt (KESP:B1).

BATSON
Edward, m. by 1 Oct 1706, Amy (or Ann), admx. of James Martin of CV Co. (INAC 26:55, 303; MCHR PC:605: PCJU PL#2:170, 185).

BATTEE
Benjamin, m. in Aug 1717, Ann Evans (AAJA:51#1).
Ferdinando, m. on 11 Dec 1718, Elizabeth Wooden (AAAL 2:16).

BATTEN
Capt. William, d. by 1662, having m. by c1651, Margery [-?-], she m. 2nd, [-?-] Ashcom, and had a dau. Lydia Ashcomb, and 3rd, by 1666 John Bowles (*ARMD* 53:269, 57:1151; MPL AB&H:202).

BAUGHER
[-?-], m. by 1707, Ann, relict of Charles Egerton (SMRR:1).

BAULDING
[-?-], m. by 1684, Elizabeth [-?-], formerly Dorrell (AALR IH#1:225-228).

BAXTER
Edward, m. by 29 April 1701, Margaret, admx. of Edward Cocknall of CV Co. (INAC 21:323).

Richard, m. by 1718, Ellinor, admx. of John Biscoe of SM Co. (MDAD 1:200-1; SMWB HH:190).

Roger, of KE Co., m. on 6 d, 11 mo., [1651?] Mary Crouch. She was the widow of the late George Crouch (*ARMD* 54:38, 45).

Thomas, of KE Co., m. on 19 Dec 1668, Hannah Fordah (*ARMD* 54:87).

Thomas, m. Elizabeth, widow and extx. of Thomas Marsh of QA Co.; she m. 3rd, by 28 Oct 1718, George Commerford (MDAD 1:208, 364; 6:413).

BAYLE
William, d. by 2 Aug 1709, having m. Elizabeth, sister of Charles James; they had a son William, who would be five years next Aug; she m. 2nd, Philip Kennard (KELR JS#N:141).

BAYLEY. See BAILEY.

BAYLOR
[-?-], m. by 16 May 1717, Bridget, dau. of Thos, Millmon of DO Co. (MWB 14:456).

BAYLY. See BAILEY.

BAYNARD
James, m. on about 33 years earlier (before 23 Aug 1714; say c1689), by Rev. James Clayland, at the house Richard Dudley in TA Co., to Elizabeth Blackwell (QALR ETA:62, cites a deposition by Rev. James Clayland).

Robert, m. by June 1714, Sarah (lately Hall), admx. of Richard Hall (QAJR June 1714:284).

Thomas, planter, m. on 19 d. 2 m., 1704, Esther Pratt, at Tuckahoe Meeting House (TATH).

BAYNE(S)
[-?-], m. by Jan 1679/80, Elinor, admx. of Matthew Hill of CH Co. (MDTP 11:284).

Dr. Christopher, m. by 1697, Elizabeth Higham (PGLR A:186).

Epsworth (Beyne), m. on 26 May 1717, Kenrick Rumney (AAAL 1:38).

Capt. Jno., m. by 1688, Ann Smallwood, relict of Thomas Gerrard of SM Co. (MDTP 14:67, 109; Cotton cites INAC 10:179; Hodges cites Judgements 6:307-317, 7:188, 15:232; CHLR R#1:256).

Ralph, Passenger on the *Ark/Dove*, d. by 24 April 1655, leaving a widow Elizabeth [-?-], who m. 2nd, by 9 Aug 1658, John Tonge of the Parish of St. Thomas, Southwark, Surrey, Citizen and Merchant Taylor (*NFMP*:174 cites *ARMD* 65:181).

Smallwood, m. by 1709, Charity Courts, dau. of Col. John Courts of CH Co. (MWB 12:208).

BAZEMAN
Joseph, m. on 13 July 1707, Mary Persias (AAJA:34 #8).

BEACH
Elias (Beech), m. by 25 March 1659, Sarah, dau. of William and Sarah Coale of St. Jerome's, SM Co. In 1679, she was named as a sister and admx. of Richard Cole (MWB 1:335; MDTP 3:251, 4B:28, 8:338; INAC 6:282).

BEADLE. See BEEDLE.

BEALE
John, of Resurrection Hundred, CV Co., m. on 30 July 1674, Joane Tyler, relict & admx. of George Reade of Resurrection Hundred, CV Co., and relict and extx. of Robert Tyler of Resurrection Hundred, CV Co. (MDTP 7:15).

John, m. by 22 June 1700, Eleanor, widow of 1st, John Stone, and 2nd, Hugh Tears, and dau. of Walter Bayne. (CHLR Z#2, 485; MDTP 19a:75, 78; INAC 33B:131).

John, m. on 19 Aug 1708, Elizabeth Norwood (AAAN:7).She was sister of Andrew Norwood (MCHR PC:825).

John, m. by 12 May 1718, [-?-], extx. of Francis Crompton of CH Co. (MINV 1:488).

Capt. Richard, m. by 1684, Audrey, sister of William Godwin (*ARMD* 5:421).

William, m. by 23 July 1712, Elizabeth, extx. of Ninian Beale of PG Co. (INAC 33B:17).

BEALL
[-?-], m. by 31 Dec 1711, Elizabeth, dau. of Samuel Magruder (INAC 33A:38).

James, Jr., m. by 27 Jan 1717, Mary, dau. of Archibald Edmondston (PGLR E:550, F:25).

Ninian, m. by 1669, Ruth, dau. of Richard and Jane Moore of SM Co. (Fresco cites *ARMD* 10:267).

William, m. by 20 May 1712, Elizabeth, extx. of William Beall (INAC 33A:179).

BEAN
John, m. by Dec 1687, Ann Gerard, dau. of Thomas Gerard of SM Co. (MDTP 14A:17; MDTP 13:519 says she was the relict and extx. of Thomas Gerard).

Capt. John (Beane), of CH Co., m. by Oct 1696, Margery, relict of Thomas Gerard of SM Co. (MDTP 16:197).

BEANES
William, m. by 22 Nov 1708, Elizabeth, admx. of Capt. James Bigger of PG Co. (INAC 29:31).

BEANS
Nathaniel, m. by April 1701, Ann, dau. of John Latham (MDTP 19A:5).

BEASON. See BESSON.

BEASWASSICKS
   William, m. on (date not given), Elizabeth Midland (KESP:B1).

BEAUCHAMP
   Edmond, m. 11 June 1668, Sarah Dixon, dau. of Ambrose and Mary Dixon (SOLR:IKL).
   Robert, m. by 28 May 1713, Elizabeth, admx, of Richard Tull, Jr., of SO Co. (INAC 34:229).
   Thomas, m. 9 Sep 1692, Mary Turpine (SOLR:IKL).

BEAVEN
   Charles, m. by 1713/ Mary, dau. of Thomas Lamar (Warrant Record AA(#7):221).
   John, m. by 3 Nov 1692, Sarah, widow of Benjamin Bennett (BALR RM#HS:361).

BEAVER
   Francis, m. in Feb ---, Elizabeth Sharby (KESP:B1).

BEAVIS
   Nathaniel, m. by 3 June 1701, Ann, dau. of John Latham, who lately died intestate (MDTP 19A:5).

BECK
   Edward, Jr., m. by 4 April 1710, Mary, widow and extx. of William Price of KE Co. (INAC 31:55).
   Edward, m. by 19 May 1712, Mary, dau. and heir of Robert Neeves (KELR JSN:282).
   Jonathan, m. by 3 Feb 1703, Mary, extx. of John Atkey (MDTP 9B:21).
   Jonathan, m. by 14 June 1704, Mary, widow of John Atkinson, all of CE Co. (CELR 1:394).
   Matthew, m. on 14 Sep 1713, Mary Ashly (KESP:B2).
   Richard, m. by 16 Aug 1687, Mary, sole heiress of Robert Page (TALR 5:115).
   Vivian, m. on 6 Sep ---, Sarah Randall (KESP:B1).0 He m. the widow of Robert Randall by 15 March 1703, [-?-] (MWB 3:64).
   Vivian, m. by 28 May 1718, Elizabeth, admx. of Richard Barker of CV Co. (INAC 38A:43).
   Vivian (Beek), m. by 10 Sep 1717, Dorothy, admx. of Thomas Hynten of CV Co. (INAC 37B:170).

BECKETT
   Humphrey d. by 1712 leaving a son John, and a widow Hester who m. Hugh Abrahams. Beckett may have been the father [or father-in-law] of Elizabeth Becraft and Mary Rodecy (Ref. not clear: Hodges cites Wills? 1:?67).
   Humphrey, m. on 28 Aug 1712, Dorcas Brown (AAAL 2:9).

BECKWITH

[-?-], m. by c1677, Elisabeth, relict and admx. of Thomas Skinner of DO Co. (INAC 5:150).

Charles, m. by 1697, Eliza Hill Keen, widow of Richard Keen, and dau. of Francis Hill of SM Co. (MDWB 2:325, 7:295); MDTP 16:91; 17:319, 321; 19a:161).

Charles, m. by 1717, Ann, dau. of Christian Barbara Cooper of SM Co. (MWB 14:651; SMWB PC#1:179; MDTP 23:126).

George, of CV Co., m. by Oct 1657, Frances, dau. of Nicholas and Jane Harvey, dec. (*ARMD* 10:259, 548, 65:679; MWB 6:1; INAC 9:476; MCHR PC:433).

Nehemiah, planter, m. on 10 d. 5 m., 1712, Frances Taylor, both of DO Co., at the meeting house at Transquaking, DO Co. (TATH). She was a dau. of John Taylor of DO co. (Warrant Record AA(#7):366).

BEDDINGFIELD

Anthony, m. by 31 May 1705, Mary, dau. of William Jones, Sr., of AA Co., planter (MWB 3:489).

BEDWORTH

Richard, of AA Co., d. by 26 Feb 1683, having m. Sarah, mother of Abraham, Richard, and John Thornberry; she m. 2nd, Matthew Axon (MWB 4:16, 89).

BEECH. See BEACH.

BEECHER

John, m. by 21 Feb 1693, Edith, widow of Christopher Gist, and of Joseph Williams (BALR RM#HS:417; MDTP 15C:88).

John, m. by 25 April 1702, Susannah, admx. of Thomas Heiford of AA Co. (INAC 21:342; AAJU TB#1:559).

BEECKE

Elias, d. by 21 Feb 1675, having m. Elizabeth Loquer, sister of Thos. Loquer (MDTP 7:306).

BEEDLE

Edward, d. by 30 Dec 1696, leaving two daus.: Martha, extx. of George Goldsmith, and wife of John Hall, and Mary, widow of George Utie (BALR IS#IK:241, 245; BACP G#1:201).

Henry, m. by 12 Nov 1673, Sophia, extx. of Richard Wells of AA Co. (*ARMD* 51:427; 65:145).

John, Jr., m. by banns on 2 Feb 1715 by Mr. Sewell, Mary Mounce (CESS).

Thomas (Beadle), m. by banns on 1 Jan 1717, Elizabeth Boulding, spinster (CESS).

William, m. on 23 Dec 1703, Mary Williams (AAAL).

BEEK. See BECK.

BEESLEY
Abraham, m. on 22 Aug 1717, Mary Neal (TAPE).

BEESTON
William, m. by banns on 19 Dec 1706 by Rich. Sewell, Sarah Chisups, spinster (CESS).

BEETENSON
Edmund, m. by 31 July 1680, Lydia, relict and extx. of Thomas Watkins of AA Co. (INAC 7A:172; MPL 24:287, 28:148).

BELAINE
George, m. (before 1676) Elizabeth, relict of 1st, Francis Posey; she m. 3rd, by Aug 1676, Alexander Smith (MDTP 11:172).
John, m. by 12 April 1669, [-?-], widow of Francis Posey (CHLR H#1:248; MDTP 11:100, 172).

BELCHER
John, banns pub. Feb., m. on 16 March 1706, [-?-], Widow Perkins (HAGE:18). She was Mary, admx. of Richard Perkins (BAAD 2:88; INAC 28:260).

BELL
[-?-], m. by 13 Nov 1687, Mary, sister of Arnold and Thomas Parramore of SO Co. (MWB 6:32).
Adam, d. by 1718 having m. Ann, sister of Richard Hopewell; Ann also m. Thomas Aisquith (Hodges cites SMWB PC#1:247; MDAD 6:133).
Andrew, m. on 30 Oct 1703, Mary Boucher (AAJA:28#3).
Anthony, m. 25 Dec 1687, Abigail Roatch (SOLR:IKL).
David (Beall), m. by c1701, Rose, admins. of George Bruise [Bruce?] of AA Co. (INAC 20:117).
John, m. by 16 March 1700/1, Sarah, dau. of Sarah Peerce, and granddau. of Thomas Sprigg (PGLR A:362).
John, m. on 2 April 1703, Susanna Higgdon [*sic*] (TAPE).
John, m. by 24 July 1710, Elinor, widow and acct. of Nicholas Baker of PG Co. (INAC 32A:32).
Matthew (Bell?), of CV Co., m. by July 1668, Mary, admx. of Thomas Johnson (MDTP 13:373).
Richard, m. on 28 Aug 1704, Jane Denhoe, spinster (CESS).

BELLOWS
Francis, m. in Nov ---, Margaret Ayures (KESP:B2).

BELT
John, and Lucy Lawrence filed their intentions to marry on 2 d., 11 m., 1701, and on 30 d., 11 m., 1701/2, with consent of their parents (WRMMa). John, m. 10 Feb 1701 at a Quaker meeting "connivingly," Lucy Lawrence the betrothed

wife of Joseph Tilly, "which action is contrary to the law of God and man" (AAAL 1:21(2)).
    Joseph, of PG Co., m. by 10 March 1706, Hester, dau. of Ninian and Ruth Beall of PG Co. (PGLR C:186).

BENGER
    Robert (Benjar), m. by 29 Feb 1677, Katherine, admx. of John Shadwell (BAAD 2:41; INAC 4:631, 632; 7A:9; MDTP 9:335).
    Robert, of BA Co., m. by April 1678, [-?-], dau. of Margaret Therrell of BA Co. (MDTP 10:36).
    Robert, of CE Co., m. by May 1688, [-?-], relict of Nicholas Shaw (MDTP 14:72).

BENHAM
    William, m. by Feb 1686, [-?-], distributive heir of Maj. William Coursey of TA Co. (INAC 10:155).

BENJAR. See BENGER.

BENNET(T)
    [-?-], m. by 2 April 1718, Mary, dau. of George Young of CV Co. (MWB 14:613).
    Disborow, m. on 21 April 1676, Mary Wells (*ARMD* 54:318). He d. by Feb 1677/8 when his admx., Mary, admx. of Tobias Wells, had m. [as her third husband] Lewis Blangy (*ARMD* 67:208; MDTP 9:184). She was mother of Mary, Tobias, Sarah, and John Wells (MWB 5:294).
    James, m. on 12 Sep 1708, Mary [-?-] (KESH:6).
    John, on 28 Jan 1683/4, banns of matrimony were published for him and Sarah Furnis (SOJU O#7:18). **John, m. on 6 Feb 1683, Sarah Furnis.** She was a dau. of William Furnis (*ARMD* e90 (SOJU L):18; *ARMD* e91 (SOJU AW reverse):49).
    John, m. by 8 June 1689, Sarah, widow of John Homewood (AALR IH#1:298; TALR 5:342).
    Peter, m. by Aug 1717, [-?-], widow of Benjamin Peck (TAJR FT#1).
    Richard, m. by 1665, Henrietta Maria Neale, dau. of Capt. James Neale (MWB 1:278).
    William, m. on 6 Nov 1713, Ann Chinton (AAAN:9).

BENNISON
    Richard, m. by 12 March 1705, [-?-], mother of Mary Ball, who m. as her third husband, Edward Peake (AALR WT#2:336).

BENSON
    [-?-], m. by 25 April 1693, Grace, dau. of Robert Houston of SO Co. (MWB 2:407).
    Edward, m. on 15 --- 1714, Hannah Hammond, widow of Charles (AAAN:22). She was the extx. of Charles Hammond (AAJU RC:269).
    George, m. May 1682 Anne Roberts (SOLR:IKL).
    John, m. by 1696, Elizabeth, dau. of Thomas Smith of CV Co. (MWB 5:148).

Philip, m. on 23 Sep 170-, Ann Citto (KESP:B2).

BENTHAM
Richard, of St. Jerome's Neck, SM Co., m. between 1675 and 1686, Sarah, widow of William Cole. She also m. William Cole and Alexander Younger (Hodges cites Prov. Court WRC#1:4, 407, 416; MDTP 4B:29).

BENTLEY
Stephen, m. by Nov 1693, Ann, relict of Phillip Pissions(?), and formerly wife of William Pearle (BACP F#1:300, 307).
Stephen, m. by 19 Jan 1714/5, [-?-], mother of William Pearle (MCHR CL:109).
William (Bently), m. by 13 Jan 1706, [-?-], dau. of Daniel Norris of KE Co. (MWB 12:242; KELR G#1:108-111).

BENTLY. See BENTLEY.

BENTON
Mark, m. by c1702, Mary, admx. of John Dobbs of TA Co. (INAC 23:87).
Peter, m. by July 1713, Comfort, extx. of Isaac Coston (PCJU VD#1:334).

BERAUS
William, m. by 20 Dec 1715, Mary, dau. of Walter Lane, planter, of SO Co. (MWB 14:282).

BERBERFIELD
Henry, m. by 21 May 1689, Elizabeth, sister of William Parker of CV Co. (AALR PK:66).

BERKHEAD. See BIRCKHEAD.

BERKUM
Roger, m. 10 Dec 1681, Lucia (or Anna) Jones (SOLR:IKL).

BERREY. See BERRY.

BERRY
[-?-], m. by 12 Aug 1679, Margaret, sister of Thomas Marsh of KE Co. (MWB 10:52).
[-?-], m. by 2 Feb 1697, Mary, dau. of Thomas Hillery of CV Co. (MWB 7:321).
[-?-], m. by 23 Jan 1717, Margaret, dau. of Duncan Monroe of QA Co. (MWB 14:595).
Edmund, m. on 23 Nov 1708, Mary Procter (TAPE).
George, m. on 6 Feb 1714 Mary Cox (SJSG:5).
George, d. by 21 Sep 1717, having m. Mary, dau. of Simon Pierson (MWB 14:545).

Henry, m. 2 June 1700, Susanna Clements, servant of Joseph Hanslap (AAAL 1:21(1)).

James, m. by 1686, Anne, relict of John Wynne of SM Co. (INAC 9:132).

James, of TA Co., boatwright, m. on 14 d. 2 m., 1686, Sarah Woolchurch, spinster, at the house of Henry Woolchurch, TA Co. (TATH). She was a dau. of Henry Woolchurch (TALR 5:258). Berry d. by 14 March 1697, and his widow Sarah m. 2nd, Henry Parrott (TALR LL#7:195).

James, of CV Co., m. by July 1686, Ann, admx. of James Milson (MDTP 13:371).

James, m. by 10 Aug 1686, Ann, relict and extx. of Thomas Baker of CH Co. (INAC 9:131).

James, of TA Co., planter, m. on 11 d. 12 m., 1691, Elizabeth Pitt, at the house of John Pitt (TATH).

John, carpenter, m. on 10 d. 8 m., 1711, Ann Pratt, both of TA Co. (TATH). She was a dau. of John Pitt, merchant, of TA Co., who named his grandson James Berry in his will (MWB 14:377).

John, m. on 27 Dec 1711, Esther Foster (KESP:B2).

Nathaniel, m. on 8 July ---, Jane Hem (KESP:B1).

Samuell, m. on 28 Oct 170-, Martha Griffith (KESP:B2).

Thomas, boatwright, m. on 4 d. 3 m., 1699, Sarah Godard, both of TA Co., at Third Haven meeting house (TATH).

Thomas, m. by 16 Oct 1703, Honrica, dau. of Henry Stockett (AALR WT#2:79).

William, marriage contract dated 8 Jan 1669, to marry Margaret Preston (*ARMD* 57:469). She was the widow of Richard Preston (MDTP 3:297).

BESON. See BESSON.

BESSON
    Capt. Thomas, m. by 27 March 1679, Hester, widow of Henry Caplin of AA Co. (*ARMD* 51:262).

    Thomas, Jr., m. 5 March --- in South River, MD, Margaret Saughier, b. 11 --- 1646 in VA, dau. of George Saughier ("Jones Bible Records," *MG* 2:107).

BESTON
    George, m. by 9 April 1699, Jane, relict and admx. of James Taylor of CE Co. (INAC 18:224).

BESWICK
    [-?-], d. by 23 Aug 1714, having m. Ann, sister of Richard Carter of MD (AALR IB#2:170).

BETTS
    George, m. 7 Nov 1669, Bridget Bossman (SOLR:IKL).

BETTY
    Arthur, m. by 26 Feb 1713/4, [-?-], mother of Joseph, Benjamin, and James Woodard, and Martha Person, Mary Parck, and Rachel Vickers (MWB 13:667).

BEVAN
Thomas, m. by 12 Oct 1691, Pretitia, or Pretiosa, extx. of William Ramsey of AA Co. (TALR 5:331; AALR IH#3:91 states she was the dau. of Ramsey).

BEVEN
Richard, m. by 11 June 1703, Jane, extx. of William Bayly of PG Co. (INAC 24:16).
Rowland, on 27 Dec 1670, the bands [*sic*] of matrimony were published between him and Margarett Price both of this County; on 1 Jan 1670 a Certificate [was] past out for the said Rowland Bevend & Margarett Price none having to this day alleged any thing against them upon record (*ARMD* e86 (SOJU DT#7):53).
Rowland (Bevels), m. 4 Aug 1672, Mary [Beware?] (SOLR:IKL).

BEVINS
[-?-], m. by 1 March 1711/2, Elizabeth, extx. and relict of Thomas Strickland, dec. (KELR JSN:277).
Thomas (Bevings), m. on 8 July 1700 [-?-] [-?-] (HAGE:11).

BEYNE. See BAYNE.

BIBBY
John, m. on 12 Nov ---, John [*sic*] [Joan?] Mackarthy (KESP:B1).

BICKARDIKE
Richard, m. on 16 Oct 1704, Ann Smith (AAAN:19

BIDDINGFIELD
Anthony, 12 Feb 1701, Mary Throgdon or Hogdon, widow (AAAL 2:2).

BIDDLICUM
Mr. William, of "Wincansun in the County of Loundin, [This may have been in Co. Somerset, Eng.]" m. by 9 Aug 1677, Mary, sister and heir of John Vining of Chester R., planter (KELR K:31).

BIGGER
James, m. by 10 Aug 1686, Margaret, extx. of James Nuthall (INAC 9:98; 10:184).
Col. John, m. by 9 Oct 1702, Ann, widow and admx. of William Head of CV Co. (INAC 22:42; MWB 14:14).

BILLINGSLEY
Francis, m. by 1670, Martha Merritt of CV Co. (Hodges cites Prov. Court J or JJ: 185).
Francis, m. by 1713, Susannah Gover, of CV Co. (Hodges cites Rent Roll 1:2).
James (Billingslea), m. by 7 Dec 1663, Susannah, sister of Richard, John, Anne, and Sophia Ewen, and Eliza Talbott, and Susanna Burgess (MWB 1:99).

BILLITER
    Thomas, m. on 14 Aug 1715, Sarah King (TAPE).

BINLEY
    John, m. by 1686, Blanche, relict of Wm. Stanton (Hodges cites "Liber 9":124).

BIRCH
    [-?-], m. by 10 March 1716/7, Mary, dau. of Mary Rose of Chaptico Hundred, SM Co. (MWB 15:376).

BIRCKHEAD
    Abraham, and Rebecca Billingsley, filed their intentions to marry on 18 d., 10 m., 1691 (WRMMa). She was a dau. of Francis Billingsley of CV Co. (MWB 7:163).
    Nehemiah (Birkhead), m. in 1682, Elizabeth Sloper (WRMM).
    Nehemiah, and Sarah Hutchins filed their intentions to marry on 1 d., 9 m., 1706, and 29 d., 9 m., 1706 (WRMMa).
    Nehemiah, m. on 24 d., 6 m., 1712, Margaret Johns (WRMM).
    Solomon, and Anne Child filed their intentions to marry on 24 d., 1 m., 1703/4, and on 21 d., 2 m., 1704 (WRMMa).

BIRD
    John, m. by Nov 1680, Eliza, extx. of Henry Lewis (*ARMD* 69:270, 366; INAC 7B:8; MPL LL:842, 15:565).
    John, m. by Nov 1684, [-?-], wid. of James Armstrong (BACP D:212).

BIRK
    Tobias, m. on 2 May 1708, Ann Bromigan (AAAN:7).

BIRUM
    William, m. in July ---, Hannah Chandler (KESP:B1).

BISCO(E)
    James, m. by 9 July 1686, Sarah, admx. of Charles Priest of SM Co. (INAC 9:45).

BISHOP
    [-?-], m. by 15 Feb 1702/3, Abigail, dau. of Thomas Poynter, Sr., of SO Co. (MWB 12:9).
    [-?-], m. by 30 Jan 1709, Rebecca, dau. of John Batie of AA Co. (MWB 14:391).
    Benoni, m. by 22 Oct 1677, Sarah, relict and extx. of Benjamin Hancock of TA Co. (INAC 4:452).
    David, on 8 Aug 1671, banns of matrimony were published for him (certificate given 30 Aug 1671) and Sarah Persell (SOJU DT#7:182).
    Emanuell, m. on 30 May 1705, Sarah [-?-] (AAAN:19).
    Henry, of VA, m. by 1672 Ann, mother of David, William, and Mary Bowen (MPL 17:388).

William, m. by Jan 1708/9, [-?-], widow of Thomas Lucas (MDTP 21:78).

BITTISON
[-?-], m. by 12 June 1682, Lydia, mother of Thomas Watkins, and dau. of John Baldwin of South River, AA Co. (MWB 4:43).
John, m. 21 Dec 1672, Mary Bowen (SOLR:IKL).

BLACKFAN
[-?-], m. by Aug 1676, Mary, relict of Thomas Stone of CH Co. (MDTP 8A:171).
John, m. by 1682, Mary, widow of Joseph Manning (Cotton cites INAC 7C:253).

BLACKISTON(E)
[-?-], m. by 27 Nov 1712, Sarah, dau. of Thomas Joce of KE Co. (MWB 13:486).
[-?-], m. by Nov 1712, Anne, sister of Luke Guibert (MDTP 22:276).
Ebenezer, of CE Co., m. by 13 Oct 1679, [-?-], admx. of William Pike of AA Co. (INAC 6:474).
John, of SM Co., m. by 16 Feb 1713, Ann, dau. of Joshua Guibert of SM Co. (MWB 13:593, 14:224). She was a sister of Luke Guibert, and a dau. of Elizabeth Guibert of SM Co. (MDTP 22:276; MWB 14:224).
Capt. Nehemiah, m. by 1669, Elizabeth, dau. of Thomas Gerard (Hodges cites MWB 13:593; Prov. Court NN:784; MDCR 3:1014; MDTP 19A:153).
Capt. Peter (Blackstone), m. on 17 March 1701, Elizabeth [-?-] (TAPE).

BLACKLEACH. See BLACKLEDGE.

BLACKLEDGE
Benjamin (Blackleach), m. by 1687, Hannah, b. c1671, dau. of William and Lucy Gallaway of CE Co., and sister of James and William Gallaway. She m. 1st, c1727, [-?-] Clove of KE Co. (KELR JS#X:409, 416; CELR 2:19).

BLACKMAN
Wm., m. by 1703, Sissly, widow of Jno. Kelly (SMWB HH:120; MDAD 13:319).

BLACKMOOR
William, m. by 6 Aug 1703, Sislly, widow and admx. of John Kelly of SM Co. (INAC 24:210).

BLACKSTON(E). See BLACKISTON.

BLACKWELL
Thomas, m. by Dec 1692, Sarah, widow of John Dorsey of AA Co. (INAC 10:314; MDTP 15A:3).
Thomas, m. by March 1699, Sarah, extx. of [-?-] Newton, widow of John Newton (MDTP 17:273).

BLADEN
William, m. by 29 April 1696, Ann, dau. of Mary, and sister of Joseph Vanswearingen, widow of SM Co. (MWB 13:557; SMWB PC#1:190; Hodges also cites Judgements 22:186, and *ARMD* 25:265).

BLAKE
Charles, m. by 1697, Henrietta Maria, dau. of Philemon and Henrietta Maria (Neale) Lloyd, of QA co. (MDTP 17: 3, 4, 5, 6).
John, m. by Sep 1708, Elizabeth co-exec. of Thomas Pointer (MDTP 21:57).
Thomas, m. by 6 Oct 1694, Jane, admx. of Robert Webb of CV Co. (INAC 13A:209).
Thomas, m. by 13 Oct 1697, Jane, admx. of Edward Isaack of CV Co. (INAC 15:230).

BLAND
Thomas, m. by 30 Aug 1675, Damaris, relict and extx. of Nicholas Wyatt of AA Co. (INAC 2:246; *ARMD* 51:153; 66:xxix, 247; MDTP 7:59, 8:46, 75, 87, 94; MDTP 7:57).

BLANDEL
Laurence, m. on 27 April 1712, Elizabeth Hesket (AAJA:41 #16).

BLANEY
David, d. by 11 Sep 1700, when his extx. Catherine had m. William Alderne (INAC 20:54).

BLANFORD
[-?-], m. by 27 June 1709, Eliza, sister of Martha Lamar and of Richard Bevan (MWB 13:30).
Thomas, m. by 13 June 1678, Tabitha, relict and extx., of William Mills of CV Co. (INAC 5:146).

BLANGEY
Jacob, m. on 27 May 1703, Elizabeth Merriken, dau. of Joshua Merriken, Sr. (AAMA:81; INAC 38A:75).

BLANGY
Lewis (sometimes written as Blaney), m. by 24 May 1678, Mary, admx. of Tobias Wells of KE (INAC 5:193; *ARMD* 67:28). He m. by 30 July 1679, Mary, relict of Disborough Bennett of KE Co. (INAC 6:261, 7A:33; *ARMD* 51:205; 68:49; MDTP 9:184).

BLAY
Edward, m. between 1686 and 1695, Barbara, dau. of James Ringgold. She also m. Josias Lanham (MWB 4:232; MDTP 16:84).
Edward, m. by March 1695/6, Ann, relict of Robert Burman (MDTP 16:142).

Edward, of CE Co., m. by 7 April 1697, Anne, extx. and widow of Henry Staples (KELR M:62b).

BLEAMER
John, m. on 2 Aug 1718, Jane Cotter (TAPE).

BLINKHORNE
Robert, m. by 8 Oct 1701, Martha, extx. of John Holloway of CV Co. (INAC 21:145, 28:158).

BLIZARD
George, m. on 16 Oct 1684, Susanna, dau. of John Cane (CHLR S:286).
George, m. by 16 June 1704, Sarah, dau. of Benjamin Aydolett (Idolett) of SO Co. (MWB 3:262).
John, m. by 16 June 1704, Mary, dau. of Benjamin Aydolett (Idolett) of SO Co. (MWB 3:262).

BLO(O)MFIELD
John, m. by 6 Dec 1671, Elizabeth (nee Younge), relict of Luke Barber of SM Co. (*ARMD* 5:98, 102, 15:21, 51:334; INAC 1:192).

BLUNDELL
Richard, m. by 21 March 1704/5, Dorothy, admx. of Michael Taney of CV Co. (INAC 25:139; MDTP 19B:80).

BLUNT
Richard, on 12 Feb 1675 named a dau.-in-law Grace Harrington (INAC 2:113).
Richard, m. by 14 Feb 1675, [-?-] widow of William Howard of CE Co. (MDTP 7:258).

BOANAM. See BOWMAN.

BOARMAN
Capt. [-?-] (Boreman), m. by 9 Jan 1675, Mary, dau. of Thomas Matthews of CH Co. (MWB 5:53).
Maj. [-?-], m. by 16 June 1696, [-?-], relict of Nicholas Clouds who was a legatee of John Gouldsmith of SM Co. (INAC 13B:112).
Robert (Bourman), m. by 1688, Anna, widow and extx. of Henry Staples of TA Co. (Cotton cites INAC 10:340, 11:515),
Maj. William, m. by 1686, 1st, Mary, dau. of Col. John Jarboe, and 2nd, Jane [Cane?] (Hodges cites Prov. Court WRC#1:396, 398, FF:489).
William, m. by 27 Nov 1683, Jane, dau. of James Neale (MWB 4:40).
Maj. William, m. by 1698, Catherine, dau. of Baker and Ann (Calvert) Brooke (Hodges cites SMWB PC#1:114; MDTP 13:?; and Kilty)
William, Jr., m. by 11 Oct 1701, Mary, dau. of Joseph Pile of SM Co. (INAC 21:149, 26:192).

BODELL
Thomas, m. [by c1666?], Jane (or Jone), relict of Stephen Clifton of CV Co.
(MDTP 2:106).

BODY
Peter, m. 28 Dec 1686, Frances, dau. of Stephen Cannon (SOLR:IKL).
Philip, m. by c1696, Sarah, admx. of Thomas Robinson of CV Co. (INAC
13B:103).
Philip, m. by 9 April 1707, Sarah, sister of John Godsgrace (INAC 26:340).

BOLTICK
[-?-], m. by 26 March 1718, Mary, dau. of John Nicholson of QA Co. (MWB
14:595).

BOLTON
[-?-], m. by 10 Feb 1684, Elizabeth, late wife of Richard Bennett of AA Co.
(BALR RM#HS:110).
John, m. by Nov 1685, Dorothy Crandon (BACP D:358).

BOND
Jeremiah, m. by 1718, Anne, admx. of George Hoskins (MDAD 1:41).
John, m. by 26 Feb 1712/3, Mary, admx. of Samuel Standiford (BAAD 1:370,
2:172; INAC 34:56).
Peter, m. by June 1678, Alice, widow of William Drury (*ARMD* 67:407). Drury
had bequeathed the greatest portion of his estate to his daughter Christian Drury
(MDTP 10:191). Hugh Merriken was brother of the half blood to Christian Drury, dau.
of said William (MDTP 10:192).
Richard, of CV Co., m. on 24 d., 7 m. (Sep), 1702, Elizabeth Chew of AA Co.
(WRMM). She was the extx. of Benjamin Chew (MDT{P 22:423).
Stephen, m. 6 June 1673, Jane Sewell (SOLR:IKL). He d. by 1678, having m.
Jane, mother of Mary Sewell (MPL 15:523, 18:35, 37).
Thomas, m. 20 Sep 1700, Ann Robison of BA Co. (AAAL 2:1).
William, m. by 8 March 1710, Mary, heir of William Westbury (BALR TR#A:63).

BONFF
Thomas, m. by 19 Feb 1704, [-?-], relict and admx. of Joseph Wickes of KE Co.
(INAC 25:171).

BONNER
Henry, m. by Dec 1670, Eliza Storey, admx. of Walter Storey (*ARMD* 51:37, 44).
Henry, m. by 1 Sep 1674, Elizabeth, widow of John Taylor (*ARMD* 60:579).

BONNES
John, in Jan 1693/4, posted an affidavit granting his wife Mabel freedom to go
where she pleases; this was an agreement to separate and not trouble or molest each
other (SOJU LD:75).

BOOKER

[-?-], m. by 20 June 1713, Eliza (of Nanjemy, CH Co.), mother of William, George, and Henry Brett, Mary Gray, and Margaret Duninton (MWB 13:512).

John, m. by Aug 1693, Ann, extx. of Richard Price (MDTP 15A:62; INAC 13A:14).

John, m. by 8 July 1718, Eliza Brothers of AA Co. (MDAD 1:11).

Richard, m. on 5 Dec 1700, by Mr. Benjamin Nobbs, minister, Sarah [-?-] (TAPE).

Thomas, planter, m. on 3 d. 11 m., 1696, Ellinor Orum, both of TA Co.; dau. of Andrew Orum, at the meeting house near Tuckahoe Creek (TATH).

BOON(E)

John, m. by 5 June 1707 Jane, widow of John Durham, and sole heir of Francis Trippols(?) (BALR RM#HS:553 and IR#AM:60).

Robert, m. on 17 Sep 1702, Elizabeth [-?-] (AAMA:81).

Robert, m. by Sep 1707, Eliza, dau. of Richard Moss (AAJU TB#1:616)

William, m. by 8 Aug 1705, Margaret, extx. of William Purnell of TA Co. (INAC 26:21).

William, m. by 1 March 1709/10, Margaret, dau. of William Jump of QA Co. (MWB 13:414).

BOOTH

John, m. by 24 Feb 1663/4, [-?-], relict of Thomas Ringe (MDTP 1E:91).

John, m. on 19 Sep 1712, Margaret Gilberd (TAPE).

Peter, m. by Nov 1709, Margaret, admx. of Thomas Surman or Sermon, and mother of Peter, John, Alexander, Thomas, Isaac, Rachel, and Edward Sermon (MWB 13:415, SOJU 1707-1711:276).

Robert, m. on (date not given), Sarah Filmoore (PGKG:241).

BOOTHBY

Charles, m. by 1 July 1718, Margaret, extx. of Alexander Stuart of AA Co. (MDAD 1:20).

Edward, m. by 7 Sep 1686, Elizabeth, widow of Col. Nathaniel Utie of BA Co., and of Henry Johnson (INAC 12:143, 145, 19½b:67, 28:143; BAAD 2:118).

BORDLEY

Stephen, m. on 14 Oct 1700, Ann Hynson (KESP:B1). She was a dau. of John Hynson of KE Co. (KELR JD#1:64).

Thomas, m. on 26 Dec 1708, Rachael Beard (AAAN:7).

BORING

John, m. by 1677, Margaret, widow of Roger Sidwell of BA Co. (MDTP 9:337; INAC 6:423).

John, m. by 15 Sep 1711, Mary, dau. of John Kemp who left Claybank to his dau. Mary (MWB 4:239; BALR TR#A:171).

BORK
[-?-], m. by 6 Oct 1717, Cislye, mother of Edward, Elizabeth, Ann and Rachel Alford (MWB 14:455).

BORMAN. See BOWMAN.

BORRIS
William (Borritt), m. on 21 Feb 1703, Mary Walker (AAJA:28#11).

BORRITT. See BORRIS.

BOSMAN
[-?-], m. by 13 April 1717, Sarah, dau. of Randall Revell, yeoman of SO Co. (MWB 14:622).
George, m. by 10 June 1690, Jane, relict & extx. of Mr. William Jones (SOJU 1691-1692: 19).

BOSTICK
Samuel of CE Co., m. by 20 May 1709, Jane, dau. of Thomas King (CELR 1:502).

BOSTOCK
[-?-], m. by (no date), Elizabeth, widow of John Nicholson of AA Co. (AALR IH#1:219, 229).

BOSTON
[-?-], m. by 19 March 1707/8, [-?-], dau. of Joseph Benton of Annmessex, SO Co. (MWB 13:206).
Henry, m. 19 May 1675, Elizabeth Rogerson (SOLR:IKL).
Isaac, m. by 20 Nov 1695, Eliza, dau. of Samuel Long of SO Co. (MWB 7:169).
Capt. Samuel, m. by 1676, Mary, dau. of Capt. George Goldsmith (MDTP 8:467). He d. by Aug 1677, having m. Mary, "relict and extx." of Capt. George Goldsmith (MDTP 4C:11). She was the mother of Michael Rochfort (MDTP 8A:476).

BOSWELL
[-?-], m. by 3 March 1716, Mary, dau. of Rosamond Machetee, widow of Patrick Machetee of CH Co. (MWB 14:236).
Thomas, m. on 20 Nov 170(?), Mary Marcey (KESP:B2).

BOTELER
Edward, m. by 12 Oct 1707, Anne, dau. of George Lingan of CV Co. (MWB 12:248).
Henry, m. by 1705, Catherine, dau. of George and Ann Lingan of CV Co. (INAC 26:45; MDAD 1:289).

BOUALCH
 Hezekiah, m. on 30 July 1707, Matthew [Martha?] Brewenton (AAAN:1).

BOUCHELLE
 Lege de la (Bouchele), of Bohemia River, CE Co., m. by 30 May 1698, Anna Margaret Conte, mother of Sibilla Heselrigg, who recently m. Henry Slyter (MWB 6:388).
 Peter, m. on 28 March 1716, Mary Hayatt, spinster (CESS).

BOUCHER
 [-?-], m. by 20 Jan 1712, Ann, mother of Thomas, Randolph James, and George Egerton and Mary Underwood (MWB 13:491).

BOUGHTON
 [-?-], m. by 17 Feb 1697, Catherine, sister of Parthenia Burditt (MWB 6:75).
 Richard, m. by 24 June 1668, Verlinda, admx. of Thomas Burditt and mother of Elizabeth, Francis, Parthenia, and Sarah Burditt, and sister of Samuel and Nathaniel Eaton (CHLR C:270; *ARMD* 60:133; MDTP 13:130).

BOULD
 John, m. by 1682, Jane, sister of Cuthbert Scott of SM Co. (MDTP 15:14, 61).

BOULDIN
 Richard, m. by banns on 17 Jan 1716 by Mr. Sewell, Mary Hewes (CESS).

BOULS. See BOWLES.

BOUNDS
 [-?-], m. by 3 Nov 1713, Sarah, dau. of Richard Stephens or Stevens of SO Co. (MWB 13:686).

BOURK
 John, m. by 19 Nov ----, Cecelie, admx. of John Alford of DO Co. (INAC 32C:112).

BOURNE
 [-?-], m. by 1698, Elizabeth, extx. of John Hambleton (INAC 15:97).
 Jesse Jacob, and Hannah Nellis, both of Patuxent Meeting, filed their intentions to marry on 12 d., 1 m., 1713/4, and 9 d., 2 m., 1713/4; he produced a certificate from London (WRMMa).
 Samuel, m. by June 1680, [-?-], relict of Thomas Billingsley of CV Co., who died leaving daughters Elizabeth and Sarah (Warrant Record CB#1:56).

BOUSTEAD
 William, m. by 3 Nov 1708, Mary, admx. of John Cooke of TA Co. (INAC 29:127).

BOURMAN. See BURMAN.

BOWDELL. See BOWDLE.

BOWDITCH

Robert, of SO Co., m. by 2 Nov 1710, Anne, possibly mother of Joanna and Rebecca Clarke, who Bowditch called daus.-in-law (MWB 14:257). **N.B.**: On 6 July 1714, Andrew Wilson of SO Co. named Robert Bowditch his brother-in-law, and named Robert's wife Anne (MWB 14:182).

BOWDLE

[-?-] (Bowdell), m. by 29 April 1711, Katherine, dau. of Mary Sargeant of QA Co, (MWB 13:315).

Loftus, m. on 27 Feb 1716, Ann Thomas (TAPE).

Thomas (Bowdell, Bowtle), of CV Co., m. by 1664, Jane Turner, relict of Stephen Clifton (MPL 8:427; PCJU FF; MDTP 2:106; *ARMD* 49:440).

Thomas, m. by May 1684, Phoebe Loftus, who had been appointed extx. of Timothy Goodridge of TA Co. (MDTP 13:119).

Thomas, m. on 6 Dec 1709, Sarah Gorsuch (TAPE).

BOWDY

[-?-], m. by 6 Nov 1711, Rosamond, heir of Richard Unitt of KE Co. (INAC 33A:164)

Richard, m. by 8 June 1709, Elisabeth, extx. of John Cracknall of CE Co. (INAC 29:320, MWB 13:377)

BOWEN

[-?-] (Bowing), m. by 9 May 1711, Eliza, dau. of John Dossett of PG Co. (MWB 13:274).

[-?-], m. by 17 July 1718, [-?-], dau. of Edward Hammon, Sr., of SO Co. (MWB 14:674).

Benjamin, m. by April 1703, [-?-], widow and relict of Nathaniel Ruxton of BA Co. (MDTP 19A:16).

Benjamin, m. by Nov 1710, Rosanna, widow of James Robertson (BACP IS#B:187).

George (Bowin), m. on 27 March 1706, Elizabeth Gibbs [or Marr] (AAJA:32 #5).

John, Jr., m. on 7 Sep 1699, Milcah Claxton (AAJA:6#6). She was Milcah, dau. of Robert Clarkson of AA Co., who was the son and heir of Robert Clarkson (BALR RM#HS:549; AALR WT#2:202, 216).

Jonas, of BA Co., m. by 26 March 1699, Martha, mother of Lawrence Wolden (MWB 6:228).

Jonas (Bowin), m. by 6 Oct 1702, Anne, admx. of William Story of BA Co. (INAC 23:96).

Thomas, m. on 13 March 1717/8, Elizabeth Swilloven (AAAL 2:14).

BOWERS
James, m. on 9 Nov 1697 by Rev. Richard Sewell, Margaret Cock (CESS).

BOWIN, BOWING. See BOWEN.

BOWLES
[-?-], m. by 23 March 1707, Margaret, former wife of William Burden of CE Co. (CELR 2:112).
[-?-], m. by 1717, Catherine, sister of Edward Dickinson (MWB 14:458).
Isaac, m. on 20 Sep ---, Mary Rease (KESP:B1).
Isaac, Jr., m. by 1704, Mary [-?-], b. c1689; by 1746 she had m,. [-?-] Davis (KELR JS#25L430).
Isaac, m. by 7 July 1708, Mary, dau. of Thomas Kear, whose extx. m. William Dixon, in Dixon's acct. (INAC 28:160).
James, m. by 14 June 1718, Jane, sister of Anne Lowe, late of SM Co., but now of PG Co. (MWB 15:115).
Jno. (or James), m. by 1662, Margery, widow of 1st, William Batten of CV Co., and 2nd, [-?-] Ashcomb (*MHM* 3:58; MPL ABH: 202; *ARMD* 51:68, 70; 53:269; 57:151; MDTP 15C:77½, 78 gives his name as James).
John (Bouls), m. by May 1699, Cecilia, relict of George Hardesty (MDTP 17:320).
John, m. on 4 Sep 170-, Margaret McNieu (McNeill?, McNiett?) (KESP:B1).

BOWLING
James, m. by 1692, Mary, dau. of Col. Thomas and Elinor (Hatton) Brooke; Mary m. 2nd, Henry Hall, and 3rd, Henry Witham (SMWB PC#1:84; MWB 16:354, 527, 18:492).
James, d. by 1692/3, having m. Mary, dau. of Henry Darnall (SMWB PC#1:84).
John, m. by 1694, Mary, dau. of William and Mary (Hussy) Longworth (MWB 2:282, 13:253, 301MDTP 22:38).

BOWLY
Solomon, m. on 13 April 17--, Kath. Eads (KESP:B2).

BOWREY
[-?-], m. by 11 Oct 1703, Elizabeth, dau. of Walter and Sarah Quinton (TALR 9:199).

BOX
Thomas, d. by 10 June 1709 when his admx. Jane had m. Thomas Hinde (INAC 30:437).

BOY
John, m. by 11 Oct 1698, Jennet, relict and admx. of John Knight of CH Co. (INAC 18:790).

BOYCE
James, m. on 22 July 1713, Mary Meek (AAAN:9). She was the extx. of John Meak or Meek of AA Co. (INAC 35A:127).
John, m. by May 1698, [-?-], admins. of Joseph Moseley of TA Co. (MDTP 17:135).
Roger, m. by 8 April 1703, Mary, extx. of James Sewell, who had been admin. of Bridget Hedger of CV Co. (INAC 23:27).
Thomas, m. by Nov 1718, Mary, extx. of John Meek (AAJU RC:270).

BOYD
[-?-], m. by 1674, Anne, widow of John Neale (Cotton cites INAC 1:145).
Abraham, m. on 16 Oct 1705, Mary Gray (AAAL 1:32(2)).
Benjamin, m. by 1681, Elizabeth, widow of Humphrey Jones (of AA Co.?) (MPL 24:400).
James, m. by Feb 1673/4, Ann, widow of John Norwood of AA Co., and mother of Andrew Norwood (*ARMD* 65:192; INAC 1:48, 159).
John, m. on 28 March 1706, Eleanor FitchEdmunds (AAAL 1:32(2)).

BOYDEN
[-?-], d. by 2 Feb 1688, having m. Deborah [-?-], widow of Thomas Impey (TALR 5:242).

BOYER
William, m. on 26 Dec 1688, Phillis Holeger (CESS).

BOYSE
John, m. 21 Aug 1701, Mary Jolly (AAAL).

BOYSS
William, of Enemessicke, SO Co., m. by Jan 1666, [-?-], sister of Jane Bellamin (MDTP 2:143).

BOZMAN
Thomas, m. on 27 May 1715, Mrs. Mary Glen, widow of the Rector of St. Peter's Parish (TAPE). She was the admx. of Wm. Glen of TA Co. (INAC 37A:2, 38C:2).

BRABANT
Wm, m. on 24 April 1706, Mary Gyatt (CVCH).

BRACE
William, m. on 30 June 1715, Ann Lam-(?) (KESH:16).

BRADAY
John, marriage contract dated 6 June 1680, Sarah, dau. of John Richardson of DO Co. (*ARMD* 70:158, 159).

BRADBURY
Jacob, planter, m. on 19 d. 12 m., 1692, Ann Jadwin, spinster, both of TA Co., at Tuckahoe Meeting House (TATH).
Roger, m. on 16 Oct 1704, Mary Man [or Marr] (TAPE).

BRADCUTT
Richard, m. on 27 Feb 1715, Eliza Cook (PGQA:1).

BRADDIS
Thomas, m. on 1 Jan ---, Sarah Baker (KESP:B1).

BRADFORD
John, m. by 18 April 1713, Joyce, widow and admx. of Mr. James Butler of PG Co. (INAC 34:176; MPL RY#1:415).

BRADLEY
Francis, m. by 2 July 1707, Rebecca, dau. of Evan Morley (QALR ETA:3).
John, m. 28 Nov 1698, Ann Stiffin (AAAL 1:10).
Robert, m. by 1687, Sarah, dau. of Richard Hall of CV Co. (Hodges cites Prov. Court PL#8:80).

BRAINTHWATE
Wm., m. by 1649, Helenor Stephenson, who came into the Province with Sir Edmund Plowden (*ARMD* 1:524; Warrants 2:556).

BRALL
David, of AA Co., m. by Sep 1705, [-?-], widow of George [Bruens?] (MDTP 19B:82).

BRAMSTEAD
Thomas, m. by 1657 Mary [-?-], later Mary Cole, maidservant (*NFMP*:194 cites *ARMD* 10:549-156).

BRAND
Samuel, d. by Dec 1688, having m. Mary, dau. of John Hammond. She m. as her 2nd husband, Richard Ascue (MDTP 14:124).

BRANGWELL
Peter, m. by 30 April c1683[?] Elizabeth Kemb (BACP D:94).

BRANNACK
Edmund, m. by 10 Nov 1675, [-?-], legatee of Alexander Roche of Barbados, merchant (INAC 1:449).

BRANNAN
Philip, banns pub. Feb 1699/1700, Susannah Thomas (HAGE:8).

BRASHIER
Samuel, Jr., m. on 17 Dec 1717, Eliza Brashier, dau. of Benjamin (PGQA:2).
Thomas, m. on 11 Sep 1711 by Rev. Jona' White, Anne Venman (PGQA:1).
She was the extx. of John Venman of PG Co. (INAC 33A:161).

BRATTEN
Nicholas, m. on 21 Feb 1709, Mary Wood (AALR 2:6).

BRAWNER
John, m. on 8 Jan 1716, Mary Dunning or Downing (PGKG:241, 258).

BRAY
Pierce, m. by Aug 1694, Mary, widow of Archibald White (SOJU LD:113).

BREAD
John (Breed, Broad), Gent., m. by Oct 1677, Jane, widow and extx. of Dr.
Thomas Matthews, and mother of Ignatius, William, Victoria, Jane, and Anne Matthews
(MDTP 9:351; CHLR H:45; INAC 4:379; *ARMD* 51:242; Warrant Record CB#4:228).

BREATTON
John, m. by 2 April 1709, Katherine Hutchins (in 1709 acct. of Edward James of
Kent Island) (INAC 29:218)

BREDELL
Isa[i]ah, m. by 3 July 1712, Margaret, admx. of James Gray (INAC 33B:180).

BRENT
Capt. George, m. by 1687, Elizabeth, widow of Col. William Chandler, and dau.
of Henry and Jane (Lowe) Sewell (Pro. Court WRC#1:448; INAC 14:127; MDTP 17:31;
MWB 14:63, 28:61).
Col. Giles, m. by 1644, Mary Kittamaqund, only dau. of the Tayac or Emperor of
the Piscataway Indians; he m. 2nd, c1655, Frances, widow of Dr. Jeremy Harrison, and
dau. of Thomas Whitgreave of Staffs. (*ARMD* 3:162; *MHM* 3:60; *VMHB* 16:96, 97,
211).
Henry, m. by Nov 1681, Ann, extx. of Baker Brooke, and dau. of Leonard Calvert
(*ARMD* 70:79, 157; INAC 9:390; Fresco cites SMWB PC#1:114; MTDP 13:??). He d.
by 31 Oct 1709 when his admx. Ann had m. Richard Marsham (INAC 30:221).

BRENTON
John, m. by 1715, Mary, dau. of John Wadmor of CV Co. (MCHR 3:24-25).

BRETT
George (or Britt), m. by 9 July (c1710), Susanna, admx. of Joseph Cooper of CH
Co. (also in admin. acct. of Hon. Philip Lynes of CH Co.) (INAC 32C:65, 128).

BRETTON
William (Britton), m. by 1637, Mary, dau. of Thomas Nabbs (MPL 1:18, 68).
William (Britton), of Little Britain, MD, on 10 July 1651 was about to marry Mrs.
Temeprance Jay (*ARMD* 65:684).

BREWEN
John, m. by Oct 1710, [-?-], admx. of Elizabeth Goldsborough (MDTP 21:271).

BREWER
John, m. on **14 Feb 1704/5, Dinah Battee** (AAAL 1:27). She was a dau. of
Ferdinando Battee, of AA Co. (MWB 3:744).
Joseph, m. on 18 Dec 1715, Jane Rutland (AALR 1:38).
William, m. by 1684, Grace, dau. of Thomas Thomas, and sister of William
Thomas (Fresco cites MWB 1:412, 4:107; SMWB PC#1:57; Judgements 7:156).
William, m. on 14 Feb 1715/6, Martha Skeys (AALR 1:38).

BREWIN
[-?-], m. by 29 April 1711, Priscilla, dau. of Mary Sargeant of QA Co, (MWB
13:315).

BREWSTER
William, m. on 26 June 1716, Jane Banister (PGQA:1).

BRIAN
Nathaniel, m. by 2 Nov 1695, Frances, heir (sister?) of Richard Charlett of
Patuxent River (Hodges cites Pro. Court WRC# 1:772).

BRICE
John (Brise), m. on 16 Nov 1703, Sarah Worthington (AAMA:81). She was the
widow of Capt. John Worthington, and a dau. of Matthew Howard (AALR IH#1:128,
137, 143; INAC 25:52, 54).

BRIDGIN
Robert, m. by 6 April 1685, Mary, dau. of Simon and Virtue (Vowles) Reader of
SM Co.; Mary m. 2nd, by 1686, John Shanks (MWB 4:147; SMWB PC#1:565-57;
MDTP 13:236, 389, 419).

BRIGGS
Charity [*sic*] , m. on 20 April 1704, Bridgitt Jones (AAAL 1:26).

BRIGHT
Thomas, of KE Co., m. on 11 May 1662, Elizabeth Cripes (or Crisp) (*ARMD*
54:186). He m. 2nd, by 1680, Cecilie Evans (MPL WC#2:212).
William, m. on 6 June ---, Sarah Thorn (KESP:B1).
William, m. by 1708, Mary, dau. of John Raley or Ryley (SMWB PC#1:1:162;
MWB 12, pt. 2: 57; MDTP 21:319, 22:104, 251).

BRIGHTWELL
[-?-], m. by 13 Nov 1681, Catherine, dau. of Eliza, widow of Robt. Lashley of CV Co. (MWB 2:196).
Richard, m. by July 1686 [-?-], heir of the Widow Trueman of CV Co. (MDTP 13:375).

BRIMER
William, m. on 16 Sep 1712, Katherine Campbell (AAAN:9).

BRIN
John, m. on 28 April 1709, Ann Abbott (TAPE). She was the admx. of John Abbot of TA Co. (INAC 32C:87).

BRISCOE
Jno. (or Biscoe), m. by c1707, Sarah Jackson, dau. of Thomas, of SM Co. (Hodges cites Rent Roll # 1:3, 12).

BRITT. See BRETT.

BRITTINGHAM
Samuel, m. by 1 July 1718, Elizabeth, admx. of William Powell of SO Co. (MDAD 1:175).

BRITTON. See BRETTON.

BRIUM
John, m. by 19 May 1709, Anne, extx. of John Abbott of TA Co., and dau. of John Barker (MWB 12:80, INAC 29:282, 32A:28, 32C:87).

BROAD
John, m. by Nov 1692, Barbara, relict of Dennis Garrett (BACP F#1:276).

BROADACRE
Thos., m. by 19 June 1677, Mary, widow of James Oliver of TA Co. (MDTP 9A:180).

BROADLY
George, m. on 6 Dec 1698, Joane Killingsworth (AAJA:5#1).

BROCKETT
Samuel, m. by 21 Feb 1660, Ann, dau. of John Abbott of Isle of Kent, MD (*ARMD* 41:422).

BROCKSON
John, m. by 1 May 1699, Bridget, admx. of Thomas Moore of CH Co. (INAC 18:231).

William, m. by 20 July 1698, Elizabeth, relict and extx of Thomas Nicholson of CE Co. (INAC 16:118).

BROOK. See BROOKE.

BROMFIELD
 Peter, m. on 28 Dec 1718, Barbara Bennett (PGQA:2).

BROOKBAND
 William, m. by 9 May 1698, Ann, dau. of Mary the wife of William Hodgson of SM Co.(MWB 6:135).

BROOKE
 Baker, m. by 1662, Ann, Calvert, dau. of Leonard Calvert; she m. 2nd, Henry Brent, and 3rd, Col. Richard Marsham (Fresco cites SMWB PC#1:1:114; MDTP 13:7; Kilty, p. 62).
 Baker, m. by 1697, Katherine, dau. of Richard Marsham of SM Co.; she m. 2nd, by 1711, Samuel Queen of SM Co. (MWB 13:514; Fresco cites SMWB PC#1:114, 176; Judgements 55:4176; *MHM* 1:184-185).
 Clement, m. by 1704, Jane Sewell, dau. of Maj. Nicholas and Susanna (Burgess) Sewell (Fresco cites SMWB TA#1:66; MWB 4:242; MDCR 2:800; Judgements 32:763; AALR WT#2:222).
 Clement, m. by 28 April 1711, [-?-], dau. of Henry Darnall of AA Co., who called the husband his son-in-law (MWB 13:233).
 Francis, m. by 19 Jan 1652, Ann Boulton (*ARMD* 10:215).
 Henry, m. by 1650, Jane, widow of David Wickliffe (MPL ABH:49).
 John, m. by 1677, Rebecca Isaac, sister of Edward Isaac of CV Co. (INAC 4:238).
 John, m. by Feb 1688/9, Katherine, admx. of Robert Stevens (*ARMD* 51:327).
 John, m. by Dec 1717, Judith, widow of John Newman (MDTP 23:107).
 Leonard, m. by 1716, Eleanor Neale, sister of Raphael Neale of SM Co. (SMWB PC#1:232; MWB 14:487).
 Robert, m. by 29 Oct 1705, Grace, admx. of John Boone of CV Co. (INAC 25:121).
 Roger, of CV Co., Gent., m. by 1670, Dorothy, dau. of James Neale of CV Co., Gent. (MPL 16:3).
 Maj. Thomas, d. by 1676 having m. Eleanor, dau. of Richard and Margaret [-?-] Hatton, and niece of Thomas Hatton, Secretary of MD (Hodges cites MWB 5:123, 18:492).
 Thomas, of Kent Island, m. by 7 Oct 1664, [-?-], relict of Walter Jenkin (MDTP 1E:47). She was Sarah, mother of three daus. named Jenkins (MPL 10:541).

BROOK(E)S
 [-?-], m. by 16 May 1708, Anne, dau. of William Boarman of CH Co. (MWB 12, pt. 2:108; MWB 13:360).
 Francis, m. by 25 Nov 1652, Mrs. Ann Boulton (*ARMD* 10:215; Proprietary Records F&B:381).

Henry (Brooks), m. by 7 Sep 1650, Jane, widow of David Wickliffe (MPL ABH:49, 3:62).

Henry (Brooks), m. on 22 Jan 17--, Ellinor Fitchwaters (KESP:B2).

Dr. John, m. by May 1695, Mary, dau. of William Worgan (MDTP 16:62).

John, m. by 26 Sep 1707, Jane, admx. of Paul Burrows of CH Co. (INAC 27:109).

John, of Ingleby, Co. Derby, [Eng.], m. by 25 Feb 1714, Mary, widow of Stephen Parker, and dau. of John Hopkins of Finden, and sister of Philip Hopkins of MD (KELR BC#1:45, 47).

Joseph, m. on 19 Nov 1704, Anne Rice (AAAL 1:27).

Robert, d. by Feb 1677/8, when his admx. [-?-], had m. Thomas Cosden (*ARMD* 67:204).

Thomas, m. by banns on 4 April 1713, by Mr. Sewell, Mary Currey, widow (CESS). Thomas, of CE Co., d. by 1 Sep 1716 having m. [-?-], widow and admx. of Thomas Currier (INAC 37A:193)

BROOKSON

Jno. (Broxson), m. on 15 Nov 1697, by Rev. Richard Sewell, Briggett Moor, widow (CESS).

William (Broxson), m. by 10 April 1700, Elisabeth, widow and admx. of Thomas Nicholson (in acct. of Peter Sesserson of CE Co.) (INAC 19½B:52; CELR 1:467).

BROOM

Joseph, m. by 23 Sep 1707, Isabella, admx. of David Dean of QA Co. (INAC 27:208).

BROOMFIELD

Francis, m. in Oct ---, Elizabeth Ward (KESP:B1).

BROTHERHOOD

Henry, m. on 14 Feb 1704/5, Joan Lester (AAAL 1:27).

BROUGHTON

John, m. 26 Feb 1684, Elizabeth, dau. of William Bradshaw (SOLR:IKL).

John, m. by 23 March 1704, [-?-], granddau. and heir of John Holland of CV Co. (INAC 25:142).

BROUTON

John, m. by 15 April 1714, [-?-], dau. of John Wadnor and his wife [-?-], who had been a dau. of John Hollins (MCHR CL:24).

BROWN(E)

[-?-], m. by Nov 1677, Katherine, extx. of Arthur Wright of KE Co. (MDTP 9A:415; INAC 7A:269).

[-?-], m. by 20 June 1686, Katherine, dau. of John Summerland of Severn R., AA Co. (MWB 4:234).

[-?-], m. on 2 June 1712, Elizabeth Slayfoot (KESP:B2).

[-?-], m. by 20 Dec 1716, Mary, dau. of William Wintersell (MWB 14:241).

[-?-], m. by 1 Dec 1717, Martha, dau. of Thomas Holbrook of SO Co. (MWB 15:15).

Daniel (Browne), m. on 9 June 1698, Sarah Tucker (AAJA:3#10).

David, m. by 11 Nov 1696, Winifred, widow and sole heir of Capt. William Thorn (SOLR 7:440).

Edward, of KE Co., m. on 28 Oct 1668, Sarah Williams (*ARMD* 54:87). [-?-], m. by 24 Jan 1684, [-?-], dau. of Morgan Williams of KE Co., by whom he had a son Morgan Brown (MWB 4:156).

George, m. by 12 Sep 1686, Elizabeth, admx. of Robert Neiwes (INAC 9:77).

Gerrard, m. by Oct 1674, Martha, relict of William Allen of CH Co. (*ARMD* 60:588).

Henry, m. by 27 Dec 1703, Sarah, dau. of Blanch wife of Thomas Ryder of AA Co. (MWB 11:403).

Henry, m. on 18 April 1705, Hannah Moss (AAMA:82). She was the extx. of Ralph Moss of AA Co. (MDTP 19B:38, INAC 26:324).

Isaac, m. on 13 July 1713, Elinor Campell (SJSG:19R).

James, and Joyce Briant: their banns of matrimony published in 1666 (*ARMD* 57:80).

James, m. by Feb 1692, Anna, relict and extx. of Thomas Pue of CV Co. (MDTP 15A:16; INAC 13A:222).

John, m. by May 1666, Elizabeth, relict and extx. of John Lumbrozo of Nanjemy (MDTP 1F:92).

John, m. by 31 March 1668, Mary, mother of Alice Clarke (MDTP 2:473).

John, m. 16 Sep 1668, Sarah Minard (SOLR:IKL).

John, of AA Co., d. by 30 Dec 1673; had m. [-?-], dau. of Robert Clarkson (INAC 1:166).

John, m. on 10 Feb 1704, Mary Wilson (TAPE).

John, son of Thomas, m. on 18 Nov 1705, Elizabeth Sicklemore (HAGE:24).

John, m. by 15 March 1706, Elizabeth, admx. of Thomas Rennolds of SM Co. (INAC 26:158).

John, m. on 17 Nov 1709, Sarah Herrington (AAJA:38 #10).

John, m. by 7 May 1710, Johannah, extx. of Nicholas Fountain of SO Co. (INAC 31:88).

John, m. on 31 Aug 1710, Ester Cook (TAPE).

John, m,. by 7 June 1710, Verlinda, admx. of Samuel Taylor of PG Co. (INAC 31:132; PGLR F (Old 6):790).

John, m. on 10 April 1716, [-?-] [-?-] (AAJA).

John, mariner, m. on 14 April 1718, Anne Sanderson (AAAN:38). John, of CV Co., m. by 9 Dec 1718, Elizabeth, dau. of James White of AA Co. (PGLR F (Old 6):675).

Mark, m. on 8 Nov 1716, Susanna Fowler (PGQA:1). She was the widow and extx. of Thomas Fowler of PG Co. (INAC 38A:104).

Morgan, of KE Co., carpenter, m. on 7 d. 10 m., 1715, Rebeckah Darden, of TA Co., at Tuckaho Meeting House (TATH).

Nicholas, m. by Oct 1680, Ann, orig. admx. of Dennis English (MDTP 12A:162).

Peregrine, of St. Catherine Cree Church, London, deposed on 8 Dec 1703 that he had m. the sister of James Frisby of CE County, who d. leaving a will dated 10 Sep 1702 (*AWAP*).

Peregrine, m. by 23 Feb 1711, Margaret, dau. of Joseph Brock (Sherwood. *American Colonists in English Records*. 167).

Richard, m. on 31 Dec 1704, Grace Fairbrother?] (AAAN:19).

Robert, m. on 27 Jan 1700, Mary Tyndall (AAJA:22#7). She was the dau. and heir of Thomas Tindale of AA Co., dec. (AALR IB#2:248).

Robert, m. 18 June 1702, Katherine Parnell, widow of James (AAAL 1:21(2)).

Samuel, m. on 2 Jan 1709/10, [Mary?] Skelton (HAGE:26).

Thomas, m. by 1 Jan 1676/7, Mary, relict of William Stacey of CV Co. (MDTP 8A:355).

Thomas, m. on 26 July 1692, Alice Horton (CHLR Q#1:18).

Tho., m. on 23 Jan 1700, by Mr. Nobbs, minister, Mary [-?-] (TAPE).

Thomas, m. on 13 Feb 1704/5, Elizabeth Stephens, widow (AAAN:19). She was the widow of Charles Stephens (*MRR*: AA Co.:214; AAJU TB#1:571).

Thomas, Jr., m. by 17 Sep 1710, Elizabeth, dau. of John Sisson (AALR PK:267; MPL DD#5:633, PL#3:173).

Thomas, m. on 24 Dec 1712, Neomi Ladmore (TAPE).

William, in March 1663/4 was about to marry Elizabeth Darnell (*ARMD* 49:171).

William, m. by Aug 1693, [-?-], admx. of William Ferguson of CV Co. (MDTP 15A:64).

William, m. by 29 May 1695, Jane, widow of 1st, William Frizzell, and 2nd, Patrick Duncan, dec. (AALR IH#1:199, WH#4:107).

William, m. on 31 Aug 1710, Margery Jones (AALR 2:6).

William, m. by 14 Feb 1712, Mary, admx. of Joseph Vickers of TA Co. (INAC 34:138; MDTP 22:252).

William, m. by June 1716, Elizabeth Walter, widow (QAJR).

BROWNING

George, m. on 19 June 1701, by banns, by Richard Sewell, Mary Kennard (CESS). She was the widow of 1st, Nathaniel Howell, and 2nd, Richard Kennard. She m. 4th, on 26 Oct 1714, Matthew Howard (MWB 6:5, 50, 21:422; CELR 1:301; INAC 36C:128; KESH; KELR JS#W:45; ESVR 1:29, 39, 40).

Thomas, m. by Feb 1695, Anne, relict and admx. of Darby Noland (INAC 13B:19).

Thomas, m. on 17 --- 1700, Mary Ward (KESP:B2).

Thomas, m. by [c1709], Mary, poss. dau. of Martha Gibson who called Browning her son-in-law (KELR JS#N:137).

BROXSON. See BROOKSON.

BRUEN

[-?-], m. by 15 Sep 1713, Priscilla, dau. of John Serjeant, dec. (QALR ETA:181).

BRUFF

Thomas, m. by Oct 1688, Rhoda, extx. of James Earle of TA Col. (MDTP 14:102).

Thomas, m. on 28 Jan ---, Alse Wickes (KESP:B1). He m. by 19 Feb 1704, Alice, relict and admx. of Joseph Wickes of KE Co. (INAC 25:171, 27:204; KELR GL#1:28/50; MDTP 19B:41).

Thomas, m. on 8 June 1705, Catherine Cu--- (AAAN:19).

BRUSSE

Thomas, of Annapolis, gent., m. by 17 April 1710, Catherine, relict of James Cullen and mother of John Cullen (AALR PK:139).

BRYAN

Daniel, banns pub. 17 Oct 1703, m. on 28 Nov 1703, Ann Veares (HAGE:17).

Edward, m. on 3 Dec 1697, Mary Vickars, widow of Francis Vickars (TAPE).

BUCHANAN

Archbald, m. on 9 April 1705, Mary Prebble (HAGE:22). She was the widow of Thomas Preble [*sic*] (BAAD 2:233; INAC 25:415).

BUCK

Edward, m. by Feb 1711/2, Jane, admx. of John Anderson (MDTP 22:85; BAAD 1:223).

John, d. by Dec 1687, having m. [-?-], sister of George Benson of AA Co.; she m. 2nd, Walter Phelps (MDTP 14A:17).

John, m. on 20 Dec 1705, Penelope Martin (AAAN:1; AAMA:85).

BUCKENALL. See BUCKNALL.

BUCKERFIELD

Henry, m. by 11 Aug 1681, Elizabeth, dau. of William Parker and sister and heir of William Parker; her father's widow Grace m. by that date Edward Lloyd (PCLR WRC:209/218; AALR PK:66).

BUCKINGHAM

John, m. in Jan 1697, Frances Hooper (AAMA:84).

Thomas, of KE Co., carpenter, m. on 3 d. 12 m., 1697, Catherine Parrat, of TA Co., at Tuckahoe Meeting House (TATH).

Thomas, of TA Co., m. by 26 Aug 1701, Katherine, sister of Elizabeth Taylor of TA Co. (KELR JD#1:5).

BUCKLEY

[-?-], m. by 15 Sep1718, Elizabeth, widow of John Currier of TA Co. (MDAD 1:353)

BUCKNALL
Thomas (Buckenall), m. by 27 March 1676, Eliza [or Mary?], widow of Edward Wheelock of AA Co., and mother of Edward Wheelock (INAC 2:18; MDTP 4C:122, 8:19, 9:159; MWB 4:20).
Thomas, banns pub. July 1701, Elizabeth Griffis (HAGE:11).

BUCKNELL
Thomas, pub. banns on 9 Nov 1704, m. on 13 Dec 1704, Elizabeth Burk (HAGE:22).

BULLEN
[-?-], m. by 10 April 1706, Margaret, dau. of Ralph Dawson, Sr., of TA Co. (MWB 12:31).
John, m. on 13 May 1703, Mrs. Margaret Knowles (TAPE).

BULLERY
Francis, m. by May 1696, Ellenor, relict and admx. of Edward ffrawner [Brawner?] of CH Co. (MDTP 16:167).

BULLIN
Henry, m. on 14 Dec 1704, Mary Clemence (TAPE).

BULLOCK
Henry, m. on 25 April 1696, Mary [-?-] (TAPE).
Joseph, m. on 24 Oct 1704, Anne Mackey (TAPE).

BULPITT
John, m. by 11 Nov 1676, Anne, relict and legatee of Thomas Henfrey (INAC 5:359).

BUMNALLEY
Andrew, m. on 6 May 1707, Elizabeth Blackett (CVCH).

BUNNELL
John, m. by 1 Oct 1707, Rebecca, widow and admx. of William Welch, Sr., of AA Co. (INAC 27:133, 28:334).

BUNTON
Joseph, m. by Oct 1713, Mary, dau. of Samuel Farmer of TA co. (PCJU VD#1:516-517).

BURAD
Darley (or Darby), m. on 7 Oct 1701, Grizell [-?-] (TAPE).

BURCH

Christopher, m. by 5 Nov 1707, Tabitha, dau. of Jeffrey and Alice Mattershaw (QALR ETA:7).

John, m. by 29 Aug 1711, [-?-], admx. of James Harlene of PG Co. (INAC 32C:148). Elsewhere, she is named as Elisabeth, admx. of James Harling of PG Co. (INAC 35B:24).

BURCHFIELD

Thomas, m. on 30 June 1709, Mary Wilson (HAGE:26).

BURD

Nicholas, m. by 29 July 1709, Mary, admx. of Walter Watkins of SM Co. (INAC 30:20).

BURDEN

John, m. on 20 June 1703, Rosannah Haines (TAPE).

William, of CE Co., m. by 24 March 1693, Margaret, mother of Thomas and Mary Smith (MWB 7:25).

BURDIT

Thomas, d. by June 1688, having m. Verlinda Eaton, sister of Nathaniel and Samuel Eaton. She was about to marry Richard Boughton (*ARMD* 60:133).

BURGAN

Sutton, m. on 6 Jan 1708, Susannah Morris (KESP:B2).

BURGEN

Philip, m. by (date not given), the relict of Robert Saunders (*ARMD* e73:179, cites Council Book CB#1).

BURGESS

[-?-], m. by 8 Sep 1702, [-?-], dau. of Francis Gunby (MCHR PC:494).

[-?-], m. by 7 Jan 1709, Mary, dau. of William Brown of TA Co. (MWB 12, pt. 2:120).

Charles, m. 26 Oct 1703, Elizabeth Hanslap, widow of Joseph (AAAL 1:26; MWB 3:416).

Edward, m. on 12 Jan 1713, Sarah [-?-], widow (AAAN:9). She was prob. Sarah, extx. of Thomas Major, to whom he was m. by Nov 1718 (AAJU RC:270).

James, m. on 12 Nov 1716, Rebecca Burk (AAAL 2:11).

John, m. by 20 0Oct 1671, Amy, widow of John Tucker (or Tinker; she m. 3rd, William Eagle) (*ARMD* 51:259; MDTP 5:114; Warrant Record CB#1:16).

Richard, m. on 13 May 1703, Mary Slater (TAPE).

Robert, of Lynn, MA, m. by 12 Sep 1677, Sarah, sister of Thomas South of KE Co., dec. (KELR F:60).

Samuel, m. on 19 April 1716, Elizabeth Durdain (AALR 1:38). She was the extx. of John Durden (AAJU VD#1:538).

William, m. 13 Aug 1697, Ann Watkins (AAAL 1:5).

BURGH
William, m. by Sep 1665, Elizabeth, widow of John Billingsley (MDTP 1F:1).

BURK(E)
[-?-], m. by 7 Sep 1708. Eliza, sister of William Pearcifield [?] of KE Co. (MWB 13:190).
Edward, m. by 3 Aug 1713, Jane, admx. of John Anderson of BA Co. (INAC 35B:15).
Henry, banns pub. 1 Jan, m. on 6 Jan 1706/7, Easter Pine (HAGE:18).
John, m. on 18 April 170-, Elizabeth Pearse (KESP:B1).
John, m. on 29 Dec 1712, Elizabeth Booth (KESP:B3).
Thomas, m. by 29 Nov 1714, Jane Carter (DOLR Old 4:107, 6:250).
William, m. by 1663, [-?-], widow of Major Billingsley (MPL 6:212).

BURKETT
[-?-], m. by 12 July 1701, Rebecca, dau. of Francis Billingsley of CV Co. (INAC 21:102).2

BURKIT
Robert, m. on 1 Oct 1716, Mary Wharton (SJSG:9).

BURLE
John, m. on 9 Oct 1711, Elizabeth Hammond (AAMA:83).
Stephen, m. on 14 Feb 1709, Sarah Gosling (AAMA:83).

BURMAN
Robert (also Bourman, Burnam), m. by May 1688, Anne, extx. of Henry Staples of TA Co. (MDTP 14:69; INAC 9:515, 10:336).

BURN
[-?-], m. by 17 Aug 1717, Mary, dau. of Peter Faulkinn of QA Co. (MWB 14:438).
Richard, m. by Nov 1682, Elizabeth, widow of Thomas Bell of AA Co. (Warrant Record CB#1:260).

BURNWELL
James, m. on 31 July 1709, Elizabeth Slater (TAPE).

BURRIDGE
[-?-], m. by 18 Jan 1681, Grace, dau. of Samuel Lane of AA Co. (MWB 2:185).

BURRILL
Samuel, m. on 16 April 1704, Anne Tooly (AAAL).

BURROSS
[-?-], m. by 2 Sep 1717, Mary, dau. of George Powell of QA Co. (MWB 14:393).

BURROUGHS
Richard, m. by March 1716/7, Eliz., dau. of John Brown (BACP IS#IA:93).
William, m. by 1 June 1696, Ann, widow of Peter Barnett of AA Co. (MPL 40:389).
William, m. 25 Nov 1700, Mary Cox (AAAL 2:1).

BURROWS
James, m. on 25 July 1718, Mary Brown (PGQA:2).

BURTON
Joseph, m. 29 July 1703, Sarah Westall (AAAL 2:4).

BUSH
John, m. on 11 Sep 1715, Mary Harlett/Hurlett (TAPE).

BUSHAW
John, m. by 1712, Phebe, dau. of Roger Phillips (SOLR 11 (KL):84).

BUSSEY
Edward, m. on 10 Aug 1701, Martha Evans (CVCH).
Paul (Busey), m. by 1716, Sarah Whipps, dau. of John and Elizabeth, of AA Co. (MWB 14:172, 173; MDTP 30:172).

BUSSNON
Thomas, m. by 8 July 1686, Elizabeth, dau. of John Morris of TA Co. (INAC 9:49).

BUTALL
Thomas, m. on 12 Aug 1705, Elizabeth Merritt (AAAL 1:27).

BUTCHER
[-?-], of Goose Grave Northamptonshire, Eng., m. by 8 Dec 1713, Eliza, sister of John Brice of AA Co. (MWB 13:589).

BUTLER
Cecil, m. by 1705, Margaret, dau. and heir of Robert Carville (SMRR:1; Prov. Court TL#2:890).
Charles (Buttler), m. by 4 July 1665, Alice, relict of William Phillips (MDTP 1E:142).
James, m. on 12 June 1706, Joyce (or Joan) Carroll (AAAN:1). The jurors of the Provincial court indicted Butler because his former wife, Hannah, was still alive, and she had not been beyond the seas for seven years, nor absent from him for seven years altogether (*CMSP: Black Books* #20).

Rupert, m. on 3 July 1711 by Rev. Jona' White, Ann Harris (PGQA:1).

BUTLERS
 Thomas, living near the head of Rumley Creek, m. on 23 Jan 1695 Mary Burthell (HAGE:2).

BUTSON
 Thomas, m. by 13 May 1714, [-?-], dau. of Edward Fisher of SM Co. (INAC 36B:75).

BUTTERAM
 John, m. by 8 March 1710, Elizabeth, heir of William Westbury (BALR TR#A:63).
 John, m. on 8 Sep 1714 Jane Mayer (SJSG:7).
 Nicholas, m. by 13 Nov 1679, Elizabeth, widow of Andrew Henderson, and mother of Roger Moore (*ARMD* 51:303, 315).

BUTTLER. See BUTLER.

BUXTON
 Francis, m. by 28 July 1685, Mary wife of George Parker of CV Co. (MWB 4:307).

BYRN
 James, m. by 27 April 1714, Elizabeth, dau. of Mary Connell and sister of William Connell (CHLR F#2:31).
 Michael (Byrne), m. by 12 Nov 1718, Sarah, dau. of Stephen Whetstone (KELR BC#1:346).

CADE
 Thomas, m. by 8 July 1701, [-?-], relict and extx. of Timothy Gunter of CV Co. (INAC 20:204).

CADREY
 John, m. by 5 Aug 1713, Mary, dau. of Lambrock Thomas of SO Co. (MWB 13:543).

CADY
 Robert, of CH Co., m. by March 1670/1, Ellenor, widow of [-?-] Corner or Conner (*ARMD* 60:328).

CAGGE
 Robert (Cogge?), m. by 1687, [-?-], relict of Mark Child of BA Co. (MDTP 14A:11).

CAHEE. See COHEE.

CALHOUN
John (Colehoune), m. in June 1676, Jane Carter (SOLR:IKL).

CALLOWAY
Antho, of KE Co., m. on 10 Sep 1658, Martha Thomas (*ARMD* 54:129).
John, Jr., m. on 25 Dec 1709, Mary Gould (WIST).
Peter, on 26 March 1667, banns of matrimony were published for him and Elizabeth Johnson (SOLR O#1:62).

CALVERT
Benedict Leonard, m. by 1698, Lady Charlotte, eldest. dau. of Edward Henry Lee (Fresco cites Prov. Court DD#4:226, but described Ed. Hen. Lee as being of SM Co.).
Charles, 3rd Lord Baltimore, m. by 1666, Jane, widow of Henry Sewell of Mattapany, and dau. of Vincent and Anne (Cavendish) Lowe of London (MDTP 1F:106; Prov. Court S:809; *MGSB* 18 (No. 1)).
William, d. by 26 Sep 1688, leaving a son Charles, and a widow Elizabeth, dau. of William Stone, dec. (CHLR P:35).

CALVEY
Henry, m. by April 1715, [-?-], admx. of William Sledmore (MDTP 22:460).

CAMDEN
John, m. on 28 Dec 1718, Ester Wood (PGQA:2).

CAME(?)
James (Caine or Keene), m. by Feb 1666/7, Elinor, widow of William Bosman (*ARMD* 57:157; on p. 198 her name is given as Mary).

CAMERON
John, m. on 12 Dec 1716, Margaret Mackellton (SJSG:9).
John, m. by 1719, Margaret, widow and admx. of Daniel Maccen of BA Co. (MDAD 3:25).

CAMMELL
John, m. by 30 Oct 1682, Elizabeth, relict and admx. of William Savin of CE Co. (INAC 8:282).

CAMPBELL
James, m. by 31 Jan 1708, Margaret, extx. of Lovering Millward of KE Co. (INAC 29:77)
Martin, barber, m. by 14 Dec 1703, Mary, dau. of Elizabeth Dermont wife of John Dermont and sister of Robert Downes, Jr., son of Robert Downes, Sr. [It is not clear if Robert Downes' sister was Elizabeth Dermont or Mary Campbell] (CHLR Z:86).
Patrick (Cammel), m. by 1663, Susanna Acheson (MWB 1:390; MPL 6:123).
Thomas (Cambel), of SM Co., m. by 1716, Jane, dau. of Mary Green (SMWB PC#1:205, 284).

CAMPISON
Leonard, m. on 26 Dec 1677, Margaret Morgan (SOLR:IKL).

CANBEE
Robert? of CE Co., m. by April 1684, Abigail, sole dau. of Roland Williams (MDTP 13:113).

CANDRY
John, on 28 Jan 1683/4, banns of matrimony published for him and Mazy Nuttley (*ARMD* e90 (SOJU L):18).

CANMAN. See CARRMAN.

CANNEDAY
John (Canaday), m. on 31 May 1701, Elizabeth Douge (KESP:C1).
Roger, m. on 6 Nov 170-, Jane Dane (KESP:C3).
William, on 26 April 1668, banns of matrimony were published for him and Anne Fisher (SOLR O#1:112).

CANNON
James, m. by 20 May 1700, Rose, dau. of Robert Pope of DO Co. (MWB 11:133; DOLR Old 5:24).
Thomas, of BA Co., d. by 18 July 1682, having m. Henrietta, widow of Edward Swanson; she m. 3rd [-?-] Reeves (INAC 7C:183, 8:275).
Thomas, of DO Co., m. on 14 d. 3 m., 1712, Betty Cox, at Transquaking Meeting House (TATH).
William, m. on 18 Feb 1695 Mary Willing (HAGE:2).

CANTWELL
Edward, banns pub. Aug and Sep 1699, m. 5 Dec 1699, Joan Chattum (HAGE:7).

CAPES
John, m. on 8 April 1696, Mary [-?-] (TAPE).

CARBERRY
[-?-], m. by 16 Feb 1713, Eliza, widow of Thomas Turner and dau. of Joshua Guibert of SM Co. (MWB 13:593).
John Baptist, m. by 19 June 1692, Elizabeth, relict of Cuthbert Scott of SM Co., and dau. of Luke Guibert (SMWB PC#1:188, 207; INAC 14A:4, 15:38; MDTP 14A:4, 10, 22:189, 272, 279).

CAREY
Edward, m. on 10 Dec 1680, Katherine Ferrill (or Fervill) (SOLR:IKL).

CARLETON
 Arthur, of CE Co., m. by 17 June 1687, Elizabeth, widow of John Morgan (TALR 5:88).

CARMAIN
 Josias, m. on 6 Nov 1715, Sarah Brown (TAPE).

CARMICHAEL
 John, m. by 30 Aug 1710, Margaret, admx. of John Williams of SM Co. (INAC 31:366).
 John, m. by 12 Aug 1715, admx. of William Duff of SM Co. (INAC 36C:61).
 John, m., by 10 Aug 1715, Anne, admx. of William Merrell of SM Co. (INAC 36C:280).

CARR
 Francis, m. by 25 May 1709, Elizabeth, admx. of Henry Sarsenett of SO Co. (INAC 29:292).
 George, m. on 20 Jan 1715, Jilian Harrison (TAPE).
 Peter, m. [-?-], the relict of 1st, Thomas Petite, who d. c1650, and 2nd, John Guy (*ARMD* e73:186).
 Peter, m. by Nov 1683, [-?-], relict of Henry Lilley (Warrant Record CB#4:130.
 Robert, m. by 15 March 1713, Rachel, admx. of Robert Hannon of KE Co. (INAC 35A:108).
 Thomas, son of Walter and Lartha, m. on 22 d., 9 m., 1705, Elizabeth Price, dau. of Mordecai and Mary (WRMM).
 Walter, m. by 1685, Latha [Juliatha], extx. of Thomas Daborne (PCJU DS#A:251).

CARRADINE
 Peter, m. by 7 April 1665, [-?-], relict of William Wright (*ARMD* 49:584).

CARRELIN
 [-?-], m. by 8 May 1710, Ellinor, dau. of Denum Glandman, Sr., of SO Co. (MWB 13:260).

CARRMAN
 Thomas (or Canman), m. on 9 May 1706, Frances Bright (AAAL 1:32(2)).

CARRIL. See CARROLL.

CARROLL
 [-?-], m. by 17 Feb 1712/3, Elinor, dau. of Mary Vansweringen, widow of SM Co, (MWB 13:557).
 Charles, m. by 1689, Martha, widow of Robert Ridgely, and widow and extx. and extx. of Anthony Underwood (INAC 10:329). He m. 2nd, by 28 April 1711, Mary, dau.

of Henry Darnall of AA Co., who called Carroll his son-in-law (MWB 13:233; MDTP 14A:8, 13; Judgements 1:565, 777, and 4:12).

James, m. on 12 Jan 1707, Margaret Miller (KESP:C3).

John, of CE Co., m. by Oct 1680, Anne, relict of William Savin (MDTP 12A:163).

Peter, m. on 4 May 1710, Mary Renshaw (HAGE:27).

Thomas, Jr., m. on 19 Oct 1686, Rebecca Walton (SOLR:IKL). She was the mother of John, William, Steven, Fisher Walton, who are not yet of age; their father left a will; Rebecca is also the mother of Mary Carroll . (SOJU 1689-1690:179, *eARMD* 106).

CARTER

[-?-], m. by 1676, Mary, mother of Sarah Thomas (MPL WC#2:16).

[-?-], m. by 13 March 1715/6, Sarah, dau. of John Burroughs, of SM Co. (MWB 14:641).

Edward, m. on 17 Nov 1709, Isabella Hamilton (TAPE).

George, on 14 Aug 1677, banns of matrimony were published for him and Mary Nicholson (SOLR O#7:121r). **George, m. on 4 Sep 1677, Mary Nicholson** (SOLR:IKL).

Henry, m. by 26 Aug 1684, Sarah, relict of John Evans, and mother of James Evans (KELR K:105).

Henry, glazier, m. by Aug 1704, Anne, admx. of William Jeffreys of AA Co. (AAJU G:555; INAC 26:33).

John, m. on 9 Aug 1710, Mary Lisbey (AALR 1:37).

John, m. by 1715, Margaret, dau. of John and Mary Burroughs (SMWB PC#1:226).

Philip, of SO Co., m. by 1682, Mary, mother of Sarah Thomas (MPL WC#4:282).

Richard, d. by 23 Aug 1714, leaving a widow Elizabeth, a dau. Frances who m. Richard Colville of the Inner Temple, London, and sisters, Mary Morell, and Ann Beswick, both widows, and a brother Thomas Carter (AALR IB#2:169, 170).

Richard, d. by 22 Feb 1715, leaving a widow Elizabeth, sister of Thomas Rasin of KE Co. (TALR RF#12:371).

Sparrow, m. on 18 May 1716, Elizabeth Sanders (AAAL 1:38).

CARTWRIGHT

[-?-], m. by 13 March 1715/6, Margaret, dau. of John Burroughs, of SM Co. (MWB 14:641).

Charles, m. by 11 July 1692, Sarah Harrison, sister of Robert Harrison (MWB 6:7).

CARVILLE

Alexander, m. on 1 March 1714/5, Mary Haley (AALR 1:38).

John, m. by 10 July 1701, Mary, dau. of James Phillips of BA Co. and his wife Susanna, who later m. [-?-] Arnold. Mary was a sister of Anthony Phillips of BA Co. (INAC 20:229; BALR HW#2:57; MWB 6:81, 12:304).

Robert (Carvele), m. by 7 March 1686, [-?-], admx. of James Bodkin the Younger of SM Co. (INAC 9:219).

CARY

Lawrence, m. by 10 June 1702, Mary, dau. of Richard Everitt of AA Co. (AALR WT#1:330).

Robert (Cavy), m. on 10 April 1710, Elizabeth Ingrum (AALR 1:38).

Robert, m. by 16 Oct 1710, Sarah, admx. of John Tryall (INAC 32A:7). She was the mother of Joseph and Elizabeth Tryall (or Thrill) (QAJRh; MWB 14:72).

CASE

John, m. on 3 April 1711, Grace Young (AALR 2:7). She was admx. of Richard Young (MDTP 22:74, 151).

CASLEY

John, m. on 3 May 1712, Elizabeth Heborn (KESH:11).

CASSEY

James, m. by 24 Nov 1681, Elizabeth, relict and admx. of Charles Barden (INAC 7B:166).

CASTEPHENES

Robert, m. by 12 Aug 1715, [-?-], widow of Robert Smith of CE Co. (INAC 36C:158).

Thomas, m. by 12 Aug 1715, [-?-], widow of Robert Smith of CE Co. (INAC 36C:158).

CATLIN. See CATTLIN.

CATRICK

Robert, m. 1 Jan 1696, Mary Mose Booth (AAAL).

CATTLE

James, m. by 4 Feb 1697, Eliza, sister of Thomas Burford of CH Co. (MWB 6:93).

CATTLIN

[-?-] (Catlun), m. by 19 March 1707/8, Jane, dau. of Joseph Benton of Annamessex, SO Co. (MWB 13:206).

Robert, m. by 14 May 1675, Anne, extx. of Patrick Robinson of SO Co. (MDTP 6:463).

Robert, on 9 Jan 1676/7, banns of matrimony were published for him and Elizabeth Curtis (SOLR O#7:70r). **Robert, Jr., m. on 15 Feb 1676, Elizabeth Curtis** (SOLR:IKL).

CATTON

William, m. on 6 June 1717, Mary Strahan (als. Storton), both of Westminster Parish (AAAN:32).

CAULK
		Isaac, d. by c1704, having m. Mary, dau. of Francis Finch (KELR GL#1:22/44).
John, m. on 7 Feb 1713, Sarah Joce (KESP:C4).

CAUSIN(E)
		Nicholas, m. c1649, Jane, widow of John Cockshot (MPL ABH:22, 59, 207, 4:27).

CAUTHEIM
		Matthew, m. by 1694/5, Mary, admx. of William Needham of CV Co. (INAC 10:440).

CAVE
		William (Cave?), m. by May 1688, Mary, relict of John Diamint of BA Co. (MDTP 14:72).

CAVELL
		William of SM Co., m. by June 1714, Catherine, dau. of coheir of Robert Joyner of SM Co. (Warrant Record AA#1:303).

CAVEN
		Patrick, m. by April 1701, Mary, extx. of George Prouse of TA Co. (MDTP 18B:29; INAC 26:209, 27:226; DOLR 6 Old:239).

CAVINAUGH
		[-?-], m. by 1 Dec 1718, [-?-] {Margaret?], dau. of Gilbert Turberville of SM Co. (MWB 15:122).

CAVY. See also CARY.

CAWARDIN
		Peter, m. by 14 May 1675, Dorcas, dau. of John Lawson of SM Co. (MDTP 6:465).

CAWOOD
		Stephen, m. by 1696, Mary, dau. of John Cox (MDJU 30:24, 240).

CAWSINE. see CAUSIN.

CEAMP. See KEMP.

CECIL(L)
		John, m. on --- 1718, Elizabeth Sallers (PGQA:2).
		Joshua, m. 30 July 1701, Mary, extx. of William Selby of PG Co. (INAC 20:237).
		William, m. by 1714, Catherine, dau. of Robert Joyner of SM Co. (Warrants AA#7:303).

CEELY
John, of AA Co., d. by 14 Feb 1691 having m. Mary, sister of James Rigby (MWB 6:15).

CEMEY
Walter, m. by 1 Feb 1698/9, Elizabeth, dau. of Henry Griffith (DOLR Old 3:51; Old 5:108).

CEMP. See KEMP.

CERMIKEALE. See also CARMICHAEL.

CHADBOURNE
William, m. by 13 Dec 1674, [-?-], relict of Richard Foxon or Fexton (BAAD 2:202; *ARMD* 51:475; INAC 1:147).

CHAMBERLIN
John, m. by banns on 6 Feb 1713 by Richard Sewell, Jane Ashford, spinster (CESS).

CHAMBERS
[-?-], m. by 24 Nov 1702, Anne, dau. of James Sanders of AA Co. (MWB 12:125).
Richard, on 14 March 1675/6, banns of matrimony were published for him and Mary Ivery (SOJU O#7:39). Richard, m. on 24 May 1676, Mary Ivery (SOLR:IKL).
Samuel, merchant, m. 23 July 1700, Anne Gassaway, widow of Capt. Nicholas (AAAL 1:21(1)). She was the admx. of Capt. Nicholas Gassaway (INAC 20:41).

CHAMBLEY
Francis (Champly, Chamby), m. by March 1685/6, Barbara, relict of Charles Cullen (MDTP 13:300).
John, banns pub. 1 Oct 1708, and m. ---, Margery Cheek (HAGE:24).

CHAMPE
[-?-], m. by 1 Jan 1674, Eliza, sister of Thomas Sparrow of AA Co. (MWB 2:76).
William, of SM Co., d. by Oct 1668; left widow Fortune Mitford, now wife of Marmaduke Simm (*ARMD* 57:358).

CHANCE
Richard, m. on 10 June 1704, Ellin Peirceson (TAPE).

CHANCELLOR
John, on 24 Oct 1676, banns of matrimony were published for him and Abigail Harrington, all of Wicomico Hundred (SOLR O#7:60r).

CHANCEY
George, m. after 1700, [-?-], dau. of William Hollis (*MRR*:23).
Mr. George, m. on 22 June 1706, Mrs. Smith (HAGE:18). She was Sarah, admx. of Benjamin Smith (BAAD 2:71; INAC 28:25).

CHANDLER
Job (or John), m. by May 1659, Ann, sister of Simon Overzee (*ARMD* 53:460). She was a dau. of Sarah Yardley (MWB 1:97; CHLR B:274-5).
Richard, m. by Oct 1684, Elizabeth, relict and admx. of John Hamilton of CH Co. (MDTP 13:167, 361; INAC 8:221).
Robert, m. on 5 May 1713, Elizabeth Bryon (AAAN:9).
Col. William, d. by March 1687, having m. Mary, dau. of Henry and Jane (Lowe) Sewell; Mary m. 2nd, Capt. George Brent (MWB 14:63, 28:61; INAC 14:127).
William, m. on 8 Feb 1713/4, Ann Laswell (AAAN:22).

CHANNELL
Henry, m. on 2 Feb 1706, Margrett Ryley (KESP:C2).

CHAPLAIN
James, m. on 20 Feb 1704, Elizabeth [-?-] (TAPE).

CHAPLIN
[-?-], m. by 8 Sep 1710, Susanna, dau. of John Kemball of DO Co. (MWB 13:346).
James, planter, d. by 8 Nov 1717, when his widow had m. William Aires (TALR 12:305).
William, m. by 1651, Elizabeth, mother of Alice Bancroft (MPL ABH:273).
William, m. by Sep 1663, Mary Richardson (Richard Smith informed the court that Capt. Thomas Manning married them without license or banns) (*ARMD* 49:43).
William, of PG Co., m. by c1716, Elizabeth, dau. of Hugh Riley/Ryley of PG Co. (PGLR F:579).

CHAPMAN
Edward, m. by 22 March 1702, Mary, admx. of Henry Chappell of AA Co. (INAC 23:102).
Edward, of SO Co., m. by 21 Sep 1716, Mary, dau. of Richard Harris (MCHR CL:307).
Richard, m. by 8 June 1714, Mary, dau. of John Robson (DOLR Old 2:9, 4:94, 6:219).

CHARLESON
Charles, m. on 14 Nov 1689 Dorothy Musgrave, widow (CHLR P#1:208).

CHARLEWORTH
Robert, m. by [c1702/3], Elinor, extx. of George Eyres (MWB 3:112).

CHARLTON
Thomas, m. on 13 Feb 1715/6, Mary Fowler (AAAN:29).

CHARMES
Maunders, m. by 2 Nov 1716, Bridgett, dau. of Nicholas Richardson, chirurgeon, of SM Co. (MWB 14:304; MDTP 23:84).

CHARNOCK
Anthony, m. on 14 May 1717, Hannah Hollingsworth (AAAN:32).

CHEAPMAN
John, of Bush Creek, banns pub. June 1701 Hannah Markum (HAGE:11).

CHEENEY. See CHENEY.

CHENEY
Charles, m. 15 July 1701, Ann Pattison (AAAL 2:2). She was the relict and extx. of Gilbert Pattison of AA Co. (INAC 25:327).
Charles (Cheeney), m. by 31 May 1705, Anne, dau. of William Jones, Sr., of AA Co., planter (MWB 3:489).
John, m. by May 1674, Jane, admx. of Henry Hough of CV Co., chirurgeon (*ARMD* 65:301, 329).
John, m. on 3 Jan 1705/6, Mary Beadle (AAAL 1:32(2)).
John, m. on 22 Sep 1709, Elizabeth Tylley (or Tilley) (AALR 1:37). She was the admx. of Charles Tilley of AA Co. (INAC 31:135, 32B:126, 33B:172).
John, m. on 24 July 1718, Anne Burgess (AAAL 2:15).
Richard, d. by Aug 1694, having m. Eleanor, mother of John Pindle (MDTP 15C:115).
Richard, m. on 11 Dec 1707, Rachel Nicholson (AAAL 1:36).
Thomas, m. 19 Aug 1697, Sarah Westall Booth (AAAL 1:5).She was a dau. of George Westall [or Eestall] (MWB 11:191).
Thomas, m. on 7 June 1716, Susannah Hooper (AAAL 1:38, 2:11).

CHERRY
Oliver, m. on 5 July 1718, Rebekah Holland (AAAN:39).

CHESELDINE
Kenelm, m. by 28 Sep 1712, Mary, dau. of Thomas Gerard formerly of Westmoreland Co., VA (CHLR D#2:24; MDTP 23:154, 361).

CHESHERE
John, m. on 18 July 1706, Hannah Gott (AAJA:33 #1).

CHESHIRE
Richard, m. by 3 Oct 1696, Mary, extx of Samuell Raniger of AA Co. (INAC 14:61).

William, m. by 20 Dec 1682, Mary, prob. dau. of John Tennison of SM Co., who named William Cheshire as his son-in-law (MWB 4:16).

CHESTER
William, m. by 1697, Ann, dau. of John and Eliza Green (SMWB PC#1:99, 174).

CHEVERELL
John, m. by 1702, Jane, dau. of Edward and Mary Morgan of SM Co. (SMWB PC#1:129, 159, 273).

CHEW
Benjamin, of AA Co., m. on 8 d., 10 m. (Dec), 1692, Elizabeth Benson of CV Co., at the home of Richard Harrison, father-in-law of said Elizabeth Benson (WRMM).
John, and Elizabeth Harrison filed their intentions to marry on 19 d., 1 m., 1707/8, and 20 d., 6 m., 1707 (WRMMa).
Joseph, of AA Co., m. by 17 Dec 1673, Margaret, relict and admx. of Thomas Miles (or Mills), innholder, of AA Co. (MDTP 6:56).
Joseph, of CV Co., m. on 17 d., 9 m., 1685, Mary Smith of said Co. (WRMM). He m. 2nd, by c1688, Elizabeth, relict and extx. of Seaborne Battee of AA Co. (INAC 10:313, AALR PK:469-474). She was a dau. of Henry Hanslap of AA Co. (MWB 6:163).
Joseph, bapt. 21 Jan 1710), m. on 23 Jan 1710, Mary Ford (AAJA)
Samuel, m. by 1658, Ann, dau. of William Ayres (Hodges cites Judg. 65:210).
Samuel, m. by 2 Feb 1699/1700, Ann, extx. of Dr. Alexander Chappell (MDTP 17:251).
Samuel, and Mary Harrison filed their intentions to marry on 15 d., 5 m., 1703, and on 13 d., 6 m., 1703 (WRMMa). She was a dau. of Richard Harrison of CV Co. (MWB 14:142).
Samuel, and Elizabeth Coale (a widow with children) filed their intentions to marry on 19 d., 3 m., 1704, and on 16 d., 4 m., 1704 (WRMMa).
Samuel, son of Benjamin (dec.) and Elizabeth, on 7 d., 8 m. (Oct) 1715, Mary Galloway, dau. of Samuel and Ann (WRMM).
William, son of Samuel, dec., m. on 20 d., 10 m. (Dec), 1690, Sydney Wynne, of AA Co., dau. of Thomas and Martha, dec., of PA (WRMM).

CHIBSEY
Edmond, m. by 20 May 1694, Jane, dau. of George Robins of TA Co. (MWB 7:90).

CHICISK
Thomas, m. by 12 Aug 1706, Elizabeth, admx. of Daniel Jenkinson of CH Co. (INAC 25:386).

CHICKLY
James, m. 29 Jan ---, Sarah Cheney (AAAL).

CHIELY
Samuel, m. by 1687, Elizabeth, relict of William Marshall of CV Co. (MDTP 14:11, 45, 86).

CHILCOCK. See CHILCOTT.

CHILCOTT
James (Chilcock), m. in 1698, Mary Tindale (AAJA:4#8). She was the extx. of William Tindall (MDTP 17:92).

CHILCUTT
Anthony, of DO Co., m. by May 1685, [-?-], widow of James Harper (MDTP 13:236).

CHILDS
Henry (Child), Jr., and Margaret Preston, both of Herring Creek MM, filed their intentions to marry on 23 d., 11 m., 1709/10, and 17 d., 12 m., 1709/10 (WRMMa).
Nathaniel, m. on 25 Oct 1704, Elinor Stutson (KESP:C2).
William, m. on 9 Feb 1715/6, Mary Cook (AAAN:29).

CHILTON
Cuthbert, m. on 29 July 1703, Mary Baker (CVCH).

CHING
John, m. on 8 Jan 1700, Ann Skidmore (AAMA:81). She was the admx. of Samuel Skidmore of AA Co. (INAC 23:68).

CHINTON
Hugh, of CV Co., innholder, m. by 12 Nov 1711, Elinor, dau. of Richard Hooper (DOLR Old 4:75, 6:184)

CHISSAM
John, m. on 31 Aug 1678, Abigail Bell (SOLR:IKL).

CHITTAM
John, m. by April 1686, Dorothy, widow of [-?-] [-?-] (MDTP 13:334).

CHITTIM
George, m. on 22 Nov 1705, Sarah Mallbey (AAJA:31 #19).

CHOCKE
John, m. on 14 Oct 1703, Margaret Tudor (AAJA:28#2).

CHRISTIAN
Christian, m. on 16 Aug 1707, Margaret Wessels (KESP:C3).

CHRISTISON
Wenlock, of Miles R., of TA Co., m. by 27 Feb 1678, Eliza, mother of Samuel, Peter, John, and Eliza Harwood, whom Christison named as sons-in-law and dau.-in-law in his will (MWB 2:89).

CHRISTOPHER
John, m. by 1710, Mary, dau. of John Rixon (SOLR 10 (CD):597).

CHUBB
John, m. by May 1707, Isabella Be...ly of Philadelphia (PCJU PL#1:142).

CHUMBLY
Francis, m. by 11 May 1685, Barbara, widow and extx. of Charles Cuiles of CH Co. (INAC 9:6).

CLACKSON. See CLARKSON.

CLAGETT
[-?-], m. by 26 Nov 1714, Deborah, dau. of the Hon. John Dorsey of BA Co. (MWB 14:26).
John, m. by 1714, Verlinda, dau. of John and Ann Sollers (INAC 36A:155).
Capt. Thomas, m. by 2 Oct 1674, Mary [sometimes given as Margaret], widow of Richard Hooper of CV Co. (INAC 1:80; MDTP 5:1, 289). Mary was late wife of Richard Hooper, and mother of Sarah and Elizabeth Hooper (*ARMD* 67:115).

CLARK(E)
[-?-], m. by 26 July 1658, Jane, relict of Nicholas Cawsine, and mother of Mary Adams and Jane Cockshutt (*ARMD* 41:171).
[-?-], m. by 24 July 1675, Rachel, dau. of Richard Beard of AA CO. (MWB 2:143).
[-?-], m. by 12 Oct 1696, Julian, dau. of Thomas Mudd of CH Co. (MWB 7:265).
[-?-], m. by 28 Nov 1709, Grace, dau. of James Greenwell of SM Co. (MWB 13:725).
[-?-], m. by 6 Oct 1710, Mary, dau. of Richard Tull of SO Co. (MWB 13:258).
[-?-], m. by 19 Jan 1711, Elizabeth, kinswoman of Capt. Lawrence Draper (BAIN 3:216).
[-?-], m. by 10 March 1716/7, Mary, dau. of Mary Rose of Chaptico Hundred, SM Co. (MWB 15:376).
Benjamin, of AA Co., m. by Feb 1692/3, Thamar, widow of James Hackett, and dau. of Edward Selby, Sr., late of AA Co. (MDTP 15A:4; AALR IH#3:86, WT#1:51).
Benjamin, m. by 1714, Judith, widow of Robert Parker and dau. of Thomas Mattingly, Sr. (SMWB PC#1:192; MDTP 21:210).
Benoni, m. by 22 Feb 1696, [-?-], dau. of Jacob Young of CE Co. (MWB 7:277).
Edward, m. by 1667, Ann, dau. of John Shircliff (MPL 8:502, 10:474).
Edward, m. by 1714, Henrietta, dau. of Thomas Walker (SMWB PC#1:325).
George, m. on 2 May 1711, Margaret Screech (TAPE).

George, m. by 30 Sep 1717, Susannah, sister of John Mason of SM Co. (MWB 14:648). She was the dau. of Susanna, the widow of Robert Mason, Gent., of SM Co. (MWB 14:341).

George, m. by 1718, Hannah, dau. of Peter Watts (SMWB PC#1:249).

Henry (Cleark), m. on 5 Dec 1706, Katherine Brion (AAAL 1:33).

Henry, m. on 21 d. 2 m., 1708, Sarah Parratt at Tuckahoe Meeting House (TATH).

John, m. by 19 March 1674/5, [-?-], widow of John Elly of CV Co. (INAC 1:195).

John, m. on 24 Oct 1704, Martha Shepard (TAPE).

John, m. on 2 Dec 1708, Alce Withers (AALR 1:36).

John, m. on 16 Oct 1713 or 1714, Elizabeth Draper (HAGE:30, 33).

Jonathan, m. by 21 May 1717, Elizabeth, admx. of John Freeman of SO Co. (INAC 38A:152).

Matthew [or Matthias], m. by 1706, Eliza, widow of Job Barnes of AA Co. (AAJU G:670; AALR IB#1:150, IB#2:118-120).

Neale, m. 17 Oct 1699, by Mr. Gresham, Jane Jones (AAAL 1:12). She was a dau. of William Jones, Sr., of AA Co., planter (MWB 3:489).

Philip, m. by 30 March 1686, Hannah, admx. of George Mecall or Mackell of SM Co. (INAC 13A:285; MDTP 13:313, 16:115).

Richard, m. by 14 Aug 1679 (immediately after Street's death), Susanna, extx., of Francis Street of CV Co. (INAC 6:294).

Richard, m. on 11 Aug 1713, Eleanor Selman (AAAL 2:10).

Robert, m. by 1654, Winifred Seyborne, late wife of Gov. Thomas Greene (MPL ABH:403;rants ABH:6, 12, 67, 7:427, 12:560).

Robert, m. by 1684, Sarah, dau. of Abraham Combs of SM Co. (MDTP 13:243).

Robert, m. by 9 Oct 1714, Elizabeth Mattingly, dau. of Thomas and Elizabeth (SMWB PC#1192, 302; MINV 16:653; MWB 14:222).

Robert, m. on 18 Feb 1717/8, Sillinah Smith (HAGE:34, 80).

Samuel, m. on 25 Sep 1717, Mary Clark (KESP:C4).

Thomas, m. by 1693, Ann Barber, sister of Edward Barber of SM Co. (Hodges cites MDAD 5:408).

William, m. by 3 Jan 1708, Mary, heir of James Homewood, and sister of Thomas Homewood (MWb 12, pt. 2:189; AALR IB#2:108).

CLARKSON
[-?-], m. by 29 March 1714, Eliza, dau of Thomas Hagoe (Hague?) of CH Co. (MWB 14:213).

[-?-] (Clackson), m. by 8 Nov 1683, Johanna, dau. of Thomas Hooker of West River, AA Co. (MWB 4:28).

William, m. on 22 Nov 1713, Elizabeth Hagian (PGKG:242).

CLARY
John, m. on 30 Dec 1705, Elizabeth Haly (AAAN:1). [This name has been misread by several transcribers, but an examination of the original register shows the name was actually Clary].

CLAWE
William, m. by 27 May 1677, Sarah, widow of William Cole (*ARMD* 51:498).

CLAYLAND
Roger, m. by Oct 1713, Elizabeth, extx. of Moses Harris of TA Co. (MDTP 22:268; INAC 35A:128).
William, m. by 3 March 1714, Anne, dau. of Edward and Elizabeth (Comegys) Fry (MCHR CL:46).

CLAYTON
David, m. on 8 June 1717, Elizabeth Selby (AAAN:32).
Solomon, m. by 19 Feb 1714, Ann dau. of Edward Smith, dec., and his wife Ann, now wife of [-?-] Marshall (QALR I(J)KA:32).
William, of TA Co., m. by Aug 1682, Margaret, relict and admx. of Jno. Greene (MDTP 12B: 178).
William, m. by 1 April 1708, Joan, extx. of Robert Gough of QA Co. (INAC 28:84, 29:279).

CLEARK. See CLARK.

CLEFTON. See CLIFTON.

CLEGATT. See CLAGETT.

CLEMENCE
Henry, m. by 2 Jan 1703, Sarah, admx. of John Hews of CE Co. (MWB 3:370)

CLEMENTS
[-?-], m. by 3 March 1716, Rosamond, dau. of Rosamond Machetee, widow of Patrick Machetee of CH Co. (MWB 14:236).
[-?-], m. by 3 March 1716, Elinor, dau. of Rosamond Machetee, widow of Patrick Machetee of CH Co. (MWB 14:236).
Andrew, m. by banns on 20 Nov 1718, by Mr. Sewell, Kathrin Sefferson (CESS).
John, the Elder, d. by 1676; his widow, Mary Inchbudd, m. 2nd, James Derumple (*ARMD* 38:130-131, 70:38).
Lambert, m. on 24 July 1715, Sarah Dawson (TAPE).
Michael, m. 1 Nov 1713, Elizabeth Jonson, spinster (CESS).

CLIFF
Samuel, m. on 24 Nov 1715, Catherine Hues (TAPE).

CLIFT
John, m. by 1 Oct 1694, Elinor, mother of Roger Bradberry (TALR LL#7:107).
John, m. on 28 Aug 1701, Elizabeth [-?-] (TAPE).

CLIFTON

[-?-] (Clefton), m. by 12 Jan 1707, Sarah, dau. of Samuel Collings, bricklayer of Pocomoke, SO Co. (MWB 12:262).

James, m. by 1674, Ann, sister of George Brent, Gent. (MPL 6:26, 19:382).

Stephen, m. by 11 June 1663, d. by 1665, having m. Jane or Joan Turner, dau. of William Turner; she m. 2nd, Thomas Bowdell/Bodell of CV Co. (PCJU FF:---; MDTP 2:106; *ARMD* 49:440; MWB 1:202).

CLIMER

Charles, m. on 1 Jan 1709, Johannah Neale (TAPE). She was a dau. of Francis Neale, Sr., planter, of TA Co. (MWB 14:168).

John (Clymer), d. by 1 June 1685, having m. Ann, widow of Philip Stevenson of TA, and mother of Thomas Stevenson (TALR 5:15).

CLIMPS

Thomas, m. on 13 Jan 1701, Mary Dollin (AAMA:81).

CLIPSHAM

Thomas, m. by Oct 1678, Susanna, relict and extx. of John Cage of CH Co. (MDTP 10:300; INAC 7A:151).

CLOATHER. See CLOTHIER.

CLOCKER

Daniel, m. by Oct 1658, Mary, relict of James Courtney (*ARMD* 41:185).

Daniel, m. by 17 Dec 1675, Patience, sister of Mary [-?-], who m. William Baker of SM Co. (MDTP 7:180).

CLOTHIER

Lewis, d. by 23 Dec 1684, having m. by 12 Aug 1680, Susanna, dau. of Robert Knapp of TA Co. (MWB 2:188; TALR 4:343).

Robert (Cloather), m. by 6 Nov 1702, Jane, dau. of Robert Kemp of TA Co. (MWB 11:324).

CLOUDER

[-?-], m. by July 1678, Temperance, relict of John Ashberry of CH Co. (MDTP 10:185).

CLOUDS

[-?-] (Cloudes?), m. by July 1678, Temperance, widow of John Ashberry (MDTP 10:185).,

Nicholas, m. by 16 June 1696, [-?-], legatee of John Gouldsmith of SM Co. (INAC 13B:112).2

Richard, m. by 16 June 1696, Judith, extx. of John Gouldsmith, and widow of John Joy (INAC 13B:112; Hodges cites SMAD HH:96).

CLOVE
[-?-], m. sometime after 1687, Hannah, b. c1671, widow of Benjamin Blackledge of KE Co., and dau. of William and Lucy Gallaway, and sister of James and William Gallaway (KELR JS#X:409, 416).
John, m. on 15 July 1714, Hannah Blackleat (KESP).

COAD
John, m. by 1670, Susanna, widow of Robert Slye, and dau. of Dr. Thomas Gerard of St. Clement Manor (Fresco cites Prov. Court MM:403, 412, 419-420; MDCR 3:753, 1092, 1093).

COAL(E)/COLE
[-?-], m. after 1657, Mary [-?-], maidservant, formerly the wife of Thomas Bramstead (*NFMP*:194 cites *ARMD* 10:549-156).
    Edward, m. Eliza, widow of Capt. Luke Gardiner, and dau. of Robert Slye (MWB 1:422; Hodges cites Pro Court DD#2:396).
    Edward, Jr., of SM Co., m. by 25 May 1716, Ann, dau. of James Neale, Sr., of CH Co. (PGLR F:529).
    John, m. by 1691, Judith, dau. of John and Margaret Gouty (DOLR Old 5:81).
    John, m. by 1697, Margaret, widow of John Atkins of AA Co. (MDTP 17:49).
    Philip, m. on 6 d., 1 m. (April), 1697, Cassandra Skipwith (WRMM). She was a dau. of George Skipwith (MRR: AA Co.:114).
    Richard, m. by 27 June 1719, Mary, dau. and the only heir apparent of Renatus Smith (QALR I(J)KA:236; *ARMD* 34:35; 38:325).
    Robert, m. by 9 March 1677 as her 2nd husband, Ann Rennalls, sister of George Rennalls, and had m. 1st, John Medley, who d. by Aug 1677, and 3rd, [perhaps by 1693] Charles Daft (INAC 4:624, 13:293, 624; MDTP 4C:36, 14:8).
    William, m. by 9 Sep 1674, [-?-], dau. of Philip Thomas of AA Co. (MDTP 7:63).
    William, m. by June 1679, Margaret, extx. of Michael Rochford (*ARMD* 68:221, 69:26; INAC 7A:144, 371).
    William, m. by 4 Oct 1688, Ann, relict of David Adams of BA Co. (MDTP 14:99).
    William, Jr. , m. on 30 d., 5 m. (July), 1689, at the house of Richard Johns, Elizabeth Sparrow, of the Clifts (WRMM).
    William, and Sarah White, filed their intentions to marry on 29 d., 4 m., 1716, and 27 d., 5 m., 1716 (WRMMa).

COALE. See also COATE.

COATE
John (or Coale), m. on 14 April 1707, Mary Daveridge (KESP:C2).

COAT(E)S
Leonard, of AA Co., m. by 7 June 1679, Martha, admx. of William Russell (*ARMD* 68:208; INAC 6:232, 362; &A:258).

COATSWORTH
Caleb (Coakworth), Dr. of Physic, London, m. by June 1705, Susannah, only sister of Roger Newman (MWB 3:258; MDTP 19B:56).

COBB
James, m. on 30 Oct 1709, Rebecca Emerson (HAGE:26). She was the relict and admx. of John Daniell of CV Co., and extx. of James Empson (Emison) of BA Co. (INAC 9:27 32A:23; BAAD 2:147).

COCKAYNE
Samuel, of Co. of York, Eng., m. by 15 April 1710, Ann, surviving dau. of the elder bro. of Richard Carter of TA Co., MD, dec. (TALR RF#11:136).

COCKEE. See COCKEY.

COCKERIN
John, m. by 27 March 1714, Elizabeth, admx. of Denis Connelly of TA Co. (INAC 35A:37).

COCKEY
Edward, of St. Margaret's, Westminster, Parish, m. on 1 Aug 1717, Rhoda Harris, widow, of Kent Island (AAAN:33).She was the admx. of Isaac Harris of QA Co. (INAC 39C:135).
Joshua, m. by 20 June 1716, Sarah, dau. of John Ray of AA Co., dec. (AALR IB#2:283).
Thomas, m. by Dec 1700, Elizabeth, extx. of Richard Moss of AA Co. (MDTP 18B:27; INAC 23:15).
William, of Severn, AA Co., banns of marriage pub. 29 Sep 1668, for him and Frances Vincent of Somerset Co. (*ARMD* 454:729; SOLR O#1:136),
William, m. by 1707, Mary Crouch (MRR: AA Co.:254).

COCKS. See COX.

COCKSHOTT or COCKSHUTT.
Rev. Thomas (sometimes Cockshutt), m. by 1 Oct 1708, Anne, widow and extx. of Joseph Hall (INAC 28:351, 32A:74, 35A:14, which gives Joseph's name as Hale; MDTP 31:299).

CODD
Col. St. Leger, m. by (c1697), Anna, widow of Maj. Joseph Wickes of KE Co. (INAC 15:217).
Saint Leager (Cood), m. on 18 Oct 1700, Mary Francis (KESP:C1).
St. Leger, m. by 26 Aug 1703, Mary, dau. of Hans Hanson of CE Co. (MWB 3:264; INAC 25:86).

COHEE
    Nicholas (Cahee?), m. on 11 Dec 1701, Sarah [-?-] (TAPE).

COHOW
    [-?-], m. by 4 Jan 1717, Martha, dau. of William Harde of CH Co. (MWB 14:714).

COLBOURNE
    Francis, m. on 9 May 1708, Deborah Beamish (AALR 1:36).

COLBRON
    Joseph, m. on 21 Oct 1710, by Rev. Jona' White, Mary Stone (PGQA:1).

COLCLOUGH
    Maj. George, m. by Jan 1660/1, Elizabeth, widow of Simon Overzee (*ARMD* 41:403).

COLE. See COAL(E)

COLEGATE
    Richard, m. by 5 Aug 1707, Rebecca, dau. of Eleanor Herbert   (BALR RM#HS:569).

COLEHOUNE
    John, on 16 June 1676, banns of matrimony were published for him and Jane Carter (SOJU O#7:43).

COLEHOUNE. See also CALHOUN.

COLEMAN
    Elias, m. by Jan 1665/6, Ann Stevens (*ARMD* 57:4).
    Joseph, m. on last d., 6 m., 1712, Mary Thomas, both of AA Co. (WRMM).
    Thomas, m. by Dec 1699, Mary, admx. of Jonathan [Lamary?] (MDTP 18A:49).

COLLE
    Edward (Cole), m. by 23 May 1713, [-?-], heir of Nicholas Power of SM co. (INAC 35B:67).

COLLETT
    John, of BA Co., d. by 1693/4, leaving an admx. Elizabeth who was also widow of Miles Gibson, and formerly widow of Henry Hazlewood (INAC 12:150).

COLLIER
    Francis (Collyer), m. by March 1695, Sarah, admx. of John Evans of CV Co. (INAC 13B:91, 18:160).
    Giles (Colliar), m. by 12 Dec 1688, Grace, step-dau. of Alexander Smith, planter (CHLR Q:2).

James, m. by 26 March 1674, [-?-], widow of Edward Ayres of Bush River, BA Co. (MDTP 6:178).

James, of SO Co., m. by 8 Dec 1708, Mary, dau. of George Betts, whom Collier called father-in-law (MWB 12, pt. 2:90).

John, d. by about March 1673, having m. Ann, widow of James Stringer of AA Co.; she m. 2nd, William York (MDTP 6:148).

John, m. by March 1684/5, Sarah, admx. of George Hooper. She later m. by 1 April 1693, John Hall (BALR HW#2:38; BACP D:252).

John, m. by 1 June 1686, Sarah [-?-]; they are called bro. and sister in the undated will (proved on that date) of Abraham Holman of BA Co. (MWB 4:219).

Matthew, m. by 20 Aug 1702, Alice Austin (KELR JD#1:55). She was widow of Samuel Austin, and mother of Margaret Watson and Hannah Phillips (QALR IKA:221).

Robert, m. on 2 March 1675, Elizabeth Dashiell (SOLR:IKL).

COLLIES

James, m. by 1674, Elizabeth, widow of Edward Ayres (MDTP 6:178).

COLLIN(G)(S)

[-?-], m. by 18 March 1715, Mary, dau. of James Truett, Sr., of SO Co. (MWB 14:581).

Cornelius, m. on 3 March 1700, by Mr. Nobbs, minister, Sarah [-?-] (TAPE).

Cornelius, m. by 14 July 1716, Sarah, dau. of John Cox (TALR RF#12:247).

Edmund (Collins), m. entered on 16 Nov 1682, Honora [-?-] (SOLR:IKL).

Francis, m. by c1692, Sarah, extx. of [-?-] Evans (PJCU DSA:32).

James, m. by banns on 1 Aug 1717 by Mr. Sewell, Ellinor Ozey, widow (CESS).

Matthew, m. by Nov 1710, Ursula Griffin (QAJR Nov 1710:115).

Richard, m. by April 1678, Sarah, extx. of William Hambleton of TA Co. (MDTP 10:41; INAC 6:309).

Robert, m. on 1 Jan 1704/5, Mary Watson (CVCH).

Samuel, m. on 3 Sep 1680, Margaret Hodson (SOLR:IKL).

William, m. on 12 Oct 1699, Martha Pratt (KESP:C1).

COLLISON

George, m. by 6 Nov 1702, Eliza, dau. of Robert Kemp of TA Co. (MWB 11:324).

William, m. on 3 Dec 1713, Susanna Adams (SJSG:20R). She was admx. of William Adams (BAAD 1:212, 256; 2:127).

COLLYER. See COLLIER.

COLT

Robert, m. by 16 Oct 1708, Dorothy, widow and extx. of Walter Smith (INAC 29:12; QALR ETA:171).

COLVILLE
Richard, of the Inner Temple, London, m. by 2 March 1713, Frances, dau. of Richard Carter, late of MD (AALR IB#2:169).

COMAGIS. See COMEGYS.

COMBE(S)
Abraham, m. by 8 April 1684, Margaret, admx. of Edward Fishwick of SM Co. (INAC 8:247).
Edward, m. on 28 July 1697, Judith [-?-] (TAPE).
John, m. by 1676, Mary, dau. and heir of Edward Rose, dec. (*ARMD* 66:490).
William, m. by 5 Jan 1678, Elizabeth, dau. and heir of Edward Roe (TALR 3:283).

COMBERFORD
George (Commerford), m. on 4 Nov 1717, Elizabeth Marsh, widow (AAAN:35). She was the widow and extx. of Thomas Marsh of QA Co., and widow and admx. of Thomas Baxter of QA Co. (MDAD 1:208, 364; 6:413). She was the dau. of Major John Hawkins (MWB 14:385).

COMEGYS
[-?-], m. by 30 Oct 1711, Judith, widow of Edward Combes of TA Co. She m. by 4 May 1719, David Robinson (MDAD 1:408).
Cornelius, m. 1 Oct 1679, Mary, relict and admx. of James Kenneday of KE Co. (INAC 6:458).
Cornelius, m. by [c1712] Rebecca [-?-], relict and extx. of 1st, John Campbell and KE Co., and 2nd, Benjamin Smith of CE Co. (INAC 33A:244).
Edward (Comagis), planter, m. on 17 Nov 1717, Mary Harwood (AAAN:35).
William, m. on 14 Dec 1709, Mary [-?-] (KESH:9). She was prob. Mary, widow of Moses Alford of KE Co. (PCJU TP#12:369; INAC 31:238)
William (Coegeies), m. by 22 April 1710, Mary, sister of Edward Venitt of KE Co. (IMWB 13:33).

COMES
John, m. by banns on 31 Dec 1715, by Mr. Sewell, Sarah Newman, spinster (CESS).

COMING(S)
Nicholas, m. by 13 April 1702, Margaret, widow of Leonard Camper of TA Co. (INAC 21:330).

COMMERFORD. See COMBERFORD.

COMMON
[-?-], d. by 15 June 1715, leaving a widow Jane, mother of John Higgins (TALR RF#12:204).

CONANT
    Robert, m. on 9 May 1705, Sophia Harrington (AAJA:31 #2).

CONAWAY. See CONNOWAY.

CONNARD
    Philip, m. on 17 Dec 1677, Mary [Dance?] (SOLR:IKL).

CONNELL
    Thomas, m. by 1717, Mary Ogden (CH Court Records, I#2:249).

CONNER
    Arthur, m. on 11 Oct 1710, Margaret Pollard (TAPE).

CONNIEW
    [John?], m. on 18 Sep 1673, Dorothy Bundick (SOLR:IKL).

CONNILL
    [-?-], m. by 28 March 1715, Eliza, dau. of Robert Collson, Gent., of CH Co.
(MWB 14:50).

CONNOR
    James, m. on 1 Jan 1705, Elinor Flanagan (KESP:C2).
    John, m. by 22 Aug 1713, Margaret, extx. of James Tyer of CH Co. (INAC 34:31).
    Philip, m. on 4 March 1700, Jane Harris (KESP:C1).

CONNOWAY or CONAWAY.
    James, m. on 11 May 1714, Sarah Chappell (AAMA:84).
    John, m. on 17 Aug 1714, Ann Aegillston (Eagleston) (AAAN:22).

CONSTABLE
    [-?-], m. by 23 March 1699, Grace, called sister in the will of John Humbe of CV
Co. (MWB 6:212).
    Henry, m. by 26 Sep 1682, Katherine, extx. of James Rigby of AA Co. (INAC
7C:335; 10:245).
    Henry, m. by Aug 1688, Catherine, extx. of Rowland Nance of AA Co. (MDTP
14:89).

CONTEE
    Mr. John, m. by 16 Oct 1704, Charity, widow and extx. of Col. John Courts. He
m. 2nd, Mary [-?-] (MWB 3:386, 12:276).
    Peter, of Barnstaple, Devon, m. by 16 Oct 1703, Frances, dau. of Henry Stockett
(AALR WT#2:79).

CONWELL
    Anthony, and Elizabeth Talbott filed their intentions to marry on 9 d., 5 m., 1708 (WRMMa).

COOD. See CODD.

COODE
    Col. John, m. by 8 Dec 1674, Susannah, widow of Robert Slye, and dau. of Thomas Gerard; she m. Coode as her 2nd husband (Hodges cites Pro. Court MM:403, 412, 419, 420; MCHR 3:1092-1093; Judgements 1:122; *ARMD* 65:506; 69:136).

COOK
    Edward, m. by c1677, Katherine (or Alice), admx. of Henry (or Robert) Montague of TA Co. (INAC 5:150, 6:468; *ARMD* 69:59, 142).
    Edward, m. by c1681, Katherine, extx. of Dr. Robert Winsmore of DO Co. (INAC 7B:47).
    John, of Findren, Eng., m. by 15 Oct 1700, Ann, niece and residuary legatee of George Robotham of TA Co. (TALR 9:70).
    John, m. on 17 Aug 1702, Catherine [-?-] (TAPE).
    John, m. on 31 Oct 1706, Catherine Squibb (AAAN:1).
    William, m. on 12 Aug 1711, by Rev. Jona. White, Eliza Anderson (PGQA:2).
    William (Coock), m. on 27 Aug 1713, Sarah Garrett (HAGE:30).

COOK. See also CORK.

COOKE. See COOK.

COOKSON
    William, m. on 31 May ---, Margrett Petterson (KESP:B3).

COOLE
    [-?-], m. by 9 July 177, Eliza, dau. of Thomas Ford of QA Co. (MWB 12, p. 2:197).

COOLEY
    Daniel, m. on 23 Oct 17--, Elizabeth Watson (KESP:C2).
    Daniel, m. by 22 April 1714, Elizabeth, dau. of Henry Gott of KE Co. (Warrant Record AA(#7):289).
    George (Cooly), m. by 26 April 1709, Mary, extx. of Ralph Dawson, Sr., of TA Co. (INAC 29:277).

COOMES
    Richard, of CH Co., m. by 1697, Clare Green, dau. of Clare Green (CHWB 11:315).

COOPER

[-?-], m. by 5 Oct 1717, Christina Barbara, mother of Nicholas Guyther, Ann Beckwith, Dorothy Leigh, and grandmother of Richard Beard (MWB 14:651).

George, m. on 31 Dec 1700, Mary Moss (KESP:C1).

John, of CV Co, granted a marriage license on 4 Aug 1666 to marry Elisabeth Holland of CV Co. (MDTP 2:172).

John, banns of marriage pub. on 28 May 1667 for him and Susanna Brayfield (*ARMD* 54:671; SOLR O#1:62).

John, m. by 27 May 1710, Susannah, relict and admx. of John Shareman of CH Co. (INAC 31:287).

Richard, m. on 12 Feb 1701, Mary [-?-] (TAPE).

Robert, of SM Co., m. by Dec 1692, Patience, widow of James Yore, dec., and of Daniel Clocker (MDTP 14A:9, 15A:16, 22).

Tho., m. by 1707, [-?-], kin of Hugh Benson (SMRR:7).

Thomas, m. by 5 Aug 1713, Mary, admx. of William Bright of SM Co. (INAC 35B:95).

Walter, d. by 10 Sep 1651, having m., prob. as his second wife, Anne, sister of John Depotter and William and Thomas Deynes, and cousin of Richard Bridgman, both of Amsterdam (MWB 1:29).

COP

Henry, m. by c1652, [-?-], widow of [-?-] Bury (MPL ABH:276).

COPAS

John, m. by Nov 1685, Ann, widow of Matthew Wood (BACP D:356).

COPEDGE

John, m. by 14 Jan 1683, Eliza, dau. of Eliza Eareckson (MWB 4:37).

John, of TA Co., m. by 2 Sep 1698, Mary, relict and admx. of Allan Smith of KE Co. (INAC 16:171).

COPPING

John, m. by lic. 14 May 1703, Margaret Atkey, dau. of John Atkey (CESS).

John, of CE Co., m. by 25 Sep 1704, Angelica [?], sister of Mary Atkey, and dau. of John Atkey of CE Co. (CELR 2:58).

COPUS

John, m. by Nov 1685, Sarah Teale, mother of Ales Teale (BALR TR#RA:338).

CORBIN

[-?-], m. by 21 April 1718, Jane, dau. of William Wilkinson of BA Co. (MWB 14:603).

CORD

Thomas, banns pub. July 1698, m. on 4 Aug 1698, Hannah Matthews (both of this parish) (HAGE:2).

CORDEA
Mark, on 10 Jan 1673, made a prenuptial agreement with Hester Lecompte, widow and extx. of Anthony Lecompte of DO Co. (MDTP 6:63).

CORDWARDIN. See CAWARDIN.

CORK
[-?-] (Corke), m. by 6 July 1695, Sarah, dau. of Nicholas Allom of CE Co. (MWB 7:96).
William (Cook?), m. on 4 Aug 1705, Anne Whitehead (KESP:C2).

CORKER
Thomas, m. by Jan 1675/6, Elizabeth, dau. of Clement Theobald of CH Co. (MDTP 7:147).

CORKERIN
[-?-], m. by 21 Jan 1693, Ellinor, sister of Jane Linsey and of Thomas Butler (MWB 7:15).
James, m. on 22 Dec 1715, Susannah Baley (TAPE).

CORNE
Thomas (Conn), m. by Aug 1714, Elizabeth, extx. of John Mortimore (BACP IS#B:566); INAC 36C;23 states that John Mortimore was of CV Co.; see also AAJU VD#1:392).
Thomas, m. by Dec 1714, Elizabeth, extx. of Jno. Bigger of CV Co. (MDTP 22:374).

CORNELIUS
Hugh, m. by 1665, Mary, mother of Mary Coke (MPL 8:130).
John, m. on 27 Feb 1717, Sarah White (AAMA:90).
John, m. on 6 Feb 1718, Sarah White of Westminster Parish (AAAN:36).
Peter, m. by 11 June 1713, Margrett, extx. of Anguish Morah (INAC 34:4½).

CORNELL
Joseph, m. by 13 Aug 1686, Margrett, admx. of Robert Worrall of CH Co. (INAC 9:76).

CORSE
James, Jr., m. on 23 d. 3 m., 1710, Ann Beck, both of KE Co. (KECE).

COSDEN
Alphonso, m. by 10 June 1685, Anne, dau. of Christopher Beanes (BALR IS#H:101).
Thomas, m. Feb 1677/8, [-?-], admx. of Robert Brooks (*ARMD* 67:204).

COSLEY
William, m. on 26 Dec 1709, Mary Ellis (HAGE:26).

COSTIN
Stephen, m. by 10 June 1690, Comfort, dau. of William Furnis (*ARMD* e106: SOJU 1689-1690:87).

COSTLEY
James, m. on 2 Aug 1714, Elinor Chisnald (HAGE:32).

COTTINGHAM
John, m. by 21 Feb 1702/3, Mary, dau. of Philip Conner, Sr., of SO Co. (MWB 3:491).
Thomas, m. on 8 July 1666, Mary, dau. of Ambrose Dixon (SOLR:IKL).

COTTMAN
Benjamin, m. by 1699, [-?-], widow of William Robinson (Cotton cites INAC 19½B:105).
John, m. by July 1711, [-?-], extx. of John Waters of SO Co. (MDTP 22:28).

COTTON
William, of Findren, Eng., m. by 15 Oct 1700, Ann, niece and residuary legatee of George Robotham of TA Co. (TALR 9:70).

COTTRELL
James, Gent., m. by 2 Nov 1705, Elizabeth, dau. and coheir of Thomas Burford (CHLR Z:240).

COULBOURNE
William, m. on 15 June 1678, Anne Revell (SOLR:IKL). She was a joint heir of Randall and Katherine Revell of SO Co. (SOJU AW:44).

COULSON
James, m. on 14 Sep 1714, Elizabeth Bayley (TAPE).

COUNTIS
[-?-], m. by 31 July 1705, Mary, dau. of Henry Green of KE Co. (MWB 12, pt. 2:25).

COURSEY
Henry, m. by 28n Jan 1667, [-?-], relict of Richard Harris (MDTP 2:360).
Henry, d. by 13 Jan 1702, having married Eliza [-?-], a widow (MWB 11:262).
Thomas, m. on 17 Oct 1699, Ann Harris (KESP:C1).
William, m. by 2 June 1673, Juliana, relict and extx. of John Russell, Gent. (TALR 2:104).
William, m. Nov 1698, Elizabeth, admx. of Vincent Lowe (PCJU WT#3:515).

Col. William, m. by 23 April 1717, Eliza, sister of John Hawkins of QA Co. (MWB 14:535).

COURTNEY

James, was granted a license dated 23 May 1639, to marry Mary Lawne (*ARMD* 4:52; Proprietary Records F&B:137).

Thomas, m. Sarah, widow of John Anderton and sister of Thomas Taylor of CV Co. (*ARMD* 49:211).

Thomas, m. by 22 Oct 1692, Eleanor, niece of Fobbs Roberts of SM Co. (MDTP 14A:7).

Thomas, d. by 25 May 1708, when Mary, his admx., had m. Robert Hagar of SM Co. (INAC 28:218).

COURTS

John, m. by 15 Feb 1683, Charity, dau. of Robert Henley of Pyckywaxen, CH Co. (MWb 4:31).

COUSINS

Edward, m. on 27 April 170-, Elizabeth Fisher (KESP:C3).

COVAN

John, m. on 8 March 1680, Elizabeth Carr (SOLR:IKL).

COVELL

Jonathan, m on 14 Dec 1707, Mary Caine (AAAL 1:36).

COVIL

Abraham, of SM Co., m. by April 1684, [-?-], relict and admx. of Edward Fishwick of SM Co. (MDTP 13:113).

COVINGTON

[-?-], m. by 23 April 1717, Sarah, sister of John Hawkins of QA Co. (MWB 14:535).

Nehemiah, m. on July 1667, [Anne?] Ingram (SOLR:IKL).

Thomas, banns of marriage pub. 30 June 1668 for him and Susanna Cooper (*ARMD* 54:712; SOLR O#1:116).

COWARDEN

Thomas, m. on 12 April 1716, Frances Ambrose (KESP:C4).

COWDRY

John, on 8 Jan 1683/4, banns of matrimony were published for him and Mary Nuttley (SOJU O#7:18).

COWING

John, m. on 25 Sep 1712, Susanna Teague (HAGE:33).

COWLEY

George, m. by Aug 1707, Mary, extx. of Ralph Dawson (TAJR 1706-1708).

Thomas, m. by Jan 1706, Sarah, extx. of Emanuel Bishop of AA Co. (AAJU TB#1:461).

COX

Benjamin (Cocks), m. by 25 April 1701, Elizabeth, dau. of Henry Rigg of CE Co., whose widow Ann renounced the right to admin. her husband's estate (MDTP 19A:4).

Charles, m. on 13 Sep 1702, Mary, dau. of John Preston (TAPE).

Cornelius, of Alluster, Warwickshire, skinner, m. by 16 March 1716/7, Margaret, sister of Edward Cooper of CE Co. (MWB 14:345).

George (Cocks), m. by Dec 1684, Mary, sister of William Wright of SM Co. (MDTP 13:190).

Gessery, m. on 25 July 1709, Susannah Melleway (TAPE).

Henry, m. by 22 April 1652, [-?-], wife of Robert Ward, by whom she had three children (*ARMD* 10:161; Proprietary Records F&B:299).

John, m. by banns on 20 April 1717, by Mr. Sewell, Rose Davis (CESS).

Joseph, m. after 30 May 1685, but before 28 March 1729 Sarah Hunter (KELR I:39).

Philip, m. by 22 Oct 1697, Sarah, widow of John Johnson (who was a nephew of Fobbe Roberts, and who d. leaving an infant dau. Sarah) of SM Co. (MDTP 14A:7, 16:210).

Thomas, m. by Aug 1681, Rebecca, sister and heir of Daniel Clarke (of SO Co.) (MPL 29:203; Warrant Record CB(#3):180).

Thomas, m. on 8 Nov 1706, Johannah Clark (TAPE).

Thomas, m. on 4 Dec 1714, Elizabeth Clarkson (WIST).

William, m. by 20 April 1717, Catherine, admx. of Derick Ramsey of CV Co. (INAC 38A:36).

COZENS

[-?-], m. by 2 May 1713, Elizabeth, dau. of Thomas Taylor, of KE Co. (MWB 17:76).

COZINE

George, m. on 30 Jan 1696, Ann Johnson (CESS).

CRABB

Ralph, m. on 22 Aug 1716 Priscilla Sprigg, dau. of Col. Thomas (PGQA:2).

CRAFFORD

James, m. on 12 Feb 171-, Frances Ringgold (KESP:C3).

Richard, m. on 17 Sep 1709, Mary Covene (CVCH).

CRAFT

Robert, of CH Co., d. by 1718, when his admx. Mary had m. Thomas Allen (MDAD 1:301, 360).

CRAMPTON
   Joseph, banns pub. in "Pesusie" [Spesutia] 20 Aug 1703, m. on 19 Oct 1703, Mrs. Mary Costley (HAGE:17).

CRANDELL
   Francis, m. on 25 Sep 1707, Esther Hill (AAAL 1:36).

CRANE
   Thomas, m on 16 Sep 1707, Elizabeth Ensor (AAAL 1:36). She was the widow and admx. of John Inser [*sic*] of AA Co. (INAC 32A:80).

CRANFORD
   [-?-], [or Crawford], of CV Co., m. by Jan 1680/1, Mary, relict of John Ricks or Ricko (MDTP 12A:213).
   Nathaniel, m. by 15 Sep 1686, Martha, admx. of John Gill (INAC 9:89).
   William, m. by 15 May 1705, Anne, extx., of Ignatius Sewell of CV Co. (INAC 25:124, 367).

CRANLEY
   Michael, m. by 1658, Mary, widow of Thomas Gregory (*ARMD* 41:193).

CRANS. See CROSS.

CRAPPER
   Edmund, m. by [June 1711], Hannah, extx. of Charles Rackcliffe (SOJU 1707-1711:462).

CRASE. See CROSS.

CRAWFORD
   [-?-], m. by Aug 1682, Ann, extx. of John Clarke of CV Co. (MDTP 12B:279).
   [-?-], m. by 1694, Sarah, dau. of John White (PCJU TL#1:86).
   Adam, m. on 16 April 1714, Mary [-?-] (KESH:15).
   Lawrence, m. by 15 Nov 1690, Sarah, admx. of Jno. Thomas (*ARMD* e191 (SOJU AW, 1690-1691):12).
   Lawrence, m. by Nov 1692, Sarah, admx. of John White (SOJU 1692-93:136). John White left orphans William, Tabitha, and Priscilla (SOJU LD:99, 162).

CRAWLEY
   Daniel, m. by 13 Dec 1701, Joan, extx. of Christopher Brumbridge of BA Co., and admx. of John Boy of BA Co. (INAC 21:173, 252).

CRAWS. See CROSS.

CRAYCROFT
Ignatius, m. by Feb 1686, [-?-], distributive heir of Maj. William Coursey of TA Co. (INAC 10:155).
Ignatius, of CV Co., Gent., m. by Aug [168-?], Sophia, sole dau. and heir of Henry Beedle, of AA Co., Gent., dec., who was a son of Julian (TALR 9:98; PCLR WRC#1:696; MDTP 13:388).

CRAYERS
Ignatius, m. by 14 March 1708, Sophia, dau. of Henry Parker (QALR ETA:48).

CRAYKER
Samuel (Croyker), m. by 19 Sep 1687, Mary, relict and admx. of George Sealey of DO Co. (INAC 9:430; MDTP 14A:4).

CREED
William, m. by 16 Feb 1701, Mary, admx. of John Kenneday of CV Co. (INAC 21:179).

CRESSY
Samuel, m. by 2 Sep 1673, Susanna, widow of William Robinson (MDTP 6:1; *ARMD* 51:184).

CRIBB
Richard, webster, m. on 11 d. 12 m., 1701, Ann Estell, spinster, both of TA Co., at meeting house near Tuckahoe Creek (TATH).
Richard, m. by 5 Nov 1711, Anne, dau. of John Ashdell (TALR RF#12:67).

CRITCHETT
William, m. by 1718, Frances Watkins (SMWB PC#1:232).

CROCKER
William, m. by 30 July 1709, [-?-], relict of Christopher Kirtly of CH Co. (INAC 30:17).

CROCKETT
John, and Mary Coale, filed their intentions to marry on 1 d., 4 m., 1716, and 29 d., 4 m., 1716 (WRMMa).

CROMP. See CRUMP.

CROMWELL
Richard, of BA Co., m. 26 Oct 1697, Ann Besson, b. 26 Dec 1670, dau. of Thomas and Margaret ("Jones Bible Records," *MG* 2:107).
Thomas, and Jemima Murray, widow, filed their intentions to marry on 5 d., 8 m., 1705, and 2 d., 9 m., 1705; the Meeting to inquire into the care of James

Murray's children (WRMMa). Thomas, m. by 2 March 1707, Jemima, relict and extx. of James Murray of BA Co. (INAC 28:46, 30:206; BAAD 2:207, 208).

CRONEAN
    [-?-], m. by 16 July 1717, Margaret, dau. of Anne Dawson, widow of DO Co. (MWB 14:731).

CROOK(E)
    James, m. on 27 Dec 1716, Sarah Burgess, widow (AAAN:29).
    John, m. by July 1685, Sarah, extx. of George Powell of CV Co. (MDTP 13:247, 393; INAC 9:137).
    Robert, d. by 23 April 1700, when his extx. Parnell (mother of Elizabeth Larramore), m. Henry Eldesley (INAC 19½B:29; CELR 2:1).

CROPER
    Edmond, m. by 31 Jan 1713, Hannah, admx. of John Bradley of SO Co. (INAC 35A:284).
    Edmond, m. by 2 Jan 1715, Hannah, admx. of Charles Rackcliffe of CE Co. (INAC 36C:283).

CROSHAW
    William, m. by 19 Sep 1682, Elizabeth, relict and admx. of Thomas Russell of BA Co. (INAC 7C:330); She m. 3rd, by Aug 1685, William Harris (BACP D:385).

CROSHIER
    John, cordwinder, m. by 16 March 1713, Mary, dau. of Ralph and Elizabeth Elston (TALR RF#12:158).

CROSS
    John, m. by 30 Aug 1688, Ellinor, dau. of Edward Selby of AA Co. (MWB 6:17).
    John (Crase?), m. on 7 July 1715, Mary Tro--- (AAAN:22).
    Robert, m. on 20 July 1710, Anne Bourd, both of Westminster Parish (AALR 1:37; AAMA:84).
    Robert (Craws), m. on 28 Nov 1712, Hannah Gosnell (AAMA:84). She was a legatee of William Gosnell of AA Co. (INAC 33B:169).
    Thomas, m. by Jan 1693/4, Anne, admx. of John Wood (SOJU LD:163).

CROUCH
    [-?-], m. by 7 March 1703, Susanna, dau. of Mary Rockhold (MWB 3:248).
    [-?-], may have m. by 1698, Mary, extx. of William Sutton of AA Co., and granddau. of Maurice Baker (Cotton cites INAC 16:199).
    George, m. c1640, [-?-], servant of Richard Howbyn or Hawlyn (MPL 3:19, ABH:45).
    James, m. Mary, dau. and surviving heir of William Hill. They had a son James, and Mary m. John Rolls (by whom she had a son John). She m. 3rd, by 20 May 1713, Philip Jones of AA Co. (AALR IB#2:93).

James, m. by 1 Sep 1711, Anne, admx. of John Ching of AA Co. (INAC 32C:146).
Wedge, m. on 24 Dec 1713, Mary Hurtt (KESP:C4).
William, m. on 16 March 1702, Susannah Howard (AAMA:82). She was the extx. of John Howard of AA Co. (INAC 25:61, 27:9). William d. by 8 Oct 1713, leaving two children: James and Hannah; his widow Susannah m. 3rd, James Smith (AALR IB#2:129).

CROULEY. See CROWLEY.

CROW
John, m. by banns on 19 Oct 1713, by Mr. Sewell, Martha Newman, spinster (CESS).
William, m. on 24 May 1702, Mary Unick (KESP:C1). She was admx. of John Unick of KE Co. (INAC 24:177; KELR GL#1:27/49).

CROWDER
Joseph, on 13 March 1689/90, banns of matrimony were published between him and Susan: Hides (*ARMD* e106: SOJU 1689-1690:58).

CROWLEY
Bryan, m. by 20 July 1680, Anne, relict and admx. of William Wilson of CV Co. (INAC 7A:147).
Daniel, m. by 11 Feb 1709, Elinor, relict and admx. of Evan Jones of TA Co. (INAC 31:93).
David (Crouley), m. on 15 d. 1 m., 1699, Mary Everett, both of CE Co., at Cecil Meeting House (KECE).
David (Crowly), m. on 22 Sep 1711, Mary Beck (KESP:C3).
James, m. by 9 Oct 1695, Jane, extx. of Benjamin Pride (INAC 10:448).

CRUCHLEY. See CRUTCHLEY.

CRUDGINGTON
Roger, m. on 24 Nov 1718, Dinah Simons (AAJA:52#14).

CRUMP
Thomas (Cromp), m. 6 April 1703, Elizabeth Boughton or Bolton (AAAL 1:26).

CRUTCHLEY
Thomas (Cruchley), m. by 12 June 1682, Margaret, dau. of John Baldwin of South River, AA Co. (MWB 4:43).

CULLAM
George, m. by 1707, Eliza, widow of John Attwood (AAJU IB#1:504, 649, 693, 744).
James, m. by c1697, [-?-], legatee of Mark Cordea of SM Co. (INAC 15:40).

CULLEN
George, m. on 1 Oct 1673, Avis Grottin (SOLR:IKL).
John, m. on 12 Oct 1694, Mary [-?-] (SOLR:IKL).

CULPEPER
Michael, m. on 14 Jan 1705, Elliner Fidgarill [Fitzgerald?] (CVCH).

CULVER
Henry, m. by c1693, Rebeccah, widow and admx. of William [or Guy] Finch of CV Co. (INAC 10:333; MDTP 15A:23).
John, m. on 2 Dec 1711, Martha Coppinger (AALR 1:38).

CUMBER
John, of West River, AA Co., d. leaving a will dated 20 Nov 1676, by which he left everything to his wife Judith who m. 2nd, William Parker (AALR PK:66).

CUMMINGS
Michael, m. by 27 Sep 1707, Mary, dau. of Thomas Lurkey (TALR RF#12:32).

CUNNINGHAM
Daniel, m. by June 1678, Bridget, dau. of John Potts (*ARMD* 67:449).
Daniel, m. by Aug 1678, [-?-], dau. of Mrs. [-?-] Edwards (*ARMD* 15:179).
John, m. by 1 Feb 1704, [-?-], widow and admx. of Richard Franklin (INAC 25:164).
John, m. on 2 Oct 1716, Sarah Pinckney (AAAN:29).

CURIER
William Coulbourne, m. in June 1683, Elizabeth, dau. of John Ellis, Jr. (SOLR:IKL).

CURREY
John, m. by 7 March 1695, Elizabeth, dau. and legatee of Guy White (of CV Co.?) (INAC 13B:91).

CURRIER
Daniel Larke, m. on 19 May 1710, Millescent Fletcher, widow of St. Anne's Parish (AALR 2:6).
Thomas, of CE Co., d. by 13 March 1713, [-?-], dau. of William Husband, who as the widow's father, signed the inventory as next of kin (INAC 36A:34).
William, m. on 26 Dec 1713, Mary George (CENE).

CURTIS
[-?-], m. by 30 May 1699, Jane, dau. of Susannah, widow of Thomas Vaughan, of TA Co. (MWB 6:286).
Daniel, m. on 1 July 1666, Mary Greene (SOLR:IKL).
James, m. on 2 Feb 1685, Sarah, dau. of Charles Hall (SOLR:IKL).

Michael, m. by 20 March 1693, Sarah, widow and extx. of Justinian Gerard of SM Co. (INAC 12:63, 13A:220, 24:13; SMRR:10).

CUSACK
Michael, m. by 14 Jan 1702, [-?-], relict and extx. of John Smith of SM Co. (INAC 23:35).

CUSADAY
Owen (Custody), m. by March 1713, Bridget, admx. of Henry Phillips of SO Co. (SOJU 1707-1717:269).

CUTCHIN
Robert (Cutcheon), m. by 17 March 1701, Dorothy, admx. of Moses Groome of BA Co. (INAC 21:246, 27:27; BAAD 1:83).
Thomas, m. on 28 Oct 1713, Jane Hicks (SJSG:20R; see also BACP IS#B:633).

DABB(S)
John, of KE Co., m. in 8 mo. 1655, Nan Eares (*ARMD* 54:38).
John, m. by 10 April 1674, [-?-], widow of 1st, Andrew Ellenor, and 2nd, Macom Mehenny (*ARMD* 51:113). He d. by 11 June 1700, leaving a widow Mary, mother of John Meconikey and of John and Mary Dabbs (TALR 8:48).

DABRIDGECOURT
John (sometimes given as Dabridge), m. by 28 July 1679, Ann, extx. of Edward Clark of SM Co., and dau. of John Shercliff (INAC 6:217; MPL 8:502, 10:474).

DAFT
Charles (Darft), m. by 7 June 1696, as her 3rd husband, Ann Rennalls, sister of George Rennalls, and widow of 1st, John Medley, who d. by 1693; she m. 2nd, Robert Cole (INAC 13:293, 624, 13B:107; MDTP 14:8).
Charles, m. by 22 April 1710, Elizabeth, extx. of William Spinke of SM Co. (INAC 31:129).

DAILEY/DALEY/DALY
Bryan, m. by 1663, [-?-], relict of Nicholas Keyton (*ARMD* 57:394, 424). Elsewhere his name is given as Nicholas Keeling (MPL 6:36). Keyton's orphans were wards of William Calvert (*ARMD* 57:244, 425).
Bryan, m. by 1680, Rebecca, widow of John Askin, and dau. of George Wright; she m. 3rd, Jno. Seamans (MWB 2:82, 4:51; Hodges cites PCLR WRC:429; *ARMD* 70:369).
Bryan, of SM Co., m. by Aug 1682, Rebecca, relict and admx. of Philip Land (MDTP 12B:164).
Bryan, m. by 1696, Rebecca, dau. of Edward Simmons (INAC 9:53).

DAKINS
Thomas, of SM Co., m. by Oct 1684, [-?-], relict of Daniel Hammond (MDTP 13:167).

DALE
William (Dale?), m. by April 1686, [-?-], eld. dau. of George Watts of TA Co. (MDTP 13:318).

DALLAHIDE
Francis (Dellehede), m. by 14 Nov 1700, Sarah, extx. of Thomas Heath of BA Co. (INAC 20:68).

DALTON
Richard, m. by 5 July 1708, Mary, admx. of Daniel Connolly of PG Co. (INAC 28:157).

DANDE
Ralph, m. on 23 Sep 1714, Mary Fox (HAGE:32).

DANDRIDGE
John, m. in Nov 1703, Joanna Hall (AAMA:82).

DANGERMAN
Christopher, m. by 19 Nov 1704, Mary, extx of Richard Pollard of CV Co. (INAC 25:142).

DANIEL
Edward, m. on 11 Oct 1703, Ruth Sacum (KESP:20).
Wm. (Daniell), m. by 28 March 1715, Frances, dau. of Robert Collson, Gent., of CH Co. (MWB 14:50).

DANNELLY
Patrick, of DO Co., m. by 12 March 1697/8, Ann, dau. of William Dorrington of DO Co. (MDTP 17:206).

DANSEY
John (Dansy), m. by 16 July 1689, Jane, widow of Richard Flower, and of Edw. Knight, and mother of Elizabeth Flower, and Elinor, John, and Rebecca Knight (CHLR P:180).
John (Danzey), m. by 8 April 1712, Martha Earle, widow of Charles Ashcom of SM Co. (MWB 14:465; MDTP 25:110, 175; MCHR PC:879, 2:878; SMRR:13; INAC 25:35, 34:156).

DANVIL
Robert (Danvil?), m. by 23 April 1676, Johanna, dau. of Alexander Dhynyosa (PCLR WRC:42).

DARBY
[-?-], m. by 29 March 1689, Ann, dau. of Edward Mann of TA Co. (MWB 7:272).

DARE
Nathaniel, m. by Dec 1685, Elizabeth, widow and extx of Thomas Banks of CV Co. (PCJU DS#A:477; INAC 13B:1; MDTP 13:262).
Patrick, m. on 10 April 1705, Sarah Todd (AAAN:19).

DARLING
John (Daring), m., by 9 June 1696, Martha, relict and admx. of John Miller of CE Co. (INAC 13B:113; MDTP 16:179).

DARNAL(L)
Col. Henry, m. by 1678, Elinor, widow and extx. of Thomas Brooke, and dau. of Richard Hatton (MPL 10:541, 15:561; MWB 5:123, 18:492).
Col. John, m. by 1684, Susanna Maria Bennett, dau. of Richard Bennett; she m. 2nd, Col. Henry Lowe (MWB 4:186; MDTP 20:43; INAC 14:117; Prov. Court TL 2:108; MPL NS#8:595).
John, of CV Co., d. by 4 Sep 1688, having m. Susan dau. of Nicholas Allome; she m. 2nd, Henry Lowe (MPL 32:593).

DASH
[-?-], m. by 12 Nov 1677, Elizabeth, relict and extx. of John Mackark or Markart of SM Co. (INAC 4:529; MDTP 9A:409).
Oswell, m. by 7 March 1711, Elizabeth, admx. of Joseph Powell of SM Co. (INAC 33A:181).

DAUZEY
[-?-], of CV Co., m. by Feb 1677/8, Martha, relict and admx. of Thomas Morris (MDTP 9A:462).

DAVENPORT
Humphrey, m. by 2 Jan 1676, Sarah, formerly Hawkins of New York (CELR 1:81).

DAVIDGE
Robert (Davadge), imm. by 1669, and m. Sarah, dau. of Thomas Tenney (MPL 12:471).

DAVIES
Isaac, m. 12 June 1701, Mary, widow of Robert Hopper (AAAL 2:2).
Nicholas, Jr., m. by 10 July 1712, Elizabeth, extx. of Thomas Gibbings of PG Co. (INAC 33B:9).
Thomas, m. on 7 April 1708, Anne Gross (Groce) (AAAL 1:36).
William, of KE Co., m. on 18 Feb 1659, Sarah Coming (*ARMD* 54:129).

DAVIS

[-?-] (Davies), m. by 15 Nov 1677, Rebecca, relict and extx. of John Baill or Beale of SM Co. (INAC 4:537; MDTP 9A:410).

[-?-], m. by 1681, Abigail, admx. of Arthur Wright of DO Co. (Cotton cites INAC 8B:153).

[-?-], m. by April 1689, Ann, relict of George [Green?] of CV Co. (MDTP 14:139).

[-?-], m. by 13 March 1695, Eliza, dau. of John Mackeele of DO Co. (MWB 7:209).

[-?-], m. by Aug 1695, Elizabeth, widow of William Ashley (MDTP 16:88).

Edward, m. on 14 May 1711, Mary Young (KESP:21).

Edward, m. by 21 Sep 1714, [-?-], widow of Thomas Ricaud, in 1714 acct. of Benjamin Ricaud of KE Co. (INAC 36B:17)

Henry, m. on 24 Aug 1711, Ann Foxen (KESP:21). She was the admx. of George Foxon of KE Co. (INAC 35A:137)

James, on 26 April 1668, banns of matrimony were published for him and Ann Marckum (SOLR O#1:112).

James, m. on 27 Jan 1709, Panelipa [Penelope?] Reed (KESP:21).

John, m. by 1666, Mary, sister of John Harrington of SM Co.; she m. 2nd, by 1676, Morgan Jones ((MWB 5:25; INAC 2:175, 4:243; Prov. Court JJ:218; SMWB PC#1:2).

John, m. by 20 Sep 1684, Ann, dau. of Thomas Lewis of TA Co. (MWB 6:20).

John, m. by c1688/93, Ann, widow and extx. of Samuel Jackson of SO Co. (INAC 10:326).

John, pub. banns 14 Oct, m. on 12 Nov 1702, Easther Fugat (HAGE:22).

John, m. on 6 June 1703, Eleanor Spicer (AAJA:27#10).

John, d. by 8 June 1706 leaving a widow Mary who m. William Anderson, and the following children: Mary, Elizabeth, and Anne (INAC 25:418; AALR IH#I:263; AAJU IB#2:184).

John, m. by 4 March 1716, Mary, extx. of Joseph Dorrington of KE Co. (INAC 39B:52).

John, m. by 1717, Ann, dau. of Benj. and Eliz. Reeder (SMWB PC#1:258; MDTP 23:132).

Jonas, m. by 1672, Elizabeth Atlee, widow of William Durand of CV Co. (MDTP 5, pt. 3:372, 374; INAC 1:86).

Nicholas, m. on 15 Oct ---, Martha Fitchgerrald (KESP:20).

Philip, m. by 15 April 1682, Susanna, extx. of John Wedge of KE Co.; she m. 2nd, by 1698, Edward Wallwin (INAC 7C:26, 17:33).

Phillip, m. on 19 Dec 1703, Tabitha Norris (KESP:20).

Richard, on 14 March 1675/6, banns of matrimony were published for him and Elizabeth Berre (SOJU O#7:39). **Richard, m. on [c1675], Elizabeth Barry** (SOLR:IKL).

Richard, m., as a Quaker, some time before Jan 1695/6, Sarah Dorman (SOJU E#26:112).

Robert, m. by 23 Feb c1686, Elizabeth, admx. of Hugh Baker of SM Co. (INAC 9:7; SMWB HH:83; MDTP 13:282).

Samuel, m. by 1707, Elizabeth, widow of George Metcalfe (*NFMP*:238 cites SM Co. Rent Roll, p. 28).

Thomas, tailor, on 8 Nov 1670, banns of matrimony were published for him and Judith Best (SOJU DT#7:37). She had borne a child out of wedlock, named Richard Boston; the father was Henry Boston (*ARMD* e89 (SOJU O#7):115).

Thomas, carpenter, m. in Sep 1671, Judith Bloyes (SOLR:IKL).

Thomas, of Manokin, in 1676, banns of matrimony were published for him and Mary Nicholson (SOLR O#7:54r).

Thomas, m. by 1682, Mary, dau. of Thomas Thomas of SM Co. (MDTP 12B:12; PCJU TL#3:44).

Thomas, of Annemessex, m. on 7 May 1687, Sarah Guy (SOLR:IKL).

Thomas (Davis or Dance), m. by April 1689, Ann, relict of Dennis Sullivan of SM Co. (MDTP 14:145).

Thomas, tailor, m. in 1693, Elizabeth Clouder, dau. of Richard and Temperance (CHLR Q#1:21).

Thomas, and Mary Day filed their intentions to marry on 2 d., 11 m., 1701, and 2 d., 11 m., 1701 (WRMMa).

Thomas, m. by July 1710, Anne, dau. of Hester Gross (PCJU PL#3:296).

William, on 26 March 1667, banns of matrimony were published for him and Elizabeth Hooper (SOLR O#1:62).

William, m. in Aug 1667, Anne [*sic*] Hooper (SOLR:IKL).

William, m. on 17 June 1705, Joanna Everitt (AAMA:82).

William, of PG Co., m. by 9 March 1708, Priscilla, dau. of Richard True, dec. (CHLR C#2:141).

William, m. on 27 April 1718, Jane Robinson (KESP:22).

DAWKINS

James, m. by 1700, Ann Brooke, dau. of Roger and Mary (Wolseley) Brooke (MWB 4:40, 6:384; INAC 20:213, 32:25; PGLR C: 258).

Joseph, of CV Co, m. by 31 March 1685, Mary, sister of Thomas Hall of Pocomoke (MWB 4:86).

Miles, m. by 10 May 1694, Elizabeth Goldsmith, heir of John Collett of BA Co. (INAC 12:149).

Symon, m. by 1692, Elizabeth, sister of Mathew Goldsmith of BA Co. (MWB 1:548, INAC 12:149).

William, m. by 31 July 1710, Ann, dau. of Richard Smith of St. Leonard's, SM Co. (MWB 14:82).

DAWNEY

John, m. in March 1716, Lydia Swift (SJSG:13).

DAWSON

[-?-], m. by 14 June 1709, Eliza, dau. of Richard Samuel of SO Co. (MWB 13:62).

Anthony, of DO Co., m. by 28 March 1674 Rebecca, dau. of Henry Osborne of CV Co. (MDTP 6:177).

John, m. on 16 Sep 1690; Elizabeth Thirst (CHLR P#1:210).

John, of TA Co., m. by March 1694, Sarah, dau. of Bryan Omaly (MDTP 15C:38).

John, m. by 17 Oct 1710, Elizabeth, admx. of James Higgins (INAC 32A:90).

Nicholas, of PG Co., Gent., m. by 22 Sep 1708, Mary, dau. of Robert Doyne (PGLR C:224).

Ralph, m. by March 1694, Mary, dau. of Bryan Omaly (MDTP 15C:38).

Richard, planter, m. on 23 d. 8 m., 1698, Susannah Foster, spinster, both of DO Co., at the meeting house near head of Transquaking Creek (TATH).

Thomas, m. on 2 Jan 1700, Sarah Fuller (AAMA:81). She was the widow of Edward Fuller of AA Co. (MPL DD#5:517, PL#3:49).

Thomas, m. by 4 Jan 1716, [-?-], prob. dau. of Francis Meed of AA Co., who called Dawson son-in-law (MWB 14:441).

DAY

Edward, m. in April 1681, Jane Walker (SOLR:IKL). She was the relict and extx. of Thomas Walker of SO Co. (INAC 8:417; MCHR PC:278).

Edward, of SO Co., m. by June 1684, Elizabeth, relict and admx. of Thomas Walker of said co. (MDTP 13:139).

Francis, m. on 16 Nov 1710, Elizabeth Simson (AALR 2:6).

George, m. on 10 June 1669, Eleanor Ditty (SOLR:IKL).

Hezekiah, m. on 12 July 1713, Alce Bonney (SJSG:19R).

Nicholas, m. on 14 July 1707 Elizabeth Cox (SJSG:17R). She was a dau. of Christopher Cox of BA Co. (MWB 13:649).

Robert, and Sarah Meares filed their intentions to marry on 3 d., 5 m., 1698/9 (WRMMa).

Thomas, and Hannah Harris filed their intentions to marry on 15 d., 4 m., 1705, and 3 d., 5 m., 1705 (WRMMa).

DEALT

William, m. by 9 April 1703, Eliza, dau. of Richard Stallings of CV Co. (MWB 11:419).

DEAN(E)

[-?-], m. by 24 Jan 1684, Mary, dau. of Benjamin Ricaud (Richand) (MWB 4:80).

Michael, m. by 16 March 1693, Elizabeth, dau. of Edward Roper (TALR LL#7:66).

Nathan (Dan or Dean), m. by Oct 1685, Elizabeth, widow of Thomas Binks of CV Co. (MDTP 13:246).

William, m. by 26 July 1679, Sarah (age 21), admx. of Thomas Warrin of KE Co. (INAC 6:433, 434).

DEAVOR

[-?-] (Deaver), m. by 24 July 1700, Eliza, dau. of Eliza Peacock of CV Co (MWB 11:70).

Gilbert (Deavour), m. by Dec 1685, [-?-], widow of John Johnson of CV Co. (MDTP 13:269).

John, m. on 12 July 1707, Hannah Bell (AAJA:34 #7).
Richard (Devor), m. on 23 Nov 1703, Mary [-?-] (AAJA:31 #2).
Richard, m. on 16 Dec 1710, Mary Shierbott (AAJA:41 #8).
Stephen, m. on 7 Jan 1710/11, Mary Smith (AAJA:40 #1).

DEBRULER

George, m. on 23 Oct 1713, Esther Lewis (KESP:21).
John, m. on 12 April 1704, Mary Drunkord (HAGE:18).
Peter, m. on 22 Dec 1712, Margaret Skidmore (KESP:21).

DEDMAN

Thomas, m. on --- (date not given), [-?-] [-?-] (AAJA).

DEERE

John, of KE Co., m. on 22 Aug 1658, Eliz: Robinson (*ARMD* 54:129).
John (or Deen), m. by July 1659, Elizabeth Hayling, who m. 2nd, Thomas Hill (MPL 4:60, 69, 10:272).

DEGROATE

Aron, m. on 10 Nov 1697, by Rev. Richard Sewell, Mary Collens (CESS).

DEHORTY

[-?-], m. by June 1697, Margaret, mother of Joseph Blackwell who was then two years old (TAJR AB#8).

DELAFRO

Joseph, m. by 29 July 1708, [-?-], widow and admx. of George Beaston (INAC 28:326).

DELAHAY

Arthur (Delehay), m. by 1646, Mary Shepphard (MPL 7:462).
John (Delehay), m. by 1661, Jane, mother of James Sisson (MPL 4:623).
Thomas, m. on 9 July 1681, Eve, dau. of William Rich of Island Creek (*ARMD* 54:602). He m. by 15 May 1692, E--., dau. of Alice Rich of TA Co. (MWB 6:9).

DELAHIDE

Thomas, m. by Sep 1694, Anne, admx. of Alexander Addison (SOJU LD:118).

DELEVALLEE

[-?-], m. by June 1684, Ann, relict of Daniel Devine of SM co. (MDTP 13:146).

DELIMERE

David, m. on 29 Feb 1701, Elizabeth Mauldin (CVCH).

DELLAHUNT
    Thomas, m. by 20 Aug 1709, Mary, widow and admx. or extx. of Murphey Ward of PG Co. (INAC 29:424).

DELOZER
    Daniel, m. by 14 Sep 1708, Mary, dau. of John Cable (CHLR C#2:111).

DEMASTERS
    Anthony, m. by Nov 1692, Rebecca, widow of Randall Death (BACP F#1:325).

DEMILLIANE
    Gabriel, (Minister), m. on 31 Jan 1704, Ann Young (CVCH). She was a dau. of George Young of CV Co. (MWB 14:613).

DEMINGTON
    (Francis?), m. by 2 March 1718, Rebecca, dau. of Matthew Booker of CH Co. (MDAD 1:385).

DEMONDIDIER
    Anthony, m. by 2 Oct 1683, Martha, sister of Eliza Horton of London (MWB 2:289).

DEMPSEY
    John, m. after 1703, Mary Connel (*1 Harris and McHenry 65*, "John Greaves' Lessee vs. John Dempsey," *NGSQ* 53:200).

DENAR
    John, of SO Co, m. by 1671, Elizabeth, mother of William Empson (MPL WT:326).

DENNIS
    [-?-], m. by 1687, Anne, extx. of Thomas Banks of CV Co. (INAC 9:475; PGJU SS:50).
    Christopher, m. by 7 March 1678/9, Anne, widow of [-?-] Nowell (*ARMD* 68:129).

DENT
    [-?-], m. by 17 Oct 1718, Elizabeth, dau. of George Short of CH Co. (MWB 15:315).
    George, m. by 9 May 1715, Anne, dau. of William Herbert of CH Co. (MWB 14:661).
    John, of "Anstruther," Newtown Hundred, SM Co., d. by 1712, having m. Mary, dau. of John and Ann (Spink) Shercliff, and niece of Henry Spink (MCHR 2:862; MDTP 22:115, 444; SMWB PC#1:181; MCHR PC:861).
    John, m. by 1716, Anne, dau. of John Bayne of "Locust Thicket" of CH Co. (Warrant Record BB(#6):26).

Peter, m. by 25 Feb 1710, Jane Pitman (MWB 13:207).

Thomas, m. by 29 May 1663, Rebecca, dau. of William Wilkinson (MWB 1:190).

Thomas, d. by 21 May 1677, when his relict and extx. Rebecca m. [-?-] Addison (INAC 4:74; *ARMD* 67:1).

William, m. on 8 Feb 1684, at the house of Mrs. Ann Fowke, Elizabeth, dau. of Mrs. Ann Fowke (CHLR P#1:208).

DENTON

[-?-], m. by 9 Feb 1710, [-?-], dau. of Oliver Wilington of DO Co. (MWB 13:355).

James, of BA Co., m. by Nov 1675, [-?-], relict of Thomas Daniell who died about 10 years earlier (MDTP 7:140; 9A:514; BACP D:164; INAC 5:25).

DEPOST

Martin, m. on 16 Jan 1697, Temperance Holt (or Hoff) (HAGE:2).

DERMOT

Charles, m. by 1 May 1694, [-?-], widow of John Gulder, in the admin. acct. of James Phillips of BA Co. (INAC12:135).

DeROCHBRUNE

Lewis, Doctor of Physique on Kent Island, m. by 18 June 1706, Mary, dau. of John Wallton (TALR 10:8).

DERRICK

John (Darick), m. on 17 Dec 1713, Susannah Rickard (KESP:21). She was the admx. of Benjamin Ricaud (INAC 37A:12).

DE(R)RUMPLE

James, m. after 1676, and by Oct 1678, Mary (Inchbudd), widow and extx. of John Clements the elder of TA Co. (*ARMD* 38:130-131, 68:49, 69:234, 70:38; DOLR 4 Old:37).

John, m. on 10 July 1718, by Rev. Thomas Cockshutt, Grace Constable (CVCH).

William, m. by 9 May 1706, [-?-], widow and extx. of John Sollers of CV Co. (INAC 25:324).

William (Dorromple), of CV Co., m. by 12 Jan. 1716, Judith, admx. of Charles Swarmstead of CV Co. (INAC 38A:64, 67).

DEUCEY [*sic*]

[-?-], m. by 4 Jan 1715, Margaret, dau. of John Bowen, planter, of AA Co. (MWB 14:94).

DEVAGH

John, m. by 7 Nov 1694, Elizabeth, dau. of Edward Ayres (BALR RM#HS:439).

DEVEGA
John, m. by Sep 1693, Elizabeth, admx. of William Dison (or Deyson) (BACP G#1:103; MDTP 16:170).

DEVERAN
Manus (Devoran, Devren), m. by 7 Feb 1708, Dinah, widow of 1st, [-?-] Nuthead (AALR WT#2:684, 685). Manus d. by 21 Feb 1710, when his widow Dinah, mother of William Nuthead, had m. [-?-] Sebastian [Oely?] (AALR PK:364).

DEVERAX
John, m. by 1671, Elizabeth, mother of William and Mary Empson (MPL 16:501, 16:309).

DEVERGE
James, m. by 23 June 1704, Barbara, extx. of Thomas Collins (KELR JD#1:164).

DEVINISH
Robert, m. on 25 April 1705, Elizabeth Whitehead (KESP:20).

DEW
Patrick, of CV Co., m. by 17 July 1716, Anne, mother of Robert Leafe (MWB 14:308, 314).

DIAPER
William, m. on 11 Feb 1703/4, Rose Hopper (AAAL 1:26).

DIAS
Thomas, m. in Sep 1674, Jane Pelingham (SOLR:IKL).

DICK
[-?-], m. by Nov 1683, Mary, widow of Thomas Alcock (MDTP 13:74).
Henry, m. by 3 June 1712, Margaret, extx. of William Gaskin of PG Co. (INAC 33A:233).

DICKINSON
Edward (Dickenson), m. on or by 14 Jan 1666, Elizabeth Dickenson, *als* Denson (*ARMD* 54:653).
Henry, m. on (date not given), Sushanah [*sic*] Saratt (PGKG:245).
James, son of William and Elizabeth, m. on 21 d., 9 m. (Nov), 1717, Hannah Coale, dau. of William and Elizabeth (WRMM).
John, planter, m. on 23 d. 7 m., 1692, Rebeckah Thomas, both of TA Co., at the house of John Dickinson (TATH).
Samuel, m. on 4 d. 11 m., 1710, Judith Troth, at Treadhaven Meeting House (TATH).

William, of TA Co., m. on 16 d. 10 m., 1680, Elizabeth Powell of TA Co., at Howell Powell's (TATH).

DICKS
Robert, m. by 1 March 1676, Elizabeth, kinswoman of William Ford of DO Co. (DOLR 3 Old:133).

DICUS
William (Dicas), m. on 25 Dec ---, Elizabeth Ambrose (KESP:20).
William, m. on 21 Dec 1710, Mary Smith (KESP:21).

DIGG(E)S
Charles, of PG Co., m. by 28 Aug 1707, Sophia, dau. of Ignatius Craycroft of PG Co., Gent. (PGLR C:191).

Charles, m. by 25 Oct 1717, Susanna Maria, dau. of Henry Lowe, Sr., Gent., of SM Co. (MWB 14:453). She was also sister of Anne Lowe, late of SM Co., but now of PG Co. (MWB 15:115).

Edward, m. by 28 April 1711, Elizabeth, dau. of Henry Darnall of AA Co. (MWB 13:233).

William, m. by 24 Aug 1681, Elizabeth, relict and admx. of Jesse Wharton, and dau. of Henry and Jane Sewell (INAC 7B:144; Judgements 6:7870, 791; MWB 1:225, 665, 7:282, 13:96).

DIKE(S)
John, of AA Co., m. by 13 Oct 1705, Abigail, only dau. and heir of Samuel Mitchell of AA Co. (AALR WT#2:300).

Mathew, m. by 20 April 1684, Mary, relict of Thomas Alcock of CH Co., and mother of Thomas Alcock (INAC 8:291, 15:359; CHLR Q:62).

DILL
John, m. on 7 April 1702, Sarah [-?-] (TAPE).

DILLAHAY
Thomas, m. by Aug 1691, Elizabeth, relict of Michael Hastead (CHLR Q:39).

DILLINGHAM
Robert, m. on 8 March 1708/9, Jane Bagster [Baxter] (AALR 2:5).
[Roger?], m. by Aug 1715, [-?-], sister of Sarah [Bourton?] (AAJU VD#1:90).

DILLON
Lawrence, m. by 17 Sep 1710, Mary, dau. of George Cox of SM Co. (MWB 13:145).

DIREKSON
William, m. on 26 Aug 1701, by license, by R. Sewell, Marack Care (CESS).

DIRRICKSON
Andrew, m. by 20 Jan 1703/4, Temperance, dau. of Samuel Hopkins, Sr., of SO Co. (MWB 13:417).

DISHAROON(E)
John, m. by 11 June 1705, Margaret, admx. of John Stevens of SO Co. (INAC 25:284).
Lewis (Dissuroon), m. on 20 Nov 1703, Jane Cox (WIST).

DISHOONE
[-?-], m. by 9 June 1675, Anne, relict and extx. of William Anderas (or Andrews) of AA Co. (MDTP 6:508).

DISTANCE
Ralph, m. on 13 May 1711, Sarah Whetstone (KESP:21).
Ralph, m. on 21 April 1712, Elizabeth Frahill (KESP:21).

DIXON
Andrew, of CV Co. d. by March 1683 having m. Lavinia, mother of Samuel Bagby (MDTP 13:22).
Edward (Dison), m. on 28 April 1702, Annie Collett (AAJA:25#6).
George, m. on 22 Jan 1708, Mary Petty (or Betty?) (PGKG:252).
Rich., m. on 5 Jan 1711/2, Alce Mackelfresh (AALR 1:38).
Robert, m. on 20 April 1703, Ruth Manning (CVCH). She was the widow of John Manning, who was exec. of John Manning (INAC 32A:34).
Thomas, m. on 12 Aug 1672, Christianna Potter (SOLR:IKL).
Thomas, m. by 25 Feb 1685, Sarah, admx. of John Gwinn of CH Co. (INAC 9:19).
Thomas, m. by 6 March 1704, Anne, relict and admx. of Samuel Compton of CH Co. (INAC 25:123).
William, of TA Co., m. on 8 d. 4 m., 1680, Elizabeth Christison (erroneously transcribed as Cristerson) of TA Co., at the house of Elizabeth Christison (TATH). She was the extx. of Wenlock Christison of TA Co. (*ARMD* 70:254). In Aug 1682 William and Elizabeth named their "brothers" John Gary, and William [Sharpe?] (MDTP 12B:168).
William, of TA Co., m. by 30 Oct 1696, Eliza, mother of John Harwood and sister of John Gary (MWB 7:264).
William, m. by 30 Oct 1702, Marrah, relict and extx. of Thomas Keare of CE Co. (INAC 23:103, 28:160).

DOANE
[-?-], m. by july 1679, Sara, admx. of Thomas Warren of KE Co. (MDTP 11:137).

DOB(B)S
[-?-]. m. by 1666, Aninking, relict of Mekin Mekenny of KE Co. (MPL 10:312).
[-?-], m. by Dec 1676, Ann... , formerly the wife of Andrew Ellenor (PCLR WRC:44).

John, m. by 27 July 1666, Anna, relict of Macam Macenna of KE Co. (MDTP 1F:124).

John, of TA Co., m. by 14 May 1697, Mary, relict and admx. of John Mecomkin (or Meconikin) of KE Co. (INAC 14:140). Mary, admx. of John Dobbs of TA Co., m. by c1702, Mark Benton (INAC 23:87).

William (Dobb), m. by June 1718, Priscilla, admx. of John Mills (MDTP 23:200).

DOBSON
Samuel, m. by April 1662, [-?-], mother of Mary Stratton (*ARMD* 53:214).

DOCKERRY
John, m. by 11 Nov 1717, Salome, admx. of James Roberson of PG Co. (INAC 37B:208).

DOCTON
Thomas, of AA Co., m. by 11 July 1676, [-?-], kinswoman of William Pagett of AA Co. (MDTP 8A:159).

DODD
Peter, marriage contract, 19 Sep 1685, with Elizabeth, mother of William and Richard Chance (TALR 5:36).

Richard, m. by 4 Feb 1697, Jane, sister of Thomas Burford of CH Co. (MWB 6:93; CHLR Z:240).

DODDRIDGE
William, m. by 23 Dec 1717, Lettice, dau. of Abraham Taylor (BALR TR#RA:435).

DOLEY
John, m. on 21 Oct 1705, Margaret Hard (AAAL 1:32(2)).

DOLPHIN
Thomas, m. in 1698, Elizabeth Edwards (AAJA:4#10).

DONAHOE
[-?-], m. by 27 Feb 1691, Arcadia, dau. of William Turville of SO Co. (MWB 7:85).

John, m. on 25 June 1704, Mary Conner (KESP:20).

John, m. on 11 Aug 1709, Elinor Sullivan (KESP:20).

DONNAVAN
Daniel, m. by c1694, Mary, extx. of James Derrumple of TA Co. (INAC 13A:207).

DONNEY
John, m. in Nov 1705, Hannah Dart (AAMA:82).

DONNING
Stephen, m. on Jan ---, Mary Greenwood (KESP:20).

DORING
[-?-], m. by 4 Feb 1707, Naomi (formerly) Willimot, admx. or extx. of John Willimot of CV Co. (INAC 28:6).

DORMAN
Henry, m. by 12 Aug 1699, Mary Heath (SOLR 7:519).
John, m. by 9 Nov 1675, Sarah [-?-], sister of Eliza [-?-] who m. 1st, John Teague, and 2nd, Richard Turner (*ARMD* e89 (SOJU O#)7:20).
Robert, on 27 Nov 1666, banns of matrimony were published for him and Elizabeth Knight (SOLR O#1:41).
Selah, m. by 20 July 1695, Jane, heir of Roger Sidwell (BALR RM#HS:507, TR#RA:325).

DORMOND
[-?-], m. by 11 Aug 1715, Catran, dau. of Edward Stevens of SO Co. (MWB 14:290).

DORMONT
[-?-], m. by Dec 1696, Mary, relict of Abraham Hollins of CE Co. (MDTP 16:209).

DORRELL
John, m. on 31 Dec 1672, Sarah Percell (SOLR:IKL).
Matthew, m. on 19 Aug 1672, Philippa Gillman (SOLR:IKL).
Nicholas, m. by 13 Sep 1687, Christian, relict and admx. of Andrew Peterson of CE Co. (INAC 9:409).

DORRINGTON
[-?-], m. by 8 Oct 1674, Dorothy, widow of Henry Robinson of CV Co. (INAC 1:83).
Francis, m. by 17 June 1678, Sarah, dau. of James Humes of CV Co. (*ARMD* 67:381; INAC 6:259).
Joseph, m. on 18 Sep 1705, Mary Shield (KESP:20).
Philip, m. on 2 Aug 1708, Elizabeth Hutchins (KESP:20).
William, m. by 21 March 1656/7, Anne, widow of Capt. Peter Johnson of Patuxent, who made a deed of gift to her children, Peter, James, Mary, and Cornelia (MWB 1:64; *ARMD* 10:491).
William, m. by 14 Jan 1687, Elizabeth (now dec.), sister of William Winsloe (DOLR Old 1:106).

DORSEY
[-?-], m. by 13 March 1695, Mary, dau. of John Mackeele of DO Co. (MWB 7:209).

Caleb, m. on 24 Aug 1704, Elinor Warfield (AAAN:19).

Edward, m. by 1676, Sarah, dau. of Nicholas Wyatt (MDTP 8:46, 75, 87, 94; AALR WT#2:574).

Edward, m. after 1690, Margaret, poss. dau. of John Larkin; She m. 2nd, John Israel (INAC 26:147, 27:59).

John, of Middle Neck, m. 22 Aug 1702, Comfort Stimson, also of Middle Neck (AAAL 1:21 (2)). She was a dau. of John Stimson (AALR IB#2:469).

John, m. on 8 April 1708, Honor Sta--- (AAAN:1).

Nicholas, m. on 20 Dec 1709, Frances Hughes (AAAN:9).

DOSSEY

James, m. by 23 Oct 1679, Martha, extx. of Thomas Morris of CV Co. (INAC 6:500).

DOTTRIDGE

William, m. on 18 Sep 1717, Lettis Taylor (SJSG:11). She was a dau. of Abraham Taylor of BA Co. (MWB 15:196).

DOUGHERTY

Cornelius, d. by May 1688, having m. [-?-], dau. of Cornelius Ward of SO Co., who called him son-in-law (MDTP 14:78).

DOUGHTY

[-?-], m. by 5 Nov 1662, Ann, mother of Thomas Burdett and "cousin" of Elizabeth Calvert (*ARMD* 53:289-281).

Enoch, blind, son of Rev. Francis Doughty, claimed in Sep 1661 he was m. to Elinor Empson, and he had sent a note to his father by Richard Watson, to forbid the banns between Elinor Empson and any other person (CHLR A:157).

Francis, on 3 Dec 1659 was called bro.-in-law by William Stone in the latter's will (MWB 1:89).

DOUGLAS

Col. John, d. by 13 Jan 1678/9, having m. [-?-], sister of Henry Bonnde (Bond) (MDTP 10:334).

Joseph, m. by 10 May 1702, Penelope, dau. of Penelope Land of CH Co. (MWB 11:299).

Patriarch [Patrick?] (Duglis), m. on 26 Dec 1707, Margaret Bruer (AAJA:35 #2).

William (Douglass), m. by 8 June 1716, Mary, dau. of Catherine Knowles, widow of BA Co. (MWB 14:230).

DOVERGE

James, m. by 23 June 1704, Barbara, widow and extx. of Thomas Collins of KE Co. (KELR JD#1:164).

DOWDELL

John, of DO Co., m. on 9 May 1697, by Joseph Leech, minister, Ellinor [-?-] (TAPE).

John, m. by 27 Aug 1705, Judith, extx. of Col. John Thompson of CE Co. (INAC 25:83).

DOWELL

Edward of BA Co., m. by 30 Oct 1690, [-?-], mother of Oliver and Unity Harrod (BALR RM&HS#1:332).

John, m. by 1711, Mary, dau. of John Tydings (MWB 6:40; AA Co. Rent Roll B#2:423).

Phillip, m. by 5 Feb 1683, Mary, dau. of Richard Tydings of AA Co. (INAC 26:160; BALR TB#E:522).

Philip, m. on 11 June 1702, Mary Tydings (AAJA:25#15).

DOWN(E)S

Mr. Abraham, m. by July 1711, Elizabeth, widow and extx. of William Wadsworth of CV Co. (MDTP 22:30; INAC 33B:66).

Abraham, m. by July 1711, [-?-], widow and extx of William Wadsworth of CV Co. (MDTP 22:30).

Darby, m. in March 1712, Ann Westbrook (AAMA:84).

George, on 12 June 1677, banns of matrimony were published for him and Anne Bossman (SOLR O#7:100r).

John, of TA Co., m. by 8 Nov 1704, Margaret, dau. of Ralph Hawkins, the elder, dec. (TALR 9:241).

John, m. by March 1711/2, Mary, admx. of Christopher Durbin (BACP IS#B:308; INAC 33A:212).

Thomas, m. by 25 Oct 1699, Susanna, dau. of Stephen and Clare Gary (DOLR Old 5:146).

DOXEY

John, m. by Feb 1677/8, [-?-], relict of John Biscoe of SM Co. (*ARMD* 57:253).

Thomas (Doxie), m. by 12 Feb 1667, [-?-], relict of John Biscoe or Briscoe (*ARMD* 57:253; MDTP 2:347).

Thomas, m. by 1669, Ann, widow of Robert Hooper of SM Co. (MPL 12:267; INAC 1:335).

DOYLE

[-?-], m. by Nov 1716, Margaret, mother of Christopher Reny (QAJRh).

John, m. on 1 April 1700, Jane Blaisdaile (KESP:20).

DOYNE

Ethelbert, m. by 13 May 1707, Jane, relict and extx. of Peter Johnson of SM Co. (INAC 26:323).

Capt. Joshua, m. by 1688, Jane Matthew of SM and CH Cos. Fresco cites Warrant Record CB#4:315).

Joshua, m. by 3 Dec 1713, Mary, dau. of Nicholas Power of SM Co. (INAC 35A:15).

Robert, m. by Oct 1677, Mary, admx. of Jno. Thomas (*ARMD* 67:47, 68:1).

Robert, m. by 1696, Ann Burford, dau. of Thomas and Ann Burford of CH Co., she m. 2nd, by 1696, George Plater, 3rd, John Rousby (Fresco cites Warrant Record CB#4:376; BFD 1:38; INAC 15:31; MWB 4Z:235, 17:132; *AMG* 16 Jan 1752).

DOZEN
Peter, m. on 25 Nov 1711, Elizabeth Nobel (KESP:21).

DRANE
William, of KE Co., m. by April 1681, Christiana, widow of Thomas Warren, and dau. of Thomas Hill of KE Co. (Warrant Record CB#1:143).

DRAPER
John, m. on 17 Nov 1709, Abigail Symmons (AAJA:38 #11).
Lawrence (Dreper), m. on 24 Dec 1713, Mary Drew (HAGE:31).

DREGORS
Devorex (Dreiger), m. by Nov 1690, Sarah, widow and admx. of Henry Bishop, dec. (SOJU AW 29; *ARMD* e191; INAC 28:78).

DREW(E)
Anthony, m. by 1687, Mary Ann, dau. of George Uty of BA Co. (MDTP 14A:48; INAC 12:147).
Anthony, m. on 17 May 1709, Margaret Brown (HAGE:26).
Emanuel (Drewe), m. by 1658, Elizabeth Maurice (MPL Q:71).

DREWRY
William of AA Co., m. by 22 Aug 1676, Alice, mother of Stephen Gill (MWB 3:109).

DRIGGERS
Thomas, b. c1644, slave in Northampton Co., VA, m. by 23 April 1688, Sarah King, free woman, dau. of "King Tobey Negro," and who was in SO co. by that date (Heinegg:107 cites SOJU AW:47).

DRINER
[-?-], m. by Feb 1699, Levina, 4th dau. of Thomas Pattison, Sr., of DO Co. (MWB 11:129).

DRISCOLL
Moses (Driskell), m. on 4 Feb 1713, Katherine Elgin (WIST).

DRISKILL
Dennis, m. by Nov 1690, Honor, relict of Anthony Austin (SOJU AW 28, 139).

DRIVER
[-?-], m. by 21 Jan 1701, Levinia, dau. of Ann Pattison, widow of Thomas Pattison of DO Co. (MWB 11:301).

DRUNKKORD
James, m. by banns 22 Dec 1700, Mary Greenfield (HAGE:10). She was a dau. of Thomas Greenfield of BA Co. (MWB 3:470).

DRURY
William, d. by July 1678, having m. as his 1st wife, Christian, widow of John Merriken and mother of Hugh Merriken. Drury m. 2nd, Alice [-?-], who m. 2nd, [-?-] Bond (MDTP 10:192, 196, 197; *ARMD* 51:300).

DRYDEN
George, m. by 18 May 1710, Isabella, relict and admx. of Justinian Aylmer (who was admin. of Benjamin Robinson) (INAC 31:279, 33A:123; MDTP 22:71).

DUCKETT
Richard, m. 26 Jan 1698/9, Charity Jacob, dau. of John and Ann (AAAL 1:11).

DUCKWORTH
John, m. by 23 May 1695, Ann, dau. of Ann Hopewell (Fresco cites Judgements 5:384, MDCR PC:302; SMWB PC#1:355).

DUCOUDRY
Francis, m. on 31 March 1703, Hellin Councill (KESP:20).

DUDDIN
William, m. on 5 Feb 1705, Elinor Ducoudry (KESP:20).

DUDLEY
Thomas, m. by 18 June 1707, Susannah, dau. of Samuel Wasley, dec. (TALR RF#11:4).

DUDNEY
Roger, pub. banns on 10 Aug and m. on 10 Sep 1708, Jane Leak (HAGE:24).

DUERTY
John, m. on 13 Oct 1704, Johanna Peurisably [*sic*] (KESP:20).

DUFFEY
Daniel, m. on 25 June 1713, Elizabeth Rogers (KESP:21).

DUHATAWAY
Jacob, son of Jacob and Margaret, late of AA Co., dec., m. on 16 d., 9 m.

(Nov), 1712, Elizabeth Parrish, dau. of Edward and Mary (WRMM).

DUKE

James, m. by 31 March 1685, Mary, dau. of Joseph Dawkins of CH Co. (MWB 4:86).

James, m. by 13 April 1714, Dorothy, extx. of Thomas Jones of CV Co. (INAC 35A:113).

DUKES

Robert, m. in April 1674, Elizabeth Dixon (SOLR:IKL).

DULANY

Darby (Dullany), m. by 11 Oct 1711, Katherine, extx. of Edmond Goodman of KE Co. (INAC 32C:79, 34:192).

John, m. on 7 Sep 1718, Mary Wilkinson (KESP:22).

DULEY

John, m. on 9 Jan 1717, Elizabeth Barnet (TAPE).

DUNAVIN

Dennis (Denaven), m. on 3 Oct 1711, Rebecca Howard (AALR 1:37).

DUNCAN

Cornelius, m. by April 1696, Jane, relict and admx. of John Bould of CH Co. (MDTP 16:150).

John (Dunkin), m. by 26 March 1694, Ann, dau. of John Mould (BALR RM#HS:422).

Patrick, m. by June 1684, Jane, widow of William Frizzell, and mother of John Frizzell (AALR WH#4:107).

DUNCKLY

Basill, of Barbados, m. by 20 Oct 1705, [-?-], niece of Randolph Brandt of Potomac River and of Marcus Brandt, of Barbados, dec. (CHLR C#2:31).

DUNDANE

George (or Dundasse) of SM Co., d. by June 1676, Elizabeth, extx. of Patrick and Helena Forrest of SM Co. (MWB 5:21; MDTP 8A:56, 115-116).

DUNFORD

John, m. on 2 Nov 1712, Honour Coflin (KESP:21).

DUNIVAN

Cornelius, m. by c1695, Jane, admx. of John Bould of CH Co. (INAC 13B:6).

DUNMAN

Henry, m. on 23 Oct 1712, Elizabeth Willis (KESP:21).

DUNN
[-?-], m. by 1 June 1653, Joan, dau. of William Porter (*ARMD* 54:17 cites KELR A:140).
David, m. on 23 Dec 1710, Sarah Lee (KESP:21).
John, m. on 2 June 1716, Mary Walker (AAAN:29).
Robert, m. by Oct 1656, Joan Hood, dau. of William Porter of KE Co. (KELR D:70).
Thomas (Dunn or Donn), m. by 16 April 1689, Ann, relict of Daniel Sullivan of SM Co. (MDTP 14:145).

DURAND
William, of TA Co., filed his intention to marry, 2 Aug 1672, Elizabeth Aylee (MDTP 5:372). The marriage contract was dated 2 Aug 1672, to Elizabeth Ayler (TALR 1:209).

DURBIN
John (Derbin), m. on 20 Aug 1715, Abrillah Scott (SJSG:19R).

DURBUROW
John, m. by 1695, Ann Hopewell (PCJU TL#1:384).

DURDEN
John (Durdaine), m. 26 Aug 1703, Anne White (AAAL 1:26). She was a legatee of Samuel White of AA Co. (INAC 27:10).
John, m. on 7 Jan 1713/4, Elizabeth Fowler (AAAL 2:10).
Stephen (Durdan), of TA Co., planter, m. on 11 Jan 1695, Rebeckah (Woolchurch) Anderson, relict of Thomas Anderson, at the meeting house near Tuckahoe (TATH). She was the widow of James Anderson, and dau. of Henry Woolchurch (MDTP 16:117).
Stephen, of TA Co., planter, m. on 2 d. 9 m., 1715, Rebeckah Hosher, dau. of Henry Hosher of KE co., dec. (TATH).

DURHAM
James, m. by 5 June 1693/4, Elizabeth, dau. of John Lee (BALR RM#HS:630).
James, m. by 2 Oct 1707, Margaret, extx. and widow of William Galloway, and sister of Abraham Enloes (BAAD 2:182; BINV 1:6; BACP IS#B:125; INAC 27:197, 33A:90).
John, m. by Nov 1683, Jane, admx. of William Choice (BACP D:13, 14).
Richard (Duram), of CV Co., d. by 3 Dec 1699, Alice, widow of Nicholas Furnies (MWB 11:73; INAC 8:267).

DUSON
William, m. 31 Dec 1700, Katherine Botham (AAAL).

DUVALL

[-?-], m. by 16 Feb 1698, Eliza, dau. of William Ijams (Eyoms) of AA Co. (MWB 11:358).

John, of AA Co., m. between 19 Aug 1685 and 17 Aug 1689, Eliza, dau. of William Jones (*ARMD* 40:88; AALR IH#1:66).

Lewis, 5 March 1699, Martha Ridgely (AAAL 1:21(2)).

Mareen, m. by 28 March 1699, Frances, dau. of Mary Yate of AA Co (MWB 6:212).

Mareen, 21 Oct 1701, Elizabeth Jacob (AAAL 1:21 (2); 2:2).

Samuel, m. 18 June 1697, Elizabeth Clarke (AAAL). She was the widow of Daniel Clarke of AA Co. (MDTP 17:35).

DWAIN

Dennis, m. by 7 Sep 1709, Mary, admx. of Alexander Fraser of DO Co. (INAC 30:171). She was the mother of Alexander Fraser (MWB 12, part 2:1).

DYER

Cornelius, m. by 19 March 1715, Ann, admx. of Anthony Graberd of CV Co. (INAC 37A:28; MDTP 22:478 gives his name as Green).

Nathaniel, m. on 14 Feb ---, Elizabeth Staying (KESP:20).

Patrick, m. on 12 Oct 1702, Comfort Barnes (PGKG:242).

Thomas, m. by 19 June 1703, Elisabeth, widow of Nicholas Dowall or Dowdall of CE Co. (INAC 25:381)

DYKES

Mathew (Dikes, Dyke), m. by 1697, Elizabeth, dau. of Mathew and Mary Allcock (MWB 6:91; INAC 15:359).

DYNES

[-?-], m. by Oct 1678, Mary, relict of Richard Dod of CE Co. (MDTP 10:293).

EADKIN

[-?-], m. by 2 Feb 1717/8, Mary, dau. of John Shakley or Shekertie (MWB 14:523).

EADS

Henry (Eades), m. on 17 Sep 1696, Elizabeth [-?-] (CESS).

Thomas, m. on 19 Dec 1704, Katherine Layton (KESP:24).

Thomas, m. on 5 Jan 1705/6, Mary Steal (KESP:24).

EAGER

[-?-], m. by 12 July 1688, Mary, widow and extx. of Thomas Bucknall of AA Co. (INAC 10:70).

George, m. on 24 Aug 1705, Hannah Pennington (AAAN:19). She was a dau. of Thomas Pennington and sister of William Pennington (AALR IB#2:321).

EAGLE

Robert, m. March 1695/6, Mary, relict and extx. of James Oroack and Jacob Paine [Bene or Preene] of AA Co. (INAC 13B:91, 92; MDTP 16:144).

William, m. by 1676, Emma (or Amy), relict of 1st, John Tucker, and 2nd, John Burgess of TA Co. (INAC 2:110; *ARMD* 66:433; 67:24, 162; Warrant Record CB#1:61).

EARECKSON

Charles, m. by 24 Aug 1708, Elizabeth, dau. of John Wilson of QA Co. (MDAD 58:302).

EARICKSON

Matthew, m. by 15 Sep 1713, Catherine, dau. of John Serjeant, dec. (QALR ETA:181).

EARLE

[-?-], m. by 20 Sep 1669, Anne, dau. of George Watts (TALR 1:83).

[-?-], m. by 7 Jan 1717, Anne, dau. of Simon Carpenter and sister of Mary and William Carpenter (QALR IKA:179).

John, of TA Co., m. by (date not given), [-?-], daughter and sole heiress of John Burges (*ARMD* e73:184).

Joseph, m. by [c1707], Elizabeth Bowery, dau. of Walter and Sarah Quinton (TALR 9:199, 11:46).

Michael, m. by 23 Dec 1695, Ann, sister of Jane Coursey of TA Co. She was the dau. of Eliza Coursey, who was a widow of Henry Coursey, of TA Co. (MWB 7:229, 11:262).

Michael, of QA Co., d. by 12 Oct 1710, having m. Elizabeth, dau. of Col. Henry and Elizabeth Coursey (INAC 32A:8).

Thomas (Earl), m. on 25 Nov 1717, Welthon Wiggins (TAPE).

EARLY

John, m. by 24 Nov 1717, Eliza, mother of [-?-], who m. Richard Woodland (MWB 14:411).

EARNSHAW

John, m. on 25 Nov 1701, Elizabeth Clerk (AAMA:81).

EARP

John (Arpe), m. on 29 July 1704, Rebecca [-?-] (AAAN:19).

EASON

Samuel, m. on 20 Dec 1716, Sarah Johnson (TAPE).

EASTGATE

Caleb, m. by 20 June 1681, Sarah, formerly wife of William Elingsworth (TALR 4:43).

EATON
Jeremiah, of KE Co., m. by Nov 1673, Mary, admx. of Thomas Ingram of KE Co., and widow of Robert Vaughan and mother of William Vaughan (*ARMD* 51:106, 65:163, 178).

EAVES
George, m. on 23 Sep 1714, Mary Costley (HAGE:32).

EDELEN
[-?-], m. by 29 March 1714, Sarah, dau of Thomas Hagoe (Hague?) of CH Co. (MWB 14:213).
Christopher, m. in 1707, Jane Jones (PGKG:254).
Edward, m. by 30 July 1708, Elizabeth, extx., of Moses Jones of PG Co. (INAC 28:259).
Richard, m. by 1714, Susannah Green, sister of Wilfred Green of CH Co. (?CH INAC 1812: 15:306).
Thomas, son of Richard, m. on 9 Feb 1719, Mary Blanford (PGKG:246).

EDEN
Henry, m. by 17 July 1716, Eliza, extx. of Joseph Sanders of AA Co. (INAC 37A:122).

EDGAR
John, m. by Jan 1703/4, Mary, admx. of James Rounds (AAJU G:304)
John, m. by 11 Sep 1704, Mary, widow of William Round ((MPL 21:242, IB#IL#C:237; SOLR 8 (GI):75).

EDGE
Aaron, m. on 28 Aug 1703, Ann Pew (TAPE).

EDION
[-?-], m. by 1696, Alice, admx. of Benj. Cargill (INAC 13B:116).

EDLOE
Joseph, m. 1641, Eleanor Forringham (MPL 4:79).

EDMONDS
Richard, m. by 1694, Elizabeth, widow of Miles Gibson, and formerly widow of Henry Hazlewood (INAC 12:151).

EDMONDSON
[-?-], m. by 7 Nov 1709, Sarah, dau. of Dorothy Stevens of DO Co. (MWB 13:194).
James [but see John, below], of TA Co., planter, m. on 18 d. 10 m., 1691, Magdalen Stevens, of DO Co., spinster, at the house of Dorothy Stevens, in Great Choptank, DO Co. (TATH).

John, of TA Co., planter, m. on 28 d. 3 m., 1685, Susannah Omeli, at Bettey's Cove Meeting House (TATH).
John [but see James, above], d. by 7 Nov 1709, having m. Magdalen, dau. of Dorothy Stevens of DO Co. (MWB 13:194). Magdalen m. 2nd, Jacob Loockerman, and was the sister of John Stevens of DO Co. (QALR ETA:198).
Thomas, planter, m. on 7 d. 6 m., 1699, Mary Grasum, relict of Robert Grasum, all of TA Co., dec. (TATH).
William, m. on 25 d., 12 m., 1692, Sarah Sharp, both of TA Co., at the house of William Sharp (TATH).She was a dau. of William Sharp (TALR LL#7:182).
William, of DO Co., planter, m. on 3 d. 11 m., 1716, Margaret Berry, dau. of James Berry, late of TA Co., dec., at Treadhaven meeting house (TATH).

EDNEY
Henry, m. by Nov 1718, Elizabeth, extx. of Joseph Sanders of AA Co. (INAC 37B:218; AAJU RC:271).
Robert, m. by 6 Jan 1715, Rachel, formerly Robinson, and dau. of Rachel Free-borne of Annapolis (AALR IB#2:262, 268; PCJU VD#2:451). She was the admx. of Thomas Robinson (AAJU VD#1:339).
Thomas, m. by 1685, Margaret, extx. of Nathan Smith (PCJU DS#A:163).

EDWARDS
[-?-], m. by c1676, Anne, relict and admx. of Daniel Murphey of SM Co. (INAC 4:206).
[-?-], m. by 10 Oct 1710, [-?-], dau. of Robert Thornwell of DO Co. (MWB 13:606).
[-?-], m. by 29 Oct 1717, Elizabeth, sister of William Banks of Second Creek, TA Co. (MWB 14:721).
Alexander, m. by 3 March 1707, Mary, extx. of John Anderson of DO Co. (INAC 28:105).
Cadwallader, m. on 12 April 1710, Mrs. Catherine Bourn (AAAN:9).
George, of TA Co., m. by 4 Nov 1716, Sarah, dau. of John Wootters (TALR 12:271).
John, of CV Co., m. by Oct 1692, [-?-], widow of Andrew Abington, late High Sheriff of CV Co.; she m. 3rd, Samuel Watkins of CV Co. (MWB 6:39, 377; MDTP 16:29, 30; *ARMD* 8:405).
John, m. on 15 Dec 1709, Sarah Beetle (KESP:24).
Richard, of PG Co., m. by 23 June 1677, Hannah, widow and extx. of John Potts (*ARMD* 67:438; INAC 4:83, 7C:87; PGLR A:133).
Symon, m. by 15 Oct 1678, Susanna, coextx. of Demetrius Cartwright (*ARMD* 68:51; 70:43, 154).
William, m. on 21 Aug 1705, Susanna Piarissin (KESP:24).

EDWIN
[-?-], m. by 24 Jan 1684, Mary, dau. of Benjamin Richand (Ricaud) (MWB 4:80).
William, lic. to marry dated 26 March 1637/8, Mary Whitehead (*ARMD* 4:24).
William, m. on 14 Dec 1714, Mary Lewis (KESP:24).

EGERTON
[-?-], m. by Nov 1706, Mary, widow of William Hinton, and mother of William Hinton, Jr. (AAJU TB#1:452).
Charles, d. by 1702, having m. Mary, dau. of James Neale; she m. 2nd, by c1710, Jeremiah Adderton (MCHR 2:659-664; MDTP 28:474; MWB 15:90; MDAD 1:34, INAC 28:221, 32B:11; PGLR A:449).
Charles, m. by 1699, Ann, dau. of John Hall of SM Co. (SMWB PC#1:123).

ELDER
John, m. on 19 Oct 1708, Mary Morris (AAAN:7).
William, m. by 1713/4, Elizabeth, dau. of Thomas Lamar (Warrant Record AA#1:221).

ELDESLEY
Henry, m. by 23 April 1700, Parnell, execs. of Robert Crook (INAC 19½B:29). Parnell was the mother of Elizabeth Larramore (CELR 2:1).

ELDRIDGE
Jeremiah (or Elridge), m. by 10 May 1694, Elisabeth, admx. of Henry Devine of CV Co. (INAC 13A:310; MDTP 16:60).

ELGATE
William, m. by March 1692/3, Anne, dau. of Richard Bright (SOJU 1692-93:173).

ELLENOR
Andrew, of KE Co., m. on 5 d., 3 mo., 1656, Anicake Hanson (*ARMD* 54:38).

ELLERY
Henry, m. by April 1659, Elizabeth, widow of William Stephenson (*ARMD* 41:283; SMWB PC#1:6).

ELLIOT(T)
[-?-], m. by 17 June 1706, Elizabeth, dau. of Henry Carter of TA Co. (MWB 12:92).
Edward, m. by 14 Aug 1674, Elizabeth, relict of Henry Frith (MDTP 6:270).
Edward, m. by 1 Oct 1703, Mary, admx. of Peter Haddaway of TA Co. (INAC 24:190).
Henry, m. by 10 July 1678 ("immediately after death"), Jane, widow and admx. of John Halfhead of SM Co. (*ARMD* 51:221; INAC 6:222).
William, of KE Co., m. by 1 June 1653, [-?-], widow of William Porter, and mother of Joan Dunn (*ARMD* 54:16, 17; KELR A:75).
William, m. by 9 March 1718, Mary, extx. of Thomas Baxter of QA Co. (MDAD 1:364).

ELLIS

[-?-], m. by 16 Sep 1717, Hannah, dau. of John Chaires, Sr., Gent., of QA Co. (MWB 14:594).

Christopher, m. by 23 Jan 1702, Mary Brashier, as named in the nuncupative will of William Osborne of CV Co. (MWB 11:314).

Hugh, d. by 31 Aug 1698, having m. 1st, by July 1688, Elizabeth, extx. of Mordica Hunton of CV Co. Ellis left Ruth wife of John Manning as his extx. (MDTP 14:84, 17:197; INAC 16:230).

James, of AA Co., d. by 25 Aug 1693, having m. by Aug 1686, Mary, widow of Maj. John Welsh, and mother of Robert Welsh (MWB 2:238; MDTP 13:390; INAC 9:210).

John, Jr., m. in Sep 1686, Mary, widow of Thomas Shiletto (SOLR:IKL).

John, m. on 2 April 1703, Margaret Coffin (KESP:24).

Peter, Gent., m. by Aug 1679, Elizabeth, admx. and widow of William Palmer of BA Co. (INAC 6:462; *ARMD* 69:272, 70:134; MDTP 11:154; Warrant Record CB#4:220).

Thomas, m. by 15 Nov 1715, Elizabeth, admx. of Joseph Langleley of KE Co. (INAC 37A:110).

ELLON

William, m. 8 Jan 1695, Ann [-?-] (AAAL).

ELMED

[-?-], of CE Co., m. by Oct 1677, Jane, relict of John [Crow?] (MDTP 9A:400).

ELLT

Henry, m. on 21 June 1703, Elizabeth Topin (CVCH).

John, m. by 19 Nov 1717, Martha, extx. of John Davis of CV Co. (INAC 37B:184).

ELMES

William, of CE Co., m. by Oct 1677, Jane, relict and extx. of John Crouche (MDTP 9A:400).

ELSBERRY

Thomas, m. by 1 March 1711, Margaret, extx. of William Hadden of TA Co. (INAC 33A:104).

ELSTON

Ralph, Jr., m. on 24 Nov 1681, Elizabeth Bridges, dau. of Richard Bridges (*ARMD* 54:604).

ELTONHEAD

William, m. by Nov 1649, [-?-], widow of [-?-] Smith, Gent., and of Capt. Philip, Taylor, and mother of Thomas Taylor (MDAD 4:527; *ARMD* 49:99; Proprietary Records Z&A:558).

ELWES

Thomas, grocer of London, m. by 4 April 1668, Ann, dau. of John Thurmar of CV Co. (MDTP 2:313; MWB 1:311).

ELZEY

Arnold, Jr., m. by Nov 1710, [-?-], relict of John Fisher (SOJU 1707-1711:422).

EM(M)ERSON

Nicholas, m. by 16 Oct 1679, Elizabeth, mother of Richard Beck (*ARMD* 51:536).
Thomas, m. by 15 Sep 1713, Mary, dau. of John Serjeant, dec. (QALR ETA:181).
Tobias, pub. banns 10 Dec 1704, m. on 15 Jan 1704/5, Mary Bur (HAGE:22).

EMERTON

John, m. on 21 Jan 1698, Mary Herrington (AAJA:5#3).

EMMERTON

John, m. on 15 Jan 1712/13, Sarah Armstrong (AAJA:42 #15).

EMMITT

[-?-], m. by 3 Nov 1713, Eliza, dau. of Richard Stephens or Stevens of SO Co. (MWB 13:686).

EMORY

[-?-], m. by 4 May 1671, Anne, dau. of Robert Smith of TA Co. (MWB 1:466).
Arthur (Emery), m. by 4 Sep 1676, Catherine, widow of John Wright of TA Co. (MDTP 8A:183).
Daniel (Emery), m. 28 Nov 1703, Mary Smith (AAAL 1:26).
John, m. by 31 Oct 1710, Ann, dau. of Thomas Thomas of TA Co. (INAC 32A:92).

EM(P)SON

James, m. by 9 July 1686, Rebeccah, relict and admx. of John Daniell [or Darnall] of CV Co. (INAC 9:27). Rebecca, extx. of James Empson (Emison) of BA Co., m. by 9 Oct 1710, James Cobb (INAC 32A:23; BAAD 2:147).

ENGLAND

Isaac, of Duck Creek in New Castle Co. on Delaware, m. on 12 d. 6 m., 1714, Elizabeth Hoodt, of Sassafras River in CE Co., at Cecil Meeting House (KECE).
Thomas, m. by 16 June 1716, Ursula, admx. of Darby Mitchell of SM Co. (INAC 38B:13).

ENNALLS

John, m. by 3 Jan 1698, Elenor, extx. of John Southey (INAC 18:154).
Joseph, m. by 24 Jan 1692/3, [-?-], dau. of John Brooke (MWB 13:142).

ENNETT
William, m. on 10 Jan 1709/10, Joan Leatherwood (AAAN:9).

ENSOR
John, m. 14 May 1700, Elizabeth Hines (AAAL).
John, m. 14 May 1700, Elizabeth Evans, widow (AAAL 1:21 (1)).
John, m. by March 1709, Elizabeth, admx. of Abraham Enloes (BACP IS#B:133).

ERECKSON
John, m. on 24 Feb 1714, Elizabeth Trew (KESP:24).

ERICKSON
Matthew, m. by March 1713/4, Katherine, lately called Katherine Bowdle, extx. of Mary Sergeant, widow (QAJR March 1713/4:256).

ERPE
John, of Findren, Eng., m. by 15 Oct 1700, Mary, niece and residuary legatee of George Robotham of TA Co. (TALR 9:70).

ERWIN
Patrick, m. by 11 July 1711, Elizabeth, admx. of George Willson of SO Co. (INAC 32C:123).

ETIE
Nathan, m. by 9 March 1702, Elizabeth, sister of Benoni Fanning and dau. of John Fanning who had m. Alice, widow of James Walker (CHLR Z:35).

ETTLAND
William, m. on 19 Nov 1705, Mary Gore (KESP:24).

EUBANKS
Richard, m. by 1 Nov 1713, Ann, dau. of John James of KE Co. (MWB 13:662).
Thomas, Jr., m. on 11 d. 5 m., 1717, Jean Clother, widow, at Treadhaven meeting house (TATH). She was the admx. of Robert Clothier of TA Co. (MDAD 1:125).
William, carpenter, m. on 9 d. 6 m., 1704, Hannah Tall, both of TA Co. at Tuckahoe Meeting House (TATH).

EVALL
Samuel, m. on 25 Oct 1713, Sarah Randall (KESP:24).

EVANS
[-?-], m. by 17 July 1682, Margaret, relict and extx. of Samuel Lane (INAC 8:267).
[-?-], m. by July 1682, Mary, relict of Anthony Lamb (MDTP 12N:129).

[-?-], m. by 15 June 1684, Mary, admx. of Richard Pedder of KE Co. (INAC 8:244; MDTP 13:6).

[-?-], m. by 27 March 1695, Mary, dau. of Walter Powell of SO Co. (MWB 7:131).

[-?-], m. by 19 May 1718, Jane, mother of Richard and Thomas Harrison (CHPR B:24, 68).

[-?-], m. by 20 Sep 1718, Mary, dau. of William Bedder, Sr., of SO Co. (MWB 15:18).

Benj., m. by 1686, Mary, relict and extx. of John Bowling (INAC 9:32; MDTP 13:181, 189).

Benjamin, m. by Jan 1688/9, [-?-], the widow of William Rought or Routs (MDTP 14:131).

Charles, m. by 1692, Anne, widow of Leonard Green of CH Co. (CHLR Q#1:39).

Edmond, m. by 1716, Abigail Whipps, dau. of John and Elizabeth, of AA Co. (MWB 14:172-173; MDTP 30:172).

Edward, m. on 22 May 1677, Mary Daniell (SOLR:IKL).

Evan, m. on 15 Sep 1713, Sarah Ambrose (KESP:24).

Griffith (Evens), m. on 17 Feb 1704, Eliz. Curtis (TAPE).

Job, m. by 9 June 1700, Sarah, admx. of John Perry (INAC 19½B:126; AALR WT#1:55).

John, m. by 21 Nov 1676, Sarah, relict and extx. of Guy White of CV Co. (INAC 3:111; 7A:177).

John, d. by 1700 having m. Elizabeth Vansweringen; she m. 2nd, Jacob Williams (SMWB TA#1:51; Fresco also cites *CSM* 29 (May 1981)5).

John, m. by Feb 1709/10, Mary, widow and admx. of Edward Shipham (SOJU 1707-1711:323).

John, m. on 7 July 1713, Rebecca Comegys (KESP:24).

John, of KE Co., clothier, m. by 6 Nov 1713, Rebecca, widow of Benjamin Smith, of Biddeford, Devon (CELR 2:245).

John, of VA, m. by 21 Sep 1716, [-?-], widow of Richard Harris (MCHR CL:307).

Nicholas, m. by Oct 1695, Susanna, dau. of Thomas Walker of SO Co. (MDTP 16:110).

Nicholas, m. by 20 Jan 1699, [-?-], relict of Mr. John Hennett, in inventory of William Monteith of SO Co. (INAC 37A:76).

Owen, m. by 17 Jan 1717, Catherine, admx. of William Thomas of SM Co. (INAC 39C:121).

Richard, m. on 14 March 1704/5, Hester Dunton (AAAL 1:27).

Rowland, m. on 2 Jan 1716, Joan Washfield (TAPE).

Samuel, m. by [c1716], Jude, admx. or extx. of George Husband (INAC 36C:266).

Thomas; on 9 Sep 1673 "the Commrs: ordered that a writ be issued forth against Thomas Evans & Mary his pretended wife alias Mary fflint and alias Mary Smith in the Lord Proprietary's Suit & to summon ffrances Roberts John ffeilld John Winsor and Benjamin Cottman as evidences" (*ARMD* e87 (SOJU AZ#8):256).

Thomas, d. by 1 Oct 1707, having m. by 1 Oct 1707, [-?-], relict of Zorobabel Wells of TA Co. (INAC 27:130).

Thomas, m. on 3 Jan 1714, Patience Jackson (TAPE).

Lieut. William, m. by 21 June 1650, [-?-], widow and extx. of William Thompson (*ARMD* 10:23).

William, m. by 1651, Ann Shercliff (Warrant Record 1:251).

William, m. by 4 April 1713 Sarah, extx. of John Ryan of DO Co. (Warrant Record AA#1:113).

EVERARD
Lawrence, m. in 1714, Sarah Slyng (AAAN:22).

EVEREST
Thomas, m. by 12 May 1681, Hannah, daughter of Richard Ball by his wife Mary Humphreys (BALR RM#HS:7, 74, 75, BALR IR#AM:135, 176).

EVERETT
[-?-], m. by 23 Jan 1717, Jane, dau. of Duncan Monroe of QA Co. (MWB 14:595).

Henry, m. by 11 Sep 1683, Mary, dau. and sole heiress of Patrick Hall of AA Co., dec. (AALR WH#4:122).

Richard (Everit), of AA Co., d. by 2 Jan 1709, when his extx. Damaris had married [-?-] Hall (INAC 30:236).

EVERTON
Jeremiah, m. 21 March 1702, Hannah Irish (AAAL 1:26).
Thomas, m. in April 1686, Ann Wood (SOLR:IKL).

EVITT
Arthur, on 26 April 1668, banns of matrimony were published for him and Mary Gray (SOLR O#1:112).

EWENS
John, d. by 3 April 1686; m. Sarah, widow of Alexander Gordon; she m. 3rd, Robert Franklin, and 4th, John Willowby (AALR WH#4:256).

EWINGS
John, m. by 29 Jan 1708, Elizabeth, sister of Moses Groome (BALR RM#HS: 633).

EYRE
Thomas, of Northampton Co., VA, m. by 23 Nov 1697, Jane, dau. and heir of John Severn (PGLR A:72).

FABS
John, m. on 30 Nov 1708, Ann Snow (TAPE).

FAIRBANK
John, m. on 14 Jan 1700, Mary [-?-] (TAPE).

FAIRBROTHER
John (Fairborough), m. by 27 Aug 1688, Jane, relict and extx. of William Mitchell of AA Co. (INAC 10:160; MDTP 14A:64; AALR WT#2:453; IB#2:259).
Richard, m. by 9 Dec 1718, Rachel, dau. of William Warner, Sr., of DO Co. (DOLR 7 Old:73).
Thomas, m. on 5 June 1712, Mary Fuller (AALR 1:38).

FAIRFAX
John (Fairerfax), m. by 16 March 1712, Rachel, extx. of Daniel Murphy of CH Co. (INAC 34:145).

FALKNER
[-?-], m. by 23 June 1697, Mary, mother of William Moore (PGLR A:52).

FALLOWFIELD
Wharton, m. on 8 Nov 1706, Catherine Hughes (TAPE).

FANNING
John, m. by 9 March 1702, Alice, widow of James Walker (CHLR Z:35).
John, m. on Dec --- (year not given), Mary Davis (KESP:25). Married by 9 June 1703, she was the sole extx. of David Davies of KE Co. (KELR JD#1:101).
Richard, m. on 27 Jan 170-, Alse Welsh (KESP:25).

FARFARR
William (Forfare), m. by 11 Aug 1713, Elinor, admx. of John Harriman (INAC 34:29; BACP IS#B:598).

FARMER
Gregory, m. on 27 Aug 1703, Sarah Hews (HAGE:17).

FARRELL
Patrick, m. by 14 July 1711, Mary, admx. of Patrick Trover of CH Co. (INAC 32C:167).

FARINGTON
Matthew, of Lynn, MA, m. by 12 Sep 1676, Sarah, dau. of Martha Potter, dec., and grandchild of Robert Burgess of Lynn, MA, and wife Sarah (KELR F:60).

FARROW
George, m. on 30 Oct 1715, Sarah Carroll (KESP:26).

FATHERY
John, m. by 27 Feb 1716, Dorothy, admx. of John Russell of SM Co. (INAC 39B:57).

FAUCITT
[-?-], m. by 2 March 1686, Eliza, dau. of Alexander Williams of SO Co. (MWB 4:268).

FEAY
George, m. by 17 Nov 1701, Elizabeth, dau. of William Jump of QA Co. (TALR 9:106; MWB 13:414).

FEDDEMAN
Richard, m. by 23 March 1709, Elizabeth, dau. of Henry Frith (TALR RF#11:116).

FELKES
Edward, m. by 8 Dec 1703, Ann, former wife of Stephen Johnson, and kinswoman of Moses Groome (MWB 3:366; BALR IR#PP:171, HW#2:119; BAAD 2:27; INAC 28:23).

FENCH
John, m. by 7 Feb 1717, Elizabeth, extx. of Thomas Hackett of DO Co. (MDAD 1:120).

FENDALL
James, of Bright Helmstone, Co. Sussex, Eng., m. by 3 Oct 1710, Elizabeth, dau. of Richard Brocklesby, of Cork, and sister of Edward Brocklesby who was sent to MD. and of Thomas Brocklesby of Cork (KELR JS#W:101).

FENWICK
Cuthbert, antenuptial contract dated 1 Aug 1649 to m. Jane Eltonhead, widow of Robert Morryson (*ARMD* 41:262; MPL ABH:94, 243, 1:110, 179, 285; PCJU S:218).
Cuthbert, m. by 1715, Elizabeth Brooke, dau. of Robert and Grace (MWB 14:207, 19:888; MDTP 28:463; MINV 15:603).

FERGUSON
[-?-], m. by 13 June 1711, Elizabeth, admx. of John Howerton of CV Co. (INAC 32C:58).
Hugh, m. by 20 May 1701, Ann, sister of James Bussey of All Saint's Parish, CV Co. (MWB 11:80).
John, m. by 24 Sep 1703, Elizabeth, widow of John Howerton of CV Co. (MWB 3:34; INAC 26:96).
John, m. by 29 Dec 1707, Elizabeth, dau. of John Phillips of Hungar River, DO Co. (MWB 12:212).
John, m. on 29 Nov 1715, Mary Williams (PGQA:2).
Robert (Farguson), m. by 2 June 1699, Margrett, widow and admx. of James Pargrave of SM Co. (INAC 19:172).
William (Farguson), m. by 21 Sep 1674, Elinor, relict of Thomas Phelps of AA Co. (MDTP 6:282).

William, m. by Sep 1687, Jane, relict and admx. of Patrick Dunkin of AA Co. (MDTP 14A:1; INAC 10:52).

FERNLEY
Henry (or Hernley), m. by April 1698, Mary, admx. of John Brown or Broome of CV Co. (MDTP 17:79, 285).

FERILL
Samuel, m. on 3 April 1716, Margaret Wright (AAAL 1:38).

FERRILL
Daniel, m. on 19 Dec 1703, Agnes Scott (KESP:25).

FERRY
John, of BA Co., m. by 1 March 1688/9, [-?-], widow of [-?-] Boreing, and mother of John, James, Thomas, and Mary Boreing (MWB 6:227).

FEWE
[-?-], m. by Nov 1678, Mary, relict of Francis Finch of KE Co. (MDTP 10:320).

FFOOKES
Simon, m. by Nov 1688, Elizabeth, admx. of Samuel Hutton of TA Co. (MDTP 14:119).

FIDDIS
John, m. on 7 Jan 170-, Elizabeth Mitchell (KESP:25).

FIELD
Matthew (Feild), m. by 1705, Joan, widow of Henry Bowers (or Bowse) of DO Co. (MDTP 19C:157, 175; INAC 28:201).
Thomas, m. --- Sep 1696, Ann Douglas (AAAL).

FIELDING
James, m. by Aug 1690, Katherine Kennedy (DOJR).

FILLINGHAM
Richard, m. by 1 Sep 1703, Martha, admx. of John Wade of KE Co. (INAC 24:18).

FINCH
John, m. by 25 Sep 1707, Elizabeth, dau. of George Prouse of DO Co. (INAC 27:226).

FINECAN
Peter, m. on 4 Jan 17--, Mary Bateman (KESP:25).

FINLEY
Charles (Fenaly), m. on 11 April 1711, Elizabeth Harris (PGKG:259).
Robert, m. by 20 May 1709, Jane, widow of William Hemsley (TALR RF#11:78;
MDTP 22:13).

FINCOMB
William (ffincomb), m. on 24 --- 1714/5, Jane Wells (AAAN:22).

FISH
Edmond, m. by 3 Oct 1704, Elisabeth, admx. of William Worgan of TA Co.
(INAC 25:154; MDTP 19B:28).
John, m. by 5 Dec 1680, when William Stephens named Fish as his son-in-law,
and Fish's wife Mary in his will (MWB 2:116).

FISHBORN
Ralph, m. on 9 d. 9 m., 1673, Sarah Lewis, both of TA Co., at Betty's Cove
Meeting House (TATH).

FISHER
[-?-], m. by 22 March 1676/7, Anne, widow of William Burgess of SM Co. (INAC
3:124).
[-?-], m. by 11 Nov 1696, Sarah, dau. of John Power of KE Co. (MWB 7:276).
[-?-], m. by 16 Feb 1707/8, Mary, dau. of Thomas Vickers, Sr., of PG Co. (MWB
13:272).
Alexander, m. by 23 Oct 1676, Eliza, dau., of Robert Winsmore of DO Co. (MWB
5:252).
Alexander, m. by 10 Oct 1709, Mary, extx. of Thomas Newton of DO Co. (INAC
30:170).
Alexander, m. by 1718, Mary, dau. of John and Abigail Pritchett; she m. 2nd,
Petegrew Saldsbury (MWB 17:322; MDAD 1:108; and MDTP 24:136, 250, 437).
Edward, of DO Co., planter, m. on 1 d. 8 m., 1699, Frances Willis, relict of
Richard Willis, DO Co., at the meeting house near Tuckahoe Creek (TATH).
Francis, Negro slave of Thomas or John Beale, m. by c1702, Mary Molloyd, b.
c1680 (Heinegg:123 cites AAJU 1734-6:83, 1743-4:11).
John, m. by 15 Aug 1695, Elizabeth, extx. and widow of Tobias Miles of CV Co.
(INAC 10:432; (MDTP 16:42).
John, m. on 20 Feb 1717, Sarah Bryney (TAPE).
Simon, m. on 8 Aug 1698, Elizabeth Taylor (TAPE).

FISHWICK
Edward, m. by 1682, Margaret, widow and admx. of Thomas Bassett of SM Co.;
she later m. Abraham Combes (Cotton cites INAC 7C:197, 198, 8:288).

FITZGERALD
Edmund (Fitzjarrall), m. on 20 Nov 1715, Margaret Clark (TAPE).

Morris, m. by 12 Oct 1696, Rachell, in whose right he was exec. of Abraham Sacote of CH Co. (INAC 14:72). The name may have been Abraham Laproate of CH Co. (MWB 3:404).

FITZHERBERT
John, m. by 24 May 1673, Mary, dau. of Giles Brent (*ARMD* 65:123, 124).

FITZSIMMONS
Nicholas, m. by Sep 1693, Martha, extx. of Joseph Heathcote (BACP G#1:116, 152). She was a dau. and extx. of Thomas Morgan of BA Co. (MWB 7:392; MDTP 17:69).

FLETCHER
Michael, m. by 1 Nov 1713, Dorothy, sister of Thomas Smithson of TA Co. (MWB 13:649).
Joseph, m. on 10 Feb 1701, Elizabeth [-?-] (TAPE).

FLINT
Cornelius, m. on 30 Jan 1710, Anne Lane (TAPE).

FLOWER(S)
John, m. by 26 April 1703, Elizabeth, widow of Edward White who had been admin. of John Salisbury (INAC 23:56).
Lambrook, of DO Co., m. by 10 Dec 1714, Patience, dau. of Benjamin Palmer (MPL EE#6:279, CE#I:22).
Ralph, m. on 20 Oct 1709, Mary Harris (AAJA:38 #6).

FLOYD
William, m. on 13 Jan 1714, Magdilane Johnson (KESP:26).

FLUTCHER
William, m. on 16 Nov 1672, Mary King (SOLR:IKL).

FLYE
Richard, of London, m. by 26 May 1704, Elizabeth, sister of John Bird, dec. (MWB 3: 638; INAC 32C:153).

FLYN
Cornelius, m. by 27 July 1711, Anne, admx. of Timothy Lane of TA Co. (INAC 32C:80).

FOGG
David, m. by 17 Jan 1677, Susanna, sister of Thomas King of CH Co. (MWB 9:54).

FOLLIAR
Giles, m. by 3 Feb 1678, Grace, dau. of John Belaine (CHLR H#1:248).

FOLLON
[-?-], m. by 8 Sep 1710, Frances, dau. of John Kemball of DO Co. (MWB 13:346).

FOLSON
[-?-], m. by 24 July 1717, Amy, dau. of Cecily Manders, widow of Kent Island, QA Co. (MWB 14:686).

FOOKES
Herman, m. by 12 Nov 1688, Elizabeth, admx. of Samuel Hatton of TA Co., and mother of Richard, Elisabeth, and Sarah Gorsuch (INAC 10:184).

FORBES
George, of SM Co., m. by Jan 1717/8, Mary, sister of Kenelm Cheseldyne (MDTP 23:154).

FORBEY
Thomas, of TA Co., died by 11 May 1685, having m. Hannah, mother of Hannah, Thomas, and Roger Baxter (MWB 4:181).

FORD
Ambrose, m. by c1694, Jane widow of [-?-] Walker, dau. of John Coppin of TA Co. (INAC 13A:215).
Edward, m. by 20 Feb 1698, Eliza, sister of Charles Allison of CH Co. (MWB 7::398).
James (ffoard), m. on 15 July 1711, Elizabeth Preston (AAMA:85).
John (Foord), m. by c1695, Diana, relict and extx. of Robert Jarvie [or Jarvice] of CV Co. (INAC 13B:88, 29:391).
Robert, m. by 20 June 1709, Rachel, dau. of John Briscoe of KE Co. (MWB 14:71).
Thomas, m. on 1 Jan 1711/2, Leah Price (AALR 1:38). She was a dau. of Mary Price, widow, of AA Co. (MWB 14:628
William, m. by 20 Dec 1673, Sarah, dau. of Richard Preston, and sister of James Preston of CV Co. (MPL WC#2:264; MWB 1:574, 9:84).
William, m. on 6 Dec 1697, Elizabeth Groves (KESP:25).
William (Foard), and Hannah Galloway, dau. of Samuel Galloway, were m. without the consent of Meeting, and disowned on 7 d., 5 m., 1710 (WRMMa).

FOREMAN
Arthur, m. on 13 May 1699, Mary Read (KESP:25).
Arthur, m. on 2 June 1715, Honour Miller (KESP:26).

FORNEY
Dr. Michael, m. by 1692, Muriel, sister of John Abington (MDTP 16:64).

FORREST
Richard, m. by 1711, Christian Watts (SMWB TA#1:200; INAC 9:382, 383).

FORSTER
Ralph, m. by 4 June 1708, Elisabeth, extx. of John Green of SM Co. (INAC 28:215).
William, m. by c1693, Dorothy, extx. of Michael Minock of CH Co. (INAC 13A:145).

FORTUNE
Mary, admx. of Robert Fortune of TA Co. Co., m. by 4 May 1704, Thomas Sockwell (INAC 24:285).

FOSEY
Mary, admx. of John Fosey of SM Co., m. by 30 May 1709, William Sikes (INAC 29:296).

FOSTER
Christopher, d. by 13 May 1706, having m. Elizabeth, mother of John and Mary Steed (QALR ETA:58).
John, m. by Aug 1678, Mary, extx. of William Chandler of AA Co., who d. leaving a dau. Mary (MDTP 10:201).
John, m. on 15 Feb 1709, by Rev. Mr. Owen, Eliza Green (PGQA:1).
John, m. on 9 Jan 1710, Alice Dixon (TAPE).
Richard, m. by Feb 1660, Ann, sister of Thomas Jackson (MDTP 1C:16).
Richard, m. on 11 March 1704/5, Eliz. Purnell (AAJA:30 #19).
Richard, m. on 12 May 1715, by Mr. Sewell, Sarah Kare, spinster (CESS).
William, m. by 1694, Dorothy, execs. of Michael Minnock (INAC 13A:145).
William, m. by 1717, Ann, widow of [-?-] Ashman, and of Henry Hardy. She was the mother of John Ashman and of Mary wife of Richard Ankrum (INAC 20:195; MWB 14:424).

FOULKS
[-?-] (Foulkes), m. by 20 Feb 1695, Sarah, dau. of William Dorrington of DO Co. (MWB 7:290).
Thomas, of DO Co., m. by Oct 1677, Sarah, relict of Thomas Fisher (MDTP 9A:398; *ARMD* 69:269).
William, of Accomack Co., VA, m. on 2 d. 6 m., 1694, Mary Foster, Jr. (TATH).

FOUNTAIN
Marcy, m. on 14 Sep 1686, Mary, dau. of John Bossman (SOLR:IKL).

FOWKE
[-?-], m. by 1673, Ann, wife of Job Chandler (MPL ABH:269, 15:181).
Col. Gerard, of Westmoreland Co., VA, m. by July 1662, [-?-], widow of Job Chandler of Portobacco (CHLR A:216; *ARMD* 53:222).
Gerard, m. on 31 Dec 1686 Sarah, dau. of Thomas Burdett (CHLR Q#1:12).

Richard (Fouckes), m. by Feb 1663/4, Anne, widow of Humphrey Haggett (*ARMD* 49:8, 35, 165, 53:481).

Thomas, of "Pungatage," m. by 1665, Anne, widow of Nicholas Waddylowe (MPL 10:463).

Thomas (Ffouller), m. 15 Oct 1697, Susan Ijams (AAAL).

FOWLER

Charles, m. by 12 May 1699, [-?-], dau. of Mordecai Hinton (INAC 18:143).

Daniel, m. on 23 Dec 1711, Ann Devor (AAJA:41 #9).

Edward, m. by 1693, Alice, relict and extx. of Thomas Willin of SO Co. (MDTP 15A:60; INAC 13A:196).

Peter, m. by c1701, Elizabeth, extx. of George Selley of CV Co. (INAC 21:99).

Peter, m. on 10 Oct 1704, Agnes Gray (CVCH).

Robert, m. on 18 April 1688, Mary Wheeler, widow (*ARMD* 54:602).

William, m. by 1694, Alice, widow and admx. of Thomas Willin (Cotton cites INAC 13A:196).

FOX

Henry, m. by 1678, [-?-], dau. of Walter Hall (SMWB PC#1:30).

Henry, m. by 1680, Hester, dau. of Anthony LeCompte (MCHP 1273).

Job (Foxe), of SO Co., m. by July 1711, Eliza, admx. of John Porter of SO Co. (MDTP 22:39).

Thomas, m. by June 18704, Hannah, admx. of Samuel Biggs (AAJU G:436).

FOXWELL

James, m. by 9 Oct 1704, Eliza, dau. of Richard Kendall, planter, of DO Co. (MDTP 19C:170).

FRAHILL

David, m. by 1 June 1708, Elisabeth, admx. of William Powell of KE Co. (INAC 28:226).

FRANCHEY

David, m. on 29 July 1703, Elizabeth Powell (KESP:25).

FRANCIS

John, m. on 14 Nov 1703, Elizabeth Wink (KESP:25).

Thomas, m. by 15 June 1676, Sarah Shaw, widow and admx. of John Shaw of AA Co. (INAC 2:171; 5:379).

Major Thomas (Frances), son of Thomas, d. by 1698, having m. Mary, dau. of Hance Hanson of CE Co.; she may have m. 2nd, Samuel Young (CELR 2:16; AALR WT#1:28; INAC 16:61).

FRANKLIN

[-?-], m. by 21 April 1718, Bridgett, dau. of Edward Wale of SO Co. (MWB 14:620).

John, m. Sarah, widow of Alexander Gordon, and 2nd, John Ewens, whom she m. by 3 April 168-; she m. 3rd Robert Franklin, and 4th John Willowby (AALR WH#4:256).

Jno, m. by 14 Aug 1690, Rhodiah Fosset, extx. of John Cropper of SO Co., dec. (SOJU 1689-1690:166, *ARMD* e106).

Robert, d. by 3 April 1686; m. Sarah, widow of 1st, Alexander Gordon and 2nd, John Ewens; she m. 4th John Willowby (AALR WH#4:256).

Robert, of AA Co., m. on 19 d., 10 m. (Oct), 1697, Artridge Giles (WRMM).

Thomas, m. on 27 May 1711, Grace Currant (CVCH).

FRASER

Alexander, of DO Co., d. by 7 Sep 1709 when his admx. Mary had m. Dennis Dwain (INAC 30:171).

Dr. Alexander, m. on 27 July 1718, Elizabeth Thomas (AAAN:39).

FRASHIERS

Robert, m. on 30 Oct 1704, Mary [-?-] (AAAN:19).

FRASIER

Daniel, m. by 1 Oct 1712, Margaret, extx of Edward Baxter of CV Co. (INAC 33B:51).

FRAZER

Alexander (ffrazzer), m. on 20 Aug 1711, Mary Stoops, widow (CESS).

John, m. by 13 Jan 1709, Anne, dau. of Mary who was now the wife of James Smallwood, Gent. (CHLR C#2:154).

John, m. by April 1712, Ann, dau. and devisee of Giles Blizard (PCJU TP#2:481).

John, d. by 6 Jan 1717, having m. Mary, widow of Dennis Duskin (BALR TR#RA:523).

FRAZIER

[-?-], m. by Jan 1684/5, Elizabeth, widow of Dennis Hurley of SM Co. (MDTP 13:200).

Alexander, m. by Dec 1708, Sarah, relict of Thomas Starling of AA Co. (*ARMD* 27:235).

Robert, of SM Co., m. by Aug 1686, Elizabeth, late wife of Dennis Hurley (MDTP 13:396).

FRED

James (Fend?), m. on 18 March 1704/5, Ann Dunn (AAJA:30 #20).

FREEBORNE

Thomas, m. by Oct 1709, Rachel, extx. of Robert Proctor (PCJU PL#3:51).

FREEMAN

[-?-], m. by 24 July 1700, Ann, dau. of Eliza Peacock of CV Co (MWB 11:70).

[-?-], m. by Dec 1717, Ann, relict and extx. of Stephen Morris of CVH Co. (MDTP 23:157).

John, banns pub. 13 June 1671, m. on 2 July 1671, Rachel Moodey (SOLR:IKL; SOJU DT#7:133).

John, m. on 7 Oct 1713, Mary Smithers (AAAN:9). She was the admx. of Christopher Smiders [*sic*] of AA Co. (INAC 35A:39).

Joseph, m. on 14 Feb 1673, Mary Robbins (SOLR:IKL).

William, m. by 12 Sep 1709, Elizabeth, extx. of Thomas West of SO Co. (INAC 31:67; SOJU 1707-1711:423).

FRAY
    Charles, m. on 29 Oct 1716, Mary Tibbals (TAPE).

FREEBORNE
    Thomas, m. by Jan 1703/4, Rachel, extx. of Richard Kilburne, and "mother-in-law" [i.e., step-mother] of William Kilburne (AAJU G:278, 284).

FRIEND
    James (or Howard), m. by March 1683/4, Jane, relict of Ambrose Gillett (BACP D:141).

FRIGGETT
    [-?-], m. by 2 May 1713, Ann, dau. of Thomas Taylor, of KE Co. (MWB 17:76).

FRISBY
    James, of CE Co., m. by 1659, Rebecca Ringgold (Hodges cites KE Co. Debt Book, No. 22:10).
    James, of CE Co. m. by 20 July 1688, Sarah, sister of Thomas Read (TALR 5:181).
    Capt. James, m. by lic. on 9 Feb 1713/4, by Rev. Richard Sewell, Ariana Vanderhyden, spinster (CESS).
    William, m. by 12 May 1702, Rachel, admx. of Robert Acheson of KE Co. (INAC 23:92).

FRIZEL/FRISELL/FRISSILL/FRIZELL/FRIZZELL
    James, m. by Nov 1692, Mary, extx. of William York; mother of William York (BACP F#1:316; MDTP 16:171).
    John, m. in Nov 1721 Providence Dallahide (SJSG:13).
    Thomas, servant, of CH Co., m. by 24 Nov 1658, Hanna Glossington, servant (*ARMD* 53:28; CHLR A:33).
    William, m. by 1663, Anne Potter, whom he transported into the Province c1649 (AALR WH#4:270; MPL 5:507, 8:491, 607).

FRITH
    Henry, m. by 8 Feb 1701/2, Rebecca, dau. of John Price of Buttibrooke (Bolingbrooke?), TA Co. (MWB 11:257).

Henry, m. by 1 Sep 1707, Rebecca, extx. of Thomas Clements of TA Co. (INAC 28:20).

FROGGITT
John, m. on 25 July 170-, Ann Hoock (KESP:25).

FRY
Edward, m. by 25 Oct 1696, Elizabeth, dau. of Cornelius and Rebecca Comegys (KELR M:54).

FUCATT
Peter, m. by 4 July 1694, Frances, dau. of John Mould (BALR RM#HS:419).

FULSER
John?, m. by 23 Jan 1713, [-?-], admx. of Thomas Owen of CE Co. (INAC 36A:31).

FULLER
Edward, m. by 25 Aug 1686, Sarah, admx. of Thomas Tucker of AA Co. (INAC 9:141).

Robert, of AA Co., m. by Aug 1686, Sarah, relict of Thomas Tucker (MDTP 13:397).

FULSTON
Richard, m. by 8 May 1716, Sarah, admx. of William Scott of KE Co. (INAC 37A:111)

FURBEY
Thomas, Quaker, of TA Co., m. by c1684 Hannah, relict and extx. of Thomas Baxter of KE Co. (INAC 8:245)

FUSTON
John, m. on 1 Oct 171-, Jane Jinkins (KESP:25).

GADSBY
John, m. by April 1698, Joanna, admx. of George and Elizabeth Norman (MDTP 17:86; INAC 20:109, 22:66).

GAILLES
Mark, m. on 29 May 1707, Hannah Ryley (AAAL 1:33).

GAINE
William (Caine?), m. by May 1688, Mary, relict of John (Diamint?, Dimmitt?) of BA Co. (MDTP 14:72).

GAINES
    Richard, m. by 1664, [-?-], the widow of Andrew Warner (MPL 7:81).

GAITHER
    Benjamin, m. on 8 Sep 1709, Sarah Burgess (AALR 1:36).
    Edward, m. on 21 Feb 1709/10, Mary Duvall (AALR 1:37).
    John, m. 21 Aug 1701, Jane Buck (AAAL 1:21(1)).

GALAHAW
    [-?-], m. by 3 March 1716, Katherine,   dau. of Rosamond Machetee, widow of Patrick Machetee of CH Co. (MWB 14:236).

GALE
    [-?-], m. by 14 Dec 1714, Elizabeth, sister of William and Joshua Cromwell, and John Ashman of BA Co. (MWB 13:732).
    John, m. by [c1697], Margaret, relict of John Atkins of AA Co. (INAC 15:179; MDTP 17:49).

GALEY
    Thomas, m. by 15 Feb 1674/5, Mary, extx. of John Lewger (*ARMD* 65:521).

GALLOWAY
    James (Gallaway), Jr., m. by banns on 22 Feb 1718 by Mr. Sewell, Mary Beck, widow (CESS).
    John, son of Samuel and Ann, m. on 31 d., 5 m. (July), 1718, Mary Thomas, dau. of Samuel and Mary (WRMM).
    Peter, son of Samuel and Ann, m. on 19 d., 11 m. (Jan), 1715, Elizabeth Rigbie, dau. of John and Elizabeth, late of AA Co., dec. (WRMM; see also admin. acct, of John Gassaway of AA Co.: INAC 39C:99).
    Richard, m. on 10 d., 10 m. (called Dec), 1686 (or 1696?), Elizabeth Lawrence, widow (WRMM). She was the extx. of Benjamin Lawrence (INAC 13B:95, 14:148).
    Richard, Jr., m. on 29 d., 7 m. (Sep), 1715, Sophia Richardson, dau. of William and Margaret (WRMM).
    Samuel, of AA Co., m. on 12 d. 2 m., 1705, Sarah Pope of CE Co., at Cecil Meeting House (KECE). She was the dau. of Matthew Cope or Pope of CE Co. (MDTP 22:427).
    William, m. c1659, Lucy Child, who had been a servant (MPL 4:59).

GALSY
    Thomas, m. by 1674, 1674, Martha, dau,. of John Lewger of SM Co. (Hodges cites MPL ABH:150, 12:502; Prov. Court M:508).

GAMBOL
    William, m. 15 July 1703, Sarah Harper (AAAL 2:4).

GAMBRILL
[-?-], m. by 10 Dec 1691, Eliza, sister of Thomas Hobbs of SO Co. (MWB 6:34).
[-?-], m. by 20 Aug 1716, Anne, dau. of John Marriott of AA Co. (MWB 15:1).

GAMES
Richard, m. by 1664, [-?-], widow of Andrew Wardner (MPL CC:71, 7:81).

GARDINER/GARDNER
Alexander, of AA Co., m. by 24 Feb 1707, Mary Gibbs, widow, mother of Edward Gibbs (AALR WT#2:599, WH#4:141).
Alexander, m. by 13 March 1713/4, Frances Tyler (or Taylor), dau. of Robert of AA Co. (MWB 14:87).
Benjamin, m. on 19 Feb 1705, Ann Hall (AAMA:83).
Benjamin, m. on 27 Dec 1714, Sarah Petebone (AAMA:84).
John, m. by July 1688, Constant, relict of John Riggs of CH Co. (MDTP 14:83).
Jno., m. on 27 Jan 1704, Ann Birmingham (CVCH).
John, m. by 1712, Sarah, sister of Richard Sorrell of AA Co., and dau. of John Sorrell, who was a bro. of Richard Sorrell, dec. (MDTP 22:338, 23:5).
John, m. by 29 May 1713, Elizabeth, dau. of John Larkin (*AAAH*; MWB 3:272).
Luke, m. by 7 June 1656, Eliza, sister of William Johnson of SM Co. (MWB 1:133: Prov. Court S:1078).
Luke, d. by 1674, having m. Elizabeth Hatton; she m. 2nd, Clement Hill who d. 1708 (MWB 1:631, 9:16).
Luke, widower, m. by 1670, Eliza, dau. of Robert Slye; she m. 2nd, Edward Cole (MWB 1:422; Pro Court DD#2:396).
Luke, m. by 1691, Ann, dau. of Joseph Pile of SM Co. (INAC 6:64, 14:100, 21:149, 26:192).
Luke, m. by 1705, Elizabeth, sister of Peter Mills (SMWB PC#1:145).
Richard, m. by 1687, Elizabeth, dau. of Clement Hill (SMWB PC#1:63).
William, of CV Co., m. by 1695, Rosamond Archer, dau. of Henry and Alice Archer of AA Co. (INAC 13:186, 296; AALR WT#2:463).
William, m. on 7 Nov 1698, Ann Archer (or Fecher) (AAJA:63A). She was a dau. of Henry and Alice Archer of AA Co. (Warrant Record AA(#7):8; AALR WT#2:462).

GAREY
Stephen, of DO Co., d. by March 1685/6, having m. Clare [-?-] (MDTP 13: 301).
William (Gary), m. by 20 Aug 1689, Grace, dau. of George Aldridge (TALR 5:243).

GARNER
John, m. 14 Oct 1697, Mary Welch (AAAL 1:5).
John, m. on 6 Feb 1704/5, Sarah Rockhold (AAAN:19).
Matthew, m. by 27 July 1709, Elizabeth, admx. of John Winall of CV Co. (INAC 29:424).

GARRETT
Jacob (Garratt), m. by banns on 22 Sep 1717, by Mr. Sewell, Margaret Wisecarvor, spinster (CESS).

James, m. by 11 Aug 1675, Johanna, dau. of George and Mary Peake of BA Co. (INAC 1:409).

GARRETTSON
Garrett, Gent., m. on 5 Dec 1702, Mrs. Elizabeth Freeborne, spinster (HAGE:15).

GARTRILL
John, of AA Co., m. by March 1697/8, [-?-], sister of William Johnson of AA Co. (MDTP 17:139).

Lawrence (Gatrell), m. by April 1708, Margaret, admx. of [Thomas Robinson] (MDTP 21:6).

GASH
Thomas, m. on 22 Dec 1715, Hannah Gilbert (HAGE:35).

GASKING
John, m. by 18 Sep 1718, Anne, sister-in-law of William Greenwood of London (TALR 12:362).

GASSAWAY
Thomas, of AA Co., m. by 7 Jan 1702, Susannah, dau. of Henry Hanslap of AA Co. (MWB 3:8; AALR PK:99).

GATTERIDGE [*sic*]
Henry, m. by 24 July 1697, Mary, admx. of extx. of David Floyd of PG Co. (INAC 15:281).

GATWARD
Thomas, m. on 4 Nov 1707, Rebeckah Gott (AAJA:35 #9).

GAUTHERIN
Mathew (Gautheim), m. by [c1695], Mary, admx. of William Needham of CV Co. (INAC 10:440; MDTP 16:39).

GAY
John, m. by 3 Sep 1701, Frances, evidently an heir of Nathaniel Ruxton (BALR HW#2:90).

GEE
John, m. by Sep 1663, Hen. MacDonall (formerly servant to Robert Slye); marr. performed by John Legatt without a license (*ARMD* 49:42, 85).

GEFF
William, d. by 10 April 1710, when his widow Elizabeth had m. John Olwell of AA Co. (BALR TR#A:162).

GEORGE
Robert, m. on 10 d. 1 m., 1699, Barbara Evert, of KE Co., at Chester Meeting House (KECE).

GERARD
John, d. by 1710, having m. Jane Johnson, sister of James Johnson (Hodges cites Judgements 15:232).

John, m. by 1712, Jane, dau. of Thomas Orrell of CH Co. (CHLR D#2, part 2:20).

Justinian, d. by 1688, having m. Sarah, widow of Wilkes Maunders; Sarah m. 2nd, by 1707, Michael Curtis (SMWB PC#1:69, Judgements LD:1).

Thomas, m. by 11 Aug 1659, Susan, sister of Abel Snow (*ARMD* 41:373).

Thomas, m. on or after 1671, Rose, widow of John Tucker (SMWB PC#1:58; ARMD 41:372; Prov. Court 5: 10, 43).

Thomas (Gerrard), of SM Co., d. by 1688, having m. Ann Smallwood who m. 2nd, Capt. Jno. Bayne (MDTP 14:67; Hodges cites Judgements 6:307-317, 7:188, 15:232; MDTP 14:109; CHLR R#1:256).

GERMAIN
John, Jr., m. by Nov 1709, Anne, dau. and heiress at law of Henry Bishop, who was son and heir of Henry Bishop (SOJU 1707-1711:276; Warrant Record BB(#8):29).

GIBBS
Edward, m. by 14 Oct 1697, Mary, elder dau. of James Smith of AA Co. (INAC 15:180).

John, of CE, m. by Oct 1678, Anne, relict and admx. of Edward Best of KE Co. (INAC 5:301; MDTP 10:292).

Robert, m. by Oct 1672, Elizabeth, extx. of Henry Webb, and dau. of Margaret wife of Thomas Thatcher by her first husband, Jacob Sheafe of Boston (MDTP 5:481).

GIBSON
[-?-], of KE Co., m. June 1678, Hannah, sole extx. of John White (MDTP 10:160); she was also admx. of Jacob Johnson of KE Co. (INAC 6:605).

[-?-], m. by 9 April 1717, Alice, dau. of John Marritt of SM Co. (MWB 14:340).

Mr. Jacob, m. by 20 Oct 1715, Alice, sister and coheir of Richard Woolman, dec. (TALR RF#12:239; INAC 37C:143).

John, m. by 6 July 1692, Rosamond, dau. and heir of Edward Normand, dec. (TALR NN#6:26).

Miles, m. by 19 May 1676, Anne, dau. of Thomas Thurston (BALR G#J:330).

Miles, d. by 1693/4, having m. Elizabeth, widow of Henry Hazlewood, and of Richard Edmonds. In 1693/4 she was also the admx. of John Collett of BA Co. (INAC 12:149, 150, 151).

Robert, m. by May 1688, Martha, widow and extx. of William Oderry of CE Co. (MDTP 14:72; INAC 10:332).

Mr. Robert, of Spesutia Hund., Gent., m. on 15 Dec 1702, Mrs. Mary Goldsmith, spinster (HAGE:15).

Woolman, m. on 18 April 1718, Sarah Clements (TAPE).

GIDDENS

Thomas, m. by Feb 1709, Eliza, dau. of Benja. Sommers of SO Co. (MWB 14:132).

GIFFORD

Henry, of CH Co., m. by Aug 1687, Elizabeth, sister of Thomas Gibson of CH Co. (MDTP 13:508).

GIDENS

[-?-], m. by [c1712], Elizabeth, sister of Henry Gutteredge (INAC 33A:176).

GILBERT

Jonathan, m. by 1673, Elizabeth, dau. of Luke Barbour of SM Co. (MDTP 6:64).

Thomas, banns pub. April, May 1700, m. 27 May 1700, Sarah Bedford (HAGE:9).

Thomas (Guilber?), m. on 1 April 1703, Hannah Ashford (HAGE:17).

GILES

Ishmael, m. on 25 Dec 1711, Anne Thornbury (AALR 1:38).

Jacob, of West River, son of John and Mary, dec., m. on 8 d., 11 m. (Jan), 1701, Elizabeth Arnell (or Arnold), dau. of Richard and Martha, dec. (WRMM).

John (Giles?), of TA Co., m. by June 1686, Ann, widow of John Humberton (MDTP 13:307).

John, m. on 1 Oct 1695, Sarah Welsh (AAJA:1#9). She was a daughter of John Welch (BALR TR#A:5).

John (Gyles), m. on 9 Nov 1710, Rachell Griffith (AAJA:44 #17).

Nathaniel, and Elizabeth Harris filed their intentions to marry on 3 d., 10 m., 1703, and 31 d., 10 m., 1703 (WRMMa).

GILGO?

John, m. by April 1708, Sarah, extx. of William Scott (MDTP 21:7).

GILGORE

John, of Kent Island, m. by June 1706, [-?-], mother of Mary Ponder or Peadder); said Mary had an Aunt Griffin (TAJR 1706-1708).

GILL

[-?-], m. by 1717, Jane, sister of Peter Bond (Hodges cites Liber 14:432).

John, m. by Nov 1698, [-?-], sister of William Bates of AA Co. (MDTP 17:213).

John, m. by 29 Nov 1705, Jane, admx. of John Farthing of AA Co. (INAC 25:116).

Stephen, m. on **16 Dec 1708, Elizabeth Hubbert** (AAAN:7).

William, m. by 11 April 1698, Elizabeth, admx. of Francis Higham (INAC 16:73).

GILLET

Thomas, m. on 17 Oct 1685, Jane Blades (SOLR:IKL).

GILLEY

William, m. by (date not given), Eliza, widow of Christopher Baynes of CV Co. (Hodges cites Judgments, 3:379, 385).

William, m. by April 1698, Elizabeth, admx. of Francis Higham (MDTP 17:81).

GILLIAN

Thomas, of DO Co., m. by 1694, Mary [-?-], who m. 2nd, William Heather, and 3rd, John Wade, surgeon of Bloomsbury, near Mulberry Fields, SM Co. (Fresco cites INAC 13A:116, 301, 302; MDTP 16:59).

GILLIBOURNE

Thomas, m. by March 1691/2, Mary, relict of Timothy Pinder (BACP F#1:164).

GINDER

[-?-], m. by 7 Sep 1704, [-?-], widow and admx. of Robert Craine of SM Co. (MWB 3:420).

GIST

Christopher, d. by 21 Feb 1693, when his widow had m. John Beecher (BALR RM#HS:417).

Richard (Geist), of BA Co., m. on 7 d., 10 m. (Dec), 1704, Zipporah Murray, also of BA Co. (WRMM). She was a sister of Josephus Murray (BALR TR#A:140, 444).

GITTINGS

[-?-], of TA Co., m. by 20 Oct 1718, Mary, mother of Edward Harding and Sarah Lovdy (MWB 15:236).

John, of CV Co., m. March 1666, Margery Molllings, sister of Margaret, wife of Walter Hall of SM Co.; he m. 2nd, Margaret Reade, widow (MDTP 8:135, 136; *ARMD* 57:203, 383; MDTP 2:147).

Philip (Gittins), m. by 9 May 1704, Ann, dau. of Thomas Sprigg of PG Co. (MWB 3:448).

GLADMAN

William, late of King William Co., VA, m. by 5 Oct 1702, Mary, relict of John Jordan of AA Co. (AALR WT#1:308).

GLANN

James, m. by banns on 23 May 1717, by Mr. Sewell, Mary Newman, widow (CESS).

GLANVILL
William, m. by 26 March 1697, Mary, dau. of John Hinson of KE Co. and his wife Ann (KELR M:13, JD#1:64; MWB 3:656).

GLASPILL
William, m. by [c1710], Mary, dau. of Thomas Winn of KE Co. (KELR JS#N:274).

GLEN
Rev. William, Rector of St. Peter's Parish, m. on 15 Aug 1709, Mary Allen (TAPE).

GLOVER
John, m. on 29 July 1717, Eliza Henricks (TAPE).
Mark, m. on 31 Oct 1706, Jane Wood (AAJA:33 #8).
Richard, m. on 23 Nov 1717, Mary Jones (CVCH).
Thomas, m. by 1706, Winifred, dau. of Joseph Fowler (SMWB PC#1:174, 358).
Thomas, m. on 24 July 1712, Mary Farrell (AALR 2:9).
William, m. by 2 Oct 1700, Mary, admins. of Arthur Oneale of CH Co. (INAC 20:178).

GODDARD
Elias, of DO Co., planter, m. on 29 d. 3 m., 1692, Jone (Wright transcribed this as Jane) West, of TA Co., spinster, at Tuckahoe Meeting House (TATH).
Elias, d. by May 1696, having m. [-?-], dau. of Thomas Shillington, on whose property Elias lived; Elias left a dau. and extx. Christian (MDTP 16:174).
George, m. on 4 July 1679, Judith Goodin (SOLR:IKL).
George, m. by 1 July 1718, Elizabeth, admx. of Peter Casley of SO Co. (MDAD 1:170).
Thomas, of CV Co., d. leaving a will dated 5 March 1679, naming his wife Amy Cooper *als.* Goddard (MWB 4:159).

GODDIN
Michael, m. by 26 July 1704, Mary, extx. or admx. of Nicholas Cornwell of SO Co. (INAC 25:144).

GODFREY
George, m. by 1 June 1681, Mary, relict of John Payne (CHLR I:122).

GODMAN
Humphrey, m. on 10 Feb 1710/11, Mary Kirkland (AALR 1:37).
Thomas, m. by 27 Sep 1706, Mary, widow and extx. of James Ringgold of TA Co., and dau. of Moses Harris of TA Co. (INAC 25:423, 33A:202, 35A:128; MWB 13:455; MDTP 22:268).

GODSGRACE
John, m. on 27 Dec 1713, by Rev. Gabriel DeEmmilaine, Mary Grover (CVCH).

GODSHALL
[-?-], m. by 19 Oct 1677, Sarah, relict and extx. of Henry Barnes of CH Co. (INAC 4:431).

GODSON
[-?-], m. by 1677, Sarah, widow of Henry Barnes of CH Co. (MDTP 9:374).
Peter, chirurgeon, 6 July 1654, "about to marry" Jane Moore of CV Co., widow of Richard Moore (*ARMD* 10:395, 396).

GOFF(E)
[-?-], m. by 10 April 1676, Mary, relict and admx. of Lt.-Col. John Jarboe of SM Co. (MDTP 8A:27).
Bartholomew, m. by 1699, [-?-], widow of Thomas Hide of PG Co. (Cotton cites INAC 19½B:4; PGLR C:64).
Stephen, m. by 1676, Mary, extx. of John Jarboe (*ARMD* 66:398).
Thomas, m. by 15 April 1691, Sarah, relict of John Ingrum (TAJR April 1691).
Thomas, m. by 29 May 1699, Hannah, extx. of Thomas Hill of PG Co. (INAC 19½B:4).

GOFORTH
[-?-], m. by 9 Dec 1712, Sarah, dau. of Jno. Preston of TA Co. (MWB 13:665).

GOLAIAH
John, of CV Co. m. by 1 Jan 1682, Margaret, mother of John King (MWB 4:299).

GOLD
Joseph, m. on 22 Dec 1715, Margaret Danielson (PGQA:2).
Robert, m. by 25 June 1668, Ursula, widow of Roland Haddaway (MDTP 3:1).

GOLDHAWKE
[-?-], of KE Co., m. by 27 April 1671, Mary, dau. of Joseph Wickes, and sister of Joseph and Rachel Wickes (MWB 1:464).

GOLDSBOROUGH
[-?-], m. by 17 Aug 1717, Margaret, dau. of Peter Faulkinn of QA Co., (MWB 14:438).
Nicholas, b. c1640/1 at Melcolm Regis, Dorset, m. 1659 at Blandford, Dorset, [-?-], dau. of Abraham Howes of Newberry, Co. Berks (Goldsborough Bible, cited in "Robert Goldsborough of Ashby and His Six Sons," *MG* 2:2).
Robert, son of Nicholas, m. 2 Sep 1697, Elizabeth, dau. of Nicholas and Ann [-?-] Greenberry (Goldsborough Bible, cited in "Robert Goldsborough of Ashby and His Six Sons," *MG* 2:2, 6).

GOLDSMITH

George, d. by 30 Dec 1696, leaving an extx. Martha, who was a dau. of Edward Beedle, and who m. 2nd, John Hall (BALR IS#IK:241, 245; BACP G#1:201; INAC 15:184).

Capt. Samuel, d. by 1678, having m. Johanna, mother of George Wells (Cotton cites INAC 5:11).

William, m. by 26 Feb 1707, Elizabeth, extx. of Robert Ridgely of SM Co. (INAC 28:74).

GOLDSON

[-?-] (Goulson), m. by 30 Nov 1674, Alice, widow of James Godscrosse (INAC 1:136).

GOOD

John (Good?), and Anne (Farlow or Fowler) had their banns of matrimony published on 2 April 1689 (MDTP 14:140).

GOODIN

Abraham, m. on 11 Nov 1708, Susannah Watkins (TAPE).

William (Gooding), m. on 17 June 1705, Grace Hearle of Queen Anne's Parish in PG Co. (AAAL 1:27).

GOODMAN

Edmond, m. by 15 May 1697, Sarah, relict and extx. of Andrew Toulson of TA Co. (INAC 14:114).

John, m. on 4 Nov 1711, by Rev. Jona' White, Leah Davis (PGQA:1).

William, m. by 1699, Ruth, dau. of John Larkin (INAC 8:202, 13A:141, 200; AALR WT#1:10-11).

GOODRICK

Edmund, m. By 23 Jan 1706, Ruth, extx. of William Clarkson of PG Co. (INAC 26:147).

George, m. by April 1658, Ursula, widow of Capt. William Lewis (*ARMD* 41:58).

Henry (Goodrich), of AA Co., m. by [c1666], Katherine, widow of Paul Kinsey (MDTP 2:120).

GORDING

John, m. on 12 Feb 1711, Jean Sanders (TAPE).

GORDON

Adrian, m. by 23 Oct 1690,. Mary, dau. of Michael Disharoone of SO co. (MWB 7:386).

Alexander, d. by 3 April 1686; his widow Sarah m. 2nd, John Ewens, 3rd, Robert Franklin, and 4th, John Willowby (AALR WH#4:256).

GORLY

John, m. by 9 July 1686, Barbara Chapman, admx. of Richard Chapman and of William Hensey of CH Co. (INAC 9:44, 54; MDTP 13:372).

GORMACK

Michael, m. by May 1696, Judith, admx. of Andrew Peterson of BA Co. (MDTP 16:170).

GORMAN

[-?-], m. by 1 April 1705, Mary, dau. of William Galloway of BA Co. (MWB 3:469).

[-?-], m. by 23 Feb 1704/5, Judith, dau. of Elizabeth Snowdell of BA Co. (MWB 3:436).

GORSUCH

Charles, of TA Co., m. by 8 Dec 1679, Sarah, heir of Thomas Cole (BALR IR#PP:46, IR#AM:185).

Charles (Gossidge), of BA Co., son of John and Ann, of the Kingdom of Eng., dec., m. on 15 d., 12 m. (Feb), 1690, Ann Hawkins, dau. of John and Mary, of AA Co. (WRMM).

Charles, m. on 12 June 1700, by Mr. Nobbs, minister, Sarah [-?-] (TAPE).

Loveless, of TA Co., m. on 23 Oct 1679, Rebeckah Preston of DO Co., at the house of Howell Powell (TATH).

Lovelace, of DO Co., planter, m. on 11 d. 6 m., 1696, Hannah Walley, late of PA, at the meeting house near Tuckahoe (TATH).

Lovelace, of DO Co., m. by 20 July 1705, Hannah, aunt of John Berry (MWB 12:46).

Richard (Gossutch), m. on 3 Dec 1696, Eliza Martin (TAPE).

GOSLIN

Thomas, m. by 12 May 1699, [-?-], dau. of Hugh Ellis (INAC 18:43).

GOSNELL

William, m. by 10 Aug 1703, Sarah, dau. of Eliza Baker of AA Co. (MWB 11:394; INAC 26:339).

GOSS

John, d. by 1675 having m. Jane Mackall; she m. 2nd, John Waughop or Warhop (MDTP 7:110-111; SMWB PC#1:16, 17).

GOSTWICK

[-?-], m. by 30 March 1695, Mary, dau. of Nicholas Corbin of BA Co. (MWB 7:297).

Thomas, m. in Sep 1717, Elizabeth Yanstone (BAPA).

GOTT

Richard, m. by 14 Aug 1686, Hannah, dau. of Thomas Pratt of AA Co. (MWB 4:250).

Richard, m. by 12 Feb 1702, Eliza, dau. of Anthony Holland, she m. 2nd, by 13 March 1717, Thomas Woodfield of AA Co. (MWB 11:316; BALR TR#A:544).

GOUGH

[-?-], m. by 28 Sep 1711, Elizabeth, now age 28, formerly the wife of George Medcalfe (MCHR PC:751).

Stephen (Goffe), m. by 22 June 1677, [-?-], extx. of John Jarboe (*ARMD* 67:130).

William, of CV Co., d. by June 1680, m. by 1679, Hester, dau. of John Larkin; she m. 2nd, Nicholas Nicholson, and 3rd, John Baldwin (MWB 14:30; INAC 7A:118, 10:225, 13A:313; *ARMD* 69:337-339, 70:292; AALR IT#5:18, 29; SY#1:62-63).

GOULD

Christopher (also Gold), m. by 11 Oct 1712, Sarah, widow and extx. of William Bolton of QA Co. (INAC 33B:179; QAJRh).

GOULT

George, planter, m. on 6 d. 3 m., 1691, Mary Sockwell (Wright transcribes this as Lockwell), spinster, both of TA Co., at the house of William Sockwell (TATH).

GOVANE

James (Jeames), m. on 4 Aug 1711, Mary Hornwood [*sic*; actually Homewood] (AAMA:83). She was Mary, extx. of Thomas Homewood of AA Co. (INAC 33B:75).

James (Jeams), m. on 15 July 1713, Elizabeth Hammond (AAMA:83). She was the extx. of William Hammond of AA Co. (MDTP 22:455).

GOVER

Ephraim, and Mary Harper filed their intentions to marry on 15 d., 4 m., and 3 d., 5 m., 1705 (WRMMa).

Robert, m. on 5 Dec 1695, Elizabeth Cotten (AAJA:1#10).

Robert, and Susanna Billinglsey filed their intentions to marry on 8 d., 10 m., 1699; an inquiry was to be made into the care of her children (WRMMa).

Samuel, and Elizabeth Roberts, with consent of their parents, filed their intentions to marry on 14 d., 4 m., 1706 and 12 d., 5 m., 1706 (WRMMa).

GRACE

Abell, m. on 14 d. 5 m., 1709, Lydia Eubanks, at Treadhaven Creek meeting house (TATH).

William, m. on 15 Dec 1709, Elizabeth Hearse (AAJA:38 #16).

GRADDE

Edmund, living on the Bay side, m. on 10 March 1697, Jellen Dunawin (HAGE:2).

GRAHAM

Robert, m. by 23 Feb 1677/8, Ann, extx. of George Mackall (*ARMD* 67:208; 68:15, 85; INAC 13A:285).

GRANGE

John, m. by March 1681/2, [-?-], widow of Richard Higgins of AA Co. (Warrant Record CB(#3):204).

GRANGER

Benjamin, m. by 1678, [-?-] Avery, dau. of John (*ARMD* 51:527; MCHR PC:138, 141).

Benjamin, m. by 1687, Margaret, mother of Trustrum Mago (DOLR 4 Old:195).

GRANT

Alexander [Garit], m. on 17 Nov 1709, Mary Hambleton (AALR 1:37).

John, m. by 25 May 1711, Mary, extx. of George Higgans of SM Co. (INAC 32C:97).

GRASON

George, m. by 18 March 1702, Sarah, sister of Andrew Skinner of TA Co., ship carpenter (TALR 9:152

GRAVES

Alexander, m. by c1703, Mary, legatee of Walter Tolly of KE Co. (INAC 23:17)

Geo., of SM Co. m. by 1646, Margaret Alvey, (dau. of Margaret?) (Hodges cites Liber 24:422).

Samuel (or Simon), m. by 1676, Alice, co-extx. of Demetrius Cartwright; Alice later m. John Gyatt (*ARMD* 66:470, 68:51; 70:154).

GRAY

David, m. on 14 Dec 1703, Penelope Parsons (AAAL 1:27).

Francis, m. by lic. 26 Nov 1636, Alice Boreman (*ARMD* 4:51). Francis, had a license dated 26 Nov 1638, to marry Alice Moreman (MPL 1:134).

George, m. by 1699, Margaret Beckwith, widow of Michael Taney and Joakin Kenstead (or Kierstead), and dau. of George and Francis Harvey Beckwith (INAC 9:476, 32B:129; MWB 6:1; MCHR PC:433).

George, m. on 4 April 1711, Jane Wilson (TAPE).

James, m. on 21 March 1696 by Col. Casparus Aug. Herman, Alice Wood (CESS).

James (Grey), m. on 27 May 1701, by banns, by Rev. Richard Sewell, Minister of N. and S. Sassafras Parishes, Hono Kannington (CESS).

John (Grey), 9 Dec 1701, Mary Hendy (AAAL 2:2).

John, m. by 4 Oct 1710, Mary, extx. of Richard Nelson of CH Co. (INAC 32A:35).
John, m. on 14 Feb 1717, Ann Hopkins (AAMA:87).
Miles (Grey), m. in 1663 or 1664, in Hungar's Parish, Northampton Co., VA, Ann [-?-]; by March 1674/5 they were living in SO Co., MD (AZ#8 (*ARMD* e87):490).
William, m. on 16 Oct 1705, Martha Duke (CVCH).
Zachariah, m. on 19 Dec 1719, Mary Demitt (BAPA).

GREEN(E)

[-?-], m. by 31 March 1668, Mary, dau. of John Browne of AA Co. (MWB 1:320).

[-?-], m. by April 1681, Eliz., alias Potter (*ARMD* 70:34).

[-?-], m. by 5 May 1700, Elizabeth, dau. of Anthony Demondidier (BALR HW#2:51).

Charles, of King's Lynn, Norfolk, Eng., m. by 17 Sep 1697, Elizabeth, dau. of James Truman (PGLR A:97).

Christopher, m. by 1688, Ann, widow of Edward Jones and John Harbottle of AA Co. (MDTP 14A:68, 81, 17:248).

Francis, Jr., m. by 1714, Charity Hagoe, dau. of Thomas and Mary Hagoe of CH Co. (MWB 14:213).

Henry, m. by 1684/5, Alice, widow of Albert Johnson of TA Co. (MDTP 13:229; INAC 9:436).

Henry, of TA Co., m. by 3 July 1701, Lucy, widow of Thomas Seward and Griffin Jones, who d. by 10 Aug 1702; Lucy Green recorded the births of several children of Thomas and Lucy Seaward [Seward?] and of Griffith and Lucy Jones (KELR GL#1:7, 35).

Henry, m. on 3 March 1711/2, Anne Purdy (AALR 1:38). She was the extx. of Henry Purdy (AAJU RC:271).

Henry, m. by 23 Nov 1715, [-?-], dau. of Thomas Bayley of QA Co., who called the man his son-in-law (MWB 14:113).

Hugh, m. on 18 July 1717 Susanna Holland (PGQA:1).

James, m. by 1684, Elizabeth Tennison, widow of John Tennison of SM Co. (PCJU DSA:101).

John, m. by 1714, Elizabeth, dau. of William Watson of DO Co. (MWB 14:182, MDTP 23:309).

Joseph, m. by 1693, Sarah, widow of Michael Crawley of CV Co. (MWAR BB:335; MWB 6:33).

Joshua, m. by 1686, Jane Chandler, sister of William Chandler, niece of Richard Chandler of CH Co. (MDTP 17:105-108; CHWB A:107).

Peter, m. by 1702, Anne, dau. of John Bowles (MWB 3:253).

Philip, m. on 25 Oct 1711, Sarah Seaborn (AALR 1:38).

Richard, m. on 17 April 1704, Margery Standbridge (AAJA:1#10).

Thomas, m. 1st, Mrs. Ann Cox, and 2nd, Mrs. Winifred Seyborn (who had transported herself in 1638 and her two children in 1644). She m. 2nd, by 1654, Robert Clark (MPL ABH: 6, 12, 67, 403; Proprietary Records Z&A:346).

Thomas, on 2 April 1643 swore there was no impediment to his marrying Millicent Browne (*ARMD* 4:192).

Thomas, transported by 1653, m. by 1653, Jane, widow of Nicholas Harvey, Gent., a passenger on the *Ark* and the *Dove* (MPL ABH:3,7, 62; *ARMD* 41:249). By 5 Oct 1657 Thomas and Jane were living in Lower Norfolk Co., VA (Proprietary Records A&B:336).

Thomas, m. by 22 Feb 1709, Mildred, extx. of William Shercliffe of SM Co. (INAC 31:40).

William, m. by Jan 1660/1, Elizabeth, extx. of Henry Potter (*ARMD* 41:394). She was born within five miles of Norwich, and was the widow of [Henry?] Potter (*ARMD*49:53, 217, 232).

William, banns pub. on 27 Nov 1666, m. on 2 Feb 1666/7, Elizabeth, widow of Mark Manlove (SOLR:IKL, O#1:41; see also MDTP 2:58).

GREENBERRY
Charles, m. by 4 March 1700, Rachel, dau. of Thomas Stimpson and of Rachel, who was the widow of [-?-] Kilburne (AALR IH#1:222, IH#3:2, WT#1:118).

GREENFIELD
[-?-] [Thomas?], m. by 20 Feb 1703, Martha, sister of Thomas Hollyday of PG Co. (MWB 11:279).

[-?-], m. by 6 Dec 1708, Susannah, dau. of Kenelm Cheseldyne of SM Co. (MWB 12:307).

John, m. by 1672, Martha, dau. of Nathaniel and Ann Truman (MWB 1:509, 4:65, 14:703).

Thomas, m. by 8 March 1675, [-?-], dau. of Robert Skinner of CV Co. (MWB 4:230).

GREENIFF
John, m. by 4 Nov 1703, Ruth, extx. of Edward Dorsey, son of Capt. John (INAC 24:178; BAAD 2:228).

John (Griniffe), of AA Co., m. by 30 Oct 1708, Katherine, mother of John and Edward Dorsey (MWB 12:323).

GREENING
Albert, m. on 7 Jan 1710/11, Alce Moore (AALR 2:7). As Albertus Greening, he m. by 5 April 1711, Alice, extx. of Edward Moore of AA Co. (INAC 32B:57, 34:61).

GREENWELL
[-?-], m. by 26 Jan 1716, Catherine, sister of John Wiseman of SM Co., whose mother Katherine, m. Richard Shirley (MWB 14:238).

James, son of John, d. by 1714, having m. by 27 March 1698, Grace, dau. of Henry Taylor, Sr.; she m. 2nd, Lawrence Galle or Galley (Fresco cites SMWB TA:57, 89, MWB 11:58; MDTP 22:359).

John, m. 1st, Mary [-?-], and 2nd, by 1654, Bridget Seaborne (MPL Q:208).

GREENWOOD
Bartholomew, m. on 5 Aug 1709, Mary Brown (TAPE).

GREEVES

James, m. on 8 April 1707, Catherine Barton (CVCH). She was the widow and extx. of William Barton of CV Co. (INAC 28:354).

Robert (Greves), m. on 7 Nov 1707, Margaret Howe (CVCH).

GREGORY

Charles, chirurgeon, m. by 22 March 1676, [-?-], extx. of John Pipper (INAC 2:145).

GRESHAM

[-?-], may have m. by 1698, Rebecca, called Rebecca Gott Gresham, legatee of Robert Gott of AA Co. (Cotton cites INAC 17:158).

GRIBLE

Robert, m. by 1681, Margaret, mother of Edward Young, from VA (MPL WC4:155).

GRIFFIN

[-?-], m. by 16 Jan 1715, [-?-], dau. of Mathew Smith, planter, of QA Co., who named a grandson James Griffin in his will (MWB 14:200).

Philip, m. by 18 May 1697, Jane, relict and extx. of Richard Rawlings of AA Co. (INAC 14:115, 19½B:146).

Philip, of AA Co., m. by 13 June 1700, Eliza, only dau. and heir of Thomas Scott (AALR WT#1:70).

Philip, of AA Co., m. by 20 Nov 1700, Eliza, mother of Sarah Fisher (MWB 11:19).

Samuel, m. by 1655, Alice, sister of Robert Taylor of Patuxent; she m. 2nd, Geo. Reed (*ARMD* 9:282, 414; MPL ABH:312, 7:1664; MWB 1:128).

Thomas, m. by Nov 1676, Elizabeth, dau. of William Cole of SM Co. (MDTP 8A:294).

GRIFFITH

[-?-], m. by 30 Dec 1695, Sarah, dau. of John Howard of AA Co. (MWB 7:164).

[-?-], m. by 10 Nov 1705, [-?-], dau. of Eleanor Howard of AA Co. (MWB 13:255).

Charles, planter, m. on 29 Aug 1717, Mary Mercer, widow (AAAN:33). She was the extx. of Jacob Mercier of AA Co. (MDAD 1:18).

Henry, m. by 1 Sep 1699, Elizabeth, widow of Francis Tassell (DOLR Old 5:140).

John, m. on 3 Aug 1695, Sarah Fowler (AAJA:1#6).

Orlando, m. on 6 June 1717, Catherine Howard (AAAN:32). She was the dau. of John Howard (*Md. Court of Appeals Reports* 2:418, 421; *ARMD* 38:378).

Samuel, m. on 26 Nov 1702, Sarah Evans (AAJA:26#3). She was a dau. of Lewis Evans of AA Co. (MCHR CL:340).

GRIGGS

George, m. by 2 June 1718, Sarah, admins. of John Dorsey or Doxey of SM Co. (MDAD 1:34).

John, m. by Oct 1676, Mary, extx. of Richard Keene (*ARMD* 66:399, 456, 67:52, 68:20; MPL 15:387).

GRILLE

William, m. in June 1667 Idy? Gradlowe (CHLR C#1:253).

GRIMES

Archibald, m. by 11 July 1713, Isabel (Esable), admx. of Charles Habitt of DO Co. (INAC 35B:10).

John, m. on (date not given), Elizabeth Fosters (AAAN:22).

Nicholas, m. in 1714/5, Elizabeth Toole (AAAN:22).

GRININ

Samuel, m. on 1 March 1714, Ann Twine (SJSG:6).

GRODTWELL

George, of CH Co., d. by 13 June 1678, Mary, sister and admx. of Richard Foulkes of CV Co.; she m. 2nd, William Ward of CH Co. (MDTP 10:138).

GROOME

Moses, m. by 11 Aug 1701, Elizabeth, admx. of William Ebdell [poss. Ebden?] (INAC 20:254).

Moses, had a kinswoman Ann, former wife of Stephen Johnson, who m. by 11 Feb 1704, Edward Felkes (BALR IR#PP:171, HW#2:119; BAAD 2:27; INAC 28:23).

GROSS

[-?-], m. by 10 Jan 1691, Hester, dau. of Nicholas Gassaway of AA Co. (MWB 2:228).

[-?-] (Grosse), m. by 9 Feb 1716, Sarah, dau. of Charles Paul, Sr., of DO Co. (MWB 14:410).

GROVER

John, of CV Co., m. by Aug 1682, Katherine, widow and admx. of John Wynnall of CV Co. (MDTP 12B:168; INAC 7C:227).

GROVES

James, m. by Oct 1710, Katherine, extx. of William Barton (PCJU PL#3:527).

William, m. on 27 Sep 1705, Isitt Rouse (AAAL 1:27).

William, m. on 15 Jan 1712/13, Mary Trot (AAJA:41 #14).

William, m. by 5 Oct 1714, Mary, dau. of Patrick Hall of AA Co. (AALR IB#2:193).

GRUDGEFIELD
[-?-], of London, m. by 3 April 1679, Katherine, sister of Thomas Notley of SM Co. (MWB 10:97).

GRUNDY
Robert, Gent., marriage contract dated 2 Feb 1688, Deborah Boyden, widow, formerly wife of Thomas Impey, Gent. (TALR 5:242; INAV 15:80), widow of Daniel Carnell (*ARMD* 8:395), relict and extx. of Maj. John Stanley of TA Co.
Robert, m. by 2 Feb 1702, Judith, dau. and heir of Richard Gurling, dec. (TALR 9:147; INAC 13B:10; 15:81). (See also *Md. Court of Appeals Reports* 1:50).
Robert, m. on 6 Jan 1703, Margaret Pemberton (TAPE). She was the mother of James, Benjamin, and John Pemberton (MWB 14:700).

GRUNWYNN
Thomas, m. by 2 Nov 1700, Elizabeth, widow of John Evans of SM Co. (MDTP 18b:16).

GUDGEON
Robert, m. by 3 Sep 1703, [-?-], admx. of Moses Groome (INAC 23:165).

GUGAT
John, m. by 14 June 1678, Alice, widow of Samuel Graves of CV Co. (MDTP 10:149).

GUIBERT
Joachim (Fresco transcribes this as Jonathan), m. by 13 Jan 1673/4, Elisabeth, eldest dau. of Luke Barbier (MDTP 6:68).
Joshua, m. by 1709, Elizabeth Gerard (Fresco cites (SMWB PC#1:188; *ARMD* 12:viii, and 51:xlvi; Prov. court MM:784; MDCR 3"1094; MDTP 19A:153).
Joshua, of SM Co., Gent., m,. by 1 Dec 1716, Ann, dau. of William Boarman, Gent. (CHLR H#2:45).
Thomas, m. by 1693, Elizabeth Barber, sister of Edward Barber of SM Co. (MWB 2:287; Fresco cites MDAD 5:408).

GUILDER
Henry, of CE Co., m. by 10 Dec 1705, Mary, dau. of Peter Clawson of CE Co. (CELR 2:72).

GUINN
Richard, m. by 21 Oct 1677, Susanna, relict and extx. of William Neale of AA Co. (MDTP 9A:361; INAC 4:567).

GUISHARD
Samuel (Gushard), m. on 2 Nov 1704, Ann Gongo (AAJA:47#17). She was a dau. of Ann Gongoe (*MRR*: AA Co.:115).

GUITON
Timothy, m. by May 1698, Elizabeth, extx. of Henry Dickson of CV Co. (MDTP 17:254).

GULLETT
William (Gullick, Gullus), m. on 1 Nov 1674, Susanna Mills (SOLR:IKL).

GUMLEY
John, of New Castle Co., PA [*sic*], m. on 29 d. 4 m., 1704, Deborah Barbor of CE Co., at Cecil Meeting House (KECE). She was a dau. of James Barber of KE Co. (MWB 14:285).

GUNBY
[-?-], m. by 25 July 1673, [-?-], dau. of George Goodrick of CH Co. (MWB 5:91).
Francis, on 14 Nov 1676, banns of matrimony were published for him and Sarah Kirke (SOLR O#7:62r).

GUNNELL
George, m. by 28 July 1679, Jane, admx. of Thomas Overton of BA Co., the father of Nathaniel Overton ("m. immediately after death") (MPL 20:49; INAC 6:225; BAAD 2:72; *ARMD* 67:254, 320; Warrant Record CB(#3):36).

GUNTHROPE
[-?-], m. 29 June 1715, [-?-] , sister of John Salter of QA Co., by whom he had a son Jonathan of Ratcliffe Cross, London (MWB 14:77).

GUTRIDGE
George (Goodricke), m. by June 1658, [-?-], widow of Capt. William Lewis (*ARMD* 10:523).
Henry, m. by 20 March 1697, Mary, admx. of David Floyd of PG Co. (INAC 15:281, 16:680).

GUY
John, m. some time after 1650, [-?-], the relict of Thomas Petite, who d. in 1650; she later m. Peter Carr (*ARMD* e73:186).

GUYATT
John (Gyatt), m. by 4 Aug 1679, Alice, extx. of Demetrius Cartwright, and widow and admx. of Samuel Graves (*ARMD* 70:154; INAC 6:271; MDTP 10:149).

GUYTHER
Owen, m. by 14 Sep 1677, Elizabeth Davis or Davies, dau. of the wife of Morgan Jones of SM Co., and heir of John Davies (INAC 4:243; MDTP 9A:451).
William, Jr., son of Nicholas Guyther II, m. by 16 March 1705/6, Mary, dau. of Robert Crane; she m. 2nd, by 4 Nov 1707, Marshal Lowe; and 3rd, by 20 Nov 1706, Edward Morgan (SMWB PC#1:139, 156; INAC 27:232).

GWIN

John, m., by 25 April 1700, [-?-], widow and extx. of Thomas Tallor or Fallar of CH Co. (INAC 19½B:113; MDTP 18A:69).

William (Gwyn), m. on 3 Aug 1697, Sarah [-?-] (TAPE). She was the widow of William Anderson of TA Co.; she m. 3rd, Walter Quinton (MDTP 17:218, 18:15).

GYRLING

Richard, m. on 22 March 1667, Elizabeth Moorey (*ARMD* 54:602).

HABERDINE

John, m. on 23 Dec 1706, Elizabeth Barrington (AAAL 1:33).

HACK

John, of TA Co., m. by Sep 1686, Bridget, relict of David Johnson (MDTP 13:401).

HACKET(T)

[-?-], m. by 10 Feb 1708, Esther, dau. of Richard Jones of QA Co. (MWB 12:355).

James, m. by 30 Aug 1688, Tamer, dau. of Edward Selby of AA Co. (MWB 6:17). She m. 2nd, Benj. Clark of AA Co. (AALR IH#3:86, WT#1:51).

John, m. by 26 Nov 1707, Elizabeth, relict and extx. of John Hambleton (INAC 27:260). She was the mother of John Hawkins Hambleton (QAJRh).

John, m. by banns on 13 Feb 1711 by Rev. Richard Sewell, Anne Evins, spinster (CESS).

John, m. by June 1716, [-?-], mother of John Hawkins Hambleton (QAJRh).

Lawrence, m. on 15 Oct 1704, Anne Potts (TAPE).

Michael, m. on 28 July 1709, Mary Bowles (KESP:33). She was the admx. of Isaac Bowles, Jr., of KE Co. (INAC 31:233)

Theophilus, m. by 20 July 1680, Alice, relict and extx. of Edward Skidmore of AA Co., and mother of Michael Skidmore (INAC 7A:139; MWB 2:293).

HACKNEY

Joseph, m. by 1718, Margaret, sister of Adam Bell (Hodges cites SMWB PC#1:247; MDTP 6:325, 404, 498, 498).

HACKS

Jeremiah (Harks), m. by [c1704], Mary, admx. of John Clarke of BA Co. (MWB 3:417; BAAD 2:107).

HADAWAY

George, m. by 8 Sep 1700, Sarah, dau. of Eliza Oakley of TA Co. (MWB 11:33).

HADDEN

John, m. on 24 Feb 1717/8, Amy Short (AAAL 2:14).

William, m. by Aug 1707, Margaret Burt, admx. of Henry Burt (TAJR 1706-1708).

HADDOCK

[-?-], m. by 14 April 1713, Sarah, dau. of Richard Marsham of PG Co. (MWB 13:514).

James, Gent., m. by 5 June 1711, Sarah, widow of William Barton (MCHR PC:604, 740; INAC 34:109, 36B:203; MDTP 22:117).

Thomas, m. by 6 April 1685, Mary, dau. of Thomas Doxey of SM Co. (MWB 4:132).

HAGAN

James, m. by 1694, Elizabeth, dau. of William and Mary (Hussey) Langworth (Hodges cites SMWB PC#1:86; PGLR F:415).

James [?], of CH Co., m. by 1707, [-?-], dau. of William Langford (SMRR:11).

HAGAR

Robert, m. by 25 May 1708, Mary, admx. of Thomas Courtney of SM Co. (INAC 28:218).

HAGERTY

John, m. by 5 May 1708, Honor, admx. of Thomas Davis of CH Co. (INAC 28:120; PCJU VD#2:328).

Robert (Hagartee), m. by 13 Aug 1717, Mary, admx. of Robert Gosting of CH Co. (INAC 37B:224).

HAGLEY

[-?-], m. by April 1684, Margaret, relict and admx. of Bartholomew Henrickson (MDTP 13:119).

HAGUE

[-?-], m. by 19 May 1718, Elizabeth, sister of Thomas Harrison (CHPR, 1717-1735, 24).

HAILEY

Clement (Haly), m. by 4 Dec 1677, Mary, relict and admx. of Edward Connery (*ARMD* 67:218; MDTP 9A:397).

Darby (Heley), of CE Co., m. by Oct 1694, Elizabeth, relict of Thomas Strickland (MDTP 15C:248).

Robert, m. by 1664, Sarah Bachelor, widow of Francis, of CV Co. (MDTP 1:33, 56).

HALE

Edward, m. by 11 Sep 1689, Jane, dau. of John Sesson of AA Co., dec. (AALR IH#1:91).

George, of KE Co., m. on 10 May 1660, Margrett Hill (*ARMD* 54:186).

James, of SM Co., m. by Sep 1685, Hannah, extx. of Robert Browne (MDTP 13:251).

Patrick, m. on 17 Dec 1709, [-?-] [-?-] (HAGE:26).

William, m. on 27 Feb 1718, Mary Hippy (AAAN:36).

HALFHEAD

John, m. 1st, Anne [-?-], a free woman, and 2nd, by 27 Feb 1649, Julian [-?-], servant to Mrs. White (Proprietary Records Z&A:579).

John, d. 1675, having m. Jane Maddox, who m. 2nd, Henry Elliott (INAC1:500, 6:222; Warrants ABH:35, 15:434, Q:208).

HALL

[-?-], m. by 19 April 1712. Mary, dau. of Benja. Sauser of SO Co. (MWB 14:121).

Capt. Alexander, m. on 3 July 1709, Mable Knowles (TAPE).

Aron, m. by c1698, [-?-], admx. of John Edwards (INAC 16:230).

Benjamin, m. by July 1693, Mary, relict and extx. of James Bowling of CH Co. (MDTP 15A:44; INAC 14:105; *ARMD* 77:92).

Charles, Jr., m. on 31 Oct 1693, Martha Davis (SOLR:IKL). She was a dau. of Richard Davis of SO Co., dec. (INAC 17:132).

Charles, m. on 5 Jan 1700, Elizabeth Smithers (AAJA:22#5).

Edward, m. by 25 Jan 1652, Rebecca, widow of George Manners (*ARMD* 10:216). She m. 3rd, by 15 May 1657, Thomas Orley (*ARMD* 10:505).

Edward, m. by c1699, Sarah, admx. of Jonah Winfield of CV Co. (INAC 19:161).

Edward, m. 1st, Jane, dau. of John Sisson, by whom he had a son John, and 2nd, by 11 Oct 1710, Dorcas [-?-] (AALR PK:305).

Edward, m. on 17 Nov 1709, Deranirah Everit (AAAN:9). She was extx. of Richard Everit of AA Co. (INAC 30:236).

Edward, m. by 10 Nov 1710, Sarah, extx. of William Ridgaway of TA Co. (INAC 32B:42).

Edward, m. on 9 Feb 1713/4, Sarah Wood (AAAN:22).

Edward, m. on 31 Oct 1717, Avarilla Carvill (HAGE:39).

Edward, m. on 24 July 1718, Elizabeth Topping (AAAN:39).

Elisha, of CV Co., m. by July 1699, Sarah, relict of Jonas? Winfield of CV Co. (MDTP 17:340).

Elisha, of CV Co., m. by 10 March 1713, Sarah, dau. of   Richard Hooper of CV Co. (DOLR 6 Old:214).

Henry, minister of St. James' Parish, 5 Feb 1701, Mary Duvall, dau. of Mareen Duvall, merchant of this Parish (AAAL 2:2). She was a dau. of Mareen Duvall of AA Co. (AALR IH#1:221).

John, m. by 1688, Sarah, widow and admx. of John Collier of BA Co., and admx. of George Hooper. Sarah was the mother of Isabella Hooper, and sister of Ann Collier (BALR HW#2:38). She was also also extx. of Abraham Holman of BA Co. (INAC 10:168, 169, 12:133).

John, living on the north branch of the head of Bush River, m. on 18 July 1693, Martha Gouldsmith (HAGE:2). She was the widow and extx. of George Gouldsmith of BA Co., and dau. and coheir of Edward Beedle (INAC 10:454, 15:182, 184, 19:171, 19½B:69; BALR IS#IK:241, 245).

John, living at Bush River, m. on 6 May 1697, Ann Hollis (HAGE:2).

John, m. on 19 Oct 1710, Hannah Everet (AALR 2:6).

Joshua, m. by 28 April 1693, Margaret, widow and extx. of John [or Joseph] Isaacs (INAC 10:333; MDTP 15A:24).

Patrick, d. by March 1683, having m. Mary, widow of James Maxwell. She later married Jno. Spencer (MDTP 13:21).

Philip, m. on 25 Dec 1705, Margaret Boyse (AAAL 1:32(2)).

Richard, of TA Co., m. on 21 d. 2 m., 1680, Sarah Rastoe, of MD, at the house of Thomas Taylor, TA Co. (TATH).

Richard, of TA co., blacksmith, m. on 6 d. 6 m., 1699, Jane Judkins, relict of Obadiah Judkins, at the meeting house near Tuckaho Creek (TATH).

Richard, son of Elisha and Sarah of CV Co., m. on 4 d., 7 m. (Sep), 1712, Mary Johns, widow of Aquila, late of CV Co. (WRMM).

Richard, m. by 23 June 1714, Faith, dau. of Faith Gongo (AALR IB#2:158).

Robert, m. on 18 Oct 1682, Elizabeth Mackettrick (SOLR:IKL).

Walter, m. by 30 April 1658, [-?-], relict of Henry Fox (*ARMD* 41:79).

Mr. Walter, m. by 1663, [-?-], relict of John Lloyd, Gent. (MPL 5:393-395).

Walter, m. by 1678, Margaret Mollings, who m. 2nd, by 1680, James Patterson, Margaret was a sister of Margery, wife of John Gittings (Hodges cites Prov. Court TL#2:275; PCJU 1:354, 355; MDTP 8A:135; SMWB PC#1:30).

William, m. on 14 Jan 1716, Mary Edwin (KESP:34).

HALLOWES

John, on 1 June 1639 declared his intention to marry Restitua Tew, and swore there was no impediment to the marriage, which was performed the following day by Mr. Thomas White (*ARMD* 4:52).

HALPIN

John, m. by 2 June 1703, Elizabeth, widow of John Allford, Sr. (DOLR 6 Old:21).

HAMBLETON

Edward, m. by 1695, Elizabeth, dau. of John Elliott of TA Co. (MWB 3:653, 7:187).

Edward, m. on 27 Nov 1701, Elizabeth [-?-] (TAPE).

Edward, m. by 1702, Elizabeth, dau. of Walter Quinton (TALR 9:123). In 1716 she was listed as a sister of Walter Quinton of QA Co. (MWB 14:240).

John, m. by 26 Dec 1655, Temperance, dau. of Richard Moore (*ARMD* 10:433).

John, m. by 25 March 1679, Ann, extx. of John Avery (*ARMD* 10:433).

HAMBLIN

Benjamin, m. on 28 Feb 1717, Sarah Dowlin (KESP:34).

George, on 14 March 1670/1, banns of matrimony were published for him and Margaret Pepper. A certificate was issued on 5 April 1671 (SOJU DT#7:122). On 10 April 1671 John Pepper wrote: "Mr. Beauchamp this is to let you understand that I do give my free Consent that George Hammell Shold take my Daughter to wife & therefore I pray doe that favour as to Send y Certificate by the Bearer hereof In witness hereof I doe hereunto Sett my hand the tenth day of Aprill this note may be you discharge to keep you harmless" /s/ John Pepper (SOJU DT#7:160).

HAMILTON
  [-?-] (Hamiltowne), m. by 6 May 1695, Eliza, dau. of John Ellett of TA Co. (MWB 7:187).

HAMM
  John, m. by 24 April 1701, Mary, relict and admx. of John Eldridge of CE Co. (INAC 20:189)
  John, m. on 16 Nov 1703, Holinor Hollins (CESS).

HAMMELL
  George, had written permission of John Pepper to take Pepper's dau. to wife, according to a note written by Pepper to Mr: Beauchamp on 10 April 1671 (*ARMD* e86 (SOJU DT#7):155.160).

HAMMERSLEY
  Francis, m. by 29 Dec 1697, Margaret, dau. of Randolph Brandt of CH Co. (MWB 6:232).

HAMMOND
  [-?-], m. by 1677, Elinor, widow of Abraham Bowman (or Newman) (INAC 4:590; MDTP 9A:455).
  [-?-], m. by c1679, Mary, relict and admx. of Thomas Roper of AA Co. (INAC 6:418, 10:315).
  [-?-], m. by 29 July 1701, Hannah, dau. of Philip Howard of AA Co. (MWB 11:153).
  [-?-], m. by 15 Feb 1702/3, Parthenia, dau. of Thomas Poynter, Sr., of SO Co. (MWB 12:9).
  Charles, m. on 24 Oct 1715, Rachel Greenberry (AAMA:84). She was the dau. of John Stimson (AALR IB#2:469). She was the relict and widow of Charles Greenberry (MCHR CL:275).
  John, d. by 9 Feb 1663/4, when his admx. Ann had m. Pope Alvey (*ARMD* 49:121-122; Hodges cites Pro Court FF:30; MWB 10:17; MPL ABH:338, 12:550).
  John, m. by 5 Nov 1697, Ann, dau. of Nicholas Greenbury of AA Co. (MWB 7:314; INAC 21:327; AALR IB#2:534).
  Thomas, of BA, Gent., m. by 21 Feb 1693 Rebecca, widow of Thomas Lightfoot or Lytfoot, and dau. of John Larkin (BALR RM#HS:417; INAC 13B:23, 24; MWB 5:186).
  Thomas, of William, m. on 6 Jan 1714, Jane Lillingstone, dau. of Rev. John (AAMA:86).
  Thomas, m. by 19 May 1715, Jane, extx. of John Wells of QA Co. (INAC 36B:173, 37c:148; MDAD 1:21).

HAMNER
  William, m. by 6 Feb 1712, Catherine, dau. of Thomas Collins of KE Co., dec. (QALR ETA:169).

HAMPTON

[-?-], m. by Nov 1705, Mary, mother of William Felkes (AAJU TB#1:114).

John, m. by Aug 1708, Mary, extx. of James Round (SOJU 1707-1711:229).

John, m. by July 1708, Mary, admx. of John Edgar, merchant (PCJU PL#2:145; SOJU 1707-1711:316).

John, m. by June 1713, [-?-], admx. of William Dickenson (MDTP 22:244).

HANBY

Francis, m. by 13 Nov 1695, Alice, mother of Samuel Barker (CHLR S:431).

HANCE

Benjamin, m. by Aug 1711, Sarah, admx. of William Parker of CV Co. (MDTP 22:65).

Benjamin, and Mary Hutchins filed their intentions to marry on 3 d., 6 m., 1711, and last day, 6 m., 1711 (WRMMa). Mary Hutchins was a legatee of Thomas Godwin of CV Co. (INAC 33A:231).

John, m. by Feb 1674/5, Sarah, widow and admx. of Sampson Waring of CV Co. (*ARMD* 65:530; INAC 4:230).

John (Hans), m. by 2 Aug 1687, Mary, relict and extx. of Christopher Kellett (INAC 9:363; MDTP 13:504, 14A:57).

John, of CV Co., m. by 14 Feb 1708/9, Sarah, mother of Robert Roberts and John Claw (MWB 12, pt. 2:47).

HANCOCK

[-?-], m. by 11 June 1670, Rebecca, sister of Nathaniel Stinchcomb of AA Co. (MWB 1:585).

[-?-], m. by 16 May 1717, Charity, dau. of Thos. Millmon of DO Co. (MWB 14:456).

Stephen, (sometimes written as Hancox) of AA Co., d. by 27 Sep 1703, when his admx. Rebecca had m. [-?-] Aldridge (INAC 24:182; AAJU IB#1:561).

HANDY

Samuel, m. in March 1679, Mary Sewell (SOLR:IKL).

HANGE

John (or Hauge), m. by Dec 1711, [-?-], admx. of John Hambleton (MDTP 22:710).

HANKINGS

John, m. on 11 Sep 1708, Mrs. Eliza Needles (TAPE).

HANKS

Peter, m. on 20 Aug 1704, Mary Beez (AAAN:19).

HANNES

Miles, m. on 24 Nov 1698, Elizabeth Kelly (HAGE:6).

HANITT
William, runaway, m. by 17 June 1703, Frances, runaway, relict and extx. of John Buttler of SM Co. (INAC 24:32).

HANNAH
Robert, m. by 5 March 1710, Rachel, admx. of Thomas Covington of KE Co. (INAC 32B:251).

HANSLAP
Joseph (Handslap), m. 10 Aug 1699, Elizabeth Thomas (AAAL 1:15).

HANSON
Frederick, m. on 14 Feb 1711, Mary Lowder (KESP:33).
George, m. on 22 Jan 1711, Mary Hurtt (KESP:33).
George, m. on 17 Sep 1713, Jane Hynson (KESP:34).
Hance, m. on 29 March 1679, Martha Wells Ward (KESP:31). She was the relict of John Wells of KE Co. (MPL WC#2:414).
Hance, m. on 29 May 1707, Anne Hamer (KESP:32).
John, m. by Nov 1693, Mary, extx. of William Winslow (SOJU LD:49).
John, Jr., m. by 22 April 1707, Elizabeth, extx. of Samuel Luckett of CH Co. (INAC 27:12, 29:234).
Jonathan, of BA Co., son of Timothy and Barbara, of Philadelphia Co., PA, m. on 29 d., 5 m. (July), 1718, Mary Price, dau. of Mordecai and Mary (WRMM).
Patrick, m. by 23 Dec 1665, Katherine, dau. of Macam Macenne (MDTP 1F:122-123).
Randolph, m. by 1662, Barbara, widow of James Johnson of Poplar Hill, and dau. of Richard and Margaret Hatton, and niece of Secretary Thomas Hatton (*ARMD* 10:12; SMWB PC#1:15, 30; SMWB 6:235).
Samuel, m. by 2 Oct 1707, Elizabeth, extx. of Benjamin Warren of CH Co. (INAC 27:132, 32A:37).
Thomas (Handson), of BA Co., m. by 4 July 1696, Sarah, dau. of John Ray of AA Co. (INAC 13B:105; MWB 14:6).

HARBERT
Mr. Alexander, m. by 24 Sep 1717, Mary, extx. of Col. James Smallwood of CH Co. (INAC 37B:135).
Charles, m. on 25 Aug 1718, Margaret Tucker (TAPE).

HARBETT
John, m. on 5 June 1718, Ann Bullock (TAPE).

HARBOTTLE
John, of AA Co., m. by April 1698, Ann, relict of Henry Francis of the same county (MDTP 17:80).

HARBUYT
Jno., m. on 21 July 1706, Rebecka Williams (CVCH).
William (Harbut), m. by 1677, Eleanor, widow of John Anderton and dau. of James Pattison (MDTP 6:83, 85).

HARDAGIN
Edmond, m. on 30 Dec 1714, Catherine Jenkins (TAPE).

HARDEN
Henry, m. on 6 Jan 1713, Elizabeth Glover (TAPE).
Joseph, m. on 7 Aug 1718, Martha Fromelier (TAPE).

HARDESTY
Francis, m. on 13 Jan 1703/4, Ruth Gather (AAAL 1:26). She was the admx. of John Gaither (AAJU TB#2:64).

HARDIKIN
Edward, m. on 8 June 1718, Elizabeth Alford (TAPE).

HARDING
John, m. by May 1685, Elizabeth, widow of Morgan Penury? Pusey? Persy? of CE Co. (MDTP 13:238, 309).
John, m. on 17 Jan 1711/2, Margaret Watts (AALR 1:38). She was admx. of Francis Watts of AA Co. (INAC 34:28).
Robert, m. on 9 April 1702, Elizabeth [-?-] (TAPE).

HARDISTY
Francis, m. by 17 June 1707, Ruth, relict and admx. of John Gaither of AA Co. (INAC 27:13).

HARDMAN
Jeffrey, planter, m. on 21 d. 6 m., 1692, Elizabeth Booker, spinster, both of TA Co., at Betteys Cove Meeting House (TATH).

HARDY
Henry, m. by 24 Oct 1673, Jemima, extx. of Thomas Pearcy of CH Co. (MDTP 6:19).
Henry, m. by July 1686, Mary, admx. of William (Warder or Wardrop) (MDTP 13:360).
Henry, m. on 21 Aug 1694, Elinor, dau. of John Cumpton of SM Co. (CHLR Q#1:23R).
Henry, m. by c1700/1, Ann, extx. of Richard Ashman of CH Co. (INAC 20:195). She m. 3rd, by 1717, William Foster (MWB 14:424).
William, m. by 19 May 1709, Mary, extx. of Henry Poulter of SM Co. (INAC 29:299).

HARE
      Edward (Harry), m. by 14 June 1713, Lydia, admx. of Zachariah Brown of BA Co. (INAC 34:9).

HARGRAVE
      [-?-], of Newcastle-Upon-Tyne, m. by 1 July 1710, Catherine, dau. of the elder bro. of Richard Carter of TA Co., MD, dec. (TALR RF#12:9).

HARMAN
      Robert, m. by 17 June 1710, Rachel, admx. of Thomas Covington of KE Co. (INAC 31:235).

HARMER
      Godfrey, m. by 20 June 1662, Mary, dau. of Oliver and of Johanna Spry of TA Co., who named her dau. Mary Harmer and grandchildren, Sarah, Eliza, and Mary Harmer (BALR RM#HS:4; MWB 2:349; MDTP 7:54).

HARNEY
      James, m. by 31 July 1716, Mary, admx. of Jos. Kinnimont of TA Co. (INAC 37A:134).
      Timothy, of SO Co., m. on 1 Dec 1682, Elizabeth Green (SOLR:IKL).

HARPER
      Daniel, m. by 11 April 1713, Mary, admx. of James Munkister of CH Co. (INAC 34:136).
      Edward, m. on 4 April 1682, elsewhere the date is given as 13 May 1682, Lydia Hudson (SOLR:IKL).
      Edward, m. by 22 May 1716, [-?-], widow of Thomas Watts of CE Co. (INAC 37A:95).
      John, m. on 12 Dec 1717, Anne Crawley (AAAN:35).

HARRINGTON
      [-?-], may have m. by 2 April 1662, Anne, sister of Robert Cole of St. Clement's Bay, SM, Co., who called Anne Harrington sister in his will (MWB 1:182).
      Charles, m. by 26 Oct 1675, Mary, widow and extx. of James Stockley of CV Co. (INAC 4:511).
      Cornelius, m. by July 1708, Rebecca, admx. of Evan Miles (MDTP 21:39).
      John , m. by 29 May 1665, Mary, relict of Francis Mugg (MDTP 1E:124; *ARMD* 57:302).
      John, m. on 2 Sep 1712, Sarah Phillips (TAPE).

HARRIOT
      Oliver, m. by 9 Oct 1710, Ann, admx. of Lawrence Richardson (INAC 32A:24, 32C:135; BAAD 2:2).
      Oliver, m. on 13 Oct 1717, Susanna Morrow (SJSG:10).

HARRIS

[-?-], m. by 20 Oct 1677, Jacqueline, relict and extx. of James More (or Moore) of CV Co. (INAC 4:450).

[-?-], d. by 16 May 1681 having m. Sarah, widow of Walter Jenkins and of Thomas Brookes (MWB 4:157).

[-?-], m. by 23 Feb 1715, Sarah, dau. of Elizabeth Bourn, widow and extx. of Samuel Bourn, Gent., of CV Co. (MWB 16:50).

[-?-], m. by 5 Dec 1717, Elizabeth, dau. of George Ransom of PG Co. (MWB 14:663).

Daniel, m. on 23 May 1709, Elinor Fitchgerald (KESP:32).

Edmund, m. on 12 May 1706, Elizabeth Wright (AAJA:32 #8).

Edward, m. by June 1718, Frances, extx. of Daniel Johnson of BA co. (MDTP 23:23:193).

George, and Anna Young filed their intentions to marry on 25 d., 12 m., 1703, and on 24 d., 1 m., 1703 (WRMMa). She was a dau. of Arthur Young of CV Co., (MWB 13:249).

Henry, of TA Co., d. by 10 Oct 1709, when his extx. Mary had m. Pierce Welsh (INAC 30:176).

Isaac, m. by 13 Aug 1703, Rhoda, widow and admx. of Tobias Wells of TA Co. (INAC 24:17).

Isaac, m. by 26 May 1710, Rhoda, dau. of Susanna Workman (who later m. Benjamin Ball) of Kent Island (QALR ETA:62, 106).

James, m. on 2 April 1701, Elizabeth Jones (KESP:31). She was the dau. of Edward Jones, chirurgeon (CELR 2:301; MPL 35:406).

James, m. by 2 Nov 1718, Bathsheba, dau. of James Barlow (BAAD 2:311).

John, m. by Sep 1691, Mary: Barnett (SOJU AW:156). Elsewhere her name is given as Bennett (SOJU 1691-1692:143).

John, m. on 21 or 24 Oct 1702, Mary [-?-] (AAAN:9).

Joseph and Ann Young filed their intentions to marry on 27 d., 6 m., 1714, and 22 d., 8 m., 1714 (WRMMa).

Peter, m. by 28 June 1698, Mary, extx. of John Davis of SM Co. (INAC 16:64).

Richard, m. by 1648, Mary, dau. of Humphrey and Blanche [-?-] Howell of SM Co. (*ARMD* 10:159, 305, 514).

Richard, m. on 17 Jan 1682, Susanna Richardson (SOLR:IKL). She was a widow of [-?-] Richardson, and mother of William Richardson (*ARMD* e106: SOJU 1689-1690:112).

Richard, and Elizabeth Webb filed their intentions to marry on 20 d., 4 m., 1701; with the consent of their respective mothers at a meeting on 15 d., 6 m., 1701 (WRMMa).

Thomas, m. on 20 July 1704, Mary Mitley (AAJA:29 #5). She was the extx. of Christopher Mitley of AA Co. (INAC 25:337).

William, m. on 5 March 1676, Alce Roberts (SOLR:IKL).

William, m. by 11 Sep 1684, Elizabeth, relict and admx. of Thomas Russell, and widow of William Croshaw (INAC 7C:330, 8:214; BACP D:385).

William, m. by March 1684/5, [-?-], relict and admx. of William Hollis (BACP D:240).

William, m. on 8 Dec 1702, Elizabeth Rose (AAJA:26#4).
William, and Elizabeth Young, filed their intentions to marry on 24 d., 6 m., 1716, and 21 d., 7 m., 1716 (WRMMa).

HARRISON
[-?-], m. by 13 Nov 1673, Sarah, admx. of Alexander Towerson (MDTP 6:32) [But see the following entry].

[-?-], of Kent Island, m. by 14 March 1678, Sarah, mother of Andrew and Alexander Tolson (KELR K:48; MWB 4:77; INAC 7C:176).

[-?-], m. by 19 Feb 1694, [-?-], widow of [-?-] Hall (in inv. of John Abington of CV Co.) (INAC 13A:320).

Amos, m. on 6 Nov 1703, Jillion Batton (TAPE).

Charles, m. by Sep 1696, Joanna, relict and extx. of Anthony Arnold, and mother of William Arnold (MDTP 16:187; AALR WT#2:304).

Francis, m. on 9 July 1681, Mary, dau. of William and Alice Rich of this Parish (TAPE; MWB 6:9).

Francis, m. by Sep 1685, Margaret, widow and extx. of Robert Robbins of CH Co. (MDTP 13:252).

Francis, m. in 1716, Dorothy Lowe (TAPE).

Dr. Jeremy, of Eng. and Westmoreland Co., VA, d. by 1655, having m. Frances Whitgreaves; she m. 2nd, by c1655, Gov. Giles Brent (*ARMD* 3:162; *MHM* 3:30; *VMHB* 16: 7, 96, 211).

John, Jr., on 10 Jan 1670/1, banns of matrimony were published for him and Judith Godfrey. A certificate was issued on 2 Feb (SOJU DT#7:68). **They were m. on 18 Feb 1670** (SOLR:IKL).

John, m. by Aug 1686, Martha, extx. of Thomas Baker of CH Co. (MDTP 13:392; INAC 9:463).

Richard, m. by 13 April 1681, Elizabeth, relict and extx. of John Benson, merchant, of CV Co. (INAC 7B:43B).

Richard, of CV Co., m. on 7 d., 3 m. (May), 1695, Elizabeth Hall (WRMM).

Richard, Jr., and Elizabeth Hall, dau. of Elisha Hall, with parents' consent, filed their intentions to marry on 21 d., 11 m., 1706, and 21 d., 12 m., 1706 (WRMMa).

John, m. on 26 Dec 1710, Sarah Gilbard (TAPE).

Samuel, and Elizabeth Parrott filed their intentions to marry on 28 d., 2 m., 1699 (WRMMa). She was the widow and extx. of Gabriel Parrott of AA Co. (MWB 3:233).

Samuel, m. by 7 May 1716, Sarah, dau. of Elisha Hall of CV Co. (MWB 14:317).

William, planter, m. on 20 d. 2 m., 1699, Elizabeth Dickinson, both of TA Co., at the meeting house near Choptank River, TA Co. (TATH).

William, m. on 2 Nov 1710, Sarah Cook (TAPE).

HARRY
William, m. on 12 Dec 1710, Mary Peacock (KESP:33).

HART

[-?-], m. by 4 May 1703, Sarah, dau. of John Scutt of BA Co. (MWB 11:339).
Gilbert, m. by 26 July 1712, Helen, admx. of John Simmons of SM Co. (INAC 33B:135).

HARTLEY

Joseph (Hearthy), m. on 16 Dec 1707, Mary Ann Fanton (KESP:32).
Joseph, m. on 6 May 1714, Ann Spiring (KESP:34).

HARVEY

Timothy (Harney?), m. on 26 Dec 1682, Elizabeth Greene (SOLR:IKL).

HARWOOD

[-?-], m. by 13 May 1705, Elinor, relict of Richard Attwood of SM Co. (INAC 25:51).
John, m. on 19 June 1707, Johanna Scorch (AAAL 1:33).
Peter, carpenter, m. on 20 d. 7 m., 1690, Elizabeth Taylor, spinster, both of TA Co., at the meeting house in Tuckahoe Creek (TATH).She was a sister of Thomas Taylor of TA Co. (MWB 13:298).
Robert, promised by 25 Sep 1657 to marry Elizabeth Gary, whose mother Judith had m. 2nd, Peter Sharpe (Proprietary Records A&B:314).
Thomas, m,. on 11 Sep 1718, Sarah Belt (AAAL 2:16).

HASFURT

George, m. on 8 Oct 1674, Clements Kerne or Keene (SOLR:IKL).
George, m. on 29 Nov 1677, Elizabeth Hudson (SOLR:IKL).

HASHAND

Darby (or Hash?), m. on 27 April 1703, Dorothy Judar (KESP:32).

HASKINS

George (or John), m. by 1718, [-?-], widow of Zachariah Bond of SM Co. (Hodges cites HH:336).

HASELDINE

Richard, m. by 1687, [-?-], relict of Francis Crookes (MDTP 14A:1).

HASLEWOOD

[-?-], m. by c1680, Elizabeth, widow and extx. of John Collett of BA Co. (INAC 7A:361).
John (Hazlewood), m. by 1676, Ann, widow of Jno. Avery (MCHR PC:138, 141).
James, m. by April 1708, Mary, admx. of Henry Whittacre (MDTP 21:17).

HASLOW

[-?-], m. by 15 Nov 1712, Dianna, sister of Nathaniel and George Childs of CE Co. (INAC 36A:11)

HASSARD

Edward, banns were pub. 8 Dec 1671, m. in Feb [1671/2], Anne Carr (SOLR:IKL).

HASSELL

[-?-], m. between 1708 and 1719, Katherine Hutchings, dau. of William and Gillion Hutchings (SMWB PC#1:153, 251; TA#1:28).

HASTE

Daniel, m. on 2 Aug 1580, Sarah Rogers (SOLR:IKL).

HASTINGS

George, m. on 6 May 1714, Mary Higly (KESP:34).

George, m. by 3 Aug 1714, Mary, granddau. of Mary, widow of Isaac Bowles (KELR BC#1:28).

Henry, m. by 10 Sep 1651, [-?-], dau. of Walter Cooper, who m. 2nd, Anne [-?-] (MWB 1:29).

Michael, m. by Nov 1688, [-?-], relict of Francis Petite of BA co. (MDTP 14:121).

HASWELL

John, m. on 17 July 1689, Elizabeth Mechathen (or as Snogorgill a runaway servant of Jacob Preen). Preen wanted her returned. James Sclater, minister, certified that John Haswell mariner and Elizabeth Mechathen then Passenger in the Turkey Merchant were married according to the laws of England in Virginia on 17 July 1689 (*ARMD* e106: SOJU 1689-1690:39, 40).

HATCH

John, m. by 3 July 1710, Sarah, admx. of Edward Jones of BA Co. (INAC 31:321; BAAD 2:158).

HATCHMAN

Thomas, m. on 8 Aug 1718, Elizabeth Taylor (AAAL).

HATFIELD

William, Jr., m. by 16 Nov ----, Adling, "natural dau." of Arthur Whitely (DOLR 6 Old:123).

HATHERLY

John, m. on 21 Dec 1704, Elizabeth Ewyrins (AAAL 1:27).

HATTEW

Joseph (or Hatlew), m. on 4 Sep 1712, Ann Spiring (KESP:34).

HATTON

Joseph, m. on 17 Oct 1710, Lucy, dau. of Francis Marbury (PGKG:239).

Richard, m. by 11 Dec 1674, Ann, dau. and heir of John Price (*ARMD* 51:445; MPL 19:375).

Samuel, m. by Oct 1678, [-?-], admx. of Richard Gorsuch (*ARMD* 68:88).

Thomas, m. by 1701, Susannah Blackstone, sister of John (MWB 11:120).

William, m. by 29 May 1663, Eliza, dau. of William Wilkinson (MWB 1:190).

HAUGE

John, m. by 20 Feb 1711, Elizabeth, admx. of John Hamilton of CH Co. (INAC 33A:122).

HAWKER

[-?-], m. by 1659, Patience, widow of Henry Needham (MPL 6:31, AA:328).

William, m. on 26 Jan 1708/9, Sarah Price (AALR 1:36).

HAWKINS

[-?-], m. by 30 June 1702, Mary, sister of Edward James of TA Co. (MWB 3:272).

Augustine, d. by 10 Nov 1700, having m. Susanna, widow of John Smick or Sivick (son of William Sivick) and dau. of Walter Carr. She m. 3rd, Thomas Tracy (AALR WT#1:131, WT#2:115; MCHR PC:538).

Henry, m. by 26 June 1683, Elizabeth, extx. of Francis Wyne of CH Co. (INAC 8:56).

Henry, m. by March 1693/4, [-?-], widow of Alexander Smith of CH Co. (MDTP 15C:132).

John, Gent., m. by 10 June 1681, Frances, formerly Grose (TALR 4:46).

John, m. by 1686, Elizabeth, widow of John Eustis (INAC 9:122).

John, Jr., and Sarah Norris, filed their intentions to marry on 21 d., 8 m., 1715, and 18 d., 9 m., 1715 (WRMMa).

John, m. on 23 Dec 1718, Rebecca Emson (HAGE:36).

Joseph, m. by 30 May 1699, Elizabeth, relict and admx. of Christopher Rowles of AA Co. (INAC 18:194). Elsewhere his name is given as Charles [*sic*] Rolls [Rowles] (AALR WT#1:201).

Joseph, m. by 27 Feb 1702, Elizabeth, extx. of Philip Griffin of AA Co. (INAC 23:72).

Robert, m. on 15 Nov 1709, Ann Preble (HAGE:33).

Thomas (Hawkines), m. on 30 d., 5 m. March [*sic*], 1704, Elizabeth Giles, dau. of Richard and Margaret Arnell (WRMM). She was the widow of Jacob Giles (MDTP 21:157).

William, m. by 9 Sep 1679, Ann, admx. of Stephen White of AA Co. (INAC 6:441).

HAWLEY

Jerome, a passenger on the *Ark/Dove*, d. 1638, in MD, having m. Eleanor, widow of Thomas Courtney, Esq. (*NFMP*:228).

HAWRET
 Peter, m. by 15 Aug 1716, Elizabeth, admx. of Alexander Standish of CH Co. (INAC 37C:136).

HAY
 [James?] (Hey), m. by 6 Dec 1708, Mary, dau. of Kenelm Cheseldyne of SM Co. (MWB 12:307).

HAYCROFT
 Thomas, of CE Co., m. by 18 Oct 1712, Sarah, dau. and heiress of William Mansfield, late of CE Co. (CELR 2:225).

HAYES
 Edmund, m. by Nov 1710, Mary Mencham, formerly bound to Nathaniel Ruxton (BACP IS#B:87).
 James (Hays), m. by 1708, Mary, dau. of Kenelm Cheseldine of SM Co. (SMWB TA#1:151).
 John, m. by 6 Jan 1699, Abigail, widow of Thomas Scudamore (or Skidmore), and dau. of John Dixon (BALR TR#RA:418; Hodges cites Prov. Court LR EI#10:745).

HAYET
 John, m. by 20 Sep 1708, Mary, dau. of William Smith of CE Co. (MWB 13:113).

HAYFIELD
 James, m. on 24 Dec 1711, Anne Philpott (AALR 1:38).

HAYLEY
 [-?-], of CE Co., m. by Dec 1683, Margaret, widow of Bartholomew Hendrickson (MDTP 13:78).

HAYMAN
 Henry, m. on 24 Aug 1687, Mathewe [Martha?], dau. of Thomas Standridge (SOLR:IKL).

HAYMORE
 John, m. on 32 July 1705, Elizabeth Browne (KESP:32).

HAYNES
 William, m. on 4 Aug --- (year not given), Mary Schooling (KESP:32).

HAYWOOD
 William, m. by May 1701, Hannah, relict of Nathaniel Hillen of CE Co. (MDTP 18B:32).

HAZARD
 [-?-], m. by 8 Dec 1703, Anne, dau. of William Cord of SO Co. (MWB 12:40).

HAZELL

John, of London, m. by 31 Jan 1692 in the Parish Church of St. Swithins, London, Dorothy, widow of Robert Baldin of CE Co. (KELR M:29).

John, m. on 7 Nov 1724 Mary Nevitt (CVCH).

HEAD

[-?-] (Heade), m. by 1 July 1718, Ann, extx. of Robert Monroe, chirurgeon of AA Co. (MDAD 1:10).

Adam, m. by 14 June 1699, Ann, relict and admx. of John Sewell of SM Co. (INAC 19:58, 29:102; SMRR:13).

William, m. by 28 Oct 1665, [-?-], relict of Henry Carlile (MDTP 1F:6).

William, d. by March 1675/6, having m. Elizabeth, dau. of Edward Coppidge of KE Co. (MDTP 7:321).

William, m. at some time before 5 June 1679, [-?-], widow of Henry Carline; by that date William had m. as his 2nd wife, Elizabeth Cash (*ARMD* 51:278).

HEARD

[-?-], m. by 28 Nov 1709, Mary, dau. of James Greenwell of SM Co. (MWB 13:725).

[-?-], m. by 16 April 1717, Elizabeth, dau. of Edward Cole of SM Co. (MWB 14:644).

William, m. by 4 March 1664, Bridget, dau. of Katherine Yowkins, and sister of Mary Yowkins (MDTP 1E:104-105).

HEARNE

Thomas, m. by 9 Feb 1712/3, Sarah, dau. of Thomas Newbold, of SO Co. (MWB 13:533).

HEATH

James, of KE Co., m. by 12 Oct 1702, Hannah, dau. of William Crump, dec. (KELR JD#1:93).

James, m. by June 1712, Mary, extx. of Dr. Edward Chetham of QA Co. (MDTP 22:116; INAC 35A:73; MPL EE#6:222, RY#1:246).

HEATHER

Ephraim, m. by 18 Aug 1708, Ann, relict and admx. of Daniel Selby of SO Co. (INAC 28:289).

William, m. by 1695, Mary, widow of Thomas Gillian; she m. 3rd, John Wade, chirurgeon of Bloomsbury, near Mulberry Fields (INAC 13A:116, 301, 302; MDTP 16:59).

HEATHMAN

Alexander, m. by 1717, Frances, sister of Charles Payne of SM Co. (SMWB PC#1:233-237).

HEBB
Thomas, m. by 28 Oct 1716, Frances, dau. of Edward Halyard (Hilliard, Halyard) of SM Co. (MWB 14:306; SMWB PC#1:239; SMWB TA#1:46, 162).
William, m. by 15 Feb 1717, Priscilla, dau. of John Miller, planter, of SM Co. (MWB 14:462).

HEBEDINE
Thomas, m. on 11 Aug 1706, Elizabeth Raymie (CVCH).

HEBRON
Thomas, m. by 6 Nov 1711, Katherine, extx. of Richard Unitt of KE Co. (INAC 33A:164).

HEDGE
Henry, banns pub. Whit Sunday and Monday and Tues. in Whitsun week, 1700, m. 25 May 1700, Mary Parker (HAGE:9, 10).

HEDGES
John, of Bristol, m. by 20 Oct 1719, Anna, dau. of William Webb, mariner, of Bristol, Eng. (MWB 13:144).

HEESE
Thomas, m. by 168, Elizabeth, dau. of Thomas and Anne Doxey (SMWB PC#1:55).

HEIGHE
[-?-], m. by 22 July 1718, Mary, dau. of Mary Nichols (Nicholas) of CV Co. (MWB 16:57).
William, m. by July 1676, Sarah, widow of Edward Oisline? of the Island of Barbados (MDTP 8:164).

HELLEN
David, m. by c1694, Susanna, relict and admx. of William Molters or Melton of CV Co. (INAC 13A:219; MDTP 15C:268).

HELME
[-?-], of Parish of Wapping, White Chapel, Middlesex, d. by 22 Aug 1700, having m. Sarah, dau. of John Meekes, of Parish of St. Paul's Shadwell, chirurgeon, dec. (PGLR A:419).
John (Helmes), m. by March 1669/70, [-?-], widow of John Mills of CH Co. (*ARMD* 60:249).

HEMSLEY
Philemon, m. by 10 April 1706, Frances, dau. of Robert Noble (INAC 25:246; QALR ETA:185).
Philemon, m. by Dec 1711, Mary, admx. of Col. John Courts (MDTP 22:71, 81).

Philemon, Gent., m. by 10 March 1714, Mary, extx. of John Contee (*ARMD* 77:195; INAC 33B:123).

William, m. by March 1685/6, Cornelia, admx. of Charles Vaughn (MDTP 13:3010).

William, m. by 10 April 1706, [Jane?], widow of Robert Noble (INAC 25:246).

HEMSTEAD

Nicholas, m. by 2 Sep 1679, Elizabeth [-?-], grandmother of Enoch Spinke (BALR HW#2:159).

HENDERSON

Andrew, m. by 23 Jan 1671, Elizabeth, mother of Roger Moore (*ARMD* 51:315). She m. 3rd, by 13 Nov 1679, Nicholas Butteram (*ARMD* 51:303).

William, m. in Aug 1684, Sarah Bishop (SOLR:IKL).

HENDRICKSON

Bartlett, son of Anguett Poulson, m. by 1664, Marg. Anguette (MPL CC:458, 7:426).

Henry, m. by banns on 5 June 1717 by Mr. Sewell, Elizabeth Etherington (CESS).

HENL(E)Y

Christopher, m. on 28 Dec 1704, Ezbell Smith (KESP:32).

Daniel, m. by 22 Sep 1703, Rose, extx. of John Hoskins of SM Co. (INAC 24:172).

Darby (Heley?), m. by 1694, Elizabeth, admx. of Thomas Strickland (Cotton cites INAC 13A:213).

Darby, m. by 11 March 1694, Anne, relict and extx. of Obadia Evans of CV Co. (INAC 13B:91, 16:94).

John, m. on 3 Feb 1712, Esther Ricketts (KESP:34).

Robert, m. by 5 April 1664, Sarah, relict of Francis Batchelor (MDTP 1E:33).

HENNINGS

Philip, m. by Oct 1710, Dorothy, admx. of William Philipson of SO Co. (MDTP 21:279).

HENRIX

John, m. on 30 July 1696, Rebecca, dau. of Robert Fortune (TAPE). He was a carpenter, of TA Co.; she was a dau. of Robert Fortune of Dover, TA Co. (TALR 9:156).

HENRY

John, m. by 1710, Mary, widow and admx. of Francis Jenkins (SOLR 10 (CD):598; INAC 32C:156, 34:95).

Philomen, m. by 9 March 1715, Mary, admx. of Thomas Guilly of TA Co. (INAC 37A:11).

HEPBURN
  Patrick, marriage contract dated 15 Oct 1711, with Elizabeth Holdsworth of CV Co., widow of Samuel Holdsworth (PGLR F:147).

HERBERT
  Alexander, m. by 20 Oct 1705, Mary, admx. of Philip Mason (INAC 25:82).
  William, m, by 23 Sep 1697, Ellinor, widow of John Angell, and dau. and extx. of James Pattison of SM Co. (MWB 6:85; MDTP 17:67).

HERNE
  William, m. on 31 Dec 1672, Katherine Mallis (SOLR:IKL). William Herne, of Matapeney, on 9 Aug 1671 caused his banns of matrimony to be set up this morning at the Court: house with one Katherine Mathis, widow. The Court being informed that the said Katherine "goeth under the notion" of John Pikes wife of Matapaney ordered the banns to be taken downe & orders that the said William Herne be taken into safe custody until he gives in Security for his good behavior (SOJU DT#7:193).

HERRING
  Bartholomew, m. 1st, Ann [-?-], who d. by 1653, and 2nd, by 1653, Margaret [-?-] (MPL ABH:313).
  Simon, of AA Co., m. by June 1680, [-?-], relict of Richard Horner of AA Co., whom d. leaving a son Richard (Warrant Record CB(#3):56).

HERRINGTON
  Cornelius, m. by 25 April 1701, Rathvael (Rachael?), dau. of Thomas Jones (BALR HW#2:105).

HERVEY
  Samuel, m. in 1715, Mary Watts (AAAN:22).

HESELDINE
  [-?-], m. by 7 Dec 1710, Anne, sister of Samuel Holdsworth of CA Co. (MWB 13:159).

HEYDEN
  [-?-], m. by Oct 1685, [-?-], widow of Henry Ward (MDTP 13:255).
  [-?-] (Haydon), m. by Dec 1688, Penelope, extx. of John Tongue of CV Co. (Warrant Record CB(#4):346).
  Francis, m. by Jan 1676/7, Tomlin [Thomasine?], sister of Thomas Butler of CH Co. (MDTP 8a:359).
  Samuel, m. on 23 Jan 1679, Ruth Miver (SOLR:IKL).

HEYLEY
  [-?-], m. by 31 Oct 1677, Mary, relict and admx. of Edward Conary or Connery of SM Co. (INAC 4:522).

HICKMAN
  Samuel, m. by Oct 1688, Elizabeth, relict of Thomas Brayne of CV Co. (MDTP 14:102).

HICKS
  James, m. on 23 July 1710, Sarah Dowling (KESP:33).

HIGGENBOTHOM
  Richard, on 14 Aug 1677, banns of matrimony were published for him and Dennis Fountain (SOLR O#7:121r).

HIGGINBOTHAM
  [-?-], m. on 31 May 1718, Mary [-?-] (KESP:35).
  Oliver, m. on 3 Feb 1708, Elizabeth Stevens (KESP:33).

HIGGINS
  John, m. by 2 June 1699, [-?-], dau. of Richard Jones of CH Co. (MWB 6:368).
  John, m. on 21 Nov 1709, Mary Bullock (TAPE).
  Nicholas, m. on 25 Nov 1714, Elizabeth Woolman (TAPE).

HIGGS
  Dr. John, of CV Co., m. by 1674 (when he immigrated), Mary, mother of John Thadlet (MPL 19:17).

HIGHAM
  Francis, of CV Co., m. by 1686, Elizabeth, widow and extx. of Francis Fooks (MDTP 13:366).

HIGHLAND
  John, of BA Co., m. by Dec 1665, Mary Dorrington, widow (MPL 9:496).

HILL
  Abell, m. on 10 July 1711, Susanna Gott (AALR 1:37). She was a dau. of Richard Gott of AA Co. (MWB 14:33).
  Clement, m. by 28 April 1711, Anne, dau. of Henry Darnall of AA Co. (MWB 13:233).
  George, m. on 6 Dec 1711, Joan Britain (KESP:33).
  Giles, m. by 29 Nov 1700, Elizabeth, widow of Justinian Tennison, and dau. of John and Abigail Shanks of SM Co. (MCHR PC:474; MDTP 13:280; Fresco cites Judgements 19:301; SMWB PC#1:45, 1111; and MWB 3731, and 4:159).
  Hasidia, of KE Co., m. on 26 April 1659, Ann Sheares (*ARMD* 54:129). As "Azadiah" Hill, he d. by Jan 1660, having m. by Sep 1659, Ann, relict of Joseph Seares (MDTP 1B:70, 1C:16).
  John, m. in Sep 1674, Alce Brangeman (SOLR:IKL).
  John, m. by 15 July 1704, Mary, widow and admx. of Richard Wallis of PG Co. (MWB 3:377).

Johnson, m. by 15 Nov 1696, [-?-], relict and admx. of John Tarr of SO Co. (INAC 15:144).

Matthew, m. by 12 April 1670, Edith, eldest dau. of Walter Beane of CH Co. (MWB 1:386). Elsewhere she is called Eleanor, dau. of Walter and Eleanor Bayne of CH Co., and widow of John Stone (Hodges cites Judgements 6:792, 21:514-516). She later m. Hugh Tears, and by 22 June 1700, John Beale (CHLR Z#2:485; MDTP 19a:75, 78).

Richard, m. by 22 May 1666, Milcah, relict of Robert Clarkson (MDTP 1F:79).

Richard, m. by 13 Aug 1688, Martha, dau. of Edward and Ann Smith of SO Co. (MWB 6:29; SOJU AW:69).

Robert, m. by Nov 1710, Tabitha, admx. of Lawrence Rile of SO Co. (MDTP 21:297; INAC 38A:148).

Thomas, m. after July 1659, Elizabeth Hayling, widow of John Deere (MPL 4:69, 10:272).

Thomas, Jr., of KE Co., m. on 4 d., 1 mo. [March], 1655, Margaret Balie. She was age 21 on 1 Feb 1655 (*ARMD* 54:38, 48, 109).

Thomas, m. by April 1661, Elizabeth Robinson (*ARMD* 54:216-217).

Thomas (Hills), m. by 28 April 1661, Elizabeth, widow and extx. of John Deere (*ARMD* 54:217).

William (Hills), of CH Co., m. on June 1667, Edith or Idy Hadlowe (*ARMD* 60:116; CHLR P#1:204).

William, m. by 1 July 1699, Sarah, admx. of William Wilson of PG Co. (INAC 19:171).

William, m. on 2 March 1701, Margaret Man (AAAL 1:26(2)).

William, m. Mary, widow of James Crouch (*q.v.*), John Rolls (*q.v.*); she m. 4th, by 18 June 1706, Philip Jones (AALR IB#2:93, IH#1:263; INAC 20:239).

HILLEARY

[-?-], m. by 2 April 1718, Eleanor, dau. of George Young of CV Co. (MWB 14:613).

HILLEN

John, m. by 25 Sep 1707, Mary, admx. of Thomas James of BA Co. (INAC 27:210).

HILLIARD

Daniel, m. in 1703, Elizabeth Worrill (AAMA:84).

Isaac, on 14 Nov 1676, banns of matrimony were published for him and Mary Thomas (SOLR O#7:62r).

John, on 14 Nov 1676, banns of matrimony were published for him and Alce Roberts (SOLR O#7:62r).

HINDERSON

John, m. on 1 July 1680, Elizabeth Barnabe (SOLR:IKL).

HINES
[-?-], m. by 10 Oct 1710, [-?-], dau. of Robert Thornwell of DO Co. (MWB 13:606).

Thomas, m. by 7 May 1714, Jane, extx. of Thomas Box of PG Co. (INAC 35A:342, 36B:182 gives his name as Hinds).

HINESLEY
Thomas, age c70, on 18 March 1718 deposed that about 40 years ago [c1678], he married [-?-], dau. of Nathaniel Cleave (MCHR CL:453).

HINGHAM?
Andrew, m. by July 1708, Mary, admx. of Benjamin Nobbs (MDTP 21:41).

HINKS
William, m. on 14 Feb 1715/6, Elizabeth Bri-? (AAAN:29).

HINTON
[-?-], m. by Jan 1679/80, Alice, admx. of Francis Sourton of SM Co. (MDTP 11:280).

John, m. on 22 June 1707, Elizabeth Cocksider (AAAL 1:33).

Thomas, m. by 1666, Grace, sister of John Walker, and widow of James Adwick of SM Co. (MDTP 1F:88, 89).

Thomas, m. by 5 April 1705, Dorothy, extx. of Richard Fowe of CV Co. (INAC 25:134).

Thomas, m. on 28 Aug 1718, Rachel Howard (AAAN:39).

HITCHCOCK
George, m. by 29 July 1713, Mary, admx. of Teage Tracey of BA Co. (INAC 35B:29).

William, m. on 7 Sep 1716, Ann Jones (SJSG:9).

HOADES[?]
John, m. by March 1705/6, Anne, extx. of Thomas [Hunter?] (AAJU TB#1:196).

HOBBS
John, m. on 20 Aug 1704, Mary Wilde (CVCH).

HOBSON
Thomas, of TA co., m. by Feb 1679/80, [-?-], relict of Clair or Cloris Odoree, a Frenchman naturalized (Warrant Record CB#1:17).

HODGE
George (Hodg), m. in 1712, Elizabeth Stanton (AAMA:84).

HODGES
John, m. on 10 May 1699, Mary Newes (KESP:31).

Robert, m. by 21 Sep 1714, Tamar, dau. of Mary [Edwin?), sister. of dec., in 1714 acct. of Benjamin Ricaud of KE Co. (INAC 36B:17).

HODGSON
Richard, of CH Co., m. by April 1681, [-?-], relict of Thomas King (Warrant Record CB#1:141).
Richard, m. by 27 Jan 1713, Elizabeth, extx. of John Banister of CH Co. (INAC 35A:59).

HODSON
John, m. by Aril 168, Rebecca, relict of James Agg of DO Co., who d. intestate (MDTP 13:324).

HOGAN
Humphrey, m. on 10 Jan 1713, Rebekah Murphy (AAAN:9).
James, m. on 30 Jan 1706, Ellin V. Dwyer (TAPE).

HOLBROOK
Joseph (Holbencke), m. on 4 Feb 1686/7, Temperance Wade (AAAL).
Joseph, m. on 8 Aug 1711, Dorothy Callingswood (AALR 1:37).
Joseph, m. on 4 Oct 1716, Mary Mon-? (AAAL 2:11).
Thomas, on 8 Aug 1676, banns of matrimony were published for him and Alce Leverton (SOJU O#7:45).

HOLBURT
Samuel, m. on 5 Oct 1718, Jane Grey (AAAN:40).

HOLDEN
William, m. on 8 June 1718, Rachel Ducktree (KESP:35).

HOLDING
John, of SM Co., m. by 16 Nov 1678, Rebecca, dau. and coheir of Samuel Neale of SM Co. (MDTP 10:323).
Richard, m. by 8 July 1710, Elizabeth, admx. of Caleb Cockerell of QA Co. (INAC 31:293).

HOLDSWORTH
John, m. by 19 Aug 1690, Isabel (now dec.), extx. and relict of George Abbott, and admx of William Martin of CV Co. (MDTP 16:8; INAC 12:127; 13A:230).
Thomas (Holsworth), m. by 3 Oct 1696, Elenor, relict and extx. of Thomas Parsloe of CV Co. (INAC 14:92).
Mr. Thomas, m. on 1 Jan 1712, Rebecca (elsewhere given as Barbara) Smith (CVCH).

HOLEBANK
Benjamin, m. on 25 Nov 1711, Mary Prise (KESP:33).

HOLFWORTH

Samuel, m. by Oct 1696, Eleanor, relict and extx. of Thomas Parrlow of CV Co. (MDTP 16:196).

HOLIDAY

William, m. on 2 June 1694, Katherine Russell (AAJA:1#8).

HOLING

William, m. on 3 Aug 1709, Mary [-?-] (PGKG:239).

HOLLAND

Anthony, m. by 12 Feb 1702, Isabel, now dec., dau. of Thomas Parsons of AA Co. (MWB 11:316; (AALR IB#2:231).

Benjamin, m. on 6 Jan 1703, Mary Wilson (AAJA:28#7).

Capell, m. on 27 May 1718, Katherine Elvidge (Eldridge) (AAJA:52#3).

Francis, d. by 12 Feb 1688/9, leaving a minor child who was a grandchild of William Meares of CV Co. (MDTP 14:132).

Francis, m. by 28 Feb 1716, Susannah, dau. of George Utie (BALR TR#A:472).

John, on 14 Nov 1676 banns of matrimony were published for him and Alice Roberts both of SO Co. (*ARMD* e89 (SOJU O#7):44).

John, m. on 11 Dec 1701, Ann Spicer (AAJA:24#3).

Michael, m. 18 June 1688, Penelope, dau. of William Coulborne, Sr. (*ARMD* e106: SOJU 1689-1690:27).

Otho, m. by c1684, Mehitable, dau. of John Larkin; she m. 2nd, c1703, John Pierpoint (BALR RM#HS:62; MCHR PC:668; AALR IB#2:545-546).

Otho, m. by 2 May 1714, Margret, dau. and extx. of John Leach, Gent., of CV Co. (INAC 36B:247, 37A:26).

Otho, m. on 9 Dec 1718, Mary Howard, widow (AAAN:41).

Richard, m. by 1 Jan 1682, Hannah, relict and extx. of Thomas Alexander of TA Co. (INAC 8:5; *ARMD* 70:338).

Thomas, son of Anthony and Isabella, late of AA Co., m. on 3 d., 2 m. (April), 1712, Margaret Waters, dau. of John, late of AA Co., dec. (WRMM).

William, m. by 21 March 1698/9, Margaret, dau. of Margaret Gill of AA Co. (MWB 6:236).

William, of AA Co., Esq., m. by 30 Aug 1703, Margaret, only dau. and heir of Francis Holland the Elder, Gent., late of AA Co., dec. (AALR WT#2:87).

William, m. by 1 July 1718, Margaret, admx. of Henry Schoolfield of SO Co. (MDAD 1:176).

HOLLEGER

[-?-] (Holeger), m. by 29 Dec 1704, Jane, dau. of John Hynson of KE Co. (MWB 3:656).

Philip, m. by 4 Oct 1692, Mary, dau. of Jeremiah Haslin (AALR IH#3:91).

HOLLENWORTH

John, of CV Co., m. by 1665, [-?-], widow of Gabriel Golden (MPL 9:240).

HOLLICE
Henry, m. on 14 July 1711, Elizabeth Caudry (AALR 1:37).

HOLLIDAY
Thomas, m. by 1686/1713, Mary, dau. of Thomas Truman (Hodges cites Judgements 3:571; MDTP 13:375, 383, 384; PGLR E:252).

HOLLINGSHEAD
Obadia, m. on 5 Jan 1704/5, Mary Bur-? (AAAN:19).

HOLLINGSWORTH
[Charles?], m. by 2 July 1666, Damaris, dau. of Robert Martin (TALR: 1:51, 81).
Charles, Jr., m. by 24 Nov 1702, Alice, dau. of Thomas Weather, late of KE Co. (KELR JD#1:91).
James, m. on 27 Feb 1714, Ann Chitching (HAGE:32).
William, m. by 30 Aug 1704, Margaret, extx. of Claudius Dutitre of TA Co. (MWB 3:421). He d. by 15 July 1709 when his admx. Margaret had m. William Jackson (INAC 30:233).
William (Hollinsworth), m. by 22 Sep 1709, Sarah, poss. dau. of William Boulton of QA Co., who left personalty to his son-in-law William and William's wife Sarah (MWB 13:7).

HOLLINS
John, of TA Co., m. by March 1681/2, Mary Gouldson (kin of Gabriel Gouldson of CV Co.) (Warrant Record CB#1:208).
John, m. by banns in Nov 1709, by Mr. Sewell, Abigail Bateman, widow (CESS).
John, m. by 15 April 1714, Mary, widow of Gabriel Boulden or Goulden (MCHR CL:24).

HOLLIS
Henry, m. by 10 Dec 1679, Elizabeth, widow of John Grammer of CV Co. (*ARMD* 51:302; Warrant Record CB#1:276).
James, m. on 25 March 1706, Sarah Clarke (KESP:32).
Thomas, m. on 11 Aug 1715, Ann Green (KESP:34).
William, m. by 11 June 1694, Mary, dau. of Abraham and Sarah Clark (BALR RM#HS:401).
William, m. on 6 March 1708, Sarah Morgan (KESP:33).

HOLLOWAY
John (Halloway), m. by May 1688, Martha, relict and extx. of Samuel Vines of CV Co. (MDTP 14:71; INAC 10:349).

HOLLUM
John, m. by 20 Dec 1715, Joana, dau. of Walter Lane, planter, of SO Co. (MWB 14:282).

HOLLY
John, m. on 4 March 1712, Hester Birch (PGKG:248).

HOLLYHOCK
Joseph, m. on 5 Nov 1704, Elizabeth Saint (KESP:32).

HOLMEARD
Mr. James, m. by 8 Aug 1711, Mary, widow and admx. of John Hallum of PG Co. (INAC 32C:31).

HOLMES
Charles (Holms), m. on 25 Dec 1716, Barbary Williams (TAPE).
Nicholas (Hoolms), m. on 24 Oct 1710, Ellinor Jones (TAPE).
Richard, m. on 25 Sep 1703, Eve Delehay (TAPE). She was the extx. of Thomas Delahay of TA Co. (INAC 28:230, 31:109).
Thomas (Holms), m. on 8 Jan 1707, Mary Rosann (AAAN:9).
Thomas, m. on 8 Jan 1708/9, Mary Rossier (AAAN:1).
William, m. by 10 July 1681, Frances, late wife and extx. of William Lucas of SM co. (PCLR WRC:202/211).
William (Holms), m. by 1695, Sibilla, widow and extx. of Edward Barber or Barbier of SM Co. (MDTP 15:182; INAC 13A:252).
William, m. on 8 May 1711, Mary Pottenger (AALR).

HOLSHOT
John, m. on 10 Aug 1701, Dorothy Ireland (CVCH).

HOLSILL
[-?-], m. by 15 Nov 1718, Ruth, dau. of George Miller, of PG Co. (MWB 15:38).

HOLT
Joseph, m. by 1703, Eleanor, widow of Samuel Abbott, of TA Co. (MWB 11:320; MDTP 19A:172-173, 19C:106, 207, 231).
Robert, m. by 28 June 1662, Christian Bonfield. This may have been a bigamous marriage as Holt already had a wife named Dorothy (*ARMD* 3:463, 41:150).

HOLWOOD
James, m. by 30 Jan 1715, Elizabeth, relict and admx. of Philip Pealey of CH Co. (INAC 37A:18).

HOMEWOOD
John, m. by 16 May 1674, Sarah, dau. of Thomas Meeres of Severn R., AA Co., and sister of John Meeres (MWB 2:3, 72).

HOOD
Casper (or Jasper Hoodt), of Philadelphia, tailor, m. by 25 Feb 1703, Sarah, only dau. and heir of John Van Heck of CE Co. (CELR 1:374; KELR JSN:125).

Robert, m. by 26 Oct 1677, [-?-], widow of John Rye (in admin. accts. of John Powell of CE Co. and Stephen Whetstone of KE Co.) (INAC 4:505, 609).

Thomas, m. on 30 July 1707, Elizabeth Battee, widow (AAAL 1:36). She was the extx. of Ferdinando Batty [Ferdinando Battee] (INAC 29:120, 226).

HOOK

Roger, m. on 15 Feb 1696, Ann Taylor (TAPE).

William (Hooke), m. by April 1715, Elizabeth, extx. of John Coode of SM Co. (MDTP 22:455; INAC 36C:66).

HOOPER

[-?-], d. by 1 April 1693, when his widow Sarah, mother of Isabella Hooper, m. John Hall (BALR HW#2:38).

Henry, m. Nov 1660, Susan, widow of Richard Gott of Herring Creek, AA Co. (MDTP 1D:61).

Henry, m. on 4 July 1669, Elizabeth Denwood (SOLR:IKL).

Richard, of DO Co., m. by Oct 1703, Ann Donnelly, dau. of William Dorrington (MDTP 20:10; DOLR 6 Old:242). She was a sister of William Dorrington of DO Co. (MWB 14:246).

Robert, m. on 16 April 1718, Deborah Lee (AAAL).

HOPE

George, m. on 21 Dec 1703, Dorcas Turner (AAAL 1:26).

George, m. on 27 May 1706, Judity Clark (AAAL 1:32(2)).

HOPEWELL

Francis, of CV Co., m. by 29 May 1674, Anne, dau. of William Whittle (MDTP 6:238).

Hugh, Jr., m. by 19 Sep 1696, Eliza, dau. of Francis Hill of SM Co.; she m. 2nd, Richard Keen of CV Co., and 3rd, Charles Beckwith (MWB 7:295; Fresco also cites MDTP 16:91, 19A:161, 17:3190, 321; MWB 2:325, 7:295).

HOPKINS

[-?-], m. by 23 July 1707, Elizabeth, dau. of John Debruly of KE Co. (MWB 13:34).

[-?-], m. by 8 March 1708/9, Jennet, dau. of William Noble, Sr., of SO Co. (MWB 12, pt. 2:167).

[-?-], m. by 15 June 1717, Margaret, dau. of Rich. Johns of the Cliffs, CV Co. (MWB 14:532).

Charles, m. by 5 July 1711, Mary, admx. of William Wainwright or Windight of SO Co. (MDTP 21:341; INAC 32B:269).

Gerard, and Margaret Johns filed their intentions to marry on 6 d., 10 m., 1700 (WRMMa).

Jarret, of AA Co., m. by Jan 1671, Thomasine, widow of Andrew Baker of AA Co. (MDTP 5:197).

John, m. on 27 Dec 1713, Ann Hickambottom (SJSG:20R).

John, m. on 19 Nov 1717, Elizabeth Dunning (PGKG:247).

Joseph, m. by 15 Oct 1706, [-?-], dau. of Joseph Fowler of SM Co. (MWB 12:101).

Joseph, m. by 2 Feb 1713/4, Sarah, dau. of William Pearce of KE Co. (KELR JSN:367).

Nathaniel, m. by 11 Feb 1718, Dennis [sic], dau. of Matthew Scarbrough of SO Co. (MWB 18:294).

Philip, m. by 29 Aug 1682, Anne, extx. of Nehemiah Covington of TA Co. (INAC 7C:262).

Philip, of CH Co., m. by May 1688, Elizabeth, dau. of Archibald Wahob of Portobacco, CH Co., and sister of Margaret, wife of John Lemair (MWB 4:23; MDTP 13:78, 14:72-73). [See Philip Hoskins below].

Philip, m. on 24 March 1705, Johanna Piner (KESP:32).

Thomas, m. by 29 Aug 1671, Alice, widow of William Wenham (MDTP 4A:13).

Thomas, Jr., m. by c1698, Elizabeth, relict and admx. of Jacob Abrahams of TA Co. (INAC 16:176; see also MDTP 17:199).

Thomas, m. by 26 June 1699, Elizabeth, admx. of Mortough Horney of TA Co. (INAC 19½A:109, 174).

Thomas, m. by Aug 1707, Anna, extx. of Alexander Ray (TAJR 1706-1708).

William, m. on 31 March 1700, Dorothy Willis (KESP:31). She was the extx. of John Willis of CE Co. (INAC 29:81)

William, of AA Co., m. by 26 July 1702, [-?-], mother of Thomas Browne, and grandmother of William and Henry Lewis (MWB 11:212).

HOPPER

Dave, m. by 31 March 1717, Rachel Barton, admx. of Elizabeth Barton of CH Co. (INAC 39C:134).

James, m. on 5 May 1709, Elizabeth Pattison (AALR 1:36).

HORNE

Edward, m. by 22 Feb 1701, Sarah, dau. of Susanna Miles of SM Co. (MWB 11:207).

John, m. by 1717, Winifred, dau. of John Wheatley (Fresco cites MDAD 23:150).

William, m. by 5 Nov 1684, Mary, coheir of Thomas O'Daniel (BALR RM#HS:101).

William (Horne?), m. by April 1687, [-?-], relict of John Peake or Pake of SO Co. (MDTP 13:479).

William, m. on 28 Oct 1697, Sarah Franklin (AAJA:3#8). She was a sister of Robert Franklin (MDTP 17:213).

HORNEY

[-?-], m. by 4 Aug 1718, Margaret, relict of Joseph Kinnimont (TALR RF#12:334).

Murty, m. by Feb 1692/3, Elizabeth, dau. of Wenlock Christison (MDTP 15A:10, 68).

HOROHON
    John (Horrohone), m. on 22 Dec 1709, Mary Clifford (TAPE). She was the admx. of Daniel Clifford of TA Co. (INAC 31:306).

HORSEY
    Isaac, m. on 7 Aug 1688, Sarah [-?-] (SOLR:IKL).
    Nathaniel, m. by 11 Feb 1690/1, Sarah, joint heir of Randall and Katherine Revell of SO Co. (SOJU AW:44).
    Stephen Horsey, m. by 11 Feb 1690/1, Hannah, joint heir of Randall and Katherine Revell of SO Co. (SOJU AW:44).

HORSLEY
    Richard, of DO Co., m. on 9 May 1697, Mary Lirkey [Lucy H. Harrison read this as Vickery] (TAPE).

HORSSMAN
    Thomas, m. on 19 Sep 1681, Jane Edgar (SOLR:IKL).

HORTON
    Robert, of SM Co., m. by 1 Nov 1703, Margery, relict of Richard Gardiner of SM Co. (PGLR C:87a).
    William, m. on 18 Dec 1707, Mary Davis (AAAN:1).

HOSIER
    Henry, m. by 13 Jan 1673, Mary, dau. of Lewis Stephens of Chester River (MDTP 6:258).
    Henry, m. by Feb 1686/7, Rebecca, dau. of Stephen Keddy or Kadday of KE Co. (KELR M:15; MWB 4:251).

HOSKINS
    Edward, m. on 8 April 1705, Mary Prise (KESP:32).
    George, m. by 28 June 1718, Ann, admx. of Zachariah Bond of SM Co. (MDAD 1:41).
    Philip, m. by 14 Nov 1682, Elizabeth, dau. of Archibald Wahop of Portobacco, CH Co. (CHLR K:36; MWB 4:23). She was the admx. of Margaret Lemar (INAC 10:353). [See Philip Hopkins above].
    Philip, m. by 15 Dec 1698, Ann, widow and extx. of Thomas Mudd of CH Co. (INAC 18:126).
    William, m. by April 1715, Ann, extx. of William Taylor (MDTP 22:455).

HOUGHTON
    William, m. by 24 May 1718, Ann, extx. of Robert Catherwood of SO Co. (MDAD 1:88).

HOULDSWORTH
Samuel, of CV Co., m. by 11 May 1695, Helena, relict and extx. of Thomas Parslow (MCHR PC:322).

HOULT
Joseph, m. on 27 March 1703, Ellin Abbott (TAPE).
Robert, m. by 1662, Christian Bromfield (MDTP 1:19, 29).

HOULTINS
Toles, m. by c1697, [-?-], dau. of Cornelius Mulraine (INAC 15:245).

HOULTON
William, m. by 12 June 1718, Ann, extx. of Joseph Goutee of DO Co. (MDAD 1:106).

HOUSE
William, Jr., m. by 9 Sep 1682, Ursula, extx. of Amos Bagby of CV Co. (INAC 7C:309).

HOW
Thomas, m. by 1 March 1718, Elizabeth, admx. of John Easterling of CV Co. (INAC 39A:51).

HOWARD
[-?-], m. by Aug 1687, Hannah, extx. of William Young of KE Co. (MDTP 13:501).
[-?-], m. by 16 Oct 1704, Hannah, dau. of Edward Dorsey of BA Co. (MWB 3:725).
[-?-], m. by 30 Dec 1717, Sarah, dau. of Peter Smith, Sr., of SM Co. (MWB 14:653).
Benjamin, m. on 27 Jan 1716, Catherine Buck (AAMA:87).
Charles, m. on 1 Aug 1715, Mary Selby (AAAN:22).
David, m. by 5 Feb 1701, Eliza, dau. of William Allen of TA Co. (MWB 11:166).
David, m. by 17 May 1706, Alice, admx. of Thomas Wilson of SO Co. (INAC 26:164).
David, m. on 27 July 1711, by Mr. Macankie, Catherine Barley (AAJA:41 #1).
Edmund, m. on 26 May 1681, Margaret Dent (SOLR:IKL). She was a sister of Peter Dent; their son William Stevens Howard called Peter Dent his uncle (SOJU 1707-1711:147).
Edward, m. by 1705, Mary, dau. of Thomas Melton, Sr.(MDTP 23:84, 89, MWB 12:58; MCHR CL:467).
George, m. by 25 May 1708, Mary, relict and admx. of Darby Conner of SO Co. (INAC 28:214).
George, m. by 30 Sep 1715, Sarah, admx. of William Hall of SO Co. (INAC 37A:89).
Job, m. on 29 April 1704, Anne Howell (TAPE).

John (Havard), m. by c1666 or later, Susan, widow of Charles Stevens of AA Co. (MPL 9:448, EE:436, 10:499). He d. leaving a widow Susannah who m. 3rd, William Crouch, and 4th, by 8 Oct 1713, James Smith (AALR IB#2:129).

John, m. by July 1688, Ellinor, extx. of John Maccubbin (MDTP 14:83).

John, m. by 23 April 1702, Katherine, heir of Col. Nicholas Greenberry of AA Co. (INAC 21:327).

John, m. on 6 Jan 1704, Mary Milnes (TAPE).

Joseph, m. on 12 Dec 1706, Anne Burrass (AAAL 1:33). She was Anne, relict and admx. of William Burroughs of AA Co. By a former husband she was the mother of Anne Barnett (AALR WT#2:580; INAC 28:41). See also the admin. acct. of Thomas Frisby (MDAD 1:182).

Joseph, m. on 28 Sep 1708, Margery Keith (AAAN:7).

Matthew, m. on 26 Oct 1714, Mary Browning, widow (and admx.) of George Browning. She was the widow of 1st, Nathaniel Howell, 2nd, Richard Kennard, and 3rd, George Browning; she was a dau. of Richard Pullen (MWB 6:5, 50, 21:422; CELR 1:301; INAC 36C:128; KESH; KELR BC#1:61, 69, JS#W:45; ESVR 1:29, 39, 40).

Thomas, m. by 24 May 1699, Mary, admx. of Stephen Mannkin of CH Co. (INAC 19:35).

Thomas, m. by 31 Jan 1714, Elisabeth, relict and extx. of Charles Brandt, of CH Co. (INAC 36B:97).

William, m. on 4 Jan 1673, Mary Hobday (SOLR:IKL).

William, m. on 6 Nov 1712, Elizabeth Seeney (KESP:33).

HOWARTON
     William, m. on 19 Jan 1695, Katherine Ridge (AAJA:2#9).

HOWELL
     [-?-], m. by 23 Feb 1715, Mary, dau. of Elizabeth Bourn, widow and extx. of Samuel Bourn, Gent., of CV Co. (MWB 16:50).

Humphrey, m. by 14 Nov 1651, Blanch, widow of John Harrison, Roger Dixon, and Roger Oliver, and mother of Mary Harrison, and William Oliver (Proprietary Records F&B:231).

Nathaniel, m. by 2 April 1687, Mary, dau. of Richard Pullen (MWB 6:5, 50). She m. 2nd, Richard Kennard, 3rd, by 19 Aug 1703, George Browning, and 4th, on 26 Oct 1714, Matthew Howard (MWB 6:5, 50, 21:422; CELR 1:301; INAC 36C:128; KESH; KELR JS#W:45; ESVR 1:29, 39, 40).

Septimus, of DO Co., m. by Aug 1710, [-?-], widow of Thomas Taylor (MDTP 21:270).

Thomas, m. by 9 May 1673, Ellinor, relict of Humphrey Warren of Hatton's Point, CH Co. (MDTP 5:439).

HOY
     [-?-], m. by 9 May 1711, Frances, dau. of John Dossett of PG Co. (MWB 13:274).

HUBBARD
John, m. by 13 Nov 1681, Margaret, relict of John Leekins of BA Co. (INAC 7B:157).
Nathaniel, of Goodman Fields, Parish of St. Mary's White Chapel, Mddx., Eng., m. by 9 Aug 1717, Eleanor, dau. and co-heir of Matthew Hill of MD, Gent. (CHLR H#2:88).

HUCKER
Robert, of PG Co., m. Amy (dec. by 20 April 1711), dau. of William Selby (MWB 13:286).

HUDD
[-?-], may have m. by 1 Oct 1650, Jeane, dau. of William Porter, whose will, proved on the above date named a dau. Jeane Hudd (MWB 1:27).

HUDSON
[-?-], m. by 2 Feb 1703/4, Ann, dau. of John Worth of KE Co. (MWB 3:254).
[-?-], m. by 5 March 1717, Mary, widow and extx. of Isaack Seserson (TALR RF#12:319).
David, m. by 11 Jan 1706, Amy, admx. of Armwell Shewell of SO Co. (INAC 26:320).
Hugh, m. on 5 Feb 1709, Catherine Donagun (TAPE).

HUFF
John, m. on 25 Nov 1706, Ann Morgan (KESP:32).

HUGG
Thomas, m. by 6 Dec 1710, Johanna, relict and admx. of John Polk of SO Co. (INAC 32B:245).

HUGGINS
John, m. on 27 April 1700, Elizabeth Morley (AAJA:7#5).

HUGHBANKS
Richard, m. by 3 Nov 1714, Elisabeth Tilton, who was due a portion, in the 1714 admin. acct. of John James KE Co. (INAC 36B:150).

HUGHES
Charles (Hughs), m. by 8 Feb 1694, Abigail, relict and admx. of George Carter of CV Co. (INAC 13A:220).
George (Hues), m. on 16 Feb 1716, Eliz. Simmons (TAPE).
John (Hugh, Hughson), m. by 1698, Ann, admx. of John Tillotson, who left five children (INAC 16:66; MDTP 16:266).
John, m. on 20 Jan 1703, Elizabeth Wilson (TAPE).
John (Hues), m. by 10 June 1715, Rebecka, admx. of Thomas White of CV Co. (INAC 36B:200). She was also admx. of Ralph Bagnall of CV Co. (INAC 36B:238).

John, m. on 20 Nov 1710, by Rev. Jona' White, Sarah Holland (PGQA:1).
Samuel (Hewes), m. by April 1701, Ann, relict of Lawrence Lawrenson (MDTP 19A:4).
Samuel (Hughs), m. on 27 Feb 1714, Jane Watkins (HAGE:32).
Thomas (Hughs), m. on 21 Sep 1703, Mary Whiborn (AAJA:28#1).
William (Hughs), m. on 25 Nov 1716, Elizabeth Croley (AAAN:29).

HULL
Joseph, m. on 28 Aug 1712, Hannah Shapely (KESP:33).

HUMBES
[-?-] [poss. James], m. by 8 Oct 1674, Sarah, dau. of Cornelius Regan of CV Co., whose account named dau. Sarah Humbes, and James Humbes was exec. (INAC 1:85).

HUMPHREYS
Joseph (Humpheris), m. on 18 Jan 1708/9, Ell-? Masksfield (AAAN:1).
Richard (Humphris), m. on 13 May 1703, Mary Barwell (AAMA:81). She was a dau. of John Barwell of AA Co. (MWB 12:214).
Richard (Humphris), m. by 12 July 1715, Elizabeth, admx. of Henry Jones of BA Co. (INAC 36C:48).
Robert, of KE Co., m. on 2 Sep 1664, Elizabeth Bromton (*ARMD* 54:186).

HUMPHRY
Thomas, m. on 29 April 1674, Mary King (SOLR:IKL).

HUNGERFORD
[-?-], m. by 19 April 1703, Margaret, sister of William Barton of PG Co. (MWB 3:643).
Thomas, m. by 1717, Mary, dau. of Thomas Smoot (MWB 14:658; MDTP 27:66).

HUNINGS
Philip [Hunings?], m. by April 1780/9, Dorothy, admx. of William Philipson (MDTP 21:98).

HUNT
[-?-], m. by 6 July 1651, Katherine, mother of William and Thomas Daynes, and of a dau., [-?-] Edmonds (MWB 1:30).
Jobe, and Sarah Day, filed their intentions to marry on 15 d., 9 m., 1717, and 13 d., 10 m., 1717 (WRMMa).

HUNTER
[-?-], of London, m. by 6 May 1711, Mary, sister of Anthony Smith of AA Co. (MWB 13:331).
Richard, m. by 20 March 1707, Elizabeth, extx. of Thomas Thomas of QA Co. (INAC 28:35).

Thomas, m. by 1718, Margaret, dau. of Thomas and Margaret (Bell) Hackney (SMWB PC#1:247).

Timothy, m. on 26 Jan 1703, Mary Robinson (TAPE).

William, of Piscataway Parish, PG Co., marr. lic. application approved, 22 Nov 1711, Rebecca Dillum (PGLR F:155).

HURLEY

Richard, m. by July 1708, Katherine, extx. of John Wiseman (MDTP 21:43).

HURLOCK

Abraham, m. by 20 Sep 1702, Eliza, dau. of Daniel Walker, Sr., of TA Co. (MWB 3:189).

George, in March 1686 brought testimony of his marriage to Eliza Potter, dau. of John Coppin and his wife Sarah (TAJR: Jan 1686, March 1686).

James, m. on 19 Dec 1710, Sarah Foard (TAPE).

HURST

John, m. in May 1718, Mary ffincke (AAMA:85).

HURTT

Daniell, m. on 21 Jan 1704, Rebecca Moss (KESP:32).

Morgan, m. on 2 Feb 1714, Mary Prise (KESP:34).

HUSBAND(S)

James, m. by lic. on 1 Jan 1717 by Mr. Sewell, Alice Parr (CESS). She was the admx. of Ezekiel Parr of CE Co. (MDAD 1:348).

William, m. by Oct 1684, Mary, admx. of William Bowin (MDTP 13:182; INAC 9:27).

HUSSEY

Thomas, m. by 13 Aug 1666, Joan or Johanna Porter, widow of John Nevill (*ARMD* 60:27; MPL ABH:24; CHLR C:61).

HUST

Emanuel, m. by 1 March 1715, [-?-], admx. of John Hudson of KE Co. (INAC 37A:106).

HUTCHESON

Vincent, m. on 22 April 1716, Rachel Nobleman (KESP:34).

HUTCHINS

[-?-], m. by 30 Aug 1715, Elizabeth, dau. of Edward Talbott, dec. (MPL EE#6:40, PL#3:496).

Francis, of CV Co., dec., m. by 10 Dec 1678, Elizabeth, dau. of John Burrage, dec. (AALR IH#3:85, WT#2:72).

Francis, m. by 23 Feb 1708/9, Eliz., dau. of John Welsh (AALR WH#4:47).

John, and Elizabeth Talbott, Jr., filed their intentions to marry on 8 d., 7 m., 1704, and 6 d., 8 m., 1704 (WRMMa).

Thomas (Huchings), m. on 28 Nov 1703, Mary Cox (TAPE).

HUTCHINSON
 [-?-], m. by 9 Dec 1712, Mary, dau. of Jno. Preston of TA Co. (MWB 13:665).

HUTCHISON
 [-?-], m. by 9 Dec 1712, Mary, dau. of Jno. Preston of TA Co. (MWB 13:665).
 John, m. by banns on 27 June 1716, by Mr. Sewell, Mary Pirkens (CESS).

HUZZ
 Thomas, cooper, m. by 26 Nov 1708 Katherine, widow of Joseph Pond of TA Co. (TALR RF#12:23).

HYATT
 [-?-] (Hyat, Hyett), m. by 2 June 1715, Barbara, dau. of Thomas and Barbara Jackson of QA Co. (MWB 14:156, 15:201).
 Seth, of PG Co., m. by 9 Feb 1718, Alice, dau. of Clement and Alice Davis (CELR 3:193).

HYDE
 Henry, d. by 29 Oct 1675 having m. Frances Goss, dau. of John and Jane (Mackall) Goss; Jane m. 2nd, John Warhop

HYNDE
 Thomas, m. by 8 April 1713, Jane, dau. of Edward Phoenix of PG Co. (MWB 13:677).

HYNES
 Col. John, m. by 1697, Anna, widow of Major Joseph Wickes (Cotton cites 15:218, 219).

HYNSON
 Charles, m. on March 1687, Margaret Harris (KESP:31). She was a dau. of William Harris of CE Co. (KELR M:116b)
 Henry, m. by 21 Nov 1701, Mary, widow and extx. of Andrew Price of TA Co., and mother of Thomas Price (INAC 22:76; TALR RF#11:107).
 Henry, of KE Co., m. by 19 Dec 1702, Mary, dau. and heiress at law of Thomas Stagwell, dec. (TALR 9:193).
 John, m. by 8 May 1694, Anne, admx. of Jonathan Grafton of KE Co. (INAC 12:128).
 Mr. John, m. on 1 June 1695, Mary Stoop, dau. of Mr. Jno. Stoop (CESS).
 Nathaniel, m. on 6 Aug 1714, Mary Kelley (KESP:34).
 Thomas, Jr., m. after 15 March 1663, Anne Gaine. Anthony Purss, Constable of Chester Hundred, had reported them for committing fornication Contrary to the Laws of

the Province and whereas the said Mr. Thomas Hynson, Jr., had come into Court being very sorrowful for it, and hath now made her his lawful Wife, The Court for his Punishment have thought fit, and hereby orders that he be suspended from setting in this County Court for one year and a day, or until further order from the Governer and Council; and it is further ordered that he bring his wife to the next Court held for Talbott County (*ARMD* 54:366).

Thomas, m. on 19 Oct 1710, Wealthy Ann Tildon (KESP:33).

IDOL
Samuel, m. on 1 Jan 1716, Esther Walton (AAAL).

IJAMS
Richard, m. on 16 Jan 1706/7, Anne Cheney (AAAL 1:33).
William, m. by 1 March 1674, Elizabeth, dau. of Richard Cheney of AA Co. (AALR IH#1:50).
William, m. 27 Aug 1696, Elizabeth Plummer (AAAL).

ILLIS?
Richard, m. by Dec 1688, Jane, relict of Domindigo Gambrall (MDTP 14:129).

IMPEY
[-?-] [poss. George], m. by 18 Feb 1681, Deborah, sister of John Sprigly of AA Co. (MWB 2:186).

INCHBUD
[-?-], m. by 10 Dec 1698, Mary, dau. of Joseph Wiggott of Great Choptank R., TA Co. (MWB 2:336).

INDREL
John, banns of marr. announced c1681/2, to Elinor Abnanathan (SOJU 1691-2:147).

INGERSON
Daniel, m. by 16 Aug 1695, Seth [*sic*; Faith?], admx. of Henry Pratt of TA Co. (INAC 10:420, 18:187; MDTP 16:91).

INGLESBY
[-?-], of CH Co., m. by Feb 1679/80, Bridget, relict of Edward Philpott (MDTP 11:324).

INGLISH
James (English), m. in Sep 1681, Sarah Bee (SOLR:IKL).
James, of So Co., m. by 18 June 1718, Mary, admx. of Alexander Gibbons of SO Co. (MDAD 1:162).
William, of CE Co., m. by 22 July 1688, Katherine Plaine (MWB 6:12).

INGRAM

[-?-], m. by 16 Jan 1715, Mary, dau. of Mathew Smith, planter, of QA Co. (MWB (MWB 14:200).

Abraham, m. by Aug 1707, Ellinor, admx. of John Genner (SOJU 1707-1711:31).

Daniel, m. by May 1699, Seth, relict of Henry Pratt of TA Co. (MDTP 17:282).

James, m. in Aug 1682, Mary Askewe (SOLR:IKL).

James (but see John, below), m. by Nov 1718, Mary, extx. of James Homewood AAJU RC:269).

John, of KE Co., m. on 10 Aug 1669 Hannah Jenkins (*ARMD* 54:186).

John, m. on 20 Oct 1680, Sarah Prince (SOLR:IKL).

John, m. on 10 Jan 1704, Mary Brington (KESP:41).

John, m. on 3 Sep 1705, Mary Homewood (AAMA:82). She was the extx. of James Homewood of AA Co. (INAC 25:411, 38A:65). She was a dau. of Capt. Peasley (MDTP 22:381, 401; MWB 12:321).

John, m. by 21 Sep 1714, Mary, niece of dec., in 1714 acct. of Benjamin Ricaud of KE Co. (INAC 36B:17).

Robert, d. by 24 Jan 1709, when his admx. Mary had m. John Williams (INAC 31:50).

Thomas, m. by 13 Sep 1699, Mary [-?-], widow of Capt. Robert Vaughan (a passenger on the *Ark and Dove* expedition to MD in 1634) (MWB 1:408).

Thomas, of PG Co., d. by Jan 1717/8, having m. Hannah, dau. of Hannah (or Honour) Herbert (MDTP 23:153).

INNIS

Samuel, m. by 13 Aug 1688, Mary, dau. of Ann Smith of SO Co. (MWB 6:29).

Thomas (or Innes or Jains), m. by 1658, Ann, widow of Elias Beech (MPL R:10b, 4:19).

William, m. by 31 May 1712, Jane, admx. of John Green of SM Co. (INAC 33B:16, 34:55).

INSHBORD

[-?-], m. by 15 March 1715, Mary, one of the legal reps. of John Clements of TA Co. (DOLR 7 Old:50).

INSLEY

Andrew, m. in or after 1668, Margaret Jones, whom he had transported (MPL 6:27, 11:507).

IRELAND

Robert, m. on 7 Nov 1704, Joan Butcher (KESP:41).

Samuel, m. on 1 Jan 1715, Anne White (TAPE).

William, m. on 15 Oct 1704, Ann [-?-] (TAPE).

IRVING

John (Erving), m. by 26 March 1709, Frances, dau. of Geo. Betts of SO Co. (MWB 13:381).

ISHAM

     James (Isum), m. on ---- Elizabeth Robinson (SJSG:11).

     James, m. by 22 July 1707, Julian, widow of Abraham de Lappe (INAC 27:28; BALR HW#2:291, TR#A:455).

ISRAEL

     John, m. by 15 Feb 1706, Margaret, widow and extx. of Col. Edward Dorsey of AA and BA Co., and poss. dau. of John Larkin (INAC 26:147, 27:59; AALR WT#2:471).

IVY

     Anthony, m. by 17 Feb 1708, Ann, only dau. and heiress of Robert Smith of TA Co. (QALR ETA:32; KELR JSN:117).

JACKS

     [-?-], m. by 7 Nov 1715, Eliza, widow of Jno. Powell, and mother of Jno. Powell, Jr. (MWB 14:227).

     Thomas, m. on 9 Nov 1704, Elizabeth Walters (AAAL 1:27).

JACKSON

     [-?-], m. by 12 July 1694, Mary, dau. of Thomas Plummer of AA Co. (MWB 7:56).

     [-?-], m. by 7 April 1703, [-?-] , dau. of Edward Fry of KE Co. (MWB 3:255).

     [-?-], m. by 12 Dec 1706, Hannah, dau. of Edward and Alice Sissons (MWB 12:89; SMWB PC#1:173).

     [-?-], m. by 30 April 1717, Rachel, dau. of James Atkinson, of SO Co. (MWB 17:88).

     Barnaby, m. by 1657, Margaret, dau. of George Goodrick and sister of Robert Goodrick; some time before 8 Sep 1702 she m. 2nd, George Thompson (MPL 4:22, R:11b; MCHR PC:494).

     Henry, m. by 24 Jan 1704, Mary, sister of William Kimball of BA Co. (MWB 3:432).

     Philip, m. by 25 Jan 1702, Ann, dau. of John Davis, of KE Co., planter (KELR JD#1:76).

     Richard, m. on 5 May 1715, Ann Froggett (KESP:41).

     Robert, of Bush River, banns pub. July and Aug 1699, m. on 24 Aug 1699 Isabel Hooper of Cranbury Hall (HAGE:7).

     Samuel, banns pub. Nov 1698, m. 11 Dec 1698, Sarah Mathews (HAGE:5, 6).

     Samuel, m. by 3 March 1714, Sarah, admx. of William Davis of SO Co. (INAC 36B:343).

     Simon, m. by May 1688, Elizabeth, eld. dau. of John Chadwell (MDTP 14:72).

     Thomas, of CV Co., m. by April 1679, Mary, dau. of William Harbud (MDTP 11:28).

     Thomas, m. on 25 July 1703, Mary Kembal (HAGE:17).

     Thomas, m. on 12 Dec 1709, Mary Blackiston (KESP:41).

William, m. by 15 July 1709, Margaret, admx. of William Hollinsworth of TA Co. (INAC 30:233).

JACOB(S)
Benjamin, m. on 1 May 1711, Alice Westals (Westal) (AALR 1:37).
John, m. by 1 March 1674, Anne, dau. of Richard Cheney (AALR IH#1:47).
John, m. on 4 July 1706, Mary Swanson (AAAL 1:32(2)).
Joseph, m. on 1 Oct 1706, Elizabeth Jones (AAAL 1:33).

JADWIN
Bartholomew, of TA Co., m. on 26 d. 4 m., 1680, Ann Estell, of MD, spinster, at the house of John Jadwin (TATH).
Jeremiah, of TA Co., planter, m. on 9 d. 9 m., 1701, Isabel Harrison at Third Haven meeting house (TATH).
Robert, planter, m. on 11 d., 12 m., 1699, Martha Wootters, spinster, all of TA Co. (TATH). She was a dau. of John Wootters, Sr., of TA Co. (MWB 11:157).
Robert, m. on 17 June 1715, Elizabeth Hill (TAPE).

JAMES
[-?-], m. by 3 June 1679, Anne, relict and admx. of Edward Lowder of KE Co. (INAC 6:72).
Anthony, m. on 13 May 1703, Sarah Pingstone (TAPE).
Charles, of BA Co., Gent., m. by March 1670, Elizabeth, dau. and sole heir of Leonard Strong of AA Co., merchant (MPL 14:40; *ARMD* 51:142; MDTP 5:32).
Charles, m. by 30 April 1705, Mary Burford, extx. of Daniel Clarke of DO Co. (INAC 25:63).
Edward, of KE Co., m. by Oct 1684, Catherine, relict of Thomas Browne (MDTP 13:169).
John, m. by c1695, Ann, extx of Richard Whitton of CE Co. (INAC 13B:3).
John, son of Joseph, m. on 19 Dec 1708, Jane Carter (TAPE).
Joseph, m. by 1676, [-?-], widow of Peter Underwood (MPL 19:590).
Joseph, m. on 10 Aug 1710, Elizabeth Shepherd (TAPE).
Richard, a Manny Indian, m. on 26 Aug 1688, Honor [-?-] (SOLR:IKL).
Richard, m. on 11 June 1702, Sarah Taylor (TAPE).
Richard, m. on 4 April 1714, Elizabeth Rae (KESH:13).
Thomas, m. by 20 Feb 1682, Sarah, relict and admx. of Gyles Stevens of BA Co. (INAC 8:3).

JAMESON
Thomas, m. about 10 Nov 1698, by Rev. William Hunter, Mary Matthews, sister of Jane [-?-], who m. by 1738 Henry Wharton (CHLR G#3:370). Mary was the relict of Ignatius Matthews (INAC 19½A:107).

JARBOE/JERBOE
John, m. by 1668, Mary, dau. of Walter and Frances Peake (Fresco cites MPL 8:88, Hodges, and Index to Warrants and Assignments 1688:46).

Peter, d. by 8 Nov 1699, having m. Ann, dau. of John Nevett (INAC 19½B:120).

JARVIS
[-?-], m. by 29 Dec 1680, [-?-], dau. of William Kent of TA Co., who named his grandchildren William and Mary Jarvis (MWB 2:130).

JAVERT
John (Jawert), m. by 1 Dec 1704, Katherine, widow of Augustine Hermann (MDTP 23:4). She was the admx. of Col. Casparus Hermann of CE Co. (INAC 25:167; 34:142, 153). She was the mother of Ephraim Augustine Hermann (CELR 2:291).

JAY
William, m. on 6 Dec 1705, Sarah Wilder (AAAL 1:32(2)).

JEDBERRY
John, m. by 17 April 1676, [-?-], sister of Robert Taylor of CV Co. (MDTP 8A:46).

JEFF
William, living at the head of Swan Creek, m. on 12 Aug 1697, Ruth Matthews (Mathews) (HAGE:2).
William, banns pub. May 1701, m. 29 May 1701, Elizabeth Aishley (HAGE:11).

JEFFERYS
[-?-], of Dorsetshire (Eng.), m. by 4 March 1667, Ann, sister of Henry Coler or Coller of Bristol City and of CV Co. (MDTP 2:108).

JEMINEY
James, m. on 26 Feb 1717, Sarah Cox (TAPE).

JENIFER
Daniel, m. by Sep 1669, Mary, extx. of Lieut. William Smythe or Smith of SM Co. (*ARMD* 51:327; MPL 20:48).
Michael, m. on 9 Jan 1718, Mary, dau. of George and Susanna Parker (CVCH).

JENKINS
[-?-], m. by 1710, Mary, sister of Robert King (SOLR10 (CD):541).
[-?-], m. by 16 April 1717, Mary, dau. of Edward Cole of SM Co. (MWB 14:644).
[-?-], m. by 16 April 1717, Susanna, dau. of Edward Cole of SM Co. (MWB 14:644).
Enoch, m. on 26 Jan 1718, Ann Clarvo (PGKG:246).
Francis (Jenckins), m. on 12 April 1672, [-?-], widow of Henry Weedon (SOLR:IKL).

Francis, m. by Nov 1675, Lucy, extx, of James Weedon (SOJU L (Rev) 21; *ARMD* e 89).

John (Jenkinson), m. 1st, by 1654, Ann [-?-], and 2nd, by 1658, Joan, widow of Thomas Bachelor (MPL Q:53, R:29b, 150b, 4:63, 375; *ARMD* 41:96).

John (Jenkings), m. on 5 Nov 1704, Frances Pollett (AAAL 1:27).

Richard, m. by 18 Aug 1687, Ann, relict and extx. of William Graves of CV Co. (INAC 9:477).

Thomas, m. by 5 May 1711, [-?-], dau. of Matthew Lewis of TA Co. (MWB 13:457).

William, m. on 26 Aug 1674, Ann Stadley (SOLR:IKL).

William, of SO Co., m. by 14 Nov 1689, Alce, the relict of John Hill deceased, and mother of Alce Hill (*ARMD* e106: SOJU 1689-1690:4).

JENKINSON

Emanuel (Wright transcribed this as Jenkins), planter, m. on 1 d. 9 m., 1704, Elizabeth Jadwin, both of TA Co. at Tuckahoe Meeting House (TATH). She was a dau. of John Jadwyn or Jadwin of TA Co. (MWB 12:136).

John. See JENKINS.

Robert, m. by 14 March 1690, Mary, widow of [-?-] McCotter (TALR 5:288).

Samuel, m. on 1 d. 10 m., 1679, Elizabeth Morgain of TA Co. (TATH).

JENNER

John, m. by Sep 1692, Magdalina, widow of James Traine (SOJU 1692-93:49).

JENNINGS

[-?-] (Jenings), m. by 3 Feb 1717/8, Elizabeth, dau. of Barbara Jackson, widow of QA Co. (MWB 15:281).

Henry (Jenings), of SM Co., m. by July 1710, Eliza, extx. of William Goldsmith (MDTP 21:263; PCJU TP#2:37, PL#3:374).

Henry, m. by 1716, [-?-], sister of John Beall of SM Co. (MWB 14:302).

JERRCONS

Edward, m. on 13 May 1711, Elizabeth Piscood (CVCH).

JERVIS

Edward, m. on 20 July 1708, Mary Wade (KESP:41).

James, m. in Sep 1709, Sarah Smith (KESP:41).

JOBSON

John, m. on 23 July 1711 by Mr. Sewell, Hester [or Heather] Hollyday, widow (CESS). She was Heather, relict and admx. of Samuel Hollyday of CE Co. (INAC 33B:86; MDTP 22:61).

JOCE

Thomas, m. by 28 Sep 1685, Anne, admx. of Samuel Tovey of KE Co. (INAC 9:15, 32C:100).

JOHNS

Aquila, of CV Co., m. on 16 d. 9 m., 1704, Mary Hosier, of KE Co., at Chester Meeting House (KECE). She was a dau. of Henry Hosier of KE Co. (MWB 13:192).

Isaac, son of Richard and Elizabeth, of CV Co., m. on 25 d., 10 m., 1712, Ann Galloway, dau. of Samuel and Ann (WRMM).

Kensey, son of Richard, and Elizabeth Chew, dau. of Benjamin, filed their intentions to marry on 24 d., 9 m., 1710, and 22 d., 10 m., 1710 (WRMMa).

Richard, of CV Co., m. by Sep 1676, [-?-], relict of Thomas Sparrow of AA Co. (MDTP 8A:209; *ARMD* 51:228).

Richard, Jr., and Priscilla Hutchins filed their intentions to marry on 4 d., 7 m., 1707, and 3 d., 8 m., 1707 (WRMMa).

JOHNSON

[-?-], m. by 2 Oct 1662, Eliza, dau. of Thomas Turner of St. Winifred's, SM Co. (MWB 1:169).

[-?-], m. by 2 Jan 1703, Rachel, dau. of Thomas Robertson of AA Co. (AALR WT#2:150).

[-?-], m. by 17 Aug 1716, Susannah, relict of John Raymond of AA Co. (AALR IB#2:296).

[-?-], m. by 12 March 1708/9, Hannah, dau. of Jacob Lusby of AA Co. (MWB 12, pt. 2:121; MDAD 1:235).

[-?-], m. by 30 Dec 1717, Mary, dau. of Peter Smith, Sr., of SM Co. (MWB 14:653).

Albert, of TA Co., d. by 1686, leaving a widow who was the widow of Henry Green (Cotton cites INAC 9:436).

Andrew, m. on 25 Jan 1707/8, Elizabeth Vetherall (AAMA:84).

Anthony, m. on 3 March 1699, Catherine Smith (*1 Harris and McHenry* 281, "Johnson and Johnson's Lessee vs. Howard," cites a now missing Register of marriages, births, and burials, of St, Paul's Parish, BA Co., in *NGSQ* 53:201-202).

Frederick, m. by 25 Feb 1642, [-?-], widow of Richard Stevens (*ARMD* 4:185).

Henry, m. by June 1677, Elizabeth, extx. of Nathaniel Utie (*ARMD* 66:364, 67:14).

Jacob, pub. banns on 12 Nov 1704, and m. on 11 Jan 1704/5, Alice More (HAGE:22).

James, m. by 27 Jan 1649, Barbara Hatton, kinswoman of Thomas Hatton, Secretary of the Province (MWB 1:26; *ARMD* 10:12).

Jeremiah, m. by March 1683/4, Lucy, admx. of James Gilstrope of CV Co. (MDTP 13:92; INAC 9:135).

John, m. by 1687, Mary, sister of Fobbs Roberts (MWB 4:282, 6:4).

John, m. on 7 Feb 1704, Shusannah [sic] Benstead (TAPE).

John, m. by 8 July 1707, Mary, admx. of John Medcalf of SM Co. (INAC 27:151).

John, m. on 27 May 1711, Mary Williams (AALR 1:37).

John, m. on 12 Jan 1713, Sarah Jones (TAPE).

Joseph, m. on 5 July 1713, Ann Tod (HAGE:30).

Robert, m. by 14 Aug 1703, Elizabeth, dau. of Thomas Hide (PGLR C:64).

Robert, m. on 11 Jan 1716/7, Rebekah Ragg (AAAN:29).

Samuel, m. on 17 Feb 1708, Ann Nelson (AAAN:7).

Thomas, m. by Jan 1688/9, Mary, dau. of Roger Baker, whose sister was the mother of Thomas [Bowman?] of London (MDTP 14:130).

Thomas, m. by 28 Nov 1699, Mary formerly Hays, admx. of Charles Hays of PG Co. (INAC 19½B:5, 21:336).

Thomas (Jonson), m. on 16 Oct 1701, Rachel Robeson (AAMA:84).

Thomas, m. on 18 April 1706, Dorothy Chittham (CVCH).

Thomas, m. by 5 Nov 1712, Elizabeth, admx. of John Paule of SO Co. (INAC 34:154).

Thomas, m. on 3 Sep 1716, Mary Enlowe (SJSG:9).

William, died by 1656, having m. Emma Langworth, sister of James Langworth; she m. 2nd, Thomas Turner, who d. 1663, and 3rd, William Roswell of SM Co. (SMWB PC#1:94; MDTP 13:136; Prov. Court BB:38, S:1078.

William, of Ratcliffe in Old England, m. on 26 Dec 1682 [*sic*], Sarah Edmondson, dau. of John and Sarah Edmondson, at the house of John Edmondson (TATH).

William, m. by May 1686, Katherine, relict of William Sertgerson of SM Co. (MDTP 14:86).

William, m. by 18 Sep 1703, Sarah, admx. of William Browne of CV Co. (INAC 24:171).

JOHNSTON
Nathan, m. on 30 Oct 1716, Magdalen Poulson (CENE).

JOLLY
Edward, m. by 1675, Margaret [-?-], who m. 2nd, John Stevens (MCHR1:159).

JONES
[-?-], m. by Oct 1677, Elizabeth, widow and extx. of William Cross of CV Co. (MDTP 9A:372, 460).

[-?-], m. by Feb 1678/9, Honoria, relict and extx. of John Ware of Rappahanock Co., VA (MDTP 10:352).

[-?-], m. by Aug 1679, Love, admx. of Constant Daniell of SM Co. (MDTP 11:148).

[-?-], m. by 15 April 1689, Ann, admx. of Richard Weaver (INAC 10:231).

[-?-], m. by 22 July 1695, Dinah, admx. of William Drake of CE Co. (INAC 13A:380; 13B:10).

[-?-], m. by 1 Sep 1701, Jane, dau. of Edmond Brannock of DO Co. (MWB 3:18).

[-?-], m. by [c1703/4], Ann, widow of John Robinson (MWB 3:73).

[-?-], m. by 19 Oct 1709, Sophia, dau. of John Pooly of TA Co. (MWB 12, pt. 2:237).

[-?-], m. by 4 July 1710, Elizabeth Mash (MCHR PC:668).

[-?-], m. by 1 Jan 1713, Barbara, mother of Richard Chapman, Ann, wife of John Suttle, Thomas Goletie and William Chapman (MWB 13:640).

[-?-], m. by 1 Feb 1717, Sarah, relict of Walter Meeks (KELR BC#1:348).

[-?-], m. by 2 Sep 1717, Jane, dau. of George Powell of QA Co. (MWB 14:393).

Andrew, m. on 13 Jan 1680, Elizabeth Winder (SOLR:IKL).

Cadwallader, m. on 23 April 1702, Mary Ellis, spinster (HAGE:14).

Cadd[wallader], m. on 7 May 1704, Mary Pool or Powell (HAGE:22, 69).

Charles, m. on 8 Dec 1681, Grissegon Barre (Berré) (SOLR:IKL).

Charles, m. by 26 March 1708, Jane, admx. of Bowles Tyer of CH Co. (INAC 28:102, 29:60).

Christmas, m. by 15 Sep 1716, Elisabeth, admx. of James Harrison of TA Co. (INAC 37C:153).

David, m. by 16 Jan 1678, [-?-], relict of Capt. Thomas Todd of BA Co. (INAC 7A:279).

David, m. by 1687, [-?-], widow of Dennis Husculaw of SM Co. (MDTP 14A:39).

David, m. on 22 Oct 1706, Margaret Morley (AAJA:33 #7).

Edward, of KE Co., m. on 10 May 1661, Margrett Hale (*ARMD* 54:186).

Edward, m. in 1669, Mary Barnaby, widow (SOLR:IKL). She was the relict of James Barnaby (*ARMD* e86 (SOJU DT#7):196/200).

Edward, m. by 9 Oct 1682, Mary, relict and admx. of William Brockhurst (Brochas) of CE Co. (INAC 8:271), 13A:210).

Edward, m. by 1696, Ann, widow of Christopher Green (MDTP 14:65, 81, 17:248).

Edward, m. by 18 Sep 1704, Elizabeth, dau. of Philip Lewin of PG Co. (PGLR C:123b).

Edward, m. on 29 Jan 1710, Susannah Bell (TAPE).

Evan, m. on 6 Oct 1709, Ann Drincall (AAJA:38 #4).

Evan, m. on 28 May 1713, Mary Bradford (PGKG:239).

George, m. by 1690, Joanna, widow of Orlando Ultrajactrius (MDTP 16:10).

Griffith, m. by 2 March 1688, Lucy, widow of Thomas Seaward [Seward?]; Lucy later m. Henry Green; on 3 July 1681 Lucy Green recorded the births of several children of Thomas and Lucy Seaward [Seward?] and of Griffith and Lucy Jones (KELR GL#1:7, 35; MDTP 14A:53).

Griffith, m. on 15 Dec 1709, Frances Butler (TAPE).

Griffith, m. on 18 Dec 1712, Sarah Porter (KESP:41). She was a dau. of Giles Porter (INAC 36B:60).

Henry, m. by 21 June 1699, Elinor, dau. of Edward Owen, and sister of Richard Owens; they had a son William Jones (AALR PK:221-226).

Henry, m. by 1 Oct 1711, Joan (Jone), admx. of Edward Lappis of KE or CE Co. (INAC 33A:10).

Jacob, on 9 Jan 1676/7, banns of matrimony were published for him and Elizabeth Stevens (SOLR O#7:70r).

James, of Northumberland Co., VA, m. by 1694, Rebecca, dau. of John Waughop of Piney Point (Fresco cites Prov. court WRC#1:698).

John, living on Swan Creek, m. on 8 July 1695, Martha Loveill (HAGE:2).

Jno., m. on 13 Aug 1695, Mary Machahay (CESS).

John, m. by 24 April 1701, Elizabeth, admx. of Woolfran Hunt of AA Co. (INAC 20:192, 249; AALR IB#2:501, 561).

John, m. by 19 Dec 1702, Elizabeth, relict and admx. of William Simpson of CH Co. (INAC 23:65).

John, m. on 21 Oct 1704, Mary Darby (KESP:41).

John, m. by 3 Nov 1712, Ann, extx. of Henry Guttereg (or Guttridge) of PG Co. (INAC 33B:178, 34:67, 36c:39).

John, m. By 5 June 1713, [-?-], relict and extx. of John Gawdard [Goddard?] of SM Co. (INAC 34:175).

John, m. by 29 July 1713, [-?-], relict of William Steward of SM Co. (INAC 35B:108).

Joseph, m. on 16 Feb 1703/4, Elizabeth Elder (AAAL 1:26).

Joseph, son of Griffith and Joan of Phila. Co., PA, merchant, m. on 8 d., 4 m., 1704, Margaret Birckhead, dau. of Nehemiah (WRMM).

Joseph, m. on 10 Dec 1704, Mary Pybern of PG Co. (AAAL 1:27).

Joseph, m. on 22 Oct 1712, Mary Harwood (AAJA:42 #6). She was the admx. of Richard Harwood of AA Co. (INAC 35A:27, 36B:226; AAJU RC:269, which gives his name as Norwood, 270).

Leonard, m. by 4 Nov 1702, Ann, dau. of Robert Collier of SO Co. (MWB 1:290).

Lewis, m. by June 1689, Katherine, widow of Wm. Searson (MDTP 14:80, 151).

Morgan, m. by Nov 1672, Mary, widow of John Davis or Davies, and dau. of John Harrington (*ARMD* 65:137; INAC 2:175, 4:243; MDTP 9A:451; SMWB PC#1:2).

Morgan, may have m. by 5 Jan 1685/6, Johanna, dau. of Henry Hosier, Sr., of KE Co., who calls them son and dau. in his will (MWB 4:247).

Morgan, m. by 1716, Jane Whipps, dau. of John and Elizabeth, of AA Co. (MWB 14:173; MDTP 30:172).

Morgan, m. by (date not given), Elizabeth, admx. of Edward Platford of CV Co. (INAC 38A:50).

Moses, m. by Nov 1688, Katharine, relict and extx. of James Wheeler of CH Co. (MDTP 14:119, 15A:28; INAC 9:188; 10:364; CHLR Q:53).

Nathaniel, m. by 10 Oct 1688, Susanna, legatee of John Kirk of DO Co. (INAC 10:171).

Phillip, m. by 9 July 1686, Susan, admx. of John Clarke of CV Co. (INAC 9:46).

Philip, m. on 3 Jan 1700, Mary Rowles (AAMA:82). She was Mary, dau. and surviving heir of William Hill. Mary was the widow of James Crouch (by whom she had a son James) and John Rolls (by whom she had a son John) (AALR IB#2:93, IH#1:263; INAC 20:239).

Philip, m. by 16 Feb 1704, Jane, extx. of George Blacketor of CV Co. (MWB 3:399).

Philip, m. by 10 Aug 1703, Mary, legatee of Elizabeth Baker of AA Co. (MWB 11:394; INAC 26:339).

Richard, m. by 15 Nov 1675, Elizabeth, relict and admx. of Richard Stevens of TA Co. (INAC 1:461; MDTP 7:125).

Richard, m. by 17 Oct 1688, Elizabeth, admx. of William Vaughan (INAC 10:181).

Richard, m. by 15 Aug 1699, Anne, relict and admx. of William Burgess of AA Co., son of Col. William Burgess (INAC 19½B:153, 20:43; AALR WT#1:97, WT#2:222).

Richard, Jr., of AA Co., m. by 30 Sep 1714, Ann, mother of John, Nicholas, Gassaway, and Elizabeth Watkins (MWB 13:684).

Richard, m. on 18 Feb 1717, Jane Sweringen (PGQA:1).

Richard, m. on 15 July 1718, Elizabeth Clark (AAAL 2:15).

Rise, m. on 25 Oct 1713, Sarah News (KESP:41).

Robert, m. on 27 June 1703, Ann Yates (TAPE).

Robert, planter, m. on 24 d. 9 m., 1709, Anne Lewes, at Treadhaven meeting house (TATH).

Roger, m. on 24 June 1704, Mary Carr (TAPE).

Samuel, on 14 Aug 1677, banns of matrimony were published for him and Mary Davis (SOLR O#7:121r).

Samuel, m. in Nov 1691, Mary Flannakin (SOLR:IKL).

Stephen, m. on 26 Oct 1707, Rebekah Darby (AAAL 1:36).

Thomas, of BA Co., m. by April 1676, [-?-], relict of Walter [Marcanallie?] of BA Co. (MDTP 8:23).

Thomas, m. by 15 Oct 1675, Sarah, dau. of William Crouch of AA Co. (MWB 5:163).

Thomas, m. by 16 May 1676, Jane Gray, admx. of Alexander Winsore (INAC 5:99, 102).

Thomas, m. by 1696, Mary, formerly Harrison, who was mentioned in the will of Edward Dowse (BALR RM#HS:524).

Thomas, m. on 12 July 1702, Mary Willis (KESP:41).

Thomas, m. on 9 Dec 1705, Mary Barker (AAAL 1:32(2)).

Thomas, m. on 11 May 1708, Mary Tillard (KESH:11).

Thomas, m. by 29 June 1708, Ephia (or Esther?), extx. of Francis Bright of QA Co. (INAC 28:130, 29:412, 32A:11; MDTP 21:26, 292).

Thomas, m. by 9 July 1710, Mary, dau. of George Green of KE Co. (KELR JS#N:197).

Thomas, m. by April 1711, [-?-], admx of Samuel Tovey of KE Co. (MDTP 22:2).

William, m. on --- (date not given), Hannah Norris (AAJA:49#6).

William, of TA Co., m. on 24 d. 12 m., 1679, Sarah Hall (TATH).

William, m. by 9 Aug 1686, Mary, relict and admx. of William Hitchcock of CV Co. (INAC 9:136; 14:97).

William, m. by 23 Aug 1696, Sarah, dau. of Sarah Yewell of TA Co. (MWB 6:127).

William, m. on 5 Jan 1700, by Mr. Benjamin Nobbs, minister, Honora [-?-] (TAPE).

William, m. on 21 March 1702, Alse Smith (AAMA:82). She was formerly Alice Smith, but dau. and heiress of Tobias Butter, late of AA Co., dec. (AALR WT#2:107, 109).

William, m. by 12 Oct 1704, [-?-], widow and acct. of Christopher Horrell (MWB 3:385).

William, m. on 13 Feb 1710/11, Susan Jacob (AALR 2:7).

William, m. on 25 Nov 1711, Mary Cooper (TAPE).

JORDAN

John (Jordain, Jurdan), of KE Co., m. by 14 May 1697, Charity, dau. and extx. of Richard Tydings of AA Co. (INAC 14:143, 26:160; MDTP 14:156).

Capt. John (Jordain), m. by May 1669, Elizabeth, widow of Col. William Evans; she m. 3rd, Cuthbert Scott (INAC 6:363, 359; *ARMD* 51:284).

Tho., d. by 29 May 1665 having m. Sarah, relict of John Elzey, Gent. (MDTP 1E:124).

Thomas, m. by 21 Dec 1681, Eliza, sister of George Billingsley of Upper Norfolk, VA (MWB 4:118).

JOSEPH

William, m. by 25 April 1703, Elizabeth, dau. of Luke Gardiner of SM Co. (MWB 33:470; SMWB PC#1:145).

JOWLES

Col. Henry, m. by 17 March 1679, Sybil, relict and extx. of William Groome of CV Co. (INAC 6:683; PCLR WRC:98; *ARMD* 67:434).

Henry Peregrine, m. by 1717, Dryden, sister of Kenelm Cheseldine (PCJU 19:465, 467; MCHP 8).

JOY

John, d. by 1696, Judith, dau. of John Goldsmith; she m. 2nd, Richard Cloud (SMAD HH:96).

Peter, m. by 1663, [-?-], dau. of Daniel Goldson (Goulson) (*ARMD* 49:36, 78).

JOYCE

Thomas, m. on 22 April 1716, Eliza Cheeny (PGQA:1).

JOYNER

William, m. by 10 April 1674, Sarah, dau. of Andrew Ellenor (*ARMD* 51:113).

JUB(B)

Robert, m. on 6 July 1704, Elinor [-?-] (AAMA:81). She was Elinor, admx. of Jonathan (or John) Neale of AA Co.; and admx. of Robert Neale (MWB 3:414; INAC 27:57, 32C:58; MDTP 22:15; AAJU TB#1:616).

JUDD

Michael, after 8 April 1676 and before 9 April 1685 m. Jane, widow of William Ebden, and mother of William Ebden, Jr. (BALR IR#PP:8, RM#HS:130).

JUDKINS

Obadiah, m. on 9 d. 11 m. [or 11 d. 9 m.], 1669, Joan Davis, both of TA Co., at Betty's Cove Meeting House (TATH).

Obadiah, Jr., of TA Co., planter, m. on 22 d. 7 m., 1672, Elizabeth Parratt, spinster, at the house of Obadiah Judkins, Sr. (TATH).

Obadiah, of TA Co., m. on 16 d. 10 m., 1680, Joan Huntingdon, spinster, at Howell Powell's (TATH).

JUDRELL
John, banns of Matrimony with Elinor: Abnanachan published 1st time on 12 Jan 1691/2 (SOJU 1691-1692).

JUMP
Thomas, m. by 18 June 1718, Alice, admins. of John Wooters of QA Co. (MDAD 1:277).

JUSTIS
Henry, m. by 10 March 1709, Mary, admx. of Michael Liuge of CH Co. (INAC 31:76).

KALE
Thomas, of AA Co., d. by 24 Oct 1709 when his admx. Mary had m. Peter Anderton (INAC 30:239).

KANERY
Richard, 22 Aug 1655, was about to marry Mary, extx. of John Hodger (*ARMD* 10:419).

KEARE
Robert, m. on 30 Oct 1713, Rachel Hannah (KESP:43).

KEATING
John, m. on 21 Oct 1713, Sarah Schooling (KESP:43).

KEECH
[-?-], m. by 12 June 1716, [-?-], dau. of Eliz. Hawkins, widow of CH Co. (MWB 14:510).
James, m. by 27 Jan 1697, Eliza, dau. of John Courts of CH Co. (MWB 11:246).
John, d. by April 1712, Elizabeth (poss. dau. of Hugh Tears); she m. 2nd, William Middleton (MDTP 22:98; INAC 33B:131).

KEEF
Cornelius, m. on 16 Nov 1707, Dianna Cockarill (KESP:43).

KEELING
[-?-], m. by 28 Feb 1697, Mary, sister of George Robotham of TA Co. (MWB 7:358).

KEEN(E)
Edward, of CV Co., d. by 19 Oct 1675, having m. Susanna, mother of Susan Hunt

(MWB 2:405). Susanna was also the widow and admx. of William Hunt (INAC 3:97).

James (Keen), m. by 30 Sep 1708, Susanna, relict of John Shareman, mentioned in acct. of John Bead of CH Co. (INAC 28:343).

John, m. by 23 May 1687, Ann, extx. of Hugh Hopewell of CV Co. (MDTP 16:7; INAC 13A:312).

John, Jr., m. by 14 Nov 1716, Mary, extx. of James Mosley of DO Co. (INAC 38B:17).

Richard, of CV Co., m. by 1697, Elizabeth, widow of Hugh Hopewell of SM Co., and dau. of Francis Hill; she m. 3rd, Charles Beckwith (Fresco cites MWB 2:2:325, 7:295; MDTP 16:91, 17:319, 321, 19A:161).

Timothy, m. on 14 May 1709, Mary Moone (HAGE:26).

William (Keen), Jr., m. 14 July 1692, Sarah Ackworth (SOLR:IKL:3).

KEIRSTEAD

Joakim, m. by 1699, Margaret Beckwith, widow of Michael Taney. She was a dau. of George and Francis Harvey Beckwith, and m. 3rd, George Gray (INAC 9:476, 32B:129; MWB 6:1; MCHR PC:433; Warrants 7:62; MCHR PC:433).

KEITH

Alexander, m. by 26 Feb 1708/9, Christiana, dau. of William Farfarr (BALR RM#HS:636).

KEIVE

John, m. on 25 Nov 1705, Catherine ffahee (AAAN:19).

KELK

Richard, m. on 9 April 1708, Katherine [-?-] (AAAN:1). She was the widow and admx. of James Shirley of AA Co. (INAC 28:296).

KELLOW

John, m. by 1697, Mary, dau. of Thomas and Hannah Hide of PG Co. (Hodges cites MWB 6:80).

KELLUM

[-?-], m. by 18 March 1715. Tabitha, dau. of James Truett, Sr., of SO Co. (MWB 14:581).

KELLY

Dennis, m. by 2 April 1709, Ann Kinbow, in 1709 acct. of Edward James of Kent Island (INAC 29:218).

Patrick, m. on 15 Nov 1701, Elizabeth Simmons (CVCH).

KEMBAL(L)

[-?-], m. by 1 June 1691, Jone, mother of John and William Jones of DO Co. (DOLR 4½ Old:29).

Jno. (Kimball), m. by June 1678, [-?-], extx. of William Jones (*ARMD* 67:419).

John, Jr., m. on 16 April 1703, Elizabeth Gilbert (HAGE:17).

Rowland, m. on 15 May 17-- [prob. before 1717], Hannah Jackson (HAGE:37).

KEMBLE

William, m. by 27 March 1716, Mary, dau. of Humphrey Jones (BALR TR#A: 389).

KEMP

[-?-], m. by 11 Nov 1685, Eliza (Ceamp or Cemp), dau. of Edward Webb of TA Co. (MWB 4:206).

John, of BA Co., m. by 1 Dec 1686, Sarah Wichell (MWB 4:239).

John, planter, son of Robert Kemp and his wife Elizabeth, dec., m. on 1 d. 11 m., 1705, Mary Ball, dau. of Thomas Ball and Susanna, his wife, both of TA Co., at the house of John Kemp, TA Co. (TATH).

William, m. on 27 May 1715, Hannah Warren (CVCH).

William, m. on 11 d. 5 m., 1717, Martha Eubanks, Jr., at Treadhaven meeting house (TATH).

KEMPERSON

Stephen, m. by 1 Oct 1701, Mary, admx. of William Rabbitts of TA Co. (INAC 21:110).

KEMPSTON

[-?-], m. by 23 Oct 1716, Ann, sister of Septimus Nowell, of Great Choptank Parish, DO Co. (MWB 14:175).

KENDLE

[-?-], m. by May 1697, Jane, relict of John Quatermus of DO Co. (MDTP 16:236).

KENELAGH

Dominick (Kenslagh), m. by 30 Aug 1708, Margaret, admx. of Daniel Kelly of KE Co. (INAC 28:295).

KENNARD

[-?-], m. by 11 April 1688, Sarah, relict and extx. of Capt. Joseph Hopkins of CE Co. (INAC 9:508).

Philip, m. on 8 Dec 1708, Mary Bally (KESP:43).

Philip, of KE Co., m. by 2 Aug 1709, Elizabeth, widow and relict of William Bailey, mother of William Bailey, and sister of Charles James (KELR JSN:141).

Philip, m. by 14 Sep 1714, [-?-], mother of Joseph Hopkins (MCHR CL:322).

Richard, m. Mary, widow of Nathaniel Howell, and dau. of Richard Pullen. She m. 3rd, by 19 Aug 1703, George Browning, and 4th, on 26 Oct 1714, Matthew Howard (MWB 6:5, 50, 21:422; CELR 1:301; INAC 36C:128; KESH; KELR JS#W:45; ESVR 1:29, 39, 40).

KENNEDY
	Michael (Kanady), m. by 15 June 1709, [-?-], admx. of Thomas Messer of DO Co. (INAC 29:397).

KENNERLY
	Joshua, m. by 4 May 1710, Martha, dau. of Thomas Everendon of DO Co. (MWB 13:56).
	Joseph, miner, m. on 14 d. 9 m., 1711, Mary Stevens, both of DO Co., at Transquaking meeting house (TATH).

KENNETT
	Jasper, m. by 14 Feb 1718, Elizabeth, dau. of Richard Brightwell (PGLR F (Old 6), 765).

KENNY
	Darby, m. by 25 Nov 1710, Mary, extx. of James Willistone of QA Co. (INAC 32A:92, 33A:220).

KENT
	Absolom, m. by 20 Dec 1710, [-?-], dau. of William Wadsworth of CV Co. (MWB 13:200).
	Henry, Jr., m. by 12 April 1677, Martha, sister and extx. of Benjamin Brasseur of CV Co. (INAC 3:165).

KENTON
	William (Kenten), of Lancaster, VA, carpenter, m. on 13 d. 2 m., 1687, Mary Parratt, relict of Henry Parratt, dec., of TA Co. (TATH).
	William, carpenter, m. on 1 d. 3. m., 1698, Rebeckah Dudley, spinster, both of TA Co. (TATH).

KEON
	[-?-], m. by 1711, Hannah, widow of Lodowick Williams, and mother of Edward Williams (BALR TR#A:135).

KERBY
	Nathaniel, m. on 3 June 1707, Elizabeth Deale (AAAL 1:33).
	William, m. by 14 Oct 1717, Frances, admx. of Thomas Locar of SM Co. (INAC 39C:118).

KERSEY
	[-?-], m. by 7 Oct 1714, Mary, dau. of John Dickinson of TA Co. (MWB 14:582).
	[-?-], m. by 2 Feb 1717/8, Tabithey [Tabitha], dau. of John Shakley or Shekertie (MWB 14:523).
	John, m. on 8 Nov 1705, Elizabeth [-?-] (AAAN:19).
	Philip (Kersie), m. on 20 Dec 1710, Mary Alexander (TAPE). She was the acct. of John Alexander of TA Co. (INAC 32C:88, 33A:109).

KERWICK
[-?-], m. by 9 Jan 1696, Eliza, dau. of William Parrott of TA Co. (MWB 7:271).

KETERING
John, of SM Co., m., by Nov 1678, Rebecca, dau. and coheir of ?? (MDTP 10:323).

KEYS
John, m. by 11 Feb 1702, Elizabeth, widow and admx. of Henry Pennington of CE Co. (INAC 23:99).

KEYTON
Theophilus (Kitten?), m. by 1687, [-?-], relict of John Buck of AA Co. (MDTP 14A:17).

KIBBAL
[-?-], m. by 3 Oct 1705, Patience, dau. of James Wetherby, Sr. (MWB 13:44).

KIBBLE
John, m. on 27 Feb 1672, Abigail Horsey (SOLR:IKL).

KILBOURNE
[-?-], m. by 6 Feb 1698, Rachel, admx. of Robert Proctor of AA Co. (INAC 17:176).

[-?-] (Kilburne), d. by 4 March 1700, leaving a widow Rachel who was the mother of three daus.: (1) Rachel, wife of [-?-] Greenbury, (2) Comfort, wife of [-?-] Stimson, and (3) Ruth, wife of [-?-] Williams (AALR WT#1:118).

Charles (Kilburne), m. on 18 April 1708, Elizabeth Welply (Wellplay) (AAAN:7). She was the extx. of Andrew Wellpley of AA Co. (INAC 29:429). She was the widow of 1st, Andrew Norwood, and 2nd, Andrew Welply (MCHR PC:825).

Francis, of CH Co., m. by March 1670/1, Eliza, widow and admx. of Daniel (or Donnell) Johnson (*ARMD* 51:66, 379, 60:333, 65:69; MPL 16:595).

KILE
[-?-], m. by 18 March 1698/9, Flora, mother of Ralph Hawkins (MWB 6:231).

KILLETT
John, d. by 31 March 1686, having m. [-?-], sister of John Sewall? Swall? of CV Co. (MDTP 13:314).

KILLIARD
[-?-], m. by 17 Dec 1689, Mary, dau. of George Hamlin of SO Co. (MWB 6:37).

KILLINGSWORTH
[-?-], m. by 5 Jan 1709, Eliza, dau. of Jno. Wood of CH Co. (MWB 14:106).

KIMBALL
John, Jr., m. on 6 Nov 1717 by Mr. Sewell, Rebecca Atkins (CESS).
Richard, m. by Feb 1675, Joan, the relict of Alex'r Jemison, late of SO Co., dec.
(*ARMD* e89:19).

KIMBLE
Richard, m. on 18 Oct 1674, Jane Jemison (SOLR:IKL).

KING
[-?-], m. by 8 Sep 1705, Margaret, admx. of John Grigs of SM Co. (INAC 25:47).
[-?-], m. by 7 Nov 1716, Ann, dau. of Nicholas Cooper of CH Co. (MWB 14:193; INAC 37A:219).
Andrew, m. by 1 Sep 1705, Mary, relict and admx. of Benjamin Nobbs of TA Co. (INAC 25:425, 27:221, 28:234).
Elias, m. on 24 Dec 1699, Mary Tildon (KESP:43).
Francis, m. on 26 Sep 1717, Mary Sprigg, dau. of Col. Thomas Sprigg (PGQA:2).
Henry, of BA Co., m. by 15 April 1698, Tabitha, dau. of Jane Long of BA Co. (MDTP 17:87).
James, m. on 2 Sep 1708, Sarah Denny (KESP:43).
John, m. by 23 Aug 1666, Elizabeth, dau. of Andrew Skinner (TALR 5:78).
John, of Morumsco, m. on 11 Feb 1672, Elizabeth Crew (SOLR:IKL).
John, m. on 6 April 1687, Elizabeth Ballard (SOLR:IKL).
John, m. by June 1710, Ursley, admx. of Andrew Whittington, dec. (SOJU 1707-1711:420).
Mark, m. by 4 May 1671, Eliza, dau. of Robert Smith of TA Co. (MWB 1:466).
Peter, of CE Co., d. by 26 Dec 1713 having m. Susannah Slover (MWB 13:707).
Richard, m. by 2 Nov 1695, Katherine, heir (sister?) of Richard Charlett of Patuxent River (Hodges cites Pro. Court WRC#1:772).
Robert, m. by 13 June 1704, Mary, extx. or admx. of John Gibson of CH Co. (INAC 25:146).
Samuel of KE Co., m. by Jan 1668, [-?-], widow of Nicholas Pickard (*ARMD* 54:255).
Thomas, of BA Co., m. c1669/73, Joane Strand, who had immigrated from VA (MPL 17:443).
Thomas, of CH Co., m. by 17 Jan 1677, Joanna, mother of Eliza and Philip Jones (MWB 9:54).
William, m. by 22 Jan 1680, Margaret, relict of Ishmael Wright of CV Co. (INAC 7A:334; MDTP 4A:2).

KININGTON
Thomas, m. on 15 June 1695, Hannah Trego (HAGE:1).

KINGSBERRY
Dr. James, m. by 28 April 1705, Elizabeth, extx. of Richard Evans of CV Co. (INAC 25:60).

KINNEMONT
Joseph, m. on 29 June 1707 in St. Michael's parish, Margaret Ray, dau. of Alexander Ray and Anna his wife. In June 1708, Kinnemont was presented [indicted] that the said Anna Ray was his natural sister (TAJR 1706-1708).

KINSBY
Robert, m. on 1 Aug 1710, Mary Wood (HAGE:27).

KINSEY
Francis, m. on 14 Oct 1708, Margrett Morris (KESP:43).
Paul, m. by Dec 1661, [-?-], relict of William Bisse (MDTP 1E:26).

KIRBY
Thomas, m. by 1675, Mary Brown, dau. of William and Margaret Brown of SM Co. (Fresco cites Prov. Court NN:4).
William, m. by 17 Nov 1718, Frances, admx. of James Watts of SM Co. (MDAD 1:322).

KIRCOM
[-?-] (Kircam), m. by 2 Jan 1709, Africa, dau of Stephen Durdin, of TA Co. (MWB 13:20).
[-?-], m. by 7 Aug 1710, Alice, widow of Matthew Jenkins of TA Co., dec. (QALR ETA:73).

KIRK
[-?-], m. by 13 March 1695, Sarah, dau. of John Mackeele of DO Co. (MWB 7:209).
George, m. on 9 Dec 1705, Mary Hill [or Kilk] (AAJA:31 #21).
James (Kirke), m. by 15 July 1699, [-?-], dec., widow and admx. of William Spikeman (INAC 19:169).
John, d. by March 1678, having m. Mary, dau. of William Slade (MDTP 10:11).
John, m. by Nov 1684, Joan, dau. of Esther Hepworth or Hopworth of SO co. (*ARMD* 17:314).

KIRKHAM
James, planter, m. on 11 d. 6 m., 1703, Affrica Dordon, both of TA Co., at Tuckahoe Meeting House (TATH).

KNAP
Henry, m. by 16 Sep 1671, Mary, sister of John Parker of SO Co. (MWB 1:5109).

KNIGHT
Mr. Stephen, m. by lic. on 24 Feb 1708, by Rich. Sewell, Sarah Robinson (CESS).
Thomas, m. on 28 Nov 1718, Susanna Simpson (HAGE:37).

KNIGHTON

Thomas, m. by 2 Jan 1687, Dinah, sister of Seaborn Battee of AA Co.; she m. 2nd, by 1696, Anthony Smith (MWB 4:286; INAC 13B:15).

Thomas, m. on 3 Dec 1700, Dorothy Wood (AAJA:21#13).

KNOTT

Francis, may have m. by 2 April 1662, [-?-], dau. of Robert Cole of St. Clement's Bay, SM, Co., who called Knott his son-in-law (MWB 1:182).

KNOWLAND

Stephen, m. by 31 March 1708, Mary, admx. of Dennis Connell of CH Co. (INAC 28:119).

LABAT

David, m. by Aug 1703, Ruth, admx. of John Boyce of AA Co. (AAJU G:192).

LABEY

Thomas, m. on 6 Aug 1708, Sarah Pindell (AALR 1:36).

LACECY

John, m. on 25 March 1706, Mary Vinicomb (AAAL 1:32(2)).

LADD

Richard, Gent., m. by Nov 1673, Rosamond, extx. of Joseph Horsley, dec., of CV Co. (*ARMD* 51:190 65:138; INAC 5:71).

LADDEMORE

Alexander, m. by 16 July 1700, Mary, dau. of Thomas Wildes of TA Co. (INAC 20:40).

LAERTHY

Philip, m. on 18 May 1703, Cath. Toomey (KESP:45).

LAKE

Henry, on 13 Nov 1683, banns of matrimony were published for him and Mary Cooke, both servants of Thos. Cottingham (SOJU O#7:11). Henry, m. on 25 Dec 1683, Mary Cooke (SOLR:IKL).

LAKING

Abraham, m. on 10 Oct 1717, Martha Lee (PGQA:1).

LAMB

Francis, m. on 3 April 1714, Rosamond Beck (KESP:45).

John, merchant, 25 July 1701, Elizabeth Belt, widow of John (AAAL 1:21 (1)).

John, m. on 16 April 1703, Katherine Galloway (AAMA:81).

LAMBERT

[-?-], m. by 8 Aug 1713, Ann, relict of John Cowell of MD (AALR IB#2:114).

John, m. by 15 Jan 1664, Eliza (or Ellinor), dau. of John Nevill (MWB 1:222). Elsewhere she is named as Ellinor, dau. of John Nevill (*ARMD* 60:49, 278; CHLR D:74).

John, on 13 April 1676, was about to marry Sarah Barker, to whom he conveyed a half parcel of land (CHLR F:182).

LAMPTON

Mark, of CH Co., m. by 1708, Ann, dau. of John and Margaret Tant of SM Co. (MWB 11:274, 12:327; SMWB PC#1:300).

LAMPIN

Thomas, of SO Co., m. by 1673, Elizabeth, mother of Elizabeth Crowder (MPL LL:819).

LANCASTER

Henry (Lankaster), m. on 15 Jan 1697, by Rev. Richard Sewell, Anne Satchell, widow (CESS).

LAND

[-?-], m. by 1695, Penelope, widow and admx. of Richard Long (Cotton cites INAC 10:389).

George, m. by 4 April 1709, Dianah, relict and admx. of John Ford of CV Co. (INAC 29:138).

John, m. by Nov 1708, Katherine, admx. of Edward Boarman (MDTP 21:74).

LANE

[-?-], m. by 1 Feb 1711, Frances, dau. of Thomas Roe, Sr., of QA Co. (MWB 13:408).

[-?-], m. by 10 Sep 1713, [-?-], dau. of Richard Harrison of CV Co. (MWB 14:142).

Dennis, m. on 26 April 1702, Honora [-?-] (TAPE).

Dutton, m. by 5 Feb 1683, Pretiosa, dau. of Richard Tydings (BALR TB#E:522).

George, m. on 20 Oct 1678, Dennis [*sic*] Fountaine (SOLR:IKL).

John, m. by 1683, Mary, admx. of John Markes (*ARMD* 70:333; MDTP 13:423).

Samuel, physician of AA Co., Gent., m. by 14 June 1679, Margaret, relict and admx. of John Burridge of AA Co. (INAC 6:136; MDTP 4A:9).

Timothy, m. on 11 April 1674, Mary Ball (SOLR:IKL).

Timothy, m. by 12 Dec 1696, Margaret, relict and extx. of Capt. Henry Alexander of TA Co. (INAC 14:50; TAJR AD#8:469, 575).

Walter, m. on 16 April 1684, Sarah Wilson (SOLR:IKL).

LANG

John, m. on 1 Jan 1712, Catherine Howard (AAJA:41 #13).

LANGFORD
John, m. on 24 Aug 1714, Ann Ralph (WIST).

LANGLEY
Charles, m. by July 1698, Ann, relict and extx. of John Brashere of CV Co. (MDTP 17:173).

LANGREENE
James, m. on 1 Dec 1684, Alce Primme? (SOLR:IKL).

LANGWORTH
James, m. by 7 June 1656, Agatha, sister of William Johnson of SM Co. (MWB 1:120, 133).
William, of SM Co., m. by 7 Feb 1693, Mary, dau. of Thomas Hussey (MWB 2:282; Fresco cites SMWB PC#1:86 to show that he m. by 1693, Ann, sister of Thomas Luckett of SM Co.).

LANHAM
[-?-], m. by 18 May 1686, Barbara, dau. of James Ringgold of KE Co. (MWB 4:232).
[-?-] (Lenham), m. by 11 Dec 1713, Mary, dau. of Thomas Dickeson of PG Co. (MWB 18:340; PGLR F (Old 6):545).
John, Jr., m. on 14 Feb 1708, by Henry Acton, Justice of the Peace for PG Co., Mary Dickinson (PGKG:245).
Josias, m. between 1686 and 1695, Barbara, dau. of James Ringgold. She also m. Edward Blay (MWB 4:232; MDTP 16:84).

LANSLY
Charles, m. by 10 March 1697, Ann, extx. of John Brasseur of CV Co. (INAC 16:73).

LANT
Lawrence, m. by Feb 1718/9, [-?-], extx. of Joseph Edwards of SM co. (MDTP 23:310).

LARAMORE
[-?-] (Larrimore), m. by 12 March 1700, Eliza, dau. of Henry Eldezly of CE Co. (MWB 11:45).
Roger, m. by lic. on 17 Feb 1707, Margaret Dare, Jr. (CESS).
Thomas (Laremore), m. on 4 Aug 1680, Katherine [-?-] (SOLR:IKL).
Thomas, m. by 14 July 1710, [-?-], extx. of Robert Hopkins, Sr., of SO Co. (INAC 31:276).

LARGE
Robert, m. by 4 March 1671, Elisabeth, widow of John Stockes of SM CV Co. (MDTP 5:245).

LARKIN
Jeremiah, m. on 16 Aug 1702, Margaret Brown (AAJA:25#19).
Nicholas, m. on 14 Feb 1709/10, Margaret Gott (AAJA:38 #24).
Thomas (Larkins), m. 20 Sep 1697, Margritt Gassaway (AAAL 1:6).

LARY
Darby, m. by 26 Oct 1709, Sarah, extx. of Darby Hern of KE Co. (INAC 31:54).

LASHL(E)Y
[-?-], m. by 16 Nov 1703, Alice, widow of John Chapman (MWB 3:99).
John, m. by 15 Sep 1704, Alice, extx. or admx. of John Chipman of PG Co. (INAC 25:148).

LATCHAM
[-?-], m. by 6 Oct 1710, Eliza, dau. of Richard Tull of SO Co. (MWB 13:258).

LATEN
Will., m. on 13 March 1669, Sarah Shirtt, widow (*ARMD* 54:601).

LATHAM
Joshua (Lathom), m. by banns on 30 Aug 1716, by Matt. Vanderheyden, Mary Kare, widow (CESS). She was the admx. of Thomas Kar (MDAD 1:351).

LATHAN
Joshua, m. by banns on 16 Feb 1714/5, by Mr. Sewell, Anne Laurance (CESS).

LATTIMORE
James, m. by 29 Dec 1697, Mary, dau. of Randolph Brandt of CH Co. (MWB 6:232).
William, of KE Co., m. by Feb 1709/10, [-?-], widow of Christian Christian, who had m. [-?-], sister of Gerardus Wessells (MDTP 21:2080.

LAVONE
Dennis, m. on 7 Nov 1709, Catherine Waley (TAPE).

LAWE
Richard, on 14 March 1675/6, banns of matrimony were published for him and Anne Smith (SOJU O#7:39).

LAWES
John, on 13 June 1671, banns of matrimony were published for him (certificate was given 4 July 1671) and Katherine Nelson, widow (SOJU DT#7:133). She was the widow of John Nelson and mother of John and Bridget Nelson (*ARMD* e 87 (SOJU AZ#8):177-178).

LAWLER
David, m. in 1715, Elizabeth Polson (AAAN:22).
Henry (Lawlor), m. on 6 July 1704, Bridget Carmacker (KESP:45).

LAWRENCE
[-?-], m. by 8 Jan 1716, Mary, dau. of James Willson of QA Co. (MWB 14:593).
Benjamin, son of Benjamin and Elizabeth, m. on 6 d., 11 m. (Jan), 1702, Rachel Mariarte, dau. of Edward and Honor, of AA Co. (WRMM; INAC 25:414).
Henry, in May 1672, banns of matrimony were published for him and Elizabeth Williams (SOJU AZ#8:84). Henry m. on 4 July 1672, Elizabeth Williams (SOLR:IKL).
Henry, m. by 2 May 1682, Frances, extx. of Henry Hyde (*ARMD* 70:193). She was a dau. of John Goss of SM Co. (Warrant Record CB#1:258).
John, carpenter, m. on 9 d. 7 m., 1702, Martha Wilson, both of TA Co. at Tuckahoe Meeting House (TATH).
Richard, m. on 25 Dec 1702, Constance Merry (KESP:45).
Richard, m. on 21 Dec 1704, Mary Wilson (KESP:45).
William, m. by 22 Jan 1663, Mary, dau. of Anne Beach (PCLR BB:111).
William, m. by 2 Oct 1669, Mary, relict of William Elliott of KE Co. (MDTP 4A:1).

LAWS
John, of SO Co., m. by 8 Feb 1674/5, [-?-], relict of John Nelson of SO Co. (MDTP 6:348).

LAWYER
William, m. by 30 Oct 1696, Grace, admx. of John Barnes of DO Co. (INAC 14:67).

LAXTON
Thomas, m. on 14 Sep 1708, Elizabeth Wilson of PG Co. (AAJA:36 #2).

LAYFIELD
George, m. by Aug 1693, Ann, extx. of William Stevens. In Sep 1693 she is called Elizabeth (SOJU LD:20, 39). George, m. by 25 Nov 1695, Elizabeth, extx. and sole heiress of William Stevens (SOLR 7:363).
George, of Pocomoke, SO Co., m. by 27 March 1703, Priscilla, dau. of John White (MWB 3:497).

LAYHER
William, m. on 20 Nov 1707, Mary Joyner (KESP:45).

LAZELL
Michael, m. on 26 Dec 1705, Martha Cook (KESP:45).

LAZZEIUR
    Joseph, 19 April 1702, Susanna Webb (AAAL 1:21(2)).

LEACHMAN
    Andrew, m. on 8 May 1712, by Rev. Jona. White, Ellinor Burke (PGQA:2).

LEAGE
    John, m. on 31 Oct 1703, Elizabeth Millin (AAJA:28#4).

LEAK(E)
    Henry, m. on 7 June 1705, Elizabeth Ward (AAAL 1:27). She was a dau. of Robert Ward of AA Co. (MWB 2, pt. 12:192).
    Robert (Leake), m. by 1711, Jane, dau. of John and Abigail Pritchett of DO Co.; she m. 2nd, Timothy Macnamara (MWB 17:322; MDTP 24:308).

LEAKINS
    John, m. by 18 Sep 1703, Elisabeth, admx. of John Enlow of BA Co. (INAC 24:235).

LEBATT
    David, m. by 29 April 1703, Ruth, admx. of John Boyce of TA Co. (INAC 23:32).

LeCOMPTE
    Anthony, m. c1661, Esther Dottando (Doatloan, Dotlando) of Dieppe, Normandy (Fresco cites SMWB PC#1:53; Prov. Court TL#2:722)
    Peter, m. by 10 June 1717, Elizabeth, dau. of Rebecca Brannock (DOLR 7 Old:49).

LEE
    Charles, m. by 1718, Mary, dau. of William and Barbara (Johnson) Fielder (Fresco cites MDTP 24:162; SMWB PC#1:240).
    Edward, 2 Oct 1701, Anne Vandobender (AAAL 1:21(2)).
    Hugh, m. by 1650, Hannah, widow of Richard or Robert Heuett; Lee was d. by 30 July 1663, and his widow m. William Price (*ARMD* 49:35, 54:22, 57:177; MPL 3:17, ABH:44, 6:216; KELR A:98).
    James Lee was presented by the CH Co. Jury of Inquest on 1 Oct 1662 for having two wives (*ARMD* 53:217).
    James, m. by 15 May 1707, Margaret, admx. of John Wilson, Jr. of AA Co. (INAC 26:312).
    John, m. on 2 May 1706, Ann Green (KESP:45).
    Oliver, m. on 6 Feb 1708, Ellinor Barker (TAPE).
    Philip, m. by 29 Dec 1713, Sarah, dau. of Thomas Brooke (PGLR F:312).
    Richard, m. on 25 d. 8 m., 1668, Joan Lippett, both of TA Co., at the house of Peter Sharp (TATH).
    Robert, m. on 16 April 1704, Elizabeth Munday (CVCH).

Samuel, m. by Feb 1694/5, Susanna, admx. of Edward Baxter of SM Co. (MDTP 15C:276; INAC 14:148).

Thomas, m. by 18 Nov 1693, Jane Farrington, dau. of Robert Farrington, dec., and Anne, who m. 2nd, Robert Morecocke (TALR LL#7:53).

Thomas, m. by Dec 1699, Alice, extx. of William Burman (MDTP 18A:58).

Thomas, m. on 8 May 1701, Elizabeth Shelds (HAGE:11).

William, m. by May 1676, Judith, relict of James Chancelor of CH Co. (MDTP 8A:102).

LEES

Thomas, m. by 6 April 1685, Eliza, dau. of Thomas Doxey of SM Co. (MWB 4:132).

Thomas, m. on 2 Jan 1704/05, Mary Symmons (AAJA:30 #8).

LEG

William, m. by 18 June 1715, Penelope, dau. of Thomas Tanner of QA Co. (INAC 36B:162).

LEGO

Benjamin, m. by 25 Sep 1707, Mary, extx. of William Hill of BA Co. (INAC 27:211).

LEIGH

John, m. by 5 Oct 1717, Dorothy, dau. of Christina Barbara Cooper, widow, of SM Co. (MWB 14:651).

LEISETT

[-?-], m. by Oct 1688, Ann, relict of Thomas Colsen or Cosden of CV Co. (MDTP 14:116).

LEISITCH

[-?-] (Leisitch?), m. by March 1688/9, Margaret, widow of John Blomfield (MDTP 14:137).

LEMARE

John (Lemaire), m. by 1 Dec 1683, Margaret, dau. of Archibald Wahob of Portobacco, CH Co. (MWB 4:23; MDTP 13:78). She was a sister of Elizabeth, wife of Philip Hopkins of CH Co. (MDTP 14:72-73).

LEMARR

John, m. on 21 Jan 1714, Susanna Tyler (PGQA:1)

LEMASTER

John, m. by 30 July 1711, Christian, extx. of Samuel Cooksey of CH Co. (INAC 32B:267).

LENNOX
Richard, m. by 6 March 1705/6, Mary Richardson (BALR IR#AM:40).

LEONARDSON
Leonard, of SM Co., in his will dated 24 March 1640, named his mother as Alice Cales (MWB 1:5).

LESTER
Peter, m. on 8 May 1713 [-?-] [-?-] (HAGE:31).

LETCHWORTH
Joseph, m. by 8 March 1675, Mary, dau. of Robert Skinner of CV Co. (MWB 4:230).

LETTON
Richard, m. on 18 April 1689, at the home of Ann Lambot, widow, Honor Durdin, widow (WRMM).

LEVITT
Robert, marriage contract dated 12 Aug 1713, with Elizabeth Clarke, widow, sister-in-law of Benjamin Lawrence of AA Co. who posted bond (PGLR F:368).

LEWEN
Richard, and Mary Child, with consent of Henry Child, filed their intentions to marry on 30 d., 9 m., 1705, and 28 d., 10 m., 1705 (WRMMa).
Robert, banns of marriage pub. 30 June 1668 for him and Anne Nolton (*ARMD* 54:712; SOLR O#1:116).

LEWES
[-?-], m. by 28 April 1709, Sarah, dau. of Rowland Beavens of SO Co. (MWB 12, pt. 2:100).
Thomas, m. on 3 June 1695, Anne Parsons (SOLR:IKL).

LEWIN, Robert. See William Stevens.

LEWIS
[-?-], m. by 12 June 1716, Eliza, dau. of Eliz. Hawkins, widow of CH Co. (MWB 14:510).
Charles, m. by 1 Nov 1709, [-?-], dau. of William Troth, planter, of TA Co. (MWB 13:178).
Henry, of AA Co., on 12 June 1677, banns of matrimony were published for him and Elizabeth Boston of SO Co. (SOLR O#7:100r). Henry, m. by 8 April 1686, Abigail, extx. of Robert Thomas of SM Co. (INAC 9:31, 217; 13A:257).
Henry of BA Co., m. by 13 Dec 1700, Sarah, dau. and heir of William Jones who d. leaving a will dated 22 March 1684 (AALR WT#1:105, WT#2:527).

James, m. by 2 Sep 1686, Katherine, extx. of Edmond Townhill of AA Co. (INAC 9:327).

John, m. by 17 Feb 1703, Ann, extx. of Joseph Pettibone of AA Co. (MWB 3:132).

John, of DO Co., cooper, m. on 2 April 1717, Elizabeth Winsley (AAAN:292).

Thomas, m. on 14 Feb 1702, Eliner Stoaks (KESP:45).

William, had a license on 2 Nov 1638, declared his intention to marry Ursula Gifford, and swore there was no impediment to their marriage (*ARMD* 1:133; MPL 1:133).

William, m. by (date not given), Katherine, admx. of Joseph Saratt of PG Co. (INAC 38A:117).

William, m. by May 1707, Ann, extx. of Joseph Pettibone (AAJU TB#1:561).

LEYCOCKE
John, m. by 16 July 1694, Elizabeth, relict of John Talley (MDTP 15C:108).

LIBBEY
John, m. on 1 Jan 1712, Amy [Emy] Elizabeth Cathrop (TAPE). She was a sister of Lemmon John Catrup (TALR 12:273).

LICENCE
Peter, m. on 27 Dec 1711, Elizabeth Waney (AALR 1:38).

LIDDELL
William, m. by 10 Aug 1697, Jane, relict of Nicholas Terrett (MDTP 17:26).

LIDYATE
John, of CV Co., d. by 20 March 1693/4, having m. Jane, widow of Edward Hurlock (MDTP 15C:36).

LIFELY
Marke, m. on (date not given), Sarah Hancock (AAAN:22).

LIGHT
John, m. in 1680, Elizabeth Greene (SOLR:IKL).

LILE
[-?-], m. by 30 Nov 1674, Mary, relict and admx. of Michael Farmer of CV Co. (INAC 1:135).

LILLINGTON
[-?-] (Lillingston), m. by 23 Dec 1695, Mary, sister of Jane Coursey of TA Co. (MWB 7:229).

John (Lillingston), m. by April 1682, Margaret, relict of Matthew Ward of TA Co. (Warrant Record CB#1:212).

John, m. by May 1689, Elizabeth, relict of John Taylor of BA Co. (MDTP 14:148).

LIMES
Robert, m. on 22 June 1712, Margaret Stevens (AAJA:42 #3).

LINCKHORNE
John, m. on 3 Sep 1687 by Rev. Richard Sewell, Elizabeth Browning (CESS).

LINDSEY
David, in 1676, banns of matrimony were published for him and Sarah Connard (SOLR O#7:54r). On 17 Sep 1676 Philip Connard father of Sarah, forbade the banns, then gave his consent (SOLR O#7:59r). David, m. on 5 Oct 1676, Sarah Connard (SOLR:IKL).

John, m. by 22 Oct 1689, Elizabeth, mother of Thomas Chitterley (TALR NN#6:1).

Thomas, m. by Nov 1680, Katherine, widow of 1st, William Stanley, who left three small children, and 2nd, widow and admx. of Robert Morrice of CE Co. (MDTP 13:113; Warrant Record CB#1:94).

Thomas (Lyndsey), m. by 1 Oct 1688, Jane or Joan, widow of Richard Jones, and mother of Richard and Anne Jones; she was also relict of Robert Potts (INAC 10:160; CHLR Q:18, 60).

LINES
Thomas, m. 4 March 1702, Elizabeth Vincett (AAAL 1:26).

LINLEY
John, m. on 13 June 1708, Mary Webb (KESP:45).

LINSEY
[-?-], m. by 21 Jan 1693, Jane, sister of Ellinor Corkerin and of Thomas Buttler (MWB 7:15),

Thomas, m. by 16 Aug 1684, Katherine, admx. of Robert Morris of CE Co. (INAC 8:213).

LINTHICUM
Ezikia (Linsicom), m. 5 Oct 1697, Milcah Francis (AAAL 1:5).

Thomas, m. by 1651, Deborah, dau. of Simon and Madaline Abott of SM Co.; she also m. either before or after Linthicum, Leonard Wayman (Fresco cites Warrants 4:68; Prov. Court PL#8:479).

Thomas (Linsicom), m. 22 June 1698, Deborah Wayman (AAAL 1:7).

LINTON
[-?-], m. by 7 Aug 1716, Susannah, dau. of William Parsons of Town Point, CE Co. (MWB 14:299).

LIPER
    Edgar, m. on 30 Oct 1713, Elizabeth Pritchet (HAGE:30).

LIPTROT
    Jno., m. on 2 Sep 1704, Mary Lunt (TAPE).

LISTER
    Thomas, m. in Sep 1682, Abigail London (SOLR:IKL).

LITTLE
    [-?-], m. by April 1680, Elizabeth, widow of David Holt, who died and left four small children, and who was the son of Thomas Holt (Warrant Record CB#1:159).
    [-?-] (Litle), m. by 12 Jan 1689, Hester, dau. of Anthony Arnold of AA Co. (MWB 2:204; INAC 11A:5).
    Samuel, m. by 22 July 1717, Elisabeth, admx. of James Maccoby of CV Co. (INAC 39C:44).
    Thomas, and Elizabeth Day filed their intentions to marry on 7 d., 5 m., 1710, and 2 d., 7 m., 1710 (WRMMa).

LITTON
    Edward (Litten), m. by 1688, Catherine, sister of John Acton (MWB 6:1; MDTP 17:289).
    Richard, m. by Aug 1693, [-?-], admx. of John Darden of AA Co. (MDTP 15A:64).

LITTOUR
    Richard, m. by c1693, Honora, relict and admx. of John Durdaine of AA Co. (INAC 10:360).

LIUGE
    Michael, of CH Co., d. by 10 March 1709, when his admx. Mary had m. Henry Justis (INAC 31:76).

LLEWELLIN
    John, of SM Co., m. by Dec 1678, Audria [-?-] (Hodges cites Judg. 7:160).
    John, m. by Oct 1692, Audrey, widow of William Cocks (*ARMD* 8:397).
    Richard, son of John and Audrey, m. by 1706, Jane Orrill (Fresco cites MDTP 19C:118, MPL C#3:2; Prov. Court WRC#1:216).
    Samuel (Luellen), m. on 10 March 1684, Anne Kelly (SOLR:IKL).

LLOYD
    [-?-], m. by 27 Nov 1683, Henrietta Maria, widow of [-?-] Bennett, dau. of James Neale (MWB 4:40). She was the dau. of Ann Neale, sister of James and Anthony Neale, and mother of Richard Bennett and of Philemon Lloyd (MDTP 17:92).
    [-?-], m. by 14 Feb 1710/11, Sarah, dau. of Nehemiah Covington of SO Co. (MWB 13:549).

Edward, m. by 11 Aug 1681, Grace, widow of William Parker of St. Mary's Whitechapel, Mddx., whose dau. Elizabeth m. by that date Henry Buckerfield (PCLR WRC:209/221).

John, m. by 12 Oct 1702, Hannah, dau. of William Crump, dec. (KELR JD#1:93).

Capt. Philemon, m. by 26 July 1675, [-?-], legatee of Henry Hawkins of TA Co. (INAC 1:384).

Philemon, m. on 11 April 1709, Mrs. Margaret Freeman "so called" (AAAN:7). She was the admx. of Mr. John Freeman (MDTP 22:73).

William, m. on 9 April 1707, Grisell Johnston (PGKG:241).

LOCK

Daniel, m. on 5 Aug 1718, (Mary) Ducker (TAPE).

Dr. William (Loch), m. on 18 Sep 1710, Mary Biggs (AAJA:39 #9). Dr. William (Loch), of AA Co., chirurgeon, m. by 10 Nov 1710, Mary, relict of Seth Biggs (INAC 32A:81, 33A:237; AALR IB#2:259).

LOCKER

John, m. on 31 Aug 1713, Magdalen Ray (PGKG:254).

Thomas, m. on 13 Jan 1716, Elinor Evans (PGKG:246).

LOCKERMAN

Jacob (Lookerman), m. on 26 April 1711, Magdalen Edmondson (TAPE). She was the relict and admx. of James Edmondson, and a dau. of Dorothy Stevens and sister of John Stevens of DO Co.; she m. Edmondson by 10 March 1713 (TALR RF#12:55; MDTP 22:450; MDAD 1:98; QALR ETA:198; *ARMD 77:152*; TAJR FT#1).

LOCKWELL

Thomas, m. on 11 July 1703, Massy Fortune (TAPE).

Thomas, m. on 25 Nov 1718, Mary Barrett (TAPE).

LOCKWOOD

Robert, m. by Nov 1671, Ellinor, extx. of Nicholas Waterman of AA Co. (MDTP 5:131).

Robert, m. by Aug 1686, [-?-], mother of Francis Price, infant, who had been named exec. of Robert Phillips of AA Co. (MDTP 13:387).

LODERFORRESTER

Peter, m. on 30 Nov 1704, Mary Nelson (AAAL 1:27).

LOGGINS

Thomas, of TA Co. m. by 30 May 1676, Elizabeth, widow of John Henrix, and mother of John, Thomas and Henry Henrix (MDTP 8A:108; TALR 4:117).

LOGON

Alexander, m. on 12 May 1711, Christian Grant (AAAN:9).

LOGOZ

Barnaby, m. on 19 Nov 1704, Mary [-?-], of PG Co. (AAAN:19).

LOKER

Thomas, m. by 25 July 1700, Frances, dau. of William Aisquith of SM Co. (MWB 15:55).

LOLLAR

Henry (or Lolly), m. by 14 June 1705, [-?-], widow and extx. or admx. of Dennis Carmack of CE Co. (INAC 25:382).

LOMAX

Aaron, m. by 18 May 1711, [-?-], admx. of Thomas Palmer of PG Co. (INAC 32C:153).

Osborne, m. by 1683, Elizabeth Smith, extx. of Archibald Waughop (Fresco cites MWB 1:127; INAC 19:158; *MHM* 16:304).

LONEY

William, m. by 13 April 1703, Jane, dau. of Thomas Overton (BALR RM#HS:386, HW#2:220).

LONG

[-?-], m. by 4 Jan 1716, Susannah, dau. of Francis Meed of AA Co. (MWB 14:441).

[-?-], m. by 2 Sep 1717, Eliz., dau. of George Powell of QA Co. (MWB 14:393).

Samuel, m. on 15 Feb 1667, Jane Michell or Minshall (SOLR:IKL).

Samuel, m. on 22 Feb 1693/4, Elizabeth King (SOLR:IKL).

Thomas, m. on 29 Dec 1709, Elizabeth Nun (TAPE).

LONGLEY

Joseph, m. on 27 Feb 1708, Rachel Roberts (KESP:45).

LONGMAN

Daniel, of AA Co., m. by 1686, Martha, widow of Richard Arnold (MDTP 13:309).

LORD

James, m. by 13 Sep 1700, Judith, admx. of Samuel Martin of TA Co., who was the eldest son of Thomas Martin (INAC 31:89; Warrant Record AA#1:168).

LORKITT

John, m. by 19 Sep 1692, [-?-], dau. of Richard Green [Gwinn?] of BA Co. (MWB 6:48).

LOSLEY

Henry (Loallis), m. by 14 June 1705, [-?-], widow of Dennis Cormack of CE Co. (INAC 25:118).

LOUDRIDGE

William, m. on 20 March 1674, Katherine Jones (SOLR:IKL).

LOUGHTON

Joseph, m. on 4 Aug 1701, Mary Smith (KESP:45).

LOVE

John, m. on 10 Feb 1704, Mary [-?-] (TAPE).

John [Jone], m. on 26 June 1713, Anne Preston (TAPE). She was a dau. of John Preston (MCHR CL:23).

John, m. in 1718, Rebecca Stapleford (TAPE).

Thomas, m. by April 1683, [-?-], dau. of John and Judith Goldsmith (Fresco cites SMWB PC#1:44).

Thomas, m. by March 1684/5, Lucie, widow of Samuel Dobson of SM Co. (MDTP 13:223).

William, m. on 27 April 1706, Arabella Walston (HAGE:18).

William, m. on 2 Jan 1710, Anne Bell (TAPE).

LOVEDIE

John, m. on 11 April 1703, Sarah Harden (TAPE).

LOVLY

Deliverance, of KE Co., m. on 24 Aug 1658, Eliz. Ward (*ARMD* 54:129). She was a widow of Thomas Ward (MPL Q:359).

LOWD

Thomas, m. on 18 April 1703, Catherine Gilmor (TAPE).

LOWDEN

Thomas, m. on (date not given), Eliza Walker (PGKG:242).

LOWE

Charles, m. by 20 June 1700, [-?-], relict of Thomas Johnson of SO Co. (INAC 19½B:156).

Henry, m. by 4 Sep 1688, Susanna Maria, widow of John Darnall (INAC 14:117). Other sources say she was a dau. of Nicholas Allome (MPL 32:593). If she was the widow of John Darnall, she was a dau. of Henrietta Maria Lloyd (INAC 10:230; 14:117; CELR 1:125).

John, m. on 2 d. 12 m., 1700, Mary Bartlett, both of TA Co., at Readhaven [*sic;* more likely Treadhaven] meeting house (TATH). She was a dau. of Thomas Bartlett of TA Co. (MWB 13:451; MWB 13:451).

Marshall, m. by 4 Nov 1707, Mary, extx. of William Guyther of SM Co., and of Robert Crane of SM Co. (INAC 27:232, 233).

Col. Nicholas, m. by 1676, Elizabeth, dau. of Edward Roe of "Dover" (Fresco cites MWB 15 5:58, 15:248; Rent Rolls of TA and QA Cos.)

Thomas (Loe), m. by 24 April 1702, Elizabeth, admx. of John Sheilds of BA Co. (INAC 21:372).

Thomas, m. by Oct 1713, [-?-], admx. of George Snowden of SM Co. (MDTP 22:269).

Vincent, m. by 2 Dec 1674, Eliza, dau. of Seth Foster of TA Co. (MWB 2:348, 6:7; MDTP 7:25).

William, m. by 22 July 1707, Anne, dau. of Abraham Delap of BA Co. (INAC 27:28).

William (Lough), m. on 6 July 1710, Temperance Pickett (HAGE:27).

LOWRIE

William, m. by 14 July 1709, [-?-], dau. of Robert Jarvis, mentioned in acct. of John Ford (INAC 29:391).

LOYD

John, m. by 11 Sep 1695, Hannah, legatee of William Crump (KELR GL#1:2c).

Richard, m. by 1665, [-?-], widow of Thomas Phillips (MPL 8:482).

LUCAS

Charles, m. on 20 Nov 1718, Eliza Evans (PGQA:2).

LUCKETT

[-?-], m. by 6 Feb 1699, Eliza, dau. of Thomas Hussey of CH Co. (MWB 11:43).

Samuel, of CH Co., m. by Aug 1686, [-?-], admx. of John Gardiner (MDTP 13:405).

Samuel, Sr., of CH Co., d. by 28 April 1709, when his extx. Elizabeth had m. John Hanson, Jr. (INAC 29:234).

Thomas Hussey, m. by 23 Dec 1717, Elizabeth, dau. of Juliana Price, widow (CHLR H#2:140).

LUDDALL

William, m. by 4 Jan 1698, Jane, admx. of Nicholas Terrett of AA Co. (INAC 17:152).

LUDDINGHAM

John, of TA Co., m. by 6 Jan 1717, Mary, sister of Henry Henrix (MWB 14:556).

LUDLEE

William, m. in Jan 1713/14, Eliz. Trott (AAJA:44 #13).

LUDLUM

William, m. on 13 Jan 1703, Sarah Little (AAJA:28#8).

LUDWIG
William, m., by 10 Aug 1715, Elisabeth, admx. of Thomas Trott of AA Co. (INAC 36B:233).

LUELLIN
[-?-], m. on 2 July 1702, by Mr. Nobbs, minister, Mary [-?-] (TAPE).

LUFF
Stephen (Lufte), m. by Jan 1682. Sarah, widow of Charles Ballard, and mother of Arnold Elzey (MDTP 13:1, 9). She was also a mother Jarvis Ballard of DO Co. (DOLR 6 Old:37).

LUMBROZO
Dr. Jacob, married by 1666, Elizabeth Wiles (George Ely Russell, "Portuguese and Spanish Colonists in 17th Century Maryland." *TAG* 76 (April 2001): 139-140).

LUMOS
Aaron (or Lumas), m. by 26 Aug 1710, Elizabeth, widow of Thomas Palmer of PG Co. (INAC 32B:30, 33A:115).

LUNN
Edward, of AA Co., m. by Sep 1679, Elizabeth, relict of William Cooke (MDTP 11:194).
Thomas, m. by 27 March 1679, Dianah, relict of Oliver Holloway (*ARMD* 51:269).

LUSBY
John, m. on 1 July 1702, Eleanor Cross (AAAN:1).
Robert, m. by 20 Sep 1700, [-?-], dau. of Stephen Johnson of BA Co. (MWB 11:150).
Robert, m. on 21 Aug 1707, Mary Baldwin (AAAN:1). She was a dau. of John Baldwin, Gent., of AA Co. (MWB 14:30).
Robert, m. by 8 April 1718, Mary, dau. of Lawrence Draper of BA Co. (MWB 13:559).

LUSTHEAD
Richard, a passenger on the Ark/Dove, m. by 10 March 1650/1, [-?-], a sister of Luke Gardiner (MPL 1:168).

LYAL
John, m. on 2 Feb 1717, Ann Muture (HAGE:67).

LYFOOT
[-?-], m. by 2 Feb 1697, Eliza, dau. of Thomas Hillery of CV Co. (MWB 7:321).

LYLE

Samuel, m. by 15 Feb 1699, Ann, dau of John Sallers of CV Co. (MWB 6:353).
William, d. by 9 Oct 1696, leaving a relict and admx. Priscilla, who had m. Henry Dykes, and 3rd, Edward Ball (INAC 14:85, 86, 19:166, which gives Henry's name as Dukes).

LYNN

Francis, d. by 5 March 1714, having m. Marjery, admx. of Richard Thomas and of John Thomas of CH Co. (INAC 36B:95, 99).
Michael, m. by 16 March 1699 Mary, dau. of the dec. wife of Robert Benson of CH Co. (MWB 6:369).

LYON

Daniel, m. on 30 Sep 1708, Mary Rouse (AAJA:36 #4).

LYTFOOT

Thomas, m. by 29 April 1685, Rebecca, dau. of John Larkin; she m. 2nd, Thomas Hammond (BALR RM#HS:417; INAC 13B:23, 24; MWB 5:186).

M'ALPINE

Andrew, m. on 24 Feb 1718, Deliverance Pomfret (AAAN:36).

M'CAN

Edward, m. by 18 Jan 1708, Elisabeth, extx. of David Murphey of KE Co. (INAC 29:82).

M'CANAN

Cornelius, m. on 13 March 1708/9, Ann Thornton (AAJA:36 #14).

M'CARTY

Daniel (Mackarte), banns pub. on 25 Dec 1703, m. on 23 Jan 1703/4, [-?-] Woolsher (HAGE:17).
Daniel (Mackarte), m. on 15 April 1707, Elizabeth Matthews (KESP:48).
Daniel, m. on 20 Jan 1714, Sarah Morris (HAGE:33).
John (Mecartee), m. on 29 May 1718, Elizabeth Taylor (TAPE).

M'CHALY

Thomas, 23 Dec 1701, Elizabeth Ridgely (AAAL 1:21(2)).

M'CLAYLAND

Fenley, m. on 6 Oct 1704, Ann Wadson (TAPE).

M'CLENAHAN

Thomas, m. by 7 Sep 1705, Elizabeth, dau. of Thomas Crompton (TALR 10:32).

M'CLESTER
Joseph, m. by April 1711, [-?-], extx. of James Dashiell of SO Co. (MDTP 21:340).

M'COMAS
Alexander, m. on 19 Nov 1713 Elizabeth Day (SJSG:20R).

MACONCHIE
Rev. William, m. by 12 Dec 1713, Mary, dau. of John Hanson of CH Co. (MWB 13:719).

M'CRAH
Owen, m. on 23 April 1676, Mary Benderwell (SOLR:IKL).

M'CUBBIN
Samuel, m. on 20 Oct 1702, Elizabeth Prise (AAJA:25#21). She was Elizabeth, relict and admx. of Edward Price of AA Co. (INAC 26:143).

William, m. by 5 May 1703, Sarah [-?-]; they were execs. of George Westall of AA Co. (INAC 19A:168).

Zachariah, m. on 20 July 1704, Susanna Nicholson (AAAL 1:26).

M'DANIEL
Arthur, m. by 10 Sep 1708, Elisabeth, admx. of John Sweetnam of KE Co. (INAC 29:36).

Charles, m. by 29 March 1714, Ann, dau. of William and Susannah Edwards of Turner's Creek of KE Co. (KELR BC#1:3; CELR 2:262).

Daniel (Magdaniel), m. on 23 May 1702, Ann [-?-] (TAPE).

David, m. in 1715, Sarah Jones (PGQA:1).

M'DONALL
Hen., formerly servant to Robert Slye, marr. by Sep 1663 to John Gee performed by John Legatt without a license (*ARMD* 49:42, 85).

M'DONNELL
Arthur, m. on 25 --- 1705, Ellin Owens (TAPE).

M'DOWELL
[-?-], m. by Aug 1679, Elizabeth, relict and admx. of William Standley of Patuxent River, CV Co. (MDTP 11:153).

Henry (McDowall), d. By 5 Jan 1687 leaving a widow Eliza, dau. of John Hambleton (MWB 4:281).

John, m. by 1692, Frances, dau. of George Abbott of CV Co. (MWB 14:124; INAC 13A:230).

John, m. by May 1696, Mary, relict of John White of CV Co. (MDTP 16:162).

William, m. by 1658, Mary Brood (or Brooder) (MPL Q:205, 317).

M'FARLAND
Alexander, m. by 11 April 1688, Elisabeth, extx. of Mathew Selly [or Selby] of AA Co. (INAC 9:518; MDTP 14:131).

M'GILL
David, m. on 6 March 1708/9, Grace Boon (CVCH).

M'GINNIS
Patrick, m. by Sep 1701, Sarah, extx. of Robert Goldsborough (MDTP 18B:101).

MACKALL
James, m. by 1701, Ann, widow and extx. of James Dawkins of CV Co. (MDTP 19:91; INAC 23:25).
James, m. by 31 March 1709, Ann, dau. of Roger Brooke, dec., of CV Co. (PGLR C:258).
John (M'Kall), m. by 1716, Elizabeth Brady (or Bready), dau. of Owen and Elizabeth Brady (Fresco cites SMWB PC#1:201; MWB 14:282, 16:452; MDAD 1:31; MDTP 13:313).
John, m. by Dec 1718, [-?-], extx. of George Parker (MDTP 23:293).

M'KEE
Henry, m. by 20 July 1708, Rebecca, extx. of John Summers of PG Co. (INAC 28:263).

M'KENNY
Alexander (McKenney), m. on 4 Sep 1710, Catherine Plunkitt (CVCH).
Macom (Mahenny), m. by 10 April 1674, [-?-], widow of Andrew Ellenor (*ARMD* 51:113).

M'KENZIE
Colin, of SM Co., m. by Feb 1681/2, Elizabeth, dau. of Bartholomew Phillips of SM Co. (Warrant Record CB(#3):194).

M'KETTRICK
John, banns of marriage pub. on 28 May 1667 between him and Mary Allen, widow (*ARMD* 54:671; SOLR O#1:62).

MACKEY
[-?-], m. by 10 April 1709, Eliza, dau. of John Williams of CH Co. (MWB 12, pt. 2:58).
Daniel, m. on 9 Nov 1704, Alice Goodwell (AAAL 1:27).
Henry (Mackie), m. by 11 April 1709, Rebecca, extx., of John Simmons of PG Co. (INAC 31:140).
James, m. by 24 May 1714, Ann, extx. of Thomas Williams of CH Co. (INAC 35A:380).
James, m. by April 1715, [-?-], admx. of John Ellis of PG Cop. (MWB 22:458).

M'KNITT
John, m. on 28 March 1683, Jane Wallis (SOLR:IKL).

M'LAMY
Owen, m. by 15 July 1699, [-?-], admx. of John Hammon (INAC 19½A:106).

M'LANDER
Nicholas, m. on 16 Aug 1714, Elinor Hogin (KESP:49).

M'LANE
[-?-], m. by 9 June 1697, Sarah, dau. of Thomas Morgan of BA Co. (MWB 7:392).

MACKLEN
Daniel, m. by Feb 1696/7, Margaret, extx. of William Burden of CE Co. (MDTP 16:218).

MACKLIN
Robert, m. by 21 July 1684, Mary, admx. of Francis Asbury (or Ashbury), dec. (KELR K:78).

M'LOUGHLIN
Kalum (or Kenelm) (Mackloglin), m. by 1 Oct 1672, Mary, admx. of James Lindsey of CH Co. (MDTP 5:389; Warrant Record CB(#3):82).

Kenelm, of CH Co., m. by Feb 1677/8, [-?-], mother of Elizabeth Lindsey, whom MackLoughlin calls daughter-in-law (MDTP 9A:458).

Kenelm, m. by 19 June 1713, Elizabeth, widow of Giles Glover and, mother of William Glover (MCHR CL:15).

M'MANUS
John, m. by 27 March 1712, Lisha, admx. of William Simson of SO Co. (INAC 33A:239).

M'MERE
Jeremiah, m. by Jan 1670/1, Philise, mother of John Howard (*ARMD* 60:281).

M'MILLION
George, of CH Co., m. on Jan 1669 Grace Carr (CHLR P#1:205; *ARMD* 60:221).

McNAMARA
Timothy, m. by 17 Feb 1680 (immediately after death of the deceased), Sarah, relict and admx. of Lewis Griffin of DO Co. (INAC 7A:377; PCJU TL#3:399).

Timothy (M'Nemarra), m. after 1711, Jane, widow of Robert Leake, and dau. of John and Abigail Pritchett of DO Co. (MWB 17:322; MDTP 24:308).

M'NAWHAWN
Martin, m. on 17 Dec 1707, Mary Murphy (KESP:48).

M'NEALE
Daniel, m. by 15 Feb 1696, Margaret, relict and extx. of William Burdin of CE Co. (INAC 15:51).

M'NEER
John, m. on 16 June 1700, Joan Cossinger (KESP:47).

M'SALL
Thomas, m. by 28 April 1705, [-?-], admx. or extx. of Charles Powell of DO Co. (INAC 25:50).

MADDIN
John, m. on 21 Sep 1707, Kather. Flanakin (KESP:48).
Timothy, m. by 9 Feb 1715, Elizabeth, widow of William Marshall and legatee of Randall Condew (KELR BC#1:132).

MADDOCK
[-?-] (Maddox), m. by March 1677, Jane Elliott, relict of John Halfhead (MDTP 9A:519).
[-?-] (Maddocks), m. by 16 March 1685/6, Mary, dau. of James Smallwood (CHLR M:27).
Edward, m. by 27 Sep 1678, Hannah, admx. of Henry Frankham of CH (INAC 5:285; 7C:95; MDTP 13:56).
Edward (Maddox), apothecary, m. by 12 Nov 1678, Margery, relict and extx. of Matthew Stone (CHLR H#1:75, I:125).
Nath., m. by July 1716, [-?-], admx. of Henry Scholfield (MDTP 23:62).
Rice (Maddookes), m. by 1 Jan 1657/8, Anne, relict of John Dandy (*ARMD* 41: 13).

MADDY
John, of BA Co., m. by Feb 1711, Ann, extx. of Robert Gardiner of BA Co. (MDTP 22:81, 82; INAC 33A:231).

MADE
William, m. on 18 Dec 1692, Jane Hambelton (KESP:47).

MAGEE
George, Negro, m. by 1702/5, Maudlin Magee, white woman (Heinegg:128 cites SOJU 1702-1705, in KELR G#1:251).

MAGGS
Daniell, m. on 19 July 1703, Grace Canfield (KESP:47).
Daniell, m. on 15 Oct 1713, Wealthy Ann Evans (KESP:49).

MAGISSON
  John, of KE Co., m. on 9 May 1665, Jane Shears (*ARMD* 54:186).

MAGLAVIN
  William, m. on 4 April 1714, Eynor James (KESH:13).

MAGNOR
  James, m. on 27 Dec 1702, Mary Prise (KESP:47).

MAGHOIN
  [-?-], m. by 11 April 1714, Jeane, dau. of Philip Cox, of Harris Hundred, SM Co. (MWB 15:48).

MAGRAH
  John (Magraugh), m. by 11 Dec 1717, Mary, admx. of Patrick Moreland of CH Co. (INAC 39C:117).

MAGRUDER
  [-?-], m. by 4 Nov 1713, Elinor, dau. of Robert Wade of PG Co. (MWB 13:612).
  Alexander, m. by 7 Dec 1699, Ann, extx. of Thomas Hutchinson (INAC 19½A:102, 28:1).
  John, m. on 1 Dec 1715, Susanna Smith (PGQA:1).
  Nathaniel, of PG Co., m. by 19 May 1713, Susannah, dau. of Giles Blizard of CH Co., dec. (PGLR F:241).
  Ninian, of PG Co., m. by 10 Aug 1711, Elizabeth, dau. of John Brewer (AALR PK:399).

MAHALL
  Timothy, m. by 6 Aug 1717, Sarah, widow and admx. of Jeremiah Macknew of PG Co. (INAC 37B:190).

MAHAN
  Edward, m. by 1 July 1718, Ann, admx. of Samuel [Greening] (also given as Grinning or Gunning) of BA Co. (MDAD 1:23).
  Robert (Mahaune), m. by 6 April 1711, Elizabeth, admx. of John Simpson of CH Co. (INAC 32C:127).

MAHER (O'MAHER)
  Gabriel, d. by 12 Jan 1709, having m. Ann, widow of Robert Husse of CE Co. (CELR 2:136).

MAHINNEY
  Timothy, m. on 17 July 1709, Hannah Neal (TAPE).

MAHONY
  Dennis (Mahoney), m, by 1707, Mildred, dau. of William and Mildred Shercliff

(Fresco cites SMWB PC#1:125, 149).

Thomas, m. by 1714, Jane, dau. of Philip Cox; she m. 2nd, John Dean, and 3rd, by 1733, William Abell (Fresco cites MDTP 24:300, 25:71-76, 26:220-223).

Timothy, d. by 4 Aug 1714, having m. Elizabeth, dau. of John Smith of SM Co., and leaving a son Dennis (CHLR F#2:25).

MAKEALL
David (Macall), m. by 3 July 1708, Cornelia, extx. of Thomas Phillips of DO Co. (INAC 28:200; MDTP 21:41).

MAKEWAY
Patrick, m. on 29 Sep 1705, Elizabeth Martin (TAPE).

MALLETT
John, m. by 14 Aug 1677, Hannah his wife alias Manlove, dau. of Mark Manlove late of this Co., dec. (*ARMD* e89 (SOJU O#7):97).

MALLING
John, m. by 1683, Elizabeth, dau. of Ralph Williams (AALR IT#5:72-77).

MALOHAN
[William?], m. by 10 Jan 1716, Liza, dau. of Owen Bradey of SM Co. (MWB 14:284).

MALOW
[-?-], m. by 5 Jan 1715, Margaret, dau. of John Alward of CH Co. (MWB 14:81).

MALOY
Charles, m. by June 1718, Rachel, admx. of Edward [Cath?] of QA Co. (MDTP 23:193).

MANDERS
William, m. on 7 Oct 1714, Ann Darley or Darbey (AAAN:22).

MANHEE
Thomas, m. by 29 Dec 1712, Jane, admx. of David Watson of SM Co. (INAC 33B:157).

MANLOVE
John, m. on 9 Aug 1672, Elizabeth Lee (SOLR:IKL).

Mark, in May 1672, banns of matrimony were published for him and Eliz: Greene (SOJU AZ#8:84; SOLR:IKL). **Mark, m. on 4 April 1672, Elizabeth Greene** (SOLR:IKL).

Thomas, banns of marriage pub. on 30 July 1667, between him and Jane De Lamas (or Jane Lamar (*ARMD* 54:679; SOLR O#1:79). **Thomas, m. in 1667, Jane Dillamas** (SOLR:IKL). She was a sister of William Boist, dec. (*ARMD* e87 (SOJU

AZ#8):150).
William, on 8 Aug 1676, banns of matrimony were published for him and
Mary Robbins (SOJU O#7:45). William, m. on 1 Nov 1676, Alce [*sic*] Robins
(SOLR:IKL).

MANN
John, m. by Sep 1687, Sarah, execs. of Tho. Cox (TAJR Sep 1687).

MANNER
William, m. by 24 Aug 1698, Lydia, widow of George Newman of CH Co., dau.
of Margery [-?-], who m. 2nd, William Ballin (MCHR PC:395).

MANNING
[-?-], m. by Feb 1677/8, May [Mary?], relict and extx. of John Blackfan of CH Co.
(MDTP 9A:475).
[-?-], m. by 21 Jan 1701, Priscilla, dau. of Ann Pattison, widow of Thomas
Pattison of DO Co. (MWB 11:301).
Cornelius, m. by 1703, Mary, dau. of John and Katherine (Miles) Wiseman
(MWB 3:242).
Cornelius, m. by Sep 1716, Mary Simeon (dec.?), admx. of George Simeon [or
Simson]. (PCJU VD#2:345).
John, m. by 31 Aug 1698, Ruth, relict of Hugh Ellis, whose first wife Elizabeth,
was extx. of Mordecai Hunton of CV Co. (INAC 16:230, 18:143).
John, m. by 1713, Eleanor Van Swearingen, dau. of Mary and sister of Joseph
Van Swearingen (Fresco cites SMWB PC#1:190, Judgements 2:186).
Thomas, m. by 22 June 1687, Priscilla, admx. of John Taylor of DO Co. (INAC
9:314); MWB 11:129.

MANROW
Duncan, m. by 13 Feb 1710, Sarah, admx. of Henry Everet of QA Co. (INAC
32B:35).

MANSELL
George, of AA Co., Gent., m. on 7 March 1714, Sarah Norwood (PGKG:240).
John, m. by 1642, Ann Pike (or Peake) (MPL ABH:34, 58, 150).
Vincent, d. by 1687, having m. Jane, dau. of Justinian Tennison, Sr. (MDTP
14A:37).

MANSFIELD
Vincent, m. by 22 March 1675/6, [-?-], dau. of Richard Foster of St. Clement's
Manor, SM Co. (MDTP 7:358).

MARBURY
Francis, m. by 25 Aug 1704, Mary, dau. of Francis Green (CHLR Z:70).
Francis, m. on 14 Sep 1714, Frances Heard (PGKG:245).

MARCH
John, m. on 24 June 1702, Ellinor Anderson (KESP:47).

MARCHMENT
Samuel, m. on 25 March 1685, Mary Wharton (SOLR:IKL).

MARCY
Jonathan, m. on 25 Nov 1701, Mrs. Ann Collyer, spinster (HAGE:14).

MARIARTE
Edward (Maryartee), m. on 5 Feb 1705/6, Rachel Grey (AAAL 1:32(2)).

MARKINS
Thomas, m. by 1661, [-?-], widow of [-?-] Day (MPL.4:580).

MARLER
John, m. by 31 Aug 1717, Margaret, legatee of John Allwood of CH Co. (INAC 37B:92).
Jonathan, m. by c1665, Eleanor Baynes (Pro Court FF:778).

MARLETT
John, banns of marriage pub. on 28 May 1667 between him and Hannah Manlove (*ARMD* 54:671; SOLR O#1:62).

MARLOY
Ralph, m. on 22 May 1717, Anne, dau. of John and Mary Middleton (PGKG:254).

MARRETT
John, m. by 29 May 1708, Frances, admx. of John Price of SM Co. (INAC 28:222).

MARRIOTT
John, m. by 9 Aug 1684, [-?-], aunt of John Buck, who was a son of John Buck, dec. (AALR IH#3:73).
Mark, m. by 18 Jan 1716/7, Sarah, sister of Alexander Fisher of DO Co. (MWB 14:249).

MARRITT
John, m. on 5 (or 25) June 1667, Hannah Manlove (SOLR:IKL).

MARROT
Jno., m. on 19 April 1707, Mary Miller (TAPE).

MARSH
Edward, m. on 21 Sep 1711, Cathrine Wiggins (TAPE).

George, m. on 15 Aug 1681, Elizabeth Davis (SOLR:IKL).

James, m. on 14 July 1699, Alce Gale (AAJA:5#4).

Robert, of KE Co., m. by 25 Aug 1701, Rachel, dau. of William Rogers (KELR JD#1:13).

Thomas, of KE Co., m. by 12 Aug 1679, Jane, dau. of John Clements (MWB 10:52).

Mr. Thomas, m. by 23 April 1717, Eliza., dau. of John Hawkins of QA Co. (MWB 14:535).

Thomas, of QA Co., m. Elizabeth [-?-], widow and admx. of Thomas Baxter of QA Co.: she m. 3rd, by 28 Oct 1718, George Commerford (MDAD 1:208, 364; 6:413).

MARSHALL

[-?-], m. by 4 Aug 1712, Ann, admx. of William Lewis of AA Co. (INAC 33B:22).

Charles, Gent., m. by 26 July 1706, Anne, widow and extx. of Edward Smith of KE Co. (INAC 25:332; QALR I(J)KA:32; QAJRh).

Edward, m. by 4 March 1716, Anne, admx. of William Lewis (INAC 37C:113).

Nicholas, m. by 11 Nov 1701, Elizabeth, late wife of John Lewis of TA Co. (TALR 9:80).

Thomas, Negro, m. 25 Dec 1700, Mary [Marshall?], Negress (AAAL 1:22(1)).

William, m. by 1650, Katherine, widow of Thomas Hebden (MPL 3:199-200, ABH:912, 125).

William, of CH Co., m. by 22 April 1673, Katherine Ebden (MWB 1:592).

William, m. on 19 June 1718, Mrs. Mary Wells (HAGE:36).

MARSHAM

Richard, m. by Jan 1697/8, Ann, admx. of Henry Brent late of CV Co., dec. Brent d. intestate (PGCP A:274; INAC 15:186, 17:144, 23:22, 30:221). She was a dau. of Gov. Leonard Calvert, and had m. 1st, by 1662, Baker Brooke, and 2nd, Henry Brent (Fresco cites SMWB PC#1:114; MDTP 13:7).

MARTIN

Charles, m. on 25 Aug 1701, Elizabeth [-?-] (TAPE).

Francis, m. in Nov 1683, Mary Roatch (SOLR:IKL).

George, m. by 14 Nov 1715, Dorothy, extx. of Mr. John Paynter of SO Co. (INAC 37A:35).

Henry, of TA Co., m. some time after 1708, [-?-], widow of David Rogers of TA Co. (QAEJ: John Moore).

John, d. by 24 Feb 1675, when his widow and admx. Mary, m. Jasper Allen: she m. 3rd, by 10 March 1676, [-?-] Taylor (INAC 2:187).

John, m. by c1682, Mary, relict and admx. of Richard Hall of CH Co. (INAC 7C:163).

John, m. on 14 Aug 1714, Mary Holloway (AAAN:22).

Thos., m. on 11 Feb 1701, Ann [-?-] (TAPE).

Thomas, m. on 19 Dec 1717, Jane Thomas (TAPE).

William (Martine), m. by 4 July 1660, [-?-], mother of Mathew [Martha], Dorothy, and Margaret Needham, who Martine called daus.-in-law (MWB 1:126).

William, m. by July 1686, Frances, dau. of George and Isabel Abbott; she m. 2nd, John Holdsworth (MWB 4:124; MDTP 13:232, 361, 15C:111, 16:8; INAC 13:230, 35:33).

William, m. by 1693/4, Isabel, widow of George Abbott; she later m. John Holfworth (Cotton cites INAC 12:157). [**N.B.**: These two marriages require additional study--RWB].

Wm., m. on 21 Oct 1705, Elizabeth Chapple (CVCH).

William, m. on 9 June 1709, Phebe Bowdle (TAPE).

William, m. by Aug 1714, Rebeckah, now dec., mother of Maurice Lane et al (QAJRh).

MARTINDALE
[-?-], m. by 15 Sep 1682, Ruth, relict and admx. of Thomas Vaughn of SM Co. (INAC 7C:328).

MASCALL
Richard, m. by June 1671, Katherine, widow and relict of Henry Gutterick of AA Co. (MDTP 5:68).

MASLIN
Thomas, m. on 4 Dec 1711, Jane Britain (KESP:48).

MASON
[-?-], m. by 10 Oct 1712, Mary, dau. of John Pigman of PG Co. (MWB 15:83).

Edward, m. by 15 May 1695, Alice, relict and admx. of Henry Archer of AA Co. (INAC 13A:296).

George, m. by 31 July 1713, Ann, extx., of Paine Turberville of SM Co. (INAC 35B:62).

John, m. by 1713, Mary, dau. of Joshua and Elizabeth Guibert of SM Co. (MWB 14:224; Fresco also cites SMWB PC#1:18, 207; MDTP 22:273, 285; Prov. Court DD#2:393).

Lemuel, of Elizabeth River in Lower Norfolk co., VA, m. by 1 June 1678, Ann Sewell, b. c1634/5, sister and heir to Mr. Henry Sewell, dec., and dau. of Henry Sewell, dec. (DOLR 4 Old:5, 6).

Phill. (Mayson), m. on 10 Jan 1713, Eliza Duning (PGKG:253). She was Elizabeth, extx. of Turrin Dunnings of PG Co. (INAC 35A:6).

Samuel, m. by 1699, Mary, admx. of Christopher Mires (INAC 19½B:68; MDTP 18A:48).

Stephen, m. on 22 April 1717, Jane Gregory (AAAN:29, 31).

Thomas, m. by 15 Sep 1688, Margaret, relict of Robert Weld of TA Co. (MDTP 14:93).

William, m. on 18 Aug 1680, Anne Deane (SOLR:IKL).

MASSEY
Jno., m. by Jan 1682/3, [-?-], relict of William Cane (MDTP 12B:310).

John, m. by Sep 1706, Sarah, possibly a sister of William and Stephen White of

SO Co. (PCJU PL#1:16, 17).

Nicholas, marriage recorded in Aug 1688 to Margaret Morgan (TAJR Aug 1688).

Peter, m. by 19 Feb 1705/6, Sarah, dau. of Daniel Toas, and sister of John Toas (CELR 2:81, 176).

MASTERS

Thomas, banns pub. on 28 April 1706, Margaret Jones (HAGE:18).

MATHER

George, m. on 14 Aug 1708, Susanna Story (AALR 1:36).

MATHES

William, m. on 29 Jan 1701, Ann [-?-] (TAPE).

MATKIN

Theodore, m. by [c1707/8], Hannah, extx. of Philip Talle of DO Co. (INAC 28:87).

MATTHEWS

[-?-], m. by 13 Oct 1684, Jane, dau. of Henry Adams, of CH Co. (MWB 4:205).

Auriah, m. on 7 Nov 1703, Sarah Gannon (TAPE).

Giles, m. by 1657, Elizabeth Maurice (MPL Q:71).

Ignatius, m. by 10 March 1697, Mary, dau. of Joshua Doyne of SM Co. (MWB 6:169).

Roger, m. on 14 Nov 1710, Mary Carvil (HAGE:33).

Thomas, of CH Co., m. by 1676, Jane, dau. of John and Jane Cockshott of SM Co. (Fresco cites MDCR 3:707; MWB 5:80, 11:205).

Thomas, d. by 30 Sep 1703 having m. Sarah, dau. of William Boarman; she m. 2nd, [-?-] Mudd, and 3rd, John Sanders (CHLR Z:127).

Thomas, m. by 31 May 1715, Hester, admx. of Edward Chapman of CH Co. (INAC 36B:330; MDAD 3:332).

Thomas, m. by 14 Jan 1717, Esther, dau. of Joseph Manning of CH Co. (MWB 14:447).

MATTINGLY

[-?-], m. by 16 April 1717, Ruth, dau. of Edward Cole of SM Co. (MWB 14:644).

Thomas, m. by 7 Oct 1681, Mary, extx. of John Suttle of SM Co. (INAC 7B:150).

MATTOCKS

Edward, m. on 12 Oct 1714, Elizabeth Smith (AAMA:84).

MATTOX

Henry, m. by Oct 1688, Elizabeth, admx. of John Mitchell (MDTP 14:98, 14A:10).

Jonas, m. by banns on 22 April 1711, Ann Bentley (CESS).

MAUD
        Daniel (Wright transcribes this as Hand), mariner, of the City of London, m. on 17 d. 6 m., 1710, Magdalen Stevens of TA Co. (TATH).

MAUGHLIN
        Richard, m. on 25 Oct 1711, Kath. Ferrill (KESP:48).

MAUHANE
        Edward (Mauhon) , m. on 1 Jan 1704, Honour Allsen (KESP:47).
        Thimithy [*sic*], m. on 7 April 1716, Sarah Macknew (PGKG:247).
        Thomas (Mauhawn), m. on 12 April 1716, Mary Moore (KESP:49).

MAUNDERS
        Wilkes, d. by 1707, having m. Sarah Tucker, widow of Justinian Gerard who d. 1688; she m. 3rd, by 1707, Michael Curtis (Fresco cites Judgements LD:1, 8:174; MWB 7:129; and SMWB PC#1:69).

MAXFIELD
        Robert, m. on 2 Oct 1702, Ann Park (KESP:47). She was a dau. of Robert Park who m. Mary [-?-] (KELR JS#N:250; MWB 17:171).

MAY
        John, m. by 18 Sep 1717, Mary, dau. of Jeremiah Sampson of St. Mary's, London, Rotherhithe, Surrey, mariner (MWB 14:493).
        Roger, m. Ann Phillips (poss. of SM Co.) (Warrants 1:134).

MAYNARD
        Henry, m. on 17 Feb 1703, Sarah Hopkins (AAMA:82). She was the widow and extx. of Robert Hopkins of BA Co. (INAC 28:41).
        Thomas, m. on 25 Aug 1693, Ann Smith (CVCH).

MAYO
        Joshua, m. on 10 July 1707, Hannah Searson (AAAL 1:36).

MEAD
        Benjamin, m. on 18 Nov 1708, Elizabeth Dawdridge (AAMA:83).
        Edward, m. on 13 Oct 1713, Darcass Ewins (SJSG:20R).
John (Meades), of AA Co., m. by Sep 1705, Amy, admx. of Thomas [Shuter?], chirurgeon (PCJU TB#2:151).
        Joseph, m. on 14 Dec 1711, Eleanor Hacket (AALR 2:8).

MEAKIN
        William (Meakins), m. by 18 March 1683, Eliza or Margaret, dau. of Robert Beard of SM Co., by whom he was the father of William and Robert Meakin (MWB 4:178).

MEDCALFE
>John (Metcalfe), m. by 23 April 1701, Lydia, dau. of Thomas Crutchley (AALR WT#1:229).
>John, m. by 9 April 1716, Mary, widow of Richard Butt of PG Co. (INAC 36C:169; MDAD 1:188).

MEDLEM
>**Henry, m. on 5 Dec 1706, Naomi Prentice** (AAAL 1:33).

MEDLEY
>John, m. by 1677, Anne Cole (MDTP 4C:36). She was Ann Rennalls, sister of George Rennalls; she m. 2nd, Robert Cole, and 3rd, Charles Daft (INAC 13:293, 624; MDTP 14A:8).

MEE
>George, m. by 1651, Katherine, mother of John Vanhack (MPL ABH:173, 201).

MEEK(S)
>Francis, of CH Co., m. by July 1686, Mary, relict of Richard Pinner, dec. (MDTP 13:373).
>**Francis, m. on 3 Jan 1704, Mary Smith** (KESP:47).
>Francis, m. by 19 June 1713, [Mary?], sister of William Glover, and dau. of Giles and Elizabeth Glover (MCHR CL:15, LP#3:15).
>**John, m. on 4 Dec 1716, Hannah Brown** (AAAN:29).
>**Walter, m. on 27 March 1700, Jane Reed** (KESP:47).

MEEKIN(S)
>Richard, m. by 14 Oct 1701, Mary, admx. of Charles Staplefort of DO Co. (INAC 21:143).
>William, m. by 1707, [-?-], dau. of Robert Beard (SMRR:11).

MEERS.
>**Abraham (Mears), m. on 7 Sep 1704, Martha Killinworth** (AAJA:29 #11).
>John, m. by 9 Sep 1674, [-?-], dau. of Philip Thomas of AA Co. (MDTP 7:63).
>**Jno., m. on 8 Dec 1715, Jane Gilberd** (TAPE).
>**William, of CV Co., planter, m. on 1 d. 9 m., 1679, Elizabeth Webb, of TA Co., at King's Creek, TA Co.** (TATH).

MEHENNY
>Macom, d. by 1674, having m. [-?-], widow of Andrew Ellenor; she m. 3rd, by 10 April 1674, John Dabb (*ARMD* 51:113).

MEKIN
>John, m. by 6 Feb 1676, Rebecca, sister and extx. of Daniel Clocker (INAC 3:68).

MELLING
John, of London, Eng., innholder, m. by 9 Oct 1683, Elizabeth, dau. of Ralph Williams of AA Co., dec. (AALR IT#5:72).

MELSON
John, on 9 Jan 1671/2, banns of matrimony were published for him (certificate granted 31 Jan 1671/2) and Elizabeth Painter (SOJU AZ#8:43). **John, m. on 4 April 1672, Elizabeth Painter** (SOLR:IKL).

MELTON
Thomas, m. by 25 March 1707, Mary, dau. of William Shercliffe of SM Co. (MWB 12:157).

MERCHANT
James, m. on 25 April 1709, Jean Steuart (TAPE).

MERCIER
Francis, m. on 7 June 1713, Margaret Weldon (AAAN:9).

MERIDAY
Henry (Merriday), and Ann Stratton, on 15 Jan 1702/3 had a certificate of banns of matrimony granted to them (AAJU G:12).
Henry (Merriday), m. on 29 Oct 1711, Sarah Aldridge (AAMA:85).
Henry, m. by 7 Oct 1718, Sarah, dau. of Thomas Aldridge of AA Co. (MDAD 2:341).
John, m. by 11 Sep 1695, Mary, legatee of William Crump (KELR GL#1:3a).

MERRICK
James, m. on 10 Dec 1713, Elizabeth Barron (TAPE).
John, m. by 20 Sep 1702, Jane, dau. of Daniel Walker, Sr., of TA Co. (MWB 3:189).

MERRIDAY
[-?-], m. by 7 Oct 1718, Sarah, dau. of Thomas Aldridge of AA Co. (MWB 14:678).
John, m. by 23 Nov 1715, [-?-], dau. of Thomas Bayley of QA Co., who called the man his son-in-law (MWB 14:113).

MERRIKEN
Hugh (Merike), m. on 20 Nov 1716, Sarah Burley (AAAN:29). She was dec. by 27 Sep 1717 and had been the extx. of Stephen Burle of AA Co. (AAJU RC:268, INAC 37B:31).
Hugh m. by 23 Dec 1719, Anne, extx. of George Westall of BA Co. (MDAD 2:372; MDAD 3:18).
John (Merekin), m. on 26 Sep 1710, Mary Stephens (AAMA:83).

Joshua (Merricke), m. by 26 Feb 1696, Grace, dau. of Richard Bayly of AA Co. (MWB 7:247).

Joshua, m. on 16 Feb 1709/10, Elizabeth Ewins (HAGE:26).

Joshua, m. on 24 June 1718, Dinah Day (SJSG:11).

MERRITT

John (Meritt) m. by 10 Sep 1707, Frances, widow and admx. of John Price of SM Co. (INAC 27:154).

Samuel, m. on 29 Nov 1705, Phebe Millward (KESP:48).

MERRYMAN

[-?-] (Merriman), m. by 14 Jan 1709, Jane, admx. of Joseph Peake of BA Co. (INAC 30:253).

John, m. by 12 April 1802, Martha, dau. of Martha Bowen, widow of BA Co. (MWB 3:2).

Samuel, m. by April 1710, Mary, relict of [-?-] Thomas Eager (MDTP 21:222, 22:227).

Samuel, m. by 19 Nov 1709, Mary, dau of Humphrey Boone and sister of Robert Boone of BA Co. (MWB 12, pt. 2:205; INAC 32B:249).

MERSON

William m. by 26 Sep 1706, Priscilla, extx. of Katherine Murphey of TA Co. (INAC 25:429).

MESEX

Lewen (or Julien), m. on 29 April 1674, Sarah Convention (SOLR:IKL).

MICHALL

John, m. on 2 Sep 1704, Grace Billiter (TAPE).

MIDDLETON

[-?-], m. by 26 Dec 1711, Penelope, dau. of William Hatton of PG Co., dec. (PGLR F:206; MWB 13:432).

Lutener, m. on 6 Aug 1705, Elizabeth Miller (KESP:47).

Robert, m. by Feb 1684, Mary, dau. of John Wheeler (CHLR L:52).

William, m. by April 1712, Elizabeth, admx. of John Keech of CH Co. She may have been a dau. of Hugh Tears (MDTP 22:98; INAC 33B:131).

MIDFORD

Jno., m. on (date not given), Jaine Hyland (CESS).

MIDIATE

Mathew, m. by 17 June 1707, Judith, legatee of Samuel White of AA Co. (INAC 27:10).

MIGRAUGH
    John, m. on 26 Sep 1708, Ann Lee (AAAN:7).

MILBOURNE
    Ralph, m. by 27 Oct 1709, Mary, dau. of Henry Hall of SO Co. (MWB 12, pt. 2:180).

MILES
    [-?-], m. by 20 April 1709, Mary, dau. of William Pecket of BA Co. (MWB 13:132).
    Charles, m. by 18 Dec 1718, Rachel, admx. of Edward Brosbank of KE Co. (MDAD 2:259).
    Henry, on 28 Jan 1667/8, banns of matrimony were published for him and Mary Barnabe, widow (SOLR O#1:90).
    John, m. by 1677, Mary, dau. of George Beckwith (MDTP 9:242; INAC 4:179 says she was Mary Parker).
    Thomas, of AA Co., m. on 23 d., 10 m. (Dec), 1714, Elizabeth White, widow, of PG Co. (WRMM).
    Thomas, of AA Co., m. on 27 d., 4 m. (June), 1704, Ruth Jones, dau. of Joseph and Elizabeth, of AA Co. (WRMM).

MILLAM
    Edmund, m. by 9 Aug 1711, Jane, admx. of Nicholas Cock of SM Co. (INAC 32C:94).

MILLER
    [-?-], m. by 5 Sep 1717, Margaret, dau. of William Barton, Gent., of CH Co. (MWB 14:658).
    [-?-], m. by 5 July 1718, Elizabeth, dau. of John White of SO Co. (MWB 18:5).
    Arthur, m. on 23 July 1705, Sarah Jones (KESP:47).
    Jacob, m. by 20 Nov 1710, Margret, extx. of William Hungerford of CH Co. (INAC 32B:9).
    James, m. by 27 April 1705, Jane, admx. of Jeremiah Shermedine of CV Co. (INAC 25:127, 26:110, 27:80).
    John, m. by 7 June 1706, Sarah, admx. of Benjamin Cassock of CH Co. (INAC 26:36).
    John, m. by April 1708, Sarah, admx. of James Smith (MDTP 21:18).
    Jonathan, m. on 6 Nov 1708, Mary Baxton [or Batton] (TAPE).
    Michael, m. by Oct 1671, [-?-], widow of John Stevens of KE Co. (MDTP 5:91).
    Michael, of KE Co., m. by 1678, [-?-], widow and extx. of Robert Hood (MPL 16:41).See also acct. of Christopher Andrews of KE Co. (INAC 6:617).
    Michael, Jr., m. by c1697, Martha, dau. of Maj. Joseph Wickes of KE Co. (INAC 15:217).
    Nicholas, m. on 15 Dec 1708, Ellinor Wateman (KESP:48).
    Richard, m. by Oct 1677, Gweltian, widow of Richard Graves of TA Co. (MDTP 9A:348).

Robert, m. by 9 Dec 1712, Eliza, dau. of Jno. Preston of TA Co. (MWB 13:665).
William, m. on 21 Oct 1707, Grace Young (CVCH). She was a dau. of George
Young of CV Co. (MWB 14:613).

MILLERT
Christopher, m. on 14 Oct 1705, Elizabeth Harris (AAAL 1:27).

MILLS
[-?-], m. by 25 Oct 1662, Mary, eld. dau. of Richard Willan (MDTP 1D:146).
David, m. by 25 Sep 1707, Mary, dau. of George Prouse of DO Co. (INAC
27:226).
David, m. by 29 Aug 170-, Isabel, sister of John Anderson and dau. of William
Anderson of TA Co. (TALR 9:327).
David, m. on 24 Jan 1716, Elizabeth Elston (TAPE).
James, m. on 19 Oct 1711, Sarah Slater (TAPE).
Nicholas, m. by 13 May 1706, [-?-], dau. of Susanna Heard, widow of John Heard
of SM Co., who called Mills son-in-law (MWB 12:199).
Peter, of Brittons Bay, SM Co., m. by 1667, Mary, dau. of John Shircliff (MPL
10:477).
Peter, m. Frances, widow of Ignatius Wheeler and dau. of Robert Slye (Warrants
10:474, 477, MPL ABH:150; Hodges cites Pro. Court DD#2: 339-401; Wills 6:296;
INAC 19½:15).

MILNS
David, m. on (date not given), Mary [-?-] (TAPE).

MILSON
Samuel, m. on 7 May 1703, Elizabeth Brady (or Bradley) (KESP:47). She was
the mother of David Bradley, now 5½ years old (KELR GL#1:14).

MILTON
Abraham, m. on 10 June 1713, Barbara Everett (KESP:49).

MINISHAL
Randolph, m. in 169-, Alice Potter (SOLR:IKL).

MISHUE
William, m. in or after 1679, Sarah Newton, extx. of Samuel Pritchard (MPL
WC#2:41. 116. 256). He d. by 6 March 1701, having m. Sarah, mother of Sarah Ryan,
Thomas Newton, and Eliza Winsmore (MWB 11:239).

MISKILL
[-?-], m. by 11 May 1711, Ann, dau. of George Spicer of PG Co. (MWB 13:268).

MITCHELL
[-?-], m. by Jan 1688/9, Ann, extx. of James Scott of TA Co. (MDTP 14:130).

[-?-], m. by 7 Nov 1700, Susanna, dau. of Ursula Moore of AA Co., whose will named her husband Mordecai Moore, and her sons Benjamin and Charles Burgess (MWB 11:309).

Edward, m. on 21 Nov 1706, Grace Lewis (AAAL 1:33).

George, banns pub. 29 Sep 1668, Isabell Higgens (*ARMD* 54:729; SOLR O#1:136).

Henry, m. by Oct 1659, Grace Molden (*ARMD* 41:338).

John, of St. Michael's R., m. by 28 Feb 1676/7, Ann, mother of John, Grace, Benjamin, George, Mary, and Thomas Aldridge, and of John Bulpit (TALR 3:46).

John, m. by 20 Feb 1695, Jane, the dau. and heir of Frances Lombard (KELR M:25, 61).

John, m. 14 July 1700, Susanna Burgess, dau. of Col. William (AAAL 1:21(1)).

Walter, d. by 21 Feb 1702/3, having m. Ellinor, dau. of Philip Conner, Sr., of SO Co. (MWB 3:491).

Capt. William, m. on 10 April 1652, by Rev. William Wilkinson, Joane Toast [but there appears to have been some question as to the marriage's validity (Proprietary Records F&B:315).

William, m. on 12 Nov 1702, Alice [-?-] (TAPE).

William, d. by 23 Aug 1706, having m. 1st, Elizabeth, only dau. and heir of John Mott, and 2nd, Jane [-?-], who m. as her 2nd husband [-?-] Fairbrother (AALR WT#2:453).

MITCHELLER
Alexander, on 14 Nov 1676, banns of matrimony were published for him and Anne Surnam (SOLR O#7:62r).

MITFORD
[-?-], m. Fortune, widow of William Champe; she m. 3rd, by Oct 1668, Marmaduke Simm (*ARMD* 57:358).

MITLEY
Christopher, m. on 7 Jan 1700, Mary Cashmore (AAJA:22#6).

MOBBERLY
John, Jr., m. on 11 Feb 1711/2, by Rev. Jona' White, Rachel Pindell (PGQA:1).

John, Sr., m. on 28 Feb 1716, Susanna Scaggs, widow of Aaron Scaggs (PGQA:2).

MOCKBEE
Brock, m. on 22 Dec 1715, Eliza Beckett (PGQA:1).

MOCKDELL
Williiam, m. by c1699, Ann, admx. of Benjamin Hunt of DO Co. (INAC 18:191).

MOGBEE
[-?-], m. by 5 March 1712, [-?-], dau. of Edward Brock of PG Co., who named his grandchildren Brock Mogbee and Matthew Mogbee in his will (MWB 13:723).

MOHAWNY
Dennis, m. by 25 March 1707, Mildred, dau. of William Shercliffe of SM Co. (MWB 12:157).

MOLL
John, m. on 13 June 1711, Mary Whitworth (KESP:48).

MONCASTER
John, m. by 6 Dec 1703, [-?-], widow and extx. of James Hakson of CH Co. (MWB 3:51).

MONDAY
Robert, of St. Michael's Parish, m. on 15 Dec 1700, Catherine Hogill (TAPE).

MONEY
Robert, m. by banns on 4 Oct 1706, Margaret Dorrell, spinster (CESS).

MONK
Gilbert, m. on 12 Feb 1703, Margrett Bullock (KESP:47).
Gilbert, m. on 25 May 1708, Mary Kelly (KESP:48).
Henery, m. on 2 Dec 1708, Honour Connor (KESP:48).
Samuel, m. on 21 Oct 1698, Ann Skinner (AAJA:63a#11).

MONOUGH
John, m. by 9 July 1686, [-?-], who was paid her thirds out of the estate of George Newman of CH Co. (INAC 9:52).

MONROE
George, m. by 10 Aug 1667, Dorothy, dau. of Robert Cager of SM Co. (MWB 1:293; MDTP 2:189).

MONTAGUE
Will (Munttegue), m. on 12 Oct 1668, Elizabeth Morgaine (*ARMD* 54:601).

MONTGOMERY
Hugh, m. by c1693, Catherine, extx. of George Parker (INAC 10:355, 20:67).
Robert, m. on 12 Aug 1717, Alice Smith, widow (BAPA).

MONUS
Robert, m. by 31 May 1712, [-?-], dau. of Nicholas Dorritt, in 1712 acct. of Christopher Mounce of CE Co. (INAC 33B:85).

MOOLSON
   Thomas, m. in 1669, Ann Taylor (SOLR:IKL).
   Thomas, m. by 1678, Rachell [-?-], alias Mason, alias Williams (MPL LL;755, 15:507, WC#3:29).

MOOR(E)
   [-?-] (More), m. by 16 Sep 1712, Sarah, dau. of Col. James Smallwood of CH Co. (MWB 14:31).
   Alexander, m. by c1694, Sarah, widow and admx. of John Coppin of TA Co. (INAC 13A:215).
   Edward, m. 4 Dec 1700, Alice Withers (AAAL 1:21(1)).
   Francis, m. on 27 April 1705, Elizabeth Stogdon [*sic*] (AAJA:31 #5). She was the admx. of John Stockdon of AA Co. (INAC 25:62).
   John, m. on 25 Oct 1685, Anne Mitchell (SOLR:IKL).
   John, m. by 8 May 1702, Margrett, dau. of Jenkins Morris of SO Co. (INAC 21:352).
   John, m. on 7 Nov 1706, Eliza Danielson (PGQA:1).
   Jno., m. by 13 April 1716, Priscilla, dau. of John Smith of CH Co. (MWB 14:195).
   Joseph, m. on 29 March 1703, Sarah Watts (TAPE).
   Martin, banns of marriage pub. 26 March 1667, between him and Margaret Cornelius (*ARMD* 54:666; SOLR O#1:62). Martin, m. on 13 April 1667, Margaret Cornelius (SOLR:IKL).
   Dr. Mordecai, (later styled merchant of AA Co.), m. by 4 March 1688, Ursula, widow of Col. William Burgess and mother of Charles Burgess (AALR WT#1:45; PGLR C:165a; INAC 10:193, 18:180).
   Richard, of TA Co., d. by 15 March 1705, when his admx. Joane had m. John Allen (INAC 25:432).
   Samuel, m. on 18 Nov 1708, Katherine Collins (AAAN:7).
   Thomas, m. by Feb 1677/8, Mary, admx. of Stephen Whetstone (*ARMD* 67:209).
   William, m. by 10 Sep 1698, Hannah, relict and admx. of Christopher Bettson of TA Co. (INAC 17:130; MDTP 17:219).
   William, m. on 10 May 1716, Mary Gatrill (AAAL 2:48).

MOOTH
   Thomas, of TA Co., d. by 6 April 1709, having m. Katherine, widow and extx. of William Webb of TA Co. (INAC 29:129, 136).

MORDANT
   William, m. on 22 Oct 1715, Ann Watts of AA Co. (PGQA:2).

MORECOCKE
   Robert, m. by 18 Nov 1693, Anne, widow of Robert Farrington and mother of Jane Farrington who m. Thomas Lee (TALR LL#7:53).

MORGAN

Rev. [-?-], m. by 1678, Elizabeth Jones (MPL 12:526).

David, Jr., m. by 31 Oct 1705, Grace, admx. of John Russell of CV Co. (INAC 25:132).

Edward, m. by 1708, Mary, widow of William Guyther and of Marshall Low, and dau. of Robert Crane of SM Co. (Fresco cites SMWB PC#1:139, 156, 273; INAC 27:232).

George, banns pub. Dec and Jan 1699/1700, m. 10 Feb 1699/1700, Elizabeth Smith (*HAGE:*5, 6).

James, m. on 25 Feb 1718, Mary Merriken (AAAN:36).

Philip, m. on 18 d. 12 m., 1707, Sarah Jadwin at Tuckahoe Meeting House (TATH). She was a dau. of John Jadwin (MDTP 21:56).

Richard, m. on 23 Dec 1703, Alice Butterfield (AAAL 1:26).

Richard, m. by 26 July 1708, Mary, widow and extx. of Daniel Benching of CE Co. (INAC 28:331).

Robert, m. by 20 Oct 1705, [-?-], dau. of Robert Crane of St. George's Hundred, SM Co. (MWB 12:1).

Thomas, m. on 14 Dec 1708, Margritt Ellt (CVCH).

William, m. by 29 July 1698, Elizabeth, admx. of Robert Large of SM Co. (INAC 16:184).

William, m. by 10 March 1700, [-?-], relict and admx. of William Chesham of SM Co. (INAC 21:115).

MORIATE

James, m. by 26 July 1707, Sarah, relict and extx. of William Bateman of AA Co. (INAC 27:42).

MORLIN

Jacob, m. on 19 Dec 1710, Sarah Armstrong (TAPE).

MORPHEW

John, m. on 7 March 1707, Mary Eliot (HAGE:52).

MORRELL

[-?-], d. by 23 Aug 1714, having m. Mary, sister of Richard Carter of MD (AALR IB#2:170).

MORRIS

[-?-] (Morrice), m. by 31 Aug 1701, Margaret, dau. of James Frisell of AA Co. (MWB 11:209).

[-?-], m. by 28 April 1709, Hester, dau. of Rowland Beavens of SO Co. (MWB 12, pt. 2:100).

Anthony, m. by Aug 1695, Martha, admx. of John [whose name was given as Joseph on p. 80] Light (SOJU E#26:2).

Griffin, m. on 23 July 1684, Sarah Vaus (SOLR:IKL).

Jeremiah, m. by 16 Feb 1716, Elenor, dau. of Donnack Dennis of SO Co. (MWB 14:278).

John, of CH Co., m. by 4 March 1661/2, Eleanor, widow of William Empson (*ARMD* 53:196; CHLR A:195, 210).

John, of TA Co., d. by 8 July 1686, when his widow Margaret m. Peter Anderson (INAC 9:49).

Manus, m. on 23 April 1680, Elizabeth Ellis (SOLR:IKL).

Richard, of KE Co., m. on 29 July 1668, Jeane Putbery (*ARMD* 54:186).

Richard, m. by 7 Oct 1696, [-?-], dau. of Robert Rowland (in account of Humphrey Warren of CH Co.) (INAC 14:74).

Robert, m. by 23 Feb 1677, Katharine, relict and admx. of Peter Johnson of CE Co. (INAC 4:618;(MDTP 9A:504).

Robert, d. by Nov 1680, having m. Katherine, widow of William Stanley, who left three small children. She m. 3rd, Thomas Lindsey of CE Co. (Warrant Record CB#1:94; MDTP 13:113).

Thomas, m. by 10 March 1690, Mary, dau. of Edward and Ann Smith (SOJU AW:69).

Thomas, m. by Aug 1690, Mary, relict of Samuel Innis (*ARMD* e405:60).

Thomas, living on The Level, banns pub. in June and July, m. on 14 July 1698, Elizabeth Jackson (HAGE:2).

Thomas, living on the Level, banns pub. June and July 1698, Elizabeth [-?-] (HAGE:2).

Thomas, m. on 25 Feb 1708, Ann Bradley (KESP:48).

Thomas, m. by 17 Aug 1708, Parthenia. admx. of Henry Read of SO Co. (INAC 28:295).

Thomas, m. by 28 Sep 1712, [-?-], relict and admx. of Daniel O'Bryan of CE Co. (INAC 33B:84).

William, m. on 2 July 1709, Frances Merry (KESP:48).

MORROW

Anguish (Morroe), of DO Co., on 8 Aug 1676, banns of matrimony were published for him and Rose Daniel (SOJU O#7:45). Anguish (Morrah, Murrah), m. by 1687, [-?-], relict of Thomas Daniell of DO Co. (MDTP 14A:3).

John (Morough), m. by 1686, [-?-], heir or legatee of George Newman (INAC 9:520).

MORRY

Gerald, m. by 21 Dec 1691, Susannah, dau. of William Brockas (CELR 1:493).

MORTIMER

John, m. by June 1713, [-?-], (admx.?) of John Holdsworth of CV Co. (MDTP 22:252).

MOSE

George, m. on 3 Aug 1707, Mary Gander (AAAL 1:36, states that the banns were published on Kent Island).

MOSELY

Richard, m. by 23 July 1709, Barbara, admx. of Richard Shoobottom of SM Co. (INAC 30:21).

MOSS

John (Mosse), m. by 2 Oct 1700, Margaret Hamersley, legatee of Capt. Randolph Brandt of CH Co. (INAC 20:50).

Richard, of AA Co., m. by 1 May 1675, Eliza, mother of James Crucke (MWB 5:143).

Richard, m. by 12 March 1705/6, Elizabeth, dau. of William Slaid [Slade?] (AALR WT#2:335).

MOTE

William, of AA Co., m. by Aug 1696, Susanna, relict of John Smart of AA Co. (MDTP 16:184).

MOUAT

James, m. on 20 Feb 1706/7, Sarah Bateman (AAAL 1:33).

MOULD

John, of CH Co., on 12 April 1669 was about to marry Anne, dau. of Francis Posey, and stepdau. of John Belaine (CHLR H#1:248). They were m. by June 1679 (MDTP 11:100).

MOULTON

Walter, m. on 11 Oct 1704, Lydyah Bryant (TAPE).

William, m. by 17 Feb 1704, Lydia, admx. of Robert Bryan of TA Co. (INAC 25:153).2

MOUNTFIELD

John, m. by 18 June 1698, Ann, widow of Thomas Morris (BALR IS#IK:251).

MOY

Richard, m. by 1669, Elizabeth Turpine (Fresco cites INAC 6:312, 12:122; MDTP 7:275, 284; MWB 2:371, 372, 396).

Roger, had a license dated 24 Nov 1638 to marry Ann Phillipson (*ARMD* 4:51; MPL 1:134).

MUDD

Thomas, m. by 5 April 1709, Rebecca, late Rebecca Bright (or Wright), extx. of Maj. John Lowe of SM Co. (INAC 29:177, 300; MDTP 21:96, 22:372).

MULLIKIN

James, of CV Co., d. by Oct 1667, having m. by 1650 Mary, mother of James Demaall (*ARMD* 57:215; MPL 7:498).

James, m. by 1659, Mary Weylett (MPL R:67a-b, 4:147).

James, m. by 23 May 1698, Jane, sister of George Prather of PG Co. (MWB 6:123).

John, m. by Aug 1707, Sarah Mtchell, admx. of William Mitchell, dec. (TAJR 1706-1708).

John (Mullakin), Jr., of TA Co., m. by 4 Sep 1716, Alice, dau. of John Mitchell (MWB 14:561; TALR RF#12:334).

Patrick (Mullican), m. on 6 April 1671, Elizabeth Kindcade (*ARMD* 54:602).

Thomas, m. on 25 Oct 1714, by Rev. Jona' White, Eliza Wilson (PGQA:1).

MUMFORD

[-?-], m. by 18 March 1715, Sarah, dau. of James Truett, Sr., of SO Co. (MWB 14:581).

MUNFORT

John, m. on 2 Jan 1706/7, Elizabeth Lee (AAAN:1).

MUNKISTER

[-?-], m. by Sep 1671, Elizabeth, widow of John Charman (*ARMD* 60:346).

James, m. by Nov 1671, Elizabeth, widow and relict of John Chagreman, planter of CH Co. (MDTP 5:123).

MURCOT

John, m. on 28 April 1709, Anne Norvill (AALR 1:36).

MURPHY

[-?-], m. by April 1684, Mary, relict and admx. of John Grey of AA Co. (MDTP 13:110).

[-?-] (Murphey), d. by 21 April 1703 having m. Katherine, mother of George, Patrick, and Andrew Sexton, and of William Bachelor (MWB 3:459; TALR 9:320).

Charles (Murphey), m. on 1 Jan 1714, Mary Thompson (TAPE).

Daniel, of SM Co., m. by 4 Aug 1675, Anne relict of Peter Roberts of SM Co. (MDTP 7:42).

Edward, of Cecil Co., m. by 2 Oct 1715, Jane, dau. of Thomas Greenfield (BALR TR#A:376).

James (Murphey), of TA Co., m. by 13 Oct 1682, Mary, dau. of Richard Richardson, dec., and sister of George Richardson, dec. (DOLR 4 Old:99).

James (Murfey), m. on 1 Jan 1712, Margaret Hynson (KESP:48).

John (Murphey), m. on 19 Jan 1700, Yther [*sic*] [Esther?] [-?-] (TAPE).

Patrick, m. by 25 Aug 1686, Mary, relict and admx. of John Gray of AA Co. (INAC 9:138).

Patrick (Murphew), m. by 11 Aug 1702, Sarah, admx. of John Copas (INAC 23:90).

Roger (Murphey), m. on 4 Aug 1715, Mary Green (KESP:49).

Thomas, m. on 1 April 1706, Martha Royall (KESP:47).

Thomas, m. by 1707, Alice, widow of Thomas Stephens, and dau. of Francs and Isabella Barnes (MDTP 19C:221).

MURRAY

James, m. by 9 June 1697, Jemima, dau. of Thomas Morgan of BA Co. (MWB 7:392). He d. by 11 Oct 1709 when his widow had m. Thomas Cromwell (INAC 30:206).

MURRY

Daniel, of Kent Co., DE, Province of PA, m. by 22 June 1715, Elizabeth, widow of Robert Surry of TA Co. (QALR I(J)KA:73).

MURWENT

[-?-], m. by 1677, Eliza, widow of Richard Blunt, of KE Co. (MDTP 9:370).

MUSGROVES

Anthony, m. on 25 Nov 1707, Margaret Deavor (AAJA:34 #15).

MYNES

Robert, m. by 27 Feb 1681, Marjory, admx. of Patrick Due or Done of CV Co. (INAC 7B:201, 8:487).

NALLE

John, m. by 29 Dec 1693, Jane, sister of William Husculah of SM Co., and dau. of Dennis Husculah (MWB 7:109).

John (Nalley), m. by 26 June 1718, Mary, admx. of Thomas Harguess of CH Co. (MDAD 1:67).

NASH

Alexander, of KE Co., m. on 20 Jan 1662, Ruth Hill (*ARMD* 54:186).

Richard(?), m. by 28 June 1670, Ann, relict of Richard Blunt of KE Co. (*ARMD* 54:289; INAC 2:113; MDTP 4C:5, 7:70).

NATION

George, m. on 15 Oct 1704, Ann White (AAAL 1:27).

NEAGLE

William, m. by 1696, Mary, widow of Henry Payne, and dau. of Ann Assiter of SM Co. (Fresco cites SMWB PC#1:82; MDTP 15C:36).

NEAL(E)

[-?-], m. by 17 April 1713, Elizabeth, dau. and coheir of John Morris of TA Co. (MPL PL#3:216).

Anthony, son of James, on 10 Oct 1681, entered into a prenuptial contract with Elizabeth, dau. of William Rosewell (CHLR K:132; MWB 7:105).

Henry (Neall), d. by 12 June 1674, having m. Anne, relict and extx. of William Tetershall (or Tattershall), Gent., of SM Co. (MDTP 6:246; INAC 1:19).

James, m. by 1644, Anne, dau. and heir of Benjamin Gill (MPL 14:145; *ARMD* 41:238, 65:325).

James, of CH Co., Gent., m. by 20 Dec 1681, Eliza, dau. of William Calvert. He m. 2nd, by 1687, Elizabeth, dau. of Capt. John Lord of VA, and 3rd, by 1706, Elizabeth, dau. of Capt. Joseph Pile of CH Co. (PGLR A:449; Fresco cites CHLR 2 (1722-1729):212, 214; Westmoreland Co., VA Wills and Deeds; *MHM* 7:2).

Jeremiah, planter, m. on 10 d. 2 m., 1717, Elizabeth Lewis, dau. of Charles Lewis, all of TA Co., at Tuckahoe meeting house (TATH).

John, m. by 1717 Elizabeth, granddau. of Thomas Smoot and of William Barton, Gent., of CH Co. (MWB 14:658).

Roswell, m. by 1713, Mary Brent (MWB 14:63).

Samuel, of TA Co., planter, m. on 2 d., 2 m., 1718, Hannah Webb, widow, of QA Co., at Tuckahoe meeting house (TATH).

NEARNE
Robert, m. by June 1711, Mary, co-extx. of Samuel Layfield (SOJU 1707-1711:480).

NEAVE
Robert, m. by 1679, [-?-], widow of William Davis of KE co. (MPL 20:158).

NEEDLES
[-?-], m. by 29 March 1689, Eliza, dau. of Edward Mann of TA Co. (MWB 7:272; TALR 9:164).

NELSON
Ambrose, m. on 5 Feb 1707/8, Sarah Du---e (AAAN:1).
John, m. on 12 Jan 1718, Frances Roades (SJSG:10).
John (Nellson), m. on 15 Nov 1719, Frances [-?-] (SJSG:14).
Thomas, m. by 1 Oct 1696, [-?-], dau. and legatee of [-?-] Johnson (mentioned in account of Joseph and Elizabeth Fry of PG Co. (INAC 14:46).
Thomas, of PG Co., m. by 10 Oct 1711, Martha, dau. of Bernard Johnson of Calvert Co. (PGLR F:156).

NESHAM
Benjamin, m. on 10 May 1680, Elizabeth Jemison (SOLR:IKL).

NETTLEFOLD
George, m. Maudlin, widow of Simon Abbott and Edmund Townhill; she m. 4th, Thomas Smithwick (Warrants 4:68; MWB 1:627, 2:363; MDTP 7:112; 9:331; AALR IH#1:172).

NEVILLE
John, m. by 14 Nov 1649, Bridget Thoresby (MPL ABH:27). He m. 2nd, by 1651, Joan or Johanna Porter. She m. 2nd, by 13 Aug 1666, Thomas Hussey (MPL ABH:24; CHLR C:61).

NEWBEE
    Bernard, m. on 19 Oct 1706, Lettice Ireland (AAAL 1:33).

NEWELL
    Henry, m. by 1 March 1700, Ann, extx. of Solomon Rolle of SM Co. (INAC 21:188).
    John (Newill), m. on 29 July 1711, Ellinor Lloyd (KESP:53).

NEWMAN
    George, m. by 29 May 1662, Lydia, dau. of William Battin of SM Co. (MWB 1:162).
    John, servant, m. 1st, Joane [-?-], servant, and 2nd, by 1666, Frances Richeson, also a servant (MPL 10:391).
    John, m. by 19 March 1695, Rebeckah, extx. of John Bearcroft of SM Co. (MCHR PC:341; INAC 14:60).
    John, m. by 9 June 1697, [-?-], admx. of William Allen of TA Co. (INAC 15:252).
    John (Newnam?), m. by 28 April 1708, Mary, admx. of James Linn of TA Co. (INAC 28:229; MDTP 21:41).
    John, m. on 9 April 1713, Elizabeth Malone, spinster (CESS).
    Richard, m. by 9 Aug 1686, Anastatia, admx of Michael Thompson of SM Co. (INAC 9:148).
    Walter, Jr., m. 31 Oct 1716, by Mr. Sewell, [-?-] ...epin, spinster (CESS).
    William, m. by 1690, [-?-], admx. of William Allen of TA Co. (INAC 15:253).

NEWSOM
    Thomas, m. in Feb 1715, Mary Finchecome (or Stinchecomb) (HAGE:35).

NEWTON
    [-?-], d. c1679, having m. Sarah, extx. of Samuel Pritchard (or Pritchett); she m. 3rd, William Mishue (MPL WC#2:41, 116, 256; INAC6:544).
    [-?-], m. by 28 April 1709, Eliza, dau. of Rowland Beavens of SO Co. (MWB 12, pt. 2:100).
    Henry, m. by 30 July 1712, Anne, only child, aged 17, of Thomas Hicks (INAC 33B:19).
    John, m. by 1 Feb 1718, Frances, admx. of Francis Bolentson of CH Co. (MDAD 1:341).1
    Richard, d. by c1709, when his widow [-?-], dau. of Gerard Brown, m. 2nd, John Woodward (CHLR H#3:432).
    Thomas, of DO Co., d. by 10 Oct 1709, when his extx. Mary had m. Alexander Fisher (INAC 30:170).

NICHOLAS
    John, m. on 25 Jan 1715, Mary Todd (AAMA:87).
    Dr. William, m. by 23 Nov 1708, Elizabeth, extx. of John Sellman, Sr., of AA Co. (INAC 29:38).

NICHOLES
    John, Sr., d. by 1700, when his widow Rebecca had m. James Anderson (DOLR Old 6:121).

NICHOL(L)S
    [-?-], m. by 14 Dec 1671, Hester, widow of Capt. Edward Maynard (MDTP 5:305).
    [-?-], m. by 2 March 1693, Mary, sister of Edward Barber of SM Co. (MWB 2:287).
    [-?-], m. by 17 Dec 1708, Grace, dau. of Mark Noble of TA Co. (MWB 12, pt 2: 19).
    John, m. by 19 May 1651, [-?-], widow of William Evans, and mother of John Evans (*ARMD* 10:87; Proprietary Records F&B:188).
    John (Nichalls), on 8 Aug 1671, banns of matrimony were published for him and Martha Popley (SOJU DT#7:182).
    Simon, m. by 15 Feb 1588/9, Jane Gaskins, legatee of William Smith of CV Co. (MDTP 14:133).
    Thomas, of CE Co., m. by 15 April 1696, Elizabeth, widow of Thomas Yerbury (MPL 37:1).
    Thomas, m. on 8 Oct 1717, Ann Davis (PGQA:1).
    William (Nichols), m. on 4 Nov 1708, Elizabeth Sellman (AALR 1:36).
    William, m. on 9 Sep 1711 by Rev. Jona' White, Mary Mockby (PGQA:1).
    William, m. on 13 Feb 1715, Ann Burrows (PGQA:1).
    William (Nichalls), m. by 23 Sep 1715, Mary, extx. of Edward Brock of PG Co. (INAC 36C:40). She was a granddau. of Edward Brock (PGLR F (Old 6), 552). She was a dau. of Edward Brock of PG Co., who named his granddau. Mary Nicholls, and her brother Matthew in his will (MWB 13:723).
    Will'm, m. on 23 Oct 1718, Sarah Simons (AAJA:52#13).

NICHOLSON
    [-?-], m. by 1693/4, Catherine, admx. of Edward Inglish and extx. of William Inglish of CE Co. (INAC 12:158).
    James, m. in 1663, Mary Price (SOLR:IKL).
    John, m. by 29 Aug 1681, Rebecca, dau. of Richard Beard of AA Co., dec., sis. of Richard Beard (AALR IH#1:106; IB#2:110).
    John, m. on 23 Dec 1708, Esther Ijams (AALR 1:36).
    Nehemiah, of SO Co., m. by April 1711, [-?-], extx. of James Collier (NMDTP 21:340).
    Nicholas, m. by 12 Sep 1682, Hester, admx of William Gough; Hester, age c55 dep. c1684, dau. of John Larkin. After Nicholson's death she m. 3rd, [-?-] Baldwin (AALR IT#5, 18, 29; INAC 7A:118, 8:267; *ARMD* 70:177).
    William, m. on 15 Aug 1704, Elizabeth Burgess (AAAL 1:26).

NICKS
    [-?-], m. by 20 Feb 1710, Phebe, dau. of John Price of TA Co. (MWB 13:568).

NIFINGER

William, m. by 16 June 1696, [-?-], legatee of John Gouldsmith of SM Co. (INAC 13B:112).

NIMMO

[-?-]?,of TA Co., m. by Nov 1680, Jane, relict of [-?-] Richardson (MDTP 12A:178).

NIOME

[-?-], m. by 1677, Mary, widow of Stephen Whetstone (INAC 4:609).

NOADES

John, m. on 6 Feb 1704/5, Ann Shooter (AAJA:30 #14). Dr. John, m. by 10 May 1706, Ann, widow and admx. of Dr. Thomas Shutter of AA Co. (INAC 25:252).

NOAKES

[-?-], m. by 5 April 1711, Rebecca, dau. of William Pritchett (MCHR PC:709).

NOALES

Thomas, d. by April 1672, Margaret, widow of Bartholomew Herring. She later m. William Argent (MDTP 5:235).

NOBBS

Mark, m. on 16 Oct 1708, Elizabeth Cooper (TAPE).

NOBLE

[-?-], m. by 26 Feb 1704, Susanna, dau. of George Britt of CH Co. (MWB 3:485).

[-?-], m. by 1707, Eliza, dau. of James Hepbron of KE Co. (MWB 12: part 2:134).

[-?-], m. by 1707, Margaret, dau. of Walter Peake of Newtown (Fresco cites SM Co. Rent Roll)

[-?-], m. by 19 March 1707/8, Eliza, dau. of Joseph Benton of Annamessex, SO Co. (MWB 13:206).

[-?-], m. by 5 April 1709, Abigail Adams, dau. of Richard and Abigail Adams of DO Co. (MWB 12, pt. 2:119).

George, Gent., m. on (date not given), Charity Wheeler (PGKG:249).

Isaac, in Jan 1675/6, banns of matrimony were published for him and Mary Robeson (SOJU O#7:27).

Isaac, m. on 9 May 1676, Mary Robinson (SOLR:IKL).

John, m. by 21 April 1711, Jane, sister of Edward Edloe, and dau. of Jos. Edloe. Edward Edloe called their dau. Henrietta Maria his niece (SMWB PC#1:80; SMRR:12; MWB 13:216).

John, m. by 7 Dec 1708, Jane, admx. of Thomas Peerce of SM Co. (INAC 29:70).

John, m. by 20 June 1718, Margaret, admx. of Peter Booth of SO Co. (MDAD 1:161).

Joseph, b. in Cockermouth, Eng., on 17 April 1689, son of Joseph and Catherine, m. on 2 Dec 1708, Mary Wheeler (PGKG:251). She was Mary, dau. of

Francis and Winifred Wheeler (PGLR F (Old 6), 671).
Mark, m. on 27 Nov 1707, Elizabeth Heaburn (KESP:53).

NOEL
Lewis, pub. banns on 25 Oct, m. on 25 Nov 1704, Mary Ferril (HAGE:22).

NOLAN
Daniel (Nowland), m. on 6 Jan 1713 by banns, Mary Hill, widow (CESS).
Henry, m. on 5 Nov 1711, Sarah Cambell [Campbell] (KESP:53).
Thomas (Nowland), m. by 1662, Jane Battin, widow of Thomas Smoote (MDTP 15C:77, 80).

NOLES
John, m. on 9 Nov 170-, Susannah Grace (KESP:53).

NORLY
Andrew, m. on 8 Sep 1708, Jane Hyssett (KESP:53).

NORMAN
George, m. by 14 Oct 1697, Elizabeth, youngest dau. of James Smith of AA Co. (INAC 15:180).
George, m. on 26 Oct 1717, Mary Wood (AAAN:34).
John, d. by c1657, having m. 1st, by 1649, Ann [-?-], widow of John Smithson; he m. 2nd, Agnes Neale (*NMFP*:260; MPL ABH:24:46).
Nicholas, m. on 11 Aug 1706, Elizabeth Howard (AAJA:33 #2).

NORRIS
Caleb, m. by 14 Dec 1706, Elizabeth, widow and extx. of John Rablin of PG Co. (INAC 26:145).
John, m. on --- (date not given), Clare Wells (AAJA:48#12).
John, m. by 13 May 1706, Susanna, dau. of Susanna Heard, widow of John Heard of SM Co. (MWB 12:199).
John, m. on 3 April 1716, Mary Newman (AAJA:49#14).
Jno., m. by 16 Nov 1716, Clare, dau. of Mary Watkins (MWB 14:678).
Thomas, and Sarah Parrish filed their intentions to marry on 26 d., 9 m., 1708, and 24 d., 10 m., 1708 (WRMMa).

NORTH
[-?-], of AA Co., m. by Feb 1677/8, Elizabeth, relict and admx. of Thomas Joyson (or Toyson) (MDTP 9A:464).

NORTON
Andrew, of CH Co., formerly of Fairfield Stope Parish, South Britain, m. by 10 Aug 1712, [-?-], dau. of Cornelius White of CH Co., Gent. (MWB 14:500).

NORWOOD
[-?-], m. by 3 Sep 1686, Sarah, dau. of Tobias Wells, in acct. of Lewis Blangy of KE Co. (INAC 9:91).
Arthur, m. by July 1679, Anne, widow of John Eason of TA Co. (MDTP 11:125, 307).
Philip, m. on 2 Jan 1704/5, Hannah [-?-] (AAAN:19).

NOUGHTON
William, m. on 12 Dec 1672, Katherine Newgent (SOLR:IKL).

NOULEN
Robert, m. on 15 Aug 1718, Rachel James (AAAN:39).

NOWELL
Henry, m. by 24 July 1699, Anne, extx. of Solomon Rutte [Rutter?] of SM Co. (INAC 19½A:153).
Henry, m. by 28 May 1715, Elizabeth, extx. of Robert Hager of SM Co. (INAC 36C:63).
Septimus, m. by Aug 1710, Jeane, sister and extx. of Thomas Taylor (MDTP 21:276, 27:96; INAC 37A:32; MWB 14:175).

NUMBERS
Peter, m. by banns on 9 Oct 1711, Ann Pennington, widow (*CESS:* 1).

NUNIN
Dennis, m. by 19 Sep 1709, Katherine, extx. of Thomas Knightsmith of BA Co. (INAC 30:18, 33A:79).

NUTHEAD
[-?-], d. by 7 Feb 1708, leaving a widow Dinah who m. 2nd, [-?-] Oely, and 3rd, Manus Devoran. Dinah Nuthead was the mother of William and Susannah Nuthead (AALR WT#2:684, 685, PK:364).

NUTTER
[-?-], m. by 5 March 1693, Eliza, dau. of Thomas Nutter of SO Co. (MWB 2:319).
Christ., m. by 11 May 1715, Sarah, dau. of William Piper of DO Co. (INAC 36B:258).

NUTTHALL
[-?-], m. by 9 May 1704, Oliver [*sic*], dau. of Thomas Sprigg of PG Co. (MWB 3:448)
Elias (Nuthall, Nutalls), m. by 28 April 1679, Elizabeth, dau. of George and Frances (Harvey) Beckwith (Fresco cites *ARMD* 8:507; Prov. Court WRC#1:524-526; INAC 6:46, 58).
James, m. by 28 April 1685, Mary, mother of John and James Boulton (MWB 4:110).

John, Jr., of SM Co., m. c1693, Mary Brent of Stafford Co., VA, according to a deposition made on 3 Aug 1717 by Rev. Nicholas Gulick. She was a sister of William Brent of Stafford Co., VA, according to a deposition of Susan Evans (MCHR CL:363).

John (Nuthall), of SM Co., planter, m. by 25 June 1700, Elinor, widow of Thomas Hillary (PGLR A:218).

NYERSBY

[-?-], m. by 2 May 1716, Sarah, dau. of Glode Lewis, Sr., of DO Co. (MWB 14:730).

OAKEY

John, of SO Co., m. by 1671, Mary, mother of Abinadab Haw (MPL 16:308).

OBRIAN

Phillip, m. on 7 Jan 1704/5, Mary Riley (AAAN:19).

ODELL

Thomas, m. by 30 April 1705, Sarah, dau. of Henry Ridgely, merchant, of PG Co. (MWB 13:89).

ODEN

Francis, m. by 5 Oct 1713, Elizabeth, dau. of John Caine (CHLR D#2:59).

OELY

Sebastian (Olley), m. on 28 April 1701, Dianah Deverin (AAMA:81). She had m. 1st, William Nuthead, and 2nd, Manus Devoran. Dinah Oely was the mother of Sebastian Oely (AALR WT#2:684, 685; INAC 21:190).

OFFETT

William, m. by 5 March 1712, Mary, dau. of Edward Brock of PG Co. (MWB 13:723).

OGG

Francis m. by 3 March 1710, Katherine, relict and admx. of Henry Roades of BA Co. (INAC 32B:48).

George, m. June 1691, Elizabeth Bagley (AAAL 1:6).

OKEE

[-?-] (Okey), m. by 27 March 1703, Rhoda, dau. of Walter Talbott of SO Co. (MWB 11:368).

John, on 4 Sep 1666, banns of matrimony were published for him and Mary Vincent, both of Manokin (SOLR O#1:29). **They were m. on 2 Oct 1666** (SOLR:IKL).

OLANDMAN

Denum (or Dennis), m. by 15 Feb 1716/7, Mary, poss. sister of William Bouland (MWB 14:495).

OLES

Robert, m. by May 1696, Margaret, admx. of William Westbury (MDTP 16:170).

OLDFIELD

George, of CE Co., m. June 1677, Petronella, admx. of John Carr (*ARMD* 66:433, 67:16).

Henry, m. on 15 July 1717, Sarah Barber (TAPE).

OLDRIDGE

Thomas, m. on 10 June 1702, Rebecca Hancock (AAMA:82).

OLESS

Robert, m. by 4 June 1695, Margaret, widow of William Westbury, and coheir of Thomas O'Daniel (BALR RM#HS:466).

OLIVELL

John, of AA Co., m. by 10 April 1711, Elizabeth, widow of William Jeffs of BA Co (BALR TR#A:162).

OLIVER

John, of CE Co., m. by 20 May 1709, Margery, dau. of Thomas King (CELR 1:502).

John, m. on 9 April 1716, Mary Isaac (PGQA:1).

Roger, d. by 14 Nov 1651 having m. by 6 March 1646, Blanch, admx. of Robert Dixon, and widow of John Harrison, and mother of Henry Harrison (Proprietary Records F&B:218, 231; *ARMD* 4:506, 10:108).

OLWELL

John, m. by 10 April 1710, Elizabeth, widow of William Geff of BA co. (BALR TR#A:162).

O'MELY

[-?-], m. by 14 March 1666/7, Ann, formerly wife of Abraham Morgan (BALR IR#PP:70).

Bryan (Omelia), of TA co., m. on 27 d. 6 m., 1676, Mary Lewis (TATH).

O'NEALE

Henry, m. by 26 April 1718, Mos---, extx. of Thomas Vinson of DO Co. (INAC 39A:55).

Hugh, m. by 26 Sep 1661, Mary, widow of [-?-] Van der Donk (*ARMD* 53:326).

Hugh, m. by 28 Jan 1663, [-?-], sister of Enoch Doughty of CH Co. (*ARMD* 53:442).

Joseph, m. by 9 Oct 1693, [-?-], dau. of Peter Lemaire of CV Co. (MWB 2:301).

Owen, d. by 19 June 1710, having m. Sarah, whose will of that date named her only son John Syms (MWB 13:75).

ORAM
Andrew, m. on 21 d. 12 m. **1678, Eliner Morris, both of TA Co., at the house of John Pitts** (TATH). She was a dau. of John Morris of TA Co. (INAC 9:49).

ORANGE
John, m. on 26 Nov 1704, Mary Wright (AAAL 1:27).

ORGAN
Matthew, m. by 27 April 1705, Katherine, extx. of John Carrington of BA Co., and widow and admx. of Turloe Michael Owen of BA Co. (INAC 25:48, 68, 27:261).

ORLEY
Thomas, m. by 15 May 1657, Rebecca, widow of 1st, George Manners, and 2nd, Edward Hall (*ARMD* 10:216, 505).

ORMAN
Thomas, m. by Aug 1693, [-?-], extx. of John Tong (MDTP 15A:67).

ORMSBY
John (Orms), had a license dated 16 Oct 1641 to marry Frances Griffin (MPL 1:149-149-150; *ARMD* 4:67; Proprietary Records F&B:149).

O'ROURKE
James, m. by March 1678, Mary, widow of John Ricks, and dau. of William Slade (MDTP 9A:499; 10:11).

ORRICK
James, m. by 15 Feb 1680, Mary, relict and extx. of John Ricks of AA Co. (INAC 7A:368).

James, m. on 23 March 1709, Priscilla Ruley (AAAN:9).

William, m. 22 Oct 1700, Katherine Duvall (AAAL 2:1).

William (Orick), m. in 1704, Hannah [-?-] (AAAN:19).

ORTON
Henry, and Mary Davis filed their intentions to marry on 21 d., 2 m., 1682, and 16 d., 5 m., 1682 (WRMMa).

Henry, of CV Co., d. by 25 July 1711, having m. [-?-], dau. of John Wilkinson (INAC 32B:228).

OSBORN(E)
[-?-], m. by 7 March 1691, Rebecca, dau. of John Hill of BA Co. (MWB 7:127).

[-?-] (Orsborne), m. by 24 July 1717, Hannah, dau. of Cecily Manders, widow of Kent Island, QA Co. (MWB 14:686).

Daniell, m. on 2 Feb 1715, Mary Tansey (AAJA:49#4).

Thomas, m. by 27 May 1710, Sarah, extx. of John Williams (INAC 31:282).

William (Osbourne), m. by 1693/4, Margaret, extx. of John Walton or Walston (INAC 12:139; MDTP 16:98).

William, m. by 29 June 1698, Hannah, admx. of Edward Owan of KE Co. (INAC 16:136).

William, m. on 24 Jan 1710, Avarilla Hollis (HAGE:55).

OTHNEEL
Philip, m. on 30 Sep 1708, Mary Dixon (AAJA:36 #3).

OTHOSON
Otho (Otterson), m. on 25 Dec 1704, in St, Stephen's Parish, by Mr. Richard Sewell, Mary Matthiason, widow (CESS). She was the extx. of Matthias Matthiason (PCJU TB#2:228).

Otter, m. by 1 Feb 1700, Elisabeth, relict and admx. of John Wheele [Wheeler?] of CE Co. (INAC 20:185).

OTTAWY
Thomas (or Harey), m. on 5 Aug 1713, Sarah Mullakin (AAAN:9).

OULFORD
[-?-], m. by 16 July 1717, Mary, dau. of Anne Dawson, widow of DO Co. (MWB 14:731).

OUTEN
[-?-], m. by 29 March 1718, Sabro, dau. of John Jones of Mattapany, SO Co. (MWB 15:46).

OVERARD
Peter, m. on 6 April 1710, Mary Morphy (AAAN:9).

OVERTON
Thomas, m. by 5 June 1676, Jane, who joined him in sale of part Beaver Neck, formerly sold by John Mascord and his wife Jane (BALR TR#RA:127, 235).

OVERZEE
Simon, d. by July 1665, when his widow Elizabeth had m. Isaac Allerton (*ARMD* 49:466).

OWEN
Edward, of New Kent, PA, bachelor, m. on 15 d. 1 m., 1684, Hannah Baxter, of TA Co., single woman, at the meeting house in Michael's River (TATH).

Richard, of KE Co., m. by 6 Oct 1677, Jane, relict and admx. of John Raven of DO Co. (INAC 4:355).

Thomas, m. in 1669, Mary Turner (SOLR:IKL).

OWENS

John, m. on 4 Feb 1705/6, Elizabeth Spicer (AAAL 1:32(2)).

Richard, m. by 1676, Mary Ann Potter, mother of Mary Buence of London, Eng. (AALR PK:221-226).

Richard, m. by 8 June 1716, Sarah, dau. of Catherine Knowles, widow of BA Co. (MWB 14:230).

Thomas, m. by Nov 1674, Mary Turner (SOJU AZ#8 (*ARMD* e87):393).

OYDOLETT

[-?-], m. by 29 March 1718, Margaret, dau. of John Jones of Mattapany, SO Co. (MWB 15:46).

PACA

Aquila, of Bush R., m. on 11 Sep 1699, Martha Phillips (HAGE:8). She was a dau. of James Phillips of BA Co. (INAC 20:229). Her mother, Susanna [-?-] Phillips, later married [-?-] Arnold of Spesutia Hundred, BA Co. (MWB 12:304).

PACKETT

Daniel, m. on 28 Dec 1717, Mary Matthews (AAAN:35).

PADDISON

John, m. by 15 May 1692, [-?-], dau. of Alice Rich of TA Co. (MWB 6:9).

John (Paddison), m. on 4 June 1714, Sarag [Sarah?] Long (TAPE).

PAGE

Jonathan, m. on July ---, Hannah Pendar (KESP:56).

Stephen, m. by [July 1691?], Bridget, admx. of Arnold Parramore (SOJU 1691-1692:131).

PAGETT

William, m. by 12 May 1679, Amy, sister of James Pascall (*ARMD* 51:263).

PAINTER

Nicholas, m. by 4 March 1679, Judith, admx. of William Parker of CV Co.; she was also admx. of John Cumber (INAC 7A:128; MDAD 69:372; *ARMD* 70:339; MDTP 14A:10).

Thomas, m. by 5 Aug 1718, Mary, admx. of Andrew Dirrickson of SO Co. (MDAD 1:216)

PAIRMAN

Henry, m. on 4 June ---, Jane Brion (KESP:56).

PAKES

Walter, m. by 1665, Elizabeth, widow of Thomas Mattingly (MPL 8:88, DD:107).

PALMER

Thomas, m. by 1707, Katherine, widow of Thomas Waughop of Piney Point, SM Co., and dau. of John Catanceau of VA (SMRR:4; Fresco cites SMWB PC#1:313, TA#1:39; MDRP 19:26, 175, 27:347).

PANTER

John, on 26 March 1667, banns of matrimony were published for him and Mary Williams (SOLR O#1:62).

PARDOE

John, and Mary Webb, filed their intentions to marry on 30 d., 6 m., 1689 (WRMMa).

John, and Levicey Webb filed their intentions to marry on 13 d., 7 m., 1700 (WRMMa).

PARKE

Robert, m. by 24 June 1684, Mary, orphan of Vincent Atchison (KELR K:69).

PARKER

[-?-], m. by 18 Oct 1714, Mary, mother of Henry, William, and John Ellt, and of Henry, Fielder, Mary, and Eliza Parker, and Margaret Morgan (MWB 14:22).

[-?-], m. on 22 June 1704, Mary Davis (KESP:56).

[-?-], m. by 9 Oct 1714, Judith, dau. of Thos. Mattingly, Sr., of SM Co. (MWB 14:222).

Gabriel, m. by 17 Aug 1715, Eliza, dau. of Thomas Greenfield of PG Co. (MWB 14:89).

George, of CV Co., m. by 9 Feb 1703, Susannah, dau. of Gabriel Parrott of AA Co. (MWB 3:440; PGLR F "Old 6").

John, m. by 10 June 1685, Mary, dau. of Christopher Beanes (BALR IS#H:101).

John, Sr., of Bush River, m. on 12 Sep 1699, Isabella Smith, of Gunpowder R., widow, (HAGE:8). She was admx. of Thomas Smith of BA Co. (INAC 28:150).

Richard, m. on 5 April 1711, Sarah Peton (TAPE).

Robert, m. by 4 Aug 1710, Judith, admx. of Benjamin Clarke, Gent., of SM Co. (INAC 31:357).

Thomas, m. by 19 Sep 1679, Elizabeth, admx. of Henry Gott of KE Co. (INAC 6:606).

Stephen, d. by 25 Feb 1714, having m. Mary, dau. of John Hopkins of Finden; she m. 2nd, by Feb 1714, John Brookes of Ingleby, Co. Derby (KELR BC#1:45, 47).

Thomas, m. on 17 Feb 17--, Martha Woodland (KESP:56). He m. by 8 Feb 1709, Martha, extx., of William Woodland of KE Co. (INAC 31:61).

William, of CV Co., m. by 8 Sep 1675, [-?-], relict of Thomas Preston (MDTP 7:80).

William, of the Clifts, CV Co., m. after 20 Nov 1676 and before 2 Dec 1678, Judith, relict and extx. of John Cumber (AALR IH#1:285, PK:66).

PARNELL
   James, 1 Sep 1701, Katherine Cheney (AAAL 1:21(2)).

PARRAN
   Alexander, m. on 16 Feb 1693, Mary Ashcom (CVCH). She was a dau. of Nathaniel Ashcom of CV Co. (MDAD 11:248; DOLR 4 Old:26; 6 Old:77).
   Alexander, m. by 29 May 1711, Mary, dau. of Arthur Young of CV Co., ()MWB 13:249).

PARRISH
   Edward, of AA Co., m. by June 1694, [-?-], dau. of Andrew Roberts (MDTP 15C:87).
   John, son of Edward and Clara, m. on 23 d., 11 m. (Jan), 1700, Sarah Horn, widow, and dau. of Robert and Sarah Franklin (WRMM).

PARROTT/PARRATT
   Benjamin, of TA Co., planter, m. on 21 d. 8 m., 1680, Elizabeth Keen, spinster, at Henry Parratt's (TATH).
   Benjamin (Parratt), planter, m. on 6 d. 2 m., 1698, Elizabeth Estell, spinster, both of TA Co., at the meeting house near Tuckahoe Creek (TATH).
   Benjamin (Parratt), planter, m. on 9 d. 5 m., 1704, Jane Clark, Jr., both of TA Co. at the Tuckahoe Meeting House (TATH).
   George (Parratt), m. on 3 d. 11 m., 1677, Elizabeth Bodwell, of TA Co. (TATH).
   Henry, of Tredaven, TA Co., m. by 20 March 1670, Elizabeth, dau. of Henry Woolchurch of Tredavon (TALR 1:141).
   Henry, of TA Co., planter, m. on 25 d. 5 m., 1683, Mary Bates, at the house of Henry Parratt (TATH).
   Henry, of TA Co., died by 22 Oct 1685 having m. Mary, dau. of Henry Woolchurch, named as the grandfather of Parratt's son Henry (MWB 4:199).
   Henry (Parratt), planter, m. on 3 d., 12 m., 1697, Sarah Taylor, spinster, both of TA Co., at the meeting house near Tuckahoe Creek (TATH). She was a sister of Thomas Taylor of TA Co. (MWB 13:298).
   Henry, m. by 14 March 1697, Sarah, widow of James Berry, and dau. of Henry Woolchurch (TALR LL#7:195).
   Will. (Parratt), m. on last day of Nov 1669, Sarah Morgaine (*ARMD* 54:602).
   William (Parratt), planter, m. on 10 d. 11 m., 1704, Susannah Silvester, both of TA Co., at Tuckahoe Meeting House (TATH).

PARRY
   John, m. on 17 Dec 1704, Elizabeth Williams (AAAL 1:27).

PARSLEY
Richard, m. by banns on 5 Aug 1716, by Mr. Sewell, Sarah Brace, spinster (CESS).

PARSONS
David (Parson), m. by May 1686, [-?-], widow of Humphrey Jones (MDTP 13:348).

Edward, d. by 1716, having m. Mary, sister of Robert Hopkins (SMWB PC#1:206).

Peter, m. on 2 May 1803, Ursula Jenkins (WIST).

Robert, m. by June 1719, Eliza, dau. of Peter Smith of CV Co. (MDAD 2:28).

Thomas, m. by 9 June 1710, Elizabeth, extx. of John Nabb of QA Co. (INAC 31:294).

PARTRIDGE
Richard, m. on 18 Nov 1671, Margaret Lee (SOLR:IKL).

PASON
[-?-], m. by 9 Oct 1704, Mary, dau. of Richard Kendall, planter, of DO Co. (MDTP 19C:170).

PATRICK
Dorman, m. by 13 Jan 1710, Eliza, dau. of Mary Swain of SO Co. (MWB 13:357).

PATTEN
John, m. on 7 Nov 1706, Charity Cheney (AAAL 1:33).

PATTERSON
James, m. by 1680, Margaret Mollings, widow of Walter Hall (Fresco cites SMWB PC#1:30; Prov. Court TL#2:725; PCJU 1:354; MDTP 13:8).

James (Paterson), m. on 15 Nov 1705, Mary Blancher (AAJA:31 #18).

PATTISON
[-?-], m. by 30 Sep 1716, Mary, sister of Richard Twiford, shipwright of AA Co. (MWB 14:116).

James, of DO Co., m. by 29 Sep 1681, Margaret, widow of Walter Hall who d. 1678 (MPL 28:202).

James, m. by 1682, Ann, widow of Pope Alvey of SM Co. (MDTP 13:8).

PAUL
John, m. by 10 Nov 1711, Elisabeth, admx. of William Bentley of KE Co. (INAC 33A:153).

PAWSON
Henry, bro. of John Pawson of the City of York, Eng., m. by 2 Aug 1677, Margaret Leeds (MWB 10:56).

PAYNE

[-?-] (Pain), m. by 16 May 1717, Elizabeth, dau. of Thos. Millmon of DO Co. (MWB 14:456).

Henry, m. by 4 Nov 1693, Mary, dau. of Henry and Anne Assiter; he d. by 1696 and she m. 2nd, William Neagle (MWB 2:251; MDTP 15C:36, 16:36; SMWB PC#1:36).

Isaac (Paine), son of Thomas, m. by 1684 Sarah Smith, dau. of Henry Smith of SM Co. (PCLR WRC:704).

Jacob (Paine), m. Mary, relict and extx. of James Oroack [Orrick?]; she m., 3rd, by 10 March 1695?, [-?-] Eagle (INAC 13B:91, 92).

John (Paine), m. 23 Sep 1667, Marie White (*ARMD 60:116;* CHLR C#1:253).

John (Pain), m. on 25 April 1705, Catherine Secum (TAPE).

Thomas (Paine), m by 1675, Jane Smalpiece, sister of John Smalpiece [sometimes written as Smalpeace] of SM Co. (MDTP 5:354, 398, and 6:497; CELR 2:41).

PEACOCK

[-?-], m. by 1695, Elizabeth, admx. of Richard Freeman (Cotton cites INAC 10:423).

Jacob, m. on 30 April 1703, Jane Kindall (AAMA:82).

Richard, m. on 19 Oct 1704, Ann Allen (KESP:56).

Richard, m. by 7 June 1710, Mary, admx. of Pearce Lamb of KE Co. (INAC 31:233).

Samuel, m. by 8 July 1711, Anne, extx. of Richard Sandsberry of CV Co. (INAC 32C:67, 33A:156).

PEAKE

Edward, m. by 12 March 1705/6, as her 3rd husband, Mary Ball, dau. of [-?-], wife of Richard Bennison, by a previous marriage (AALR WT#2:335).

George, m. by 4 Nov 1657, [-?-], relict of Robert Parr (*ARMD* 10:554).

Joseph, m. by Aug 1698, Jane, extx. of Jane Long of BA Co. (INAC 16:208).

Joseph, of BA Co., d. by 14 Jan 1709, when his admx. Jane had m. [-?-] Merryman (INAC 30: 253).

Walter, m. by 1665, Elizabeth Mattingly, widow of Thomas Mattingly (Fresco cites Warrants 8:88).

William, m. by 1708, Elizabeth, dau. of John Raley (Rylay, Ryly) of Britain's Bay, SM Co. (SMWB PC#1:162; MWB 12, part 2:57; MDTP 21:319, 22:104, 251, 324).

PEARCE

[-?-], m. by 16 March 1700, Sarah, eld. dau. of Thomas Sprigg. Her dau. Sarah m. James Bell (Beall?) (PGLR A:362).

Benjamin, m. by 16 July 1711, Mary, extx. of John Hynson of CE Co. (INAC 32C:89, 33A:221, 35A:129).

Benjamin, Gent., m. by 14 June 1717, Mary, extx. of Capt. John Hanson of CE Co. (INAC 39B:64).

Daniel, m. on 4 Feb 1704, Mary Caulk (KESP:56).

Gideon, of KE Co., Gent., m. by 9 March 1713/4, Anne, dau. and coheiress of John Wheeler of CE Co. (CELR 2:256).

Mr. John, m. on 17 June 1697, by Mr. William Dare, Margaret Blake, widow (CESS).

Nathaniel, m. on 20 Oct 1715, Sarah [-?-] (KESH:14). She was the admx. of Richard Campbell of KE Co. (INAC 38B:72).

Nathaniel, of KE Co., m. by Dec 1716, Mary, widow of Matthew Pope of KE Co., and David Young (AALR IB#2:320).

Thomas, of CE Co., m. by 29 Jan 1703, Elizabeth, widow of William Beck and mother of Jonathan Beck (CELR 2:372).

William, m. on 5 Sep 1711, Elizabeth Anderson (AALR 1:37).

PEARLE

James, m. on 2 April 1682, Mary Glover (SOLR:IKL).

William, m. by 9 Sep 1686, Elizabeth, relict and extx. of Thomas Warren of KE Co. (INAC 9:81).

PEARSON

Francis (also Person), m. by 5 Feb 1712, Elizabeth, extx. of John Lewis of PG Co. (INAC 33B:167; MDTP 22:152).

PEARSY

Daniel, m. 10 --- ---, Ann Hopper (AAAL).

PEDDISON

[-?-], m. by 9 Sep 1706, Mary, dau. of St. Leger Codd of CE Co. (MWB 12:195).

PEDINGTON

Henry, m. on 25 Aug 1674, Margaret Griffith (SOLR:IKL).

PEIRSON

Thomas, m. by 3 April 1689, Margaret, admx. of John Golash of CV Co. (INAC 10:227).

PELLEY

Richard, m. by 20 Oct 1682, Sarah, admx. of Henry Harrison of CV Co. (INAC 8:31).

PEMBERTON

John, of Tuckahoe, TA Co., cooper, m. on 11 d. 4 m., 1684, Margaret Mathews, of the same place (TATH).

PENN

Edward, m. 11 Feb 1703, Judith Deavour (AAAL 1:26).

Mark, m. by 19 Feb 1714, Jane, admx. of Abednego Jenkins of CH Co. (INAC 36B:101).

William, m. by 9 Aug 1717, Elizabeth Dutton, niece of Eleanor Hill (dau. of Matthew Hill; Eleanor had m. Nathaniel Hubbard of Eng.) (CHLR H#2:88).

PENNINGTON

Henry (Peninton), m. by banns in Dec 1708, by Rev. Richard Sewell, Elizabeth Drake, spinster (CESS). She was a dau. of William Drake (CELR 2:306).

John (Peninton), m. by lic. on 3 April 1716, by Mr. Sewell, Sarah Beedle, spinster (CESS).

Richard (Peninton), m. on 4 Sep 1711, by Mr. Sewell, Margaret Huntly, spinster (CESS).

Robert (Peninton), m. by banns on 13 Oct 1716 by Mr. Sewell, Mary Ryland, spinster (CESS). She was a dau. of John and [Alce/Alice/Else] Ryland of CE Co. (CELR 3:187).

Thomas, in Jan 1702/3 had a certificate of the banns of marriage to Ann [Ashley?] (AAJU G:12).

Titus, m. by 20 Feb 1710/11, Elizabeth, dau. of John Ray (AALR PK:332).

William, Jr., m. on 15 Dec 1706, Susannah Smart (AAMA:83).

William (Peninton), m. by banns on 14 Sep 1713 by Richard Sewell, Mary Atkey, spinster (CESS).

PENSON

William, m. by 28 Oct 1714, Elizabeth, extx. of Robert Wade of PG Co. (INAC 36B:113).

PERDUE

Jeremiah, m. by 1 Aug 1712, Sarah, admx. of John Wheate of PG Co. (INAC 33A:216, 33B:177).

PEREGOY

Henry, m. on 16 Feb 1716, Amy Green (BAPA).

PERKINS

Daniel, m. on May ---, Susannah Stanton (KESP:57).

Elisha, m. on 1 Dec 1718, Margaret Sherrell (HAGE:39).

John, m. in March 1683, Sara Roatch (SOLR:IKL).

Robert, of CH Co., m. by 30 Dec 1668, Anne, mother of Patrick Forrest (MWB 1:354).

William, m. on 3 Feb 1703/4, Martha Miles (HAGE:18).

PERRIE

Samuel, m. by 11 Nov 1713, Sarah, granddau. of William Barton, Gent. (CHLR F#2:1).

PERRY

Robert, m. by 24 Oct 1665, Margaret, relict of Bartholomew Philips of St. Clement's Manor (MDTP 1F:3).

PERSON

Symon (Pearson), m. on 23 July 1715, Sarah Schaw (Shaw) (SJSG:19R). She was admx. of Thomas Shaw (MDTP 23:50).

PETERS

Edward (Petters), m. on 9 Aug 1715, Catherine Hanning (AAAN:22).

Joseph, m. by 8 July 1686, Amy, admx. of Thomas Branson of SM Co. (INAC 9:52).

PETERSON

Andrew, m. by 23 April 1696, [-?-], admx. of Nicholas Dorrell (INAC 13B:21).

Jacob, of CH Co., m. after 1662, as his 2nd wife Elizabeth Proter [*sic*], whom he had transported (MPL 9:459).

Rozamus (Petterson), m. on 21 Oct 1705, Penelope Kimball (AAAL 1:32(2)).

PETTIBONE

[-?-], m. by 26 Feb 1696, Ann, dau. of Richard Bayly of AA co. (MWB 7:247).

Joseph, m. on 19 Dec 1717, Isabella Wilson (AAAN:35).

PETTICOATE

[-?-], m. by 16 Oct 1704, Sarah, dau. of Edward Dorsey of BA Co. (MWB 3:725).

John, m. by 1 Oct 1702, Sarah, extx. of John Norwood of AA Co. (INAC 22:40; MWB 3:131).

PEVERELL

[-?-], m. by 16 April 1804, Sarah, dau. of Hannah, wife of George Smith of BA Co. (MWB 3:238).

PHEBUS

George, m. on 14 Oct 1678, Anne Streete (SOLR:IKL).

PHELPS

John, m. on 16 Oct 1718, Susan Meek (AAAL 2:16).

Walter, m. by 1681, [-?-], widow and relict of John Buck of AA Co., and sister and only heir of George Benson (MDTP 14A:17).

Walter, Jr., m. 1 Dec 1702, Mary Cheney, Jr. (AAAL 1:26).

William, m. on 8 Aug 1706, Elizabeth Cheney (AAAL 1:32(2)).

William, m. on 11 Dec 1718, Rachel [-?-] (AAAL 2:16).

PHENIX

William, m. on 31 Dec 1702, Bridget Linsey (AAJA:26#6).

PHIGGETT

Daniel, of VA, m. by 15 April 1714, [-?-], aunt of Mary who m. 1st, Gabriel Goulden, and 2nd, John Hollins (MCHR CL:24).

PHILLIPS

[-?-], m. betw. 1705 and 1712, Cornelia, dau. of John Ross; she later m. David Macawl (DOLR 14 Old:658).

Bartholomew, m. on 16 July 1696, Mary [-?-] (TAPE).

Henry, m. on 12 Aug 170-, Jane Rawlinson (KESP:56).

James, Gent., m. in 1716 by Rev. William Tibbs, Minister of St. Paul's Parish, Johannah Kemp, widow, both of this parish (HAGE:34).

John, m. by 21 Dec 1672, Katherine, widow of John Felton, of DO Co. (MDTP 5:376; MPL Q:28, 15:290; INAC 1:238).

John, m. by 7 Aug 1705, Mary, admx. of Peter Timms of CV Co. (INAC 25:130).

John, m. 26 Sep 1710, Mary, admx. of Charles Raley of QA Co. (INAC 32A:10).

Nathaniel (Philips), m. by 23 June 1716, Elizabeth, widow of John Consyn of CE Co. (INAC 37A:95).

Robert, m. by April 1693, [-?-], widow of John Martingal (MDTP 15A:24).

Roger, m. on 22 Oct 1672, Dorothy Clarke (SOLR:IKL).

Thomas, m. by 1667, [-?-], widow of Francis Overton (MPL 11:166).

PHILPOT

Charles, m. by 1717, Elizabeth, dau. of Thomas Smoot, and granddau. of William Barton, Gent., of CH Co. (CHWB AB#3:119; MWB 14:658).

Edward, m. by 1690, Susanna (Austin), extx. of John Posey (and wife of Thomas Posey) (CHLR Q#1:26; V#1:310).

Edward, m. by 24 July 1708, Eleanor, widow of 1st, George Tubman, and 2nd, William Smallwood (INAC 28:129, 29:374, 383; MDTP 21:60).

Robert (Philpott), m. 27 Dec 1700, Anne Banks (AAAL 2:1).

Thomas (Phillpot), m. in July 1686, Mary Goldsmith (SOLR:IKL).

PHIPPARD

[-?-], m. by 9 Feb 1714, Mary, dau. of John Brown of PG Co. (MWB 14:217).

PHIPPS

Henry, m. by 12 Oct 1677, Elizabeth, widow of Dr. George Dundasse, and dau. and extx. of Patrick Forrest (INAC 4:412; Fresco cites SMWB PC#1:29, 169; MDTP 4B:35, 4C:33,36).

Robert (Phips), m. on 6 May 1696, by certificate, Ellis [-?-] (*1 Harris and McHenry* 281, "Johnson and Johnson's Lessee vs. Howard," cites a now missing Register of marriages, births, and burials, of St, Paul's Parish, BA Co., in *NGSQ* 53:201-202).

PIBORN

Richard, m. on 11 Nov 1718, Sarah Morrice (AAAL 2:16).

PICKET(T)

George, of BA Co., d. by 17 Aug 1717, leaving a widow who was the dau. of Sarah Spinks and sister to Luke Stansbury (INAC 39C:73).

Matthew, m. on 23 Dec 1711, Cathrine [-?-] (TAPE).

William, planter, m. on 21 Nov 1717, Mary **Ruley** (AAAN:35).

PICKRELL
Thomas, m. on 15 Oct 1712, Eliza **Marloy [or Marley]** (PGKG:254).

PIERCE
William, m. on 9 Dec 1714, Elizabeth **Bettson** (TAPE).

PIERPONT
John (Peirpoint), m. by March 1706/7, Mehitable, widow of Otho Holland, and dau. of John Larkin (AAJU TB#1:295, IB#2:431, 545-546; MCHR PC:668; (BALR RM#HS:62; AALR IB#2:545-546; *ARMD* 25:220).

Francis, 2 Oct 1701, Elizabeth **Mitchell** (AAAL 1:21(2)). She was a dau. of William Mitchell who d. leaving a will dated 6 Feb 1684 (AALR WT#2:498).

PIKE
William, m. 16 July 1699, Mary **Ousmore** (both were servants of Thomas Larkins (AAAL 1:15).

PILE
John, m. by 1642, Sarah Jarboe (Fresco cites MPL 1:247, 4:543; MINV 2:156).

Col. Joseph, m. by 16792, Mary, dau. of Thomas and Emma (Langworth) Turner (MPL ABH:23, 4:543; MWB 1:133, 167, 6:64, 7:245, 8:60, 139, 14:7).

PILLE
[-?-], m. by 3 May 1703, Sarah, dau. of John Lane, Sr., of SO Co. (MWB 11:353).

PINCKNEY
Mr. Henry, m. by 25 Sep 1704, Sarah, admx. of Philip Howard of AA Co. (MWB 3:401; INAC 25:45, 242, 28:35).

PINDAR
Christopher, m. by June 1710, Susanna, widow and admx. of John Gibbs, Sr., and mother of John Gibbs, Jr. (QAJR June 1710:72; INAC 32A:6).

Christopher (Pinder), m. by Aug 1711, Susannah, mother of John Caustin (QAJR Aug 1711).

PINDELL
James (Pindle), m. by April 1689, Eleanor, admx. of Richard Cheney (MDTP 14:144).

Philip **(Pindle)**, m. on 3 Aug 1709, Elizabeth **Holland** (AALR 1:36).

PINE
Francis, of KE Co., m. on 24 Feb 1669, Mary **Vicaris** (*ARMD* 54:87).

PINER

James, m. by 19 Nov 1716, Martha, dau. of Cornelius Comegys (QALR I(J)KA:93).

Thomas, m. on 8 April 170-, Rachel Glanvill (KESP:56).

PINKSTON

William, m. on 4 March 1716/7, Martha Nellson (AAAN:29).

PIPE

Job, m. by Dec 1711, Eliza, admx. of John Porter of SO Co. (MDTP 22:71).

PIPER

[-?-], m. by 2 Dec 1702, Sarah, dau of Christopher Nutter of SO Co. (MWB 11:311).

Tobias, on 8 Aug 1676, banns of matrimony were published for him and Mary Empson (SOJU O#7:45).

PITCHER

Emanuell, m. by Jan 1693/4, Jane, relict of Michael Radagh (MDTP 15C:20, 24).

PITT

John, of TA Co., planter, m. on 25 d. 6 m., 1680, Sarah Thomas, of KE Co., at the house of William Berry (TATH).

John, of TA Co., m. by 22 Nov 1699, Sarah, late wife of John Woolcott of Kent Island, dec. (TALR 8:3).

John, merchant, m. on 6 d. 9 m., 1706, Elizabeth Baynard, both of TA Co., at Tuckahoe Meeting House (TATH).

Philip, d. by 28 Jan 1698 having m. Ann, dau. of Alexander Fisher of DO Co. (MWB 6:308).

PLARING

[-?-] (Plaring?), m. by Oct 1688, Katherine, admx. of Edward English of CE Co. (MDTP 14:107).

PLATER

George, m. by Nov 1691, Anne, widow and extx. of Robert Doyne, and dau. of Thomas and Ann Burford (CHLR Q:46; 2:240).

PLATFORD

[-?-], m. by 12 Dec 1715, Elizabeth, dau. of John Mackdowell of The Clifts, CV Co. (MWB 18:358).

PLATT

[-?-], of AA Co., m. by Oct 1682, Elizabeth, relict and extx. of Robert Parnall (MDTP 12B:270).

Samuel, m. on 12 Feb 1714, Elizabeth King (TAPE).

PLOTT
William, m. by 8 June 1684, Elizabeth, extx. of Robert Parnafelt (INAC 8:236).

PLOWDEN
George, m. by 3 Aug 1717, Margaret Brent, sister of William Brent of Stafford Co., VA (MCHR CL:363).

PLUMMER
[-?-], m. by 6 June 1691, Eliza, dau. of Joseph Yate of AA Co. (MWB 2:226).
[-?-], m. by 19 April 1698, Elia, sister of John Smith of CV Co. (MWB 6:143).
Thomas, m. by 6 June 1691, Elizabeth, dau. of George and Mary Yate of AA Co. (INAC 11A:33 1/2; BALR HW#2:309; MWB 6:212).
Thomas, m. by July 1714, Mary, extx. of Ralph Stevenson (PCJU VD#1:206; INAC 36B:291).
Thomas, Jr., m. on 5 Feb 1715, Sarah Wilson (PGQA:1).

POLLARD
[-?-], m. by 7 March 1692, Martha, dau. of Francis Billinglsey of CV Co. (MWB 7:163).
Richard, m. by July 1686, Mary, admx. of William Gambell (or Gambrell) of CH Co. (MDTP 13:370, 14A:56; INAC 9:473).
Tobias, m. on 12 Nov 1701, in Dorchester Parish, Jane Robinson (DOLR 7 Old:64).

POND
John, m. on 13 Nov 1706, Margaret Powel (AAJA:33 #9).

POOER
Robert, m. on 27 June 1710, Anne Lewis (PGKG:246).

POOLE
Richard, m. 12 Aug 1703, Johanna Duvall (AAAL 2:4).

POOLEY
Nicholas, m. by banns on 9 Jan 1709, by Mr. Sewell, Sarah Reynolds, spinster (CESS).

POOR
John, m. on 10 Aug 1707, Mary Higgins (KESP:56).

POPE
Henry, m. by 1658, Annis, widow of James Bulmer (MPL ABH:50, 3:63, Q:142).
Henry, m. by 10 Jan 1663, Anne, widow of Thomas Bulmear of Patuxent (*ARMD* 10:307).
Job, m. by 24 Sep 1711, Elizabeth, admx. of John Porter of SO Co. (INAC 33A:43; MDTP 22:71).

Thomas, m. on 23 Feb 1711, Elizabeth Partridge (CESS).

William, m. by 8 d., 7 m., 1696, Sarah, legatee of John Trew of KE Co., dec. (KELR GL#1:4).

William, m. on (date not given), Martha Glanvill (KESP:57).

PORFRAY

Peter, m. by 16 Feb 1709, Elizabeth, relict and admx. of Thomas Bartlett of CH Co. (INAC 31:78).

PORTER

[-?-], m. by 19 March 1707/8, [-?-], dau. of Joseph Benton of Annamessex, SO Co. (MWB 13:206).

Hugh, m. by 16 Feb 1716, [-?-], dau. of Donnack Dennis of SO Co., who called Porter his son-in-law (MWB 14:278).

Hugh, m. by March 1717/8, Mary, extx. of Edward Bryer (MDTP 23:168).

James, m. by 30 May 1716, Mary, relict of John Roye of CE Co. (INAC 37A:96).

James, m. by 14 March 1716/7, Mary, widow of John Clements, and mother of Anne Clements (CELR 3:141).

John, m. on 25 Jan 1688, Elizabeth Gray (SOLR:IKL).

Joseph, m. on 10 d. 3 m., 1699, Susanna Wethervile, both of CE Co., at Cecil Meeting House (KECE).

PORTWOOD

John, of SM Co., m. by 1679, [-?-], mother of John Robinson (MPL WC:380, WC#2:124-125).

POSEY

John, m. by 30 May 1706, Lydia, relict and extx. of Richard Robins of CH Co. (INAC 26:45).

Thomas, m. by 1697, Susanna Austin (CHLR V#1:310).

POTT

William, m. by 6 Sep 1705, Martha, extx. of Hans Hanson of CE Co. (INAC 25:86, 28:163).

William, m. by 29 June 1711, Mary, extx. of Thomas Church of KE Co. (INAC 32C:17).

William, m. by 2 Feb 1713/4, Mary, dau. of William Pearce of KE Co. (KELR JSN:368).

POTTENGER

Robert, m. on 12 Dec 1718, Ann Evans (PGQA:2).

Samuel, m. on 11 July 1717, Eliza Tyler, dau. of Mr. Robert Tyler (PGQA:2).

POTTER

[-?-], m. by 12 Sep 1677, Martha, dau. of Robert and Sarah Burgess of Lynn, MA (KELR F:60).

[-?-], m. by Jan 1682, Elizabeth, widow of [-?-] Green and mother of Jno. Green of SM Co. (MDTP 13:4).

POTTS
    [-?-], m. on 4 June 1704, Martha Hanson (KESP:56).

POUDER
    John, of KE Co., d. by 27 Aug 1709, when his admx. or extx. Mary m. Daniel Teany (INAC 30:179).

POUNCY
    George, m. by 6 April 1687, Mary, relict of John Boswell of CH Co., and mother of Matthew, John, Mary, Martha, Michael, and William Boswell (CHLR N:206; MDTP 14A:6).

POWELL
    [-?-], m. by 3 May 1703, Eliza, dau. of John Lane, Sr., of SO Co. (MWB 11:353).
    [-?-], m. by 20 Aug 1703, Sarah, relict and admx. of Thomas Parker of CH Co. (INAC 24:231).
    [-?-], m. by 6 Oct 1710, Rachel, dau. of Richard Tull of SO Co. (MWB 13:258).
    Charles, m. by 25 June 1697, Clare, dau. of Steven Gary, late of DO Co., dec. (DOLR 5 Old:97).
    Daniel, planter, m. on 20 d. 7 m., 1684, Susannah Pitt, both of TA Co., at the house of John Pitt (TATH). She was a dau. of John Pitt, merchant, of TA Co. (MWB 14:377).
    Howell, Jr., m. on 6 d. 8 m., 1698, Joanna Pryer, spinster, at the meeting house near Choptank River, TA Co. (TATH).
    Howell, Jr., of TA Co., planter, m. on 2 d. 2 m., 1704, Esther Bartlett, at Third Haven meeting house (TATH). She was a dau. of Thomas Bartlett of TA Co. (MWB 13:451).
    Howell, m. on 2 d. 8 m., 1718, Sarah Edmundson, at Treadhaven meeting house (TATH). **Howell, m. on 2 Oct 1718, Sarah Edmondson** (TAPE).
    James, m. on 25 June 1709, Mary Sanders (TAPE).
    John, m. by 28 July 1685, Julian, admx. of Thomas Leidget of CV Co. (INAC 8:473; MDTP 13:277).
    John, m. 27 April 1703, Mary Dunstone (AAAL).
    John, m. on 21 April 1707, Elizabeth Purner (AAAN:1).
    Richard, m. in Oct 1713, Dorothy Jones (AAJA:45#23).
    Samuel, m. by Oct 1710, [-?-], admx. of Charles Fossett (MDTP 21:280).
    William, m. on 15 Dec 1709, Alice Archer (or Archur) (AAJA:38 #18).

POWER
    Nicholas, m. by c1697, Sarah, eld. dau. of Capt. Joseph Piles of SM Co. (INAC 14:98, 21:149, 26:192; MDTP 15A:2).

POYER
    Robert, m. on 4 March 1687, Rose Bayley (SOLR:IKL).

POYNTER
    Thomas, m. by 7 July 1681, Frances, dau. of William Innis, Sr., of SO Co. (MWB 4:61).

PRATHER
    Thomas, m. by 9 May 1704, Martha, dau. of Thomas Sprigg of PG Co. (MWB 3:448).

PRATT
    [-?-], m. by 1 July 1707, Jane, sister of William Cross (QALR ETA:2).
    George, of TA Co., turner, m. on 19 d. 8 m., 1682, Elizabeth Parratt, relict of George Parratt, spinster, at Tuckahoe meeting house (TATH).
    George, m. on 2 d. 5 m., 1690, Mary Parratt, spinster, both of TA Co., at Tuckahoe Meeting House (TATH).
    George, m. on 12 d. 3 m., 1700, Sarah Broadway, both of TA Co., at Tuckahoe Meeting House (TATH). George, of TA Co., d. by 9 June 1704, having m. Sarah, widow of Samuel Broadway, and mother of Sarah Broadway (MWB 3:394).
    Isaiah, planter, m. on 9 d. 9 m., 1709, Hannah Clark, at Tuckaho meeting house (TATH).
    William, m. on 6 April 1678, Elizabeth Johnson (SOLR:IKL).

PRESBURY
    James, m. on 26 Feb 1708, Martha Goldsmith (HAGE:25).

PRESTON
    James, m. in Oct 1713, Elizabeth Pritcherd (SJSG:8R).
    William, m. on 24 Jan 1710/11, [-?-] [-?-] (AAJA:40 #5).

PRICE
    [-?-], m. by 7 June 1656, Eliza, called sister Eliza Price in the will of William Johnson of SM Co. (MWB 1:129).
    [-?-], m. by 19 Nov 1685, Ann, dau. of Thomas Robinson of Nanjemoy, CH Co. (MWB 4:211).
    [-?-], m. by 15 Feb 1702/3, Rachel, dau. of Thomas Poynter, Sr., of SO Co. (MWB 12:9).
    [-?-], m. by 9 Sep 1712, Diana, dau. of Francis Harrison of CH Co. (MWB 13:504).
    [-?-], m. by 5 Aug 1713, Rebecca, dau. of Lambrock Thomas of SO Co. (MWB 13:543).
    Alexander, m. on 29 Jan 1680, Rebecca, dau. of Alexander Thomas (SOLR:IKL).
    Andrew, of QA Co., m. by 10 Oct 1707, [-?-], widow of Henry Denton of AA Co. (INAC 27:113A).

Andrew, m. by 23 April 1716, Prudence, dau. of Elizabeth Lowe of TA Co. (QALR I(J)KA:74).

David, m. by banns on 31 Dec 1715, by Mr. Sewell, Kathrin Flinn, spinster (CESS).

Edward of CH Co., m. by June 1673, [-?-], relict of John Tompkinson (*ARMD* 60:495).

Edward, m. on 29 Nov 1698, Elizabeth Lunn (AAJA:64a#1). She was the dau. of Thomas Lunn (MPL 34:182, 38:151).

Evan, m. by March 1714, [-?-], widow of Robert [Booker] who left children John, Lambert, and Margaret Booker (TAJR FT#1).

John, m. by 12 Feb 1707, Mary, extx. of James Wroth of KE Co. (INAC 28:1, 33A:167; KELR I:189, GL#2:27).

John, of TA Co., d. by 1 Oct 1707, when his relict and extx. Margery m. William Anderson (INAC 27:134, 30:165).

John, m. by banns in Nov 1714, by Mr. Sewell, Mary Davis, spinster (CESS).

John, m. by 19 June 1716, Mary, widow of John Price (KELR BC#1:142).

Steven, and Constant Horne filed their intentions to marry on 29 d., 4 m., 1716, and 27 d., 5 m., 1716 (WRMMa).

Thomas, of CV Co., m. by Feb 1687/8, Elizabeth, widow of Samuel Ramsey (MDTP 14A:42).

William, m. 1661, as her 3rd husband, Hannah, widow of 1st, Richard Heuett, and 2nd, Hugh Lee, who d. by 1661 (*ARMD* 10:542, 49:35, 54:22, 57:177; MPL ABH:44, 6:216).

William, Jr., m. by banns on 7 July 1707, by Mr. Sewell, Katharine MacCandrick, widow (CESS).

William, m. by banns on 1 Aug 1717, by Mr. Sewell, Sarah Wallis, widow (CESS).

PRIDE

Abel, m. on 17 June 1704, Margaret [-?-] (TAPE).

Jacob, m. by 16 Sep 1716, Anne, sister of Richard Woolman of TA Co. (INAC 37C:143).

PRIDEAUX

[-?-], m. by 1 July 1676, Honor, sister of Thomas Ceely of Cornwall, Eng., and SM Co. (MWB 5:33).

PRIM

Richard, on 14 Aug 1677, banns of matrimony were published for him and Alce Wilson (SOLR O#7:121r).

PRIME

Richard, m. by 1667, Ann Atkins (Hodges cites Liber 11:235).

PRIOR

[-?-], m. by 15 March 1714, Catherine, dau. of Michael Paul Vanderforth of QA

Co. (MPL PL#3:479).
Edmond, m. by 8 Aug 1701, Catherine, extx. of Arthur Emory of TA Co. (INAC 21:23).
John (Pryor), m. on 24 Dec 17--, Sarah Clark (KESP:56).
Thomas, of BA Co., m. by 7 Aug 1671, Margaret, dau. and heir of Rowland Reynolds of AA Co. (AALR IH#1:302).
William (Pryor), m. by 9 Nov 1695, Marie, dau. of Nicholas and Elizabeth Emerson (or Empson?) (CHLR M:212).

PRISE
John, m. on 21 Jan 1706, Mary Wroth (KESP:56).
John, m. on 14 Nov 1710, Margaret Huebanks (TAPE).
William, m. on 8 April 170-, Mary Hodgess (KESP:56).

PRISK
Morris, m. on 5 Sep 1703, Mary Welch (TAPE).

PRITCHETT
John, son of Michael, b. Herburn Parish, Staffs., m. on 2 March 1701, Elizabeth Bener, b. Stepney Parish, Mddx. (PGKG:239).
Thomas, m. by 1663, Charity, mother of Henry Hayler (MPL AA:357).

PROCTOR
[-?-], m. by c1688, Rachel, extx. of John Stimpson of AA Co. (INAC 10:323).
John, m. by 1686, Amy, widow of Thomas Branson (Hodges cites Liber 9:52).
Robert, of AA Co., m. by 10 Jan 1673, Elizabeth, widow of John Freeman (AALR IH#2:75).

PROFETT
Thomas, m. by May 1686, [-?-], sister of John Jones (MDTP 13:341).

PRUITE
George, m. by 14 Feb 1700, Sarah, extx. of Samuel Broadway of TA Co. (INAC 20:57).

PROUT
George [Prout?] of VA, m. by May 1697, Mary, relict and extx. of Col. William Chandler of CH Co. (MDTP 16:240).
John, m. in Sep 1674, Mary Wilkinson (SOLR:IKL).

PUCKHAM
James [an Indian baptized by John Huett, minister, on 25 Jan 1682], m. on 25 Feb 1682, Jone or Jane Johnson [Negro] (SOLR:IKL). She was a granddau. of Anthony Johnson (Heinegg:292 cites Stepney Parish, SO Co.; *ESVR* 1:137).

PULLEN

Richard, m. by 2 April 1687, Ann, mother of Ann Beck and Rosamond Queney (MWB 6:50).

PURDEW

Jeremiah (Purdue), m. by June 1712, [-?-], admx. of John Wheat of OG Co. (MDTP 22:127).

John, 31 Aug 1701, Mary Jarvis, widow (AAAL 1:21(2)).

PURDY

Henry, m. 8 Jan 1700, Anne Saunders (AAAL 1:21(1)).
John, m. on 30 Nov 1704, Mary Seamor (AAAL 1:27).
William, m. on 30 Aug 1711, Anne Mackelfresh (AALR 1:37).

PURNELL

John (Purnall), m. by Aug 1707, Tabitha, admx. of Parker Selby of SO Co. (SOJU 1707-1711:21; INAC 28:293).

Richard, d. by 14 Feb 1702, leaving a widow Mary who m. 2nd, Josias Towgood (AALR WT#2:21).

PURSELL

Patrick, m. by 10 April 1717, Mary, extx. of William Hopper of QA Co. (INAC 37B:40).

Patrick, m. by 1 Sep 1718, Mary, admx. of Edward Gray of QA Co. (MDAD 1:273). (MDTP 23:153 gives his name as Richard Gray).

PYE

Col. Edward, m. by 1686, Ann Sewall, whose next relative was Major Nicholas Sewall of SM and CH Cos. (MDTP 16:45; PCJU 1:620, 3:295, 298, 301).

Edward, m. by 1682, Ann, admx. of Benjamin Rozer (*ARMD* 70:276).

PYNER

Thomas, of KE Co., m. by 6 Aug 1705, Joanna, sister of Henry Hosier (MWB 3:729).

QUEEN

[-?-], m. by 14 April 1713, [-?-], dau. of Richard Marsham of PG Co. (MWB 13:514).

John, m. by 3 Jan 1712, Margaret, extx. of Henry Robins, who was exec. of Nathaniel Hicks of PG Co. (INAC 33B:176). John and Margaret were also administrators. of James Wilson of PG Co. (INAC 34:97).

QUINNEY

[-?-], m. by c1704, Joyce, dau. of Francis Finch (KELR GL#1:22/44).
Salathiel, m. on 5 Aug 1715, Elizabeth Jobson (AAAN:22).

QUINTON

Walter, in 1679 had an prenuptial contract with Johane Wyatt, widow of Timothy Wyatt (TALR 4:118).

Walter, Jr., m. on 18 Nov 1703, Alice Megloulin (TAPE).

Walter, m. by 1703, Sarah, widow of 1st, William Anderson, and 2nd, William Gwynn (MDTP 17:218, 18:15; TAJR 1706-1708).

RABBITS

William, m. on 3 Feb 1714/5, Rebeckah Morgan (AAAN:22).

RAFFE

Edward, m. on 6 Nov 1705, Ufley Veale (KESP:58).

RAGON

Timothy, m. on 24 Nov 1703, Mary Lary (AAMA:81).

RAIMON

John, m. on 15 Feb 1712, Susanna Drier (AAAN:9).

RAISIN

Thomas, m. on 30 Jan 1713, Mary Wismer (KESP:59).

RAKESTRAW

Richard, m. on 23 Sep 1705, Elizabeth Ward (AAAL 1:27).

RALEY

James, m. by 1692, Jane, dau. of Thomas and Jane Patterson (Fresco cites MDTP 18B:19, 33, 82, 86).

RAMSEY

[-?-], m. by 24 Nov 1707, Grace, dau. of John Chittem of PG Co. (MWB 12:234).

Charles, m. by 1 March 1679, Elizabeth, widow of John Walley and dau. of Thomas Thurston (BALR RM#HS:340, 356).

RANDALL

[-?-], m. by 8 Oct 1687, Sarah, dau. of Walter Meekes of CE Co. (MWB 6:20).

Christopher, m. in Jan 1678, by Anthony Demondidier, "contrary to the law," Johanna Norman (*ARMD* 70:121).

RANTIN

William, m. on 7 Aug 1709, Elizabeth Smith (AAMA:83).

RAOLASS

James, m. by 15 April 1710, Margrett, admx. of William Shannahave of TA co. (INAC 31:317).

RASBERRY
Thomas, m. 16 Oct 1700, Ann Lambeth (AAAL 1:21).

RATCLIFFE
[-?-], m. by 21 April 1718, Rachel, dau. of Edward Wale of SO Co. (MWB 14:620).
Emanuel, m. by Dec 1671, Anne, relict of William Black, and mother of Thomas Black (*ARMD* 5:101; MDTP 9A:517).
Nathaniel (sometimes given as Rackliffe), m. by 31 Aug 1713, Rachel, admx. of Presgrave Turvill of SO Co. (INAC 34:90, 37A:36).
Richard, of TA Co., lawyer, m. on 13 d. 3 m., 1691 Mary Caterne, spinster, at the meeting house at Tuckahoe Creek (TATH).

RATHELL
John, m. by 21 Sep 1708, Sarah, dau. of Michael Kerby of TA Co. (TALR RF#11:50).

RATTENBURY
Jno., m. 30 Dec 1701, Margaret Besson, b. 31 Jan 1673/4, dau. of Thomas and Margaret ("Jones Bible Records," *MG* 2:107).

RAVEN
[-?-], m. by 7 Dec 1708, Ester, dau. of Thomas Preston, Gent., of BA co. (MWB 13:155).

RAWBONE
[-?-], m. by 23 Nov 1675, Margaret, widow of Dr. Robert Busby [Lusby], and mother of Mary and Eliza Venus (MWB 5:215).

RAWLEY
James, m. on 15 Aug 1685, Jane Wilson (SOLR:IKL).
William, m. by 13 March 1712, Rebecca, extx. of James Anderson of DO Co. (INAC 33A:228).

RAWLIN(G)S
Aaron, m. by 19 March 1705, Susanna, dau. of Dr. William Jones (AALR IH#1:217, 330).
Daniel, m. on 12 July 1716, Mary Rumney (AAAL 2:11).
John, m. by 20 Nov 1700, Olive, dau. of Philip Griffin of AA Co. (MWB 11:19).
John, of KE, Co., m. by c1702, Jane, dau. and heir of William Haggerty (or Daggerty) of CE Co. (KELR JD#1:99).
John, m. by 14 Sep 1704, Elizabeth, extx. of Alexander Fisher of AA Co. (MWB 3:415). She was the mother of Alexander Fisher of DO Co. (MWB 14:249).
John, m. on 13 Jan 1712, Eleanor Ridgely (AAAL 2:9).
Paul, m. by 1 Oct 1696, [-?-], legatee of [-?-] Johnson (mentioned in account of Joseph and Elizabeth Fry of PG Co. (INAC 14:46). He m. by 10 Oct 1711, dau. of

Bernard Johnson of CV Co. (PGLR F:156).
   Ralph, m. on 6 June 1708, Jane Mitchell (KESP:58).
   Richard, m. on 13 Jan 1708/9, Deborah Pinch (AALR 1:36).

RAY
   Alexander (Rae), m. by 30 Aug 1687, Hannah, dau. of John Kinnamont of TA Co. (MWB 6:35).
   Daniel, m. by 7 Jan 1717, Jane, extx. of Edward Hillyard of SM Co. (INAC 39C:115).
   James (Raay), m. by 5 March 1710, Elizabeth, admx. of Archibald Bishop of CH Co. (INAC 32B:240).
   John (Rea), chyrurgeon, m. on 8 Aug 1699, Anna Mary Powell, widow (AAJA:6#4).
   John (Raye), m. by 14 July 1711, Mary, widow and admx. of John Clements of CE Co. (INAC 33A:13).

RAYMOND
   John, m. by 18 May 1713, Susanna, widow of Samuel Dryer (AALR IB#2:81).
   Jonathan, m. by 1703, Judith Brereton (Warrants BB:170).

READ
   George, m. by 1658, Alice, widow of Samuel Griffin, and sister of Robert Taylor; she m. 3rd, by 1675, John Beal (MPL ABH:312, Q:106; MWB 1:128; *ARMD* 9:282, 414).
   George, m. on 2 May 1709, Mary Tilton (KESP:58).
   George (Reed), m. by 3 Nov 1714, Elinor Tilton, who was due a portion, in 1714 acct. of John James KE Co. (INAC 36B:150).
   Henry, m. by March 1693/4, Parthenia, relict and extx. of John Smock (or Sinock) of SO Co. (SOJU LD:96; INAC 13A:190, 13B:86).
   Thomas (Reade), m. 1st, Elizabeth [-?-], who d. by 1658, and 2nd, by 1658, Elizabeth [-?-] (MPL Q:29).
   Thomas, d. by 11 Dec 1660, leaving a widow Elizabeth, who m. 2nd, Isaac Abrahams (*ARMD* 41:379).
   Will, m. on 4 April 1671, Ellenor Hurley (*ARMD* 54:602).

READING
   Thomas, m. on 11 Dec 1705, [-?-] Gittings, widow (AAAN:19). She was Kathrine, widow and extx. of Gabriel Gittings of AA Co. (INAC 28:71).
   William, m. on 4 Sep 1704, Ann Rogers (KESP:58).

REAKES
   John, m. by 10 Aug 1710, Abigail Adams, mother of Thomas Turner (DOLR 6 Old:181).

REALL

Jacob, m. by 15 Sep 1715, Sarah, admx. of Thomas Bull of CE Co. (INAC 36C:268).

RECAND

Thomas, m. by 22 June 1718, [-?-], sister of James Lewis of KE Co. (MDAD 2:252).

RECORD

Benjamin?, m. by 11 March 1679, Elizabeth Cash, widow of William Head (*ARMD* 51:267).

REDGRAVE

Abraham, m. by 27 June 1698, Margaret, relict and admx. of John Morris of CE Co. (INAC 16:126).

REEDER

Benjamin, m. by 1709, Elizabeth Attaway of SM Co. (MWB 13:54). She was a dau. of Elizabeth Attaway of SM Co. (MWB 13:54).

William, m. by 22 June 1697, Jane, dau. of John Wheeler of DO Co. (MWB 7:333).

REETE

[-?-] (or Roote), m. by 22 May 1699, Eliza, dau. of John Sheppard of SM Co. (MWB 6:237).

REEVELY

[-?-], m. by 19 June 1677, Mary, widow and extx. or admx. of William Hampstead of SM Co. (INAC 4:143).

REEVES

Edward, m. by 18 July 1682, Henrietta, widow of: Edward Swanson, Thomas Cannon of BA Co., and William Robinson (INAC 7C:183; BALR RM#HS:58).

John (Reives), m. on 4 Feb 1706/7, Elinor Murfee (AAAL 1:33).

John (Reaves), m. on 30 Nov 1707, Sarah Rawlins (AAJA:34 #16).

Thomas, m. by 9 Nov 1671, Mary, dau. of Richard Upgate of St. Clement's Manor, SM Co. (MWB 1:504).

Ubgatt, m. by 1 Oct 1696, Jane, extx. of Ignatius Causin of CH Co. (INAC 14:56, 16:6).

REGAN

Morris, m. on 15 May 1716, Elizabeth Smith (TAPE).

REGESTER

Robert (Rechester), of TA Co., webster, m. on 1 d. 11 m., 1698, Mary Booker,

relict of Thomas Booker at the meeting house at the head of Tread Haven Creek (TATH).

Robert, planter, m. on 4 d. 11 m., 1704, Sarah Neal, at Tread Haven Meeting House (TATH). She was a dau. of Francis Neale, Sr., planter, of TA Co. (MWB 14:168).

William, carpenter, m. on 2 d. 12 m., 1700, Sarah Booker, both of TA Co. (TATH).

REGNIER
Jacob, m. by April 1703, Elizabeth, extx. of James Metcalfe (PCJU TL#3:59).

RELFE
Thomas, m. on 12 March 1680, Ann Hoston {or Houston] (SOLR:IKL).

RENSHAW
[-?-] (Rensher), m. by 19 April 1712, Ann, dau. of Benja. Sauser of SO Co. (MWB 14:121).

John (Rensher), m. by 16 July 1712, Anne, admx. of Francis Roberts of SO Co. (INAC 33A:220; MDTP 22:307).

Thomas (Rensher), m. by 17 Aug 1714, Bridget, dau. of John Shiles of SO Co. (MWB 14:51).

Thomas, m. on 16 Dec 1718, Anne Charvel (AAAN:41).

William, m. by 1717, Ann, extx. of Thomas Fletchall of PG Co. (MDAD 1:3; PGLR F (Old 6), 620).

RESTING
Edward, m. on 18 March 1715/6, Mary Chaffey (PGQA:1).

REVELL
[-?-], m. by 9 June 1695, Rachell, dau. of Charles Hall of SO Co. (MWB 7:129).

Randall, m. in Oct 1682, Sarah Ballard (SOLR:IKL).

REYNARD
Joseph, m. on 23 June 1709, Mary Lusby (AAAN:7).

REYNOLDS
[-?-], of CV Co., m. by Jan 1684, Sarah, extx. of Henry Robinson (MDTP 13:204).

[-?-], m. by 1685, Sarah, extx. of Henry West of CV Co. (MDTP 13:311).

[-?-], m. by 10 Nov 1705, Sarah, dau. of Eleanor Howard of AA Co. (MWB 13:255).

Edward, m. by c1702, Mary, extx. of William Hickman of CV Co. (INAC 22:72).

John, of AA Co., m. by 11 March 1684/5, Providence, widow of Robert Davidge of AA Co. (INAC 8:45; BALR RM#HS:127, 470).

Nicholas, m. by 17 June 1718, Eleanor, admx. of Matthew Shaw of KE Co. (MDAD 1:69).

Thomas, planter, m. on 13 d 1 m., 1690, Ann Register, spinster, both of TA Co., at Bettey's Cove Meeting House (TATH).

Thomas, m. by 30 Jan 1687, [-?-], relict of William Griffith (AALR IH#1:72).

Thomas, m. on 30 Nov 1699, Sarah Griffith (AAAN:1).

William, m. on 7 Feb 1710/11, Elizabeth Lunn (AALR 1:37).

RHODES

Henry, m. 15 Jan 1697/8, Katherine Stockett (AAAL). She was an heir [prob. a dau.] of Henry Stockett (AALR WT#2:79).

William (Roades), m. on 17 Jan 1717, Mary [-?-] (SJSG:10).

RIALLS

Edward, swore there was no impediment to his marrying Anne Chapman (*ARMD* 4:272).

RICAUD

Benjamin, of KE Co., m. by 26 June 1678, Elizabeth, extx. (and mother) of Christopher Hall of Kent Co. (AALR WH#4:306).

Benjamin, m. by 10 Aug 1702, Susanna, extx. of Richard Louden of KE Co. (INAC 23:92).

Thomas, m. Nov 1718, Mary, extx. of William Edwin (MDTP 23:269).

RICE

Evan, m. by 1694, Ann Binks of CV Co. (INAC 13B:1).

Evan, m. by Sep 1694, Elizabeth, legatee mentioned in the will of Thomas Binks of CV Co. (MDTP 15C:230).

Ralph, m. by 14 Jan 1717/8, Catherine, sister of Philip Sherwood of TA co. (MWB 14:552).

RICH

Henry, m. by 28 Dec 1699, [-?-], relict of John Williams of SO Co. (INAC 19½B:87).

RICHARDS

David, m. by 20 Feb 1710, Hannah, widow and admx. of Henry Browne of AA Co. (INAC 32B:58, 33A:88; MDTP 22:41).

David, m. by 15 May 1718, Hannah, widow and extx. of Ralph Moss of AA Co. (INAC 39A:19).

David, m. on 10 Nov 1718, Anne Waters, widow (AAAN:41).

John, on 14 March 1675/6, banns of matrimony were published for him and Grace Dixon (SOJU O#7:39).

John, banns of matrimony pub. on 8 Aug 1676 for him and Elizabeth Trevett, both of SO Co. (*ARMD* e89 (SOJU O#)7:27).

John, m. by 3 March 1707, Anne, admx. of William Bradly of DO Co. (INAC 28:88, 30:162).

John, m. by April 1708, Ann, admx. of William Brady (MDTP 21:17)

John, of CE Co., d. by 28 Aug 1716, having m. Catherine, mother of Samuel Bouchille (INAC 38B:62).

Oliver, m. by Feb 1685/6, Ann, sister and coheir of William Jenkins of CV Co. (MDTP 13:290).

Thomas, m. on 25 Dec 1707, Margrett Delaine (CVCH).

Thomas, m. by 26 July 1718, Mary, extx. of William Edwin of KE Co. (MDAD 1:260).

Will, of KE Co., m. on 27 Dec 1658, Mary Short (*ARMD* 54:129).

RICHARDSON

[-?-], m. by 4 May 1698, Margaret, dau. of Eliza Smith of CV Co. (MWB 6:107).

Daniel, of AA Co., son of William and Elizabeth, m. on 4 d., 12 m. (Feb), 1691, Elizabeth Welsh, dau. of John (dec.), and Mary, of AA Co. (WRMM). She was a dau. of John Welsh or Welch (BALR TR#A:5, 33).

John, m. by 1682 [-?-], admx. of Henry Bradley (*ARMD* 70:189).

John, m. on 2 Oct 1706, Katherine Connaway (AAAL 1:33).

Joseph, son of William and Elizabeth, m. on 25 d., 8 m., 1705, Sarah Thomas, dau. of Samuel and Mary (WRMM).

Mark, m. by June 1683, Susanna, widow and extx. of George Utie (BACP D:45; INAC 10:170).

Mark (Richison), 2 Dec 1701, Mary Barrington (AAAL 1:21(2)).

Richard (Richison), m. on 3 Dec 1707, Jane Aldridge (AAAL 1:36).

Capt. Samuel, m. by 8 June 1717, Elizabeth, acct. of Parnell Rogers of CE Co. (INAC 38A:23).

Thomas, m. by 9 May 1685, Rachel, widow of John Towers (BALR RM#HS:216).

Thomas, m. on 15 Dec 1709, Bridget Clark (AAJA:38 #17).

William, m. by 1677, Elizabeth, widow of Richard Talbot (MPL 19:615, WC:480).

William, m. on 16 d., 5 m., 1689, Margaret Smith (WRMM). She was a legatee of Alice Smith (MDTP 17:184).

William, m. by 20 July 1717, Jane, admx. of William Veatch of CV Co. (INAC 39C:21).

William, may have m. by 11 Feb 1718, [-?-] dau. of Matthew Scarbrough of SO Co., who called Richardson his son-in-law (MWB 18:294).

RICKARDS

John, on 8 Aug 1676, banns of matrimony were published for him and Elizabeth Trevett (SOJU O#7:45).

RICKETTS

Jeremiah, m. on 15 Jan 1712, Ann Jones (KESP:59).

Nathaniel, m. by 4 March 1717, Elizabeth, relict of William Bateman of KE Co. (KELR BC#1:308).

Thomas, m. 10 Dec 1702, Rebecca Nicholson (AAAL 1:26).

Thomas, Sr., m. on 14 Aug 1705, Sarah Rawlings (AAAL 1:27).

RICKS

John, d. by Feb 1677/8, having m. [-?-], dau. of William Slade. She m. 2nd, James O'Rourke (MDTP 9A:499-500).

RIDER

[-?-] (Ryder), m. by 20 Nov 1674, Jane, relict and extx. of Thomas Wright of SM Co. (INAC 1:125).

[-?-], d. by 14 May 1675, having m. Jane, dau. of John Lawson of SM Co. (MDTP 6:465).

[-?-], m. by 29 March 1707, Blanch, mother of Stephen and John Burle, and of Blanch Wharton and Eliza Stanton (MWB 12, pt. 2:13).

Ric'd, of SO Co., m. by July 1711, {-?-], admx of John Henry (MDTP 22:29).

RIDGELL

Richard, m. by 1701, Elizabeth, dau. of John and Martha (Vines) Holloway, of CV Co. (INAC 21:145).

RIDGELY

Charles, m. by 26 Nov 1714, Deborah, dau. of the Hon. John Dorsey of BA Co. (MWB 14:26; INAC 25:48).

Henry, m. c1659 or later, Eliz. Howard (MPL 7:461).

Henry, m. by c1696, Mary, widow and extx. of Mareen Duvall of AA Co. (INAC 15:64, 18:183).

Nicholas (Ridgly), m. on 26 Dec 1711, Sarah Worthington (AAMA:83).

RIDGEWAY

William, m. by Oct 1701, Sarah, admx. of [Jos.?] Thompson (MDTP 19A;16).

RIDLEY

James, of TA Co., planter, m. on 28 d. 89 m., 1686, Rebecca Berry, spinster, at King's Creek meeting house (TATH).

RIGBY

Arthur, m. by 29 Sep 1701, Elinor, admx. of Andrew Orem of TA Co. (INAC 21:25).

Arthur, m. by 17 April 1714, Ellinor, dau. of John Morris of TA Co. (MPL DD#5:784, PL#3:16).

James, m. by Feb 1704, Elizabeth, dau. of Nathan and Margaret (Burrage) Smith (AALR#2:276).

John, m. by 26 Oct 1700, Eliza, dau. of Richard and Eliza Galloway (MWB 11:28).

Nathan (Rigbie), and Cassandra Coale, filed their intentions to marry on 20 d., 7 m., 1717,. and 15 d., 9 m., 1717 (WRMMa).

RIGDON
Henry, m. by 16 March 1684, Ellen, sister of Richard Ladd or Lord of CV Co., and mother of John Rigdon (MDTP 16:32-33).

RIGGALL
[-?-], m. by 2 Nov 1697, Eliza, dau. of John Holloway, of CV Co. (MWB 6:145).

RIGGIN
Teege, banns of marriage pub. on 30 July 1667, between him and Mary London (*ARMD* 54;679; SOLR O#1:79). Teague, m. in 1667, Mary London (SOLR:IKL).

RILBY
John (Rilly?), m. on 6 Sep 1714, Elizabeth Silvester (KESP:59).

RILEY
[-?-] (Ryley), m. by 6 June 1692, Jane, dau. of Jane Pattison of South River, AA Co. (MWB 2:232).
[-?-] (Reyley), m. by 21 Aug 1697, Mary, dau. of Robert Hawkshaw of KE Co. (KELR M:70).
Hugh (Ryley), m. by Aug 1698, [-?-], admx. of Martin Folkner (*ARMD* 202:359).
John (Rylie), m. by banns on 9 Feb 1713, by Richard Sewell, Mary Clements, widow (CESS).
Lawrence, m. by Sep 1706, Tabitha, poss. sister of William and Stephen White of SO Co. (PCJU PL#1:16, 17).

RINGGOLD
Charles, m. on 17 Jan 1705, Elizabeth Parke (KESP:58).
James, m. by July 1673, Mary, relict and admx. of Edward Burton (MDTP 5:522).
James, m. by 1684, Mary Spears (INAC 13:212).
James, m. by 1688, Mary, dau. of Capt. Robert Vaughan of KE Co. (MWB 4:232).
James, d. by 16 Feb 1712, leaving a widow Mary, dau. of Moses Harris of TA Co. She m. 2nd, Thomas Godman (MWB 13:455).
John, son of Thomas, m. by 1674, Elizabeth Cooke, who m. 2nd, Samuel Wheeler (INAC 1:179).
Thomas, of KE Co., m. by Nov 1657, Christian, admx. of Thomas Hill, Sr. (*ARMD* 54:121, 126).
Thomas, m. on 7 Sep 1699, Mary Tilden (KESP:58).
Thomas, m. on 1 May 1712, Rebecca Wilmer (KESP:58).

RIPETH
James (Ripworth), m. by 9 April 1717, Mary, admx. of William Eubanks of TA Co. (INAC 38A:180; MDTP 23:61).

RISWICK

John, of SM Co., m. by July 1685, Margaret, widow and extx. of Abraham Combes (MDTP 13:243).

RIVERS

Charles, m. on 26 Sep 1704, Ann [-?-] (AAMA:81).

Charles, m. by 3 July 1717, Ann Jobson (AALR IB#2:368).

RIVETT

Jonas, m. by 12 Dec 1688, Elizabeth, dau. of Alexander Smith, planter (CHLR Q:2).

RIXON

John, m. on 10 Jan 1672, Ann Davis (SOLR:IKL).

ROACH

John (Roch), m. on 4 Feb 1663, Sarah Williams (SOLR:IKL).

John, m. by 7 mo., 1717, Alice, dau. of Alice Hall of SO Co. (MWB 18:253).

ROAD

Henry (Road?), m. by Sep 1694, Parthenia, relict of John Smock of SO co. (MDTP 15C:124).

ROAE [*sic*]

Thomas, Jr., m. by 3 March 1706, Abigail, admx. of William Bell, Jr., of TA Co. (INAC 26:204).

ROAH

[-?-], m. by 9 June 1695, Alice, dau. of Charles Hall of SO Co. (MWB 7:129).

ROBERSON

[-?-], m. by 1680, Mary, relict of Thomas Dines of CH Co. (Cotton cites INAC 7A:305).

Robert, m. by 1693, Margaret, admx. of William Dunderdall of TA Co. (INAC 12:132).

ROBERTS

[-?-], m. by July 1678, Katherine, mother of Hugh [Marnecke?] of Nansemond, VA, who was the minor son of Hugh [Marnecke?] of Nansemond (MDTP 10:186).

[-?-], m. by 30 March 1695, Eliza, dau. of Nicholas Corbin of BA Co. (MWB 7:297).

[-?-], m. by 7 March 1692, Sarah, dau. of Francis Billingsley of CV Co. (MWB 7:163).

[-?-], m., by 15 Sep 1697, Ann, dau. of John Price of SM Co. (MWB 7:374).

David, m. by 10 Oct 1716, Elizabeth, widow of George Collison, Jr. (TALR RF#12:256).

Henry, m. on 10 Dec 1699, Ann Hopkins (AAJA:24#6). She was a dau. of Gerard Hopkins, named in the will of John Chappell of AA Co. (MWB 13:720).

John, m. by 2 Aug 1694, Eliza, dau. of Mareen Duvall of AA Co. (MWB 2:337).

Jno., m. on 17 Sep 1704, Deborah Roberson (CVCH).

Jno., m. on 3 Sep 1707, Grace Mannin (CVCH).

John, m. on 11 April 1705, Mary Jackson (HAGE:22). She was the widow and extx. of Thomas Jackson (BALR IR#AM:20; MDTP 19B:34).

John, m. on 5 Nov 1709, Martha Aldridg (AALR 2:5).

John, m. by 9 June 1712, Ann, extx. of John Kemball of DO Co. (INAC 34:114).

John, m. on 7 Feb 1714, Ann Richardson (SJSG:5).

Robert, and Priscilla Johns filed their intentions to marry on 3 d., 10 m., 1703 and 31 d., 10 m., 1703 (WRMMa). She was a dau. of Rich. Johns of the Cliffs, CV Co. (MWB 14:532).

Mr. Robert, m. on 15 Oct 1706, Mrs. Parks (HAGE:18).

Robert, m. by Nov 1711, [-?-], sister of the wife of John Toas (*CMSP: Black Books* #124).

Roger, m. on 23 Nov 1693, Sarah Archer (or Hecher) (AAJA:3#9).

Roger, m. on 30 Nov 1701, Anne Stanley (AAJA:24#6).

Thomas, on 8 Aug 1676, banns of matrimony were published for him and Ann Webb (SOJU O#7:45).

William, m. on 4 Oct 1704, Elizabeth Deane (KESP:58).

William, m. on 6 July 1705, Sarah Horn (AAJA:31 #15).

William, m. on 27 June 1713, Jane Squiers (TAPE).

ROBERTSON

John, m. on 1 May 1711, Ester Mattucks (AAAN:9).

Robert, m. by Nov 1698, Margaret, admx. of Jacob Seth of TA Co. (MDTP 17:217; INAC 21:343).

ROBESON

John, on 9 Jan 1676/7, banns of matrimony were published for him and Tanzine Prideaux (SOLR O#7:70r).

John, m. on 1 May 1711, Easter Mattocks (AAMA:84).

Oneall, m. on 5 Nov 1714, Martha Barns (AAMA:90).

ROBINETT

Allan, m. by 2 Sep 1701, Eleanor, dau. of John Beaman; she d. s.p. (AALR WT#1:297).

Allen, m. by 10 May 1706, Rebecca, admins. of George Williams of TA Co. (INAC 26:29).

ROBINS

George, m. c1670 [-?-], widow of Nicholas Goldsborough, and dau. of Abraham Howes of Newberry, Co. Berks (Goldsborough Bible, cited in "Robert Goldsborough of Ashby and His Six Sons," *MG* 2:2).

John, m. by 1679, Katherine, mother of Hugh, John, Katherine, and Margaret Marnacks (MPL LL:851, MPL 15:532, 570).

Robert, m. by 1657, Elizabeth, sister-in-law of William Herde (MPL 3:275-76).

Thomas, son of George and Margaret Howes Robins, m. on 3 Feb 1696, by Joseph Leech, minister, Susanna Vaughan, dau. of Thomas Vaughan (TAPE).

Thomas, m. on 6 Dec 1704, Elizabeth Allen (TAPE). She was the admx. of William Allen of TA Co. (INAC 19C:190, 192, 242, 27:224).

Thomas, m. by 4 Oct 1710, Barbara, legatee of Richard Nelson of CH Co. (INAC 32A:35).

ROBINSON

[-?-], m. by 13 Aug 1673, Tomasin, widow of Nathaniel Stinchcomb, and dau. of Joane Mastey (MWB 1:585, 586).

[-?-], of CV C0., m. by Oct 1682, Ann, admx. of James Garner (MDTP 12B:261).

[-?-], m. by 26 March 1699, [-?-], dau. of Jonas Bowen, Sr., by whom he had a son Jonas Robinbson (MWB 6:268).

[-?-], d. by 6 Jan 1715, having m. Rachel, dau. of Rachel Freeborne of Annapolis; Rachel Robinson m. 2nd, Robert Edney (AALR IB#2:262, 268).

[-?-], m. by 4 Jan 1716, Mary, dau. of Joseph Crouley, Sr., of DO Co. (MWB 14:319).

[-?-], may have m. by 22 Dec 1716, [-?-], dau. of Thomas Shaw of SO Co., who named his grandson William Robinson in his will (MWB 14:404).

Mr. Ahip, m. on 28 Aug 1697, by Rev. Mr. Richard Sewell Margaret Pryer, dau. of Thomas and Margaret (CESS).

Daniel, of CV Co., m. on 13 d., 11 m. (Jan), 1703, Sarah Neeves (elsewhere her name is given as Hughes) of AA Co. (WRMM).

David, m. on 17 Jan 1711, Mrs. Judith Combes (TAPE). She was the admx. of Edward Combs (PCJU VD#1:344).

George, m. by 13 Dec 1690, Elizabeth, relict and admx. of Paul Dorrell [or Sorrell] of AA Co. (INAC 11A:1½).

Henrietta, relict of William Robinson, m. by 6 Aug 1683, Edward Reeves (BALR RM#HS:58).

Henry, m. c1658 or later, Dorothy Leaster (MPL Q:159)l

Jacob, m. on 5 July 1714, Mary Whiticar, widow (SJSG:7).

John, m. on 21 March 1666, Elizabeth Brown (CHLR C#1:253; *ARMD* 60:116).

John, m. by 11 May 1696, Frances, relict and extx. of James Graves of CV Co. (INAC 13B:27).

John, m. on 25 April 1703, Mary Donellan (TAPE).

John, m. on 17 Sep 1711, Grace Standley (TAPE).

Richard, m. on 12 Jan 1713, Elizabeth Slade (SJSG:20R).

Richard, m. by July 1713, Rachel, admx. of Richard Sorrell (PCJU IO#1:288). [But see Thomas Robinson below].

Robert, m. by May 1694, Margaret, widow and admx. of William [Dundorath?] of TA Co. (MDTP 15C:59).

Mr. Thomas, Esq., m. on 1 July 1697, by Mr. Lehiton, Sarah, dau. of James Frisby (CESS).

Thomas, m. by 23 Jan 1713, Rachel, admx. of Richard Sorrell of AA Co. (INAC 35A:40; PCLR TP#4:64; MDTP 22:244; in INAC 35A:168, Thomas' name is given as Robins). [But see Richard Robinson above].

Thomas, m. on 30 Oct 1714, Dorothy Williams (TAPE).

Thomas Godsgrace, m. by 12 July 1714, Mary, dau. of William Sturmey of CV Co. (MWB 14:74).

William, m. on 8 Jan 1680, Elizabeth Hady (SOLR:IKL).

William, m. on 11 Dec 1704, Sarah Combest (HAGE:65).

William, m. by April 1711, Mary, admx. of William Macarty (MDTP 21:344).

William, m. on 8 Dec 1713, Mary Combest (HAGE:31).

ROBSON

[-?-], m. by Feb 1699, Eliza, 2nd dau. of Thomas and Ann Pattison, Sr., of DO Co. (MWB 11:129, 301).

[-?-], m. by 29 Dec 1707, Mary, dau. of John Phillips of Hungar R., DO Co., and sister of Thomas Phillips of DO Co. (MWB 12:212, 13:350).

Richard, m. 7 Aug 1701, Martha Roddry, dau. of Matthew and Sarah (AAAL 1:21(1)).

William, m. by 25 Jan 1700, Jane, dau. of John Pollard of Little Choptank, DO Co. (MWB 11:294). She was prob. the Jane who was admx. or extx. of Edward Wooland of DO Co. (INAC 22:30).

William, m. on 11 May 1711, Hannah Maria Younger (TAPE).

ROCHFORT

[-?-], d. by Feb 1676/7, having m. Mary, dau. and extx. of Capt. George Goldsmith; they had a son Michael. Mary m. 2nd, Capt. Samuel Boston (MDTP 4C:11, 8A:476).

ROCKWELL

John, m. on 25 May 1705, Elizabeth Morris (AAMA:82).

RODDERY

John, m. on 13 June 1706, Mary Beckett (AAAL 1:32(2)).

ROE

Edward (Rowe), m. by 5 Jan 1678, Mary, widow of [-?-] Duncombe [or Duncan] and mother of John Duncombe and Thomas Duncombe, Jr. (TALR 3:283; MWB 5:59).

William, m. on 15 May 1703, Sarah Wells (AAJA:27#9).

ROGERS

[-?-], m. by 29 Dec 1704, Elizabeth, dau. of John Hynson of KE Co. (MWB 3:656; KELR GL#1:9).

[-?-], m. by Jan 1716, Elizabeth, dau. of Susanna, the widow of Robert Mason, Gent., of SM Co. (MWB 14:341).

[-?-], m. by 30 Sep 1717, Elizabeth, sister of John Mason of SM Co. (MWB 14:648).

James [Rogers?], m. by June 1715, Mary, admx. of John Meeke (AAJU VD#1:49).

Mr. John, m. by 5 Sep 1712, Anne, dau. of Col. John Courts of CH Co. (INAC 34:75).

John (Roggers), m. on 25 April 1714, Rebeckah Stevens (SJSG:6).

Joseph, m. on 10 d. 12 m., 1688, Mary Boker, both of TA Co., at Betty's Cove Meeting House (TATH).

Matthew, m. by 1 Dec 1709, [-?-], widow and extx. or admx. of Hugh Rice of CE Co. (INAC 30:343).

ROLESTON

[-?-], m. by 14 May 1678, Eliza, sister of Jacob Singleton of CE Co. (MWB 10:34).

ROLLE

[-?-], m. by 3 June 1712, Dorothy, dau. of Richard Feddeman of TA Co. (MWB 13:567).

ROOKSBY

John, m. on 20 Jan 1705/6, Giles [*sic*] Kinedey (AAAL 1:32(2)).

ROOKWOOD

Edward, m. by 10 July 1686, Elizabeth, admx. of Capt. Henry Aspenall of CH Co. (INAC 9:55).

ROPER

[-?-], m. by 10 Oct 1676, Alice, relict and admx. of Jarvis Morgan of AA Co. (INAC 2:347).

John, 23 Sep 1701, Ellinor Carter (AAAL 2;2).

ROSE

John, m. by 27 Sep 1688, Mary, extx. of John Johnson of SM Co. (INAC 10:185; MDTP 14:94).

John, of CV Co., m. by April 1714, Frances, sister and heiress of William Dorrington, who died a minor (Warrant Record AA#1:291).

Paulus, m. on 28 July 1698, Mary Chilcott (AAJA:4#9).

Thomas, m. by 8 June 1696, Jane, admx. of Emanuel Pitcher of SM Co. (INAC 13B:109).

Thomas, m. 23 Jan 1702, Sarah Broadhead (AAAL 2:4).

ROSENQUEST

Alexander, m. on 22 Dec 1712, Hannah Smith (AAJA:42 #11). As Johanna, she was the extx. of Anthony Smith of AA Co. (AAJU RC:271; INAC 35B:73, 37A:17, 38B:86).

ROSEWELL
William, m. by 1664, Emma or Emilia, sister-in-law of James Langworth, and relict of 1st, William Johnson, and 2nd, Thomas Turner (MPL R:206b, Q:19, 4:530, 589. 7:166-7, 12:148, CC:158-9, and HH:178).

ROSS
Allen, m. by 15 Aug 1715, Jean, admx. of Woodman Stockley of SO Co. (INAC 37A:88).

John, m. by 7 June 1716, Elizabeth, widow of [-?-] Clayland, and dau. and heir of Roger Nettleship of Clerkenwell, London, Mddx. (TALR 12:245).

Reuben, m. on 5 Dec 1711, Elizabeth Harwood (AALR 1:38).

Thomas, m. by July 1696, Jane, extx. of Emanuel Pitcher of SM Co. (MDTP 16:180).

ROUNSIFER
Thomas, m. on 26 May 1705, Rose Johnson (KESP:58).

ROUSBY
Christopher, m. by Feb 1672, Elizabeth, late wife of Richard Collett (*ARMD* 65:88, 66:166).

John, m. by 28 Sep 1676, Barbara, one of daughters of Henry and Frances Morgan, dec., of KE Co.; she m. 2nd, by Sep 1687, Richard Smith (MDTP 8A:217; 14A:6; MPL 19:603).

John, m. by 14 July 1709, Anne, widow of 1st, Robert Doyne, and 2nd, widow and admx. of George Plater, of CV Co.; she was a dau. of Thomas and Ann [-?-] Burford, of CH Co. (Warrants CB#4:376; INAC 15:31, 29:391, 32B:130; MWB 4:235, 17:132)

ROWE
[-?-], m. by Oct 1677, Mary, mother and extx. of Thomas Duncombe of TA Co. (MDTP 9A:325).

ROWELL
John, on 12 June 1677, banns of matrimony were published for him and Mary Owen (SOLR O#7:100r).

John, m. in May 1686, Margaret [Gra--?] (SOLR:IKL).

ROWLAND
[-?-], m. by 12 Feb 1676, Margery, dau. of John Cage of CH Co. (MWB 5:289).

Lawrence (Rouland), of CV Co., m. by May 1682, Grace, widow of James Williams (MDTP 12B:99; INAC 8:55).

Robert, m. by 1662, Jane Batten, sister of William Batten of SM Co., and widow of Thomas Smoot (MWB 1:162; MDTP 15C:77½, 80).

ROWLES
[-?-] (Rawls), m. by 16 Oct 1676, Elisabeth, relict and extx. of William Head of KE Co. (MDTP 8A:250).

[-?-], m. by 24 Jan 1684, Eliza, dau. of Benjamin Ricaud (Richand) (MWB 4:80). Charles (Rolls), d. by 12 Sep 1701, leaving a widow [-?-], who had m. 2nd, Joseph Hawkins of AA Co.(AALR WT#1:201).

John (Rolls), m. Mary, widow of James Crouch (*q.v.*); John and Mary had a son John Rolls); she m. 3rd, William Hill, and 4th, by 18 June 1706, Philip Jones (AALR IB#2:93, IH#1:263; INAC 20:239).

John (Rolls or Rowley), m. on 5 Oct 1710, Sarah Goslinn (AALR 2:6). She was the extx. of William Gosnell of AA Co. (INAC 33B:169, 182).

John, of Kent Island, carpenter, m. by 4 July 1713, Mary, widow and extx. of Lewis DeRochbrune, surgeon, of Kent Island (INAC 34:214).

William (Rawlls), of KE Co., m. by March 1678, [-?-], dau. and extx. of Edward Coppage (MDTP 10:34).

William (Rowls), m. in 1707, Martha [*sic*] Smith (AAMA:84). She was the relict of John Smith (AALR PK:208; AAJU TB#3:104).

ROWLY

William, m. by 21 Feb [1709], Rebecca, widow of James Anderson, former admin. of John Lyon (INAC 30:327).

ROWSE

Gregory, m. by 13 May 1679, Bridget, widow of Robert Sheale (*ARMD* 51:274).

ROYSTON

Edward (Ryston), m. on 7 Dec 1698, Margaret Singly (AAJA:5#2).

George, and Rebecca Cullin, filed their intentions to marry on 28 d., 10 m., 1683 (WRMMa).

John, m. by 10 March 1697, Anne, widow and extx. of Roland Thornborough (INAC 16:25, 94).

ROZER

Benjamin (Rozier), m. by 1681, Ann Sewall, sister of Major Nicholas Sewall (CHLR L:33, Q#1:58, 60; MDTP 16:45; PCJU 1:620, 3:293).

RUFF

Richard, m. c1700, [-?-], heiress of Daniel Peverell (*MRR*:20).

RUGG

Richard, m. by Nov 1690, Mary, admx. of Thomas Cottingham (SOJU AW 28; *ARMD* e191).

RUGLISS

James, m. on 5 May 1702, Elizabeth [-?-] (TAPE).

RUMNEY

Edward, m. by 27 Feb, 12 [12th year of the reign of Queen] Anne (c1713?), Elinor, sister of William Maccubbin (AALR IB#2:194).2

RUMSEY
Charles, m. by 21 Dec 1602, Eliza, dau. of Thomas Thurston of BA Co. (MWB 6:31).
James, m. 1677, Ann, relict and extx. of John Bigger of CV Co. (INAC 4:570, 5:350; *ARMD* 66:374; MPL LL:423, 443, 461).

RUNNALLS
John, m. by 23 March 1716, Elizabeth, sister of Richard Shelvington (TALR RF#12:309).

RUNTON
Joseph, m. on 25 April 1709, Mary Farmer (TAPE).

RUSHALL
Edward, m. by 17 July 1695, [-?-], dau. of Thomas Parker of KE Co. (MWB 7:117).

RUSSELL
Abraham, m. on 26 July 1711, Jane Guildbert (or Gilburn) (AAJA:41 #4). She was extx. of William Gilburn [*sic*] (MDTP 22:65).
Brutus, m. by 20 May 1708, Mary, admx. of Richard Sothoron, and dau. of Margaret Swift, of CH Co. (INAC 28:124; CHLR D#2:142).
Brutus, m. by 10 Feb 1710, Mary, extx. of Richard Tilyard of CH Co. (INAC 32B:116).
George, d. by c1691/2, having m. Sarah, dau. of Tamasin Locatt, sister of John Milby, late of Accomack Co., VA (SOJU 1691-2:225).
John, m. by 6 Dec 1694, Rachel, dau. of John Campbell of "Poplar Hill," SM Co. (MWB 7:190).
Michael, of TA Co., planter, m. on 13 d. 11 m., 1681, Elizabeth Shaw, spinster, at the house of John Pitt (TATH).
Michael, m. by 23 March 1713, Rebeckah, dau. of Thomas Bruff, late of TA Co., dec. (QALR ETA:202).
Tho., planter, m. on 27 July 1702, Mary Cahell, spinster (HAGE:15).
Thomas, m. on 7 Nov 1714, Mary Boring (HAGE:33).
William, m. by 11 Jan 1681, Elizabeth, relict and admx. of William Hollis of BA Co. (INAC 7B:168).

RUSSUM
Thomas, m. by 14 Oct 1687, Elizabeth, one of the daus. and coheirs of John Morris of Thirdhaven (TALR 5:151).

RUTH
Edward, m. by 20 July 1699, [-?-], legatee of Thomas Parker of KE Co. (INAC 19:164).

RUTHERFORD
Richard, m. in 1715, Margaret Baker (AAAN:22).

RUTHORN
Joseph, m. by Sep 1714, Mary, extx. of John Boulin (MDTP 22:369).

RUTLAND
Thomas, m. 13 Jan 1695, Jane Linsicom [Linthicum] (AAAL). She was a dau. of Thomas Linthicum, Sr., of AA Co. (MWB 11:159).

RYALL
Jacob, m. by Dec 1714, Sarah, widow of Thomas Bull of West Elk Hundred, CE Co. (MDTP 22:371).

RYAN
[-?-], m. by 5 May 1703, Sarah, mother of James Tregow of Do Co. (DOLR 6 Old:24).

[-?-] (Reyan), m. by 7 June 1710, Sarah, dau. of James Dun of QA Co. (MWB 13:237).

John, m. by 10 Feb 1704, Sarah, extx. of Sarah Mishew of DO Co. (MWB 3:422).

John (Rion), m. on 30 Nov 1710, Mary Cobbey (AALR 1:37).

RYE
Charles, m. by 1 Oct 1703, Jane, admx. of Thomas Blake of CV Co. (INAC 24:176, 33A:172). She was the mother of Sutton and Edward Isaac (her eldest sons) and of Richard Blake (MWB 12:pt. 2:146).

RYMER
Ralph, m. by 20 June 1699, Elizabeth, admx. of Col. Nehemiah Blackiston of SM Co. (INAC 19:159)

SADLER
Giles, m. Dorothy, widow of Daniel Goldson (Goulson); she m. 3rd, by 1663, Hugh Stanley (*ARMD* 49:36, 78).

SALISBURY
[-?-], m. by June 1684, [-?-], who with Philip Smith, admin. the estate of Abraham Smith (MDTP 13:144).

Petegrew (Saldsbury, Sallesbury), m. after 1718, Mary, widow of Alexander Fisher, and dau. of John and Abigail Pritchett (MWB:17:322; MDAD 1:108; and MDTP 24:136, 250, 437).

William (Salsbury), m. on 22 Aug 1717, Mary Sherredine (TAPE).

SALLERS
John, m. by 7 June 1679, Ann, relict of Jeremiah Shulivant of AA Co. (*ARMD* 51:268).

John (Saller), m. by 2 Nov 1695, Mary, heir (sister?) of Richard Charlett of Patuxent River (PCLR WRC# 1:772).

SALLYARD
Charles, d. by 23 Jan 1709, when his extx. Katherine had m. Clement Barkston (INAC 30:341).

SALMON
Peter, of Andover, Co. Southton [Southampton?, Eng.], innholder, d. by 17 July 1688, having m. Katherine, sister of Nicholas Painter of AA Co., dec. (AALR IB#2:432, 435).

SALTER
John, m. by 1659, Jane, widow of Francis Lumbar or Lumbard (MPL 4:62, R:29b; *ARMD* 54:47).

John, m. by 26 Sep 1687, Mary, dau. of Thomas Bostick of CE Co. (MWB 6:19).

John, m. by 20 April 1700, Bridget, relict and admx. of John Sides of TA Co. (INAC 19½B:26).

SALWAY
Anthony (Salloway), m. by 22 June 1667, Martha, dau. of Richard Wells, Sr., of AA Co. (MWB 1:287).

SAMPSON
[-?-], m. by 3 Jan 1713, Sarah, dau. of Thomas Freeborne of AA Co. (MWB 13:621).

SANDERMAN
William, m. on 26 Sep 1701, Margaret [-?-] (TAPE).

SANDERS
[-?-], m. by 7 Nov 1716, Prudence, dau. of Nicholas Cooper of CH Co. (MWB 14:193).

[-?-], m. by 13 Feb 1717, Mary, dau. of Edward Rockwood (MWB 14:519).

Edward, of CH Co., m. by 5 Jan 1688, Jane, dau. of John Ocane (Ocaine) of CH Co. (MCHR PC:282; CHLR C#2:99).

Francis, m. by 29 Aug 1672, Mary, widow of Ralph Bassell of AA Co. (MDTP 5:309).

Francis, m. on 12 July 1702, Susannah Eads, servant to Geo. Symmons (AAJA:25#16).

James (Saunders), son of James, m. 23 Sep 1703, Jane Cotter, widow (AAAL 1:26). She was the extx. of William Cotter (INAC 28:42).

James, m. on 25 June 1706, Elizabeth Jones, widow (AAAL 1:21(2)). She was the extx. of William Jones of AA Co. (INAC 28:264, 30:157).

Capt. James, m. by 28 Nov 1714, Jane, admx. of James Parnall of AA Co. (AAJU RC:271; INAC 35A:261).

John, m. by 30 Sep 1703, Sarah, widow of [-?-] Mudd, and dau. of William Boarman (CHLR Z:127).

John, m. 11 Nov 1703, Rachel Davies (AAAL 1:26).

Mr. John, m. by 4 Sep 1711, Mary, extx. of Maj. William Boarman of CH Co. (INAC 32B:247, 33A:158).

Joseph, m. by 8 April 1689, Elizabeth, widow of John [Tornton?] (MDTP 14:143).

Joseph, m. by 1 Dec 1714, Elizabeth, formerly wife of Jno. Franton (MCHR CL:234).

Robert, son of James, m. last day of Aug 1698, Rebeckah Groome, dau. of Moses [and Amy Groome (AAAL 1:16).

Stephen (Saunders), m. on 15 May 1707, Rose Nelson (AAAL 1:33).

SANDERSON

Peter, m. on 14 Jan 1700 Hannah [-?-] (TAPE).

SANGSTER

James, m. on 13 Nov 1679, Mary Benston (SOLR:IKL).

SANSBURY

[-?-], m. by 28 April 1688, Katherine, sister of John Dew of CV Co. (MWB 6:44).

[-?-], m. by 20 Dec 1683, Margaret Brett of CV Co., dau. of Ann Brett (MWB 4:39).

SANSTER

[-?-], m. by 24 Oct 1709, Penelope, dau. of William Warner of KE Co. (MWB 12, pt. 2:228).

SAPPINGTON

Nathaniel, m. by banns, on 27 Dec 1713, by Mr. Sewell, Margaret Huntly (CESS).

Thomas (Sapinton), m. on 30 Jan 1717, Mary Ruttland (AAAL 2:14).

SARGENT

[-?-] (Sergeant), m. by Jan 1695, Damaris, now aged 50, widow of John Ward of CH Co., who d. about 9 years ago (MDTP 17:114).

John, m. on 2 Oct 1692, Sarah Carne (SOLR:IKL).

SARJENT

William, m. by 17 Feb 1692, Mary, relict of Charles Stephens of CH Co. (INAC 10:251).

SATER

Henry, m. by June 1718, Mary, admx. of Edward Stevenson (BACP IS#IA:316; MDAD 2:26).

SAUSER
[-?-], m. by 4 March 1710, [-?-], dau. of John Rensher or Renshaw of SO Co. (MWB 13:369).
[-?-] (Saser), m. by 5 July 1718, Susannah, dau. of John White of SO Co. (MWB 18:5).

SAVIN
William, m. on 6 Oct 1695, Sarah, dau. of Samuel and Elizabeth Hill (CESS).

SAVORY
John, m. on 27 June 1699, Ann Reeves (*HAGE:*7).
William, m. by 14 April 1709, Penelope, extx. of John Ricketts of CE Co. (INAC 29:217).

SAWS
Robert, of Aberford, Yorkshire, m. by 14 Oct 1704, Ann, sister of Robert Lockwood of AA Co., and dau. of Robert Lockwood of Aberford (MWB 12, pt. 2:75).

SAYERS
Peter (Sayer), m. by Feb 1675/6, Frances, dau. of Henry and Frances Morgan (MDTP 4B:24, 7:247).
William, m. by 6 Aug 1709, Mary, dau. of Nathaniel Teagle, late of TA Co., dec. (TALR RF#11:83).

SAYWELL
James, m. on 30 Jan 1686, by Joseph Leech, minister, Mary Price (TAPE). She was a dau. of John Price of Buttibrooke (Bolinbrooke?), TA Co. (MWB 11:257).

SAYWOOD
John, m. by 24 Sep 1703, Mary, dau. of Edward Dawson of DO Co. (MDTP 19C:154).

SCANDLEN
Michael (Scandall, Scandell), m. by 24 May 1712, Ann, b. c1678/9, acct. [and widow] of Hilary Ball of PG Co., and sister of James Wheeler (INAC 33A:211; PGLR M:28, RR:232).

SCANTLEBURY
Thomas, marriage contract, 1701, to Sarah, dau. of George Fey, late of the Parish of St. David; contract written in Latin, and Scantlebury died by 6 June 1719 (TALR RF#12:366).

SCARBOROUGH
Col. Charles, of Accomac Co., m. (date not given), Elizabeth Bennett, dau. of Richard Bennett of Nancemond Co., VA (MPL 10:3, 14:314, 19:604).

SCHOLFIELD

Henry (Scholdfield), m. by 27 March 1695, Margaret, dau, of Walter Powell of SO Co. (MWB 7:131).

SCOFIELD

Robert, m. on 14 Oct 1697, Mary Lewis (AAJA:2#12).

SCOTT

[-?-], m. by June 1693, Comfort, mother of Wrixham White (SOJU 1692-93:249).

[-?-], m. by Feb 1709, Ann, dau. of Benja. Sommers of SO Co. (MWB 14:132).

Charles, m. by June 1706, Margaret, dau. of Henry Archer (Warrant Record AA#7:8).

Cuthbert, m. by 28 Oct 1678, Elizabeth, widow of 1st, Col. William Evans, and 2nd, of Capt. John Jordaine (*ARMD* 51:284; INAC 6:368; MPL CB2:136-37).

Cuthbert, d. by 1692, having m. Elizabeth, dau. of Joshua Guibert; she m. 2nd, by 1692, John Baptist Carberry (Fresco cites MDTP 14A:10, 22, 189, 272, 2771 Prov. Court PL#1:207; SMWB PC#1:188, 207).

Daniel, m. by 3 Aug 1703, Jane [-?-] (BALR HW#2:334). On 31 May 1744 William Denton deposed that she was Jane Scott, and that she acknowledged Eliz. Shaw to be her sister on her mother's side, and they both called Deborah Benger mother (BALR TB#C:477).

Daniel, Jr., m. by 5 Sep 1707, Elizabeth, admx. of Robert Love of BA Co. (INAC 27:110, 31:84; BAAD 2:109).

Edward, m. on 17 April 1702, Martha Tildon [Tilden] (KESP:64).

Francis, m. by banns on 7 June 1715, by Mr. Sewell, Elizabeth Single, spinster (CESS).

James, m. by 30 Aug 1687, Margaret, dau. of John Kinnamont of TA Co. (MWB 6:35).

John, m. by c1686, Christian, extx. of Thomas Sterling of CV Co. (INAC 9:222, 12:138). He d. by 27 March 1711, having m. Christian, sister of William Dorrumple (MWB 13:231).

John, m. by May 1694, Sarah, extx. of Thomas Sterling of CV Co. (MDTP 15C:64).

Mr. John, m. 8 April 1711, Jane Pitman, relict and extx. of Peter Dent of CH Co. (INAC 33A:159, 34:139, 36B:295).

Thomas, of CV Co., m. by Feb 1686/7, [-?-], relict and extx. of Thomas Sterling (MDTP 13:445).

Walter, m. on 17 April 1707, by license, by Rev. Dr. Richard Sewell, Grace Rumsey (CESS).

William (Scote), m. by 1652, Sarah, relict of William Bloff or Brough; she m. 3rd, by 1665, Thomas Wright (MPL 1:300, 309, 335, AB&H:225-26, 9:250, 270, EE:237,256; *ARMD* 10:162; Proprietary Records F&B:300).

William, m. by 1652, Jane, relict of William Brough. By 1665 she had m. 3rd, Thomas Wright (MPL AB&H:225-26, 9:250, 260, EE:237, 256).

William, m. by 1709, Ann, dau. of John Cood (SMWB PC#1:152; MDCR 3:975, 97).

William, m. by 9 July 1715, Sarah, dau. of John Porter, late of Bristol, Eng., chirurgeon (KELR BC#1:73).

SCOTTEN
William, of DO Co., 13 Oct 1718, about to marry, Mary Anderton, widow, mother of Sarah and Mary Anderton (DOLR 7 Old:79).

SCRIVENER
Benjamin, m. by 4 May 1700, Grace, dau. of John Burridge (AALR WT#1:59, IH#3:77).
Richard, b. 2 April 1686, bapt. 1 Sep 1709, m. on 1 Sep 1709, Mary Burck (AAJA:17 #17).

SCRIVIN
Philip, m. on 18 Sep 1703, Mary Simmons (AAJA:27#17).

SCUDAMORE
Nicholas, m. by May 1683, Ann, relict of Henry Brough of SM Co. (MDTP 13:43).
Thomas (Skidmore), d. by 6 Jan 1699, when his widow Abigail, dau. of John Dixon, m. by 6 Jan 1699, John Hayes (BALR TR#RA:418; Prov. Court LR EI#10:45).

SCUTT
John, m. by Dec 1696, Katherine, relict of Stephen Hart (MDTP 16:214).

SEABERY
John, of CV Co., d. by April 1676, having m. [-?-], the sister of Robert Taylor of CV Co. (MDTP 8:46).

SEAGER
John, m. by 27 Sep 1714, Margaret, extx. of Samuel Southeron of SM Co. (INAC 36C:57).
Thomas, m. by Sep 1698, Margaret, admx. of John Lawrence (MDTP 17:224).

SEAMANS
John, m. by 1685, Rebecca, widow of John Askin and Bryant Dailey, and dau. of Daniel Clocker (Fresco cites INAC 3:71; Prov. Court WRC:83, 95, 429; MWB 2:83, 96, 4:51; SMWB PC#1:99). Hodges states John, m. Rebecca, dau. of George Wright, widow of 1st, by 1688, John Askin, and 2nd, Bryan Daly (MWB 2:82; Hodges cites Liber 4:51; Hodges cites Pro. Court BB WRC:429).

SEARS
William, former servant of William Parker, m. by 1663, Elizabeth Lovell (MPL 7:130).

SEARY
William, m. by 3 June 1701, Rosamond, widow and admx. of George Stevens (INAC 19A:5).

SEAWELL
Thomas, m. on 8 Oct 1677, Jeane Boist (SOLR:IKL).

SEDGWICKE
[-?-] (Sedwicke), m. by 8 April 1712, Sarah, dau. of John Dorman (INAC 33A:157).
Elisha, m. on 3 Oct 1711, Grace Amos (or Anian) (AALR 2:8).
Gabriel, m. on 30 ---- 1713, Margaret [-?-] (AAAN:22).

SEENEY
Morgan (Seiney), m. on 4 Sep 1703, Elizabeth Briant (KESP:64).

SEFFERSON
Peter (Jefferson?), m. by 1696, Mary, dau. of Andrew Peterson of CE Co. (INAC 13B:121). Peter (Sesserson), d. by 10 April 1700, leaving a relict and extx. Mary who m. John Atkins (INAC 19½B:52).

SELBY
Edward, m. by 1658, Eleanor Matthews whom he transported (MPL Q:71).
Parker, m. by Aug 1707, Martha, dau. of John Osborn (SOJU 1707-1711:127).
Samuel, m. on 12 Dec 1717, Sarah Smith, dau. of Nathan Smith of AA Co. (PGQA:2; MDAD 1:224).
William, m. by 10 July 1713, Elizabeth, legatee of Nathan Smith of CV Co. (INAC 34:215).

SELMAN
John, m. on 4 Dec 1707, Martha Groce (AAAL 1:36).
William, m. on 9 Oct 1718, Anne Sparrow (AAAL 2:16).

SELWAY
Anthony, m. c1652/8, Martha Wells (MPL Q:70, 71; Fresco cites this as Warrants Q:70, 71).

SEMMES
James, m. by 1701, Mary, admx. of John Anderson of CH Co. (PCJU WT#3:737).

SEMPHILL
Joseph, chyrurgeon, m. by 26 Feb 1683, Mary, dau. of William Finney (TALR 4:269, 5:149 gives his name as Joseph Sampele).

SERJEANT
John, m. by Dec 1677, Mary, widow of Edward Norman, and guardian of

Rosamond Norman, dau. of Edward Norman (*ARMD* 67:231).
    William, m. by 10 Nov 1692, Damaris, widow of John Ward of CH Co. (MDTP 14A:8).
    William, m. by March 1693/4, [-?-], admx. of Charles Shepherd (MDTP 15C:32).

SERTAIN
    Robert, m. by 27 June 1716, Dinah, dau. of Joan Taylour, widow (QALR I(J)KA:79).

SETH
    Jacob, m. by 1679, Barbara, dau. of George and Frances Beckwith of CV Co. (MDTP 11:271).

SEWARD
    [-?-] (Saward), m. by 20 April 1665, Mary, sister of Thomas Griffith (MWB 1:253).

SEWELL
    Charles, m. by 2 Aug 1714, Ellenor, relict of John Tasker (MCHR CL:102).
    Henry, m. by 1663 in Eng., Jane, dau. of Vincent and Ann (Cavendish) Lowe of Denby, Eng. (Fresco cites MWB 1:225; Prov. Court S:809; *MGSB* 18, No. 1).
    Henry, m. by 13 Feb 1673, Johanna, dau. of James Warner of AA Co. (MWB 1:between 614 and 619).
    Ignatius, m. by 12 May 1699, [-?-], dau. of Hugh Ellis (INAC 18:43).
    James, m. by 10 July 1701, Bridget, extx. of John Hedger of CV Co. (INAC 20:203).
    Maj. Nicholas, m. by 11 July 1685, Susanna, dau. of William Burgess of South R., AA Co. (MWB 4:242).
    Philip, m. on 10 Feb 1708, Sarah Floud (AAAN:7).
    Richard, m. on 13 June 1699, by license, by Rev. Mr. Stephen Bordley, Minister of St. Paul's Parish, KE Co., Jane Ellis (CESS).

SEXTON
    Patrick, m. by May 1680, Katherine, relict of Robert Fuller of TA Co., who left two children by a former wife, and one, born after his death, by Katherine (Warrant Record CB#1:45).

SHACKERLY
    John, m. by 1668, Phillis, widow of William Hampton, and mother of Phillis and Hannah Hampton (MPL 16:229, 17:601).

SHADOCK
    Henry, m. by 14 June 1701, Eliza, dau. of Thomas Keare of Back Creek, Bohemia Hundred, CE Co. (MWB 11:89).

SHAHAN

Darby (Shawhawn), m. on 20 Nov 1707, Sarah Meeks (KESP:64).

David, m. by 25 Sep 1713, Bridget, dau. of David Fairbank, Sr., of Second Creek, TA Co. (MWB 13:672; TA and QA Rent Roll 1:62, 163).

SHALL

Peter, m. by 1659, Breta Andrews (MPL 4:64, R"30b).

SHANKS

[-?-], m. by 5 Jan 1712, Mary, dau. of John Bailye of St. Clement's Bay, SM Co. (MWB 13:582).

John, d. by 1684 having m. Abigail Simons (SMWB PC#1:45; MWB 4:159, 9:6; 12:239).

John, of SM Co., m. by Aug 1686, Mary, relict of Robert Bridgen (MDTP 13:389).

SHANNAHANE

Peter, m. on 25 Feb 1717, Catherine Pindergrass (TAPE).

SHAPGOOD

John, m. by 1673, Susana *alias* Butcher (MPL 17:602).

SHAPLEIGH

Philip, m. by 18 Nov 1673, Joyce, relict and extx. of Daniell Holland (MDTP 6:28).

SHARP(E)

Peter, chirurgeon, m. by 6 March 1651, Judith, widow of John Garey (or Gary), and mother of Elizabeth Gary (MPL3:314; *ARMD* 10:139).

Peter, m. on 4 d. 3 m., 1704, Catherine Troth, both of TA Co., at Third Haven meeting house (TATH). She was a dau. of William Troth, planter, of TA Co. (MWB 13:178).

William, son of Peter, m. on 4 July 1673, Elizabeth Thomas, dau. of Thomas Thomas; Elizabeth acknowledged the said William to be her lawful husband in the presence of the following witnesses: Howell Powell, John Web, Wm. Stevens, Jr., Wm. Ford, Wm. Pick, Elizabeth (EP) Powell, Magdalin Stevens, Judith Sharpe, Dorothy Stevens, Sarah Dickason, Sarah Ford, and Ralph Fishborne (*ARMD* 54:603-4).

William, m. by 12 Feb 1677, Eliza, sister of William Stevens (TALR 3:114).

SHAVERS

Abraham, m. by Aug 1718, Mary, extx. of Henry Dukes (BACP IS#IA:19).

SHAW

John, m. by 21 Jan 1702, Sarah, dau. of Mary Brown of CH Co.(MWB 11:199).

Matthew, of KE Co., m. by 26 April 1714, Elinor, mother of William and Humphrey Best (MWB 14:188).

Nicholas, m. by 10 Oct 1677, Martha, widow and extx. of Thomas Middlefield of SM Co. (INAC 4:374).

Ralph, m. by c1700/1, Ann, extx. of Thomas Wakefield of CH Co. (INAC 20:194).

Richard, m. on 2 Oct 1706, Margaret Turner (AAAL 1:33). She was the extx. of John Turner of AA Co. (INAC 30:15).

Timothy, m. by 16 March 1703/4, Ann, widow of James Frizele or Frizzell (AALR WT#2:108; MPL EE#6:187, CE#1:54).

William, of CE Co., m. by March 1675/6, [-?-], relict of Thomas Middlefield (MDTP 7:339).

William, m. on 7 July 1709, Jane Cox (TAPE).

SHEALY
Daniel, on 14 Aug 1677, banns of matrimony were published for him and Elianor Harris (SOLR O#7:121r).

SHEFFIELD
John, a seaman, m. on 17 Jan 1710/11, Elizabeth Whitington of CV Co. (AAJA:40 #2).

SHEKEL
Thomas, m. on 11 Dec 1701, Mary Budd (or Budo) (AAJA:24#14).

SHELLS
Robert, m. by 19 Feb 1661/2, Judith [or Bridget], widow of John Greenhill or Greenwell (*ARMD* 41:563).

SHELTON
John, m. by July 1686, [-?-], admx. of Robert Croft of SM Co. (MDTP 13:365).

Thomas, some time before July 1662 stated he had m. Katherine Budd (CHLR A:218, 220).

SHEPHERD
[-?-] (Sheppard), m. by 10 May 1714, Catherine, of SM Co., mother of William and John Wilkinson, and of Catherine Taney (MWB 14:7).

Nicholas, of AA Co., m. by 29 Oct 1707, Joyce, mother of Anne and William Grimes (MWB 12:231).

SHEPPEY
Richard, m. by 1665, Mary Mills (MPL EE:50, 9:52).

SHERBUTT
John, m. on 14 Sep 1697, Mary Fowler (AAJA:2#11).

SHERDEMITT

John, m. by 14 Oct 1700, Margaret, extx. of Samuel Copeland of PG Co. (INAC 20:190).

SHEREDINE

Jeremiah, m. by 2 Aug 1687, Jane, widow and admx. of Nicholas Buttram of CV Co. (INAC 9:358).

Jeremiah, m. by 25 May 1709, Martha, extx. of Thomas Atterbury of CV Co. (INAC 29:398, 32B:121).

SHERWOOD

Francis, m. on 31 July 1701, Mary [-?-] (TAPE).

John, m. by April 1798, Lucy, admx. of Edward Man of TA Co. (MDTP 17:80; INAC 23:17).

John, m. on 28 Jan 1702, Elizabeth Berry (TAPE). She was the extx. of James Berry of TA Co. (INAC 23:59, 37A:7). Elizabeth may be the Elizabeth Sherwood who was advised by Third Haven MM to go to the priest by which she was married and condemn her action publicly (*QMES:*24).

John, m. by 21 Oct 1717, Elizabeth, dau. of John Pitt, merchant, of TA Co. (MWB 14:377).

John, m. on 10 Sep 1718, Penelope Skillington (TAPE).

Philip, m. by 10 June 1718, Frances, dau. of Lawrence Knowles (TALR RF#12:354).

SHIELD(S)

Bryan, m. on 24 Sep 1711, Jane Curtis (TAPE).

Edmond (Sheeld), m. by 2 June 1717, Catherine, mother of Leonard, Mary, and Susanna Malton (MWB 14:548).

John (Sheeld), living at the head of Colletts Creek, m. on 16 Jan 1696, Elizabeth Bunn (HAGE:2).

William, m. by 17 July 1695, [-?-], dau. of Thomas Parker of KE Co. (MWB 7:117).

William, m. by 9 April 1715, [-?-], heir of Elizabeth Smith of KE Co. (INAC 36B:139).

William, the younger, m. by 20 Oct 1712, Rhoda, sister and coheir of John Dammes of TA. (TALR RF#12:140).

SHILETTO

Thomas, m. on 31 Oct 1678, Mary Rogers (SOLR:IKL).

SHIPLEY

Robert, m. by 12 Oct 1710, Elizabeth, dau. of Charles Stephens (AALR PK:296).

SHIRCLIFF

John, m. by 1651, Ann Goldsborough (MPL ABH:150).

William (Shertcliffe), of SM Co., m. by 1702, Mildred, dau. of Arthur Thompson;

he d. by 22 Feb 1709, when his extx. Mildred had m. Thomas Green (SMWB PC#1:125, 149; INAC 31:40).

Wm., m. by 7 Aug 1718, Mary, admx. of Edw'd Howard of SM Co. (MDAD 1:199).

SHIRLEY

Richard, m. by 20 Sep 1705, Katherine, extx. of John Wiseman of SM Co. (INAC 25:52, 28:223). She was a dau. of Francis Miles of SM Co. (MWB 6:375, 14:238; SMWB PC#1:204).

SHOCKLY

Richard, m. on 4 Oct 1674, Ann Boyden (SOLR:IKL).

SHOLLS

Robert, m. c1661, Bridget Seaborn, widow of John Greenwell (Fresco cites Warrants Q:208; Prov. Court S:1076).

SHONBURT

Richard, m. by 12 Dec 1706, [-?-], dau. of Alice Sisons, widow of Edward Sisons of SM Co. (MWB 12:89).

SHORES

[-?-] (Shore), m. by 25 July 1678, Katheren, relict and admx. of John Lewis of SM Co. (INAC 5:240).

Edward, m. by 6 June 1710, Elizabeth, admx. of Nicholas Dun of SO Co. (INAC 31:227).

SHORT

Abraham, m. on 23 Jan 1706/7, Naomi Thurman (AAAL1 33:).

Christopher, m. by 22 June 1697, Ann, dau. of John Wheeler of DO Co. (MWB 7:333).

George, m. on 23 Dec 1705, Susanna Darnell (KESP:64).

George, m. by 5 Feb 1708, Mary, legatee of John Smith of CH Co., and by 30 July 1711, legatee of Samuel Cooksey of SO Co. (INAC 29:64, 32B:267).

John, m. by 18 May 1697, Ann, relict and admx. of Andrew Tannehill of CV Co. (INAC 14:112).

Thomas, m. by 24 May 1714, Elisabeth, legatee of Thomas Williams of CH Co. (INAC 35A:380).

SHORTER

[-?-], m. by 4 Jan 1716, Eliz., dau. of Joseph Crouley, Sr., of DO Co. (MWB 14:319).

Anthony, m. by 9 Oct 1704, Susannah, dau. of Richard Kendall, planter, of DO Co. (MDTP 19C:170).

SHUBART

Richard, m. by 1706, [-?-], dau. of Edward and Alice Sisson (SMWB PC#1:173).

SHULIVANT

Owen, m. on 11 Dec 1709, Catherine Whaley (TAPE).

SHYLES

[-?-], m. by 26 March 1709, [-?-], dau. of George Betts of SO Co. (MWB 13:381).

SIBREY

Capt. Jonathan, of CE Co., m. by Oct 1677, [-?-], relict of Thomas Howell (MDTP 9A:393).

SICKLEMORE

Samuel, m. on 8 Dec 1713, Ruth Cammel (SJSG:20R).
Samuel, m. on 12 Sep 1716, Katherine Herrington (SJSG:9).

SIKES

William, m. by 30 May 1709, Mary, admx. of John Fosey of SM Co. (INAC 29:296).

SILK

John, citizen and pewterer of London, m. by 20 Nov 1701, Mary, relict of Abraham Wild, late of the Parish of Stepney, Co. Mddx. (CELR 2:29).

SILVERO

Nicholas, in 1676, banns of matrimony were published for him and Elizabeth Barnet (SOJU O#7:54).

SILVESTER

[-?-], m. by 29 April 1697, Eliza, sister of Thomas Purnell of CV Co. (MWB 6:255).

SIMCO

George, of PA, feltmaker, m. by 26 July 1717, Jane, dau. and heiress of Robert Sims of AA Co. (AALR IB#2:397).

SIMKINS

John, m. on 19 Aug 1711, Sarah Bradley (KESP:65).

SIMMONS

[-?-] (Simons), m. by 10 July 1686, Rebecca, extx. of Bryan Daily, dec. (INAC 9:53).

[-?-] (Simons), m. by Aug 1687, Abigail, extx. of John Shanks of SM Co. (MDTP 13:504).

[-?-], m. by 10 June 1706, Barthia [Bethia?], sister of Brian Daly of AA Co. (MWB 13:252).

Charles (Simonds), m. by 5 June 1704, [-?-], admx. of Thomas Jones of BA Co. (MWB 3:413; BAAD 2:238).

John (Simons), m. by 22 Aug 1705, Mary, mother of John Tryall (TALR 9:346).

John, of PG Co., d. by 11 April 1709, when his extx. Rebecca had m. Henry Mackie (INAC 31:140).

Richard (Simmonds), m. on 30 July 1702, Alse Trew (KESP:64).

Richard, m. in Oct 1713, Sarah Thornbury (AAJA:47#8).

Thomas (Simonds), m. by 1 Oct 1688, Margaret, extx. of John Walker of TA Co. (INAC 10:158).

SIMM(S)

Anthony, m. by 1706, Ann, dau. of Edward and Alice Sisson (SMWB PC#1:173; Fresco cites Test. Proc. MC:246).

Anthony, m. by 1 Aug 1707, Anne, admx. of Michael Brown of SM Co. (INAC 27:148).

Marmaduke, m. by Oct 1668, Fortune, widow of Bulmer Mitford, and extx. of William Champe of SM Co. (*ARMD* 57:358; MPL 10:429, 12:204).

Richard, of BA Co., m. by Oct 1680, [-?-], relict of William Wignall who was killed by the Indians (Warrant Record CB(#3):86).

SIMPSON

Amos (Simson), m. on 24 April 1716, Elizabeth Duvall (AALR 1:38).

Andrew (Sympson), m. by 1703, Elizabeth, dau. of Robert and Mary Green (CHLR Z#2:71, 89).

Andrew, on 19 May 1718 was about to marry Juliana Price, widow, mother of Mary Price (CHLR H#2:173).

Thomas, m. on 7 Aug 1703, Rebecca Richardson (KESP:64).

Thomas, m. on 9 Feb 1707, Esther Moggeridge (KESP:65).

Thomas, m. on 13 Feb 1717, Mary Smith (HAGE:46).

William (Simson), m. by 1 Sep 1675, [-?-], widow of Robert Hale of TA Co., who had died 15 mos. earlier (MDTP 7:59).

SIMS

James, m. by 9 May 1701, Mary, relict and admx. of John Anderson of CH Co. (INAC 20:262).

Richard, m. by 5 April 1676, [-?-], dau. of John Taylor of BA Co. (MWB 5:26).

SINCLAIR

Laurence (Sinclear), m. by 4 Sep 1710, Anne, admx. of George Cubbidge of TA Co. (INAC 32A:22).

Michael (Sinclor), m. on 29 Oct 1700, Hannah Hoff (AAMA:81).

William (Sinclar), m. by banns on 8 April 1714, by Mr. Sewell, Rachel Denbow, spinster (CESS).

SINNOT

Garrett (Sinnett), m. on 31 Nov 1666, Alice Hunt (CHLR P#1:204).

William, m. by 27 Aug 1718, Anne, admx. of Thomas Tippins of QA Co. (MDAD 1:278).

SISK

Maurice, m. by 1 Aug 1707, Mary, extx. of William Welch of TA Co. (INAC 27:223).

SISSARSON

Richard, m. on 9 Jan 1717, Elizabeth Clifford (TAPE).

SISSONS

Edward, of SM Co., m. by Oct 1686, [-?-], relict of John Morris of SM Co. (MDTP 13:423).

SKATS

[-?-], m. by 7 Dec 1708, Sarah, dau. of Thomas Preston, Gent., of BA Co. (MWB 13:155).

SKELTON

John, m. by 9 Aug 1686, Ann, relict and admx. of Robert Croft of SM Co. (INAC 9:145).

SKERVIN

William, m. by 24 June 1718, Margaret, admx. of Alexander Brown of SO Co. (MDAD 1:163).

SKIDMORE

[-?-] (Scidomore), m. by 11 April 1688, Judith, dau. of Capt. Joseph Hopkins of CE Co. (INAC 9:508).

Josias, m. on 7 Aug 1707, Rebecca Smith (KESP:64).

SKILLINGTON

Kenelm, of TA Co., Planter, m. on 20 d. 8 m., 1692, Lydia Craxtill, late of Barbados, at the house of Thomas Skillington (TATH).

Penelope, dau. of Kenelm Skillington, on 24 d., 7 m., 1718 was reported to Third Haven MM as "not-withstanding being precautioned to the contrary, " having been married by a priest to a man not of the Society (*QMES:*34).

SKINNER

[-?-], m. by 25 Nov 1686, Ann, sister of Arthur Storer of CV Co. (MWB 6:88).

[-?-], m. by 20 Feb 1703, Ann, mother of Thomas Hollyday of PG Co. (MWB 11:279).

[-?-], m. by 25 May 1716, Ann, formerly the wife of Andrew Tannihill (MCHR CL:279).

[-?-], m. by 25 Jan 1717, Elizabeth, dau. of Mary Mackall of CV Co. (MWB 14:657).

Andrew, m. on 28 May 1669, Anne Snodon (*ARMD* 4:601).

Andrew, m. by 3 June 1712, Elizabeth, dau. of Richard Feddeman of TA Co. (MWB 13:567).

John, m. by March 1710/1, Margaret, mother of John Newman (QAJRh March 1710/11, June 1712).

Robert, m. by 10 March 1676, Anne, relict and admx. of James Trueman (INAC 3:116; PGLR A:97).

Robert (Skiner), m. by 3 Aug 1702, Anne, relict and admx. of John Taney of CV Co. (INAC 24:37, 29:17).

Robert, of CV Co., d. by 4 May 1713 having m. Ann, mother of [-?-] Greenfield, and Elizabeth Green (MWB 13:703).

William, m. on 23 Oct 1701, Elizabeth [-?-] (TAPE).

William, m. by 27 Aug 1705, Hester, extx. of Henry Fox of TA Co. (INAC 25:73).

SKIPPERS

Abraham (sometimes given as Skypers), of CV Co., d. by 6 July 1710, leaving a widow and admx. Mary, who had formerly been m. to Samuel Holdsworth, and to John Dorman (MWB 3:145; INAC 31:300-302, 33A:157).

SKIPWITH

George, m. by 21 Dec 1602, Eliza, dau. of Thomas Thurston of BA Co. (MWB 6:31; BALR RM#HS:60).

SKY

Thomas, banns pub. 5 June, m. on 23 July 1706, Elizabeth Maryfield (HAGE:18).

SLADE

George (Slayde), m. by Aug 1691, Anne, relict of George Geer (CHLR Q:410).

John, m. on 9 Feb 1709, Elizabeth Crouch (AAMA:83).

SLATER

John, m. on 15 Oct 1704, Jane Richards (TAPE).

John, m. on 11 April 1708, Margaret Pennington (AAAN:1, 7).

SLAY

[-?-], m. by 11 April 1713, Mary, dau. of William Gadds, dec. (KELR JS#N:314).

SLICE

Samuel, m. on 15 Oct 1711, Mary Chance (KESP:65).

SLYE

Clement, m. by 28 Dec 1693, [-?-], dau. of Edward Turner of SM co. (MWB 12, pt. 2:158).

Capt. Gerard, m. by 1676, Jane Saunders, SM Co. (MWB 1:422; MDCR 3:751; MDTP 19::131).

Gerard, m. by 29 Nov 1718, Mary, extx. of John Gardiner of SM Co., and dau. of Major William Boarman (MWB 20:833; SMWB TA#1:1, 157; Judgement 22:186; MDAD 1:311).

Patience [*sic*], m. by 3 Feb 1715, Susannah, admx. of Joshua Satliff (INAC 37A:22).

Robert, m. by 1674, Susannah Gerard, dau. of Thomas; she m. 2nd, Col. John Coode (Hodges cites Pro. Court MM:403, 412, 419, 420; MCHR 3:1092-1093; Judgements 1:122).

SLYTER

    Henry, m. by 30 May 1698, Sibilla Heselrigg, dau. of Anna Margaret Conte, wife of Lege de la Bouchele of Bohemia River, CE Co. (MWB 6:388).

SMALL

    John, m. by 1 March 1711, Marjery, extx. of Thomas Faulkner of TA Co. (INAC 33A:108).

SMALLPAGE

    [-?-], m. by 31 Oct 1702, Ellinor, mother of Mary Griffin and John and James Boyce (MWB 12:269).

SMALLWOOD

    [-?-], m. by 18 April 1715, Mary, widow of Giles Blizard (PGLR F:440).

    Bayne, of Port Tobacco, CH Co., m. by 28 June —, Charity, dau. of Col. John Courts (MWB 12, pt. 2:208).

    Maj. James, m. by 15 May 1695, Mary, admx. of Robert Thompson, Jr., of CH Co. (INAC 13A:310).

    James, m. by 13 Jan 1709, Mary who was the mother of Anne, wife of John Frazer (CHLR C#2:154).

    Pryor, m. by 14 June 1708, Elisabeth, extx. of Peter Mackmillion of CH Co. (INAC 28:129).

    William, d. by 24 July 1708, having m. Eleanor, widow of George Tubman; she m. 3rd, by 24 July 1708, Edward Philpot (INAC 28:129, 29:374, 383).

SMART

    John, m. by 1 Oct 1688, Susan, relict and admx. of Richard Bennison of AA Co. (INAC 10:159).

SMICK

    John [Sivick?], m. [before 1700] Susanna, dau. of Walter Carr; she m. 2nd, Augustine Hawkins who d. by 10 Nov 1700, and 3rd, by 26 April 1703, Thomas Tracy (AALR WT#1:131, WT#2:115).

SMITH

    [-?-], m. by 1665, Margaret, widow of Peter Sudberry (or Sudborough) MPL 5:257, 8:400, DD:441).

    [-?-], m. by 7 Jan 1684, Margaret Birckhead, sister of Abraham Birckhead of AA Co. (MWB 4:173).

    [-?-], m. by Oct 1688, Ann, relict of William Bonham of TA Co. (MDTP 14:103).

    [-?-], m. by 1699, Elizabeth, extx. of Archibald Van Hop (INAC 19:158).

    [-?-], m. by 10 Nov 1700, Mary, dau. of Maurice Baker of AA Co. (MWB 11:22).

    [-?-], m. by 15 Feb 1702/3, Ellianor, dau. of Thomas Poynter, Sr., of SO Co. (MWB 12:9).

    [-?-], m. by 8 Dec 1703, Bridgett, dau. of William Cord of SO Co. (MWB 12:40).

[-?-], m. by 21 Dec 1713, Elizabeth, mother of Thomas Parker and Mary Sheele (MWB 14:3).

[-?-], m. by 29 March 1714 Ann, dau of Thomas Hagoe (Hague?) of CH Co. (MWB 14:213).

[-?-], m. by 2 April 1718, Sarah, dau. of George Young of CV Co. (MWB 14:613).

Alexander, m. by Aug 1676, Elizabeth, relict of 1st, Francis Posey, and 2nd, John Belaine (MDTP 11:172).

Allen, m. by 3 Sep 1686, Mary, relict and extx. of Lewis Blangy of KE Co. (INAC 9:91).

Andrew, m. by 5 July 1712, Anne, admx. of William Richards of SO Co. (INAC 33B:174).

Anthony, m. by June 1690, Martha, dau. of Thomas Baker (CHLR Q:10).

Anthony, m. by 16 May 1696, Dinah, admx. of Thomas Knighton (INAC 13B:15).

Anthony, m. 9 Jan 1700, Johanna Hull (AAAL 1:21(1)).

Benjamin, m. on 25 Feb 1704/5, Sarah Hollis (HAGE:22).

Benjamin, of Biddeford, Devon, d. by 6 Nov 1713, when his widow Rebecca m. John Evans of KE Co. (CELR 2:245).

Casparus, m. by banns on 11 Oct 1703, Ann Robinson, widow (CESS). She was the widow of James Robinson, Jr., of CE Co. (MWB 3:378).

Caspar, m. by 7 July 1708, Anne, dau. of Thomas Kear, whose extx. m. William Dixon of CE Co. (INAC 28:160).

Charles (Smyth), m. on 16 Nov 1703, Mary Bond (KESP:64). She was probably a dau. of Benjamin Bond of KE Co. (MWB 13:659).

Charles, m. on 6 Nov 1715, Martha Parker (KESP:66).

Christopher of London, m. by 10 Feb 1691, Mary, dau. of William Hill of Transquaking River, DO Co. (MWB 2:334).

Christopher, m. by 1706, in her former husband's lifetime, Ann Foster. She was bur. 26 Oct 1706 (AAAN:23). **See SMITHERS below.**

Edward, m. by 23 Oct 1711, Margaret, admx. of Charles Jones of BA Co. (INAC 32B:270).

Edward, m. by 25 June 1711, [-?-], dau. of William Hawkins, Sr., of BA Co., who called Smith son-in-law in his will of that date (MWB 13:213).

Edward, m. on 2 Aug 1713, Mary Doulon (AAAN:9).

Francis, m. by May 1696, Eliza, admx. of Daniel Lawrence of BA Co. (MDTP 16:170).

George, m. on 3 Oct 1671, Martha Gibbs (SOLR:IKL).

George, m. by 16 May 1678, Elizabeth, widow of Anthony Brispoe; on that date, Smith was granted a patent for Crab Hill , which Brispoe had purchased some years earlier from Richard Morgan (*ARMD* 66:474-475; MPL 19:619).

George, m. by May 1694, Hannah, extx. of Daniel Peverell (MDTP 15C:65).

James, m. on 19 Feb 1703, Hannah Hurtt (KESP:64).

James, m. on 21 Jan 1705, Sarah Hynson (KESP:64).

James, m. on 6 Dec 1708, Joyce Quinney (KESP:65).

James, m. on 4 May 1710, Mrs. Susanna Crouch (AALR 1:37; AAMA:83).

James, m. by 8 Oct 1713, Susannah, widow of 1st, John Howard, and 2nd, William Crouch (INAC 25:61, 27:9; AALR IB#2:129).

Capt. John, sheriff, m. by 26 Dec 1655, Mary [-?-], widow of [-?-] Smith (Proprietary Records A&B:170).

John, m. by 1658, Margaret, widow of Francis Hunt (MPL Q:67).

John, m. by 20 Oct 1666, [-?-], widow of George Holdcraft (MDTP 2:62).

John, m. on 14 Feb 1666/7, Margaret Barber (CHLR C#3:252; *ARMD* 60:116).

John, m. by (Feb 1667?), Susanna, relict of George Holdcraft, chrurgeon of SM Co. (MDTP 2:295).

John, m. by 17 Sep 1687, Lucia, dau. of Richard Hall of CV Co. (MWB 6:13).

John, m. on 24 Sep 1699, Mary David (KESP:64).

John, d. by 18 April 1700, leaving an extx. Joan who m. 2nd, Thomas Atterbury (MDTP 18A:47; INAC 19½B:27).

John, m. on 3 June 1704, Mary Coawck? (KESP:64).

John, m. by 10 Aug 1703, Martha, legatee of Elizabeth Baker of AA Co. (MWB 11:394; INAC 26:339).

John, m. on 7 April 1708, Mary Tomon (AAAL 1:36).

John, m. on 4 Dec 1708, Mary Simpson (CVCH).

John, m. on 2 Feb 1709/10, Mary Hedge (HAGE:26). She was admx. of Henry Hedge of BA Co. (INAC 32B:270).

John, m. on 5 May 1710, Ellen Holt (TAPE).

John, m. by 9 Jan 1711, Jane, dau. and heir of Reese Hinton (CELR 2:211).

John, m. by 20 June 1711, Dorothy, admx. of Michael Taney of CV Co. (INAC 32C:139).

John, of PG Co., d. by 27 July 1710, having m. Jane, mother of William, Thomas, Jno, and Jonathan Prater [Prather] (MWB 13:623).

John, Jr., son of John Smith, on 14 April 1714, was about to marry Ann Hagan, dau. of Thomas (CHLR D#2:70).

John, m. on 17 — 1715, Isabella Moore (AAAN:22).

Joseff, m. on 12 Oct 1714, Elenor Humfress (AAAN:22).

Joseph, of CV Co., son of Nathan and Elizabeth, m. on 4 d., 3 m. (May), 1710, Laurana Richardson, dau. of Daniel and Elizabeth (WRMM).

Leven (Smyth), m. on 31 Oct 1703, Ezbell Reed (KESP:64).

Mathew, m. by 21 March 1656, [-?-], relict of Richard Manship (Proprietary Records A&B:259; MPL Q:428).

Matthew, m. by 19 Nov 1679, Elizabeth, widow of Christopher Thomas (TALR 3:315).

Matthew, m. by 4 Jan 1699, Mary, admx. of John Dine [or Vine?] of TA Co. (INAC 19½A:170; MDTP 18A:53).

Nathan, m. by 24 June 1700, Eliza, sister of William Cole of AA Co. (MWB 6:397).

Nathan, d. by Feb 1704, having m. Margaret, dau. of John Burrage; she m. 2^{nd,} Thomas Tench (AALR WT#2:276).

Oliver, m. by 8 May 1702, Mary, dau. of Jenkins Morris of SO Co. (INAC 21:352).

Ralph, m. by 21 Sep 1680, Sarah, widow of Col. John Douglass, and mother of Robert, Charles, Joseph, Eliza, and Sarah Douglass (in will of Peter Carr of CH Co.) (MWB 4:12; CHLR H:290).

Richard, m. by 1671, Elizabeth, sister of Charles Brooke (MPL 20:285; MPL 20:285; MWB 1:459).

Richard, m. by March 1686/7, Barbara, extx. of John Rousby. She was one of daughters of Henry and Frances Morgan, dec., of KE Co. (MDTP 8A:217; MDTP 13:470).

Richard, m. by 22 Nov 1710, [-?-], heir of Garrardus Wessells, in 1710 acct. of Christian Christian of KE Co. (INAC 32B:252).

Robert, m. by license dated 23 Nov 1638, Rose Gilbert, widow of Richard Gilbert. Smith swore he was not already contracted to any other woman (*ARMD* 4:51; MPL 1:133-134, 2:606, 4:193, ABH:37).

Robert, m. by 22 Dec 1690 (immediately after death of dec.), Ann, relict of Thomas Hinson. (INAC 7A:327).

Robert, m. by 19 May 1698, [-?-], dau. of John Townsend of SO Co. (MWB 6:179).

Robert, m. by 29 April 1703, Bridget, relict and extx. of Charles Jones of BA Co. (INAC 23:50).

Samuel, m. on 27 Jan 1714/5, Elizabeth Watkins (AALR 1:38).

Samuel, and Judith Hoodt, of Cecil MM, on 9 d., 11 m., 1716, declared their intention to marry (*QMES:*87).

Thomas, d. by 1649 having m. [-?-], widow of Capt. Philip Taylor; she m. 3rd, by 1649, William Eltonhead (MPL 2:558).

Thomas, of KE Co., d. by 1667/8 when his dau. Gertrude m. John Anderton (PCJU FF:548, 550).

Thomas, m. by 2 Oct 1684, Elinor, relict and admx. of Nathaniel Evitts of KE Co. (INAC 9:199, 32C:180).

Thomas, m. by 1688, Elizabeth, sister of John Acton (MWB 6:1; MDTP 17:292).

Thomas, m. by 20 Nov 1688, Anne, widow and extx. of William Boanam or Bowman or Borman of TA Co. (INAC 10:312; MDTP 15A:1).

Thomas, m. by 1707, Anne, relict of 1st, John Edwards who d. by 1700, 2nd, Samuel Watkins who d. by 1700, and 3rd, Andrew Abington (MWB 6:39, 377; MDTP 16:29, 39; SMRR:56).

Thomas, m. on 25 Feb 1715, Eliza Rigdon (PGQA:1).

Thomas, m. by 14 March 1717, Dorothy, dau. of John Stevens of DO Co. (DOLR 7 Old:53).

Walter, m. by 17 Sep 1687, Rachel, dau. of Richard Hall of CV Co. (MWB 6:13).

William, m. by 1671, Mary [-?-], sister of Hannah who m. Vincent Atcheson (MPL LL:91).

William, of TA Co., m. by Sep 1671, Elizabeth, admx. of Hopkin Davis (MDTP 5:91).

William, m. by 1681 Elizabeth, dau. of Francis Batchelor of CH Co. (MDTP 16:55, 192).

William, of Mt. Calvert Hundred, m. by 12 Jan 1681, Eliza, grandmother of Jane and William Gaskin (MWB 2:197).

William, of CV Co., m. by May 1686, Elizabeth, widow of William Hunt (MDTP 13:343).

William, m. on 2 Feb 1696, Alice Gott (AAJA:2#13). She was the relict and extx. of Robert Gott of AA Co. (INAC 17:158).

William, m. 28 Jan 1702, Elizabeth Seaborn (AAAL 1:26).

William, m. by 17 June 1703, Rachel, legatee of Samuel White of AA Co. (MWB 11:313; INAC 27:10).

William, m. by June 1710, Susanna, extx. and widow of William Crouch (MDTP 21:245).

William, m. on 13 May 1711, Elizabeth Gardner (CVCH).

William, m. by 5 May 1712, Rachel, admx. of Morris Fitzgarrell (Fitzgerald) of CH Co. (INAC 33A:189).

William, m. by 4 May 1715, Elizabeth, admx. of Mr. Richard Dallam of CV Co. (INAC 36B:250).

SMITHERS

Christopher, m. June 1708, Ann Foster (AAJU TB#1:734).

Richard, m. on 14 Feb 1700/1, Mrs. Blanch Wells, spinster (HAGE:14).

Richard (Smithes), m. on 18 Aug 1709, Philizanna Maxwell (HAGE:26).

Richard, m. by 6 May 1718, Mary, extx. of John Carvil of KE Co. (MDAD 1:147).

SMITHSON

[-?-], m. by 1638, Ann, relict of Jerome Hawley (MPL 1:152, 2:105, 123).

John, m. [by 1657] Ann [-?-], who m. 2nd, John Norman, who d. c1657 (*NFMP*:260).

Owen, m, by 14 Oct 1717, Mary, admx. of Thomas Courtney of SM Co. (INAC 37B:107; MDTP 23:137).

SMITHWICK

Thomas (Smethwick), m. by 1661, Maudlin, widow of Simon Abbott, Edmund Townhill, and George Nettlefold (MWB 1:627, 2:363; MDTP 7:112; 9:331; AALR IH#1:172).

SMOCK

[-?-], m. by 7 July 1681, Parthenia, dau. of William Innis, Sr., of SO Co. (MWB 4:61).

SMOOT

Barton, m. by 5 Sep 1706, Sarah, relict of Henry Hawkins and mother of Tubman, Elizabeth, and Elinor Hawkins (CHLR C#2:24).

Edward, m. by Feb 1684/5, [-?-], widow of John Gee of SM Co. (MDTP 13:209).

Thomas, m. by 1662, Jane Batten, sister of William Batten of SM Co. She m. 2nd, Robert Rowland (MWB 1:162; MDTP 1D:44, 15C:77½, 80).

Thomas, m. between 1688 and 1703, Eliza Barton, dau. of William and Mary Barton of CH and PG Co. (CHLR B#2:302, P#1:6; CHWB AB#3 part 1:119; PGWB 1:26-20).

William, m. by 1646, Grace Wood, mother of Elizabeth Wood (MPL ABH:230; *ARMD* 53:343).

William, d. by 11 Nov 1673, leaving a widow and extx. Mary, whose sister Hannah m. Vincent Atchison (*ARMD* 65:127, 137).

SNOWDEN

[-?-], m. by 1699, Ellinor, called Ellinor Snowden, extx. of Edmond O'Neale (INAC 11B:62).

Richard, m. by 10 Sep 1675, [-?-], one of the daughters of Magdalen, relict of Edmund Townhill (MDTP 7:120).

Richard, m. by 4 Dec 1675, Eliza, sister of John Grosse of AA Co. (MWB 5:30).

Richard, m. by 17 May 1699, Mary, dau. of Thomas Linthicum, Sr., of AA Co. (MWB 11:159).

Richard, youngest son of Richard, Jr., and Mary, m. on 19 d., 3 m. (May) 1709, Elizabeth Coale, Jr., dau. of William and Elizabeth, all now of AA Co. (WRMM).

Richard, son of Richard and Mary, m. on 19 d., 10 m. (Dec), 1717, Elizabeth Thomas, dau. of Samuel and Mary (WRMM).

SOAPER

John, of PG Co., m. by 27 Sep 1711, Mary, one of the heirs of Thomas Houser of PG Co. (PGLR F:141).

SOCKWELL

Thomas, m. by 4 May 1704, Mary, admx. of Robert Fortune of TA Co. Co. (INAC 24:285). She was the mother of Robert Fortune of TA Co. (MWB 13:560).

SOMERFORD

[-?-], m. by 26 April 1668, Sibil, admx. and widow of John Six (MDTP 2:316).

SORRELL

[-?-], m. by 21 March 1693, Eliza, sister of Michael Skidmore of CE Co. (MWB 2:293).

SOLLERS/SOLLARS

Robert of CV Co., m. by 1698, Mary, dau. of William Selby (MWB 6:215; MDTP 5:472, 542; PGLR A:427).

SOTHORON

[-?-], m. by 10 March 1716/7, [-?-], dau. of Mary Rose of Chaptico Hundred, SM Co. who named her grandchildren John Johnson Sothoron, Benjamin, and Ann and Mary Sothoron in her will (MWB 15:376).

John, of CH Co., m. by 18 March 1711, Mary, dau. of John Johnson (MWB 13:402).

Richard, m. by July 1686, [-?-], heir of the Widow Truman of CV Co. (MDTP 13:375).

Richard (Southern), d. by 20 May 1708, having m. Mary, dau. of Margaret Swift. Mary Swift Sothoron m. 2nd, Brutus Russell of CH Co. (INAC 28:124).

SOUTH

Thomas, m. by 24 July 1673, [-?-], dau. of Thomas Hinson (MDTP 5:527).

SOUTHBEE

William, m. on 29 d. 1 mo., 1668, Elizabeth Read, both of TA Co., at the house of Isaac Abraham (TATH).

William, m. on 20 d. 4 m., 1677, Joan Lee, both of TA Co., at the house of Thomas Taylor (TATH).

SOUTHCOTE

[-?-], m. by (date not given), Jane, sister of John Coursey (MWB 1:148).

SOUTHERN

Henry, m. by 20 Jan 1698, Ann, relict and admx. of George Johnson of CV Co. (INAC 17:169).

Capt. Richard, m. by 1681, Ann Lashley, dau. of Robert and Elizabeth Lashley (MWB 2:196; INAC 23:173, 24:167; MDTP 20:8; Warrants 15:400, 430).

SOUTHES

[-?-], m. by 3 May 1710, Jane, dau. of William Garnish, and niece of John Garnish of SM Co. (MCHR PC:651).

SPALDING

[-?-], m. by 16 April 1717, Honour, dau. of Edward Cole of SM Co. (MWB 14:644).

Andrew, m. on 10 April 1709 Elizabeth Chaddock (KESP:65).

SPARROW

Solomon, of AA Co., son of Thomas, dec., m. on 12 d., 6 m. (Aug), 1690, Sarah Smith, dau. of Thomas Smith, dec., and Alce (WRMM; MDTP 17:184).

Thomas, son of Thomas and Elizabeth, m. 8 June 1697, Ann Burgess, dau. of Col. William and Ursula (AAAL 1:5).

Thomas, son of Thomas and Sophia, m. 28 June 1698, Sophia Richardson, dau. of William and Elizabeth (AAAL 1:10; AALR WT#1:146).

SPEAKE

Thomas, m. by 1659, Frances, dau. of Dr. Thomas Gerard (Westmoreland Co., VA, Will Book).

SPEAKS

John, m. by 11 Aug 1685, Winifred, dau. of John Wheeler (CHLR L:178).

SPEAR

Henry, m. in 1711, Jane Calloway (WIST).

SPEARING

John, m. by 31 May 1709, Barbara, admx. of Michael Realy of CH Co. (INAC 29:396).

SPEARMAN

William, of KE Co., m. by March 1715 Charity [-?-]. On 14 d., 12 m., 1710 Cecil MM stated that Charity Spearman, widow of James Kelley, had taken a husband contrary to Truth. On 25 d., 5 m., 1711 Cecil MM referred to Third Haven MM their further proceedings against Charity "Spirman" who has taken a husband contrary to

Truth's order and run into divers other evil and light actions (KELR BC#1:115; *QMES:*30, 85).

SPEARS
[-?-], m. by 8 May 1694, Mary, extx. of James Ringgold of KE Co. (INAC 13A:213).

SPEER
Andrew, m. on 10 March 1690, Priscilla [-?-] (SOLR:IKL).

SPENCE
Magnu [Magnus], m. on 14 June 1703, Jane Whitehead (TAPE).
Patrick, m. on 24 Nov 1713, Phebe Sizzarson (TAPE).

SPENCER
Francis, m. by 21 Feb 1677, Mary, widow and extx. of John Anderson of CV Co. (INAC 5:273).
Francis, m. by 23 July 1678, Mary, extx. of Joseph Anderson of CV Co. (MDTP 10:280).
Jno., m. by March 1683, Mary, widow of 1st, James Maxwell, and 2nd, Patrick Hall (MDTP 13:21).
William, of Hunting Creek, m. by 15 Oct 1712, Isabella, widow of John McCall, and mother of Susannah McCall (DOLR 6 Old:199).

SPERNON
Joseph, m. by 14 Sep 1686, Alice, relict and admx. of Thomas Hinton of CE Co. (INAC 9:109).

SPICER
[-?-], m. by 6 July 1686, Ellinor, widow and admx. of Thomas Evans of CV Co. (INAC 9:40; Cotton states she was also the widow of Thomas Windon of CV Co.).
John, m. on 10 Nov 1709, [-?-] Hawkins (AAJA:38 #8).

SPINK
Enoch (Spinks), m. by Oct 1710, [-?-], admx. of Tobias Starnborough (MDTP 21:281).
Henry, m. by 1663, Eleanor Edwards (Hodges cites Prov. Court BB:116, 160).
Thomas, d. by 1695, having m. Jane, dau. of Jane Payne of SM Co. His widow and admx. also m. George Mackall, and m. 3rd, John Walton (or Watson). (INAC 8:155, 10:481, 13A:285).

SPOT
John (Sprot?), of CV Co., m. by June 1686, Winifred, extx. of John Mund (MDTP 13:354).

SPRACKLIN
[-?-], m. by 16 Oct 1677, Elizabeth, relict and extx. of John Macky and of Elizabeth Rawlin, both of SM Co., and extx. of Elizabeth Rawlings (INAC 4:423, 425; MDTP 9A:364).

SPREADDEX
William, m. on 9 Oct 1707, Elizabeth Hicks (AAAL 1:36).

SPRIGG
Thomas, m. by 1 July 1668, Ellinor, dau. of John Nuthall, of SM Co., dec. (MDTP 3:2). She was a sister of James Nuthall (MDTP 14:102).
Thomas, m. by 31 May 1703, Margaret, sister of Daniel Mariarte of AA Co. (MWB 3:415).

SPRIGNALL
Christopher, m. by 23 Oct 1716, Elinor, admx. of Thomas Booker of TA Co. (INAC 37C:151).
Jno., m. by Aug 1716, [-?-], admx. of Emanuel Jenkins of TA Co. (MDTP 23:61).

SPRY
Christopher, m. by 21 April 1677, [-?-], widow of Thomas Brinson (INAC 4:1).
Christopher, m. by Oct 1678, [-?-], admx. of John Hales (*ARMD* 68:80).

SPURRIER
William, m. on 7 Feb 1702, Elizabeth Turner (TAPE).

SQUIRE
John (or Squires), m. by 1716, Sarah Green, dau. of Mary, of SM Co. (SMWB PC#1:205; MWB 14:229).

STACEY
John (Staycy), carpenter, m. on 5 d. 4 m., 1695, Martha Sockwell, spinster, both of TA Co., at the house of William Sockwell (Wright transcribed this as Lockwell) (TATH).
William, m. by Dec 1674, Mary, extx. of Richard Stacey, dec. (*ARMD* 65:411).

STAFFORD
Lawrence, m. on 23 Oct 1708, Alse King (KESP:65).
Richard, m. on 5 Dec 1703, Mary Gaylor (AAAL 1:26).
William, m. by 22 Feb 1677, Sarah, widow and admx. of John Todd of AA Co. (INAC 5:2, 363; Cotton cites INAC5:363 to say she was the widow of Thomas Todd).
William, m. by 24 Sep 1678, Sarah, widow of Thomas Todd of AA Co. (MDTP 10:282).

STAGG
[-?-], m. by c1678, Margaret, relict and admx. of John Gittings of CV Co., mother

of Mary Gittings, and step-mother of John and Philip Gittings (INAC 6:1).

STAGOLL
[-?-], m. by Oct 1666, Ruth, Relict to John Morecroft (*ARMD* 57:127).

STALLINGS
[-?-], of BA Co., m. by March 1680, Mary, relict of Thomas Bworth [*sic*] (MDTP 12A:223).

STALY
[-?-], m. by 31 March 1701, Mary, admx. of Thomas Jones of BA Co. (INAC 21:161).

STANAWAY
Joseph (Stannaway), m. by 25 July 1718, Sarah, extx. of Charles Paul of DO Co. (MDAD 1:84).

STANDFORD
[-?-], m. by 24 April 1706, Margaret, dau. of Israel Skelton of BA Co. (MWB 12:15).
Jno. (Standforth, Stanford), of Herring Creek, m. by Nov 1701, Susannah, dau. of John and Elizabeth Whipps (AALR WT#1:213; MWB 14:172; MDTP 30:172).
John, Jr., m. by 30 Jan 1717, [-?-], of William Merchant of DO Co. (MWB 14:325).

STANDWORTH
[-?-], m. by 1 March 1698, Mary, widow of David Wickerly, late of TA Co., dec., and mother of David Wickerly (TALR LL#7:219).

STANFORD
Joseph, m. by Aug 1684, Mary, admx. of Alexander Addison (SOJU LD:106).
William, m. by 12 Jan 1718, Rachel admx. of Joseph Wall of DO Co. (MDAD 1:355).

STANLEY
Hugh, m. by 1663, Dorothy [-?-], widow of 1st, Giles Sadler, and 2nd, Daniel Golson. She m. 4th, by 1670, Francis Swanson (MPL AA:68, 86, 4:149, 5:195, 409, 427, 9:54, 92, 12:591, 14:214, EE:52, 86, JJ:221-2, AB&H: 142, 322-23, and KK:202; MDTP 2:163-164; *ARMD* 49:36, 78).
John (Standley), m. on 26 Aug 1713, Elizabeth Thomas (TAPE).
William, d. by 7 Oct 1672; his widow Mary m. 2nd, Christopher Andrews of KE Co. (*ARMD* 51:86).
William, m. by 19 Jan 1694, Susanna, extx. of John Wedge (KELR M:7).

STANSBY
John (Stanesby), chirurgeon, m. by 22 June 1667, Ann, dau. of Richard Wells, Sr.,

of AA Co. (MWB 1:287; MDTP 2:177).

John, d. by Dec 1671, leaving an admx. Mary who m. Richard Adams (BACP F#1:146).

Dr. John (Stanesby), m. by Aug 1675, Mary, widow of [-?-] Harmer, and dau. of Johanna Spry of BA Co. (MWB 4:755; INAC 4:564).

STANTON

[-?-], m. by 27 Dec 1703, Eliza, dau. of Blanch wife of Thomas Ryder of AA Co. (MWB 11:403).

Francis, m. by c1694, Susannah Ward, dau. of John Coppin of TA Co. (INAC 13A:215; Cotton interprets this as she was the dau. of Alexander Moore).

William, m. by 23 Aug 1686, Blanch, admx. of Stephen Binley of AA Co. (INAC 9:124).

STAPLEFORD

[-?-], m. by 25 July 1673, [-?-], dau. of George Goodrick of CH Co. (MWB 5:91).

Barnaby, m. on 29 Aug 1718, Elizabeth Reader (TAPE).

George (Staplefort), of DO co., Gent., m. by 12 March 1718, Jane, extx. of Edward Pindar, late of DO Co. (DOLR 7 Old:81).

George, m. by 11 May 1715, Jane, dau. of John Taylor of DO Co. (Warrant Record AA#1:421).

Raymond (Staplefort), m. by 1666, [-?-], widow of William May (who was the bro. of Mary Goodrick) (MPL R:12r, 4:23-2-4, 9:355, EE:341).

STAPLES

Henry, d. by Sep 1688, having m. [-?-], relict of Charles Turner of KE Co. (MDTP 14:92).

STARKEY

John, m. on 1 Jan 1707/8, Elizabeth Boyle (AAAL 1:36).

William, m. by 12 Sep 1717, Sarah, dau. of Joseph and Sarah James of TA Co. (QALR IKA:138).

STARNBOROUGH

Tobias, of BA Co., d. by [c1709], Sarah, sister of Luke Raven (INAC 29:408).

START

John, of TA Co., m. by 15 July 1717, Judith, sister and coheir of Richard Woollman, dec. (TALR RF#12:291).

STAUGHIER

John, Jr., m. on 13 May 1697, Mary [-?-] (TAPE).

STAVELY

John, of CE Co., d. by 15 June 1705, a widow, [-?-], who m. Moses Alfred or Alford (INAC 25:120, 300)

STEARMAN
    Richard, m. by Dec 1662, [-?-], widow of Edmond Brent (*ARMD* 53:304).

STEEL(E)
    Francis (Steell), m. by banns on 26 Feb 1705, by Mr. Sewell, Rebecca Peirce, spinster (CESS). She was a dau. of Thomas Peirce of CE Co., who named Steele as his son-in-law (MWB 14:274; CELR 1:495).
    John, m. on 11 Nov 1709, Mary Clark (HAGE:26).
    Matthew, m. by 1678, Restitutia Hollis, dau. of John and Restitutia Hollis of SM Co. (Hodges cites Warrants 1:138; Westmoreland Co., VA Book 9:102
    William, m. in Nov 1706, Frances Bowzer (SOLR:IKL).

STERLING
    John, banns of marriage pub. on 28 May 1667, between him and Alce Bassett (*ARMD* 54;671; SOLR O#1:62).
    Thomas, m. by 1663, Mary, widow of Benj. Brasseur of CV Co. (MDTP 1D:126, 1E:18, 20, 92, 94).

STERMEY
    [-?-] (Stirmey), m. by 17 Feb 1697, Catherine, dau. of Francis and Ann [-?-] Freeman of CV Co. (MWB 7:347,11:59).

STEVENS
    [-?-], m. by 20 Oct 1715, Mary, sister and coheir of Richard Woolman, dec. (TALR RF#12:239; INAC 37C:143).
    Edward, m. on 23 Dec 1718, Mary Gardsley (KESP:66).
    John, m. by 20 April 1671, Margaret, wife of Edward Jolley (INAC 4:398; *ARMD* 51:193).
    John, m. by May 1696, Ann, relict and admx. or extx. of Thomas Cooke of DO Co. (INAC 20:224). She was a dau.-in-law of Mrs. Judith Brooke of TA Co. (MDTP 16:162. 23:97).
    John (Stephens), m. on 19 Feb 1704/5, Sarah Brown (AAAN:19). She was a dau. of Thomas Brown, Sr., of AA Co. (AALR IB#2:117).
    John, planter, m. on 6 d. 5 m., 1709, Elizabeth Allcock (or Allcook), both of TA Co., at Tuckaho meeting house (TATH).
    John, m. by Feb or March 1710, Sarah, extx. of John Purdee of AA Co. (MDTP 21:213).
    John, m. by June 1717, Ann Cook, dau.-in-law of Judith Brooke of TA Co. (MDTP 23:97).
    Richard, m. by 28 March 1674, Katherine, widow of Henry Osborne of CV Co. (MDTP 6:177).
    Thomas (Stephens), m. by 1687, Alice, dau. of Francis and Isabella Barnes; she m. 2nd, Thomas Murphy (MDTP 19C:221).
    William?, m. by 23 March 1671/2, Mary, dau. of Dr. Peter Sharp of CV Co. (MWB 1:494).

William, of Transquaking, DO Co., upholsterer, m. on 15 d. 12 m., 1687, Jane Atkinson, relict of Thomas Atkinson, dec., of TA Co. (TATH).

William (Stewnes) (formerly called Robert Lewin), m. on 17 Aug 1688, Ann Nolton (SOLR:IKL).

William, Jr., m. on 5 d., 12 m., 1695, Elizabeth Edmondson, spinster, both of TA Co., at the meeting house at head of Treadhaven Creek (TATH). She was a dau. of John Edmondson of Tred Haven Creek, DO Co. (MWB 6:95).

William, of DO Co., m. on 6 d. 12 m., 1700, Mary Pryor, late of Phila. at the house of Dorothy Stevens, Great Choptank (TATH).

STEVENSON

[-?-], m. by 7 April 1703, Anne, dau. of Edward Fry of KE Co. (MWB 3:255).

Ralph, m. by 2 Jan 1701, Mary, dau. of Thomas Bruff of BA Co. (MWB 11:248).

STEWARD

James, m. on 21 July 1710, Rachel Wichall or Witchell in All Hallow's Parish (*AACR* 1:25).

John (Stuard), m. by 3 March 1695, Mary, relict and extx. of Robert Winsmore of DO Co. (INAC 13B:86, 87; MDTP 16:141).

John, m. by 22 June 1697, Mary, dau. of John Wheeler of DO Co. (MWB 7:333).

John, m. on 28 March 1703, Britchett [Bridget] Hughs (TAPE).

Robert (Stuard), m. on 26 Jan 1698/9, Susan Wattes (AAAL 1:11).

STEWART

Alex. (Steuart), m. by 7 July 1717, Margaret, extx. of Charles Boothby of AA Co. (MDAD 1:19).

Alexander (Stuart), m. on 15 Aug 1708, Margaret Connor (AAAN:7).

STIFFIN

John, m. 24 April 1701, Margaret Disney, dau. of William (AAAL 1:21(1)).

John, m. on 18 Aug 1709, Sarah Purdy (AALR 1:36).

STIMSON

[-?-], m. by 4 March 1700, Comfort, dau. of Rachel, widow of [-?-] Kilburne (AALR WT#1:118).

John (Stinson), m. by Sep 1677, Rachel, widow of Neal Clarke of AA Co. (MDTP 9A:295-296).

STINCHCOMB

Nathaniel, of AA Co., m. by 11 June 1670, Tomasin, dau. of Joane Mastey (MWB 1:585).

Nathaniel, m. 4 Sep 1702, Elizabeth Chappell (AAAL 2:3; AAMA:82).

STIPHIN

Mr. John, m. by 3 March 1710, Sarah, extx. of John Purdee of AA Co. (INAC 32B:37).

STIPPER
   Thomas, m. on 20 Sep 1703, Barbara Stuard (KESP:64).

STOCKDELL
   Edward, m. on 9 Aug 1693, Jane [-?-] (SOLR:IKL). She was Jean Boyce (MWB 14:121).

STOCKEN
   John, m. by 8 June 1703, Elizabeth, extx. of James Ford (INAC 23:110).

STOCKETT
   Henry, d. by 16 Oct 1703, leaving dau. Frances wife of Peter Contee, dau. Honrica wife of Thomas Berry, and [prob. a dau.] Katherine, wife of Henry Rodes (AALR WT#2:79).
   Thomas, m. by 22 June 1667, Mary, dau. of Richard Wells, Sr., of AA Co. (MWB 1:287).
   Thomas, son of Capt. Thomas, m. 12 March 1689, Mary Sprigg, dau. of Thomas (AAAL).
   Thomas, son of Capt. Thomas and Mary, m. 9 April 1700, Damaris Welsh (AAAL 1:19). She was a dau. of John Welsh (BALR TR#A:5).

STODDERT
   [-?-], m. by 30 Jan 1709, Eliz., dau. of John Batie of AA Co. (MWB 14:391).
   James (Stodert), m. on 3 March 1708/9, Elizabeth Bishop (AAJA:36 #13). James was of PG Co., and she was a dau. of Roger Bishop of AA Co. (AALR IB#2:359).

STOGDON
   John, m. on 30 March 1703, Elizabeth Ford (AAJA:27#3).

STOKELEY
   [-?-], m. by 12 Nov 1675, Mary, dau. of John Bigger of CV Co. (MDTP 7:214).
   [-?-], m. by 1675, Anne Bigger of CV Co. (MWB 2:379).

STOKER
   [-?-], d. by 11 Sep 1694 having m. Mary, widow of William Merchant and mother of Ellinor Merchant (MWB 7:55).

STOKES
   [-?-] (Stoaks), m. by 16 Feb 1707/8, Ann, dau. of Thomas Vickers, Sr., of PG Co. (MWB 13:272).
   John, m. by 29 Dec 1708, Susanna Wells, who had been a legatee of James Ives (BALR RM#HS:632, IS#G:212).
   Peter, m. by 6 Aug 1680, Ann, relict and extx. of Miles Mason, and mother of Ann Mason (INAC 7A:182; DOLR Old 14:375).

STONE

Francis, m. by license dated 28 June 1642, Deborah Paulus *(ARMD* 4:67; MPL 1:150).

John, m. by c1683, Eleanor, age 16, dau. of Walter and Eleanor Bayne of CH Co.; she m. 2nd, Matthew Hill (Judgements 6:792, 21:514-516). She m. Hugh Tears, and by 22 June 1700 John Beale (CHLR Z#2:485; MDTP 19a:75, 78).

Matthew, m. by 1717, Rachel, dau. of Thomas Smoot of CH Co., and granddau. of William Barton (MWB 14:486; CHWB AB#3: part 1:119).

Robert, m. on 23 July 1700, Ann Smith (AAJA:7#6).

Thomas, m. by May 1696, Mary, extx. of William Gaine of BA Co. (MDTP 16:170).

William, of CH Co., Gent., m. by 10 March 1698, Theodosia, dau. of Zachariah Wade (PGLR A:163).

STONEHOUSE

Thomas, m. by Sep 1685, Mary, widow of Thomas (Steed? or Wood?) of CH Co. (MDTP 13:252).

STONESTREET

Robert, m. by 5 Aug 1718, Margaret, extx. of Archibald Johnson of TA Co. (MDAD 1:241).

STOOPE

[-?-], m. by 3 April 1783, Sarah, dau. of Robert Jones (MWB 4:45).

STOREY

Joseph (Story), m. on 22 Jan 1717, Jane Soper (PGQA:1).

Walter, m. by 10 May 1702, [-?-], dau. of Penelope Land of CH Co.; she called him son-in-law in her will (MWB 11:299).

STOUR

Francis, contracted on 28 June 1642 to marry Deborah Paulus (Proprietary Records F&B: 150).

STOW

Edmund, m. by 9 Sep 1687, Jane, admx. of John King of CV Co. (INAC 9:451).

STRAND

Abraham (Strann), of BA Co., m. on 21 d. 9 m., 1672, Mary Halbrook, of TA Co., at the house of Robert Harwood (TATH).

Abraham, m. on 25 d. 9 m., 1677, Rachel Nicholson, at the meeting in Salem, NJ (TATH).

STRAWBRIDGE

John, m. by 14 Aug 1688, Honora, admx. of William Furnace of SO Co. (INAC 10:174).

Joseph, m. by 7 Sep 1696, Sarah, extx. of John Arden or Harding of BA Co. (INAC 14:152). She was the mother of Mary and Samuel Harding (MWB 6:260).

STREETER
Capt. Edward (Stroature), of Nansemond Co., VA, m. by 20 Oct 1656, Elizabeth, relict of Col. Thomas Burbage (*ARMD* 10:469; KELR C:2)).

STRINGER
[-?-], m. by 21 Sep 1685, Eliza, sister of Thomas and Nathaniel Truman of CV Co. (MWB 4:165, 5:138).

STRONG
John, m. by 4 Aug 1679, Mary, admx. of William Mackdowell of CV Co. (INAC 6:268).
Thomas, m. on 24 Sep 1711, Jane Phillips (KESP:65).

STUMP
Thomas, m. by 13 March 1717, Elizabeth, admx. of William Glover of PG Co. (INAC 39A:56).

STUPLES
Henry, m. by Sep 1686, [-?-], widow of Charles Turner of KE Co. (MDTP 13:403).

STURGES
George, m. on 22 April 1680, Frances Nicolls (SOLR:IKL).

SUDLER
James, planter of Kent Island, m. by March 1714/5, Rebecca, dau. of Elizabeth Walters, widow of Kent Island (QAJRh).
Joseph, m. by 9 Sep 1682, Cecily, relict and admx. of Thomas Bright of KE Co. (INAC 7C:304).

SULLIVAN
Daniel (Sulivant), m. on 27 Dec 1697, Elizabeth Wroth (KESP:64). She was a dau. of James Wroth (KELR GL#1:5).
Daniel (Swillaven), m. on 24 April 1705, Priscilla Stirney (CVCH). She was Priscilla, dau. of William Sturmey of CV Co. (MWB 14:74).
Darby (Sillivant), m. by 28 April 1688, Ann, sister of John Dew of CV Co. (MWB 6:44).
Darby (Sullivant), m. on 30 Dec 1714, Elizabeth Dunahoe (KESP:66).
Dennis, m. by April 1715, Agnes, admx. of Patrick Buck of KE Co. (MDTP 22:425).
Owen (Swellivant), m. on 27 Sep 1701, Dorothy Taylor, widow (HAGE:12). She was the extx. of Lawrence Taylor of [BA?] Co. (INAC 25:59).
Owen (Sillivan), m. on 24 June 1703, Mary Dedman (TAPE).

Owen, m. by 1 Nov 1704, Susannah, dau. of Jacob Seth (TALR 9:289).
Owen (Sulivant), m. on 27 June 1713, Elizabeth Mercer (TAPE).

SUMBLER
Benjamin, the banns of marriage were pub. 29 Jan 1666 between him and Izabell Wale (*ARMD* 54:657; SOLR O#1:51).

SUMET
William, m. by 27 Aug 1718, Anne, admx. of Thomas Tippins of QA Co. (MDAD 1:278).

SUMMERFORD
Jeffry, m. by 9 March 1668, Siball, relict of John Six of DO Co. (DOLR Old 1:59).

SUMMERS
Benjamin, on 18 April 1676, banns of matrimony were published for him and Deborah Wooldridge (SOJU O#7:42).
Thomas, m. on 5 June 1709, Elizabeth Perry (TAPE).
William (Summer), m. on 18 Sep 1691, Margaret Butler (SOLR:IKL).

SUMNER
Robert, m. by 14 Aug 1695, Margaret, admx. of John Sunderland (or Hinderland) of CV Co. (INAC 10:432, 14:64, 17:75).

SUNDERLAND
John, m. by 1 Aug [1679?], [-?-], widow of James Humes of CV Co. (INAC 6:259).
Josiah (Sunderlon), m. on 18 Dec 1718, Precilla Stockett (AAJA:52#15).

SUREY
Henry Surey was buried 12 January 1697 in St. James' Parish (AACR:146). He was probably married to Eliza [-?-], mother of Abraham Meares. On 23 June 1702 Eliza Surey, widow, and Abraham Meares conveyed to Thomas Miles, part of *Grammer's Parrott*, now in possession of said Surey and Meares, 100 a. (AALR WT#1: 294,WT#2:346). Elizabeth Surey of AA Co. widow, was still living on 2 Aug 1717 when she made a deed of gift of furniture and a heifer to her granddau. Rachel Voiseen (AALR CW#1:345).

SURNAM
Richard, m. on 26 --- 1664, Ann Frowin (SOLR:IKL).

SUTTON
Francis, m. on 3 Nov 1715, Elizabeth Armstrong (TAPE).
Henry, m. on 15 April 1707, Mary Robinson (TAPE).
Henry, m. on 20 July 1718, Mary Spiller (TAPE).

John, m. by 30 July 1706, [-?-], relict and extx. of Thomas Baxter of TA Co. (INAC 25:335).

John, m. by 24 June 1707, Sarah, widow and extx. of Roger Baxter of QA Co. (INAC 27:4, 32A:19).

John, m. by 5 Aug 1710, Mary, admx. of Thomas Collins of TA Co. (INAC 32A:19).

Richard, of Phila., m. on 12 d. 7 m., 1698, Mary Howell of CE Co., at Cecil Meeting House (KECE).

Thomas, m. by 31 May 1680, Hester, "very aged " extx. of Thomas Besson (INAC 7A:125).

William, d. 1698, leaving as an extx. Mary Crouch, granddau. of Maurice Baker (Cotton cites INAC 16:129).

SWAINE
[-?-], m. by 10 April 1699, Catherine, dau. of John Lee of TA Co. (MWB 6:259).

SWALLOW
John, m. on 11 Feb 1696, Alice Cox (TAPE).

SWAN
[-?-], m. by 2 April 1718, Elizabeth, dau. of George Young of CV Co. (MWB 14:613).

Edward, m. by Aug 1695, Mary, relict and extx. of Francis Buxton of CV Co. (INAC 10:474, 14:47; MDTP 16:90).

Edward, banns pub. 21 Dec 1703, and m. on 24 Jan 1703/4, Elizabeth Griffith (HAGE:17, 22).

Thomas, m. on 8 Jan 1711, Sarah May (TAPE).

SWANSON
Edward, m. by 23 Nov 1675, [-?-], relict and admx. of William Robinson of BA Co. (INAC 1:472)

Francis (Swanston), m. by 1670, Dorothy [-?-], widow of 1st, Giles Sadler, 2nd, Daniel Golson, and 3rd, Hugh Stanley (MPL AA:68, 86, 5:195,409,427, 9:54, 12:591, 14:214, EE:52, JJ:221-2, and KK:202).

Francis, m. by 12 July 1694, Susanna, 3rd dau. of Thomas Plummer of AA Co. (MWB 7:56).

SWEARINGEN
John (Sweringen), m. on 9 Feb 1715, Mary Ray (PGQA:1).
Samuel, m. on 14 Feb 1715, Eliza Farmer (PGQA:1).
Thomas, m. by 17 Nov 1716, Leady, dau. of Hugh Riley of PG Co. (PGLR F:571).

SWIFT
John, m. on 11 Sep 1703, Ann Hobbs (TAPE).
Mark, m. by 16 Feb 1698, Eliza, niece of Thomas Staley of BA Co. (MWB 11:35).

Ralph, m. on 11 April 1711, Ann Montigue (TAPE).
Richard, m. on 16 Aug 1716, Elizabeth Stacy (TAPE).

SWINBURNE

[-?-], m. by 8 June 1705, Elizabeth, mother of William Moss, Gent. (CHLR Z:201).

SWINSTIRE

John, of AA Co., m. by May 1697, [-?-], relict of Richard Deavea or Deaver of AA Co. (MDTP 16;234).

SWINSTONE

Francis, m. by 1670, [-?-], widow of Giles Sadler (MPL 12:591).

SWINYARD

John (Sweenyard), m. by 28 Oct 1712, Lucy, extx. of Francis Pottee of BA Co. (INAC 33B:65; PCJU VD#1:182).

SWORDIN

Mary, of Third Haven MM, on 31 d., 6 m., 1709, condemned her action by going to a priest to be married (*QMES:*28).

SYBERY

Jonathan, m. shortly after 8 Jan 1673/4, Frances, widow of Henry Morgan of KE Co. (MDTP 6:61).

SYKES

[-?-], m. by 10 Dec 1703, Ann, widow and extx. of [-?-] Harnung of SM Co. (MDTP 9B:19).

SYMONDS

Lawrence, m. by 1663 Seth, mother of Anthony Alexander, whom Symonds called son-in-law (MPL AA:455, 6:218).

SYMONS

Thomas (or George), m. by Feb 1698, Elizabeth, late widow of Dr. Alexander Chappell, chirurgeon (MDTP 17:253, 255).

SYNNET

Garret, m. 21 Nov 1666, Alice Hunt (CHLR C#1:253; *ARMD* 60:116).

TACKETT

Thomas, m. by 13 March 1713, Mary, extx. of William Wargen or Wargent of DO Co. (INAC 34:114, 222).

TALBOT(T)

[-?-], m. by 7 Dec 1663, Eliza, sister of Richard, John, Anne, and Susannah, widow of James Billingslea (MWB 1:99).

[-?-], m. by 1693, Elizabeth, admx. of Charles Cox of SM Co. (Cotton cites INAC 12:62).

Charles, m. on 4 June 1713, Elizabeth Wood (HAGE:30).

Edward, m. by 1697, Mary, dau. of William Cooke (AALR IB#2:179).

Edward, m. by 10 Aug 1699, Mary, dau. of Edward Sunn [Lunn?] (AALR WT#1:37).

John, of CV Co., carpenter, m. by 29 May 1697, Sarah, dau. of John Meers (son of Thomas Meers) (AALR IH#1:147).

John (Talburt), b. Pocklinton, Yorks., son of Paul, m. on 2 Feb 1696, Sarah Lockyer, dau. of Thomas (PGKG:244; PGLR A:195).

John, m. by 21 May 1701, [-?-], widow and admx. of Samuel Hayden of SO Co. (INAC 20:119).

John, and Elizabeth Galloway filed their intentions to marry on 3 d., 5 m., 1705 (WRMMa).

John, and Mary Waters filed their intentions to marry on 11 d., 5 m., 1707 (WRMMa).

John, m. by 28 Jan 1709, Lucy, extx. of Henry Green of KE Co. (INAC 31:56).

TALLE

Anthony, m. by 8 Dec 1710, Mabelow?, possibly mother of Charles and Peter Rose, whom Talle calls sons-in-law (MWB 13:462).

TANCRED

William, of Arden, Co. York, Eng., m. by 23 Aug 1714, Elizabeth, dau. of Thomas Carter, and niece of Richard Carter, of MD, dec. (AALR IB#2:170).

TANEY/TAWNEY

John, m. by 17 May 1707, Katherine, admx. of John Wilson of SM Co. (INAC 26:319, 29:393, 400).

Michael, m. by 1692, Margaret Beckwith. widow of Joakin Kierstead and dau. of George and Francis Harvey Beckwith. She m. 3rd, George Gray (INAC 9:476, 32B:129; MWB 6:1; MCHR PC:433; Warrants 7:62).

Thomas, m. by 16 May 1696, Jane, relict of Henry Truman of [TA Co.?], and mother of Thomas Truman of PG Co. (INAC 14:95, 30:266, 277; AAJU TB#1:483; MWB 14:649; PCJU PL#1:40).).

TANNER

Richard, on 8 Aug 1671, banns of matrimony were published for him and Elizabeth Tage, widow (SOJU DT#7:182).

TANT

James, m. by 13 May 1706, Mary, dau. of Susanna Heard, widow of John Heard of SM Co. (MWB 12:199; Hodges also cites SMAD HH:190, 393; MDAD 1:43, 443;

SMWB PC#1:147, 216, 334).

Thomas (Taunt), m. by 25 Nov 1672, Ann, widow of Christopher Gardner of AA Co. (MDTP 5:372).

TANYHILL

[-?-], m. by 17 Jan 1713, Sarah, dau. of Robert Orme, Sr., of PG Co. (MWB 14:41).

John, m. by 11 April 1712, Sarah, admx. of Robert Bowen of PG Co. (INAC 34:155).

TANZEY

Alexander, m. on 20 Jan 1704/5, Mary Parsons (AAJA:30 #12).

TARBLE

Thomas, m. by 1667, Elizabeth Labs (MPL 10:609).

TARENT

Leonard, of Essex, VA, m. by 4 June 1718, Mary, dau. of Robert Brooks (MWB 14:489).

TARR

John, m. by 14 Aug 1690, [-?-], relict of Thomas Proffit (SOJU 1689-90:168).

TASKER

Benjamin, m. on 31 July 1711, Anne Bladen, dau. of William and Anne (AAAN:9).

Thomas, m. by Oct 1678, [-?-], extx. of John Brooke (*ARMD* 68:43).

TATE

Thomas, m. by 19 July 1709, Susannah, mother of Thomas Alexander and grandmother of Thomas Alexander (TALR RF#11:90).

TATLOCK

[-?-], m. by 3 Oct 1709, Agnes, dau. of Edward Davis of SO Co. (MWB 12, pt. 2:237).

TATTERSHALL

William, m. by c1661, Ann, widow of John Lewger (MPL 4:568, 618; 5:472-73, AA:130).

TAVERNOR

John, of CH Co., m. by March 1679/80, Elizabeth, the widow of [-?-] Cole (*ARMD* 69:337-339).

TAYLOR/TAYLER

[-?-], m. (date not given) Alice Wells, dau. of John Wells of AA Co. (Hodges cites

Judgements 91:450).

[-?-], m. by 10 March 1676, Mary, relict and admx. of John Martin, and of Jasper Allen of CV Co. (INAC 2:187, 4:476; MDTP 8A:496).

[-?-], m. by 30 Oct 1711, [-?-], dau. of Robert Crouch of SO Co. (MWB 13:362).

[-?-], m. by 16 Sep 1712, Mary, dau. of Col. James Smallwood of CH Co. (MWB 14:31).

[-?-] (or Tyler), m. by 12 April 1714, Elizabeth, extx. of Edward Welch of BA Co. (INAC 35A:130).

[-?-], m. by 1717, Bridget Millmon, dau. of Thomas Millmon of DO Co. (MWB 14:456).

[-?-], m. by 2 Feb 1717/8, Sarah Shakley or Shekertie, dau. of John and Mary Shakley (MWB 14:523).

Abraham, m. by 19 June 1701, Jane, admx. of John Armstrong (INAC 20:253).

Abraham, m. on 20 --- ---, Dinah White (SJSG:5).

Anthony, of Annamessex, on 27 Nov 1666, banns of matrimony were published for him and Alce Bassett, also of Annamessex (SOLR O#1:41).

Anthony, m. by 1 Sep 1676, Mary Wood, dau. of Mary Wood (DOLR 3 Old:116).

Arthur, m. by 3 March 1683/4, Frances, mother of James Smithers (BALR RM#HS:68).

Francis, m. by 29 Nov 1705, Grace, extx. of Nicholas White of AA Co. (INAC 25:111).

Henry, m. Katherine, widow of George Bartlett who was said to have d. 17 Dec 1675 (MDTP 8:3, 9:452).

Henry, m. by 1686, Margaret Wynne, dau. of Thomas and Elizabeth Wynne of SM Co. (CH and SM Co. Rent Roll # 1:5; Prov. Court FF:84).

Henry, m. by 6 Dec 1694, Faith, dau. of John Campbell of "Poplar Hill," SM Co. (MWB 7:190; SMWB PC#1:90 or 191).

Hope, on 5 Feb 1683/4, banns of matrimony were published for him and Margaret Doricks [poss. Daniels] (SOJU O#7:18).

Jacob, m. by 1707, [-?-], widow of Jacob Pattison (DO Co. Rent Roll:56).

James, of TA Co., carpenter, m. on 1 d. 8 m., 1699, Isabel Adkenson (Atkinson), of DO Co., spinster, at the meeting house near Tuckahoe Creek (TATH).

John, m. by 1646, Sarah, mother of Richard Bennett of Poplar Hill, SM Co., and of Sarah and Thomas Bennett (MPL 2:220, 544, 569-570; *ARMD* 10:84; Proprietary Records F&B:184).

John, m. by 1658, Elizabeth, sister of Thomas Lomax of CH Co. (CHLR F#1:4, E#1:39).

John, whose kinsman was Thomas Harris of Swanley, Kent, Eng., m. by 1 Jan 1682, Susannah [-?-] (MWB 2:200).

John, m. by 12 Jan 1689, Anne, dau. of William Coulbourne of SO Co. (SOJU 1691-1692:5).

John, m. on 9 Nov 1713, Rachel Holmes (CVCH).

John, m. by 1718, Mary Mankin, half-sister of Thomas Howard of CH Co. (MDTP 23:166).

Jonathan, m. on 31 Oct 1706, Margaret Douglass (AAAL 1:33).

Joseph, on 14 March 1676, banns of matrimony were published for him and Margaret Rollens (SOJU O#7:39).

Lawrence, banns pub. Jan 1699/1700, Elizabeth Smith (HAGE:8).

Lawrence, m. on 7 Feb 1703/4, Agnes Montague (HAGE:18).

Richard, of AA Co., m. on 7 d., 6 m. (called Aug), 1687, at William Richardson's, Ann Trasey (WRMM).

Richard, m. on 21 Sep 1706, Anne Tatloe (AAAL 1:33).

Richard, m. by banns on June 1716, by Mr. Sewell, Anne Perrey, spinster (CESS).

Robert, m. by 1653, Mary, sister of Alce Griffin and of Ann wife of Peter Johnson (MPL 1:465-478, AB7H:140).

Robert, m. by 1676/7, Mary, widow of Joseph Allen, and dau. of Ishmael and Margaret Wright of CV Co. (MDTP 2:161, 181, 4:2, 8:495, 496).

Robert, m. by 20 March 1696, Frances, dau. of John Mitchell and his wife Jane, the dau. and heir of Frances Lombard (KELR M:25, 61).

Samuel, of PG Co., m. by 9 Jan 1702, Verlinda, dau. of Robert Doyne (PGLR C:39, Z#2:68; CHLR Z:8).

Thomas, of KE Co., m. on 2 d. 1 m., 1669, Elizabeth Marsh of Severn, spinster, at the house of John Webb at Patuxent (TATH). She was a sister of Thomas Marsh of KE Co. (MWB 10:52).

Thomas, m. by 1671, [-?-], dau. of John and Mary James (MPL 16:168).

Thomas, m. by 1680, Elizabeth, relict of Thomas Sparrow (MPL R:45b, 4:97, 20:343, WC:835).

Thomas, Jr., m. on 5 Feb 1696, Sarah [-?-] (TAPE).

Thomas, Jr., m. by c1697, [-?-], dau. of Cornelius Mulraine (INAC 15:245).

Thomas, merchant, m. on 21 d. 6 m., 1701, Elizabeth Sharp, spinster, both of TA Co., at the meeting house near Tuckahoe Creek (TATH). She was the extx. of Wm. Sharp (PCJU WT#4:258).

Thomas, Sr., of Bullenbroke, TA Co., m. on 12 Aug 1701, Elizabeth [-?-] (TAPE).

Thomas, of TA Co., m. by 26 Aug 1701, Elizabeth, granddau. of Henry Woolchurch of TA Co. (KELR JD#1:7).

Thomas, planter, m. on 3 d. 3 m., 1702, Elizabeth Dane, spinster, both of TA Co., at the meeting house near Choptank River, TA Co. (TATH).

Thomas, m. by 1703, Jane, widow of John Lane (Hodges cites Judgements 9:89).

Thomas, m. by 29 June 1706, Jane, extx. of James Marks of TA Co. (INAC 25:426). She was a dau. of John Marks, Jr. (MWB 4:76, TA and QA Co. Rent Roll 2:435). Another source states she was the extx. of James Marks, son of John (MDTP 21:86).

Thomas, m. by 9 July 1708, Elizabeth (who had been dead for about three years), extx. of William Sharp of TA Co. (INAC 28:153).

Thomas, of DO Co., m. by 10 Oct 1718, Joan, admx. of John Ennalls of DO Co. (MDAD 1:228). (MDTP 23:212/3 gives her name as Eleanor, admx. of John Ennalls).

Thomas Davis; on 8 Nov 1670 the banns of matrimony were published between Thomas Davis Taylor & Judith Best both of this [SO] County (*ARMD* e86 (SOJU DT#7):41). [N.B.: He might be Thomas Davis, tailor].

Thomas Davis, m. by 1693, Eliza, dau. of Richard and Temperance Clowder (CHLR Q#1:21).

Walter, m. by Jan 1687, the relict and extx. of David Linsey (*ARMD* e91:13; MDTP 12B:189).

William (Taylard), m. by 8 Nov 1711, Audrey, possibly mother of Richard Lluellin, whom Taylard names as son-in-law (MWB 13:338).

William, m. by 7 Sep 1715, Mary, dau. of Andrew Derrickson of SO Co. (MWB 14:127).

TEAGLE

Nathaniel, m. by 12 July 1671, Eliza Todd (in will of Richard Howard of TA Co. (MWB 1:454).

TEAGUE

John, d. by 9 Nov 1675, leaving a widow Eliza, sister of Sarah, the wife of John Dorman; she m. 2nd, Richard Turner (*ARMD* e89 (SOJU 1675-1677):20).

TEANY

Daniel, m. by 27 Aug 1709, Mary, admx. or extx. of John Pouder of KE Co. (INAC 30:179).

TEARS

Hugh, m. Eleanor, dau. of Walter and Eleanor Bayne of CH Co., and widow of John Stone. She later m. by 22 June 1700 John Beale (CHLR Z#2:485; MDTP 19a:75, 78; Hodges cites Judgements 6:792, 21:514-516).

TEDSTELL

Thomas, m. on 28 Aug 1707, Jane Eustace (AAAL 1:36).

TEMPLE

Thomas, banns pub. Jan 1698/9, m. 17 April 1699 Elenor Loreson (HAGE:6).

TENCH

Thomas, m. by Feb 1686/7, Margaret, widow of Nathan Smith, and dau. of John Burrage (MDTP 13:452; AALR WT#2:276).

TENGELL

[-?-], m. by 18 Nov 1716, Sarah, dau. of Samuel Cobb of SO Co. (MWB 14:574).

TENNISON

[-?-], m. by 30 June 1712, Mary, dau. of John Brooks of CH Co. (MWB 13:690).

Justinian, m. by 1683, Elizabeth, dau. of John and Abigail (Simon) Shanks; she m. 2nd, Giles Hill (Fresco cites SMWB PC#1:45, 111; MWB 3:731, 4:159; MDTP 13:280).

TEVIS

Robert, m. on 15 April 1707, Susanna Davies (AAAL 1:33).

THACKER
  Samuel, m. by 16 July 1711, Hester, sister of William Hawlin of PG Co. (INAC 32C:152).

THACKREL
  Thomas, m. on 9 April 1710, Mary Martin (AAAN:9).

THARP
  William, m. on 8 Jan 1709, Jane Oisbone [Oistone?] (TAPE).

THATCHER
  Thomas, clerk, of Boston, MA, m. by Oct 1672, Margaret Sheafe, widow of Jacob Sheafe, of Boston, dau. and extx. of Henry Webb, merchant of Boston (MDTP 5:481).

THICKPENNY
  Henry, m. on 5 Jan 1715, Rachel Dowden (PGQA:1).

THISELWOOD
  James, m. by 6 Nov 1707, Mary, admx. or extx. of Henry Whitaker of DO Co. (INAC 28:107).

THOMAS
  [-?-], m. by (date not given), Elizabeth, admx. of Godfrey Barnes of PG Co. (INAC 37C:130).
  [-?-], of TA Co., m. by Nov 1677, [-?-], relict of John Woolcott of KE co. (MTP 9A:441).
  [-?-], m. by 1679, Sarah, dau. of Mary, wife of Philip Carter (MPL WC2:16).
  Alexander, m. in 1678, Cicell Shaw (SOLR:IKL).
  Alexander, m. by 29 Sep 1688, Mary, relict and extx. of John Evans of SO Co. (INAC 10:176).
  Christopher, m. by 1664, Elizabeth, poss. mother of Susan and Katherine Higgins, who were called Thomas' daus. (MPL CC:512, 7:471-2, 8:207, DD:240).
  David, m. by 25 July 1706, Hannah, extx. of George Smith of BA Co. (INAC 25:330).
  Evan, m. on 8 March 1712/13, Mary Jones (AAJA:41 #16).
  John, m. by April 1698, [-?-], widow of Edward Norris of BA Co. (MDTP 17:82).
  Joseph, m. by 2 June 1699, Margaret, dau. of Richard Jones of CH Co. (MWB 6:368).
  Richard, had license dated 24 June 1641, to marry Ursula Bish (MPL 1:148).
  Robert, m. by 9 Sep 1696, Mary, extx. of John Little of SM Co. (INAC 14:89).
  Robert, m. on 18 Jan 1704/5, Jane ffreeborn (AAAN:19). She was a dau. of Thomas Freeborne of AA Co. (MWB 13:621).
  Samuel, m. on 15 d., 3 m. (May) 1688, at the home of Samuel Thomas, Mary Hutchins of CV Co. (WRMM).
  Solomon, and Rebecca Winn declared their intention to marry on 11 d., 2 m., 1685, and on 18 d., 3 m., 1685 (Third Haven MM in *QMES:*9).

Thomas, m. by 9 Sep 1651, Eliza, dau. of James Knott (MWB 1:51).

William, m. by 22 March 1665, Ann, widow of John Stevens (*ARMD* 57:10; MDTP 2:70).

William, of TA Co., m. by Nov 1686, Ann, widow of Robert [Lavrin?] (MDTP 13:429).

William, m. by Oct 1688, [-?-], relict of Robert Lambdin (MDTP 14:97).

William, m. by c1694, Mary Coppin, dau. of John Coppin of TA Co. (INAC 13A:215).

William, m. on 22 d. 11 m., 1707, Joanna Hosier, both of KE Co. (KECE). She was a dau. of Henry Hosier of KE Co. (MWB 13:192).

THOMPSON

[-?-], m. by 28 Sep 1697, Blanche, dau. of Randolph and Barbara Hinson Of CH Co. (MWB 6:235).

[-?-], m. by 6 July 1714, Margaret, widow of John Howell (MCHR CL:18).

[-?-], m. by 18 March 1718/9, Mary, dau. of William Dare of CE Co. (MWB 15:203).

Arthur, m. by 1701, Susanna, sister of John Carberry (SMWB PC#1:125).

Augustine, m. by 26 March 1713, Sarah, dau. of John Salter of QA Co. (QALR ETA:162).

Christopher, m. by c1696, Grace, widow of James Williams, and extx. of Lawrence Rouland of CV Co. (INAC 13B:26; PGLR C:96).

George, of SM Co., m. by Feb 1680/1, Margaret, widow of Barnaby Jackson and sister of Robert Goodrick (Warrant Record CB#1:120; MCHR PC:494).

James?, m. by 5 Jan 1712, Charity Bailey, dau. of John, of SM Co. (MWB 13:582).

Jasper (Thomson), m. on 29 Aug 1706, Ann Cleary (AAJA:33 #3).

John, of CH Co., m. by 1703, Mary Green, dau. of Robert and Mary (CHLR Z#1:84, Z#2:84).

John, m. by 31 Oct 1712, Jane, admx. of Cornelius Fitzgerald of SM Co. (INAC 33B:164).

Joseph, and Eliza Dawson declared their intention to marry in Third Haven MM on 23 d., 12 m., 1698 (*QMES:*19).

Richard, of Kent Island, had a license dated 24 Jan 1641 to marry Ursula Bish (MPL 1:148; *ARMD* 4:66).

Robert, m. by 5 Jan 1688, Mary, wife and extx. of Giles Blizard (MCHR PC:282).

Robert (Tomson), m. by 3 April 1708, Margaret, dau. of John Raley of SM Co. (SMWB PC#1:162; MWB 12, pt. 2:57; MDTP 21;319, 22:104, 251).

William, Sr., m. by 11 April 1681, Mary, dau. of William Britton (MWB 1:123?, CHLR Q#1:8).

William, son of William and Mary of SM Co. (she being a dau. of William Bretton), m. on 11 April 1681, Victoria Matthews, dau. of Thomas and Jane Matthews of CH Co. (CHLR Q#1:8R).

William, tailor, m. on 5 d. 2 m., 1704, Mary Hall, both of TA Co. at Tuckahoe Meeting House (TATH). She was dau. of Richard Hall of TA Co. (MWB 3:244).

William, m. by 9 Feb 1707, Elizabeth, widow and extx. of Daniel Elliott of PG

Co. (INAC 28:2).
William, d. by 1716, having m. Barbara, dau. of William Langham (SMWB PC#1:227).

THORNBERRY
[-?-] (Thornborough), m. by May 1680, Sarah, relict and admx. of John Woodhouse (MDTP 12A:38).

THORNE
William, m. by 13 Dec 1711, Mary, dau. of John Gillam of SM Co. (MWB 13:457; MDTP 24:210).

THORNTON
William, m. by 20 July 1710, [-?-], widow of Thomas Birchenall of CE Co. (INAC 32B:115).

THORNWELL
[-?-], m. by March 1706/7, Elizabeth, aged c55, former wife of Thomas Thacker (DOLR 6 Old:119).

THRIFT
[-?-], of TA Co., m. by 23 April 1711, Eliza, mother of Nicholas Brown, Susanna Kinnamont, and Sarah Conner (MWB 13:471).

THURCALL
Thomas, m. by 27 July 1686, Jane, coheir of Thomas O'Daniel (BALR RM# HS:188).

THURLOW
Richard, m. on 15 Nov 1708, Ann Holdgate (AAAN:7).

THURSTON
Daniel, m. by May 1696, Martha, admx. of Robert Cage, who was the admin. of Mark Child (MDTP 16:170).

TIBBELL
[-?-], m. by 20 Feb 1710, Eliza, dau. of John Price of TA Co. (MWB 13:568).

TIBBELS
Abraham, m. on 17 Sep 1711, Rebeckah Standley (TAPE).

TILCHBERRY
Henry, m. by 24 Feb 1707, Elizabeth, widow and admx. of John Price of SO Co. (INAC 28:106).

TILDEN
    Marmaduke, m. by 20 Aug 1712, Tabitha, dau. of William Harris of KE Co.
(MWB 13:488).

TILLINGSTON
    [-?-], m. some time before 25 d., 5 m., 1711, by a priest, Martha Baynard of
Third Haven MM (*QMES:*30).

TILLMAN
    Gydeon, m. on 15 Feb 1681, Margarett Maneux (SOLR:IKL).

TILLY
    Charles, m. by 18 June 1706, [-?-], dau. of John Gray of AA Co. (AALR
IH#1:264).
    Charles, of AA Co., d. by 26 June 1718, leaving an admx. Elizabeth who m. John
Cheney (IAC 31:135).
    Joseph, m. by 26 April 1675, Mary, widow and extx. of John Little of CV Co.
(*ARMD* 51:159).

TILTON
    Humphrey, m. by 16 Aug 1698, Mary, dau. of John James of CE Co., whose will
named his grandsons James and Humphrey Tilton (MWB 6:247).

TILYARD
    John, of KE Co., m. by 3 Nov 1698, Mary, dau. of George Green (BALR
TR#RA:308).

TINGLE
    Hugh, m. on 22 Dec 1683, Elizabeth Powell (SOLR:IKL).

TIPPENS
    William, "having run out from truth," has been married by a priest, some
time before 29 d., 10 m., 1703, to the dau. of Richard Hall (Minutes of Third Haven
MM: *QMES:*23, 26).

TIPPER
    Edgar, m. by Sep 1715 [-?-], admx. of William Pritchard (MDTP 22:491).

TIPPITT
    Nicholas, m. by 31 Jan 1708, Anne, extx. of Michael Bellican of KE Co. (INAC
29:75, 393).

TIPTON
    Jonathan, m. on 15 Dec 1709, Mary Chilcoat (AAJA:39 #19).

TISDELL

Christopher (Teasdell), m. by 15 April 1710, Mary, surviving dau. of the elder bro. of Richard Carter of TA Co., MD, dec. (TALR RF#11:136).

TOADVINE

Henry, m. by 1 Sep 1718, Alice, dau. of Thomas Dixon of Annamessex Hund., SO Co. (MWB 16:100).

Nicholas, on 24 Oct 1676, banns of matrimony were published for him and Sarah Loury (SOLR O#7:60r). Nicholas (Toadwin), m. on 15 Nov 1675 [*sic*] , Sarah Lowry (SOLR:IKL).

TOAS

John, of KE Co., m. on 14 d. 7 m., 1699, Jone Queney of CE Co., at Cecil Meeting House (KECE). She was the relict of Sutton Queney or Queeney (MDTP 18B:66).

John, m. by Nov 1711, [-?-], sister of the wife of Robert Roberts, who supported the Toas' two children after Toas ran away (*CMSP: Black Books* #124).

TOBIAS

Cornelius, m. by lic. on 24 Feb 1712, by Rich. Sewell, Eleanor Shutten, spinster (CESS).

Cornelius, m. by 15 April 1714, Ellenor, widow of Nathaniel Childs of CE Co. (INAC 36A:50).

TOBIN

Cornelius, m. by 12 June 1718, Elinor, dau. of George Strutton of CE Co. (MWB 14:627).

Walter, m. on 22 Dec 1709, Mary Shea (AAAN:9).

TOBITT

Walter, m. on 27 Dec 1709, Mary Shay (AAAN:7).

TODD

James, m. by 6 Jan 1699, Penelope, dau. of Thomas and Abigail Scudamore (her mother m. 2nd, John Hayes) (BALR TR#RA:418).

John, m. in 1710, Keatren Smith (AAMA:84).

Lambert, m. by 7 March 1704, Eliza, dau. of Mary Rockhold (MWB 3:248).

Lancelot, m. by April 1677, [-?-], only dau. of Thomas Phelps (whose widow m. William Ferguson) (MDTP 9A:44; BALR RM#HS:116).

Michael, may have m. by 19 Nov 1698, [-?-], dau. of Andrew and Elizabeth Insley, who call Michael Todd their son-in-law (DOLR 5 Old:125; MWB 6:291).

TOLLY

Thomas, m. on 6 Nov 1706, Catherine Howard (AAAN:1). She was the extx. of Samuel Howard (AAJU TB#1:703).

TOLSON
    Francis, b. at Wood Hall, Bright Church Parish, Cumberland, son of Henry, m. on 27 Sep 1707, Mary Clark, dau. of Robert (PGKG:244).

TOM
    William, m. by 31 July 1710, Elizabeth, dau. of Richard Smith of St. Leonard's, SM Co.(MWB 14:82).

TOMLIN
    Robert, m. on 2 (or 23?) Oct 1701, by Mr. Nobbs, minister, Joane [-?-] (TAPE).

TOMPKINS
    Giles, m. by 21 Jan 1702, Ann, dau. of Mary Brown of CH Co. (MWB 11:199).

TONGE
    John, of the Parish of St. Saviour Southwark, Surrey, citizen and merchant tailor, m. by Nov 1673, Elizabeth, widow of Ralph Beane of MD (*ARMD* 65:181).

TOOGOOD
    Josias (Towgood, Twogood), m. on 3 Oct 1698, Mary Purnell (AAJA:63A#9). She was the widow of Richard Purnell (AALR WT#2:21).
    Josias, m. by 17 March 1708, Mary, dau. of John Welsh (BALR TR#A:5).

TOOLE
    Timothy, m. by 22 June 1714, Sarah, dau. of John Stark of TA Co., dec. (QALR I(J)KA:3).

TOUCHBERRY
    Henry, m. by April 1708, Elizabeth, extx. of John Price (MDTP 21:8)

TOVEY
    Samuel, m. by 22 Nov 1681, Ann, mother of Richard Kane, and prob. mother of Mary Forbes, dau. of John Forbes (KELR K:2).

TOWERS
    John, d. by 9 May 1685; his widow Rachel, m. 2nd, Thomas Richardson (BALR RM#HS:216).
    John, m. by June 1693, Margaret extx. of William Galt or Gall, and mother of David Gall, aged 10 (SOJU LD:23, SOJU 1692-1693:243).

TOWNHILL
    Edmund, m. as her 2nd husband, Magdalene Abbott, widow of Simon Abbott; Townhill left a will 6 April 1661; Magdalen/Maudlin m. 3rd, by 1661, Thomas Smethwick, and 4th, by 1674, George Nettlefold (Warrants 4:68; MWB 1:627, 2:363; MDTP 7:112, 9:331; AALR IH#1:172).

TOWNLEY
Jno., m. by 8 July 1718, Mary, dau. of John Smith of PG Co. (MWB 15:205).

TOWNROE
Richard, m. by 25 Aug 1713, Alice, dau. and coheir of Samuel Farmer of TA, dec. (TALR RF#12:141).

TRACEY
Tegoe, m. on 5 Nov 1694, Mary James (AAJA:7#4).
Teague (Trasey?), m. by 6 Aug 1695, Margaret, legatee of Luke Gregory of AA Co. (INAC 10:442).
Thomas (Tracy), m. on 15 Jan 1701, Susanna Hawkins (AAJA:24#15). She was the widow of 1st, John Sivick, 2nd, Augustine Hawkins, and dau. of Walter Carr (AALR PK:102 WT#2:115; INAC 21:350; AALR PK 102).

TRAVIS
[-?-], m. by 21 Oct 1717, Mary, dau. of John Mills of PG Co. (MWB 14:664).
William, of DO Co., d. by 20 Feb 1705, having m. Eliz., dau. of William Chapling, Sr., of DO co. (DOLR 6 Old:78).

TRAWER
[-?-], m. by 16 Aug 1678, Joanna, extx. of Robert Farrer (MDTP 10:203).

TRAYMAN
James, m. on 24 Aug 1711, Elizabeth Bantom (TAPE).
Thomas, m. by 22 June 1718, Jane, admx. of John James of CV Co. (MDAD 1:93).

TREADWAY
Richard, pub. banns 7 Nov 1705, m. 17 Dec 1705, [-?-] Parker (HAGE:22).

TREGO
[-?-], m. by 16 Feb 1707/8, Sarah, dau. of Thomas Vickers, Sr., of PG Co. (MWB 13:272).

TREHERNE
George, in 1676, banns of matrimony were published for him and Anne Cameday (SOJU O#7:54). **George, m. on 29 Aug 1676, Anne Cammeday** (SOLR:IKL).

TRENNO
[-?-], m. by 3 Oct 1705, Temperance, dau. of James Wetherby, Sr. (MWB 13:44).

TREUSALE
William (Treveale?), m. by 12 Nov 1685, Mary, relict and extx. of William Luffman (INAC 8:460; MDTP 13:266).

TREVITT
    Richard, m. by 23 June 1714, Mary, dau. of [-?-] and Faith Gongo (AALR IB#2:158; his name is given as Robert in MWB 2:262)

TREW
    John, m. by 26 Sep 1679, Mary, extx. of Francis Finch of KE Co. (INAC 6:447).
    William, m. on 15 d. 10 m., 1703, Martha Pope of CE Co., at Cecil Meeting House (KECE). She was possibly an heir of John Pope of KE Co. (KELR JS#N:354).
    William, m. by 5 April 1715, Martha, "cousin" [kinswoman] of Nathaniel Howell (KELR BC#1:67).

TREWITT
    Jno. (Frewitt?), m. by July 1716, Alice, extx. of Richard Wells of SO Co.(MDTP 23:54).

TRICE
    Alexander, m. in Sep 1687, Bridgett Eley (SOLR:IKL).

TRICKY
    Thomas, m. by 24 Oct 1711, Mary, extx. of William Sparks of QA Co. (INAC 33A:26).

TRIGGS
    Richard, m. by 10 Oct 1702, Ellenor, extx. of Robert Kent of TA Co. (INAC 23:87).

TRIPPE
    Henry (Trepp), m. by 1663, Frances, widow of Michael Brooke, of CV Co. (MPL 5:59, 9:26, EE:25, 9:2; 11:347-8, and GG:288).

TRIVALLION
    John, of Charles Parish, York Co., VA, m. by 18 Dec 1699, Jane, dau. of Robert Curtis of the same parish (DOLR 5 Old:152).

TROTH
    George, m. on 22 Dec 1708, Rebecca Berry (TAPE).
    Henry, son of William of TA Co., and Elizabeth Johns, Jr., dau. of Richard Johns, filed their intentions to marry on 6 d., 5 m., 1711, and 3 d., 6 m., 1711 (WRMMa).
    William, m. on 20 Feb 1685, Isabella Harrison, widow of James Harrison (TATH).
    William, m. on 11 d. 11 m., 1704, Sarah, admx. of George Pratt at Treadhaven Creek (TATH).

TROTTER
    Walter, m. on 13 March 1704, in the Parish Church of St. Giles, Cripplegate,

London, Katherine Gallon, of St. Mary, Newington, Surrey (TALR RF#12:15). She was prob. the widow of Capt. John Gallon of Stepney, London, mariner (TALR RF#12:14, 15). Walter Trotter later settled in TA Co. (TALR RF#12:17).

TRUMAN/TRUEMAN

Edward, m. by 1697, Eliza Hutchinson, dau. of Thomas Hutchinson of PG Co. (CHLR L#2:413).

John, m. by 1685, [-?-], sister of John Makbride of SO Co. (MWB 4:215).

Thomas, m. by 20 April 1671, Mary, widow of John Bogue (*ARMD* 51:364).

Thomas, son of Mrs. Jane Taney, m. by 1717/1732, Sarah Briscoe, dau. of Philip and Susannah (Swann) Briscoe; she m. 2nd, William Stevens Howard (MWB 14:647, 21:344; CH Co. Probate Record R#2:212; MCHP # 4584).

Maj. Thomas, m. by 1681, Mary Lashley, dau. of Robert and Eliza Lashley of CV Co. (MWB 4:165; MDTP 13:375, 383, 384).

TRUNDEL

[-?-], m. by 17 Aug 1705, Mary, mother of Benjamin Thurley or Thorley, who was age 25 in Aug 1705 (MCHR PC:538).

TUCHSTONE

Richard, m. on 25 Feb 1717, Sarah Johnson (HAGE:65).

TUCKER

[-?-], m. by 7 March 1710, Ann, dau. of William Selby (PGLR F:62).

James, m. on 5 May 1709, Rebeckah Jewett [or Jewell?, Sewell?] (TAPE).

John, m. on 20 Feb 1708, Mary Lawson (TAPE).

John, of AA Co., carpenter, m. by 5 Dec 1709, Jennet, dau. of William Dorrumple of CV Co., planter (AALR PK:245).

Richard, m. on 18 April 1705, Martha Thodam (AAJA:35 #3).

Seaborne, m. by c1695, Dorothy, admx. of Charles Harrington of CV Co. (INAC 10:447; 17:74).

TULL

Richard, on 9 Jan 1671, banns of matrimony were published for him and Mathew [Martha] Rhodes (SOJU AZ#8:43).

Richard, m. on 26 Jan 1695/6, Elizabeth Turpin (SOLR:IKL).

Richard, Sr., d. by 2 May 1711, having m. Margaret, admx. of Thomas Pollett of SO Co. (INAC 32B:256).

Thomas, of Annemessex, on 4 Sep 1666, banns of matrimony were published for him and Mary Mitchell or Minshall (SOLR O#1:29). **Thomas, m. in Oct 1666, Mary Minshull** (SOLR:IKL).

Thomas, of SO Co., m. by 14 Feb 1717/8, Ann, mother of William Cox (MWB 16:117).

TULLY

[-?-] (Tulley), m. by 23 Jan 1717, Hannah, dau. of Duncan Monroe of QA Co.

(MWB 14:595).
John, m. by 8 July 1706, Mary, dau. of Edward Bennett of Quantico, SO Co. (MWB 12:113).
Stephen, m. by 8 July 1706, Jeane, dau. of Edward Bennett of Quantico, SO Co. (MWB 12:113).

TUMBLESTONE
John, m. on 16 Dec 1717, Sarah Fish (TAPE).

TURBERVILLE
Gilbert [Turberfield], m. by 6 March 1675/6, Lidia, relict and admx. of Thomas Pierse of SM Co. (MDTP 7:322; INAC 13A:221).
Payne, m. by Sep 1696, Ann, relict of Robert Taylor of SM Co. (MDTP 16:188; MWB 13:391).

TURBUTT
Samuell, m. on 30 March 1714, Rachel Goldsborough (TAPE).

TURLOE
William, aged 27, on 9 Feb 1707, bound himself to John Roe, planter, and had leave to marry Elizabeth [-?-], servant of Roe (deed gives details of Turloe's servitude) (TALR RF#11:38).
William, m. by 3 April 1708, Anne, extx. of Trustram Thomas of TA Co. (INAC 28:84).

TURMAN
Henry [more likely Truman], of CV Co., d. by 17 Jan 1709, when his relict and admx. Jane had m. Thomas Taney of CH Co., Gent. (INAC 30: 166, 277).

TURNER
[-?-], m. by 1665, Judith, dau. of Thomas and Elizabeth Mattingly (Fresco cites Warrants 8:88).
[-?-], m. by 28 April 1709, Mary, dau. of Rowland Beavens of SO Co. (MWB 12, pt. 2:100).
Bonham, m. by 10 Jan 1673, [-?-], widow of William Shirt of TA Co. (MDTP 6:63).
Edward, m. by 12 Dec 1688, Mary, dau. of Alexander Smith, planter (CHLR Q:2).
Edward, m. by 21 Sep 1702, Sarah, dau. of John Merrideth of DO Co. (MWB 11:346).
Edward (Turnor), and Lydia Durdin of Third Haven MM declared their intention to marry on 27 d., 9 m., 1712 and the following week. On 26 d., 3 m., 1714 they declared their untruth (*QMES:*31).
George (Tearner), m. by 9 Sep 1685, Ann, dau. of Joseph Hopkins (MWB 4:18).
John, m. by 9 Nov 1675, Eliza, widow of John Teague, and a sister Sarah, wife of John Dorman (*ARMD* e89 (SOJU O#7):20).
John, of AA Co., m. by July 1686, Eleanor, widow and extx. of Richard James

(MDTP 13:369; INAC 9:362, 474).

John, of CV Co., m. by Dec 1694, Mary, extx. of Robert Taylor (MDTP 15C:268).

Jno., m. on 6 Oct 1705, Elizabeth Hodges (CVCH).

John, Jr., m. on 1 July 1718, Eliza Brashier, dau. of Samuell (PGQA:2).

John, m. by 10 April 1706, Elisabeth, extx. of William Hodge of CV Co. (INAC 25:239).

Richard, m. on 8 March 1672, Elizabeth Teague (SOLR:IKL). She was the relict of John Teague (Tege) of SO Co. (MDTP 7:144).

Richard, m. by 16 Jan 1715, Elizabeth, admx. of Henry Holt of CV Co. (INAC 37A:23; 37A:28 gives his name as Henry Elet).

Thomas, m. Emma or Emilia, sister-in-law of James Langworth, and relict of William Johnson; she m. 3rd, by 1664, William Rosewell, and 4th, by 1684, William Watts (MPL R:206b, Q:19, 4:530, 589. 7:166-7, 12:148, CC:158-9, and HH:178; MWB 1:129, 133; 9:6; SMWB PC#1:94; Warrants 4:530, X:280; and MDTP 13:136).

Thomas, m. by May 1697, Elizabeth, extx. of Joshua Guybert (MDTP 16:232). She later m. by 16 Feb 1713, [-?-] Carberry (MWB 13:593).

William, m. by 1674, Joyce Bromall, widow of Richard Bromall of CV Co. (MPL WC4:147-48, 353; Warrant Record CB#1:202).

William, m. on 27 Jan 1718, Ann Maney (PGQA:2).

TURPIN

[-?-], m. by 19 March 1707/8, [-?-], dau. of Joseph Benton of Annmessex, SO Co. (MWB 13:206).

John, m. on 23 Jan 1695/6, Rebecca Bainton (SOLR:IKL).

William, m. on 6 Jan 1668, Margaret Ivery (SOLR:IKL).

William, m. by 1706, Sarah, dau. and heir of Richard Whitty (SOLR 10 (CD):26).

William, m. by 8 July 1706, Sarah, admx. of George Jones of SO Co. (INAC 25:407).

TURVILE

[-?-], m. by 21 April 1718, Eliza, dau. of Edward Wale of SO Co. (MWB 14:620).

William, m. by 12 June 1700, Elisabeth, extx. of William Tomkins of SO Co. (INAC 19½B:151).

TWIGG

John, m. by 6 June 1710, Elisabeth, extx. of Isaac Ashley of KE Co. (INAC 31:242).

TYDINGS

John (Tidings), of AA Co., son of Richard and Charity, m. on 16 d., 6 m. (Aug), 1705, Mary Ellis, dau. of James and Mary, late of AA Co. (WRMM).

TYER

James, m. by 28 Nov 1706, [-?-], dau. of Joseph Cornwell of CH Co. (INAC 26:108).

TYFERD
John, on 13 Sep 1670, banns of matrimony were published for him and Barbara Lawrence (SOJU DT#7:18).

TYLER
John, m. on 8 March 1693/4, Sarah Butter (SOLR:IKL).
Robert, m. by 28 July 1674, Joan, widow of John Beale, and George Read (INAC 1:54; Hodges cites Liber 2:346, 6:260; MDTP 7:33).
Mr. Robert, m. by Rev. Jacob Henderson on 1 or 12 June 1718, Madam Mary Todd, or Dodd, of Annapolis, widow (PGQA:2; AAAN:38).
Thomas Tyler m. on 3 d., 3 m., 1702 at Choptank Meeting, Eliza Dean (*QMES:*21).

TYNEDALE
Athelstan, upholsterer in Bristol, m. by 3 Dec 1708, Hester, sister of Edmund Howard, Gent., of CH Co. (MWB 13:632).

TYPPEN
William, m. by 28 April 1704, [-?-], dau. of Richard Hall of TA Co. (MWB 3:244).

UNDERHILL
John, m. on 14 Jan 1701, Sarah Lane (KESP:70).

UNDERWOOD
Anthony, d. by Dec 1692, having m. by 1684, Martha, extx. of Robert Ridgely (PCJU DS#A:41; MDTP 14A:8). In 1685, Martha was admx. of Nicholas [Bedrock?] (PCJU DS#A:160).
George, m. by 1712, Mary, dau. of Charles and Ann Egerton of SM Co. Anne Egerton later m. [-?-] Boucher (SMWB PC#1:172; MWB 13:491).
John, of BA Co., m. by March 1695/6, [-?-], relict of Henry Woler of BA Co. (MDTP 16:142).
Thomas, m. by 27 Aug 1710, Ann, extx. of John Dunbarr of SM Co. (INAC 31:363).

UNICK
Laughlin, m. on 13 Aug 17--, Elizabeth Tatum (KESP:70).
Richard (Unitt), m. on 19 Oct 17--, Katherine Bowdy (KESP:70). She was a dau. of Richard Boudy of KE Co. (MWB 12:171).

UPSHOTT
John, m. on 19 July 1695, in VA, Mary Thomas; a certificate was produced in SO Co. Court in Aug 1695 (SOJU E#26:6).

URINSON
Cornelius, m. by 21 March 1675/6, Elinor, mother of Andrew Powlson (CELR 1:56).

URNSER
[-?-], m. by 5 July 1718, Mary, dau. of John White of SO Co. (MWB 18:5).
[-?-], m. by 5 July 1718, Rebecca, dau. of John White of SO Co. (MWB 18:5).

USHER
Thomas, m. on 10 Nov 17---, Elizabeth Valentine (KESP:70).
Thomas, m. on 15 Jan 1702, Mary Hicks (KESP:70).
Thomas, m. by 9 Sep 1702, Elizabeth, admins. of John Clarkson (INAC 23:53).
Thomas, m. by Sep 1708, Elizabeth, extx. of John Clauson (MDTP 21:56).

UTIE
George, m. by 12 Oct 1670, Susanna, dau. of Samuel Goldsmith of BA Co. (MWB 1:442).
George, m. by 30 Dec 1696, Mary, dau. and coheir of Edward Beedle (BALR IS#IK:241, 245; INAC 15:182).
Nathaniel, m. contract dated 18 Jan 1667, to marry Elizabeth, dau. of John Carter of Lancaster Co., VA (*ARMD* 51:4).

VALENTINE
Luke, m. by 29 April 1702, Jane, relict and admx. of George Bozman of SO Co. (INAC 21:351).

VALLIANT
John, m. by 23 March 1709, Mary, now dec., dau. of Henry Frith (TALR RF#11:116).

VAN BEBBER
Matthias, m. on 17 Nov 1705, by license, Haramonica, dau. of Adam Peterson of New Castle Co., in the territories of PA (CESS).

VAN BURKELOE
Abell, m. on 7 June 1715, Catherine Herman, spinster (CESS). She was a dau. of Augustine Herman (MDTP 23:4).

VANDAN
Francis, m. by 1650, [-?-], servant of Thomas Greene, Esq. (MPL 3:20).

VAN DER HEYDEN
Mathias, m. by 10 Oct 1688, Margaret, relict and admx. of Henry Ward of CE Co. (INAC 10:172, 14:106, 24:106).

VAN DEVER
Jacob, m. by 26 Nov 1718, Jane, admx. of John Gill of BA Co. (MDAD 1:281).

VANE
John (Vain), m. on 24 April 1709, Susannah Mulvain (or Mulrain) (TAPE).
John, m. on 3 Oct 1717, Mary Arrington (TAPE).

VANHECK
John, m. by 6 Oct 1675, Sarah, dau of Thomas Howell and sister of John Howell of CE Co. (MWB 2:367; MDTP 10:127).

VAN SWEARINGEN
Garrett, m. by 13 Feb 1667, Barbara de Barrette [given elsewhere as Barburet Burrell (*ARMD* 2:105, 57:253).
Garrett, of SM Co., entered into an antenuptial contract on 5 Oct 1676, with Mary Smith, also of SM Co. (MPL 19:381).
Mr. Joseph, m. by 18 April 1718, Mary, widow and extx. of Jeremiah Adderton of SM Co., and dau. of James and Elizabeth Neale (INAC 39C:158; MDAD 1:34; MDTP 36:156).

VAUGHAN
John, m. on 30 Sep 1714, Elizabeth Stapleford (TAPE).
Thomas, m. by April 1672, Sarah, widow of Richard Russell and mother of Elizabeth Russell (*ARMD* 65:90; INAC 1:145).

VEACH
John, m. on 2 Jan 1716, Rebecka Dean (TAPE).

VEAZEY
Edward (Veazy), m. by 1 Feb 1702, Susannah, widow of Garret Morrey of CE Co. (INAC 23:101).
George, m. on 18 Nov 1708, by banns, by Rev. Dr. R. Sewell, Alice, dau. of William and Elizabeth Ward (CESS).
George, m. by banns on 3 April 1716 by Mr. Sewell, Kathrin Beard, spinster (CESS).
James, m. by banns on 20 Nov 1716 by Mr. Sewell, Mary Mercer, spinster (CESS).
Robert, m. by banns on 1 Jan 1716, by Mr. Sewell, Lucie Dermote, spinster (CESS).
William, m. by 2 June 1701, Rosamond, relict and admx. of George Stevens of CE Co. (INAC 21:13).

VEERES
Jno., m. on 30 July 1687 by Rev. Richard Sewell, Ann Winn, widow (CESS).

VEITCH
James, m. by 1658, Mary Gakerlin (MPL Q:107).

VERNON
Mr. Christopher, Gent., m. by 23 Feb 1693/4, Lois, dau. of Faith Gongo of AA Co. (MWB 2:262). She was the widow and extx. of Lewis Evans of AA Co. (INAC 31:262).

VICCARIDGE
John (Vickory), m. by prenuptial contract dated 6 Aug 1664, Mary, widow of Captain Thomas Bradnox (MDTP 1F:3, 2:74; KELR D:45, 74).

VICKERS
Francis (Vickars), m. on 3 Jan 1695, Mary [-?-] (TAPE).

Thomas, of DO Co., d. by 1710, when his dau. Elizabeth had m. James Abbott (MWB 13:272, 14:657).

VIGEROUS
[Dr. John?], m. by 11 April 1687, Ann, dau. of Edward and Ann Smith of TA Co. (MWB 4:292, 6:29; SOJU 1692-93:92).

VILLERS
Samuel, m. on 5 Feb 1710/11, Anne Swinford (AALR 2:7).

VINCENT
John, m. by 16 Feb 1705/6, Susannah, dau. of Christopher Kirkly (CHLR Z:227).

VINEY
[-?-], m. by April 1686, Thomasine, widow of Henry Kent (MDTP 13:333).

VOISEEN
Francis (Voyseen), m. on 28 Sep 1699, Mary Meeres (AAJA:6#5). She was a dau. of Elizabeth, widow of [-?-] Meares, and 2nd, Henry Surey. On that dau. Elizabeth Surey, widow conv. property to he granddau. Rachel Voiseen (AALR CW#1:345).

VOWLES
John, of CH Co., m. by Dec 1692, [-?-], sister and heiress of Cuthbert Scott (MDTP 14A:10).

Richard, m. by 9 Aug 1686, Margaret, relict and admx. of William Cole of SM Co., and dau. of John and Elizabeth Smith of SM Co. (INAC 9:143; MDTP 13:391; Fresco also cites SMAD HH: 17,87).

VRIKERS
William (Vrikers?), m. by Jan 1718, Eleanor, extx. of John Held of TA Co. (MDTP 23:194).

W[-?-]

Alexander, m. on (date not given), Elizabeth Grigg (KESP:??).

WADAAMS

Will., m. by 4 May 1717, Mary, extx. of David Jones of CV Co. (INAC 38A:48).

WADE

[-?-], m. by 9 May 1704, Elizabeth, dau. of Thomas Sprigg of PG Co. (MWB 3:448).

George, m. by 1706, Katherine Fisher, dau. of Henry Fisher of CV Co. (Warrants A:475).

John, m. by 15 May 1695, Mary, relict and admx. of William Heather, and of Thomas Gillmin [or Gillinin] of DO Co. (INAC 13A:301, 302; MDTP 16:59).

Richard, m. by 2 Oct 1701, [-?-], widow of Francis Meeke (INAC 21:47).

Richard, m. by 19 June 1713, Mary, widow of Francis Meek, and poss. sister of William Glover, and dau. of Elizabeth, widow of Giles Glover (MCHR CL:15).

Zachariah, m. by (date not given) Sarah, widow of Samuel Adams (Hodges cites Judg. 47:27, 118).

WADNIOR

John, m. by 15 April 1714, [-?-], dau. of John Hollins (MCHR CL:24).

WADSWORTH

Thomas, m. by 25 July 101, Eliza, dau. of Thomas Clagett of CV Co. (MWB 3:8).

WAGER

William, m. on 18 Feb 1704/5, Elizabeth Smith (AAAL 1:27).

WAGSTAFFE,

Charles, m. by May 1696, Mary, sister of Joseph Fary of London (MDTP 16:160).

WAILES

[-?-], m. by 14 Feb 1710/11, Eliza, dau. of Nehemiah Covington of SO Co. (MWB 13:549).

WAINWRIGHT

Mr. Thomas, of PG Co,, m. on 21 Jan 1705/6, by Rev. Mr. John Edwardson, Mrs. Susanna Richardson of Balto. (HAGE:20). She was the admx. or extx. of Mark Richardson of BA Co. (INAC 26:82, 30:152).

WAIT

Robert (Wail?), m. on 31 Dec 1713, Anne Field (AAAL 2:10).

WAKEFIELD

Abel, m. by 30 June 1712, Eliza, dau. of John Brooks of CH Co. (MWB 13:690).

WAKELYN

John, m. by 10 Feb 1704, Elinor, admx. of John Higgens (INAC 25:148).

WALKER

[-?-], d. by Aug 1692, having m. Anne, mother of Thomas, Samuel, and Charles Roberts (SOJU 1692-93:7).

[-?-], m. by 8 Feb 1704, Ann, only dau. of late William Rought of CV Co. (PGLR C:171a). Ann later m. by 1 Aug 1707, William Austin (PGLR C:210).

[-?-], m. by 13 July 1711, Mary, sister of William Jophs or Joffs (MCHR PC:744).

Daniel, m. by 4 June 1706, [-?-], dau. of Francis Sutton of TA Co. (MWB 12:103).

John, on 10 Jan 1670/1, banns of matrimony were published for him and Rachel Moody (SOJU DT#7:68). John Freeman, on behalf of Rachell Moody added these words "Rachell Moody hath nothing to Say to John Walker in the way of matrimony therefore it [the banns are] of noe effect" Feb (*ARMD* e86 (SOJU DT#7):71/68).

John, m. by Nov 1690, Mary, admx. of Thomas Carroll, Sr. (SOJU AW 28; *ARMD* e191).

John, m. 19 Feb 1696, Violet Watkins (AAAL).

John, m. on 28 Feb 1699, Margaret [-?-] (TAPE).

John, m. on 12 May 1706, Deborah Jackson [or Marr] (AAJA:323 #7).

John, m. on 12 June 1714, Mary Cox, widow (SJSG:6).

Robert, m. by March 1713/4, [-?-], mother of Sarah Poor (QAJRh).

Thomas, m. by c1670, Sarah Dawson, dau. of Henry [& Catherine?] Osborne (MPL 20:46-7; WC2:391).

Thomas, m. in Dec 1674, Jane Coppinhall (SOLR:IKL).

William, of DO Co., d. by 30 April 1711, having m. Katherine, who may have been the mother of Thomas, Alse, Anne, John, and William Vincent (MWB 13:267).

WALL

Alexander, m. by 30 Jan 1717, Mary, dau. of William Merchant of DO co. (MWB 14:325).

Thomas, of DO Co., m. by July 1688, Joan or Jane, relict of John Walker of DO Co. (MDTP 14:85, 154).

WALLACE

[-?-], m. by 5 July 1718, Grace, dau. of John White of SO Co. (MWB 18:5).

WALLAHUND

Thomas, m. by June 1712, [-?-], admx. of James Dundee (MDTP 22:118).

WALLER

Aaron, m. by 10 Nov 1711, Margaret, admx. of John Coxon of DO Co. (INAC 33A:85).

WALLEY
John, d. by 1 March 1691, having m. Elizabeth, dau. of Thomas Thurston; she m. 2nd, Charles Ramsey (BALR RM#HS:340).

WALLFORD
John, m. by Nov 1693, Mary, extx. of John Nicholson (BACP G#1:165).

WALLIS
[-?-], m. by 1706, Elizabeth, sister of John Anderson of PG Co. (*CMSP Black Books*: Item 50).
Samuel, and Frances Young filed their intentions to marry on 28 d., 1 m., 1701 (WRMMa). She was a dau. of Arthur Young of CV Co., (MWB 13:249).
Samuel, m. by 31 Oct 1704, Ann, admx. of William Pearce of CE Co. (INAC 25:120).
Thomas, m. by Nov 1710, [-?-], extx. of Peter Cambell (MDTP 21:297).

WALLOW
James, m. by 2 Oct 1716, Margaret, extx. of James Tyer of CH Co. (INAC 38B:26).

WALLS
John, m. by 8 June 1709, Elizabeth, admx. of Richard Hudson of KE Co. (INAC 29:321).

WALLWIN
Edward, m. by 1 Oct 1698, Susannah, relict and extx of Philip Davis of KE Co. (INAC 17:33).

WALMSLEY
Thomas, m. by 1669, Martha Marchant (MPL JJ:113, 12:507).
Thomas, m. by 27 Dec 1714, Katherine, sister of Robert Money (CELR 2:307).

WALSH
Benjamin, m. by 11 July 1713, Elizabeth, dau. of John Nicholson, Sr. (AALR IB#2:110).

WALSTON
William, m. on 9 Nov 1672, Ann Catlin (SOLR:IKL).

WALTERLING
Walter (Waterlin), m. by 4 May 1671, Mary, dau. of Robert Smith of TA Co. (MWB 1:466, 502).

WALTERS
[-?-], m. by 4 May 1671, Ann, dau. of Robert Smith of TA Co. (MWB 1:466).

[-?-], m. by 9 June 1675, Susanna, relict and extx. of James White of AA Co. (INAC 1:353).

[-?-], m. by 19 Dec 1715, Rebecka, dau. of Elizabeth Guibert of SM Co. (MWB 14:224).

Christopher (sometimes given as Waters), m. 16 Feb 1696/7, Elizabeth Powell (AAAL). She was the extx of John Powell of AA Co. (INAC 16:69; MDTP 18A:58).

James, m. by April 1715, Margaret, extx. of James Tyer of CH Co. (MDTP 22:455).

James, m. by 2 Oct 1716, Margrett, admx. of John Conner (INAC 38B:28).

John, m. by 14 Oct 1674, Susanna, relict and extx. of James White of AA Co. (MDTP 6:300).

Richard, m. by 9 Feb 1674/5, Mary, relict of Richard Hacker of TA Co. (MDTP 6:349; INAC 2:111).

Thomas, m. on 13 July 1713, Elizabeth Stout (SJSG:19R).

William (Walter), m. on 24 Feb 1703, Rebecca Marckum (KESP:??).

WALTHAM
John, m. on 25 May 1681, Peerse Manlove (SOLR:IKL).

WALTON
[-?-], m. by 29 March 1718, Sarah, dau. of John Jones of Mattapany, SO Co. (MWB 15:46).

[-?-], m. by 29 March 1718, Mary, dau. of John Jones of Mattapany, SO Co. (MWB 15:46).

John (Wattson), m. Jane, widow and admx. of Thomas Spinck, and dau. of Jane Payne of SM Co. (INAC 10:481).

WALWIN
Edwin, m. by c1693, Susannah, extx. of Philip Davis of KE Co. (INAC 10:412, 32C:64).

WANTLAND
James, m. on 16 Sep 1708, Mary Boyse (AALR 1:36).

WARCUP
Samuel, m. by Sep 1687, Frances, extx. of Thomas Mitchell *als* Doxey, of CV Co. (MDTP 14A:2).

WARD(E)
[-?-], of TA Co., m. by Aug 1682, Elizabeth, relict and extx. of Robert Knapp (MDTP 12B:175).

[-?-], m. Jane, dau. of John Coppin of TA Co.; she m. 2nd, by c1694, Ambrose Ford (INAC 13A:215).

[-?-], m. by Nov 1718, Elizabeth, admx. of Abraham Bently (AAJU RC:268).

Callinwood, m. 10 March 1694, Alies Larke (AAAL).

Cornelius, of Annamessex, on 27 Nov 1666, banns of matrimony were published for him and Margaret Franklin, also of Annamessex (SOLR O#1:41). Cornelius, m. in Jan 1666, Margaret Franklin (SOLR:IKL).

James, m. by 10 Dec 1714, Susannah Swanson (PGLR F:428).

John, d. by 17 July 1694, having m. Damaris Serjeant, and leaving by her a son James Ward (CHLR S:430).

John, m. on 20 Feb 1700, Elizabeth Gover (AAAL 2:1). She was the extx. of Robert Gover, the Younger of AA Co. (INAC 23:42).

John, m. on 17 July 1701, Mary [-?-] (CESS).

John, m. on 5 Dec 1706, Elizabeth Phillips (AAAL 1:33).

John, m. on 6 Nov 1711, by Rev. Jona'n White; Eliza Smith (PGQA:1).

John, m. by lic. on 2 March 1717 by Mr. Sewell, Susana Veazey, spinster (CESS).

Jonathan, m. on 28 Sep 1712, Sarah Walston (HAGE:36).

Jonathan, m. on 8 Jan 1717/8, Ann Hall (HAGE:36).

Ralph, of KE Co., m. on 20 Nov 1664, Elizabeth Bogges (*ARMD* 54:186).

Robert, Jr., m. on 5 May 1706, Rebecca Cox (AAAL 1:32(2)).

Thomas, chirurgeon, m. March 1649/50 Elizabeth, relict of Edward Commins. She m. 3rd, by 1658, Deliverance Lovely (MPL 1:399, 2:529, AB&H:27,105,128; Q:359,431, Qo:235;278: *ARMD* 10:43, 63).

Thomas, m. by 1693, Mary Vines (INAC 10:349, 21:145).

Thomas, of AA Co., m. by 13 March 1710, Elizabeth Yieldhall (AALR PK:329).

Thomas, m. by 12 Oct 1710, Rose, widow and admx. of John Doxsey of SM Co. (INAC 32B:10).

William, m. by 10 Sep 1678, Mary, sister and admx of Richard Foulke of CH Co. She was also the widow of George Credell or Grodtwell of CH Co. (INAC 5:323, 325; MDTP 10:138).

William, m. on 14 May 1718, Anne Douglas, spinster (CESS).

WARE

[-?-], m. by Dec 1677, Mary, relict of Thomas Pope of CH Co. (MDTP 9A:361, 435).

William, m. on 21 Dec 1710, Margaret Burges (AALR 2:7).

WARFIELD

[-?-], m. by 22 Nov 1709, Ruth, dau. of Thomas Crutchley of AA Co. (MWB 13:13).

Benjamin, m. by 17 June 1704, Elizabeth, dau. of John Duvall of AA Co. (AALR WT#2:153).

John (Wharfield), m. 16 Feb 1696, Ruth Gaither (AAAL). She was a dau. of John Gaither of AA Co. (INAC 27:13).

WARFOOTE

John, m. by 7 Jan 1695, Mary, extx. of John or William Nicholson [or Nicholls] (BAAD 2:33; INAC 14:154, 155).

WARING

[-?-], m. by 14 April 1713, [-?-], dau. of Richard Marsham of PG Co. (MWB 13:514).

Basil, m. on 31 Jan 1709, by Rev. Robert Owens, Martha Greenfield (PGQA:1). She was a dau. of Thomas Greenfield of PG Co. (MWB 14:89).

John, m. by (date not given), Ann, dau. of Peter and Ann Barnett (MPL 6#3:390, 391).

Sampson, of CV Co., d. by Feb 1674/5, when his extx. Sarah had m. John Hance (*ARMD* 65:530).

Sampson, and Hannah Meares filed their intentions to marry on 27 d., 1 m., 1702 (WRMMa).

WARMAN

John (Warmin), m. 20 Feb ---, Ann [-?-] (AAAL).

Stephen, m. on 2 July 1704, Hester Gross (AAAL 1:26; see also AALR IB#2:252).

WARNER

[-?-], m. by 11 April 1688, Ann, dau. of Capt. Joseph Hopkins of CE Co. (INAC 9:508).

Christopher, m. by Oct 1678, Elizabeth, dau. of Robert Downes of CH Co. (MDTP 10:308).

Gary, m. by 16 May 1764, Mary, late wife and extx of Thomas Manning, dec. (DOLR 19 Old:222).

George, m. by 1667, Elizabeth, dau. of Godfrey Bailey (MPL 20:284).

James, m. by 4 Aug 1674, Elizabeth, heir of William Harris (AALR IH#1:191).

John, m. by Oct 1678, [-?-], widow of Robert Downes of CH Co. (MDTP 10:306).

Samuel, m. by July 1686, Sarah, relict and admx. of Francis Dorrington of CV Co. (INAC 10:482; MDTP 13:372, 16:108).

Samuel, m. on 15 Aug 1715, by Rev. Jona' White; Eliza Person (PGQA:1). She was extx. of Francis Pearson of PG Co. (INAC 36C:296).

Stephen, m. by [c1709], Mary, admx. or extx. of William Dowse of DO Co. (INAC 31:104, 35B:101).

Stephen, m. by 14 April 1711, [-?-], admx. of Jethro Bruffett (INAC 32B:116).

William, m. on 10 Sep 1718, Alse Mullican (TAPE).

WARREN

[-?-], of CH Co., m. by July 1680, Margaret, relict of Robert Roelands (MDTP 12A:100).

Humphrey, m. by 29 March 1651, Susan, dau. of William Smith (*ARMD* 10:174).

Humphrey, m. by 27 July 1680, Margery, relict and admx. of Robert Rowlants of CH Co. (INAC 7A:166).

Ignatius, m. by 3 March 1673, Mary, dau. of Robert Cole (*ARMD* 51:457; MDTP 5:462).

Samuel, m. by 13 July 1699, Sarah, admx. of John Crooke or Cooke of SM Co. (INAC 19:159; MDTP 17:324).

Thomas, d. by April 1681 having m. Christiana, dau. of Thomas Hill of KE Co. (Warrant Record CB(#3):143).

Thomas, m. by 13 June 1688, Mary, dau. of William Barton, Gent. (CHLR P:6).

Thomas, m. by 30 April 1695, Rebecka, relict and extx. of Robert Cole of SM Co. (INAC 13A:292).

Thomas, m. by 1706, Honour Ferrell, widow of Patrick Ferrell (SMAD HH:132).

WARSHAM
William, m. by Sep 1703, [-?-], extx. of John Clark (PCJU TL#3:158).

WASHINGTON
Philip, m. by 14 May 1707, Alice, extx. of Peter Bond of BA Co. (INAC 26:330).

WATERMAN
[-?-], m. by 6 June 1707, Anne, dau. of John Barwell of AA Co. (MWB 12:214).

WATERS
[-?-], m. by 10 Feb 1674/5, Susanna, relict and extx. of James White of AA Co. (MDTP 6:375).

[-?-], m. by 1688, Susanna, widow of James White (INAC 2:171).

[-?-], m. by 1 Feb 1711, Mary, dau. of Thomas Roe, Sr., of QA Co. (MWB 13:408).

Alexander, m. by 1666, Margaret Hanson, heiress of Andrew Ellenor [and prob. dau. of Andrew Hanson] (MPL 10:311-312).

Christopher, m. by June 1698, Elizabeth, admx. of John Powell (MDTP 17:151).

John, m. by 1716, Rebecca, dau. of Joshua and Elizabeth Guibert (SMWB PC#1:180, 207).

John, m. on 9 Jan 1717, Ann Purnell (AAAL 1:38).

Samuel, of AA Co., m. by (date not given), Sarah, coheir of Richard Arnold of AA Co. (AALR IH#1:70).

Samuel (Watters), m. on 7 Jan 1706/7, Jane Danster (AAAN:1).

WATKINS
[-?-], m. by 10 Jan 1691, Ann, dau. of Nicholas Gassaway of AA Co. (MWB 2:228).

[-?-], m. by 1695, Alice, admx. of William Barnett (INAC 10:441).

John, m. on (date not given), Mary Warman (AALR 1:38).

John, m. by 3 July 1699, Katherine, widow and admx. of Thomas Lewis of PG Co. (INAC 19:67).

John, m. by April 1711, Grace, admx. of William Gou(l)thorpe or Gouldthrop of SM Co. (MDTP 21:284, 338; INAC 36C:67; PCJU VD#2:177).

Richard, m. by Feb 1695/6, Ann, admx. of William Overy of CV Co. (INAC 13B:4; MDTP 16:132).

Samuel, m. by Jan 1693/4, Ann, admx. of John Caine or Paine (MDTP 15C:18).

Samuel, m. by c1695, Anne, widow and admx. of Andrew Abington, and of John Edwards of CV Co., whom she m. by Oct 1692 (MWB 6:39, 377; MDTP 16:29, 30;

ARMD 8:405; INAC 10:415).

Thomas, d. by 8 July 1681, m. by 27 March 1679, Elizabeth, dau. of Henry Caplyn, dec. He m. 2nd, Lydia, dau. of John Baldwin of South River, AA Co.; Lydia m. as her 2nd husband, by 12 June 1682 Edward Beetenson (MWB 4:43; *ARMD* 51:261; Warrant Record CB(#3):104; MPL AA:198, 5:87, 541-2, WC2:334, 19:600, WC:474, 24:287, 28:148).

Thomas, m. on 8 Sep 1698, Mary Wells (AAJA:4#11). She was the widow of Richard Wells of AA Co., and dau. of Thomas Martin of AA Co. (AALR WT#1:226; MWB 3:124). She was the mother of Thomas Wells (MDAD 4:IB#2:153).

WATSON

Abraham, banns pub. 3 Feb 1705/6, m. on Margaret Ginkins (HAGE:18).

Hugh, m. by banns on 10 Jan 1716, by Mr. Sewell, Mary [-?-] (CESS).

James, m. by 17 July 1695, [-?-], dau. of Thomas Parker of KE Co. (MWB 7:117).

John, m. by May 1683, Jane, admx. of George Mackall (MDTP 13:46; INAC 8:155, 13A:285). She was extx. of Thomas Spink, and a dau. of Jane Payne of SM Co. (INAC 10:481).

John, m. by 1 Oct 1698, Mary, relict and admx. of Robert Hill of CH Co. (INAC 18:78).

John, m. on 18 Oct 1705, Margrett Peterson (KESP:??).

WATTS

[-?-], m. 19 May 1695, Margritt Purdy (AAAL). She was a dau. of John Purdy of All Hallows Parish, AA Co. (MWB 13:464).

Charles, m. by 26 March 1695, Elizabeth, relict and admx. of Absolom Tennison of SM Co. (INAC 13A:251).

James, m. by 11 May 1699, Elisabeth, admx. of Stephen Ownbey (INAC 18:162).

John, m. 31 Oct 1700, Mary Moss, als. Kattrick (AAAL 2:1).

John, m. by 3 Oct 1703, [-?-], widow of Stephen Onbee (MWB 3:158).

John, m. on 14 Dec 1703, Ann Jollett (AAAL 1:26).

John, m. on 3 July 1704, Elizabeth Hutson (KESP:??).

John, m. by 18 July 1706, Priscilla, extx. of George Layfield (INAC 26:73).

John, m. on 3 Feb 1714/5, Love Meek (AAAN:22).

Peter, m. by 4 Feb 1675/6, [-?-], dau. of Daniel Clocker of SM Co. (MDTP 7:260).

Peter, m. by 15 May 1692, Ann, dau. of Alice Rich of TA Co. (MWB 6:9).

Peter, m. by 7 July 1694, [-?-], dau. of John Evins of SM Co. (INAC 13A:190).

Richard, m. by 26 Jan 1697, Grace, dau. of Arthur Wright, and sister of Naomi Wright (DOLR 6 Old:171).

Richard, m. by 30 April 1702, [-?-], legatee of Jacob Seth of TA Co. (INAC 21:343).

Robert, m. on 10 Nov 1709, Sarah Revell (one of whom was b. 18 Dec 1687 and bapt. 10 Nov 1709 but the register does not say which one (AAJA:38 #7).

William, m. by 9 July 1686, Ann, relict and admx. of William Cannady (or Carmedy) (INAC 9:46).

William, m. on 11 Nov 1694, Margaret [-?-] (TAPE).

William, m. by 16 Oct 1697, Margaret, extx of William Bexley (or Bixby) of TA Co. (INAC 15:187).

WAUGHOP

Archibald, m. 1st, by 1669, Jane, sister of Jacob Leah, 2nd, Elizabeth Smith (Fresco cites MWB 1:127, 354, 379; INAC 19:158; *ARMD* 41:138).

John (Waghop), m. by 1654, Jane, widow of John Goss, and dau. of George Mackall (MPL AB&H:396, Q:189; 5:396,516; 8:438, AA:54,173; DD:481; MDTP 7:110-111; SMWB PC#1:16, 17)).

Thomas, d. by 1707, having m. Katherine, dau. of John Catanceau of VA (Fresco cites SMWB PC#1:313, TA#1:39; MDTP 19:175, 27:347).

Thomas (Wauhop), m. by 12 March 1718, [-?-], dau. of Peter Watts of SM Co. (MWB 15:147).

WAYE

Richard, m. by 11 Feb 171, Mary, possibly mother of Daniel Procter, a minor, whom Waye calls son-in-law (MWB 13:406).

WAYMAN

Edmond, m. on 13 Nov 1716, Mary Linciccomb (Linthicum) (AAAL 2:11).

Leonard, m. by 9 Aug 1698, Dorcas, dau. of Simon and Madelein (Maudlin) Abbott (AALR IH#1:194).

WEAVER

John, m. by 9 July 1715, Ann, dau. of John Porter, late of Bristol, Eng., chirurgeon (KELR BC#1:72).

WEBB

Edward, m. by 17 Aug 1710, [-?-], widow of William Cannon of CE Co. (INAC 32A:41).

Edward, of CE Co., m. by 15 July 1714, Mary, dau. of Robert Willen (CELR 2:271).

John, m. by 1678, Susannah, widow of Thomas Barberry of CV Co. (MPL 20:45).

John, and Hannah Parker filed their intentions to marry on 6 d., 10 m., 1700 (WRMMa).

Joseph, m. by 7 Aug 1700, Sarah [-?-]; they were heirs of Richard Allen, haberdasher of London (PGLR C:11).

Peter, late of London, Old England, merchant, m. on 6 d. 3 m., 1704, Sarah Stevens, Jr., of TA Co. at Choptank Meeting House (TATH).

Richard, in May 1672, banns of matrimony were published for him and Mary Jefferies (SOJU AZ#8:43). **Richard, m. in May 1672, Mary Jefferies** (SOLR:IKL).

Richard, planter, m. on 1 d. 3 m., 1700, Rebeckah Parratt, both of TA Co., at the meeting house near Tuckahoe Creek (TATH). She was a dau. of William Parratt, dec. (DOLR 6 Old:131).

Thomas, m. by Oct 1688, Elizabeth, relict of Nicholas Jones of CE Co. (MDTP 14:103).

Thomas, m. by 26 Aug 1707, Sarah, mother of William Jones (KELR JS#N:1).
William, m. by 19 May 1712, Sarah, sister of Seth Boggs of AA Co. (INAC 33A:237).

WEBSTER
John, Jr., m. on 28 Feb 1714, Mary MacDaniel (HAGE:32).

WEDGE
John, of TA col., m. by Jan 1678 [-?-], relict of John Chadbourne, who left orphans (MDTP 10:151).

WELCH
John, m. on 9 June 1666, Anne, relict and admx. of Roger Groce (MDTP 4B:16).
Robert, m. on 7 Oct 1701, Mary [-?-] (TAPE).
William, Sr., m. on 14 Jan 1700, Rebecca [-?-] (TAPE).

WELLBURNE
John, m. by 25 April 1715, Ann, admx. of William Price of SM Co. (INAC 36C:61).

WELLPLAY
Andrew (Welply, Wellesley), m. by 4 March 1711, Elizabeth, widow of Andrew Norwood of AA Co. (MCHR PC:825; AALR IH#1:222).

WELLS
Daniel, m. on 4 Dec 1707, Sarah [-?-] (AAAN:1).
George, 3rd son of Richard Wells of Herring Creek, on 7 Oct 1667 was about to marry Blanch, dau. of Maj. Samuel Goldsmith (BALR IS#IK:25). He m. by 12 Oct 1670, Blanch, dau. of Samuel Goldsmith of BA Co. (MWB 1:442).
George, Gent., m. by 6 July 1708, Mary, widow and extx. of Robert Gibson of BA Co. (INAC 28:142; MDTP 21:29).
John, contract of marr. 17 Aug 1671 to Ann Beedle, sister of Henry Beedle, and dau.-in-law of William Coursey (TALR 1:163). By 21 Dec 1702, Ann was admx. or extx. of Thomas Coursey of KE Co. (INAC 23:118, 27:200).
John, m. on 31 March 1709, Ann Powell (AAJA:37 #9).
John, of QA Co., m. by 10 March 1713/4, Jane, poss. dau. of Louis Blangy (MWB 14:1).
John, m. on 12 Oct 1715, by Rev. Jona' White, Margaret Parsfield (PGQA:1).
Nathan, m. on 13 Dec 1716, Mary Duckett (PGQA:1).
Richard, of AA Co., m. by 20 Jan 1681, Mary, dau. of Thomas Martin of AA Co. She m. 2nd, by 19 April 1704, Thomas Watkins (*ARMD* 70:99; AALR WH#4:54, WT#1:226; MWB 3:124).
Thomas, m. on 9 Aug 1705, Mary Hopkins (AAJA:31 #17). She was a dau. of Gerard Hopkins, named in the will of John Chappell of AA Co. (MWB 13:720).

Toby [Tobias], of KE Co., m. on 20 Aug 1665, Mary Richards (*ARMD* 54:186). She was the relict of William Richards (MDTP 1F:2).

WELNERSTONE
Walter, m. by 1686, Margaret, admx. of James Pegrane (INAC 9:55).

WELSH
Benjamin, 20 Nov 1701, Elizabeth Nicholson (AAAL 1:21(2)).

John, m. on 9 June 1666, Anne, relict and admx. of Roger Groce (MDTP 4B:16).

John, m. 13 March 1700, Thomasin Hopkins (AAAL 1:21:1 (1)). She was prob. dau. of Gerard Hopkins), named in the will of John Chappell of AA Co. (MWB 13:720). by 10 Oct 1709,

Pierce, m. Mary, extx. of Henry Harris of TA Co. (INAC 30:176).

Robert, m. on 24 Feb 1706/7, Catherine Lewis (AAAL 1:33).

William, m. on 3 d. 12 m., 1702, Dousabelle Barker, both of CE Co., at Cecil Meeting House (KECE).

WESSELLS
James, m. on 10 Sep 1707, Elizabeth Tolley (AAAL 1:36). She was a dau. of Walter Tolley, of KE Co., dec. (KELR JS#N:169).

WEST
Francis, m. on 10 Nov 1696, Sarah Harry (AAJA:1#7).

Francis, m. by 5 May 1698, Sarah, sister of Thomas Davis of AA Co. (MWB 6:202).

John, m. by Oct 1671, Ann, widow and relict of Henry Jones (MDTP 5:96).

John, of CE Co., m. on 2 d. 3 m., 1680, Joan Becrest, formerly of Salem on Delaware River, but now of CE Co. (TATH). [Records of Third Haven MM give her name variously as Beckett or Beerest: *QMES:*4]

John, m. by 11 Feb 1690/1, Katherine, joint heir of Randall and Katherine Revell of SO Co. (SOJU AW:44).

Robert, m. on 10 Nov 1695, Sarah Spinks (HAGE:46).

Stephen, m. on 21 Aug 1712, Eliz. [-?-] (AAJA:56#14).

Thomas, of SO Co., d. by 12 Sep 1709, leaving an extx. Elizabeth who m. William Freeman (INAC 31:67).

WESTAL
George, m. on 23 Oct 1711, Anne Jacob (AALR 2:8).

WESTBURY
William, m. by Feb 1677/9, Margaret, dau. and coheiress of Thomas O'Daniel; he d. by 4 June 1695, when his widow Margaret m. 2nd, Robert Oless (BALR RM#HS:466).

WESTLAKE
John (Westlocke, Westloke), of SO Co., m. by 1664, Magdalen, perhaps mother of John Manyott whom Westlake called son-in-law (MPL AA:507, 6:302-3, 7:80, 15:500. CC:69, LL:745)?

WESTLY
[-?-], m. by 1 March 1703, [-?-], dau. of John Sumers of PG Co. (MWB 12:110).

WESTRY
Michael, pub. banns 11 Nov 1705, m. on 10 Dec 1705, Jean Solomon (HAGE:22).

WETHERED
John (Witheret), m. on 1 April 1711, Rebecca fferris (AAJA:40 #13).
John (Witheret), m. on 28 Oct 1718, Mary Davis (AAJA:52#12).

WETHERLY
James, m. by 1677, Ann Ackworth (Hodges cites Warrants 15:298, 16:302).

WHALEY
Edward, m. on 9 Jan 1668, Elizabeth Ratclife (SOLR:IKL).

WHEATLEY
Thomas, m. on 15 Dec 1705, Elizabeth [-?-] (AAAN:19).
William, of SM Co., m. by Aug 1688, [-?-], dau. of Jenkin Morris (MDTP 14:14:89).

WHEELER
[-?-], m. by 21 Dec 1711, Ann, dau. of Henry Guttereg of PG Co. (MWB 13:343).
Charles, m. by 30 June 1693, [-?-], orphan of William Worgan, late of DO Co. (DOLR 5 Old:36).
Edward, m. on 10 Feb 1682, Margaret Hardy (SOLR:IKL).
Francis, m. by 1690, Winifred, dau. of Leonard and Ann Green (CHLR Q#1:39, 40, 50, S#1:398).
Ignatius, m. c1698-1703, Frances, dau. of Robert Slye; she m. 2nd, Peter Mills (Hodges cites Pro. Court DD#2: 339-401; Wills 6:296; INAC 19½:15).
James, m. by 26 Oct 1677, Elizabeth, relict and extx. of Thomas Corker (INAC 4:509; MDTP 9A:389).
Roger, m. on 16 April 1704, Elizabeth Gibson (CVCH).
Samuel, m. by 12 Feb 1674, Elizabeth Cooke, legatee of John Ringgold of KE Co. (INAC 1:178).
Samuel, m. by July 1688, Ruth, relict of John Bourchier of KE Co. (MDTP 14:88).
William, m. on 14 Nov 1706, Martha West (AAAL 1:33).
William, m. on 13 Sep 1712, Margaret King (TAPE).

WHELANE
William, m. by 10 Dec 1714, Grace, dau. and coheir of Benjamin Palmer of DO Co. (MPL EE#6:279, CE#1:22).

WHEATHERLY
[-?-], m. by 29 Oct 1713, Sybill, dau. of Thos. Hanson of BA Co. (MWB 14:6).

WHEATLEY
[-?-], m. by 4 Jan 1717, Mary, dau. of William Harde of CH Co. (MWB 14:714).

WHELLER
[-?-], m. by 11 Aug 1715, Sarah, dau. of Edward Stevens of SO Co. (MWB 14:290).

WHETSTONE
Stephen, d. by Feb 1677/8, when his admx. Mary had m. Thomas Moore (*ARMD* 67:209; INAC 4:609).
Stephen, of KE Co., m. by 13 Nov 1703, Sarah, mother of Jane and Tabitha Deane (MWB 13:32).

WHICHALEY
Thomas, m. by 29 Sep 1687, Jane, extx. of John Fanning of CH Co. (INAC 9:448).
Thomas, m. on 25 April 1694, Elizabeth, widow of Edward Ford and dau. of Thomas Alanson (CHLR Q#1:23; INAC 10:416).

WHINSELL
[-?-], m. by Nov 1688, Sarah, dau. of Richard Hooper of CV Co. (MDTP 14:188).

WHIPPS
John, m. on 14 Nov 1702, Margaret Thurston (AAJA:26#2).

WHITAKER
Charles, m. on 30 Jan 1717/8, Mary Kemball (HAGE:36).
John (Whiticar), m. on 27 April 1714, Ann Dadd (SJSG:6).
Mark (Whittacar), pub. banns 13 May 1705, m. 10 June 1705, Katherine Teag (HAGE:22).
Mark, m. on 13 Feb 1717, Elizabeth Emson (HAGE:35).

WHITBY
William, m. by 15 March 1714, Tabitha, dau. of Richard Purnell (TALR RF#12:199).

WHITCHELLY
Thomas, m. by 1687, Jane, relict of John Fanning of CH Co. (MDTP 14A:16).

WHITE

[-?-], m. by 25 June 1711, [-?-], dau. of William Hawkins, Sr., of BA Co. (MWB 13:213).

[-?-], m. by 9 April 1713, Rebecca, admx. of Ralph Bagnall of CV Co. (INAC 34:182).

Andrew, m. on 17 April 1710, Elinor Birk (AAAN:9).

Bernard, m. on 11 April 1716, Elenor Norman (AAAN:29).

Gustavus, m. by Oct 1679, Phillis, relict and admx. of Thomas Howes (or Hew) of CV Co. (INAC 6:510; 8:337).

John, m. on 7 June 1672, Sarah Keyser (SOLR:IKL).

John, m. on 6 June 1703, Elizabeth Bryan (TAPE).

John, m. on 23 April 1708, Eleanor Carty (AAAL 1:36).

John, m. on 4 Dec 1711, Mary Griffin, spinster (CESS).

Joseph, m. on 9 Feb 1709/10, Mary Gater (Gaither?) (AAAN:9).

Nicholas, m. on 24 Nov 1698, Grace Deivour (AAJA:63A#12).

Partrick [*sic*], m. on 4 March 1700, by Mr. Nobbs, minister, Elizabeth Pattison (TAPE). She was Elizabeth, admx. of John Paddison of TA Co. (INAC 21:139).

Robert, m. on 22 Sep 1709, Anne Burgess (AALR 2:5).

Samuel, m. by 1 June 1678, [-?-], widow of Silvester Abbott, Sr. (TALR 3:186).

Samuel, m. on 12 Aug 1701, Clara [-?-] (TAPE).

Samuel, m. on 18 April 1706, Rachel Gaither (AAAL 1:32). She was a dau. of John Gaither of AA Co. (INAC 27:13).

Thomas, m. on 6 Feb 1704, Mary Lane (CVCH).

Thomas, m. by 30 Nov 1707, Katherine, admx. of Charles Laine of CV Co. (INAC 27:198).

Thomas, m. by 6 March 1718, Elizabeth, extx. of Michael Williams of AA Co. (MDAD 1:372).

William, of Rappahannock R., in VA, m. on 8 d. 4 m., 1683, Martha Smith, of the same place, single woman, at the house of Howell Powell in TA Co. (TATH).

William, banns pub. June and July 1699, m. 12 Aug 1699, Ann Baker, widow (HAGE:7). She was the admx. of Samuel Baker of BA Co. (INAC 19½B:108, 20:253).

William, mariner, m. by 9 Aug 1704, Catherine, dau. of Walter Powell (MPL 21:242, CB#2:235; SOLR 8 (GI):71).

William, m. on 12 Jan 1715, Frances Boneal (TAPE).

WHITEHEAD

Charles, m. by 6 June 1692, Sarah, dau. of Jane Pattison, widow, of AA Co. (INAC 11A:45).

George, m. on 27 May 1705, Ezbell Stewart (KESP:??).

Thomas, m. on 11 Dec ----, Elizabeth Smith (KESP:??).

Thomas, m. by 6 June 1692, Sarah, dau. of Jane Pattison of South R., AA Co. (MWB 2:232).

WHITELY
Arthur, m. by 30 June 1693, Sarah, orphan of William Worgan, late of DO Co. (DOLR 5 Old:36; MDTP 16:62).

WHITTER
George, m. by 25 Aug 1710, [-?-], relict of Edward Turner of SM Co. (INAC 31:335).
William, m. by c1699, Susanna, widow and admx. of John Powell of SM Co. (INAC 19:59).

WHITTIER
Ben., m. by 1698, Ann, widow of John Powell (Cotton cites INAC 19:59).

WHITTINGTON
John (Wittington), m. on 30 Nov 1709, Eleanor Clift (TAPE).
Wm., m. by June 1688 Attalanta, extx. of Capt. Jno: Osborne (*ARMD* e91 (SOJU AW reverse):40, 99).

WHITTLE
William, m. by 1657, Susan, mother of Elizabeth and Susan Williams, and relict of Thomas Williams of VA (MPL R:63a, 4:137; *ARMD* 49:54).

WHITTON
[-?-], m. by 24 Oct 1683, Eliza, dau. of Thomas Shelton of Bohemia River, CE Co. (MWB 4:33).

WHORTON
[-?-],m. by 11 Aug 1715, Mary, dau. of Edward Stevens of SO Co. (MWB 14:290).

WICKES
[-?-], m. by Feb 1680/1, Elizabeth, relict of John Taylor who was the father of Thomas Taylor of CH Co. (Warrant Record CB#1:110).
Benjamin, m. by 5 Dec 1712, Mary, dau. and legatee of Peter Sides of TA Co., dec. (QALR ETA:158).
John (or Joseph) (Wicks or Weeks), of KE Co., m. by March 1685/6, Anne, widow and extx. of Benjamin Randall (MDTP 13:301; PCJU DS#A:48; INAC 9:5).
Capt. Joseph, of KE Co., m. on 7 d., 3 mo., 1657 Marie Hartwell (*ARMD* 54:38). She was the mother of Joseph and Mary Hartwell (MPL Q:66).
Joseph (Weeks), m. by 24 July 1673, [-?-], dau. of Thomas Hinson (MDTP 5:527).
Samuel, m. on 13 Jan 1700, Frances Wilmer (KESP:??). She was a dau. of Simon Wilmer (KELR JSN:219).

WICKHAM
Nathaniel, m. by May 1696, Sabina, extx. of Thomas Bernard (or Barnett) of PG Co. (MDTP 16:157, 17:76; INAC 21:353).

WIGHT
John, m. by 19 May 1697, Anne, relict and extx. of Thomas Gant of CV Co. (INAC 14:110).
John, m. by 13 June 1711, Ann, dau. of Thomas Greenfield of PG Co. (PGLR F:84).

WILBANCK
Helmanus Fredrick, m. by 1669, Johnakin Cremarse (MPL HH:414, 12:333).

WILDE
[-?-], m. by 11 Dec 1716, Mary, dau. of Denes Clarke of KE Co. (MWB 14:350).

WILDEY
John, m. on 10 April 1701, Martha Carr (AAJA:23#8).

WILDING
Henry (Welden?), m. by 7 March 1678, Mary, dau. of John Askew (AALR IH#1; 83).

WILEY
John (Willey), m. by c1701, [-?-], widow and admx. of Walter Carr of AA Co. (INAC 21:98).

WILKES
John, m. by 1652, Elizabeth, relict of John Taylor (MPL AB&H:229, 427).
William of SM Co., m. by 1658, Elizabeth, widow of John Taylor of Poplar Hill (MPL ABH:229, 427).

WILKINS
[Tho]mas, m. on 4 July 1716, Mary Comagys (KESP:??).

WILKINSON
Thomas, and Sarah Cox of Third Haven MM declared their intention to marry on 31 d., 6 m., 1715. On 30 d., 9 m., 1715 it was reported that their marriage was orderly accomplished (*QMES:*32).
Rev. William, m. by 1650, as his "last wife" Margaret Budden, mother of Eliza Budden (MWB 1:190; MPL ABH:49, 3:62).

WILLAN
Richard, m. by 25 Oct 1662 Sarah Holland, whom he named thus in his will (MDTP 1D:147).

WILLCOCKES
Henry, m. on 19 d. 11 m., 1669, Sarah Lewis, relict of William Lewis, both of TA Co., at Betty's Cove Meeting House (TATH; *ARMD* 54:602).

WILLER
[-?-], m. by 27 Nov 1687, Ann, dau. of Dennis Husculaw of SM Co. (MWB 4:304).

WILLERY
Philip, m. by 10 Oct 1711, Mary, dau. of Bernard Johnson of CV Co. (PGLR F:156).

WILLEY
[-?-], m. by 20 May 1700, Catherine, dau. of Robert Pope of DO Co. (MWB 11:133).

WILLIAMS
[-?-], m. by 9 Jan 1692, Elizabeth, dau. of Judith Price, widow (TALR LL#7:10).
[-?-], m. by 4 March 1700, Ruth, dau. of Rachel, the widow of [-?-] Kilburne (AALR WT#1:118).
[-?-], m. by [-?-], m. by 5 Jan 1709, Mary, dau. of Jno. Wood of CH Co. (MWB 14:106).
[-?-], m. on 25 Nov 1703, Susanna Porter (KESP:??).
[-?-], m. by 16 June 1713, Elizabeth Story (TALR RF#12:128).
[-?-], m. by 11 Oct 1718, Elizabeth, dau. of Catherine Montgomery of CV Co. (MWB 18:330).
Benjamin, m. on 17 Aug 1704, Margaret Sellman (AAAL 1:26).
Charles, on 10 Aug 1675, banns of matrimony were published for him and Mary Watson (SOJU AZ#8:551). **Charles, m. on 24 Sep 1675, Mary Watson** (SOLR:IKL).
Charles, m. by Sep 1714, Margaret, extx. of Richard Tull of SO Co. (MDTP 22:369; MDAD 1:435).
David, on 36 Nov 1667, banns of matrimony were published for him and Jane Covington (SOLR O#1:90). She was sister of the whole blood to John Coventon of SO Co. (MDTP 9A:507).
Evan, on 9 Jan 1676/7, banns of matrimony were published for him and Mary Periman (SOLR O#7:70r).
Guy, m. by 4 Nov 1702, Mary, only dau. of Christopher Rousby (KELR JD#1:88).
Guy, m. by 22 [-?-] 1702, Mary, heiress of John Paine (or Payne) (KELR JD#1:180, GL#1:32-33/54-55).
Henry, of KE Co., m. on 20 Nov 1664, Femety Albus (*ARMD* 54:186).
Henry, m. on 6 July 1707, Mary Carroll (Carril) (AAJA:34 #6).
Hugh, m. by 1 Oct 1696, [-?-], legatee of [-?-] Johnson (mentioned in account of Joseph and Elizabeth Fry of PG Co. (INAC 14:46). In Oct 1711, she was Elizabeth, dau. of Bernard Johnson of CV Co. (PGLR F:156).
Jacob, m. by 1707, Elizabeth Evans (nee van Sweringen), widow of John Evans (SMWB TA#1:51; MDTP 19C:229).
Jacob, m. by banns on 8 June 1714, by Mr. Sewell, Mary Cox, spinster (CESS).

James, m. by 1668, Mary, widow of James Mullican or Mullikin (MPL HH:442, 12:360).

James, m. by 24 April 1714, [-?-], dau. of William Tippin, planter, of QA Co. (MWB 14:11).

James, m. on 3 Nov 1715, Fortune Henricks (TAPE).

John, Jr., m. by 18 Nov 1690, Jane, dau. of James Henderson, Sr., of SO Co. (MWB 6:50).

John, m. by 3 July 1703, Sarah, sister of Henry Lindsey (CHLR Z:60).

John, m. on 6 Dec 1706, Mary Wheeler (HAGE:73).

John, m. by 16 Dec 1707, Alice, widow and admx. of Walter Quinton of TA Co. (INAC 28:21).

John, m. by 24 Jan 1709, Mary, admx. of Robert Ingram of KE Co. (INAC 31:58).

John, m. on 21 Oct 1708, Elizabeth Deal (TAPE).

John, m. by 2 Feb 1712, Alice, admx. of Nicholas Roads of PG Co. (INAC 33B:173).

John, m. by 27 Oct 1712, Mary, extx. of Joseph Trulock of KE Co. (INAC 33B:156).

Joseph, m. by 16 Jan 1682, Mary, widow and extx. of John Robinson (or Robison) of AA Co. (INAC 8:2; MDTP 13:3).

Joseph, m. on 6 Oct 1707, Esther Creed (CVCH).

Joseph, m. by 10 April 1715, Hester, admx. of Thomas Sharpley of CV Co. (INAC 36B:344).

Joseph, m. on 20 April 1710, Elizabeth Brewer (AALR 1:37).

Lodowick, m. by 23 Aug 1674, Mary, dau. of James Stringer of AA Co. (*ARMD* 51;135).

Michael, m. on 7 Feb 1672, Ann Williams (SOLR:IKL).

Nathan'll, m. by 20 Sep 1718, Elizabeth, dau. of William Bedder, Sr., of SO Co. (MWB 15:18).

Rice, m. by June 1683, [-?-], dau. of Henry Franckum, dec. (MDTP 13:56; CHLR Q:10).

Richard, m. by c1694, Sarah Ward, dau. of John Coppin of TA Co. (INAC 13A:215; Cotton interprets this as Sarah Ward, dau. of Alexander Moore).

Richard, m. on 14 Feb 1709/10, Elinour Stockett (AALR 1:37).

Robert, m. on 5 Sep 1714, Margaret Edwards (TAPE).

Thomas, m. on 10 June 1674, Frances Robinson (SOLR:IKL).

Thomas, m. by 26 March 1695, Elizabeth, sister and admx. of Francis Decoasta of SM Co., and dau. of Mathias and Elizabeth DeCoasta of SM Co. (INAC 13A:249, MDTP 14A:6, 15C:110; Prov. Court TL#2:786, 971).

Thomas, m. on 25 April 1705, Mary Carr (TAPE).

Thomas, m. by 1716, Hannah, dau. of Thos. and Sarah Beauchamp (MWB 14:359).

Thomas, m. on 2 Jan 1718, Catherine Dallas (AAAN:36).

William, m. on 26 May 1716, Jeane Asshe (Ashe) (SJSG:8).

WILLIAMSON

Alexander, m. by 27 Feb 1711, Ann, admx. of Rev. Mr. Stephen Bordley of KE

Co. (INAC 33A:171, 34:72).

David, of SO Co., m. by 1 March 1678, [-?-], eldest sister of John Covington (*ARMD* 51;302).

John, m. on 21 Aug 1709, Mary Rurk (CVCH).

John, m. on 12 Aug 1713, Jane Weatherbourn (AAAL 2:10).

WILLINGTON

Richard, m. by Oct 1686, Rachel, widow and admx. of Richard Grey of KE Co. (MDTP 13:424).

WILLIS

James, m. on 13 March 1679, Rebecca Barnabe (SOLR:IKL).

James, m. by April 1711, [-?-], admx of James Galloway of KE Co. (MDTP 22:2).

John, planter, m. on 10 d. 15 m., 1712, Margaret Cox, both of DO Co., at Transquaking meeting house (TATH).

Jonathan, m. by 29 Dec 1710, Elisabeth, admx. of James Gallaway of KE Co. (INAC 32C:20).

William, m. by 27 May 1707, Elizabeth, relict and admx. of John Ocaine of SM Co. (INAC 27:67).

WILLISEY

Joseph, m. by 7 Feb 1694, Mary, dau. of Eliza, widow of Joseph Fry, by Eliza's first husband (unnamed) (MWB 7:2).

WILLOWBY

John, m. by Feb 1685, Sarah, formerly widow of 1st, Alexander Gordon, 2nd, John Ewens, and 3rd, Robert Franklin (AALR WH#4:256; *ARMD* 17:447).

Samuel, m. by 1 April 1713, Elizabeth, extx. of Martin Skinner of DO Co. (INAC 34:113).

WILLY

John, m. by 12 Aug 1718, Katherine, dau. of Robert Pope (DOLR 7 Old:70).

WILMER

[-?-], m. by 6 Aug 1705, Ann, dau. of Thomas Pyner, of KE Co. (MWB 3:728).

Simon, d. by 17 Dec 1706, having m. Rebecca, dau. of Mary Tilghman, of TA Co., and sister of Capt. Richard Tilghman of TA Co. (KELR I:167, GL#2:16; TALR LL#7:218).

WILMOT

[-?-] (Willimott), m. by 10 Sep 1672, Anne, dau. of Thomas Arnold of CV Co. (INAC 33B:52).

Henry (Willmott), d. by 25 June 1697, having m. Susanna, dau. of Steven Gary, late of DO Co., dec. (DOLR 5 Old:97). She later m., by 25 Oct 1699, Thomas Downes (DOLR 5 Old:146).

Robert, of BA Co., m. by 9 May 1696, Jane, mother of John Copper (MWB

7:198).

William (Willimott), m. by 10 Sep 1712, Margaret, dau. of Thomas Arnold of CV Co. (INAC 33B:52).

WILSON

[-?-], m. by 20 March 1692, Margaret, dau. of William Kidd of CV Co. (MWB 6:47).

[-?-], m. by 2 Feb 1697, Frances, dau. of Thomas Hillery of CV Co. (MWB 7:321).

[-?-], of Flandren, Co. Derby, m. by 28 Feb 1697, Ann, sister of George Robotham of TA Co. (MWB 7:358).

[-?-], m. by 29 Oct 1717, sister of William Banks of Second Creek, TA Co. (MWB 14:721).

[-?-], m. by 3 June 1718, Priscilla, dau. of Absolom Kent of CV Co. (MWB 14:629).

[-?-] (Willson), m. by 4 Aug 1718, Katherine, relict of Francis Kinnimont (TALR RF#12:334).

Ephraim, m. by Aug 1710, Elizabeth, admx. of Henry Lynch, merchant (SOJU 1707-1711:420).

George, m. on 4 April 1692, Jane Cooper (SOLR:IKL).

Henry (Willson), m. by July 12696, Mary, dau of Lt.-Col. [-?-] Finney (MDTP 16:182).

James (Willson), m. by Oct 1688, Mary, relict of William Jones of CE Co. (MDTP 14:103; INAC 13A:307).

James, Jr., cordwinder, m. on 19 d. 10 m., 1716, Mary Berry, both of TA Co., at Tuckaho meeting house (TATH). She was a dau. of Thomas Berry (*QMES:*33).

John, m. by Jan 1691, Thredwith, extx. of James [Gardner?] (MDTP 16:38).

John (Willson), m. by 6 Aug 1695, Elizabeth, extx. of Luke Gregory (INAC 10:442, 14:77; MDTP 16:85).

John, Jr., m. on 28 d. 2 m., 1700, Frances Worsley, spinster, both of TA Co., at the meeting house at head of Tuckaho Creek. The minutes of Third Haven MM record her name as Woolsey (TATH; *QMES:*20).

John, m. on 16 Jan 1704, Ann Jones (KESP:??).

John, d. by 18 June 1706, leaving a widow Elizabeth, who had formerly been married to William Hempstead (TALR RF#10:4).

John, and Elizabeth White filed their intentions to marry on 11 d., 12 m., 1714/5, and 11 d., 1 m., 1714/5 (WRMMa).

Joseph, m. by 14 Aug 1694, Anne, extx. of Richard Smith of CH Co. (CHPR A:53; INAC 10:417; MDTP 16:97).

Joseph (Willson), m. by 1707, Mary, extx. of John Baly of CH Co. (INAC 27:235).

Josiah (Willson), m. by 8 April 1699, Martha, dau. of George Lingan of CV Co. (PGLR A:299; MWB 12:248).

Peter, of Sassafras, m. on 6 d., 6 m., 1681, Elizabeth Morgain, dau.in-law to Bryan Omelia, at the meeting house at Betty's Cove (TATH).

Stephen, m. by 17 June 1696, Elizabeth [-?-], who joined him in conveying land to "their daus." Mary and Elizabeth Semple (TALR LL#7:170).

Thomas, m. by Oct 1685, [-?-], widow of James Carr of CV Co. (MDTP 13:253).

William, m. on 29 Oct 1668, Mary Cotman (SOLR:IKL).

William, m. on 8 Feb 1705, Mary Williams (TAPE).

William, m. on 24 June 1709, Mary Blades (TAPE).

William, and Rachel Child filed their intentions to marry on 8 d., 2 m., 1715 (WRMMa).

WINCHESTER

Isaac, of KE Co., cordwainer, m. by 6 Oct 1673, Elizabeth, formerly Williston (AALR IH#2:188).

John, m. by 1 Oct 1662, Elizabeth, relict of Henry Stoope and John Gibson (KELR D:1).

John, of KE Co., m. on 7 Sep 1665, Janne Muntrose (*ARMD* 54:186).

WINDELL

Thomas, m. by 23 June 1696, Ann, relict and extx. of Henry Higgs of CE Co. (INAC 13B:114).

WINDLEY

Richard, m. by 5 April 1676, [-?-], dau. of John Taylor of BA Co. (MWB 5:26).

WINDSOR

John (Winsar), on 10 Aug 1675, the banns of matrimony were published for him and Elizabeth Gager (SOJU AZ#8:551).

WINE

[-?-], m. by 30 July 1710, Eliza, dau. of Edward Stockdall of SO Co. (MWB 14:121).

Henry, m. by 12 June 1716, [-?-], dau. of Eliz. Hawkins, widow of CH Co. (MWB 14:510).

WINGOD

Thomas, m. on 1 Jan 1669, Elizabeth Cooper (SOLR:IKL).

WINLEY

Richard, m. by 5 June 1695, Mary, sister of Arthur Taylor (BALR RM#HS:461).

WINN

Ephraime (Winne), Gent., of QA Co., m. by March 1711, Mary Hartshorne (QAJR March 1711:172; INAC 32C:131).

John, m. on 5 Feb 1717, Anne Smallwood (PGKG:249).

WINNALL

John, of CV Co., d. by 18 March 1709, when his admx. Elizabeth had m. Matthew

Garner (INAC 31:69).

WINNINGS
Philip (Winnings?), m. by Nov 1708, Dorothy, admx. of William Philipson (MDTP 21:71).

WINNINGTON
Robert, m. on 30 May 1705, Elinor [-?-] (AAAN:19).

WINSETT
Richard, m. by 25 July 1689, [-?-], relict and admx. of Bryan O'Bryan of SM Co. (INAC 13A:186).

WINSPEAR
William, m. on 24 June 17--, Mary Duerty (KESP:??).

WINSTANLEY
Joseph, of Barnstaple, Co. Devon, watchmaker, m. by 29 July 1715, Elizabeth, dau. of Orlando Greenslade of Maryland, merchant, dec. (AALR IB#2:256).

WINTERSELL
William, m. by Dec 1685, [-?-], widow of Henry Dat? of TA Co. (MDTP 13:268).

WINTON
Thomas, m. by 1666, Grace, widow of James Adwick, and sister of John Walker (Hodges cites Liber 1, Part F: 2:88, 89).

WINWRIGHT
Mr. John, m. in 1705, Mrs. Ann Richardson (HAGE:18).

WISE
[-?-], m. by 18 Dec 1712, Eliza, dau. of John Davis of St. Michael's River (MWB 13:497).
Richard, m. on 13 Jan 1711/12, Sarah Nichols (AAJA:33 #15).
Thomas, m. by 14 Oct 1712, Mary, dau. of John Booker of Nanjemy, CH Co. (MWB 13:587).
William, pub. banns on 30 Sep, m. on 15 Oct 1705, Margaret Osbourn (HAGE:22). She was the extx. of William Osbourn of BA Co. (INAC 25:317).

WISEMAN
John, m. by 1700, Catherine Miles, dau. of Francis Miles of SM Co. She m. 2nd, Richard Shirley (MWB 6:375, 14:238; SMWB PC#1:204).

WITCHELL
Thomas, m. on 10 d., 3 m., 1690, Mary Serson, widow (WRMM). She was the relict and admx. of Edward Sarson of AA Co. (INAC 13A:187).

WITHERED
    John, m. on 3 Oct 1695, Sarah Webb (AAJA:2#10).

WITHERLY
    James, m. by 1677, Ann, widow of Richard Ackworth (MPL 15:398, 17:34).

WITHERS
    Samuel, m. by 1660, Elizabeth, admx. of William Pell (MPL JJ:180).

WITHGOTT
    Henry, m. on 25 Aug 1703, Mary Delehay (TAPE).

WITTER
    William, cooper, m. by 21 July 1703, Margaret, widow of Walter Poore, dec., and mother of Margaret and Mary Poore (CHLR Z:100, 103).

WOLFCOMB
    Edward, m. by 8 May 1703, Rachel. extx. of Thomas Daily (MCHR PC:483).

WOLLAND
    Thomas, m. by [c1712], Margaret, admx. of James Dunn of QA Co. (INAC 33A:235).

WOLLMAN
    Richard, m. by 26 July 1675, [-?-], legatee of Henry Hawkins of TA Co. (INAC 1:384).

WOLSTON
    Thomas (Walston), m. on 16 April 1677, Ruth London (SOLR:IKL).

WOLVERTON
    Robert (Wollverton), m. by 4 April 1672, Michaell, extx. of Richard Howard of TA Co. (MDTP 5:276).
    Walter, m. by 8 July 1686, Margaret, extx. of James Pegrave (INAC 9:55).

WOOD
    [-?-], m. by 19 March 1690/1, Margaret, admx. of John Russel (MDTP 16:25).
    [-?-], m. by 13 Dec 1711, Rachel, dau. of John Gillam of SM Co. (MWB 13:457).
    [-?-], m. by 26 Nov 1716, Ann, sister of David Long of SO Co. (MWB 14:358).
    John, m. by 5 Sep 1688, Elizabeth, sole dau. of Edward Swanson (BALR IR#AM:67).
    John, m. by 1 April 1698, Joan, admx. of James Regon of CH Co. (INAC 16:247).
    John, m. on 1 July 1705, Sarah Gambill (AAMA:82).
    Dr. John, m. on 16 Nov 1709, Lydia [-?-] (TAPE).
    Joshua, m. on 15 Dec 1704, Elizabeth Pittcock (HAGE:22).
    Samuel, m. by 3 June 1718, Ann, extx. of John Davis of SM Co. (MDAD 1:54).

William, m. on 6 May 1705, Ann Hill (AAJA:31 #8).
William, m. on 1 Jan 1715, Elizabeth Low (TAPE).

WOODCOCK
William (Woodcok), m. on 24 Dec 1713, Mary Amboy (HAGE:31).

WOODEN
John, m. on 27 Jan 1716, Mary Gill (BAPA).

WOODFIELD
Thomas, of AA Co., m. by 13 March 1717, Eliza, widow and extx. of Richard Gott, and dau. and devisee of Anthony Holland (BALR TR#A:544; INAC 36C:168).

WOODLAND
[-?-], m. by 20 Nov 1708, Hannah Blackleach, dau. of Benjamin Blackleach (MWB 13:290).
William, m. on 20 Feb 1703, Sarah Blackleach (KESP:??).

WOODROFFE
William, m. by [-?-] at Cowley, Gloucs., Eng., Anna, eldest sister of Daniel Norris of KE Co. (KELR G#1:108-111).

WOODS
Robert, m. by June 1701, Ann, relict of John Johnson (MDTP 19A:6).

WOODWARD
Abraham, m. on 7 Nov 1707, Elizabeth Finloe (AAAL 1:36).
Abraham, m. on 27 -- 1715, Priscilla Orr[ick] (AAAN:22). She was the extx. of James Orrick of AA Co. (INAC 39A:16).
Benjamin, of DO Co., m. by May 1715, Mary, widow of William Seward (who left two daughters, Mary and Ann Seward) who was the heir of George Seward (*CMSP: Black Books* #133, 134).
John, m. by c1709, [-?-], widow of Richard Newton, and dau. of Gerard Brown (CHLR H#3:432).

WOOLDERTON
Richard, m. by Nov 1671, Michaell, legatee of Richard Howard of TA Co. (MDTP 5:129).

WOOLFORD
James, of SO Co., planter, m. on 3 d. 9 m., 1698, Grace Stevens, of DO Co., spinster (TATH). She was a dau. of Dorothy Stevens and sister of John Stevens of DO Co. (QALR ETA:198; MWB 13:194).

WOOLMAN
[-?-], m. by July 1679, Joan, widow of Robert Dunn of KE Co. (MDTP 11:137).

Henry, m. on 27 June 1713, Prudence Errington (TAPE).

WOOLSON
Sam., m. by 1677, Rachel Williams (MPL 15:507).

WOOLVERTON
Robert, m. by 4 April 1672, Michaell, extx. of Richard Howard of TA Co. (MDTP 5:276).

WOOTEN
Edward, m. on 5 Jan 1679, Cullett Southern (SOLR:IKL).

WOOTERS
[-?-], m. by 3 Oct 1735 Elizabeth, dau. of Ennion Williams of TA Co. On 24 d., 11 m., 1713, Eliza Wooters of Third Haven MM condemns her disobeying her father and by taking a husband by a priest (MWB 21:504; *QMES:*31).

WOOTTON
[-?-], m. by 28 June 1704, Margaret, dau. of Hellenor Neale, widow (AALR WT#2:145).

Simon, chirurgeon, m. by 24 Oct 1677, Susanna, relict and admx. of Richard Wodworth or Wadsworth of CV Co. (INAC 4:481; MDTP 9A:385).

WORKMAN
Anthony, m. by 26 July 1679, Jane, extx. of Robert Dunn of KE Co. (INAC 6:210).

WORLEYSMITH
John, of TA, planter, m. by 8 March 1715, Mary, dau. and coheir of Thomas Austen, dec. (TALR RF#12:235).

John, m. by 2 Nov 1717, Mary, dau. of Thomas Dutton (TALR RF#12:305).

WORRELL
[-?-], m. by 4 Oct 1679, Margaret, relict and admx. of Richard Ambrose of CH Co. (INAC 6:565).

[-?-], m. by 1 March 1698/9, Eliza, sister of Edward Sweatnam of KE Co. (MWB 6:249).

Thomas (Warrell), m. by 24 June 1707, Blanch Jones (SOJU 1707-1711:7).

WORRILOW
[-?-], m. by 1 Sep 1697, Eliza, sister of Capt. Richard Sweetnam of TA Co. (MWB 7:304).

Sarah Worrilow was stated by Third Haven MM on 30 d., 6 m., 1703 to have "turned her back on the truth and Friends by going to a priest to be married (*QMES:*25).

William, planter, m. on 6 d. 1 m., 1681, Margaret Pinner, spinster, both of TA Co., at Tuckahoe Meeting House (TATH).

William, m. on 10 d. 12 m., 1700, Sarah Mackee, at Bayside meeting house (TATH).

WORRING
John, m. by 23 Aug 1707, Anne, dau. of Anne and [-?-] Barnett; widow Anne later m. William Burroughs, and then Joseph Howard (AALR WT#2:580).

WORTHINGTON
John, m. by 3 Oct 1691, Sarah, dau. of Matthew Howard of AA Co. (MWB 2:222). She m. 2nd, by 25 March 1697, John Brice (AALR IH#1:144, WT#1:160; INAC 11A:28).

Thomas, m. on 23 July 1711, Elizabeth Ridgely (AAMA:83). She was a dau. of Henry Ridgely (KELR JS#W:17).

WRATTON
[-?-], m. by 27 Dec 1703, Blanch, dau. of Blanch wife of Thomas Ryder of AA Co. (MWB 11:403).

WRIGHT
[-?-] (Write), m. by 1 Dec 1717, Sarah, dau. of Thomas Holbrook of SO Co. (MWB 15:15)

Abell, m. on 12 Jan 1695/6, Katherine Clarke (SOLR:IKL).

Charles, of QA Co., m. by May 1706, Katharine, extx. of Robert Norrest (*CMSP: Black Books* #23; KELR JS#N:86).

Christopher, m. on 1 June 1673, Isabell Gradwell (SOLR:IKL).

Edward, m. by 18 Nov 1714, Elizabeth Marshall, widow (DOLR 7 Old:5).

Gustavus, m. by 9 Jan 1678, Phillis, relict and admx. of Thomas Howes of CV Co. (INAC 5:404).

Henry, m. by 23 Nov 1715, [-?-], dau. of Thomas Bayley of QA Co., who called Wright his son-in-law (MWB 14:113).

John, of KE Co., m. by 1667, Mary, widow of 1st, Philip Conner, and 2nd, Bartholomew Glevin (*ARMD* 51:165, 57:178; MPL R:30a, 4:63, 11:170, 264-265, GG:169,230; ABH:84, 12:221, 572).

John, on 12 June 1677, banns of matrimony were published for him and Mary Fox (SOLR O#7:100r).

John, m. by 14 July ---, Annapole, admx. of Thomas Hook of PG Co. (INAC 11B:72).

John, ante-nuptial contract of 16 May 1685, with Jane Claridge, widow (BALR R#HS:136).

John, m. by 1698, Ann, widow and extx. of Thomas Gant of CV Co. (INAC 14:110).

John, m. on 27 Oct 170-, Mary Paggett (KESP:??).

John, m. on 15 Oct 1707, Hannah Darling (CESS).

John, of PG Co., m. by c1715, Ann, dau. of Thomas Greenfield, Gent., of PG Co. (PGLR F:483).

Joseph, m. by 18 Dec 1710, Esther, dau. of Thomas Winn of KE Co. (KELR JS#N:249).

Philbert (Right), m. on 3 Dec 1712 by Rev. Jona' White, Esther Bycraft (PGQA:1).

Solomon, m. Jan 1717/8, Elizabeth, extx. of Robert Macklin of QA Co. (MDTP 23:153).

Thomas, m. by 1665, Jane, widow of 1st, William Brough, and 2nd, William Scott (MPL AB&H:225-26, 9:250, 260, EE:237, 256; Warrants 9:250, 270).

Thomas, m. on 15 July 1708, Diana Evans (AAAN:7).

Mr. Thomas Hynson, m. by 12 April 1715, Mary, extx. of Mr. John Coursey of QA Co. (INAC 36B:149).

William (Right), m. on 7 Dec 1669 or 27 Dec 1670, Frances Bloyse (SOLR:IKL).

William (Right), m. on 5 Sep 1714, Juliana Benbo (SJSG:7).

WRIGHTSON

John, m. by 1694, Mary, widow of Nicholas Lurkey (MWB 5:285, 7:77; MDTP 23:282; TA & QA Rent Rolls 1:15).

John, m. by 10 Oct 1698, Mary, extx. of James Sedgwick of TA Co. (KELR M:94a).

John, m. by 1 Nov 1713, Mary, kinswoman of Thomas Smithson of TA Co. (MWB 13:649).

WRINCH

[-?-], m. by 31 July 1705, Rebeckah, dau. of Henry Green of KE Co. (MWB 12, pt. 2:25).

WROTH

John, m. on 3 Feb 1705, Catherine Conaway (KESP:??).

WYATT

[-?-], m. by 16 Nov 1682, Joane, sister of William Hamstead of TA Co., by whom he had a son Timothy Wyatt (MWB 4:2).

John, m. by 29 Oct 1687, Sarah, relict and extx. of Thomas Jones of KE Co. (INAC 9:496).

Nicholas, d. c1672/3; He had come to MD from VA with his wife Damaris (an approved midwife) and her child by a previous marriage. After Wyatt's death, she m. 3rd, Thomas Bland (*ARMD* 66:xxiv).

Robert, m. by Nov 1698, Isabella, extx. of William Collier of AA Co., dec. (MDTP 17:214).

WYNNE

James, m. by 1688, Patience, widow and admx. of Daniel Clocker of SM Co. (INAC 10:232).

Thomas, m. by 1663, Elizabeth, relict of Richard Willaine of SM Co. (*ARMD* 49:300; MWB 2:296; Prov. Court FF:84, 201).

YALDING

William, on 5 Feb 1676/7, banns of matrimony were published for him and Mary Wilson (SOLR O#7:85r).

YARLEY

William, m. by 17 Sep ---, [-?-], widow of Richard Gibbs (INAC 36B:152).

YATES/YEATS

[-?-] (Yate), m. by Aug 1682, Sarah, admx. of Edward Roper of TA Co. (MDTP 12B:183).

George (Yate), m. by 10 Jan 1703, Rachel, dau. of Richard Warfield of AA Co. (MWB 11:409; INAC 25:163).

Joseph, m. on 5 Nov 1712, Mary Cowdery (HAGE:51).

Robert, of CH Co., m. by 5 Oct 1688, Rebecca, relict of James Tyre or Tyer, and extx. of Lawrence Hoskins of CH Co. (INAC 10:163, 164, 12:21).

YEO

[-?-], m. by 21 Oct 1680, Semelia, relict and admx. of Ruthen Garrettson (INAC 7A:283; BAAD 2:37).

YIELDHALL

William, m. by 23 June 1677, [-?-], one of the daus. of John Sisson (MDTP 9Al:196).

William (Yealdhall), m. on 13 Feb 1704/5, Mary Stephens (AAAN:19). She was a dau. of Charles Stephens (AALR PK:262).

YO----

William, m. in Dec 1697 by Rev. Mr. Sewell, Ann R. Jeffords (CESS) [Evidently not in Harrison or Peden].

YOE

James, d. by Dec 1692, possibly having m. Patience, widow of Daniel Clocker; she m. 3rd, Robert Cooper (MDTP 14A:9).

YONGE

Will., m. on 14 April 1670, Frances [-?-] (*ARMD* 54:601).

YOPP

[-?-], m. by 19 March 1718/9, Susanna, dau. of Isabella Drayden of CH Co. (MWB 15:1).

YORE

James, m. by 17 April 1689, Patience, relict and admx. of Daniel Clocker of SM Co. (INAC 10:232).

YORK
[-?-], m. by 24 April 1706, Hannah, dau. of Israel Skelton of BA Co. (MWB 12:15).

William, m. by 9 March 1673, Ann, widow of James Stringer and James Collier, and mother of Mary [-?-], who m. Lodowick Williams (BALR IR#AM:42; MDTP 4A:37).

William, m. by June 1692, [-?-], relict of John Wood (BACP F#1:186, 187).

William, m. by Sep 1695, [-?-], extx. of Jacob Lotton (BACP G#1:490).

YORK(EN)SON
Yorke, m. by 5 March 1697, Mary, admx. of Jonas Maddox of CE Co. (INAC 15:301).

Yorke, m. by 20 Sep 1701, Mary, relict and admx. of Jacob Archer of CE Co. (INAC 20:271; MDTP 19A:8).

YOULE
Thomas, m. by (date not given), [-?-], relict of William Smith (TALR 3:55).

YOUNG
[-?-], m. by 5 April 1676, Elizabeth, mother of Edward Packer or Parker (*ARMD* 51:192, 311).

[-?-], m. by 16 Sep 1676, Mary, relict and admx. of William Stacey of CV Co. (MDTP 8A:200).

[-?-], m. by 10 Feb 1708, Mary, dau. of Richard Jones of QA Co. (MWB 12:355).

[-?-], m. by 30 Jan 1709, Mary, dau. of John Batie of AA Co. (MWB 14:391).

Arthur, and Mary Bell or Ball from London filed their intentions to marry on 8 d., 7 m., 1704 and 6 d., 8 m., 1704 (WRMMa).

David, m. by banns on 7 Nov 1714, by Mr. Sewell, Margaret Porter, spinster (CESS).

David, d. by Dec 1716, having m. Mary, widow of Matthew Pope (or Cope) of KE Co.; Mary m. 3rd, by Dec 1716, Nathaniel Pearce of KE Co. (AALR IB#2:320; MDTP 22:427). On 13 d., 11 m., 1711, Mary Pope, now Mary Young, was charged by Third Haven MM with having taken a husband contrary to the good order of truth (*QMES:*86).

George, Sr., m. by 23 Sep 1704, Elisabeth, extx. of John Fisher of CV Co. (MWB 3:409; INAC 37B:187; MDAD 1:283).

George, Jr., m. by 14 March 1706, [-?-], a dau. and legatee of Tobias Malls or Mialls of CV Co. (NAC 26:272).

Henry, m. by June 1709, Grace, admx. of John Roberts [or Robins] of CV Co. (INAC 31:298, 32C:140; MDTP 21:264, 22:29, 143).

Jacob, m. by banns on 31 Dec 1713, by Mr. Vanderhyden, Mary Price, spinster (CESS).

John, m. on 10 Feb 1714/5, Elizabeth Frances (AAAN:22).

Lawrence, m. by 1700, Ann, dau. of John Bond (MWB 11:49; MDTP 18B:12).

Nicholas, m. by 1669, Elizabeth, widow of Edward Parker (*ARMD* 51::310; MWB 1:365; MDTP 3:396).

Richard, m. on 28 Feb 1714/5, Margaret Prindewell (Prindowell) (AALR 1:38).

Samuel, m. on 14 July 1687, Mary [-?-] (AAAN:1).

Samuel, m. by Jan 1689, Mary, admx. of Maj. Thomas Francis of AA Co. (MDTP 14:133; INAC 10:351; 16:61).

Samuel, m. by 14 May 1705, Mary, dau. of Robert Clarkson (AALR WT#2:202).

Theodorus, m. by 1678, Elizabeth Godfrey (MPL LL:724).

William, m. on 8 Jan 1706/7, Mary Bishop (AAJA:33 #15).

William, m. by 23 Feb 1715, Rebecca, dau. of Elizabeth Bourn, widow and extx. of Samuel Bourn, Gent., of CV Co. (MWB 16:50).

YOUNGER

Alexander, m. by 1676, Sarah Claw [or Cole], extx. of William Claw [or Cole] (*ARMD* 66:404, 67:88; PCLR WRC:4; MDTP 4B:29). She was the mother of Richard Cole, of St. Jerome's, SM Co., and widow of William Cole (MDTP 8A:285, 294).

William, m. on 15 Sep 1709, Hannah Moriah Cratcherwoodlayer (TAPE).

YOUP

Roger (or Youx), m. by 12 Nov 1711, Margaret, admx. of Hugh Portingall of CH Co. (INAC 33A:41; MDTP 22:71).

YOWE

James (Yowe?), m. by April 1689, Patience admx. of Daniel Clocker (MDTP 14:146).

Additions and Corrections

Some of these entries are new entries, and some expand on other entries.

AARONSON

Cornelius, m. by 1675, [-?-], relict of William Cole of BA Co. (MPL LL:411, 15:308).

ANDERSON

[-?-], m. by 1659, Amy, dau. of Nicholas Waddylove (MPL R:2b, 4:4-5, 10:463, 12:117, 118, FF:512, HH:137, 138).

ASCUE

Richard, m. by Dec 1688, Mary, widow of Samuel Brand and dau. of John Hammond (MDTP 14:124).

ATKINSON

Thomas (Adkinson), and Rachel Judkin of Third Haven MM on 20 d., 9 m., 1710 declared their intention to marry. They announced their intention at the next meeting and were given leave to marry (*QMES:*29).

BAKER

Morris, of AA Co., m. by 1671, Elizabeth, relict of [-?-] Hill (MPL WT:198-99, 16:181-82).

BALL

John, and Hester Gush of Cecil MM on 8 d., 7 m., 1708 declared their intention to marry (*QMES:*86).

BALLARD

Charles, m. by 1671, Sarah, relict of 1st, John Elzey, and 2nd, Thomas Jordain; by 1671 wife of Charles Ballard of Somerset County (MPL KK:364-365, 7:567, 598-601; 14:374-75; 17:123-24, CC:629,669-73; WT:790-91).

BARBER

James, and Barbarah Kelley of Cecil MM on 13 d., 6 m., 1712 declared their intention to marry (*QMES:*86).

BARON

Michael (Barron), m. by 1668, Gertrayt, mother of Rynier and Abraham VanHeyst (MPL HH:303, JJ:111 says the sons were his).

BAYNARD

William, and Susannah Pardoe of Third Haven MM on 24 d., 9 m., 1714 declared their intention to marry. When they declared their intention a second time they were given leave to marry (*QMES:*32).

BECKWORTH

[-?-], married by 8 May 1732, Ann, widow of John Miller of Prince George's Co. (MDAD 11:392, 393).

BELL

Mathew, cordwainer, m. by 1660, Elizabeth, relict of William Nugent (MPL 4:547).

BERRY

Susannah, of Third Haven MM, on 30 d., 3 m., 1716, was reported to have been joined to a husband by a priest (*QMES:*33).

BOND

Benjamin, m. by 1682, Elizabeth, relict of Humphrey Jones (MPL WC5:71-72, 271, 21:303-04, 400).

BOOKER

Ellen'r, widow, of Third Haven MM, was reported on 30 d., 9 m., 1715 to have gone from the truth and have taken a husband by a priest (*QMES:*32).

BOYSS

William of Ennemessicke, SO Co., m. by 1662, Mary, sister of Jane Delimus [not Bellamin], and dau. of Anthony and Jane (Butterfield) Delimus (MDTP 2:143; George Ely Russell, "Portuguese and Spanish Colonists in 17th Century Maryland." *TAG* 30 (1) (Jan 2001):52).

BROWN

James, m. by 1674, Wenifrede, widow of William Thorne MPL AA:318-19, 405, 6:19-20, 135; 7:80; 18:308, CC:70). However, see David Brown.

BULLETT

Joseph, may have m. a dau. of Capt. John Price, or have been a stepson; Price called him son-in-law (MPL 2:274,m 426, AB&H:10, 19:259, 375, EC:147, 252).

BURNETT

Richard, m. by 1659, Elizabeth, widow of Thomas Bell (MPL AA:143, WC2:16, 346-7).

BUSBY

Thomas, m. by 15 Sep 1711, [-?-], widow of John Jeffries of QA Co. (MDAD 8:16).

CANNELL
Patrick, m. by 1662, Susan(na), relict of James Acheson (MPL AA:397).

CAPE
Sarah, of Third Haven MM, on 25 d., 7 m., 1707 condemned her going to the priest for a husband (*QMES:*270.

CARNELL
Daniel, m. by 1687, Deborah, dau. of Edward Pollard of TA Co. (MWB 4:315).

CARTER
Richard [or Edward?], m. by 1658, Ann Bennett (MPL Q:147-148, 192).

CATLIN
Henry (Coplyn), m. by 1649, Jeane, possibly the mother of Richard Horner, called "son" of Henry Catlin (MPL AA:198, 5:87, 541-2, WC2:334, 19:600, WC:474).

CHESTER
Edward, of SM Co., m. by 1680, Ellinor, who may have been the mother of John Bowring and Elizabeth Bowring, who Chester called his son-in-law and dau.-in-law (MPL WC2:277, CB2:305).

CLARK
Robert, m. by 1664, Jane, widow of 1st, John Cockshott, and 2nd, Nicholas Causin (MPL 1:24, AB&H:22,59,61,207; 2;506-7; 7;132, CC:122).

CLEEVE
[-?-], dau. of Nathaniel, on 10 d., 6 m., 1680, was reported by her father to Third Haven MM as having stolen away from him and been married by James Clayland, a priest, who granted them a license and married them all in one day (*QMES:*3).

COLLIER
Francis, m. by 1681, Isabella, widow of Dr. Francis Swanson (Swanston, Swinfen, Swinston) of CV Co. (MPL CC:570, 7:520; 8:204; 10:486-87; 12:591; 14:214; 17:39, DD:237; FF:529; JJ:221-22; KK:202; WT:714; WC4:145-46).

COOKE
Mordecai, m. by 1649, [-?-], relict of [-?-] Peasley (MPL 2:526-27, 3:446-47).

COOPER
John, and Deborah Smith, of Third Haven MM, on 30 d., 7 m., 1713 declared their intention to marry. They announced their intention a second time and were given liberty to [marry] (*QMES:*31).

COVETT
   John, m. by 1651, Sarah, mother of Ann Sanders (MPL AB&H:249).

COX
   Henry (Cop?), m. by 1651, Elizabeth, mother of Paul Bury (MPL AB&H:276).

CUMBERFORD
   George, on 25 d., 1 m., 1718, was reported to Third Haven MM as having taken Mary, the 16 year old dau. of Peter Harwood, to Annapolis, where they were married by a priest. Peter Harwood was advised to engage with someone who was learned in the law (*QMES:*33).

DAVIES
   Hopkin, m. by 1662, Elizabeth [-?-], poss. mother of his "dau." Elizabeth Lee (MPL AA:318, 6:19).

DAVIS
   Oliver, m. by 1677, Rebecca, widow of James Stroud (MPL AA:456, 6:219, 7:530, 8:480, CC:548,729).

DENAR
   John (or Deverax), of SO Co., m. by 1671, Elizabeth, mother of William Empson and Mary Empson (MPL 16:309, LL:746, 15:501).

DIXON
   Isaac, and Elizabeth Harwood, Jr., of Third Haven MM on 28 d., 12 m., 1709 declared their intention to marry. They announced their intention a second time, and were given leave to [marry] with the advice of relations (*QMES:*28).

DOBB
   John, m. by 1676, Aneke or Aveke or Anikeck, relict of Andrew Ellinour (MPL Qo:239, Q:365-6; 4:61; 10:312-13; 19:385-86, R:29; FF:357-58; WC:261-62).

DURDEN
   Stephen, on 18 d., 3 m., 1685, was reported to Third Haven MM that he had brought blemish to Friends through his disorderly proceedings in taking a wife (*QMES:*9).

EATON
   [-?-], m. by 1679, Jane, dau. of Francis Leaffe of AA Co. (MPL WC2:60, [134, 228],15:489, LL:728).

EDMONDS
   Thomas, m. by 1661 Bridget, poss. mother of Gasper Guerin, who was called son-in-law by Edmonds (MPL A:511, 6:309).

ELSTON

Ralph, and Mary Ball, of Third Haven MM on 21 d.,1 m., 1694, announced their intention to marry (*QMES:*15).

ENNALS

Bartholomew (Ennalds), of DO Co., m. by 1669, Mary [-?-], poss. mother of Francis and John Howard, who he calls his children (MPL JJ:65, 12:465).

EVANS

Job, m. by 1682, Margaret, relict of John Burrage (MPL WC4:295).

EWBANCK

John, and Isabella Palmer of Third Haven MM on 26 d., 4 m. 1707 declared their intention to marry. They announced their intention a second time and were given liberty to [marry] (*QMES:*27).

FAIRBANK

David (Farebanks), of Third Haven MM, on 21 d., 1 m., 1717, was reported to have been married by a priest (*QMES:*33).

FOSTER

Seth, m. by 1669, Elizabeth, relict of Thomas Hawkins (MPL HH:489-90, 12:402-403).

FOULSHEAT

[-?-], m. by 1674, Margery, widow of Obadiah Evans (MPL 18:314, 315).

FRANCIS

Thomas, m. by 1682, Mary, dau. of Robert Clarkson, of AA Co. (MPL WC4:250).

GAMES

Richard, d. by 1664, having m. Elizabeth, relict of Andrew Wardner; she m. 3rd, Gabriel Golden, and 4th John Hollenworth (MPL 1:383, 4:4; 7:81; 9:171-2, 240, R:5a; CC:71; EE:168,228).

GLADLAND

[-?-], m. by 27 Dec 1714, Joyce, dau. of Mary Pindle, widow of PG Co. (PGLR F:429).

GLEVIN

Bartholomew, d. by 1667, having m. Mary, widow of Philip Conner; she m. 3rd, by 1667, John Wright of KE Co. (MPL R:30a, 4:63, 11:170, 264-265, GG:169,230).

GOLDEN

Gabriel, d. by 1665, having m. [-?-], relict of 1st, Andrew Wardner and 2nd,

Richard Games; she m. 4th, John Hollenworth (MPL CC:71, 7:81; 9:240, EE:228).

GOLSON
Daniel, m. by 1663, Dorothy [-?-], widow of Giles Sadler. She m. 3rd, Hugh Stanley, and 4th, by 1670, Francis Swanson (MPL AA:68, 86, 5:195,409,427, 9:54, 12:591, 14:214, EE:52, JJ:221-2, and KK:202).

GORSUCH
Charles, on 17 d., 3 m., 1678 was reported to Third Haven MM as having taken a wife contrary to the order of truth (*QMES:*2).

GRAVES
[-?-], m. by 7 Feb 1694, Eliza, dau. of Eliza [-?-], widow of Joseph Fry by her 1st husband (possibly a Johnson) (MWB 7:2).

GRIBLE
Richard, m. by 1681, Margarett, mother of Edward Young (MPL WC4:155).

GRIFFIES
[-?-], m. by 1668, Mary, dau. of Anthony Tall of DO Co. (MPL WT:746, 17:76).

GRIFFIN
[-?-], m. by 1653, [-?-], sister of Ann wife of Peter Johnson and of Mary wife of Robert Taylor (MPL 1:465-78, AB&H:140).

GRIGGS
John, m. by 1676, Mary, relict of 1st, John Hodgkins, and 2nd, Richard Keene (MPL R:210b-211a, 4:538-40; 6:211, AA:451).

GUERIN
Gasper, m. by 1661, Elizabeth [-?-], and called son-in-law by Mr. Thomas Edmonds (MPL AA:511, 6:309).

HACKETT
[-?-], m. by 13 d., 2 m., 1683, Mary, dau. of Henry Woolchurch. Mary was reported to Third Haven MM as having had a child not by her own husband (*QMES:*7).

HAINES
Elizabeth, dau. of John, of Transquaking MM, was reported to Third Haven Quarterly Meeting as like to be married by a priest. On 28 d., 7 m., 1710, her marriage by a priest was reported (*QMES:*26. 29).

HARRISON
John, m. Blanch [-?-], widow of 1st, Robert Dixon, and 2nd, Roger Oliver; she m. 4th, by 1648, Humphrey Howell (MPL 1:218, 222, 231-32, 2:362,363).

HOLLENWORTH

John, m. by 1665, [-?-], relict of 1st, Andrew Wardner, 2nd, Richard Games, and 3rd, Gabriel Golden (MPL 7:81; 9:240, EE:228).

HOMEWOOD

Thomas, m. by 1650, M. Elleson (MPL AA:383, 6:105).

HOWELL

Humphrey, m. by 1648, Blanch [-?-],widow of 1st, Robert Dixon, and 2nd, Roger Oliver, and 3rd, John Harrison (MPL 1:218, 222, 231-32, 2:362,363).

JENKINSON

Eliza, widow, of Third Haven MM, was reported on 30 d., 9 m., 1715 to have gone from the truth and have taken a husband by a priest (*QMES:*32).

JONES

[-?-], m. by 1681, Elizabeth, widow of 1st, Francis Bellows, and 2nd, Peter West (MPL WC4:71-72).

JORDAIN

Thomas, d. by 1671, having m. Sarah, relict of John Elzey; she m. 3rd, by 1671 wife of Charles Ballard of Somerset County (MPL KK:364-365, 7:567, 598-601; 14:374-75; 17:123-24, CC:629,669-73; WT:790-91).

JUDKINS

Obadiah, and Elizabeth Barden, of Third Haven MM, on 10 d., 2 m. 1680, declared their intention to marry, but the Meeting desires them to wait until her husband has been dead for 12 months (*QMES:*4).

Obadiah, and Jane Huntington, both of Third Haven MM, TA Co., were m. on 4 d., 11 m., 1681 at the house of William Southbee (*QMES:*5).

Obadiah, Jr., and Elizabeth Parratt were m. on 22 d., 7 m., 1692 in Third Haven MM [This is a correction to the marriage entry on p. 192]. (*QMES:*13).

KEENE

Richard, m. by 1676, Mary, widow of John Hodgkins of Patuxent River; she m. 3rd, John Griggs of CV Co. (MPL Qo:162, 163, Q:227,229; AB&H:141; 4:538-40; 6:211; 15:387; WC2:48, R:210b-211a; AA:451; LL:529).

KEMP

Robert, of Third Haven MM, on 6 d., 7 m, 1678, declared his intention to marry Elizabeth Webb, but the meeting advised him to forbear for the present (*QMES:*2).

KENT

[-?-], widow of [-?-] Kent., of Tuckahoe Meeting was reported to Third Haven MM on 25 d., 10 m., 1717, of having gone to a priest and taken a husband (*QMES:*33).

KINGSBURY
Robert (Kingsberry), m. by March 1652, Mary, mother of Edward and Elizabeth Wells (MPL AA:112, AB&H:385, 5:247, 454, WC4:465).

LAWRENCE
John, of Third Haven MM, on 29 d., 4 m., 1710, was reported for his having attempted several times to be married by a priest to Sarah Coughee. On 31 d., 6 m., 1710 he was disowned by Meeting for having taken a wife contrary to Truth (*QMES:*29).

LECOMPTE
Margaret, of Third Haven MM, on 31 d., 5 m., 1701, condemned her self and that spirit that drew her into the gross evil of going to a priest for a husband and marrying a man that made no profession of the blessed faith (*QMES:*22).

LEEDS
Edward, and Ruth Ball of Third Haven MM on 24 d., 12 m., 1703, declared their intention to marry; after declaring their intentions a second time, on 31 d., 12 m., 1703, they were given liberty to accomplish their intentions (*QMES:*23).

LESBY
Jacob [Lusby?], of AA Co., m. by 1681, [-?-], widow of John Hudson (MPL WC4:62).

LEWIS
Charles, appeared on 29 d., 8., 1696, before Third Haven MM and declared that he and his wife had often been grieved that they had often been married by a priest (*QMES:*17).

LIGHT
[-?-], m. by 1665, Frances, mother of Edward Williams (MPL CC:626, 7:565, 8:241, 9:304, DD:279, EE:289).

LLOYD
Richard, m. by 1665, [-?-], widow of Thomas Phillips (MPL CC:733, 8:482).

LOVELY
Deliverance, m. by 1659, Elizabeth, relict of 1st, Edward Commins, and 2nd, Thomas Ward, chirurgeon (MPL 1:399, 2:529, AB&H:27,105,128; Q:359,431, Qo:235;278).

MANNERS
George, m. by 1649, Rebecca [-?-], servant of Mr. Husband; she m. 2nd, by 1656 Edward Hall, and 3rd, Thomas Orley (MPL AB&H:4, 11, 36, 1:195, 2:201, 249, 439, 581, 3:196, 4:19).

MARSHALL

Edward, m. by Aug 1712, Ann, widow and extx. of Joseph Pettibone, and widow and admx. of William Lewis (AAJU TB#3:1, 2). [This entry expands the entry on p. 225].

MELTON

Abraham, and Mary Wyett, of Third Haven MM, on 8 d., 7 m., 1698, declared their intention to marry (*QMES:*86).

MILTON

Abraham, was reported to Third Haven MM that on 12 d., 1 m., 1713, he was visited by Friends of Chester Meeting on account of his marriage out of the good order of truth, and he has given them a paper condemning his disorderly marriage (*QMES:*87). [This refers to the marriage in June 1713 of Abraham Milton to Barbara Everett: see above].

MITCHELL

John, of Third Haven MM, was reported on 31 d., 5 m., 1700, of having taken a wife by a priest contrary to discipline (*QMES:*21). [This probably refers to the marriage of John Mitchell to Susanna Burgess in July 1700: see above]

MORGAN

[-?-], clerk, m. by 1678, Elizabeth Jones (MPL LL:781, 15:526).

Abraham, and Eliza Jenkinson of Third Haven MM on 2 d., 5 m., 1686 declared intention to marry. After declaring their intention to marry a second time, the Meeting gave them liberty to come together in marriage (*QMES:*11).

NICHOLS

John, m. by 1682, Rebeccah, dau. of Richard Beard of AA Co. (MPL WC4:251).

NIFINGER

John, m. by 1683, Judith, dau. of John and Judith Gouldsmith of SM Co.(MWB 4:15; SMWB PC#1:44).

NOBLE

John, m. by 1672, Margaret, widow of Walter Peake or Pake (MPL WT:768-69, 17:98-9).

NUNAM

John, of Third Haven MM, on 27 d., 6 m., 1696, was charged that contrary to the good order of truth has taken a wife by a priest, and not above ten days after the burial of his last wife (*QMES:*17).

OMEALIA

Bryan of Third Haven MM died by 23 d., 8 m., 1685. He married Mary, who by her will disposed of her son verbally to her bro. and sister Ralph and Sarah Fishburn (*QMES:*10).

PARRATT
Isaiah, and Hannah Clark were married 9 d., 9 mo., 1709, at Tuckahoe Meeting House (*QMES:*28).

PARSONS
John, of Third Haven MM was reported on 25 d., 10 m., 1679, to have taken a wife "contrary to Truth" (*QMES:*2).

PATRICK
Roger, m. by 1670, Ann, prob. mother of his "dau.-in-law" Sarah Harrison from Accomack Co., VA (MPL WT:338, 16:320; 17:582-83).

PEARCE
Evin, m. by 26 d., 3 m., [-?-], widow of Robert Booker (Boker) (*QMES:*31).

PHILLIPS
James, m. by 20 March 1675/6, Suzanna, widow of William Orchard and mother of Susan Orchard (MPL EE:488, 9:489; 19:257, WC:146).

PITT
John, m. by 1669, Frances, relict of 1st, Cornelius Abrahamson, and 2nd, Francis Armstrong (MPL R:69b).

John, and Rebecka Hosier, of Third Haven MM, on 13 d., 11 m., 1717, declared their intention to marry (*QMES:*86).

PRICE
Moses (Mosses), and Dorothy Rogers of Third Haven MM on 26 d., 5 m., 1689 declared intention to marry. They declared their intention a second time on 28 d., 8 m., 1689, and were given liberty by the Meeting to come together in marriage (*QMES:*12).

REASON
Philip, m. by 29 d., 10 m., 1714, [-?-], sister of George Warner of Third Haven MM (*QMES:*32).

RICHARDSON
Daniel, and Ruth Leads declared to Third Haven MM their intention to marry. Mary Ellston, mother of Ruth Leads gave her consent. The couple declared their intention to marry a second time, on 24 d., 7 m., 1712, and were given liberty to marry (*QMES:*31).

RIDLY
James, and Anna Ellitt of Third Haven MM on 21 d., 9 m., 1684, declared intention to marry (*QMES:*9).

TENNIS

John, m. by 1654, [-?-], servant to Mr. Johnson (MPL 1:631).

TRACEY

Teague (or Tego), m. on 5 Nov 1694, Mary James (AAJA:7#4). On 6 Aug 1695, Mary was one of the legatees of Luke Gregory of AA Co. (INAC 10:442).

= = 0 = =

Index